W9-CCP-197

# THE
# AMERICAN
# PRESIDENTS

GARLAND REFERENCE LIBRARY OF THE HUMANITIES (VOL. 1971)

BALDWIN PUBLIC LIBRARY

# THE AMERICAN PRESIDENTS

★ ★ ★ ★ ★ ★ ★ ★ ★ ★ ★

EDITED BY Melvin I. Urofsky

*Garland Publishing, Inc.*
A MEMBER OF THE TAYLOR & FRANCIS GROUP
NEW YORK & LONDON
2000

Published in 2000 by
Garland Publishing Inc.
A Member of the Taylor & Francis Group
29 West 35th Street
New York, NY 10001

Copyright © 2000 by Melvin I. Urofsky

All rights reserved. No part of this book may be reprinted or reproduced or
utilized in any form or by any electronic, mechanical, or other means, now
known or hereafter invented, including photocopying and recording, or in
any information storage or retrieval system, without permission in writing
from the publishers.

10   9   8   7   6   5   4   3   2   1

**Library of Congress Cataloging-in-Publication Data**

The American presidents / edited by Melvin I. Urofsky.
     p.   cm. — (Garland reference library of the humanities ; vol. 1971)
     Includes index.
     ISBN 0-8153-2184-8 (alk. paper)
     1. Presidents—United States—History.  2. Political leadership—
United States—History.  3. United States—Politics and government.
4. Presidents—United States—Biography.  I. Urofsky, Melvin I.
II. Series.
E176.1.A6566   2000
973′.09′9—dc21                                                                99-038134
                                                                                   CIP

Printed on acid-free, 250-year-life paper
Manufactured in the United States of America

# Contents

# INTRODUCTION

When the members of the Philadelphia convention of 1787 came to draft Article II of the new Constitution, that part dealing with the presidency, they had some difficulty defining the office. They were familiar with the legislative branch, since many of them had served either in the Continental Congress or in state assemblies, and Article I of the Constitution, setting forth the powers of the Congress, is detailed and fully developed.

But what exactly was a president, and what would the powers of the office be? They knew from the experience under the Articles of Confederation that the government needed an executive branch, but their memories of King George III led them to be suspicious of giving too much power to any one individual. Article II is surprisingly short, and contemporary evidence indicates that many of the delegates, assuming that George Washington would be the first president, wanted to allow him to shape the office, trusting that he would be neither an absolute monarch nor a puppet of the legislature.

One of Washington's great achievements is that he carried out the convention's implied assignment and did in fact shape the office of the presidency in ways that are still in effect today. He made it one of three equal branches of our national government—not dictatorial and not subservient to the Congress. His success in that task is one reason that various ratings of the presidents always make him one of our three greatest chief executives, along with Abraham Lincoln and Franklin Delano Roosevelt.

Presidential greatness, or lack of it, is what the following essays are about. Forty-one men have occupied the office of president of the United States, from terms that have ranged from as little to one month (William Henry Harrison) to more than twelve years (Franklin Roosevelt). Some of their names are known by every schoolchild; others would probably stump game show participants (who *is* Millard Fillmore?)

All of these men are, in one way or another, exceptional people. Although it is fashionable to talk about someone like Andrew Jackson or Harry Truman being representative of the "common folk," there was nothing "common" about either one of them. To become president requires not only great effort but achievement as well. Some of these men achieved brilliantly in one field only to find the demands of the presidency more than they could handle; the case of Ulysses S. Grant comes immediately to mind. Others found that whatever political skills they may have had in other places, they were in over their heads in the Oval Office.

To be a "great" president requires challenges, and we measure presidential achievement by how one meets those challenges. George Washington had the task of shaping the new government and protecting the fragile independence of the United States; Abraham Lincoln faced rebellion, and in preserving the Union also did away with slavery; Franklin Roosevelt had the twin challenges of the Great Depression and World War II, and if people disagree on how successful some of his programs may have been, no one questions that he galvanized the American people and led them through twelve years of continuous crisis.

Without challenges, presidential greatness is elusive. In the latter nineteenth century the country was at peace and enjoyed expanding prosperity as it went through its industrial revolution. Rutherford B. Hayes, Chester A. Arthur, and Benjamin Harrison were all competent men, and, as these essays show, had some important credits to their administration; but no matter how successful they may have been, they could not be "great" because they had no challenges of the magnitude of a civil war or major depression.

The authors of the essays in this volume were not asked to write biographies of the presidents; other sources are available for that (and there is a list of suggested additional readings at the end of each essay). Rather they were asked to evaluate these forty-one men in terms of their presidencies: Were they good, bad, or indifferent presidents? What challenges did they face and how well did they meet them? What were their most important and lasting achievements and what were their failures? No strict pattern was imposed, but rather the authors were given the leeway to answer these questions in whatever manner they thought would be most illustrative of the successes and failures of their subjects.

Some of the essays spend more time on biographical information than do others because in some cases we cannot understand how these men functioned in the Oval Office unless we know something about their background. Some take a more psychological approach, while others focus on political events or on administrative accomplishments. Taken together, the essays present unique portraits of the men who have held the highest office in the United States and of how they influenced that office—for better or for worse.

All in all, we as a nation have been fortunate in our selection of presidents. Only a few truly great men have occupied the presidency, but many of them performed their difficult task well and with honor. Only a handful have faced the threat of removal from office because of their actions—Andrew Johnson, Richard Nixon, and Bill Clinton came close, but in more than two hundred years we have never had to exercise the constitutional power of removing a president through impeachment by the House of Representatives and conviction by the Senate.

What will surprise some readers is the evaluation of presidents not normally considered in the top ranks, such as William McKinley. Others will find that some of our presidents did important things that do not show up on the radar charts of most of the public or even of many presidential students. All of them, however, have continued the task undertaken by George Washington, of creating the presidency. As the nation has grown and changed, so has this office, and each new occupant has the chance and the challenge of making that office a continuing force in our nation's development.

# Contributors

**William C. Berman**, an avid bird watcher, holds a doctorate from the Ohio State University and has taught at the University of Toronto for the past three decades. His specialty is post-1945 America, and he was most recently the author of *America's Turn to the Right: From Nixon to Bush* (1994).

**David J. Bodenhamer** is professor of history and director of the Polis Research Center at Indiana University–Purdue University at Indianapolis. In addition to more than forty articles, chapters in books, and papers, he is the author or editor of *Ambivalent Legacy: A Legal History of the South*, with James W. Ely, Jr. (1984), *The Pursuit of Justice: Crime and Law in Antebellum Indiana* (1986), *Fair Trial: Crime and Law in Antebellum Indiana* (1992), and *The Bill of Rights in Modern America: After 200 Years*, with James W. Ely, Jr. (1993).

**Alan V. Briceland** received his B.A. from the College of William and Mary and his Ph.D. from Duke. He has taught at the University of North Texas and at Virginia Commonwealth University. He is the author of *Westward from Virginia: The Exploration of the Virginia-Carolina Frontier, 1650–1710* (1987) and *1788: The Year of Decision* (1988) as well as more than a dozen articles and book chapters.

**Andrew Burstein** teaches early American history at the University of Northern Iowa. He is the author of *The Inner Jefferson: Portrait of a Grieving Optimist* (1995), and *Sentimental Democracy: The Evolution of America's Romantic Self-Image* (1999).

**John Milton Cooper, Jr.**, is E. Gordon Fox Professor of History at the University of Wisconsin-Madison. Among his many publications are *Walter Hines Page: The Southerner as American* (1977), the acclaimed dual biography of Theodore Roosevelt and Woodrow Wilson, *The Warrior and the Priest* (1983), and *Pivotal Decades: The United States, 1900–1920* (1990).

**Wayne Cutler** is research professor of history and director of the James K. Polk Project at the University of Tennessee. He earned his B.A. at Lamar University and his M.A. and Ph.D. from the University of Texas at Austin. He has worked as an editorial associate of the *Southwestern Historical Quarterly* and as assistant editor of the Henry Clay Project before taking over the Polk Project. He has served as senior editor of the fifth through ninth volumes of the Polk Correspondence series. In August 1987 he moved the Polk Project from Vanderbilt University to the Tennessee Presidents Center, which houses the editorial papers of presidents Andrew Jackson, James K. Polk, and Andrew Johnson.

**Richard J. Ellis** is Mark O. Hatfield Professor of Politics at Willamette University. He received his doctorate in political science from the University of California at Berkeley. His books include *American Political Cultures* (1993), *Presidential Lightning Rods: The Politics of Blame Avoidance* (1994), *The Dark Side of the Left: Illiberal Egalitarianism in America* (1998), and *Founding the American Presidency* (1999). He is also the co-author, with Aaron Wildavsky, of *Dilemmas of Presidential Leadership: From Washington through Lincoln* (1989).

**Paul Finkelman** is the Chapman Distinguished Professor of Law at the University of Tulsa College of Law. He is the author or editor of numerous books and articles, including *Dred Scott v. Sandford: A Brief History with Documents* (1997), a new edition of *A Brief Narrative of the Tryal of John Peter Zenger* (1997), *Slavery and the Founders: Race and Liberty in the Age of Jefferson* (1995), *Impeachable Offenses: A Documentary History from 1787 to the Present* (1999), and *Religion and American Law: An Encyclopedia* (1999).

**Paul W. Glad** is Regents' Professor of History Emeritus at the University of Oklahoma in Norman and is the author of numerous books and articles on American history, including *The Trumpet Soundeth: William Jennings Bryan and His Democracy, 1896–1912* (1960), and volume 5 of the History of Wisconsin series, *War, A New Era, and Depression* (1990).

**Robert M. Goldman** is professor of history in the department of history-political science at Virginia Union University in Richmond, Virginia. He is the author of *"A Free Ballot and a Fair Count": The Department of Justice and the Enforcement of Voting Rights in the South, 1877–1892* (1990) as well as articles on U.S. constitutional and legal history.

**Lewis L. Gould** is Barker Professor Emeritus in American history at the University of Texas at Austin. He is the author of *The Presidency of William McKinley* (1980) and *The Presidency of Theodore Roosevelt* (1981), as well as other publications on the politics and public policy of the late nineteenth century. His most recent book is *Lady Bird Johnson: Our Environmental First Lady* (1999).

**Alonzo L. Hamby**, professor of history at Ohio University, has written widely on modern America. His books include *Beyond the New Deal* (1973), *The Imperial Years* (1976), and *Liberalism and Its Challengers* (1992). He is the recipient of the Herbert C. Hoover Award and the Harry S. Truman Book Award for his 1995 book, *Man of the People: A Life of Harry S. Truman.*

**Joan Hoff**, former executive secretary of the Organization of American Historians and former co-editor of the *Journal of Women's History*, is president and CEO of the Center for the Study of the President, editor of *Presidential Studies Quarterly*, and the author of a number of books on U.S. foreign policy and politics and women's legal rights, including *American Business and Foreign Policy, 1920–1933*; *Ideology and Economics: United States Relations with the Soviet Union, 1918–1933*; *Herbert Hoover: Forgotten Progressive* (1992); *Nixon Reconsidered* (1995); and *Law, Gender, and Injustice: A Legal History of U.S. Women* (1990); *Rights of Passage: The Past, Present and Future of the ERA* (1986); *Without Precedent: The Life and Career of Eleanor Roosevelt*, co-edited with Marjorie Lightman (1984); and *For Adult Users Only: The Dilemma of Violent Pornography*, co-edited with Susan Gubar (1990).

**Robert D. Holsworth** is professor of political science and public administration and director of the Center for Public Policy at Virginia Commonwealth University. His most recent books are *Affirmative Action and the Stalled Quest for Black Progress* (co-authored with W. Avon Drake, 1996), and *Let Your Life Speak: A Study of Politics, Religion, and Antinuclear Weapons Activism* (1989). He is a frequent commentator on Virginia and national politics, appearing both on television and radio as well as in the pages of major American newspapers.

**Ari Hoogenboom** completed his Ph.D. at Columbia in 1958. In 1961 the University of Illinois Press published his dissertation, *Outlawing the Spoils: A History of the Civil Service Reform Movement*. Hoogenboom has taught since 1968 at Brooklyn College of the City University of New York (CUNY) and at the Graduate Center of CUNY. Beginning with his dissertation, Hoogenboom has been interested in Rutherford B. Hayes and has written widely about him. In forays outside of the Gilded Age, Hoogenboom has co-authored *The Enterprising Colonials* (with William S. Sachs, 1965), *A History of Pennsylvania* (with Philip S. Klein, 1973, 1980), and *A History of the ICC* (with Olive Hoogenboom, 1976). Hoogenboom received a Guggenheim Fellowship (1965–1966) and a Fulbright Award in 1991–1992 when he served as the George Bancroft Professor of American history at the University of Göttingen, Germany.

**John W. Johnson** is professor of history and head of the department at the University of Northern Iowa. A specialist in twentieth-century legal and constitutional issues, Johnson has written *American Legal Culture, 1908–1940* (1981); *Insuring Against Disaster: The Nuclear Industry on Trial* (1986); and *The Struggle for Student Rights: Tinker v. Des Moines* (1997). He has also edited *Historic U.S. Court Cases, 1690–1990* (1992), which received the 1994 Thomas Jefferson Prize of the Society for the History of the Federal Government.

**Steven F. Lawson**, professor of history at Rutgers University, has written widely on the civil rights movement. His books include *Black Ballots: Voting Rights in the South, 1944–1969* (1976), *In Pursuit of Power: Southern Blacks and Electoral Politics, 1965–1982* (1985), *Running for Freedom: Civil Rights and Black Politics Since 1941* (2nd ed., 1997), and with Charles Payne, *Debating the Civil Rights Movement, 1945–1968* (1998).

**William E. Leuchtenburg**, who has taught at New York University, Smith College, Harvard University, and, for thirty years, at Columbia University where he held the De Witt Clinton chair, has taught since 1982 at the University of North Carolina at Chapel Hill where he is William Rand Kenan, Jr., Professor of History. He has served as president of the American Historical Association, of the Organization of American Historians, and of the Society of American Historians. His books include *The Perils of Prosperity, 1914–32* (1958), *Franklin D. Roosevelt and the New Deal, 1932–1940* (1963), winner of both the Bancroft Prize and the Francis Parkman Prize, *The Supreme Court Reborn* (1995), and *The FDR Years* (1995). His volume, *In the Shadow of FDR: From Harry Truman to Bill Clinton* (1993), includes a chapter on Jimmy Carter.

**David W. Levy** is Sam K. Vierson Professor of American History at the University of Oklahoma, where his special interest is American intellectual history. He has published *Herbert Croly of the New Republic: The Life and Thought of an American Progressive* (1985) and *The Debate over Vietnam* (1991). He is the co-editor of the five-volume collection of *The Letters of Louis D. Brandeis* (1972–1978) and of *"Half-Brother, Half Son": The Letters of Louis D. Brandeis to Felix Frankfurter* (1991). He has also co-edited *FDR's Fireside Chats* (1992). Levy has won the University of Oklahoma Regents' Award for Superior Teaching and the Student Association's prize for the outstanding teacher at the University of Oklahoma.

**Jonathan Lurie** is professor of history and adjunct professor of law at Rutgers University, Newark, where he has taught since 1969. His books include *The Chicago Board of Trade, 1875–1905* (1979), *Law and the Nation, 1860–1912* (1983), *The Constitution and Economic Change* (1988), *Arming Military Justice: The Origins of the United States Court of Military Appeals, 1775–1950* (1992), and *Pursuing Military Justice: The History of the U.S. Court of Appeals for the Armed Forces 1951–1980* (1998).

**Robert F. Martin** is professor of history at the University of Northern Iowa, where he specializes in southern and Gilded Age/Progressive era history. He is the author of *Howard Kester and the Struggle for Social Justice in the South, 1904–1977* (1991) and is currently working on a biography of the evangelist "Billy" Sunday.

**Sidney M. Milkus** is professor of government and senior scholar at the Miller Center of Public Affairs of the University of Virginia. He is the author of several books on the presidency, including *The President and the Parties: The Transformation of the American Party System since the New Deal* (1993), *The American Presidency: Origins and Development* (1994), and *Presidential Greatness* (2000).

**F. Thornton Miller** received his Ph.D. in history from the University of Alabama in 1986. His publications include *Juries and Judges Versus the Law: Virginia's Provincial Legal Perspective, 1783–1828* (1994), an edition of John Taylor's *Tyranny Unmasked* (1992), and articles or chapters in a number of journals and collections. He has taught at Southwest Missouri State University since 1989.

**Herbert S. Parmet**, Distinguished Professor Emeritus of the City University of New York, is the author, among other works, of *Eisenhower and the American Crusades* (1972), *Richard Nixon and His America* (1990), *George Bush: The Life of a Lone Star Yankee* (1997), and a two-volume biography of John F. Kennedy.

**Barbara A. Perry** is professor of government at Sweet Briar College in Virginia. In 1995–96 she was a research fellow at the Virginia Foundation for the Humanities and Public Policy, where she wrote *The Priestly Tribe: The Supreme Court's Image in the American Mind* (1999). Prior to that, she served as the 1994–95 judicial fellow at the Supreme Court of the United States. Her other books include *A "Representative" Supreme Court? The Impact of Race, Religion, and Gender on Appointments* (1991) and *"The Supremes": Essays on the Current Justices of the United States Supreme Court* (1999). She is the co-author, with Henry J. Abraham, of the sixth and seventh editions of *Freedom and the Court: Civil Rights and Liberties in the United States* (1998).

**Richard M. Pious**, Adolph and Effie Ochs Professor of American Studies at Barnard College, is a prolific author on the American presidency. His works include *The American Presidency* (1979), *The President, Congress and the Constitution* (1984), and *American Politics and Government* (1986). He has written articles in numerous journals, and also the *Young Oxford Companion to the Presidency of the United States* (1993).

**Daniel Preston** is editor of *The Papers of James Monroe* at Mary Washington College.

**Leonard L. Richards** is professor of history at the University of Massachusetts, where his specialty is Jacksonian America. His publications include *Gentlemen of Property and Standing: Anti-Abolition Mobs in Jacksonian America* (1971), *The Advent of American Democracy* (1977),

*The Life and Times of Congressman John Quincy Adams* (1988), and the forthcoming *The Slave Power: The Free Negro and the Southern Domination, 1780–1860.*

**Russell L. Riley** holds a doctorate in history from the University of Virginia and is currently the director of academic programs at the Salzburg Seminar in American Studies. He has written on the presidency, political leadership, and parties and is the author of *The Presidency and the Politics of Racial Inequality: Nation-Keeping from 1831–1965* (1999).

**Greg Russell** is associate professor of political science at the University of Oklahoma in Norman and is the author, among other works, of *Hans J. Morgenthau and the Ethics of American Statecraft* (1990) and *John Quincy Adams and the Public Virtues of Diplomacy* (1995). He has published extensively in the area of political ethics and diplomatic history and is currently working on a book entitled *Theodore Roosevelt and the Soul of American Statecraft.*

**Edgar A. Toppin** is a research professor of history at both Virginia Commonwealth University (each spring semester) and Virginia State University (summer and fall). He has taught on the college level for forty years but has also spent a decade and a half as an administrator. Toppin has written many articles, some on his teaching specialty, the Civil War and Reconstruction. He is the author of ten books, among them *A Biographical History of Blacks in America since 1528* (1971) and *Loyal Sons and Daughters: Virginia State University, 1882 to 1992* (1992). Currently, he is completing a history of a historic church (Gillfield Baptist in Petersburg) and is resuming work on a biography of Luther P. Jackson, historian and civil rights activist.

**Dorothy Twohig** has served as associate and co-editor of *The Papers of George Washington* at the University of Virginia and, after 1992 until her retirement in 1998, as editor in chief of the project. She earlier worked on *The Papers of Alexander Hamilton* at Columbia University and on the staff of the *Dictionary of American Biography.* She is co-editor (with Donald Jackson) of the six-volume *Diaries of George Washington* (1976–1979) and editor of *The Journal of the Proceedings of the President* (1981).

**Melvin I. Urofsky** is professor of history and director of the doctoral program in public policy and administration at Virginia Commonwealth University. He is the author or editor of more than thirty books and over 100 articles. His most recent publications are *Affirmative Action on Trial* (1997), *Division and Discord: The Supreme Court under Stone and Vinson, 1941–1953* (1997), and *Lethal Judgments: The Supreme Court and Assisted Suicide* (2000).

**R. Hal Williams** is professor of history at Southern Methodist University, where he has also served as chair of the history department and dean of Dedman College. His publications include *The Democratic Party and California Politics, 1880–1896* (1973), *Years of Decision: American Politics in the 1890s* (1978), and *The Manhattan Project: A Documentary Introduction to the Atomic Age* (1990). He is currently at work on a biography of James G. Blaine.

**Nancy Beck Young** teaches in the history department at Southwest Missouri State University and is the author of *Texas, Her Texas: The Life and Times of Frances Goff* (1997).

★★★ 1 ★★★

# George Washington
## 1789–1797

*Dorothy Twohig*

---

*Born 22 February 1732, Pope's Creek, Westmoreland County, Virginia, to Augustine Washington and Mary Ball Washington; no formal education after age 17; married Martha Dandridge Custis, 6 January 1759; no children of their union; two children from her previous marriage; elected president 1789, receiving 69 electoral college votes, a unanimous choice (John Adams received 34 and became vice president); reelected 1792, again by a unanimous vote of the electoral college (John Adams again received the second highest number, 77); died 14 December 1799 at Mount Vernon, Virginia, and buried in family vault there.*

---

On the morning of 16 April 1789, George Washington left his Virginia estate, bidding, as he noted in his diary "adieu to Mount Vernon, to private life, and to domestic felicity; and with a mind oppressed with more anxious and painful sensations than I have words to express set out for New York . . . with the best dispositions to render service to my country in obedience to its call, but with less hope of answering its expectations." He felt, he wrote Henry Knox, "like a culprit who is going to the place of his execution: so unwilling am I, in the evening of a life nearly consumed in public cares, to quit a peaceful abode for an Ocean of difficulties, without that competency of political skill—abilities & inclination which is necessary to manage the helm." It was a triumphal journey. Everywhere along his route he met with unprecedented adulation. Escorts of citizens met him miles outside of every town and accompanied him well beyond its borders. When he stayed the night at Baltimore and at Philadelphia, elaborate festivities were prepared to honor him. At his arrival in New York City, the new nation's capital, a large ceremonial barge carried him across the Hudson to a day-long celebration.

The *Gazette of the United States* echoed general public opinion when it contended that it was "undoubtedly a new and astonishing thing under the sun, that the universal suffrages of a great and various people should centre in one and the same man; for it is evidently a fact, that, was every individual *personally* consulted as to the man whom they would elect to fill the office of President of this rising Empire, the only reply from New-Hampshire to Georgia would be Washington." A poem in the Philadelphia *Federal Gazette* lauded him as "our saviour and our guide." The *Boston Gazette* called him "the phoenix of the age." The *Federal Gazette* assured Washington that the presidential power he was about to receive was "infinitely preferable to a hereditary crown, inasmuch as it is conferred upon *merit*, by the unanimous and free suffrages of the Representatives of near three millions of affectionate and grateful People." The tributes only made Washington more uneasy, filling "my mind with sensations as painful (considering the reverse of this scene, which may be the case after all my labors to do good) as they are pleasing."

In the months before the election, Washington had been bombarded with letters from friends and political supporters urging his acceptance of the first office. Washington possessed a strong element of self-doubt. He had no doubt of his own virtue in its classic sense. But he had had serious misgivings about his abilities to surmount adverse circumstances at the beginning of the revolution—he told Patrick Henry that "from this day, I date the downfall of my

reputation"—and these misgivings were echoed twofold when he faced the presidency. Washington often commented on his "inferior endowments from nature," and it was not the first time he had been asked to assume responsibilities for which he felt ill-prepared.

And he now had a great deal more to lose. Washington had already become to his contemporaries an American version of Bolingbroke's Patriot King. Obsessed as always for reputation, he not only feared failure in his new role but was more immediately apprehensive that acceptance of the presidency would be interpreted as a repudiation of his promise to retire from public life. As he stressed to his friends, he did not really want to accept the presidency, but neither did he want to chance being defeated or even seriously challenged for the position if he did decide to stand. To a man, his correspondents argued that his fears were groundless. "You will become the Father to more than three Millions of Children," Gouverneur Morris promised him, "I form my conclusions from those Talents and Virtues which the World *believes* and your Friends *know* you possess." Even the meager criticism his support of the Constitution had evoked from its detractors redounded to his credit as a man willing to risk his reputation for the good of his country.

No president since has gone into office with the kind of public mandate Washington enjoyed. In many ways, the 1789 presidential election was more of a public anointing than a political process. In April the electoral college elected Washington, as expected, without a single dissenting vote, although the vice-presidential contest, largely between John Adams and New York governor George Clinton, was more contentious.

## THE MAKING OF CINCINNATUS
Like all presidents, Washington brought his own intellectual baggage to the office. His early education, according to the sparse information that exists, was clearly not elaborate. His father died when Washington was 11, leaving him in the care of his critical and overprotective mother and his nurturing

older half-brother Lawrence. Unlike the education in England given to his two older half-brothers, what meager education the younger George received was probably at the hands of local tutors. By the time he was 16, he had turned largely to the acquisition of such practical skills as surveying. After he moved to his brother Lawrence's home at Mount Vernon, however, young Washington moved in circles that took a classical education for granted, and he clearly absorbed many of the catchwords of the day.

He also acquired the diffident manner he would display for the rest of his life in the company of better educated men. John Adams, who did not always view Washington's fame kindly, remarked that it was beyond dispute that Washington was "too illiterate, unlearned, unread for his station." Perhaps as a defense against such opinions, Washington collected an impressive private library over his lifetime, and it is probable that he may have read in it much more widely than has been generally appreciated. A few books became central to his growing philosophy of government, public service, and leadership; for good or ill, they influenced his private and public roles for the rest of his life. One was Addison's play *The Tragedy of Cato*, which Washington had seen on stage and from which he occasionally quoted. Cato seemed to embody for him the virtues of the stoic philosophy—a noble simplicity of life, duty to the state, courage and responsibility, an acceptance of life's vicissitudes, a striving for perfection, and an unshakable integrity.

On his way to the presidency from his experience as the young commander of the Virginia Regiment during the French and Indian War and as commander-in-chief of the Continental Army during the American Revolution, Washington developed his own definitions of both public and private morality. These he based not only on classical models but on his private conceptions of honor and integrity, both for himself and for the state. Between his resignation from the Virginia Regiment in 1759 and his acceptance of the command of the Continental army in 1775, Washington deliberately

sculpted a new public image. The formerly brash young officer, impatient with his superiors, greedy for advancement in rank, determined to secure the land he felt would ensure his place in the colonial hierarchy, became, in this transformation, the temperate, dispassionate, mature figure the members of the Continental Congress found so appealing in 1775.

By 1783, Washington's reputation in the eyes of Americans as the great man of the eighteenth century was rivaled only by that of Benjamin Franklin. Contributing to that reputation were his widely known repudiation in 1782 of Lewis Nicola's scheme to create a monarchy with Washington at its head, and his skillful defusion of the Newburgh proposals. And adding immeasurably to the high regard in which he was held was his abdication of power at the end of the Revolution. As Garry Wills has observed, Washington was a virtuoso of resignations. To a society steeped in the classical concept of fame there was something essentially right in the fact that the Revolution's greatest leader should emulate the Roman Cincinnatus's return to his farm, laying aside the honors of the state.

At the time of his resignation as commander-in-chief of the army in 1783, Washington considered his retirement from public life irrevocable—to use one of his favorite phrases, he was committed to a peaceful retirement under his vine and fig tree at Mount Vernon. But although he was geographically withdrawn from the scene of politics after the war, a voluminous correspondence and almost daily visitors to Mount Vernon kept him in close contact with the state of the Union. For the first time since he had assumed command of the army, he had the leisure to contemplate the new republic. Washington's circular letter to the governors of the states at the close of the war had emphasized the scope of the opportunities facing America and his own dreams for the new Republic, but by the mid-1780s, his faith had faltered.

Washington's own tendency toward political pessimism inevitably colored his perception of the state of the nation during the

Confederation years. He viewed failure of the Revolution as the failure of his own achievements. Having devoted almost ten years of his life to creating the new nation, he now feared it was on the edge of disintegration. "I see," he wrote Jean Paul Lafayette, "one head gradually changing into thirteen." In 1786, he confided to John Jay that virtue had, in his opinion, "taken its departure from our land." Indeed, during the mid-1780s Washington echoed the view of many of the old elite that republican ideals had vanished from the new republic and that leadership now lay in the hands of selfish sybaritic men of the new order whose goals were the pursuit of luxury and self-aggrandizement. "We have probably had too good an opinion of human nature in forming our confederation," he wrote in 1786, adding that men would not "adopt and carry into execution measures . . . calculated for their own good, without the intervention of coercive power." After the Constitutional Convention, much of his optimism seems to have been restored. "I begin to look forward," he wrote Sir Edward Newenham in 1788, "with a kind of political faith, to scenes of National happiness, which have not heretofore been offered for the fruition of the most favored Nations. The natural political, and moral circumstances of our Nascent empire justify the anticipation."

## CREATING THE PRESIDENCY

If approval of Washington was universal, support for the Constitution was not, and the problems facing his new administration were overwhelming. Many Americans feared the new federal government would overpower the states, and there was strong pressure not only for a bill of rights but for a new convention to alter the Constitution itself. Hostilities with tribal groups on the northern and southern borders threatened to erupt momentarily. Economic distress with resulting unrest, was spread across all classes, and the nation faced a staggering— for the eighteenth century—foreign and domestic debt of over $50 million. And Britain on the northern frontier and Spain

on the south posed increasing threats to the new nation's borders.

Washington entered office with no specific blueprint for his presidency and with a sense of the general uncertainty about the powers and functions of the executive office. None of the delegates to the Constitutional Convention—except possibly Alexander Hamilton, James Wilson, and Gouverneur Morris—had clearly formulated ideas as to the kind of executive that would emerge from that meeting. As Madison wrote Washington "I have scarcely ventured as yet to form my own opinion of the manner in which [the executive] ought to be constituted or the authorities with which it ought to be clothed." Washington was surely aware of—and to a certain extent shared—the general Whig bias of the Revolutionary generation against the concentration of power in the executive. But he also recalled his wartime experiences with the weaknesses of the congress, and they predisposed him to accept the image of the executive office that emerged from the convention—largely a creation in committee by Morris and Wilson. Indeed, the convention perhaps devoted more time to the discussion of this issue than to any other topic. And because the debates indicated how sensitive the subject was to the delegates, Article II contains only the broadest guidelines for the executive office and its relationship to the other branches of government.

To many of the delegates, the provisions of Article II were based on the assumption that Washington would accept the office. As Pierce Butler noted—the powers of the president "are full great and greater than I was disposed to make them." As late as 1791, John Vining of Delaware noted that "while we have a Washington and his virtues to cement and guard the Union, it might be safe, but when he should leave us, who will inherit his virtues and possess his influence?" This theme surfaced often in private correspondence, especially during Washington's serious illnesses in the summers of 1789 and 1790. As presiding officer of the convention, Washington was well aware of the reservations of many of the delegates, and the most cursory examination of newspapers indicated that the general public was equally concerned. The esteem in which Washington was held undoubtedly helped mitigate the traditional suspicion with which Americans regarded the executive, and he considered it his mission to convince the public that they had nothing to fear from the new government.

Many of the affairs that occupied so much of Washington's time in the early days of the presidency appear trivial on the surface. But, as he wrote the comte de Rochambeau in the summer of 1790, "In a government which depends so much in its first stages on public opinion, much circumspection is still necessary for those who are engaged in its administration." Accordingly his earliest concern was to seek guidelines for the image the new office should project. In May 1789 he posed a series of questions to friends and political supporters, among them Adams, Hamilton, Jay, and Robert R. Livingston, asking for advice on the tone of the administration: Should he accept invitations? Should he hold levees and return visits? Should public entertainments be held? He was concerned with protecting his office from trivial demands on his time but even more with the image of the office he presented to the public. He sought, as he said, a social plan that would be designed "to preserve the dignity and respect that was due to the first Magistrate" but would not be considered "as an ostentatious imitation, or mimickry of Royalty."

## SIMPLICITY AND SOCIAL PERCEPTIONS

Washington understood, in a way that Hamilton and Adams did not, that the American people would never accept a system of even limited or mixed monarchy. Although plainly taken with the classical virtues of simplicity and austerity and the image they would portray, Washington—the product of a planter society—was not in the habit of practicing these virtues personally. From the beginning there were criticisms of the presidential household for smacking of seemingly aristocratic ostenta-

tion. The twenty-second of February had by 1791 become almost a national holiday, and critics found the occasions reminiscent of prewar celebrations of the king's birthday. Washington had, detractors said, shut himself off "like an eastern Lama." Indeed, when Thomas Jefferson arrived from France to take up his duties as secretary of state in March 1790, he was shocked at what he viewed as the monarchical trappings of the new administration. When his bows were criticized, Washington was hurt. They were, he protested, "the best I was master of; would it not have been better to throw the veil of charity over them, ascribing their stiffness to the effects of age or to the unskillfulness of my teacher, than to pride and dignity of office, which God knows has no charms for me?" Through both of his administrations there remained an undercurrent of charges of ostentation from Republican critics.

The Washingtons settled in at No. 3 Cherry Street in a house formerly occupied by the president of the Confederation Congress. Much of the furniture was owned by Congress, and Washington used at least part of it throughout both of his administrations, taking it to Philadelphia when the government moved there in 1790. When No. 3 Cherry Street proved to be too small, the presidential household moved in February 1790 to the more opulent Macomb mansion at 39–41 Broadway, just below Trinity Church. The presidential household was substantial. Martha Washington, who had not accompanied the president to New York, arrived in May with her two small grandchildren, George Washington Parke Custis and Eleanor (Nelly) Parke Custis, whom the Washingtons had informally adopted. Tobias Lear, Washington's executive secretary, and Connecticut poet David Humphreys, who had been in residence at Mount Vernon, came to New York with the president. Several additional secretaries were added to the staff over the next few months. To staff the presidential mansion, the Washingtons brought with them seven slaves from Mount Vernon, and they hired some fourteen maids and footmen in New York City.

As a matter of policy the president refused all invitations, but the family seldom lacked for diversion. Washington loved the theater and attended whenever possible, both in New York and in Philadelphia, and his household accounts indicate that the family rarely missed any local amusements of consequence. Like other members of the government, they had to adjust to life in New York. They found the capital very expensive, the weather intemperate, and the people unfamiliar—coming from the peace of a Virginia farm, the household would have agreed with John Adams that their urban neighbors "talk very loud, very fast, and altogether."

Washington eventually established what seems to have been a sensible social regimen. He held one levee a week, on Tuesday afternoons, and usually attended Martha Washington's levees on Friday nights. State dinners were usually held on Fridays, and guests tended to be evenly divided between Federalist congressmen and their opponents on the other side of the aisle. This regimen remained relatively intact after the move to Philadelphia. The food, under the supervision of Washington's steward Samuel Fraucis, offered the kind of culinary opulence Washington was accustomed to at Mount Vernon. Even so, observers such as Pennsylvania congressman William Maclay found the dinners monuments of boredom, presided over by a stiff and unapproachable president. The one bright exception seemed to be the first lady, who elicited almost universal approval, although she noted, "I live a very dull life here and know nothing that passes in the town—indeed I think I am more like a state prisoner than anything else."

## CREATING PUBLIC SUPPORT FOR THE PRESIDENCY

Unlike many of the Revolutionary leaders who aimed their arguments primarily at their educated peers, Washington set out to woo the American public and gain their support for his concept of the executive. One of the main goals of his presidency was to present the new administration in such a way as to attract the loyalty of the mass of Americans—of all factions and parties—to the new republic. The first president was acutely aware of the need of the new nation for national symbols, and he had an extraordinary grasp of the symbolic function of his office. Probably for none of his successors has this aspect of the presidency assumed a more important role. As he had in a sense created his own public persona in the Revolutionary years, he now proceeded to construct the presidency. The term *charisma* was not in vogue in the eighteenth century, but Washington entirely comprehended its function.

Recent biographers have compared this facet of Washington's character to an actor creating his greatest role. It is not a new interpretation. John Adams writing to Benjamin Rush in 1811 made much the same observation:

If he was not the greatest president he was the best actor of the presidency that we have ever had. His address to the states when he left the army, his solemn leave taken of Congress when he resigned his commission, his farewell address to the people of the nation when he resigned the presidency: these were all in a strain of Shakespearean and Garrickal excellency in dramatical exhibitions.

That is not to say that there were not occasions on which Washington lacked style. When Lafayette sent him the key to the Bastille—the symbol of oppression—in 1789, he responded with a token gift—a pair of shoe buckles.

In the first months of Washington's presidency, he gave dual billing to political and economic concerns and to establishing a public image of the executive as a force of importance equal to the legislative. He also was concerned with passing on to the public his own feelings of optimism about the new government. During the Revolution, one of his strengths had been his ability to explain the war and its political objectives to his troops. It was a policy he continued to pursue in the presidency when he developed a number of devices to dramatize the office. Both of his tours, to New England in 1789 and to the southern states in the summer of 1791 (early versions of the swing around the circle), were designed to bring the new executive power home to the people. He used the carefully constructed replies to addresses of public bodies and his annual addresses to Congress to express his optimistic enthusiasm on the prospects of the new government. In a period when much political writing not only was accessible in pamphlets and newspapers but was also read aloud in taverns and churches, his comments were widely disseminated.

Washington's attempt to refuse a salary and receive only his expenses, as he had during the Revolution, was intended to reinforce the image of an executive who was above financial considerations. Congress, remembering wartime criticism—Washington's headquarters had been frugal but not austere—refused the offer and voted him a salary of $25,000 but no expense account. Like his successors, he often found the sum inadequate. He strove, not always successfully, to give the impression that his ambitions were for his office and for the new government and not for himself or even for specific policies of his administration. He deliberately projected the image of aloofness. It is a trait that has often misled later historians into assuming that Washington was not in control of his own presidency. Nothing, in fact, could be further from he truth. If he has seemed stiff and unapproachable to posterity, it is at least partially because this was his intention in maintaining what he viewed as the dignity of his office. He had, John Adams said, the gift of silence.

Washington's game plan for reaching out to the public in no way involved sharing with them the everyday administration of government. Congressmen and senators alike complained that the president listened carefully to their comments but left them singularly uninformed as to his own opinions. William Maclay remarked during the debates on official titles for the president and vice president that the Senate had "no clew" as to the president's views. It is a trait, however invaluable to politicians, that is singularly frustrating to anyone attempting to corner the first president in his papers. Especially for the early presidency, Washington's correspondence is extraordinarily silent on such matters as the Senate debate on the removal power and other matters that closely concerned his office. He had, however, learned the value of discretion early in the war years, discovering that for a public man such a thing as a private remark did not exist. He undoubtedly did unbend in private conferences with men he trusted, but only a few tantalizing records of such conversations remain. "With me," he wrote in 1797, "it has always been a maxim, rather to let my designs appear from my works than my expressions."

Nevertheless, Washington wanted, or thought he wanted, to know how his administration was faring in the eyes of the public. As he wrote David Stuart in August 1789, "I should like to be informed . . . of the public opinion of both men and measures, and of none more than myself, not so much of what may be thought commendable parts, if any, of my conduct, as of those which are conceived to be of a different complexion." Madison, writing some years after his own retirement, observed of Washington that "although not idolizing public opinion, no man could be more attentive to the means of ascertaining it."

## STAFFING THE ADMINISTRATION

Washington was an extraordinarily successful administrator. Following the precepts of Publius in the Federalist Papers, he believed that an efficient government would be a major factor in establishing public confidence. He was able to bring to this purpose his own experience as the commander of the army and the owner of an extensive plantation. It has been aptly suggested that in his search for order Washington sometimes tended to view the world as an expanded version of Mount Vernon. One open channel in his first administration to public views of the new government was the swarm of applications for public office that bombarded him from the beginning of 1789. Nearly a year into his first administration, Washington remarked plaintively in a letter to Catharine Macauley Graham, "I walk on untrodden ground." In no instance was his ground more uncertain than in establishing a civil service for the new nation. He was under no illusion as to the significance of his initial appointments. Not only was the need to staff the civil service imperative but, as he wrote Samuel Vaughan, "Perfectly convinced I am, that, if injudicious or unpopular measures should be taken by the Executive under the new Government with regard to appointments, the Government itself would be in the utmost danger of being utterly subverted by those measures."

Although little is known of Washington's procedures in individual cases, much private consulting clearly took place, and recommendations for appointments were often made in private visits to the president. On these recommendations, as on almost all other matters at the beginning of the new government, Washington kept his own counsel concerning his intentions. Since applications had started at least seven months before his election, he had time to reflect on his procedures in nominating candidates to positions in the new government. Word went out quickly that applicants were expected to address the president directly, and he was even waylaid with requests for public jobs while traveling to New York. He wrote, "There is, I believe, no part of my administration in which I shall find myself more embarrassed than that of nominating persons to office. The pretensions will be so numerous, and many of them so nearly equal that it will require no small degree of discernment and investigation to hit upon the right."

He initially replied to applications with a standard statement that he intended to go into office unhampered by prior commitment, but in the early weeks of his first administration he ceased even to make this perfunctory reply. By the time he took office, he had developed certain criteria for applicants—the fitness of character to fill the office, the comparative merit of the claims of the different candidates for appointments, and the balanced geographical distribution of appointments. What he referred to as fitness for office did not necessarily imply technical competence; rather, it was a judgment of the candidate's integrity, standing in the community, and other personal qualifications. Washington, a man who could tip a glass of madeira with the best of them, had vivid recollections of the officer corps during the Revolution, and he was passionate on the subject of not appointing drunkards to office.

Although the inpouring letters contained the expected number of obsequious compliments to Washington and his election, they also gave him a view of a segment of society almost completely disrupted economically—and sometimes socially—by the Revolution, as well as a glimpse at the level of expectations for the new government. The applications, which often degenerated into desperate pleas for help, tended to come from the middle class—men who had frequently held some sort of office before, and often during the war, or who had served in the army—the very men whom Washington hoped to attach to the new republic. Considering the creation of a federal civil service one of his major responsibilities and one of the areas in which his administration would be most vulnerable, Washington in the first months in office repeatedly reiterated his views on presidential responsibility in making appointments—the need to be free from influence by motives of friendship or nepotism and to base his nominations on fitness for office, on comparative claims, and "on former merits and sufferings in service."

Equally important was his policy of balancing the distribution of applicants among the states. He expected these candidates to have—at the least—not been outspoken opponents of the Constitution. Generally, unless other factors prevented it, he preferred to retain officials who had served in posts under the state governments. Indeed, as he wrote Edward Stevens, "it appears to me, it will be a most unpleasant thing to turn out of office one man, against whom there is no charge of misconduct, merely to make room for another, however conspicuous his integrity and abilities may be." However, Washington did not always nominate incumbents, and unsuccessful candidates did not always take their dismissal meekly. "I have thought it my duty," he wrote the Supreme Court justices on their appointments, "to nominate . . . such men as I conceived would give dignity and lustre to our National Character."

Being familiar with the reputation of many members of the Revolutionary War officer corps and having met many prominent civilians at the Constitutional Convention, Washington had at least some knowledge of many of the candidates. In the absence of such knowledge, he resorted to his favorite procedure of soliciting advice from local acquaintances on appointments within particular states. A shadow of congressional courtesy appeared in this process, since Washington frequently consulted congressmen on appointments in their district, and they apparently also felt free to offer unsolicited advice. He consulted senators less often, commenting that their right to reject a candidate gave them enough power in the selection process. Washington's demand that the candidates apply directly for the job was obviously the most efficient way to proceed since it gave the president a pool of candidates from which to choose and whose acceptance of an offer was almost certain. It was, however, an innovation for eighteenth-century practice, which forbade presenting an appearance of lusting after power or even of being particularly concerned with rewards and emoluments for public service.

## JUDICIAL APPOINTMENTS

The ease with which Washington was able to fill vacancies during his first months in office helps explain his consternation when he ran into major difficulties with judiciary appointments in September of 1789. He considered appointments to the judiciary—"that department which must be considered as the Key-Stone of our political fabric"—to be among the most important of his admin-

istration. He evidently made extensive inquiries about potential candidates. There is perhaps more evidence for Washington's direct involvement in the judiciary appointments than in any other department, and he discussed candidates' qualifications in detail with such advisers as James Madison.

Washington sent the first judiciary appointments to the Senate without first ascertaining whether the individual appointees would accept their posts if confirmed. He was unprepared for the number of refusals he received from these appointees, among them Thomas Pinckney of South Carolina; Edmund Pendleton and John Marshall of Virginia; and Robert Hanson Harrison, Thomas Johnson, and Nathaniel Ramsay of Maryland. Some of the reluctance to serve undoubtedly was due to the general criticism of the provisions for the judiciary, which had been under fire since the Constitutional Convention. But some appointees undoubtedly hesitated to accept because of the uncertainty about whether the prestige of federal judicial appointments would equal that of state appointments. By the end of 1789, Washington was increasingly reluctant to make judicial appointments "unless I can have an assurance—or at least a strong presumption, that the person appointed will accept; for it is to me an unpleasant thing, to have Commissions of such high importance returned, and it will, in fact, have a tendency to bring the Government into discredit."

Although a history of politically correct stands was not openly stated as a condition for appointment to the new government, it was obviously important to Washington. Relatively few who had actively opposed the Constitution or who were overtly critical of the new government received posts. Over the course of both of Washington's administrations, he nominated more than 350 civil officials, not including the Supreme Court Justices and the heads of departments. By 1792, there were about 780 employees, of whom approximately 660 were employed in the Treasury, largely in Customs. Many appointees had relatively mediocre abilities, but few actually disgraced themselves.

Despite occasional rumblings in the press about what Jeffersonians later referred to as "Macadonian phalanxes" of public employees, there appear to have been relatively few public complaints about either numbers or quality of appointments. But as Washington himself observed, "Every reasonable man must conclude, that, with the best possible intentions, it will be impossible to give universal satisfaction."

## EXECUTIVE AND LEGISLATURE

The Constitution had given the president no clear instructions on a number of matters: Questions still remained concerning emergency powers, the suspension of habeas corpus, and his role in the division of powers between the branches of government. Washington proceeded tentatively and with his customary caution. "To form a new government," he had written John Washington in 1776, "requires infinite care and unbounded attention for if the foundation is badly laid, the superstructure must be bad. . . . A matter of such moment cannot be the Work of a day." Whatever Washington's uncertainties in the beginning, he was soon persuaded that his office had its own body of powers independent of the other branches of government. Even at first, his view of the presidency was never that it would be an American version of a European prime minister. And although, as usual, he is silent on the point, it is evident from his actions that he did not subscribe to the Whig theory of congressional over presidential power. But the idea of an imperial presidency was also foreign to his views of the executive role. "For the constitution of the United States, and the laws made under it, must mark the line of my official conduct," he wrote.

The relationship of the executive and the legislature were obviously of the first order of importance. Washington's policy toward the Continental Congress during the war had been notably one of public deference to civilian authority, whatever private views he held of the competence and patriotism of his congressional masters. By the end of the war he had developed considerable skill in dealing with them—a skill he hoped to bring to his relations with the new federal congress, but on new terms of equality. The distinction between what Madison called "the deliberative functions of the House and the ministerial functions of the executive powers" were ill-defined by the Constitution. Even less clearly delineated was the particular interaction between the president and the Senate, although the advice-and-consent clause appeared to Washington to mandate a peculiarly interdependent relationship. In the first days of his administration he proceeded cautiously, suggesting matters for consideration but not blueprints for policy. As usual, his papers from the summer of 1789 give very little indication of his own views.

At first, as is evident from his elaborate consultation with Senate committees on such diverse matters as whether communications should be oral or written, whether the president should wait upon the Senate or vice versa, and on such minor points as the feasibility of an executive chamber where the president could receive the Senate as a whole, Washington took the language of the Constitution on advice and consent literally. He clearly envisioned a close dialogue between equals on all aspects of treaty making. As he wrote to a committee of the Senate in August 1789, many aspects of the executive-legislative relationship called not only for consideration but for open discussion between the Senate and the Executive.

Accordingly, in August 1789, he went to the Senate chambers to pose some questions on the instructions for commissioners appointed to negotiate a treaty with the southern Indians. He then submitted seven questions. Vice President John Adams read each of the questions aloud to the senators, asking at the end of each question, "Do you advise or consent?" The senators sat there in silence until Robert Morris of New York suggested that the president's questions required further study, and he moved that they be referred to a committee of five. Washington, according to Senator William Maclay of Pennsylvania, "started up in a violent fret. 'This defeats every purpose of my coming here.'" In order to assuage the president, the Senate agreed to give its answers within three days. If Washington did not, as was widely reported in the nineteenth century, leave the Senate chambers muttering "I'm damned if I ever come back here again," he undoubtedly entertained some such sentiment.

The episode precipitated a major alteration in his views on the relationship between the Senate and the executive on the treaty-making process. By 1794, when the administration opened treaty negotiations with Great Britain, the anticipation of difficulties with Republicans and the need for secrecy surrounding the negotiation of the Jay treaty (Washington shared Hamilton's distrust of the Senate's discretion) caused him to set the precedent of executive consultation with the Senate only after the negotiation of the treaty.

In Washington's first term, a majority of both the Senate and the House were administration supporters, and most of his suggestions on such matters as Indian negotiations and the military establishment were approved. In a sense Washington, with the aid of his cabinet, had moved into what was essentially a leadership vacuum in the First Congress. He was to find it a more difficult task to deal with succeeding Congresses, although congressional votes on apportionment, on the coinage, and on the power to summon the militias expressed less disillusionment with Washington than a desire to control the executive branch. At the outset of the new government, there was considerable ambition in the Senate to exert some control over the administration through the department heads, but this ambition was not realized. More often, secretaries, especially Hamilton, campaigned for administration measures, occasionally at the president's suggestion.

In his dealings with Congress, Washington was usually careful not to tread on what he regarded as its prerogatives, although he undoubtedly allowed his congressional supporters to lobby their peers. Above all, he avoided direct confrontation. In the first administration when Madison was still his chief congressional adviser, Washington took full advantage of his services to help thwart a Senate attempt to involve itself in the removal of incumbents from office as a corollary to its role in their original appointment. Fighting with Congress, even during his second administration when political turmoil was at its height, would, however, have been an indulgence that would have violated his views of the presidential role.

Washington did sometimes violate his own rules, as in May 1790 when he attempted to persuade supporters in the Senate to reverse the House's reduction of funds for the foreign service. In general, however, he maintained his role of scrupulous noninterference in what he considered legislative prerogatives, and he was careful to project the image of an independent and equal executive. He nevertheless remained suspicious of legislative attempts to undermine the prerogatives of the presidency. As minor a matter as a House resolution in March 1792 congratulating the French government on its new constitution led to his comment that "the legislature wd soon be endeavoring to invade the executive." In 1793, his issuing of the neutrality proclamation without considering consultation with the Senate showed how far he had brought his conception of a strong and independent executive. Evidently he had few reservations about the use of his veto power; as early as July 1789, he wrote David Stuart that he had considered vetoing the tonnage bill but was deterred by remarks from members of the House that new legislation was contemplated. In 1792, he cast his first veto when the reapportionment bill was submitted for his signature. For its part, the Senate had no hesitation in rejecting nominations. Some of its members had waged a vigorous if unsuccessful campaign for Senate involvement in the removal of presidential appointees. Before the new government went into effect, the general view had been that approval of the president's appointments would be a pro forma matter. That view changed when the Senate rejected one of his first appointments—Benjamin Fishbourne of Georgia, apparently the victim of infighting among the Georgia delegation. Washington, obviously piqued, sent a stiff and defensive explanation of his nomination to the Senate.

## CONSULTATION AND CABINET

With his years of experience both as a military leader and as a successful and innovative planter, Washington was at his best as an administrator, and he saw this as one of the major functions of his office. During the war he had been accustomed to seeking advice from his general officers. His habit was to hold councils of war, a device borrowed from European military procedures and one he had used effectively as the young commander of the Virginia Regiment during the French and Indian War. It was a policy he continued to pursue with profit as president. During the first months of the presidency, before the department heads were appointed, he conferred frequently with Madison, especially on matters concerning his relationship to Congress. He also asked his advice on the discarded draft of the first inaugural address and requested that he draft other communications with Congress. Washington held frequent conversations with congressmen during the first summer of his presidency, particularly on nominations, and occasionally sought advice on appointments from trusted friends and acquaintances.

It was universally noted, however, that he kept his own counsel concerning his final decisions. During the neutrality crisis in mid-1793, undeterred by his earlier rebuff by the Senate, he attempted to recruit the Supreme Court into the pool of advisers on foreign affairs, posing a series of questions and requesting their attendance at a meeting much as if they had been cabinet members. To his dismay, the justices refused, on the grounds that their agreement would be a violation of the lines of separation drawn by the Constitution among the three branches of government. Midway through his first term, perhaps by design, he began to rely increasingly on his official family for advice.

There had been discussions in the convention on the device of a cabinet or privy council, and Article II specified opinions in writing from the department heads as a source of counsel for the president. The evolution of the cabinet as an advisory body, however, came only slowly in Washington's presidency. By early September 1789, the main departments had been established by Congress, and Washington, without conferring with the Senate, had made two cabinet appointments—Alexander Hamilton as secretary of the Treasury, and Henry Knox as secretary of war—both trusted subordinates from the war years. The State Department was left under the supervision of John Jay, secretary of foreign affairs under the Confederation government, until Washington could induce Thomas Jefferson to return from France early in 1790 to assume the post. As soon as the great departments were established, Washington's policy, as suggested by the Constitution, was to deal directly with the secretaries on matters, particularly administrative questions, that concerned their departments.

But in the midst of the heavy flow of business, some matters emerged that transcended the departments. Over the next two years, the president asked for written opinions on a number of matters from the secretaries separately—on relations between the United States and Great Britain, on the sale of Georgia lands, on the constitutionality of the Bank of the United States. Then, in the spring of 1791 when he was about to embark on his southern tour, Washington wrote to Jefferson, Knox, and Hamilton stating that if any serious matters were to arise during his absence they should "hold consultations thereon," thus providing for collective action on the part of the cabinet. If necessary, the president said, he would return to Philadelphia, but on noncrucial matters, the secretaries should agree on action, which he would validate on his return. The secretaries did in fact take such action in April 1791 on a matter concerning foreign loans—and Washington approved their decisions on his return. There is documentary evidence for several formal meetings between the president and the heads of the departments in 1791 and 1792, and it is likely that others were held. The ad hoc procedures gradually developed into genuine cabinet meetings. By the time of the neutrality crisis in 1793, cabinet meetings had become a regular function of the executive and the department heads, with the president calling the meetings, often with very little notice and with a request for the secretaries to bring with them written opinions.

The cabinet had considerable authority to act in the absence of the president, and Washington was absent a considerable amount of time—at least 180 days in his two administrations. Except for his two presidential tours, most of his time away from the capital was spent at Mount Vernon, for his view of his presidential role did not dictate the abandonment of his private affairs. He remained deeply immersed in the management of his Mount Vernon plantations and his western lands throughout both of his terms. After the war, with tobacco prices falling, he had been one of the first planters on the Potomac and Chesapeake to diversify his crops. He was deeply committed, although with varying success, to innovative use of his labor force and to experimental agriculture on his plantations. During the presidential years, he ran Mount Vernon from New York and later from Philadelphia, sending weekly instructions, in detail, in reply to his managers' reports on planting and construction, on the use of the plantation's slave labor, and on the financial state of the mills and fisheries.

The *Journal of the Proceedings of the President*, an administrative journal that Washington's secretaries kept between 1793 and 1797, indicates that virtually all correspondence and information of any importance coming to the department heads was submitted to the president for examination and decision. Thomas Jefferson, writing to Madison in 1801 in preparing his own presidential procedures, recommended Washington's methods of using the department heads as a formal advisory body, stating that by this means he was always in accurate possession of all facts & proceedings in every part of the Union, & to whatever department they related; for they formed a central point for the different branches, preserved a unity of object and action among them, exercised that participation in the gestation of affairs which his office made incumbent on him, and met himself the due responsibility for whatever was done.

Although Washington detested the squabbling between Hamilton and Jefferson—it smacked of the factionalism he abhorred—the president kept the warring secretaries on a fairly tight leash. That he was able to retain their services well into his second administration attests to his executive ability. Their successors in the second administration were competent enough, but mediocre in comparison to the constellation in the first cabinet.

## ACCOMPLISHMENTS OF WASHINGTON'S FIRST TERM

Given the degree of national divisiveness in 1787 and 1788 during the debates in the states over ratification of the Constitution, Washington's success in cementing the Union and establishing the executive as a respected and even revered icon of the U.S. constitutional system was a remarkable achievement. At the end of his first administration in 1792, he could entertain a considerable sense of gratification that administration policies for the new government had largely succeeded. Hamilton's financial system—including the funding of the debt and the controversial establishment of the Bank of the United States—had, with Washington's support, been accepted, although accompanied with ominous rumblings from critics in Congress and elsewhere. Financially and commercially the young nation seemed on an even keel. British retention of American frontier posts still rankled, and there were continuing concerns with Indian encroachments on the northern and southern frontiers. The administration's most embarrassing setbacks were the failure of two major expeditions against the Indians in 1790 and 1791 under Josiah Harmar and Arthur St. Clair. A flurry of concern arose in the fall of 1790 over the eruption of the Nootka Sound crisis between Great Britain and Spain and whether it might draw the United States into a potential conflict, but it soon evaporated. Washington was still able to maintain his stance in keeping the presidency itself above the burgeoning party affiliations. He had pursued vigorous if not always successful attempts to regularize diplomatic relations with Great Britain and to negotiate a commercial treaty with the new nation's best customer. In all, the first administration had been a mixture of success and disappointments.

But as the time for the second presidential election approached, Washington had reason to believe that he had fulfilled his commitments of holding office until the new nation, and especially the role of the executive, had been established. Now at age 60 and at the end of his first term, he hoped to return to his Mount Vernon plantation. During his first term, he had had at least two serious illnesses, one of them life-threatening, which had given rise to a flurry of public speculation about the fate of the new republic in hands other than his. Washington's decision to retire appeared firm, and he went so far as to request Madison's assistance in preparing a farewell address to the nation. He was persuaded to remain mainly by the concerted arguments, some bordering on the hysterical, of his cabinet and others that there was no viable successor and that his retirement would lead to partisan strife and eventual disunion. Washington was reelected in 1792, as expected, with all but three electoral votes, and even these three were abstentions. "It is more than probable," he admitted, "that I shold for a moment, have experienced chagreen if my reelection had not been by a pretty respectable vote."

As always obsessed with his reputation, Washington was also influenced by the things that would have been left undone on his departure. He had become intimately in-

volved with the construction of the new Federal City, to which the capital would move in 1800 after a decade's stay in Philadelphia. He had pushed for its location on the Potomac in preference to other sites, and the favorable financial aspects of its proximity to Mount Vernon were not lost on the disappointed supporters of other locations. Although authorized by Congress to supervise the creation of the new capital, Washington's involvement went far beyond his mandate, and he became enmeshed in every aspect of the city's construction, personally supervising the surveyors and the commissioners for the city, presiding over decisions on the plans for the capitol and other public buildings, and paying frequent visits to inspect progress on the site. Washington is usually not regarded as having a specific political agenda, but he would have subscribed in large part to the Federalist agenda for the country. Their fiscal policy, in which they largely succeeded, included putting the nation on a firm fiscal basis, through funding the national debt, establishing the Bank of the United States, and assuming state debts. They were less successful in establishing a national economy by aiding manufacturers, supporting the fisheries, sponsoring internal improvements, and developing western lands.

## THE SECOND TERM

There were victories even in the second administration, although in some cases the administration paid a high political price for them. One of the successes in the second administration was the effectual settlement of the Indian crisis on the Ohio frontier. After the disastrous defeat of Arthur St. Clair's forces in November 1791 by the western tribes, Washington pushed, as he always had, for the establishment of adequate military forces—preferably a national army supported by state militia—to protect the country's frontiers. Simultaneously, however, he pursued alternative courses, sending commissioners to attempt to settle differences with the tribes. Because of his experience as commander of the Virginia Regiment during the French and Indian

War and his extensive ventures in western land speculation, Washington probably knew as much about the frontier as any man of his time. Part of his dream for the future of the new country lay in the expansion of settlement into frontier areas.

One of the legacies he brought with him to the presidency was a healthy respect for the fighting abilities of Native American tribes and an understanding of their grievances unusual for his time. And his experiences with frontiersmen had not impressed him either with their sense of public responsibility or the validity of many of their complaints. As he wrote Edmund Randolph in 1795, Indians themselves "are not without serious causes of complaint, from the encroachments which are made on their lands by our people; who are not to be restrained by any law now in being, or likely to be enacted. They, poor wretches, have no Press thro' which their grievances are related." He pushed Congress to "make fair treaties with the Savage tribes by this I mean that they shall perfectly understand every article and clause of them . . . that these treaties shall be held sacred, and the infractors in either side punished exemplarily." When peace attempts broke down in early 1793, however, he made stringent efforts to support Anthony Wayne's devastating campaign against the western tribes. His victory at Fallen Timbers and the subsequent Treaty of Greenville effectually secured the northern frontiers.

## FOREIGN AFFAIRS—
## FRANCE AND GREAT BRITAIN

During Washington's first administration there were relatively few crises concerning foreign policy, and almost none caused major domestic involvement. The outbreak of war between Great Britain and France in January 1793, however, precipitated a major upheaval. The United States was almost immediately involved since, by the terms of the 1778 treaty with France, the new government was obligated not only to offer France the assistance due to any ally but to defend her West Indian possessions. Washington was dismayed that Federalist support

for Britain and Republican support for France had further polarized domestic political activities. He agreed with Hamilton that involving the country in a war with Great Britain would destroy his administration's economic platform, much of which was predicated on a thriving trade with Britain. He also was personally appalled by the excesses of the French Revolution and had little inclination to aid France's new masters. Washington viewed the French treaty, which had been a lifeline in 1778, as an albatross in 1793, when it offered the United States only the possibility of involvement in a major European war and further domestic discord.

In April 1793, after extensive consultation with the cabinet but not with the Senate, Washington issued a proclamation asserting the neutrality of the United States in the Anglo-French war. The neutrality proclamation, almost universally regarded by the Republicans as a violation of constitutional curbs on presidential powers, marked the beginning of the end for Washington's attempts to maintain a strictly nonpartisan presidency. His policies in dealing with France's army of privateers in American ports and with the antics of Edmond Genêt and the negotiation and ratification of the Jay Treaty convinced Republicans that Washington had been captured by Federalist politicians. Over the next two years, attacks by opposition politicians and press involved not only administration policies but the president himself. Washington, quite unaccustomed to such treatment, had been criticized before—during the French and Indian War and during the Revolution—but never on this personal level. He was devastated and it affected not only his personal views of his presidency but his public reactions as well. From the beginning of 1793, he moved ever closer to the Federalist camp.

## PERSONAL DISILLUSION

In mid-1796, Washington began to prepare his Farewell Address to the nation. His views of the new republic had changed drastically since Madison had drawn up a first draft in 1792. The turmoils of recent years—the neutrality crisis, the fight over the Jay Treaty, the Whiskey Insurrection, the activities of the Democratic societies— had created a public climate from which Washington felt increasingly alienated. All his fears, both for the nation and for his own reputation at the beginning of his presidency, had been realized. The personal vilification of his role had reached enormous proportions and, as he wrote Henry Know, was "couched in such exaggerated & indecent terms as could scarcely be applied to a Nero, a serious defaulter, or even to a common pickpocket." Jefferson's scathing comments on "men who were Samsons in the field and Solomons in the council, but who had had their heads shorn by the harlot England" helped cost him Washington's friendship. Increasingly, newspapers carried such reports as the list of toasts at a Lynchburg, Virginia, meeting in which attendees uncharacteristically placed their toast to Washington last, admonishing him "to remember that he [was] but a man; the servant of the people." Washington had regarded the adulation he formerly attracted as a glue to help bind the people to their government. Washington, like most people, preferred praise to blame. His extreme aversion to criticism, however, amounted almost to an obsession.

Washington was extraordinarily thin-skinned—an unusual flaw in a man of such political skill—and he would have recoiled from the modern give and take of politics. Much of this attitude goes back to his early years when he conceived not only the persona he would later develop with such skill but also the similar ideals he would pursue for the development of a national character. He dreamed of a state that would be based on the same classic axioms that had guided him in his youth. Washington had a passion for order not only in his personal life and on his plantations but on a national level as well. He was a perfectionist himself, and he sought perfection in others and in the state. Few men lived up to his expectations either privately or publicly. His philosophy of life carried over in the political arena: As he had

written to Lafayette in 1789, "Nothing but harmony, honesty, industry and frugality are necessary to make us a great and happy people." To modern observers, the development of the party system during the 1790s may seem a symptom of healthy evolution of the new republic and even a corollary to its burgeoning democracy. To Washington, it was disorder heralding a death knell; he had little conception of a responsible opposition.

When Shays's rebellion erupted in 1786, Washington, writing to Benjamin Lincoln in Massachusetts, asked "Are your people getting mad? Are we to have the goodly fabrick we were nine years raising, pulled over our heads? What is the cause of all this? When and where is it to end?" Protests in Kentucky against the Jay Treaty elicited the comment that "there must exist a predisposition among them to be dissatisfied under any circumstances, and under every exertion of government." In 1794, when he led federal troops into western Pennsylvania to put down the Whiskey rebels, Washington argued that they represented "a daring and factious spirit which . . . ought to be subdued. If this is not done . . . we may bid adieu to all government in this Country, except Mob and Club Govt."

Washington's own political philosophy came less from the philosophers of the Enlightenment than from the pragmatism of the Scottish philosophers, with their emphasis on the uniformity of human nature. It fitted in well with his own classical predilections. Far from being an egalitarian, he rarely considered that public disorders and factious behavior during his presidency might spring from the same motives that had sent him to war in 1775. In spite of the rhetoric of the Revolution, America was still in many ways a society of deference, and Washington no more questioned the political and social validity of the prevailing ideas of rule by an elite than he questioned his own position in such a society.

In the political unrest of the mid-1790s and his own sense of repudiation by his fellow citizens, Washington misread his role in the political life of the new nation. That his contributions to the creation and development of the young republic had been indispensable and unparalleled was not lost on the American people. In spite of the cavils of contemporary newspaper editors and his own fears, Washington's place was safe among American icons. But some of the political assumptions he had brought with him from his youth had lost their validity. At the time of his death in 1799, Washington retained the reverence of most Americans, but he retained it even though much of the citizenry had moved away from the kind of classical ideals and symbols for which he stood. The populist festivities at Jefferson's inauguration spoke much more to a vocal and increasingly self-important electorate than did Washington's stilted levees and his imposing European coach. But most of his fellow countrymen would surely have supported the words he wrote shortly before he went to New York in 1789: "I may err, notwithstanding my most strenuous effort to execute the difficult trust with fidelity and unexceptionability, but errors shall be of the head—not of the heart."

## BIBLIOGRAPHY

Abbot, W. W., Dorothy Twohig, Philander D. Chase, Beverly H. Runge, eds. *The Papers of George Washington*, 44 vols. to date (University Press of Virginia, 1982– ).

Boller, Paul F. *George Washington and Religion* (Southern Methodist University Press, 1963).

Decatur, Stephen. *The Private Affairs of George Washington from the Records and Accounts of Tobias Lear* (Riverside Press, 1933).

DeConde, Alexander. *Entangling Alliance: Politics and Diplomacy Under George Washington* (University of North Carolina Press, 1958).

Ferling, John. *The First of Men: A Life of George Washington* (University of Tennessee Press, 1988).

Flexner, James T. *George Washington*, 4 vols. (Little, Brown, 1965–1972).

Freeman, Douglas Southall. *George Washington*, 7 vols. (Charles Scribner's Sons, 1949–1957).

MacDonald, Forrest. *The Presidency of George Washington* (University Press of Kansas, 1974).

Miller, John C. *The Federalist Era, 1789–1801* (Harper & Row, 1960).

Phelps, Glenn. *George Washington and American Constitutionalism* (University Press of Kansas, 1993).

Schwartz, Barry. *George Washington: The Making of an American Symbol* (Free Press, 1987).

Sears, Louis Martin. *George Washington and the French Revolution* (Greenwood Press, 1960).

Smith, Richard Norton. *Patriarch* (Houghton Mifflin, 1993).

Sword, Wiley. *President Washington's Indian War: The Struggle for the Old Northwest, 1790–1795* (University of Oklahoma Press, 1985).

Twohig, Dorothy, ed. *The Journal of the Proceedings of the President, 1793–1797* (University Press of Virginia, 1981).

Wills, Garry. *Cincinnatus: George Washington and the Enlightenment* (Doubleday, 1984).

★★★ 2 ★★★

# JOHN ADAMS
## 1797–1801

*Alan V. Briceland*

---

*Born 30 October 1735 in Braintree (now Quincy), Massachusetts, to John Adams and Susanna Boylston Adams; educated at Harvard College (B.A. 1755); married Abigail Smith, 25 October 1764, Weymouth, Massachusetts; five children; elected vice president in 1788 and 1792; elected president in 1796, defeating Thomas Jefferson (who became vice president) in the electoral college, 71 votes to 68; died 4 July 1826 in Quincy, Massachusetts; buried in First Unitarian Church, Quincy, Massachusetts.*

---

Stout in stature and intellectual but blunt in manner, John Adams brought to the presidency in 1797 a set of experiences that should have prepared him to deal with the foreign relations crisis that dominated his administration. Yet, while historians have generally judged that he acted with courage and correctness in dealing with France, his contemporaries overwhelmingly condemned his actions and made him, of the first five presidents, the only one not elected to a second term. Historians Stanley Elkins and Eric McKitrick have summarized the critical question relative to Adams' presidency by asking whether Adams achieved peace with France by putting country above party at the expense of his own reelection, as he believed, or whether his "erratic executive behavior—his touchiness, vanity, impulsiveness, and failure to consult adequately with his cabinet" caused him to succeed "in spite of himself, and at unnecessary cost to both his own political fortunes and those of the Federalist party"? Could Adams, they ask, have acted in a more "deliberate and measured way ... without catching party leaders by surprise with impetuous executive decisions and without alienating sentiment for a resolute footing for military preparedness?" John Adams's presidential successes and failures were a product of his foreign affairs experience, his unique personality, and his inability to understand the role of the emerging institution known as the political party.

John Adams was born into a prosperous farm family in Braintree (now Quincy), Massachusetts, in October 1735. At Harvard between 1751 and 1755 he developed his talents for reading, writing, and self-criticism. At Worcester, while teaching in public school, he was drawn to the study of the law. He passed the bar in 1758 and returned to Braintree where he divided his time between the family farm, which he inherited in 1761, and the practice of law. In 1764 he married Abigail Smith, whose intellect and strength of will matched his own.

## FROM LOCAL TO
## NATIONAL PROMINENCE

The Stamp Act of 1765 marked a turning point not only for British America but for John Adams. While his cousin Sam Adams organized boycotts and mobs, John penned a series of articles for the Boston *Gazette*. The stamp tax was, Adams insisted, "inconsistent with the spirit of the common law and of the essential fundamental principles of the British Constitution." That fall, Adams composed a list of principles to guide Braintree's legislative delegate. The logic and power of these "Braintree Instructions" led to their adoption by forty Massachusetts town meetings. When the Boston town meeting chose Adams as one of three persons to present their petition against the tax to the royal governor, he was plucked from relative obscurity and thrust to the forefront of the revolutionary movement.

Adams, who favored reasoned protest over violent acts, was nonetheless swept into the aftermath of the 5 March 1770 deadly confrontation—later known as the Boston Massacre—in which a mob of urban workmen, bent on avenging an earlier brawl, bullied and threatened a squad of British soldiers into discharging their weapons. The soldiers were subsequently tried in Boston for manslaughter, and Adams served as their lawyer. His reputation as a friend to liberty suffered when, as a result of his skillful defense, Captain Thomas Preston was acquitted and only two soldiers were given minor sentences. Some authorities have attributed Adams's unpopular conduct in this episode to a principled belief that even the most notorious defendants deserved legal representation. Others believe that the leaders of the patriot cause were so certain of the soldiers' guilt that they sought out Adams in order to deprive the loyalists of any arguments that the trial had been unfair. But Adams's acceptance of the role may also have been his way of asserting independence from all factions, even the patriot party. Adams could work with others, but his fierce personal independence never allowed him to subordinate himself to a "party's" program.

When Virginia issued a call for colonial representatives to meet in Philadelphia in 1774 at the First Continental Congress, John Adams moved from the local to the national arena. Here his goal was to unite the other colonies in support of Massachusetts's resistance to Parliament's Coercive Acts. By 1775, well ahead of most delegates to the Second Continental Congress, Adams was leading the fight for independence from Great Britain. He also provided key legislative support for the organization of the Continental Army and the Continental Navy. From this point on, the independence and military preparedness of the United States were never far from his thoughts. When a committee was appointed to write a Declaration of Independence, he was on it. Over the course of three years he served on ninety congressional committees, many of them closely related to the conduct of war.

## REPRESENTING AMERICA ABROAD

For the better part of a decade (1778–1788), Adams was immersed in European diplomacy. Sent by Congress to strengthen American ties with France, he arrived after the French alliance of 1778 had been concluded but in time to become disillusioned by what he perceived to be French manipulation of fellow diplomats Benjamin Franklin and Arthur Lee. Returning to America, Adams became the key participant in the Massachusetts Constitutional Convention of 1779, but he was again dispatched to Europe with instructions from Congress to negotiate treaties of peace and commerce with Great Britain. Since the British were not yet willing to admit defeat in 1780, Adams, always determined to be usefully employed, established himself in the Netherlands. By 1782, two years of negotiations had produced Dutch recognition of the United States and a much needed loan of over $2 million. Although instructed by Congress to follow the French lead in negotiating a peace treaty with Britain, Adams entertained such strong suspicions of the French Foreign Minister, the Count de Vergennes, that he led John Jay and Benjamin Franklin into the separate negotiations that successfully guaranteed American independence.

After five years living in or near France, Adams assumed his next assignment, which sent him to England as the first U.S. minister to Great Britain. Having experienced French diplomatic intrigues, he now encountered British diplomatic obstinacy. Frustrated by Britain's determination not to allow an independent America to trade with British colonies, Adams asked to be recalled. Returning home in 1788 after his long residence in Europe, he believed he had sized up both the French and the English. Hamiltonians and Jeffersonians would soon be making their assessments of these nations from a distance, and they might, as Adams saw it, incautiously choose to throw themselves into the arms of one or the other of these self-interested powers. As a result of prolonged, frustrating, personal experience, Adams believed that America's interests lay in maintaining its independence from both.

## ELECTED VICE PRESIDENT, THEN PRESIDENT

The nation's new Constitution having been ratified in 1788, Adams returned shortly before the first federal elections were held. His revolutionary contributions—considered second only to those of George Washington—brought him the second highest number of electoral votes, thirty-four, which made him vice president during Washington's first term. Political parties had not yet formed, and the role of the vice president was still undefined by precedent. Confident in his own intellect (and doubtful about that of the Senate) Adams annoyed the senators by advocating—unsuccessfully—the use of monarchical titles and ceremonies and by delivering condescending lectures on how they should vote. During Washington's first term, with the Senate closely divided over the Hamiltonian economic system, Adams cast twenty tie-breaking votes. Although not elected as Washington's surrogate, Adams found himself casting his votes in agreement with the president.

Despite Adams's distaste for factions and parties, the policies of the Washington administration divided the Congress and the public into two philosophical and political camps. The Federalists, although titularly headed by Washington, were intellectually guided by Alexander Hamilton. The Republicans, organized by James Madison, were intellectually guided by Thomas Jefferson. With Washington's retirement, most Federalists rallied to Adams as being sufficiently prominent and right thinking to keep Jefferson from claiming the office. Believing that positions of trust should seek the man, neither Adams nor Jefferson attempted to influence the outcome of the 1796 election. Adams's supporters, however, branded Jefferson an atheist, while Jefferson's adherents branded Adams an antidemocratic monarchist.

Fearful of Adams's independent ways, those close to Hamilton maneuvered to replace Adams with Thomas Pinckney of South Carolina. Their machinations, however, served only to reduce Adams's electoral margin of victory to a mere three votes over Jefferson, who became vice president. Adams's interpretation of the election results provide a key to understanding his problems as president. Adams saw in the election not two parties but three. The English party, led by Hamilton, would make the United States dependent on Britain. The French party, led by Jefferson, would tie the nation to French interests. Others might label Adams a Federalist, but he saw himself as head of an independent American party.

Prior to his inauguration, Adams learned of Hamilton's efforts to deny him the presidential prize. It proved devastating to the Federalist party that neither Adams nor Hamilton were forgiving men. Had the two been able to join forces during the crisis of 1798, the nation would have been strengthened and the Federalist party might have remained a viable alternative to the Jeffersonians well into the nineteenth century.

The Hamiltonian faction of the Federalists correctly assessed the new president. His independence and prickly personality were impediments to political success under the new governmental system. Operating by his own moral and intellectual compass, Adams was neither a reliable nor a predictable party leader. He seldom looked to others for advice and, even worse for a president, was unwilling to cultivate the support of others or to compromise to gain their support for his initiatives.

## THE CHARACTER OF THE MAN

John Adams was bright but opinionated. His passionate loyalty to his own ideas engendered passionate animosity for those who disagreed with him. Adams had been elected because people recognized his honesty, judgment, and dedication to the public good, but he could be governed by his emotions as well as his intellect. He was overly sensitive to criticism and prone to self-justification. He was patient but relentless in some matters. On others, the strength of his

conviction led him to despair that others were unable to perceive what he viewed as plain facts. Yet he was always hardest on himself—so much so that, in the opinion of Elkins and McKitrick, he "could not be quite settled in his mind about the worth of any choice to be made or any end to be pursued unless it somehow held out personal disadvantage, difficulty, and even a strong prospect of failure."

John Adams was always concerned for his reputation. He believed that true fame and reputation would come only through work and dedication and that success, reputation, and wealth were worthless unless earned. His study of history had convinced him that forceful executive leadership was essential to the success of popular governments. But, also believing in the separation of powers, he was convinced that such leadership was properly used to check legislative abuse, not to build a legislative following. A president's responsibility was not to respond to popular ignorance, but to do what was right. Confident in his own judgment, he could not be swayed from it to court popularity.

In addition to his experience in European diplomacy and his knowledge of political theory, Adams brought a number of advantages to the presidency. He was a farmer who was nonetheless well acquainted with business and high finance. Having lived in Boston, New York, Philadelphia, and abroad, he was not provincial in his views. He was an avid reader and a practiced writer and was by long habit committed to filling his days with productive work. After eight years as vice president, Adams was personally acquainted with the views and personalities of virtually everyone in government. Historian Ralph Adams Brown has summarized Adams's readiness for office: "Driven by ambition, intellectual curiosity, a feeling of responsibility and concern for the welfare of mankind; aware of his ability, yet often filled with doubts and questions—Adams never backed away from a problem and made great demands upon himself."

As president, Adams looked to others for information but made his own decisions with minimal advice. Since the people and their electors had chosen him on the basis of his competence and judgment, he owed them the use of that judgment. He could not trust the advice of a cabinet more loyal to Alexander Hamilton than to himself, and he had none of the staff, bureaucracy, or experts available to modern presidents. He was not prone to quick decisions, but once having decided, he was generally so convinced of the rightness of his decision that he would persevere in it. Benjamin Rush said of Adams that he "saw the whole of a subject at a single glance, and by a happy union of the powers of reasoning and persuasion often succeeded in carrying measures which were at first sight of an unpopular nature."

## INTELLECTUAL PRINCIPLES

One of those measures, independence, underpinned his entire political career. Historian Edmund S. Morgan has said of Adams that "one can understand his subsequent role in American History only by bearing in mind how closely Adams identified himself with the independence of the United States." Having committed so much of himself to gaining independence, he remained dedicated to the equally taxing endeavor of securing independence for the long run. He was determined that the newly independent United States would not revert to dependence on another nation. Dependence in the midst of a world conflict between superpowers was both dangerous and morally debilitating. European influences would only contaminate and sap America's virtue. European rivalries and intrigues would only divide and weaken the ability of the United States to preserve a way of life based on morality, simple living, honesty, and hard work. By contrast, Adams associated Europe's way of life with the qualities of vice, luxury, corruption, and laziness.

Shortly before his inauguration, Adams wrote, "I have but few years of life left, and they cannot be better bestowed than upon that independence of my country, in defence of which that life has ever been in jeopardy." Adams's presidential goals—unity, neutrality, and military preparedness—were

a continuation of his fight for independence. With such high stakes, Adams was determined to make life difficult for anyone he believed to be undermining the independence of the United States.

A second intellectual principle guiding Adams's life—the principle of separation of powers—postulated that human nature, too often subject to the domination of passion and emotion, required regulation and control. Fearful of public prejudices and opposed to violent remedies, Adams supported strong government. Public officials should be respected. Laws, properly made, must be obeyed. Even so, Adams's concern was not governmental power but the abuse of that power. During the revolutionary struggle with Britain he had learned to fear executive dominance of the legislature. But, unlike most Americans, he also acknowledged the probability that a majority would use its dominance of the legislature to abuse the liberties of minorities. Distrusting power, he believed the protection against its misuse was a system that balanced contending interests against one another: "Power," he asserted, "must be opposed to power, force to force, strength to strength, interest to interest." He had embodied these principles in the Massachusetts Constitution of 1780 and in his *A Defense of the Constitutions of the United States of America against the Attack of M. Turgot*. Nonetheless, as important as these principles were in establishing stable governments for the American people, they hampered Adams's performance as president. Believing it wrong for the executive directly to influence the deliberations and decisions of the Congress, President Adams failed to provide necessary legislative leadership in support of his programs and party.

## POLITICAL PARTIES
## AND GOVERNMENT

Adams's intellectual Achilles heel was his misunderstanding of the importance of political parties. Most Americans in the 1790s found it difficult (and Adams found it next to impossible) to subordinate personal judgment and independence to a political party's program. The new Constitution, the structure of which had been greatly influenced by Adams's writing, required compromise and cooperation among the members of the various federal branches in making decisions, enacting laws, and carrying out policy. In short, the governmental system required people to create and work through parties.

Adams never accepted the necessity of parties, platforms, compromise, and cooperation. Thus, for all of his worldly experience, the irony was that few men came to the presidency with as little practical political experience as did John Adams. Believing the president should remain above partisan politics, he was incapable of manipulating support for his policies or of putting together a congressional majority in support of his initiatives, or of subordinating his personal views to the majority positions of his own political party.

Above all, John Adams had not accepted the presidency to serve special interests. His role, as he saw it, was not to be guided by the people so much as it was to educate and guide them. Unfortunately, he failed to understand that the people were no longer willing to defer to their betters for political guidance; they had opinions of their own. The success of his earlier campaign for "independence" had made them the masters of their government. When, ironically, he refused to acknowledge that fact, it robbed him of a successful administration.

## INHERITED PROBLEMS
The new president inherited a situation, the parameters of which had been established by his predecessor, in which foreign affairs dominated the scene. Europe was at war, yet the United States, with its army numbering less than two thousand men and its naval force composed of a single unarmed customs vessel, was virtually defenseless. British warships regularly impressed U.S. seamen. France, embittered by what it saw as a U.S. surrender by way of the Jay Treaty to British domination, was encouraging its privateers to seize U.S. ships and cargos.

As a consequence of President Washington's support for the Hamiltonian program,

Adams found few points of agreement on which to build a national consensus. While many citizens fervently believed that America needed a stronger national government, even more were convinced that it was already too powerful. The controversy over the ratification of the Jay Treaty exposed sharp divisions over foreign affairs. The economy was less than vibrant. Most important, Adams was not Washington. As respected as the new president was, he could not command the loyalty of every American in the way Washington had. Washington's retirement left a vacuum no one could have filled.

## TAKING OFFICE
The foreign affairs controversy of the Adams administration had its origins in the French Revolution. Jeffersonianism attracted Americans who conceived of the French Revolution as a popular uprising of liberty against tyranny and therefore deserving of the support of all liberty-loving people. Those who believed that the French Revolution had degenerated into tyranny and military expansionism were almost universally Federalists. Disagreement over the seriousness of the threat posed by France had further divided the Federalists into two camps, one led by Alexander Hamilton and seeking closer ties to Britain, and another led by John Adams and wanting strict neutrality.

In his 4 March 1797 inaugural address, Adams sought to assure the Republicans that he was as opposed to monarchy as they were and that he had a sincere desire to preserve U.S. ties with France dating back to 1778. He appealed for national unity in dangerous times. While the Jeffersonians praised the president's remarks, adherents of his own party were troubled. When Adams privately reached out to the Republicans by floating the idea of appointing James Madison as special envoy to France, his secretary of the treasury, Oliver Wolcott, Jr., blocked the initiative by threatening to resign. Wolcott and the Hamilton-led Federalists feared that a Republican diplomat would betray American interests.

Adams chose to keep Washington's entire cabinet—Oliver Wolcott, Jr., Timothy Pickering, James McHenry, and Charles Lee—because he valued experience, because he feared that their removals would further splinter his already fracturing party, and because noncompetitive government salaries prevented the recruitment of truly qualified applicants. This, however, proved to be a major mistake. Adams's cabinet was not only a collection of mediocre talents but was disloyal as well. Wolcott, Pickering, and McHenry looked for guidance to Alexander Hamilton. Adams compounded his error by spending the warm weather months on his Massachusetts farm, far from the seat of government in Philadelphia. Although he was in regular contact by mail, his absences nonetheless encouraged his disloyal secretaries to follow their own inclinations into policies that were not of Adams's making.

## CONFRONTING FRANCE

When Federalist Charles Cotesworth Pinckney arrived in France in December 1796 to replace pro-French minister James Monroe, the French Directory declared it would not receive him or any other U.S. ambassador until its grievances against the United States had been redressed. Relations with France deteriorated rapidly during Adams's first year in office as the Directory communicated its displeasure with U.S. trade policies, Jay Treaty concessions to Britain, and Adams's election. The French government issued a series of hostile edicts designed to punish the unruly Americans. By renouncing the principle that "free ships make free goods" (that is, that neutral ships could freely carry belligerent cargoes) and adopting in its place the principle that a single item of British origin on a U.S. merchant vessel subjected the entire cargo and vessel to confiscation, the Directory unleashed scores of French privateers bent on seizing every U.S. merchantman in the West Indies and the Mediterranean.

These French acts were simply the latest in a series of indignities imposed on the United States by Britain, Spain, France, and Algeria in little more than a decade. Adams's immediate problem was with France, but this was one element in a larger context of the general European perception that the United States could be intimidated with impunity. Knowing Americans to be incapable of offensive action against French possessions and, therefore, that hostilities would expose U.S. lives and property to attack with no option of retaliating, Adams played for time to prepare the public for the necessity of a military build-up.

Adams's cabinet, led by Francophobe Secretary of State Timothy Pickering, was anxious to turn the Directory's affront into a declaration of war until Alexander Hamilton privately warned that public opinion was not yet properly prepared. Calling Congress into special session on 15 May 1797, Adams presented a program designed to achieve peace through strength. He announced the appointment of a three-member commission, composed of southern Federalists John Marshall and C. C. Pinckney and New England Republican Elbridge Gerry. The commission's charge was to reestablish diplomatic relations with France, bring an end to the seizure of American ships, arrange for a settling of claims, and terminate the mutual defense provisions of the Treaty of 1778.

Adams firmly believed that the United States needed a permanent military establishment and that the French would have no incentive to deal with U.S. commissioners unless they thought the United States was making reasonable preparations for war. He therefore asked Congress to authorize completion of three frigates (the *Congress*, the *President*, and the *Chesapeake*) whose construction had been halted in 1796 and to allow the arming of U.S. merchant vessels. For land defenses, the president proposed enlarging the almost nonexistent army for the duration of the crisis, strengthening fortifications guarding major ports, and enacting laws for uniformly organizing, arming, and disciplining the state militias. Completion of the frigates and a little money for harbor defense was approved, but Republicans, who controlled the House, blocked the other proposals as provocative.

## THE XYZ AFFAIR

On 8 October 1797, the U.S. commissioners met briefly and unofficially in Paris with French Minister of Foreign Affairs Talleyrand. The wily foreign minister sized up the situation as providing an opportunity for both private and public gain. After leaving the three Americans to cool their heels for several weeks, Talleyrand sent emissaries to inform them that, prior to any official negotiations, the United States would have to pay a bribe of $250,000 to the Directors and make a "loan" of $12 million to the French government. To add insult to injury, Talleyrand required a public apology for allegedly offensive remarks that Adams had made to the May special congressional session.

Adams did not receive the commissioners' account of these events until 4 March 1798. Within days he informed Congress that the conciliatory U.S. initiative had been rebuffed. He again pointed to the necessity for defense expenditures and vowed that the United States would attempt no further rapprochement until France gave assurances that an ambassador would be "received, respected and honored as the representative of a great, free, powerful and independent nation."

Congressional Republicans, confident that their opponents were magnifying the gravity of French insults for political advantage, demanded proof. Knowing the correspondence substantiated his claims, Adams gladly submitted it to Congress, excising only the names of Talleyrand's go-betweens and substituting the letters *X, Y,* and *Z.* When the Senate made the documents public in April 1798, the press latched onto the letters, and the so-called XYZ Affair immediately aroused U.S. martial spirits to heights unknown since the Revolution.

The Federalists appeared vindicated. Their stock rose with the public while that of the Republicans plummeted. Adams, who had previously attended the theater in Philadelphia unacknowledged, now was greeted by audiences cheering themselves hoarse. Abigail Adams feared her husband's health would be impaired from the strain of writing replies to the many complimentary addresses he received each day. In these replies to citizen groups, the president often expressed the view that there was "no alternative between war and submission" and that the United States was "on the point of being drawn into the vortex of European war." Nonetheless, although he felt it necessary to prepare public opinion in this way for the eventuality of war, he made no move toward a declaration of war.

Adams desperately desired to unify the nation, and in the aftermath of the XYZ Affair, public opinion was more unified than it had been in years. A declaration of war by France would further unite Americans, but would a Federalist-initiated declaration unite or divide the nation? On that question, the Hamiltonian "war Federalists" and the Adams "peace Federalists" disagreed. Nonetheless, even the President understood that opportune political moments should not be wasted. France's callous obstinacy had, for the first time since there had been a federal government, created an opportunity to mount public support for an adequate national defense capability.

## CREATING A NAVY

France and John Adams created the United State Navy, but these events did not occur in a vacuum. France had not been the first nation to make war on defenseless American ships. In 1793, the Dey of Algiers unleashed a swarm of "pirates" into the Atlantic. Responding to the seizure of eleven merchantmen and the enslavement of more than one hundred Americans, Congress in 1794 had no choice but to order construction of six frigates. To pacify the measure's opponents, Congress linked continued funding to the Algerian-held hostages. Warships were the high-tech weapon of the age, and their construction took several years. Thus the six vessels were only partly completed when, early in 1796, the Washington administration decided to pay ransom to those who today would be called terrorists. To obtain the release of the hostages and safe passage for U.S. merchantmen, the United States agreed to make a cash payment and to supply Algiers with naval equipment and a thirty-two-gun ship of war. The ransom and gifts cost close to $1 million, a sum that did not escape the notice of the French Directory, which would employ the same tactics and make similar demands only two years later. (For no good reason, this response came as a surprise to members of U.S. government.)

With the signing of the Algerian Treaty, construction on three of the six frigates was halted. Fortunately for John Adams, the War Department would complete and launch the other three—*the United States*, *Constellation*, and *Constitution*—in the first eight months of his administration.

Then, shortly after the XYZ correspondence was published, Congress authorized the War Department to purchase twelve existing vessels and arm them as ships of war, a task that swamped the understaffed War Department. President Adams, who was far more interested in creating a navy than in building an army, proposed a separate Department of the Navy and signed legislation establishing it on 30 April 1798. He appointed competent and loyal Benjamin Stoddert to the new cabinet post.

In July, Congress and the president moved to put the nation on a war footing. The war Federalists, envisioning war, and the peace Federalists, seeking through strength to deter war, cooperated as Congress passed a "quasi-war" measure ordering U.S. naval vessels to capture or sink armed French vessels. The president signed legislation creating the Marine Corps and authorizing completion of the three additional unfinished frigates begun in 1794. At federal expense, cannon were mounted aboard more than a thousand merchantmen. Having begun 1798 without a single warship, the United States ended the year with a fleet of twenty. In February 1799 the *Constellation* fought, defeated, and captured the French frigate *l'Insurgente*. During the three years of the undeclared naval war with France, four U.S. squadrons operating in the Carribean captured eighty-five French vessels and recaptured some seventy former

U.S. vessels. After factoring these losses into the political equation, French authorities stopped asking for bribes and "loans" and began looking for a way out.

## THE WAR PARTY ARMS

Having cooperated to create a navy, the two Federalist factions split over the necessity of an army. The war Federalists desired a large standing army, ostensibly to repel a French invasion but actually to overawe their political opponents and, if circumstances permitted, to seize Florida and Louisiana from France's ally, Spain. Adams and the peace Federalists favored only a small army. To threaten either Republicans or Spain was beyond Adams's imaginings, and he knew the French had no invasion capability. Squandering scarce resources on a useless army when there was "no more prospect of seeing a French army here, than there is in heaven," would, he believed, once again make the United States dependent on, rather than independent of, Great Britain and her navy.

The congressional "war Federalists," on Hamilton's advice, ordered the enlistment of a ten-thousand-man "Additional Army" and increased enlisted pay by 50 percent to encourage volunteering. They also authorized, contingent on a declaration of war, a fifty-thousand-strong "Provisional Army." George Washington agreed to be the titular commander of these forces, but the work of organizing them would be left to his as yet unappointed second in command. Alexander Hamilton, desperate to resurrect his public image through military glory, demanded the post. Adams had grudgingly accepted the enlarged army but desperately sought an alternative to "General" Hamilton. When Washington forced Adams to make the appointment, Adams became ever more determined to avoid war. He was able to postpone the enlistment of the Additional Army from 1798, when it would have been recruited quickly, to 1799, when cooling of the martial ardor aroused by the XYZ furor left recruiters able to raise only a third of the authorized number.

## FEAR OF DOMESTIC REBELLION

Strange as it might seem today, the possibility of a domestic insurrection was, for Adams, a more realistic threat than that of a foreign invasion. In publicly denouncing those "who withdraw their confidence from their own Legislative Government, and place it on a foreign nation," he reflected the Federalist belief that the Republicans, America's "servile minions of France," would support the enemy against their own government. At the very time, and with the same sense of urgency, that the Federalists created the Navy and the Additional Army, they enacted four measures, the Alien and Sedition Acts, to counter the emergence of such an insurrection. Should these measures, enacted without encouragement from either Hamilton or Adams, also discomfort the unpatriotic propagandists of the Republican opposition, so much the better. The Naturalization Act extended from five to fourteen years the period of residence required to seek citizenship and the vote. The Alien Enemies Act authorized the president to imprison or deport enemy aliens in time of war. The Alien Act conferred the same powers in peace time. Neither of the Alien Acts was ever enforced.

In the fourth measure—the Sedition Act—the Federalists overreached themselves, with fatal political consequences. This assault on civil liberties provided fines up to $2,000 and imprisonment up to two years for any person uttering or printing "any false scandalous, and malicious" accusations against the president or Congress, and up to $5,000 and five years for any person involved in "conspiracies and combinations to impede the operation of Federal laws." Since misrepresentations and untruths were standard journalistic practices of that day and since what one person might consider a reasoned analysis could easily be seen by another as a scandalous criticism, this law put Republican editors and orators in imminent jeopardy. Two dozen Republicans, mostly newspaper editors, were arrested; ten, including a Vermont congressman, were convicted.

The cry of "states rights" would inevitably have reared its head eventually in antebellum America. By signing the Sedition Act, John Adams had unnecessarily and prematurely forced the question of the location of ultimate sovereignty into the open and forced James Madison (Father of the Constitution) and Thomas Jefferson (author of the Declaration of Independence) to lend their prestige to the forces of disunity by means of their authorships of the Virginia and Kentucky Resolves of 1798.

## SHOULD THE UNITED STATES HAVE GONE TO WAR?

Talleyrand and the Directory saw a need for accommodation as they learned of the belligerent mood of the American public, of the aggressive deployment of the U.S. Navy, and of shipments of cannon and shot to the United States by Great Britain. Thus when Elbridge Gerry returned from France in October 1798 and visited Adams in Quincy, Massachusetts, he carried news of a more conciliatory French attitude. U.S. ministers in Europe also relayed indications that an American envoy would now be received with respect by the French government.

The defining moment of the Adams administration occurred early in 1799. The war Federalists pressed the president to further unite the nation, establish its military on a sound footing, and discredit the Republicans as unpatriotic by rallying the country behind a declaration of war. The 1798 congressional election results demonstrated that Federalist militancy toward France was popular with the voters.

In terms of the threat to American lives and property, an outright state of war would not have been a substantial change from the existing status of quasi-war. The destructive capacity and mobility of early nineteenth-century warfare was severely limited. Except for a few undermanned (and rebellious) West Indian garrisons, French forces were tied down in Europe. Unable after Admiral Horatio Nelson's victory at Aboukir Bay to invade England, the French were equally unable to threaten North America. Without having to make a formal alliance, the United States would have had on its side the most powerful military force in the world, the British Navy.

With minimal risk and much to be gained, the war option had much to commend it. The gains, had Adams kept Hamilton in check, would have been not territorial or monetary but diplomatic, military, psychological, and political. The United States could have erased the stain of capitulating to the Barbary pirates of North Africa and instead proclaimed, by maintaining a reasonable degree of military preparedness for a nation of five million, that its citizens and property were no longer subject to seizure by international bullies. More important, before the invention of the cotton gin and its sectionally divisive impact could be felt, a no-risk, feel-good war might have altered the national psychology and engendered a sense of nationalism sufficiently well established and sufficiently strong to withstand the economic and moral issues that threatened to tear the nation apart during the first half of the nineteenth century. With the nation in the midst of a popular war during the 1800 elections, Adams probably would have been reelected, maintaining Federalist control of Congress.

## THE FAILURE OF WILL

Through continued neutrality President Adams hoped to preserve and maintain a kind of pristine U.S. independence of both Britain and France. He was so focused on independence from all things European that he failed to comprehend the adverse consequences of such a course of action. Without a war to perpetuate the feeling of nationalism, old political divisions would reappear. Without a war to justify recent tax increases and the expensive military build-up, the public mood could easily turn hostile to maintaining an adequate military establishment. Without a war to justify the Federalist-sponsored military preparations and the enforcement of the Sedition Act, Republicans might well successfully arouse public fears of waste, standing armies, and tyrannical government.

Adams did not, as is commonly misunderstood, face the simple questions of whether to put the interests of the country before the interests of his party or to put party before country. The Federalist party had come into being to advocate a program that its adherents believed would promote the national interest, and to act counter to party interests was to undermine that view of the national interest. It would also advance the Jeffersonian alternative of decentralizing sovereignty, grounding national defense on inadequate state militias, and encouraging popular loyalty to attach itself to individual states rather than to the United States as a whole.

Adams was so paralyzed by his dislike of both Britain and France that he chose pristine neutrality when confronted by the crisis moment of 1799. He oversimplified the issue to peace or war, and chose diplomatic independence rather than a war with France because war would have necessitated closer associations with Great Britain. With hindsight, one can see that by choosing negotiation, he achieved only a very temporary peace and passed up the opportunity to set America on the road to a long-term peace purchased through military deterrence. Two months after Adams left office the Pasha of Tripoli—in the grand tradition of Algeria and France—unleashed his "pirates" against U.S. commerce. Two years later, in violation of neutral rights, the British renewed their searches of U.S. ships and impressments of U.S. citizens, a practice that would culminate in the War of 1812. These events did not have to occur.

Adams cavalierly risked his own and his party's popularity because he considered neither very important. But the fate of the Federalist party was important. If the country had declared war on France, constructed several ships-of-the-line, fought principally a naval war, and concluded peace, possibly at Amiens in 1802 on the same or better terms than were recognized by the Convention of 1800, the United States might have entered the nineteenth century with a navy sufficient to prevent further harassment of its shipping and sailors. The British interference with U.S. shipping and neutral rights that precipitated the War of 1812 would then not have occurred. Had the Federalists, who championed increasingly centralized national power and responsibility, been able to maintain themselves in office for twenty or thirty years instead of twelve, sectionalism and states rights might not have become popular nineteenth-century movements. Would a unified people with a strong commitment to nationalism and to a federal government with a powerful military have allowed nullifiers and secessionists to gain respectability?

## THE CONVENTION OF 1800

On 18 February 1799, without consulting his cabinet or his party's congressional leadership, Adams submitted to the Senate the name of William Vans Murray to serve as minister plenipotentiary to France. Senate Federalists, who were in the process of enacting a bill "encouraging the capture of French armed vessels," realized that the president had undercut their preparedness campaign, and they dispatched a delegation to urge him to consider the consequences. Ever the stubborn and independent maverick, Adams replied that "I have, on mature reflection, made up my mind, and I will neither withdraw nor modify the nomination."

Adams did, however, agree to modify the nomination to the extent of including Oliver Ellsworth and William R. Davie with Murray. Then he departed for Quincy leaving the war Federalists in a cold rage and the Republicans thankful for the ineptness of their opponents. With Adams in Quincy, Secretary of State Pickering dragged out the process of preparing instructions for the American negotiators in the hope that the formation of Britain's Second Coalition against France might provide an excuse to abort the reconciliation mission. Returning to Philadelphia in the fall, Adams put an end to the delays. Murray, Ellsworth, and Davie reached Paris early in 1800 to discover that Talleyrand now served a new master, First Consul Napoleon Bonaparte.

Since Bonaparte hoped to isolate Britain diplomatically, the U.S. envoys were offi-

cially received and the negotiations begun. The three Americans sought to terminate the military commitments of 1778 and to obtain compensation for the millions of dollars of U.S. property seized by French privateers. When it became clear that Bonaparte would not bend on compensation, the Americans shamefully conceded the monetary losses in return for a mutual abrogation of the 1778 military alliance and a commercial "convention" recognizing the principle that "free ships make free goods." For all practical purposes, Adams's mission had obtained nothing of value in the Convention of 1800 except that France, which was finding it increasingly difficult to seize U.S. commerce, pledged to stop seizing it. Washington's 1793 proclamation of neutrality had effectively abrogated the 1778 treaty seven years earlier, and great-power pledges to respect neutral shipping were not worth the paper they were written on. For a second time, bullying the United States had proved very profitable.

## LOSING POPULAR SUPPORT

John Adams lost the election of 1800 by seeking peace through humble petition rather than through national strength. It did not have to be. The congressional elections of 1798, occurring during the XYZ furor, had placed both houses in Federalist hands. Even the Virginia delegation had a Federalist majority. His party was ideally positioned by late 1799, but once Adams opted for negotiations, Congress could legislate nothing of significance until the results of those negotiations were known. The Federalists had the votes, but, held in limbo by their president, they could only drift.

Meanwhile, collection began of a highly unpopular direct tax on houses, lands, and slaves that had been enacted in 1798 to pay for the defense build-up. A mob led by one John Fries forcibly removed two tax evaders from a Northampton County, Pennsylvania, jail, and President Adams ordered a portion of the Additional Army into Pennsylvania to preserve order. In the uproar that followed, the Republican press had a field day making accusations of unnecessary taxes, standing armies, and tyrannical government. Had a formal declaration of war been in place, public opinion would have condemned tax evaders, unlawful mobs, and their sympathizers as criminals and traitors. Instead, the charges gained currency in the absence of a war to validate the taxes, ships, and regiments. Adams lost to Jefferson and Aaron Burr with 65 electoral votes to their 73 each. Either New York or South Carolina, both commerce-dependent states, could have delivered the election to Adams.

Having set the stage for the emergence of localism, states rights, sectionalism, and eventually secession by handing control of the federal government to the Jeffersonians, Adams with equal lack of awareness set in motion events that would lead others to oppose secession and preserve the union. In January 1801, he nominated Virginia Federalist John Marshall to be Chief Justice of the U.S. Supreme Court. For the next quarter century, with Adams watching from retirement in Quincy, the Jeffersonian-dominated executive and legislative branches downsized the military, divested federal power to the states, reduced taxes, and severely limited the federal government's role in people's lives. The judicial branch, however, under the leadership of John Marshall, continually asserted federal authority, sovereignty, and unity. Between 1861 and 1865, those who had inherited their ideas about the Constitution from the Jeffersonian Republican tradition went to war with those who had inherited their ideas about the Constitution from the Marshall Federalist tradition. The long histories underlying both owed their existence to decisions made by John Adams in February 1799 and January 1801.

## BIBLIOGRAPHY

Adams, John. *Diary and Autobiography by John Adams.* Edited by Lyman H. Butterfield et al., 4 vols. (Athaneum, 1964).

Brown, Ralph Adams. *The Presidency of John Adams* (University Press of Kansas, 1975).

Dauer, Manning J. *The Adams Federalists* (Johns Hopkins University Press, 1953).

De Conde, Alexander. *The Quasi-War: The Politics and Diplomacy of the Undeclared War with France, 1797–1801* (Scribner's, 1966).

Elkins, Stanley, and Eric McKitrick. *The Age of Federalism: The Early American Republic, 1788–1800* (Oxford University Press, 1993).

Ferling, John. *John Adams: A Life* (University of Tennessee Press, 1992).

Fowler, William. *Jack Tars and Commodores* (Houghton Mifflin, 1984).

Hoadley, John F. *Origins of American Political Parties, 1789–1803* (University Press of Kentucky, 1986).

Kurtz, Stephen G. *The Presidency of John Adams: The Collapse of Federalism, 1795–1900* (University of Pennsylvania Press, 1957).

Palmer, Michael A. *Stoddert's War: Naval Operations During the Quasi-War with France, 1798–1801* (University of South Carolina Press, 1989).

Shaw, Peter. *The Character of John Adams* (University of North Carolina Press, 1976).

Smelser, Marshall. *The Congress Founds the Navy, 1787–1798* (University of Notre Dame Press, 1959).

Smith, James Morton. *Freedom's Fetters: The Alien and Sedition Laws and American Civil Liberties* (Cornell University Press, 1956).

Smith, Page. *John Adams*, 2 vols. (Doubleday, 1962).

★★★ 3 ★★★

# Thomas Jefferson
## 1801–1809

*Andrew Burstein*

*Born 13 April 1743 in Shadwell, Goochland County (now Albemarle County), Virginia, to Peter Jefferson and Jane Randolph Jefferson; educated at the College of William and Mary (B.A. 1762); married Martha Wayles Skelton, 1 January 1772, Williamsburg, Virginia; six children from that marriage, one or more children presumed to have been conceived with the slave Sally Hemings, after the death of Martha Jefferson; elected vice president in 1796 after polling 68 electoral college votes and losing to John Adams who had 71; elected president as a Republican in 1800, defeating the Federalist John Adams; he and his running mate, Aaron Burr of New York, each received 73 electoral college votes, sending the election to the House of Representatives, where it was resolved on the thirty-sixth ballot; reelected in 1804, along with George Clinton of New York, receiving 162 electoral college votes to the 14 received by the Federalist ticket of Charles C. Pinckney and Rufus King; died 4 July 1826 in Charlottesville, Virginia; buried at Monticello, his plantation in Charlottesville.*

Modern Americans readily associate the third president with those noble sentiments most commonly invoked to uphold the nation's idealized self-image, expressing the passionate regard for human liberty and the political philosophy that produced the first modern system of representative democracy. Thomas Jefferson, for many the apotheosis of the democratic faith, believed in the future at a time when many of his peers considered the federal Constitution and the American republic at best a noble experiment, an unfixed and uncertain enterprise.

Jefferson began his two-term presidency amid social ferment, deep political division, and domestic and international tension, some of it occasioned by his own pronouncements. Embodying the organizing spirit of the Democratic-Republican party which coalesced in the early 1790s and contested the Federalists in power, Jefferson regarded himself, somewhat disingenuously, as a harmonizer and a mirror of America's soul. Just as he feared for the life of America's first principles if a Federalist-imposed order with an overly powerful executive returned the young republic to aristocracy and effete monarchism, his Federalist opponents feared in the Republican standard-bearer a loose cannon whose airy philosophy would open the floodgates to political chaos, atheism, and immorality. As they cried out for the preservation of liberty, Jeffersonian Republicans and high Federalists each predicted dire consequences if the other's vision should prevail. The irony of Jefferson's presidency is that this most controversial of political thinkers was largely moderate in his actions. He was not a leveler. He surrounded himself with men of his own class and could not have conceived the social transformation carried out in his name by the Jacksonians in the years after his death.

Jefferson faced several crises in office which demanded precedent-setting decisions. A showdown with the courts over political appointments tested both his partisan resolve and adherence to the Constitution. The kidnapping of American seamen by Barbary pirates and later impressment by the British in American waters reflected on America's military readiness and represented key challenges to Jefferson's doctrine of peace and principled diplomacy. The acquisition of Louisiana in 1803 and the subsequent exploration of the West by the Lewis and Clark expedition set the tone for America's belief in a "manifest destiny." While Jefferson professed personal humility, reserve, and a belief in small government, he came to exemplify the way presidents could lead actively.

## THE VIRGINIA BACKGROUND

Thomas Jefferson was reared among the Virginia planter aristocracy, a highly disciplined student of languages and cultures, law and history, moral philosophy, and the natural sciences. Owner of the most impressive private library in the country, Jefferson vigorously applied his broad pursuit of knowledge to the promotion of a republican style of politics. Over a long and productive life he made little alteration when describing this vision, a view toward maintaining a common respect among the talented men who were meant to stand out among their constituents and who in turn exhibited compassion toward the whole body of citizens.

The future third president was the eldest son of frontiersman Peter Jefferson, a little educated but forward-looking man who died when his son was 14 years old. Three years later, the young scholar left Albemarle County to attend the College of William and Mary, where from 1760 to 1762 he pursued a legal career under the guidance of learned lawyer George Wythe, a highly esteemed member of the Virginia House of Burgesses. Jefferson himself became a member of that body in 1769, and he served faithfully, though without great distinction, until the British authorities dissolved the assembly in 1774. As the crisis enveloping England and the colonies intensified, the young legislator was active in establishing the Virginia Committee of Correspondence, and he justified the American cause in 1774 by authoring *A Summary View of the Rights of British America.* This bold pamphlet brought greater attention to the 31-year-old planter-lawyer and led to his selection the following year to represent Virginia at the Continental Congress meeting in Philadelphia.

The soft-spoken Jefferson let his pen convey his forceful ideas. After his heralded Declaration of Independence crystallized the sentiment of Congress, he served two one-year terms as governor of wartime Virginia (1779–1781), his first experience as an executive. A competent administrator, Jefferson was faced with a depleted treasury as the British invaded the state from the south. Narrowly escaping capture himself, the governor ended his term with his government in disarray and subsequently was compelled to answer politically motivated charges of cowardice. These attacks reinforced his conviction that politics bred bitterness and deception and that one needed always to surround oneself with a network of trusted allies. His lifelong collaboration with James Madison and James Monroe ("the two pillars of my happiness," as he later wrote) began at this time.

Intermittently serving in Congress again from late 1782 until his departure for France in mid-1784, Jefferson was concerned with such nation-building programs as systematizing coinage and settling of the West. In the latter concern, he explored questions of commercial navigation and promoted a means of land survey and sale and the states' cessions of land to the government. These efforts eventually resulted in the Northwest Ordinance, which established laws of suffrage, territorial government, and statehood. Jefferson next assumed the role of diplomat, serving as U.S. minister to the court of Versailles from 1785 to the outbreak of the French Revolution in 1789. He devoted his days largely to commercial matters, attaching himself to his revolutionary colleague John Adams, America's first minister to the former mother country.

While Jefferson was abroad, union was forged at the Constitutional Convention of 1787. Though opposed to an executive who could be reelected every four years for life,

and concerned as well about the lack of a Bill of Rights protecting personal liberties, Jefferson grew comfortable with the model of a federal republic that his esteemed friend Madison and others had labored hard to bring to life. Pressed in 1789 to serve as President Washington's secretary of state, the resourceful Virginian ended his career as a diplomat. He remained enamored with France, a nation now in the throes of a revolution he predicted would usher in an age of justice and civility; yet he had also grown nostalgic for the nurturing land and many enduring friendships of home.

## THE WASHINGTON AND ADAMS ADMINISTRATIONS

The years 1790 to 1793 were to shake his harmonious visions, as Jefferson became reacquainted with American politics. He was immediately dismayed by what he perceived to be a retreat from the republican spirit of 1776; ambitious legislators appeared easily seduced by Secretary of the Treasury Alexander Hamilton's financial schemes, which included the establishment of a Bank of the United States, refunding the national debt at par, and the assumption by the federal government of the states' revolutionary debts.

As the federal government assumed the war debts of the states, it handsomely rewarded the holders of once-depreciated notes. This enriched selfish speculators (the legislators and their friends) while failing to compensate ordinary soldiers and farmers, the original noteholders. A new moneyed elite was emerging, the secretary of state deduced, and a primary tenet of the Revolution—the virtue and disinterestedness of public servants—was being abandoned. Federalists, he believed, were now rejecting the notion of the people's sovereignty and were holding themselves above the people.

England and France went to war in 1793, further dividing the two pivotal members of the first cabinet. Jefferson became more suspicious of Hamilton when the New Yorker interfered in his domain by alerting London to their rift, proposing himself as a conduit to avoid any worsening of Anglo-

American relations. He charged that Jefferson had a "womanish attachment to France and a womanish resentment against Great Britain." Jefferson had diligently executed foreign policy, contending with Indian resistance to westward expansion of white settlers, and coping with Spain's curtailment of U.S. navigation on the strategic Mississippi River. He stood firm in his opposition to British depredations in trade. But worn from his very visible conflict with Hamilton, Jefferson retired to his Virginia plantation, Monticello, at the end of 1793, and he was no longer present in government when Federalist Chief Justice John Jay negotiated a treaty that confirmed U.S. subservience to British power. The Jay Treaty, approved by President Washington, renounced discriminatory tariffs without demanding reciprocity from England. In return, London promised little more than to evacuate forts in the old Northwest as it was meant to have done a decade earlier.

The Jay Treaty deepened Jefferson's belief that a new Tory party of "Anglomen" had arisen in America. Assisted by the efforts of then-Congressman James Madison, Jefferson became the recognized leader of the Republican party and stood as its candidate in 1796 in the first contested presidential election. He lost to John Adams, whom Jefferson acknowledged as a hero of 1776 but now considered less firmly wedded to the republican principle of elective government. As the runner-up in votes, Jefferson assumed the vice presidency. With few policy responsibilities in the Adams administration, he was hurt by the growing perception in America of French unpredictability. A Federalist upsurge, buoyed by the unstable nature of that revolution, placed Jefferson, the antiadministration leader, on the defensive. Federalists equated Jeffersonian Republicans with French Jacobins and warned that a Jefferson presidency would sacrifice order and balance to mob rule.

For his part, Jefferson reacted to repressive Federalist legislation (which had been occasioned by such extremist fears) as unforgivable abuses of power. He deemed as attacks on liberty the notorious Alien and Sedition Acts of 1798, which silenced critics of the administration under penalty of imprisonment. Jefferson made sure that encroachment by the federal government on the sovereignty of the states ("consolidation") met state protests; as the Supreme Court as yet had never overturned an act of Congress, he called forth the Virginia and Kentucky Resolutions, claiming that self-governing states had the right to resist unjust laws. The federal government was, for Jefferson, an agent of the states. He insisted that the true danger to the republic came from excessive government power rather than from unreasoning masses.

## THE REVOLUTION OF 1800

During the high tide of Federalist power preceding the election of 1800, Jefferson's public words were far less revealing than his private correspondence. A pronounced emotionalism belied his refined public persona. To Republican cohort John Taylor of Caroline he complained mightily that Federalist strongholds in the North were trouncing Virginia and the Republican South: "They ride us very hard, cruelly insulting our feelings as well as exhausting our strength and substance." Perceiving the "family pride" of New England as a potent force threatening to divide other states, Jefferson continued, "This is not new. It is the old practice of despots to use a part of the people to keep the rest in order, and those who have once got an ascendancy . . . have immense means for retaining their advantages." Bemoaning the "untoward events" which had played into Federalist hands, he ultimately urged his friend to carry on: "A little patience, and we shall see the reign of witches pass over, their spells dissolved, and the people recovering their true sight." This intense imagery was more than a literary flourish; Jefferson saw tremendous drama in political struggle and deeply personalized it.

The campaign of 1800 pitted Federalist and Republican principles against each other in an even more hysterical atmosphere than that of four years earlier. Adams and Jefferson exchanged no bitter words, seeming to have far less emotional disagreement than that which conspicuously absorbed their respective political schools. Partisan newspapers fanned the flames of intolerance, as pro-Jefferson journalists risked imprisonment by condemning efforts of the Federalist-controlled Senate to manipulate election laws. More than a hundred pamphlets were published, and the campaign literature was taunting and caustic, generating libel charges. Adams was branded "a hoary-headed incendiary" and Jefferson an atheist who had once defrauded a widow. On one occasion in 1799 Jefferson wrote his daughter that he was "environed here in scenes of constant torment, malice and obloquy," a situation that only grew worse for him. Though no stranger to controversy, the mild-mannered Virginian was obliged to turn to his more vocal allies for help in dealing with the cunning of other public men who, Jefferson surely felt, had misjudged him and his principles.

Jefferson bested Adams this time, but there was a rub. Jefferson and his presumed vice-presidential ally, Aaron Burr of New York, unintendedly received an equal number of votes. The conniving Burr refused to abide by the Republicans' will and, despite protestations to the contrary, kept the contest alive. Federalists in the House of Representatives huddled among themselves in the early months of 1801 as pivotal congressmen sought to exact concessions from Jefferson in return for a decisive vote. Jefferson resisted all such deal making, and after thirty-five ballots a single elector, James Bayard of Delaware, broke the deadlock. In the midst of this, the president-elect wrote that he felt he was "in an enemy's country." Coping with Federalists "of the violent kind . . . so personally bitter that they can never forgive me," he said he could only hope that in the future, "they will get tamed."

## "WE ARE ALL REPUBLICANS, WE ARE ALL FEDERALISTS"

On 4 March 1801, Thomas Jefferson was sworn in as the third president, completing a peaceful, if convoluted, transition of power from Federalist to Republican administrations. Attesting to the remaining discord, defeated President John Adams chose not to appear on the rostrum with his successor and was already en route home to Massachusetts. Moreover, the new chief justice who performed the swearing in was Federalist Virginian John Marshall, Adams's secretary of state from June 1800 to January 1801, who despised his distant cousin Jefferson and hoped to bear witness to the new president's rapid political demise.

Few inaugural addresses have meant as much to the course of U.S. political life as this one did. It was the same Jefferson, the bitter partisan, yet also a man struggling to convey a set of intentions different from those that the recent campaign had projected. As the new president, Thomas Jefferson stood inside the crowded Senate chamber and read his polished speech, rising to assert his belief in an optimistic view of America's destiny. The promise of 1776 was to be realized, martyrs of the Revolution vindicated, "liberty" and "virtue" preserved, and the violent tendencies of party conflict overcome. Republicans would narrow the distance between the governing and the governed, widened by the Federalists; power from above would be less felt.

Jefferson had prepared careful drafts of the inaugural message. He meant to establish the tone not just of his administration but of the new century. He was accustomed to leading with his pen: first, in nonpartisan terms, as the community-conscious clarion of virtuous republicanism and, second, as a tireless correspondent who offered to fellow Republicans, in the language of reason, subtly aggressive ideas designed to inspire forceful action while he claimed passivity, or at most "sympathy." Both Jeffersonian styles were contained in the inaugural.

"Friends and fellow citizens," he opened, declaring with republican humility a "sincere consciousness" of the magnitude of the demands of his office. America was "a rising nation, spread over a wide and fruitful land." But it was a land that had undergone upheavals, including the rancorous political struggle just ended. The election was decided nevertheless "by the voice of the nation," and so, "all will of course arrange themselves under the will of the law, & unite on common efforts for the common good." That inaugural was written not in the long, ranging paragraphs he conventionally employed in prose but rather in shorter breaths, widely spaced, with obvious pauses, and in a more open and legible hand. He proposed dramatically: "Let us restore to social intercourse that harmony and affection without which Liberty, & even Life itself, are but dreary things."

From this point in the text he moved to an equally charged reflection on the times the young nation, and the world, had passed through. Railing against political intolerance, he reached for grandeur in expression, for a splendid sound, while invoking the sensations of pain and terror—the eighteenth-century moral sublime. Citing the "throes and convulsions" of the ancient world, and the "agonising spasms of infuriated man seeking through blood & slaughter" precious liberty, Jefferson wanted to arouse sensations in his reading audience (no doubt focusing on the audience beyond those who could hear his muffled words in the Senate that day) before turning to the present. Having raised, then, images of the unbounded passion contained in that eternal contest between the best of human nature and man's dark designs, he contrasted the tranquil pursuit of reason, lauding that in *his* America, "every difference in opinion is not a difference in principle." This forceful counterposition of images led up to the most heralded words of the entire address: "We have called by different names brethren of the same principle. We are all republicans; we are all federalists."

It was the same decisive Thomas Jefferson who had been haunted by "the reign of witches" in 1798 who was now engaged in mollifying his critics and attempting to allay fears of a "democratic" administration (at that time meaning mob rule, a breakdown in the social order). Through a combination of reasoned calm and rich imagery, Jefferson intended to persuade all, political friend and foe alike, of his sober commitment to the principles of federal republican government He did not, as Peter S. Onuf points out, privilege "republicanism" over "federalism"; he was for a sound government that alone could guarantee the liberty and natural rights of individual citizens. He sought, in this much anticipated speech, to demonstrate that as fears about his political principles were wrong, so were politically inspired rumors assailing his personal morality; he had neither the libertine nor the dictator in him. As a speaker, Jefferson was unable to effect strong tones. After the inaugural, he took to sending his messages to Congress, where they were read by the clerk of the House. While a reflection on his own limitations, this departure from the first two presidents also expressed Jefferson's preference for republican simplicity over ceremonial government.

## ASSEMBLING A REPUBLICAN ADMINISTRATION

In office, Jefferson first assembled a cabinet of outstanding intellects, men who were, of course, loyal Republicans. Fellow Virginian James Madison, the wary and astute constitutional theorist and legislator, was his secretary of state and closest confidant. Albert Gallatin, Swiss-born finance expert and former Pennsylvania congressman, had shown mastery in poring over Hamilton's numbers and critiquing his complex system for managing a national debt which, to Jefferson, was "servitude." Frugality was to replace extravagance (or, in Jefferson's dire description, "licentious commerce and gambling speculations.") As treasury secretary, Gallatin quickly became as important to the president as alter-ego Madison. Gallatin was to devise and implement a decisive program for retiring the debt, taking most of the nation's naval vessels out of service, maintaining a minimal army scattered along the western frontier, and capping the federal bureaucracy at just over one hundred people. General Henry Dearborn of Maine, chosen for regional balance, served as an effective secretary of war, maintaining a watchful eye on Indian activities with regard to the Spanish and French to the south and southwest. Dearborn's fellow New Englanders Levi Lincoln of Massachusetts and Gideon Granger of Connecticut served respectively as attorney general and postmaster general.

Greatest resistance to the Jefferson administration came from New England. Corresponding with Elbridge Gerry, a signer of the Declaration of Independence from Massachusetts friendly to both Adams and himself, the new president projected a nationwide republicanization: A "revolution of sentiment" was occurring north and south, he asserted. Americans were again embracing the meaning of the Revolution, indeed were "unanimous in the principles of '76, as they were in '76." Despite having "drunk deeper of the delusion" of toryism in the 1790s, New England was already "recovering." The bitter partisan who wished to eliminate parties for the sake of union appealed to Gerry to continue to nurture the spirit of '76 in his troubled section: "You, my friend, are destined to rally them again under their former banner . . . with inflexible adherence to your own principles. The people will support you." It was precisely such an attitude—"inflexible adherence" to principles—that defined the political Jefferson.

But if they were out of office, the Federalists had not ceased breathing. Jefferson saw the alternative promoted by their dwindling numbers only as "the howlings of a ravenous crew." He described his own zeal as civilizing, and thus legitimate, theirs as unreasoning and bestial, as the word *ravenous* suggests. The harmonizing rhetoric of the inaugural address, then, was partly an act of sidestepping. Jefferson's letters reveal a disquieting capacity to cut off conversation with the opposition.

In Attorney General Levi Lincoln, Jefferson found a trusted analyst of New England affairs. In the midterm election season of 1802, Lincoln wrote Jefferson from Worcester, Massachusetts, that "the Spirit of bitterness of the opposition is as great as ever. . . . Every thing, every calumny, which malice can invent, or baseness propagate, is

put in circulation. . . . The object is to hunt down, destroy and render odious in the eyes of the people, the administration, and the whole republican character and interest."

Around this time, mercenary journalist James T. Callender charged that the president kept a biracial mistress, his own slave, and had fathered her several children. As Lincoln took up the president's interest in this matter, he shared his impression of Callender's stained character, at the same time observing that Republicans had been "too inattentive . . . too timid and accommodating to their enemies." In responding to Lincoln, Jefferson sounded his familiar theme:

> The opinion I originally formed has never been changed, that much of the body of the people as thought themselves federalists, would find that they were in truth republicans, and would come over to us by degrees; but that their leaders had gone too far over to change. Their bitterness increases with their desperation. They are trying slanders now which nothing could prompt but a gall which blinds their judgments as well as their consciences.

For Jefferson, the excesses that came about as a result of political disagreement reflected the moral instincts—the moral lapses—of individuals. The president considered that he bore no responsibility for inciting his enemies' attacks; character was evidenced not by public pronouncements but, as he later wrote, "by the tenor of my life." He had convinced both himself and his friends that as he dismissed from federal positions those Federalists for whom ample evidence of "malfeasance" existed, he did not take personal pleasure in what might be construed as royal prerogative. He claimed he only hoped to preserve "the tranquillity of the people" by granting offices to good Republicans. Moreover, he indicated that he would realize this goal through moderation, retaining significant numbers of Federalist officeholders. Jefferson professed a desire to remove from the focus of partisan debate the touchy issue he felt had been instigated by Adams's "midnight appointments" of federal judges whose views were at odds with the incoming administration.

## ATTACK ON THE JUDICIARY

The judiciary represented a major stumbling block to Jeffersonian transformation of the processes of government. Unsympathetic Federalists like Chief Justice John Marshall and Associate Justice Samuel Chase had received lifetime appointments. In a showdown over the Judiciary Act of 1801—in which Jefferson aimed to eliminate the new judgeships—and in the case of *Marbury v. Madison* in 1803—wherein the Supreme Court asserted its authority over acts of Congress for the first time—Jefferson contended with Marshall's power.

Congress had established the federal judicial system in 1789. As Americans moved, new communities formed and new states were added to the Union. Federalists proposed that circuit judges and district courts be added to lighten the burden of sitting justices. The Judiciary Act of 1801 removed a considerable amount of litigation from the state to the federal bench, thus adding to the power of the central government. This ran counter to the Jeffersonian principle: Federal courts were those furthest removed from popular consent, and Republicans viewed Federalist judges as unacceptable guardians of individual rights. Adding to the political sensitivity of the issue was the timing of this legislation granting the president authority to select numerous new judges: Federalists had pushed it through during President Adams's last months in office. Whether Adams stayed up until midnight on his last days in the President's House undoing Jefferson's triumph is less important than the result. As James Monroe put it in a letter to the incoming president on the eve of the inauguration: "The discomfited tory party . . . has retired into the judiciary in a strong body where it lives on the treasury, & therefore cannot be turned out. While in possession of that ground it can check the popular current which runs against them." He went so far as to advise suspicious Republicans to beware lest the Federalist judiciary "intrigue with foreign powers."

Despite the sweeping changes many in his party were urging, Jefferson preferred to steer a middle course rather than make removals solely on the basis of political disagreement. He truly believed the Federalists would wither away with minimal effort on his part and that there was no need to pursue amendment of the Constitution to alter the method of judicial appointments or the tenure of federal judges. Still, rather than irritate "our tried friends" for the sake of making "new converts," and perceiving, as fellow Republicans did, an arrogance on the part of some Federalist judges, the new president gradually embraced the cause of reducing the number of judgeships by repealing the Judiciary Act of 1801. A contributing factor in Jefferson's conversion was a lawsuit brought by William Marbury. Outgoing President Adams had named him a justice of the peace for the District of Columbia, and the new administration refused to issue his commission. In December 1801, Marbury decided to test the legality of that denial.

Just after New Year's Day, Senator John Breckinridge of Kentucky, a Jeffersonian stalwart, moved for repeal and a return to the original Judiciary Act of 1789. The Republican rationale was, in part, that the justice system was not so overworked that it really needed the added expense incurred by the new judgeships. Although Republicans now dominated both houses of Congress, they were less unified than the president might have hoped, and the repeal measure only narrowly passed in March 1802 after vigorous debate. At that time, the Federalist press, convinced that the Constitution had guaranteed life tenure for judges and fearing more radical measures to come, mourned: "Our Constitution is no more."

The struggle between the executive and the judiciary subsequently focused on the pending case of Marbury, who appealed to the Supreme Court on the basis of a provision in the Judiciary Act of 1789 giving the Court jurisdiction and the right to compel an executive official—in this case, James Madison—to do his duty. In ruling on the case, however, Chief Justice Marshall concluded that the First Congress had exceeded its authority by adding to the jurisdiction of the Court. The Court declared the relevant section of the Judiciary Act of 1789 unconstitutional and denied Marbury his commission. A precedent had been set: Republicans won the case, but Marshall asserted the doctrine of judicial supremacy, clearly establishing the Supreme Court's power to judge the actions of the executive. Jefferson feared that the Federalist chief justice, with whom he shared a personally rooted mutual distaste, would arrest the course of republicanization.

Frustrated by the continued outspokenness of Federalist judges, Jefferson sought the only remedy available to him: impeachment of those who could be shown to have committed "high crimes and misdemeanors." The most celebrated such effort was the trial of Marylander Samuel Chase in 1804. Justice Chase, who had presided over the sedition trial of one-time Republican firebrand James T. Callender in 1800, had turned to attacking Republican policies from the bench. Jefferson, in a blatantly partisan move, resolved to turn the tables on the judge by finding evidence of sedition in Chase's indiscreet pronouncements. The president wrote Maryland Republican Joseph H. Nicholson, then active in the impeachment of a clinically insane New Hampshire judge, asking whether Chase should go unpunished. "I ask these questions," he phrased it, "for your consideration. For myself, it is better that I should not interfere." A House committee investigated and approved eight articles of impeachment, but the result was predictable: There had been nothing unconstitutional, only unpalatable to Republicans, in Chase's behavior. He was acquitted at the end of Jefferson's first term and returned to the bench.

Jefferson's first term was distinguished by his effectiveness as a communicator. He disavowed any direct influence on Congress but nonetheless succeeded in having his policies pursued through subtle understandings reached with select Republican leaders. Senator John Breckinridge of Ken-

tucky and House Majority Leader William Branch Giles of Virginia were unerringly loyal to the president, at times even exceeding Jefferson's worried rhetoric. The *National Intelligencer*, published in Washington three times each week, defended Jefferson's position on the issues in its pages. The president lavishly entertained congressmen (at great personal expense). He hinted at what he wanted in confidential letters and in private meetings, and his lieutenants took their cue. He was the first president to behave in office as a party leader.

## BURR AND TREASON

In the wake of the Chase verdict, early into his second term, Jefferson was obliged to deal with the antics of his first-term vice president, Aaron Burr. After being dropped from the Republican ticket in 1804, Burr failed to win the governorship of New York and subsequently killed in a duel the man who had hurt his chances for that job, Alexander Hamilton. In 1805, the ambitious Burr concocted a plot by which a force of Americans would assault the Spanish and take over their American possessions. Burr allegedly saw himself establishing a new nation with himself at its head.

Jefferson described his quixotic former vice president as a "crooked gun, or other perverted machine," and wanted the conspirator punished for treason. No doubt recalling that, among his other questionable activities, Burr had been eager to compromise with the Federalists during debate over the Judiciary Act of 1801, Jefferson made his opinion clear to Congress late in 1806, as soon as he learned of the conspiracy. Some Federalists supported the president's outspokenness; others thought a chief executive should not decree guilt before the accused had received a trial by jury.

The trial opened in May 1807. Erstwhile Republican Burr found a surprising protector in Chief Justice Marshall, who brazenly subpoenaed the president. Jefferson would not appear in Court, but he agreed to turn over certain documents in his possession. Marshall orchestrated the trial in such a way that the crime of treason was too narrowly defined for the jury to find the defendant guilty. Again stymied by the Federalist-led judiciary, President Jefferson raised questions by refusing to distance himself: He coached the prosecution, corresponded with witnesses, and injudiciously winked at newspaper criticisms of the chief justice. Nevertheless, if truly embittered personally, he could have ordered Burr extradited to New Jersey to face the murder charges still outstanding since the Hamilton duel, but he did not.

## THE EMPIRE OF LIBERTY

Jefferson's approach to executive authority was formed as much in the course of conducting U.S. foreign policy as in his partisan behavior toward the high Federalists. In foreign affairs, he was a nationalist, giving much thought to America's prestige and honor and demonstrating resolve in his first months in office by announcing that he wanted to stand up to the bullying of the North African pirates who routinely collected tribute from all seagoing nations conducting commerce in the Mediterranean. In concert with his cabinet, and with due regard to congressional authority in undertaking hostilities, Jefferson moved that U.S. ship captains should be able to cruise the high seas and to search and destroy the enemy's preying vessels. Persistent activity by U.S. frigates and the blockade and bombardment of Tripoli in 1803 and 1804 led to a treaty the following year. American prisoners taken when the frigate *Philadelphia* ran aground were freed for a fraction of the $3 million dollars originally demanded by the Tripolitan pasha. The piracy of the various Barbary states thereafter came to an end for American vessels, although Europeans continued to pay tribute.

Deeply concerned since his days in the Confederation Congress with America's westward destiny, President Jefferson envisioned an "empire of liberty" in the gradual republicanization of the lands beyond the Mississippi River, presently unpopulated by white settlers. When he entered office, Spain held possession over the vast tracts known as Louisiana and the Floridas, where

Americans freely traveled and Europeans loosely ruled. A short time into Jefferson's first term, Spain ceded Louisiana to France, and Napoleon prepared to occupy the busy port of New Orleans. Jefferson was deeply concerned: "There is on the globe a single spot," he wrote Robert Livingston, then U.S. minister to France, "the possessor of which is our natural and habitual enemy. It is New Orleans, through which the produce of three-eighths of our territory must pass to market."

The president had waited, attempting to gauge Napoleon's intent before pressing with negotiations aimed at convincing Napoleon that America's continued goodwill was necessary to France, and that it would be marred by an aggressive French presence along the frontier. He wanted the usually unyielding French leader to understand how much was riding on this issue. And yet, despite his firmness, the last thing Jefferson wanted was to provoke an armed confrontation or to become embroiled in European politics by shifting alliances. Had Napoleon resisted the Louisiana Purchase, the president undoubtedly would have acquiesced to the French presence, providing American navigation rights on the Mississippi were upheld. As it was, he dispatched the trusted Monroe to join Livingston in Paris with updated instructions, including a proposal for the purchase of the city of New Orleans.

The serendipitous result of the president's tense waiting game, of course, was that just as Monroe arrived in the spring of 1803, the French campaigner, dismayed by a costly incursion in Haiti, had turned his attention to Europe and decided to sell the United States the whole of the Louisiana Territory, to the Rocky Mountains. By a stroke of the pen, America's territory doubled. Jefferson recognized an unprecedented opportunity to realize a vision he had held since drawing up plans for western settlement as a member of the Confederation Congress.

Upon learning that Napoleon wanted the agreed upon $15 million immediately, Jefferson (strongly encouraged by Secretary of State Madison) felt he had to act quickly before the unpredictable French leader changed his mind. Heralding Louisiana in his third annual message to Congress as "an ample provision toward posterity, and a widespread field for the blessings of freedom and equal laws," Jefferson pushed the treaty through the Senate for ratification. Yet he was personally troubled by a very real constitutional problem: There was no clear authority vested in the president to acquire territory from a foreign government, and these particular lands contained significant numbers of foreign citizens unaccustomed to republican government. Jefferson then went on to propose a transitional government for the newly acquired territory, whose character was more despotic than representative. Indeed, he would resettle eastern Indians across the Mississippi, although he had previously urged assimilation of tribal peoples into white republican society. He would also allow a French-inherited "assembly of notables," rather than a representative assembly, to rule in certain populated areas. Lower Louisiana, where the most brutal form of slavery was practiced, seemed far from the definition of an "empire of liberty," and Jefferson did not move to overturn that regime either. A Republican Congress narrowly passed Jefferson's plan in 1804.

Even before the transfer of Louisiana was complete, Jefferson had conceived the project of exploring this largely unknown chunk of America. In his mind, the scientific value of the proposed expedition loomed largest. He wanted to know more about Native American societies and languages, plant and animal life, and geography. But in order to appropriate funds from Congress, he stressed the commercial prospects inherent in an army-led mission of discovery. Meriwether Lewis, Jefferson's private secretary and Virginia neighbor, and frontiersman William Clark set out from St. Louis in the spring of 1804, reached the Pacific Ocean in November 1805, and returned the following year with valuable specimens, maps that featured new names, and notebooks filled with pioneering lore and poetic reflections. Only one man was lost in the round-trip journey of seven thousand miles. The lure of the West, advanced by a president who had correctly gauged the riches of the continent, would only intensify.

## GROWING CONFLICT WITH GREAT BRITAIN

The continuously unfolding drama that absorbed Jefferson during his second term was the conflict with Great Britain over commercial policy. In Paris in the mid-1780s, Jefferson had embraced the view that, despite its precarious economy, the United States should challenge Great Britain's smugness and resist trade restrictions imposed by the dominant sea power, which was wary of granting access to its various colonies. He had proposed free trade, reciprocity, and equality among seagoing nations. The "model treaty" Jefferson conceived at that time was meant to formalize this set of ideals and put the new republic on solid footing. When only Frederick the Great's Prussia signed on, the overall frustration in attempting to implement such a policy caused Jefferson to remark of Britain's bullying that "the infatuation of that nation seems really preternatural. Nothing will bring them to reason but physical obstruction, applied to their bodily senses. We must show that we are capable of foregoing commerce with them, before they will be capable of consenting to an equal commerce." Over the years, of course, Jefferson's Anglophobia had shown no signs of diminishing.

An advocate for "free commerce with all nations; political connections with none," President Jefferson was tremendously alarmed when the British he had for so long detested for their naval bullying attacked a U.S. vessel, the *Chesapeake*, off the Virginia coast in June 1807. This act occurred after a brief peace between France and England ended and war had resumed. Americans had profitably shipped goods to both sides until Orders in Council from London threatened seizure of neutral shipping. The *Chesapeake* affair was particularly egregious because the Royal Navy had dared to open fire close to America's shore (killing three and wounding eighteen) and to search for British subjects who could be impressed into serving on His Majesty's vessel. According to the British conception at this time, Americans naturalized after 1783 could still be deemed British subjects.

Knowing that the meager American navy was no match for the British, the president decided to apply economic sanctions as a means of persuading the mercantile power to come to a fair understanding. Jefferson the nationalist had high hopes and equally high confidence in the future of U.S. agriculture. Because Americans bought British manufactured goods, he expected the lure of profitable commerce to cause London to shun the risk of losing an ever-growing market and to capitulate, as it had in the 1760s. When the British showed no sign of compromise, Jefferson again made an executive decision of considerable consequence, convincing Congress at the end of 1807 to impose an embargo on virtually all U.S. exports. American vessels were prohibited from docking not merely in British ports, but in all foreign ports. The president, in a rare instance of executive shortsightedness, failed to articulate to the public what he meant to gain by enacting the embargo. He seriously overestimated the impact of his move on the intended target and underestimated its impact on the New Englanders who relied heavily on their commerce with London.

The "peaceable coercion" Jefferson favored thus backfired. The administration was seen to be interfering at all levels of society—infringing on the rights of individuals—while smugglers operated tenaciously along the Canadian frontier. Napoleon saw the embargo as more trouble for England than for France, while England itself made do. This unpopular act was repealed a few days before a fatigued President Jefferson retired to Monticello, leaving the vexatious and volatile problems of sea power, commercial expansion, and the nation's dignity to his friend and successor, James Madison.

## SIMPLICITY AND MORALITY

As president, Thomas Jefferson showed single-minded purpose, according to his ad-

mirers, or obstinacy, according to his critics. He fearlessly defined the republican spirit as one that was durable and rooted in the inherent wisdom of an honest and educable populace. It was the same enduring belief he conveyed to Madison at the end of 1787, as soon as he had been apprised of the results of the Constitutional Convention: "I think our government will remain virtuous for many centuries. . . . Above all things I hope the education of the common people will be attended to; convinced that on their good sense we may rely with the most security for the preservation of a due degree of liberty." This remained Jefferson's secular religion, ostensibly unaffected by the bitter, unrelenting newspaper attacks launched by his political enemies. Jefferson displayed a singular belief in the near-unanimous acceptance of what he could not recognize as a merely partisan cause when he wrote in 1802 to the sympathetic Joel Barlow that, except for a diminishing New England contingent, "a small check in the tide of republicanism, . . . everywhere else we are becoming one. . . . The candid federalists acknowledged that their party can never more raise its head."

In one concrete way Jefferson had succeeded in reversing the Hamiltonian Federalist program: He significantly reduced government expenditures. He had told Congress in 1801 that doing so would enable the United States "safely" to "dispense with" internal taxes, thus imposing less on citizens and removing "temptations" to use funds unprofitably for war preparations. Each year of his presidency, more and more of the national debt was retired, and upon leaving office Jefferson believed that debt, which he equated with Hamilton's "Tory" effort to undermine republicanism, would soon be extinguished. Though America was militarily unprepared for impending war with England, Jefferson was once again convinced that the republic—simple, prudent government—was being secured.

The philosophical president, a collector of Indian vocabularies and mammoth bones, saw in the abundance, in the grandeur, of the American landscape the potential for exploitation that symbolized the unstoppable American spirit. He foresaw that the small republic would grow and before long would outpace the labor-intensive lands of Europe. The sore that festered on this otherwise healthy landscape was, of course, slavery. Earlier in his career, Jefferson had strongly urged the eradication of an institution he recognized as inimical to a free society. He proposed such language in his draft of the Declaration of Independence, but in deference to the wishes of South Carolina and Georgia, the wording was deleted. Disturbingly, he was convinced that African Americans were "inferior to the whites in the endowments of both body and mind" and could not coexist peacefully when whites in America resented them. Recolonization in Africa seemed to him, and to many other liberals, the humane solution. At the same time, Jefferson had also predicted in the *Notes on Virginia*, which he authored late in the Revolution, that under republican government his countrymen, recognizing the "great political and moral evil" of the slave trade, would prohibit it through legislation.

Jefferson the slaveholder knew right from wrong, but he was unable to transcend the society that had nurtured him. Wishing blacks their deserved freedom, he termed liberty the gift of God and remarked, "I tremble for my country when I reflect that God is just." The Constitution prevented prohibition of the African slave trade for twenty years after its adoption; the slavery issue receded for Jefferson as partisan politics hardened. As president, he did recommend to Congress at the end of 1806 that at the first moment federal law allowed, these "violations of human rights" of the "unoffending inhabitants of Africa" must be ended. Jefferson was thus able during his final year in office to witness the termination of the importation of slaves.

## THE THEORY AND PRACTICE OF POWER

Jefferson's conduct in office raises a broader question that stems from the apparent contradiction between rhetorical advocacy and actual practice. The outspoken champion of individual liberty, states rights, and mild national government who moved into the President's House in 1801 proved capable of compromising his political philosophy in the face of grave executive decisions in a number of instances over the ensuing eight years. How, then, should one characterize Thomas Jefferson's attitude toward executive authority?

First, there is no reason to believe that a reflective Jefferson ever felt he had assumed arbitrary power, for he could claim that Congress had ratified his choices. He associated ambition and greed with ministerial corruption and the general tenor of British politics. His own sentiments were formed by Enlightenment values and an American's sense of the spirit of 1776. His political religion was premised on the cultivation of character and decency, over and above any legalistic definition of executive power. He assumed that all understood his republican soul as he did, that reasonable people would perceive an absence of personal motives in his actions. He was convinced that any who disputed his sense of fairness and honor were themselves perverted. A true republican, like George Washington or himself, was incapable of being seduced by power.

As president, Jefferson seems to have followed Washington's lead and felt that treaty making was most effectively undertaken with a minimum of interference. Of course, the president also found it prudent to consult the Senate, which was constitutionally charged with declarations of war and the ratification of treaties. Treating with the Barbary states, he followed constitutional procedures. In the case of the Louisiana Purchase, Jefferson perceived constitutional ambiguity. He was concerned that a constitutional amendment should precede that extensive addition to American possessions, but he ultimately rationalized the expedient acquisition of territory, recognizing that Congress would determine if and when territories were to be admitted to the Union.

Still, Jefferson's plan for Louisiana casts an ominous shadow over the president's republican credentials. He had been eager to possess the land, less forceful about republicanizing it. The Jeffersonian vision of westward expansion had always been predicated on the presence or proximity of a naturally republican population that would automatically replicate Eastern values. Jefferson now had to extemporize, faced with a population that had to be swayed from an un-American ideology. Had a Federalist president proposed such a governing arrangement as he had devised, Jefferson would probably have charged that it would lead to monarchism.

Security came first in his calculation. There could be no republicanization of Louisiana before the transition from Spanish or French forms had been made smoothly. Once again, his concern was for the transformation of character. Parallel to the Jeffersonian premise that Louisiana would witness the expansion of a republican-style agriculture and those attendant virtues that would forestall the development of a European-style, city-bred corruption, the individuals already inhabiting the new territory needed to be educated in positive American values. They would then mirror other pioneers, already armed with American principles and destined to carry on that decent tradition. Jefferson viewed the embargo crisis of his second term similarly, in that policy reflected moral responsibility as well as pragmatic calculation. His overarching concern was that the national government should act to protect Americans' freedom. He judged that his actions did just that.

Jefferson showed resolve in his approach to America's westward expansion and dealings with the European nations. His idea of an "empire of liberty" assumed a vital energy that in the long run could not be opposed by the lethargic Spanish or the inconsistent French or even the overextended British. As he persisted in conjuring greatness for his country, Jefferson tenaciously pursued commercial equality among nations. From his five years as American minister to pre-Revolutionary France, through the end of his presidency, Jefferson did not compromise on his global prescription. He held to his conviction even at the cost of domestic harmony: The 1807–1808 embargo failed to accomplish its immediate aim of compelling British moderation, and it caused hardship on significant numbers of Americans who were less convinced than the president that self-sufficiency was realizable or even desirable.

## THE MEASURE OF THE MAN

Thomas Jefferson's personality was formed by a harmony-seeking social prescription—the French and American Enlightenment. That personality was routinely strengthened by a love of reading and collecting the world's knowledge. It both framed Jefferson's idealism and made him a committed executive. His antipathy toward absolutist tyranny and commercial bullying caused him to become an impassioned advocate for human rights, highly sensitive to arbitrariness in the exercise of power. Under two Federalist administrations, Jefferson saw reason to be wary that republican methods, fairness and reason, could be easily sacrificed to private ambition as power became the exclusive tool of a self-anointed class of moneyed lawgivers. Whether or not they in fact impended, these abuses seemed very real to Jefferson as he assumed office.

Given the emotionalism surrounding his election, and the feelings of vulnerability that the 1790s provoked in him, self-preservation was a strong if subconscious motive for Jefferson as he sought to solidify his new majority. He believed in mild national government, yet his fears made it impossible for him to be in any sense a detached executive. He thought of himself as a temperate, tolerant, conciliatory man and professed not to understand why his political enemies would dispute this self-characterization. He was Anglophobic, owing to the arrogance he sensed in the British personality ("proud and hectoring," he called it), and he was pro-French only so long as France helped stave off British aggressiveness. Pleased that French liberalism had grown from America's spirit of 1776, he was equally aware that the English sense of liberty had been retained and enlarged by Americans and that

English products continued to appeal to American tastes. His countrymen did not necessarily share all of his perceptions of the conflict-ridden turn-of-the-century Western world. But he somehow believed he could rally them toward a proper, republican consensus.

Jefferson changed the office of president in terms not only of his political preferences but of his personal style. He replaced aristocratic stiffness with relative informality. As biographer Merrill D. Peterson has noted, Jefferson "substituted natural good humor and common civility for the artificial forms of foreign courts." He tried to please his guests, official or otherwise, without appearing to condescend. He dressed casually for his day and gave most the impression of a plain and friendly human being, free of conceits and cordial to the simplest of citizen callers. Yet the pleasing Virginian had a darker side, too—a profound suspicion about others' intrigue. During the politically tumultuous 1790s and the two terms of his presidency, the unmartial Jefferson frequently employed military metaphors in letters to political allies; he insisted, for example, that his enemies were lined up in a "phalanx" to oppose him.

Acknowledging in his first inaugural address that "some honest men fear that a republican government cannot be strong," Jefferson had clarified his faith:

> I believe this, on the contrary, the strongest government on earth. I believe it is the only one where every man, at the call of the laws, would fly to the standard of the law, and would meet invasions of the public order as his own personal concern. . . . Let us, then, with courage and confidence pursue our own federal and republican principles, our attachment to our union and representative government.

He meant, in the "revolution of 1800," as he later dubbed it, to make government more sensitive to the popular interest than it had been during the two administrations preceding his election. Dispensing with much of the pomp normally associated with political triumph, Jefferson felt assured that he had internalized the voice of the people. His conception of "the people" included errant Federalists and all but the most ardent anti-republicans. Federalists were enemies of the republican principle who admired the British style to the extent that they would pervert the structure and guiding principles of the U.S. government. Jefferson had battled them throughout the 1790s using the same language he had previously used to brand an unfeeling King George III and an abusive Parliament. But Federalists who had been swayed, in his words, by the "artful manoevres" of others, were still capable of being reformed, restored to their clear vision of 1776 and to upholding the healthy balance sought for in the language of the federal Constitution.

Rhetorically, then, Jefferson pronounced the republic safe, but intense hostility continued to plague him and affect his partisan movements. Harmony was deterred, in his way of thinking, by rigid identities, by sectional rivalry, and by the "spirit of party" that sapped the nation's energy, disguised true principles, and estranged friends. Significantly, he did not see himself responsible for contributing to this divisive spirit. Yet, to save the cause of liberal America from a future less democratic, Jefferson was eminently capable of resorting to the precise tactics (certainly the behind-closed-doors manipulation) he criticized in his noisy and—as he would brand them—elitist detractors. He could even, through indirection and for the greater good he perceived, impose powerfully on the lives of large segments of the population.

To this president, who did more than perhaps anyone of his generation to manipulate political language, federalism (the constitutional principle) represented institutional soundness, and republicanism (the ideal character) represented the nation's heart and soul. Combined, they were bound to produce social harmony. Federalism was a mechanism, something that was, in a Jeffersonian sense, "heart-less." Republicanism, to the at-once frustrated and optimistic, dogged yet affable president, breathed a superior, quintessential American virtue.

Because he did not equate contention between two distinct political parties as a democratic good, Jefferson could not rest. He was obsessed with his maligning enemies and ever desirous of eliminating their voice from the public forum. In his mind they were miserable obstructionists, traitors to the cause of the people's liberties, who had forfeited a role in building the nation they, as much as he, had conceived. Their "apostate" version of U.S. history, which showed Jefferson and his political allies hungry for office and dishonest in their methods, made this rigid moralist rankle.

Jefferson had to navigate tempestuous seas as he attempted from a position of military weakness to advance U.S. interests and articulate republican values. Though his presidency yielded mixed results, his grip on the American soul remained strong because his words and ideas were bold, unprecedented, and unequaled. Controversy surrounded and embroiled him as he persisted in articulating a vision, his sentimental conception that what America was destined to become depended upon the clear pursuit of right. He was convinced that he had fairly reasoned and had come to know "right." America was a fertile, promising, still largely unexplored continent. America's progress was, for Thomas Jefferson, a matter of morals and a matter of will.

## DNA SEXUALLY LINKS JEFFERSON TO HIS SLAVE

In 1998, results of a DNA study showed that one son of Thomas Jefferson's biracial slave Sally Hemings shared the Y chromosome of a Jefferson. Most scholars now presume that Eston Hemings (born 1808) was indeed the son of the president, and that in all likelihood one or more of the Monticello house servant's other children were fathered by Jefferson, though in theory they could have been fathered by other Jeffersons who shared the president's DNA profile. Rumors of a Jefferson-Hemings liaison first surfaced in 1802, but most who knew Jefferson doubted their veracity. Jefferson himself did not respond publicly to the charges during his lifetime, and they were subsequently denied by his white descendants. There remains no evidence to disclose the emotional nature of the relationship between Jefferson and Hemings, and the only direct testimony by a son of Sally Hemings, Madison Hemings's newspaper interview of 1873, suggests that Jefferson did not behave with paternal affection toward the Hemings children. Scholars are divided on the significance of this apparent reversal of the historical record.

## BIBLIOGRAPHY

Banning, Lance. *The Jeffersonian Persuasion: Evolution of a Party Ideology* (Cornell University Press, 1978).

Boyd, Julian P., et al. *The Papers of Thomas Jefferson* (Princeton University Press, 1950– ).

Burstein, Andrew. *The Inner Jefferson: Portrait of a Grieving Optimist* (University Press of Virginia, 1995).

Ellis, Joseph J. *American Sphinx* (Knopf, 1997).

Ellis, Richard E. *The Jeffersonian Crisis: Courts and Politics in the Young Republic* (Oxford University Press, 1971).

Ford, Paul L., ed. *The Writings of Thomas Jefferson* (G. P. Putnam's Sons, 1892–1899).

Gordon-Reed, Annette. *Thomas Jefferson and Sally Hemings: An American Controversy* (University Press of Virginia, 1997).

Lehmann, Karl. *Thomas Jefferson: American Humanist* (Macmillan, 1947).

Malone, Dumas. *Jefferson and His Time*, 6 vols. (Little, Brown, 1948–1981).

Mayer, David. *The Constitutional Thought of Thomas Jefferson* (University Press of Virginia, 1994)

McCoy, Drew. *The Elusive Republic: Political Economy in Jeffersonian America* (University of North Carolina Press, 1980).

McDonald, Forrest. *The Presidency of Thomas Jefferson* (University Press of Kansas, 1976.)

Onuf, Peter S., ed. *Jeffersonian Legacies* (University Press of Virginia, 1993).

Peden, William, ed. *Notes on the State of Virginia* (University of North Carolina Press, 1955).

Peterson, Merrill D., ed. *The Portable Thomas Jefferson* (Viking Penguin, 1975).

———. *Thomas Jefferson and the New Nation* (Oxford University Press, 1970).

Risjord, Norman K. *Thomas Jefferson* (Madison House, 1994).

Sheldon, Garrett Ward. *The Political Philosophy of Thomas Jefferson* (Johns Hopkins University Press, 1991).

Smith, James Morton, ed. *The Republic of Letters: The Correspondence Between Thomas Jefferson and James Madison, 1776–1826* (Norton, 1994).

Tucker, Robert W., and David C. Hendrickson. *Empire of Liberty: The Statecraft of Thomas Jefferson* (Oxford University Press, 1990).

★★★ **4** ★★★

# JAMES MADISON
## 1809–1817

*F. Thornton Miller*

---

*Born 16 March 1751 in Port Conway, Virginia, to James Madison and Nelly Rose Conway; educated at the College of New Jersey (now Princeton University—B.A. 1771); married Dolley Dandridge Payne Todd, 15 September 1794, in Harewood, Jefferson County, Virginia; no children from that marriage, but two sons from her previous marriage; ran for president in 1808 on the Republican ticket with George Clinton of New York, and defeated the Federalists, Charles Cotesworth Pinckney and Rufus King, with 122 electoral college votes to 47; in 1812 ran with Elbridge Gerry of Massachusetts and defeated DeWitt Clinton of New York and Jared Ingersoll of Massachusetts, 128 electoral college votes to 89; died 28 June 1836 at Montpelier, Virginia; buried in the family plot on his plantation there.*

---

James Madison, fourth president of the United States, was one of the most accomplished Founding Fathers and one of those presidents whose most significant contributions were made outside their tenure in the office. Madison, although re-membered most for his work on the Constitution, is also remembered for a significant presidency. He was the first wartime president. He played an important part in two key developments—territorial expansion and Indian removal. And his eight years in office were unique for another reason: The president best known as Father of the Constitution was determined to administer the office as closely as possible to the guidelines set out in the Constitution, even during a war.

Madison was born into the Virginia gentry. Unlike many of his friends, he graduated from Princeton, not William and Mary. Like other educated gentlemen of the founding generation, he saw public service as his duty and served most of his adult life in government. He was a member of the Virginia legislature, the Confederation Congress, the Philadelphia Convention, the Virginia ratifying convention, and the House of Representatives. He and Thomas Jefferson were best friends, and in the Jefferson administration, Madison served as secretary of state.

He married Dolley Payne Todd, who during the Jefferson administration had assisted the widowed president on social occasions. Known for her vibrant and charming personality, which contrasted well with her husband's, she was soon at the center of Washington high society. After the Madisons entered the White House, she carved out a role for the president's wife as the first hostess. The Madisons were very happy together, and, while in Washington, they would have their triumphs. But, after eight tumultuous years in the White House, including some spent guiding the nation through its first war, it is not surprising that the president and first lady were relieved when they could retire to Montpelier, their plantation in the Virginia piedmont.

## A STUDENT OF FOREIGN AFFAIRS

Several presidents have hoped that domestic issues would dominate their tenure in office, only to find themselves enmeshed in foreign affairs. Madison was not disappointed that foreign affairs issues would be the uppermost national concern during his two terms. Indeed, he was quite ready to devote his presidency to resolving the major foreign affairs problems that confronted the country. Madison never wanted to be just an administrator. He was thoughtful, saw problems, and devoted himself to resolving them.

During the 1780s and 1790s, Madison had concentrated his efforts on American constitutional and political development. He had not been just a political leader, however, in the movement that led to the ratification of the Constitution. He studied the history of confederations and analyzed the problems of the governmental system throughout the states, developed ideas on how to resolve the country's problems, and published his findings. He would use the same approach in 1793, when the new federal government was confronted with a war in Europe which would last intermittently through 1815. During this time, the main thread or theme running through Madison's public career was his devotion to the development of American foreign policy.

Madison was not content with opposing the Federalist administrations' foreign policy or administering foreign affairs as Jefferson's secretary of state. He made an exhaustive study of seventeenth- and eighteenth-century international law and, in 1806, published *An Examination of the British Doctrine, Which Subjects to Capture a Neutral Trade, Not Open in Time of Peace.* The work is a significant critique of British foreign policy by an author who, as the next president, would press for war against Britain.

Madison drew upon treaties, international law practice in admiralty courts, and the treatises of such writers as Grotius, Pufendorf, Vattel, and Martens to set forward the concept of the freedom of the seas. He demonstrated that international law held that if a ship were neutral during a war, the goods on board were also neutral—in other words, "free ships make free goods." This was significant because European empires had mercantilistic economies with a host of regulations benefiting their own ships and excluding foreign ships in trade between the mother country and the colonies. During war, it was not unusual for these maritime powers to relax their trade regulations so that they could use their navy and merchant marine directly in the war effort. In response to this practice, Britain issued its Rule of 1756, which stated that a neutral could not during wartime engage in a trade that was prohibited during peacetime.

The Rule of 1756 was enforced by the British Navy and Admiralty Courts but, Madison demonstrated, it was unilateral and did not become part of international law. Further, even Britain did not practice the rule. Like other maritime powers, Britain allowed her merchants to conduct foreign trade that was prohibited during peacetime. Britain was literally engaged in the same kind of trade it prohibited among neutrals. Madison asserted that Britain's ultimate goal was to monopolize Atlantic trade.

Madison worked his way through the strained opinions of the British admiralty court judges and reduced the British doctrine to interests, power, and bad arguments. He concluded that Britain's practice of enforcing her policy in her admiralty courts as if it were international law was no more than self-interested hypocrisy.

Madison had discussed the realities of interests and power in *The Federalist*. The solution was not to end interests and power but to channel and control them through a system of checks and balances. Britain had to be checked, and Madison believed the United States needed to be one of the countries that provided that check.

As Jefferson's secretary of state, Madison had watched as the British added insult to injury by seizing U.S. sailors along with ships and goods. He viewed the impressment of these sailors not only as the best example of Britain's maritime imperial arrogance but also as an assertion of power with total disregard for international law. He agreed with Jefferson that economic coercion should be tried before war, which resulted in the embargo fiasco. After Congress repealed the embargo, Madison concluded that war was the next step.

## THE REPUBLICAN NOMINATION

Madison was nominated for president in 1808 by the Republican congressional caucus. Most Republicans viewed him as the logical successor to Jefferson and an appropriate choice since he had been one of the founders of the party. The party had changed a great deal, however, since the early 1790s, when Madison first organized it in Congress as an opposition party unified by a common enemy: the Federalists, led by Alexander Hamilton. The Republicans were united against the establishment of a national bank, funding and perpetuating a national debt, increasing federal taxes, the pro-British foreign policy, and—drawing upon the fear of standing armies and the belief that liberty was best maintained by a reliance on a citizen militia—the military build-up, which they believed was expensive, unnecessary, and dangerous.

After Jefferson's so-called Revolution of 1800, Republicans cut taxes and reduced the size of the military, the federal government, and the national debt. No constitutional amendments were enacted, however, to prevent Federalist-type policies from being re-established. Disappointed, the extreme wing of the Republican party believed the party leaders had been corrupted by power, and they particularly distrusted Madison whom they saw as a moderate, uncommitted to carrying on the Revolution of 1800. By 1808, Republican opposition to the Jefferson administration and its succession through a Madison election included even John Taylor and William Branch Giles, who had originally helped Madison build the party. Nevertheless, Madison had won his party's nomination and, given the decline of the Federalists, he went on to easily win the election of 1808. Although the Republican party controlled both houses of Congress during his presidency, Madison would have continuous problems and opposition from the many factions that had grown up within the party.

Despite the disunity among Republicans, they still agreed on a great number of areas, such as reducing the size, cost, and debt of the federal government, and establishing an Indian policy that would allow expansion into their lands. Republicans gathered their strength from the South and West, which favored expansion. Madison had been an advocate for the policy goals many Republicans subscribed to: acquiring New Orleans and the Mississippi River, having full access to the Gulf of Mexico, acquiring the Floridas, and opening up for settlement territory claimed by Indians. In keeping with this policy and ideology, the Republicans sought the least expensive way to achieve their goals, preferably through peaceful negotiation or purchase, but as a last resort, through war.

## SEIZING WEST FLORIDA

Madison thought that, after the Louisiana Purchase, West Florida was the next most important area for U.S. expansion. This area of the Florida panhandle, running from the east of the Mississippi River to the Perdido River, included the area of Baton Rouge and the Gulf coast areas of the later states of Mississippi and Alabama, along with the port of Mobile. American interests in the area were obvious: Rivers of the Old Southwest, including the Alabama River system, flowed through West Florida to the Gulf of Mexico. If the region was to develop, with crops and livestock able freely to go to market, the United States needed full use of these rivers.

Madison unsuccessfully negotiated with the Spanish to acquire West Florida. Then an opportunity arose: Napoleon invaded Spain and the Spanish government collapsed. In the Spanish empire, officials in several colonies formed provisional governments, and confusion reigned elsewhere. Britain came forward as a protector for Portugal and Spain against Napoleon, with potential consequences for the United States. British interests were well served through further trade in Spanish America, and the situation in West Florida was unclear. Inhabitants in that area might set up an independent government, Britain might secure the area, or, in time, Spain might be able to reestablish its position. Madison determined that to take advantage of the moment he had to move quickly, and he ordered U.S. officials and troops in Louisiana to move into the area. He followed with a public proclamation declaring that West Florida was now part of the United States, and that taking West Florida was natural because the United States should own the land through which the rivers of the Old Southwest flowed into the Gulf.

Madison's seizure of West Florida was a bold act of imperialism, and he succeeded because the time was ripe and no one could prevent it. West Florida did not enter the United States through the sanctification of a treaty, such as Louisiana, East Florida, or Oregon, or by a treaty after a war, as in the Mexican Cession. Madison based the U.S. claim to West Florida on an interpretation of the Louisiana Purchase treaty that neither Spain nor France recognized, and neither they nor Britain acknowledged the legitimacy of the takeover. Madison made no attempt to get the action accepted by other nations, a requirement for its being recognized in international law.

Madison, however, knew he would generally get support from Republicans in Congress. West Florida had been one of their goals, and it did not matter how it had been taken, especially since so little expense was involved. Republicans had grown confident in their imperialism. There was already a sense that this taking of land to the south and west was America's destiny. Madison did not ask the people living in West Florida what they wanted, but neither had the earlier Jefferson administration asked the inhabitants of Louisiana what they wanted. Imperialist goals were not to be frustrated by the wishes of the inhabitants of the area being taken. That attitude was never more obvious than in Republican policy toward the Native American tribes.

## INDIAN POLICY

Republican Indian policy was initially peaceful: They welcomed the tribal peoples into the new nation, though on Republican terms. This was a policy of acculturation. Indians had only to give up their own tribal ways, move from communal ownership to private property, and abandon hunting and take up farming. As they moved from hunting to farming, Indians would need less land. The federal government would give them supplies during the transition and negotiate to open up for settlement former Indian-claimed territory.

Many Indians, however, were not quick to cooperate with the acculturation policy. Madison thought they possibly were too primitive to be receptive to the attempts to civilize them. Since he completely rejected any idea that Indians could organize and resist U.S. policy based on an awareness of what was in their best interests, he viewed their refusal to cooperate as confirmation of their inability to be civilized. Madison agreed with the Republicans of the South and West who wanted more land opened for settlement and were growing increasingly impatient with tribal groups who put obstacles in their way.

As the Madison administration accelerated the process of negotiating treaties with the tribes, treaty making itself changed. During the administration of George Washington, the federal government negotiated with Indians as it would have negotiated with a foreign power such as Britain or Spain. The government had proceeded as if a treaty came at the end of hostilities, as if agreements were being made that each side would be expected to comply with for a period of time, and as if a treaty were a settlement, a settling of differences, an attempt to find a resolution. Under Madison, negotiating treaties with Indians became a process. There was no attempt to find a resolution or a lasting settlement. The policy was open ended and continuous, with an obvious logical conclusion: Indians in U.S. territory must either give up their culture, adopt the settlers' culture, and become property-owning family farmers, or they must move. Failure to do one or the other would lead to war.

The acceleration of the treaty process during Madison's administration not only convinced Tecumseh and his brother, the Prophet—a Shawnee spiritual leader—that it was time to take their stand against further U.S. westward expansion but also helped them persuade other tribes and warriors to join their movement. Indians had been gathering in the Prophet's village on the Tippecanoe, a tributary of the Wabash, to

heed his call for cultural revitalization. While the Prophet preached, Tecumseh organized a military alliance among the tribes of the Old Northwest and sought and received military supplies from British Canada.

When finally confronted by a concerted military resistance from tribal peoples led by Tecumseh, Madison concluded that the Indians were inclined to fight and that British agents from Canada were inciting them to do so.

## TENSIONS WITH GREAT BRITAIN

America's problems with Great Britain continued through Madison's first term. Napoleon's attempted "blockade" of Britain also created problems for the United States and other neutral nations. After the embargo fiasco, Republicans did not give up trying to use economic coercion to protect America's commerce, at least in principle. What Congress finally settled upon was Macon's Bill Number 2, a rather feeble policy: The United States would trade with both Britain and Napoleon, but if either ended its restrictions on U.S. neutral commerce, the United States would restrict its trade with the remaining belligerent. The president was authorized to carry out this policy. Madison bowed to congressional leadership, since the Constitution placed the regulation of foreign commerce in Congress. Madison, did, however, see possibilities in the policy. He believed Britain was the main culprit and was less likely than France to take up the offer, but it was clearly in France's interest to take advantage of this situation. If France acted as expected, Madison could reinstate U.S. economic restrictions against Britain. And, if the United States acted in conjunction with Napoleon, there was the chance that Britain might alter its policy toward neutrals. If Britain did not, war was the next resort.

What could be expected in Congress was Federalist opposition and problems from factions within the Republican party, including a group led by William Branch Giles and Samuel Smith. To placate that group, Madison had already appointed Senator

Samuel Smith's brother, Robert, as secretary of state. Due to Robert Smith's mediocrity (or, rather, his incompetence) President Madison often had to rewrite Smith's diplomatic communications and eventually became, in effect, his own secretary of state (a job he was familiar with, having been Jefferson's secretary of state). When Smith criticized Madison's foreign policy among his political friends, stating that Madison was anti-British (which was generally true) and pro-Napoleon (which was generally false), Madison concluded that, given such insubordination, Smith had to go. Madison tried to remove him graciously, offering Smith another assignment. Smith then resigned and publicly criticized Madison, drawing onus upon himself and clearing the way for Madison's choice of James Monroe for secretary of state.

Robert Smith was wrong about Madison's attitude toward Napoleon. Madison thought Napoleon was exceedingly crafty and had little faith in his goodwill. As Madison expected, Napoleon seized the opportunity offered him by Macon's Bill Number 2 and announced that France would lift French restrictions upon neutral commerce, but he did not actually carry out this change in policy. Although Napoleon has often been praised for duping Madison, the president was not surprised when Napoleon's policy toward neutral ships remained unchanged. Madison could have pulled back and waited for proof that Napoleon would carry out a new policy, but he wanted to force the issue with Britain. As authorized by Macon's Bill Number 2, Madison therefore declared that, because Napoleon had announced that he would end restrictions on U.S. commerce, the United States would restrict trade with Britain. Madison notified Britain of the action and waited to hear whether that country would maintain its standing policy toward neutrals. Neither Madison nor Republican congressional leaders intended to return to the embargo of 1807. If Britain did not end its policy toward neutrals, Madison saw only one course the United States should take. He had been talking about war with Britain as a real, vi-

able, and perhaps necessary next step since the repeal of the embargo of 1807. War did not come because of a trick by Napoleon.

In the fall of 1811, Madison called a special early session of Congress and delivered his annual message. He stated that Britain, unlike France, was not responding to U.S. policy. The implication was obvious as he dealt at length with the need for military preparations. He wanted more maritime fortifications, an increase in the number of troops, longer enlistments, more training, and an increase in the manufacture of cannons and guns. He also referred to the growing activity of Indians in the Old Northwest. He stated that William Harrison, a military governor in the Old Northwest, with his regulars and militia would respond to Indians engaged in "murders and depredations." He found particularly menacing the growing number of Indians gathering at Prophetstown on the Tippecanoe.

Those Republicans in Congress who favored war with the Indians and Britain, known as the War Hawks, took Madison's speech as a signal to organize congressional support for war. Westerners, disturbed at Tecumseh's military preparations, thought war with Britain would end the Indians' ability to get supplies from Canada. The confrontation between Harrison and the Indians at Prophetstown culminated in the Battle of Tippecanoe. British supplies found in the Prophet's village after the battle convinced many westerners, Madison, and the War Hawks that the Indians were fighting for the British.

## MR. MADISON'S WAR

In the late spring of 1812, Madison presented a special message to Congress in which he listed the wrongs Britain had for years committed against the United States—seizing U.S. ships, impressing sailors, trespassing U.S. coastal waters, all in violation of international law. He stated in summary form what he had expounded on in his *An Examination of British Doctrine:* Britain wanted a monopoly control of the seas. He also charged the British with committing the worst kind of barbaric atrocity, with stepping beyond civilized bounds and the rules of warfare, by inciting the "savages" to attack Americans with their kind of "warfare which is known to spare neither age nor sex and to be distinguished by features peculiarly shocking to humanity." He regretted that the Indians' worst nature had come out despite and, indeed, in betrayal of the Americans' humanitarian efforts to civilize them.

The president declared that Britain's actions against the United States had violated American sovereignty, insulted the American flag, and compromised American independence. The United States had done everything it could, short of war, but "moderation and conciliation have had no other effect than to encourage perseverance and to enlarge pretensions. . . . We behold, in fine, on the side of Great Britain a state of war against the United States, and on the side of the United States a state of peace toward Great Britain." Should America continue to be passive, Madison asked, or should Americans act "opposing force to force in defense of their national rights"? He recommended the latter and asked Congress for a declaration of war. The House of Representatives was quick to respond, the Senate was slow—but Congress passed a declaration of war against Great Britain.

Madison would have opposition from the Federalists and from a number of factions among the Republicans, including the Clinton group in New York. In the election of 1812, Madison easily won the Republican party congressional caucus nomination for a second term, but he was opposed by De Witt Clinton, Republican governor of New York. The Federalists decided their best chance was to support Clinton. Clinton carried New York, New Jersey, Delaware, and most of New England. Madison easily won the election carrying Vermont, Pennsylvania, and all of the South and West.

Madison had found support for the war, from the electorate and Congress. Aware of the constitutional separation of powers, he would never have tried to force Congress's hand toward war. But he had been a major architect of Republican foreign policy, which set war with Britain as the final objective if all else failed. And no one was more responsible than Madison—secretary of state for eight years and president for four—for creating the image of Britain as tyrant of the seas. Madison had helped steer America in one direction, and now he would have his war. There would be no actions at the last moment like those taken by John Adams to prevent war with France. James Madison did nothing decisive or dramatic in the style of a James Polk, Abraham Lincoln, Woodrow Wilson, Franklin Roosevelt, or Lyndon Johnson. But there was much to substantiate the claim of his critics at the time: the War of 1812 was "Mr. Madison's War."

Madison had never thought of backing down and accepting British policy or accommodating it for the duration of the European wars. Realistic in many ways, such as looking at the socioeconomic interests that motivated people, political factions, and nations, Madison knew that force was necessary to achieve certain goals. War should be seen not as a threat but as the next logical step beyond diplomacy and economic coercion. In the Republican foreign policy toward Britain, war was a final step that had to be taken if Britain refused to change its policy toward the United States.

## LACK OF PREPAREDNESS

Madison was not realistic in all areas concerning war. He did not see its human side—the people who would be hurt and killed, the widows, the children losing their fathers. Madison's realism fell short in another area: He called for a declaration of war despite the country's lack of military preparedness.

The War of 1812 does not show that Republican foreign policy failed. It shows, if necessary, that Republicans were ready to go to war as the last means to achieve their objectives, defending what they saw as the principles and interests of the country. But taking this course while not making military preparations and, indeed, while reducing the military establishment the Federalists had developed was highly irresponsible.

The Republican military policy was the great failure. Jefferson, Madison, and other Republicans had placed great hope in relying on the militia and a gunboat navy during peacetime, thereby pursuing their economic objectives of holding down taxes and government expenditures while reducing the national debt. These objectives may have been appropriate for a country trying to stay out of war, but they were disastrous for a country that, while militarily unprepared, was pursuing a foreign policy wherein war was held out as a viable final option.

After the war began, the United States reaped the consequences of relying on the militia and a gunboat navy. Madison expected the militia to fight well against the Indians, as they had in the past. But in nearly all the other areas of the war with Britain, he entered the war as idealistic as Jefferson had been. He did not call for a military build-up until 1811, and then, as throughout the war, the response of the Republican Congress would prove inadequate.

### INVASION OF CANADA
There was a wide consensus among Republicans that the best way to strike militarily at Britain was through Canada, where the United States might have the advantage while Britain was preoccupied with the war in Europe. Madison agreed. If the strike was successful, territory taken in Canada could be used for bargaining purposes with Britain. And if U.S. forces seized Canadian wood and food production areas, the British West Indies would be even more dependent on U.S. trade.

The invasion failed, however, for several reasons, including a heavy reliance on militia; the New York militia's belief that its only purpose was to defend New York from an invasion; the refusal of Federalist-dominated New England states to cooperate in the war effort; and Congress's failure to establish long-term enlistments with good pay, including land, as an inducement to join the army. Republicans had not developed

the kind of standing army that could expand, train men, and launch this kind of invasion into Canada, and the United States suffered the consequences.

Initially, the only good news came from the sea, where the handful of U.S. frigates built by the Federalists were winning one-on-one battles with comparable British naval vessels. Madison enjoyed announcing the latest news of each American success, but this good news was short lived as British squadrons forced the miniature navy into port.

Things did not improve on the Canadian front. Compounding American problems was an unclear command structure that resulted at one point in a feud between two generals, James Wilkinson and Wade Hampton, and the secretary of the army, John Armstrong. The United States continued attacks into Canada in the Niagara area and above Lake Champlain into the summer of 1814, all with little success.

### MADISON AS WAR LEADER
Madison, the first wartime president, has been criticized for being a weak commander-in-chief during the war. He certainly did not provide dramatic leadership. But two points need to be taken into account in assessing his role. First, Madison, of all those who played active roles in drafting the Constitution at the Philadelphia Convention and in working for its ratification, was the only one elected president. (George Washington presided over the Constitutional Convention, but he did not play an active role in either the drafting or the ratification. Several others who drafted and ratified the Constitution served in the federal judiciary and Congress.) Madison, who generally tried to follow the Constitution as closely as possible, may well be the best example of a wartime president staying within Constitutional parameters. The Constitution assigned to Congress such important executive functions as declaring war and determining the scope and size of the military establishment. Had Congress been united and decisive in its support of "Madison's

war," problems would have been lessened. Madison was particularly aware, from his study of the history of government, that war offered executives the best opportunity to expand their powers and that a U.S. president would therefore be most likely to step beyond the Constitution during a war. It was the personal duty of the man who became known as the Father of the Constitution to stay within the constitutional bounds.

The second point that should be considered in assessing Madison as a war leader is that he did not have a commanding personality and was not a powerful orator who could inspire. He was best at perceiving problems, analyzing a situation, formulating solutions, and developing plans to meet his objectives. In military terms, he was a strategist. After the country was at war and he placed his attention on military matters, Madison was on the mark in analyzing how the United States could best use its resources to accomplish its war aims. He realized that defeating the British in Canada was not essential to U.S. strategy, and rather than concentrate the country's best forces in that theater of the war, Madison and the war department turned to America's trained regulars from before the war: Indian fighters. Militia riflemen from Kentucky and Tennessee were particularly adept at fighting Indians. He especially relied on William Harrison, who had defeated the Indian alliance at the Battle of Tippecanoe. (In time, another commander of similar background—Andrew Jackson—would emerge from the Tennessee militia.)

## WARTIME STRATEGY

Madison formulated his strategy. Harrison would fight the Indian confederation in the Old Northwest. Cannon and supplies would be sent overland to him, and a naval force would be built on the Great Lakes. This naval squadron would then take control on the Great Lakes, particularly Lake Erie, while other forces would continue to attack from the Niagara to Lake Champlain areas to keep British troops pinned down in defense of Canada. Madison saw that the best way to defeat the British Canada–Indian connection was to control the Great Lakes. If the United States could control Lake Erie and take back Fort Detroit, the British would be seriously compromised in their ability to aid the Indians.

In the fall of 1813, Oliver Perry won the Battle of Lake Erie with the Great Lakes squadron. British troops operating with the Indians in the American Old Northwest, seeing a threat to their supply line, retreated into Canada. Harrison moved to Detroit and pursued the enemy into Canada. The British continued to retreat, but Tecumseh and his warriors took their stand and were defeated at the Battle of the Thames. In the spring of 1814, Jackson defeated the Creeks at the Battle of Horseshoe Bend in Alabama. A major goal in the war had been met: ending the British-backed Indian threat.

Madison believed the best way Britain could check these gains was to send forces in Canada to the Detroit area and to revive the Indian alliance against the United States. Madison's main goal in continuing the lunges into Canada was to persuade the British that they needed to keep their troops in place to defend Canada.

## THE ATTACK ON WASHINGTON

The success in the west had made up for the problems on the Canada front, and on balance, the United States appeared to be starting to win the war. That impression changed in 1814 when, after Napoleon's defeat, Britain could dispatch fleets and armies to concentrate on the war in America. America's unpreparedness for war now hit a crisis level as a British fleet came up the Chesapeake and landed an army that marched on Washington.

Madison had earlier brought the defense of the capital to the attention of Secretary of War John Armstrong, and the president worried that Armstrong had failed to see to the adequate defense of the city. Confusion reigned as the British army approached. Only Virginia and Maryland militia were available to defend the capital, and they ran from the approaching veteran troops. Appointing John Armstrong of the New York Livingston faction of Republicans had been good politics for Madison, but the secretary of war behaved insubordinately by failing to keep the president fully informed, even though Madison had drawn up specific instructions on how the secretary was to conduct his office. Madison now confronted Armstrong and chastised him on the defense of the capital. Armstrong resigned, and Madison looked to Monroe to serve as both secretary of state and secretary of war.

What followed next was the low point in Madison's presidency. The British burned Washington's public buildings, and Congress and executive departments fled from the city. After the British withdrew, Congress ordered an investigation. Although the congressional investigation committee placed most of the blame on Armstrong, history has been less kind, holding that Madison had the ultimate responsibility.

The British march on Washington did reveal a heroic side of Dolley Madison, who secured important paintings and documents from the White House. It also revealed a stubborn side of James Madison, who remained unshaken in his resolve, sternly believing that the United States would prevail.

## THE RESULTS OF THE WAR

After the war was over in Europe, Madison reassessed the U.S. position. U.S. arms had achieved one major war aim: The British-supported Indian resistance to U.S. western expansion had been defeated. And the two other major problems with Britain—impressment and the British enforcement of the Rule of 1756 against neutrals—were removed by the end of hostilities in Europe. Madison saw no reason to continue the war with Britain after the problems that led to the war had been resolved, and negotiations were soon under way at Ghent, through diplomatic lines he had kept open. Since gaining new territory had never been a war aim, Madison was satisfied with accepting the antebellum status quo, the final terms agreed to at Ghent. For Madison, the goals for the war had been met. The United States had defended its rights, vanquished the Indians, and proven itself to be an independent nation. Any doubts that the new

nation was ready to hold its own with the rest of the world were removed by Jackson's great victory at the Battle of New Orleans. Madison submitted the Treaty of Ghent to the Senate, which quickly ratified it.

Americans, especially Republicans of the South and West, celebrating U.S. accomplishments in the West during the war had good reason to feel victorious. West Florida, the Mississippi River, and Louisiana had been secured by the Battle of New Orleans. The Indian threat to western expansion had been ended in the Old Northwest and Old Southwest. The United States would continue to grow. A patriotic and nationalistic mood swept over the nation.

## LESSONS LEARNED
## FROM THE WAR

The United States could celebrate and believe it had won the war, but Madison remembered the lessons he had learned and hoped the nation would be better prepared for the next war. He proposed to Congress the establishment of a permanent army and a renewal of the naval build-up. He also proposed that Congress enact a tariff and a national system of internal improvements, and that it recharter the Bank of the United States.

Madison's call for a tariff was based on his observation that U.S. manufacturing had made modest gains during the embargo and war years, which made America less dependent on Britain. This edge would be lost after the war if Britain could once again enter the American market with cheaper products. American infant manufacturing might not be strong enough to survive unless given some short-term protection. Congress followed Madison's recommendation and enacted a moderate tariff measure in 1816.

Madison's goal was not an industrial revolution; he envisioned little more than an extension of home industry, such as the sewing performed by women on farms. He sympathized with agrarian concerns over the ills of industrialization, such as crowded cities, and he hoped Congress would not move to a permanent or high protective tariff system, which he believed would in the long run be fundamentally detrimental to the best interests of the country. He expected tariffs would pose political and socioeconomic problems, but he did not think they posed a constitutional problem. The Commerce Clause in the Constitution made it expressly clear that Congress had authority to regulate foreign commerce.

The president also anticipated no socioeconomic or political problems from a national system of internal improvements to develop the country's infrastructure, especially transportation improvements, such as building canals, upgrading river navigation, and repairing harbors. Republicans had initiated such projects at the state level, where there would be more local control and local benefits, but they had been hesitant to do this at the federal level. Madison urged Congress to add a role for the national government, believing that a national system of internal improvements would further build the agricultural and commercial strength of the country. He believed, however, that to acquire the power to take such actions, which the Constitution did not grant to the legislative branch, Congress would have to submit to the states an amendment to the Constitution. The Republican Congress did not propose such an amendment, but it did pass legislation for national internal improvements. Madison vetoed the bill on constitutional grounds and again recommended that Congress propose an amendment to the Constitution.

Madison's postwar proposal to recharter the Bank of the United States also raised constitutional questions. In the First Congress, Madison had opposed chartering such a bank, arguing that the Constitution had not granted this power to Congress and that the Constitution would have to be amended before Congress could charter a bank. Hamilton and the Federalist supporters of the bank had prevailed, advancing a broad or loose construction of the Constitution.

Republicans were not happy with this result, for most of them preferred state banks, which favored local interests. (More agrarian Republicans stopped short even of state banks and opposed all banking.) After the Revolution of 1800, Republicans (with the obvious exception of Albert Gallatin, Jefferson's and Madison's secretary of the treasury) saw little need to continue the Bank of the United States when its corporate charter expired. When Madison failed to recommend to Congress that its charter be renewed, the first national banking system ended. He recommended recharter only after the War of 1812 caused financial problems for the federal government. Congress passed and the president signed legislation reinstating the national bank.

## CONSTITUTIONAL ISSUES

Madison had not forgotten the constitutional problems he had raised in the First Congress. He would, however, accept a historical argument, that because the Bank of the United States had been in existence for twenty years and had been generally accepted as constitutional by Congress, the president, the federal judiciary, state governments, and the acquiescence of the people, it could be accepted as constitutional, in the same way that the British accepted their unwritten constitution. Madison could not so readily apply this reasoning to a national system of internal improvements, which was not yet established. For this and other future projects linked to powers not clearly authorized by the written Constitution, he hoped that amendments would come first before the federal government took action.

Madison's long public career was distinguished by many contributions related to constitutional questions. He had written extensively on checks and balances in *The Federalist*. As president, his vetoes of acts of Congress more than tripled those of his three predecessors combined, and several (though not all) were on constitutional grounds. One such was the bill funding internal improvements. Two others involved congressional statutes relating to churches in federal territory, which Madison objected to because they violated the Establishment Clause of the First Amendment. Almost half of his vetoes were based on objections to policy or political matters, not constitutional questions. Madison was the first president who clearly used the veto as an executive check on the legislature.

## EVALUATING MADISON'S PRESIDENCY

An assessment of Madison's presidency cannot emphasize too much his conscious attempt to run the office as much as possible in accordance with the Constitution. Although he had influence in foreign affairs and was commander-in-chief during a war, Madison generally looked to Congress to determine policy. He believed that he could only make suggestions and that his main role was that of chief executive who carried out legislation. The exception to this stance was the seizure of West Florida, where he did not look to Congress for policy guidance and appeared less careful in observing constitutional bounds, apparently on the grounds that he had to move quickly and that the action would clearly benefit U.S. interests. This action demonstrated, however, that he was right to suspect that executives may overstep their bounds in military and foreign affairs. In this instance, even the Father of the Constitution may have failed to live up to his own requirements.

At the conclusion of Madison's presidency, the United States was in a wave of patriotic and nationalistic expansion and improvement. The country at least seemed to be doing better, and the future appeared a lot brighter than when he was first elected president in 1808. Madison brought in West Florida and was responsible for the defeat of the Indians in the Old Northwest and Old Southwest. Soon Indiana, Illinois, Alabama, and Mississippi would be entering the union. The country was stronger militarily, and the war had ended its problems with Britain on the seas. The Battle of New Orleans gave Americans the pride of defeating the army that had defeated Napoleon. In the War of 1812, the United States had defended its interests, rights, national independence, and sovereignty. That is how many Americans wanted to see the war. They wanted to believe Mr. Madison's War

had been a success, and they gave Madison a share of the glory. Like none of his predecessors, Madison ended his presidency more popular than ever, and many of his countrymen respected him as a successful president.

As other people have filled the office, the image of Madison's presidency has become increasingly negative. He is remembered for going into a war despite the country's lack of military preparedness, and he is blamed for the failures in the War of 1812, especially the burning of Washington. His leadership appears weak in comparison with later wartime presidents. Madison's presidency has not been remembered as he had hoped it would. He was proud of his demonstration that a president during war need not expand his powers and compromise the written Constitution.

In his last annual address to Congress, his own farewell address, Madison praised the country for maintaining its independence and the Constitution. He was happy that the Constitution had remained intact. He applauded the character of the American people, the American expansion, and the destiny of a country that stood for good government, liberty, rights, and justice. "These contemplations, sweetening the remnant of my days, will animate my prayers for the happiness of my beloved country, and a perpetuity of the institutions under which it is enjoyed."

## BIBLIOGRAPHY

Brant, Irving. *James Madison*, 6 vols. (Bobbs-Merrill, 1941–1961).

Brown, Roger H. *The Republic in Peril: 1812* (Columbia University Press, 1964).

Buel, Richard. *Securing the Revolution: Ideology and American Politics, 1789–1815* (Cornell University Press, 1972).

Clark, Thomas D., and John D. W. Guice. *Frontiers in Conflict: The Old Southwest, 1795–1830* (University of New Mexico Press, 1989).

Hickey, Donald R. *The War of 1812: A Forgotten Conflict* (University of Illinois Press, 1989).

Ketcham, Ralph. *James Madison: A Biography* (Macmillan, 1971).

Koch, Adrienne. *Jefferson and Madison: The Great Collaboration* (Knopf, 1950).

Perkins, Bradford. *Prologue to War: England and the United States, 1805–1812* (University of California Press, 1963).

Rakove, Jack N. *James Madison and the Creation of the American Republic* (Harper Collins, 1990).

Rutland, Robert Allen. *James Madison: The Founding Father* (Macmillan, 1987).

———. *The Presidency of James Madison* (University Press of Kansas, 1990).

Stagg, J. C. A. *Mr. Madison's War: Politics, Diplomacy, and Warfare in the Early Republic, 1783–1830* (Princeton University Press, 1983).

Watts, Steven. *The Republic Reborn: War and the Making of Liberal America, 1790–1820* (Johns Hopkins University Press, 1987).

★ ★ ★ 5 ★ ★ ★

# JAMES MONROE
## 1817–1825

*Daniel Preston*

---

*Born 28 April 1758 in Westmoreland County, Virginia, to Spence Monroe and Elizabeth Jones Monroe; attended the College of William and Mary; married Elizabeth Kortright 16 February 1786, New York, New York; three children; elected president in 1816 along with Daniel D. Tompkins of New York as vice president, receiving 183 electoral college votes to 34 votes for the Federalist candidate Rufus King; Federalist electors split their votes for vice president among four candidates; reelected in 1820 along with Tompkins with 231 electoral college votes to one cast for John Quincy Adams; died 4 July 1831 in New York; buried in Marble Cemetery in New York, but remains were removed to Hollywood Cemetery in Richmond, Virginia, in 1858.*

---

In 1803 William Wirt, then a young Richmond attorney, penned a series of essays on affairs in Virginia entitled *The Letters of the British Spy*. Included in these essays was a lengthy sketch of James Monroe, the governor of Virginia. Wirt portrayed Governor Monroe as a man whose "mind [was] neither rapid or rich" (a frequently quoted remark that Monroe naturally resented), but also as a man of great judgment and firm character. More to the point, however, is the concluding paragraph of Wirt's portrait:

As the elevated ground, which [Monroe] already holds, has been gained merely by the dint of application; as every new step which he mounts becomes a means of increasing his powers still further, by opening a wider horizon to his view, and thus stimulating his enterprise afresh, reinvigorating his habits, multiplying the materials and extending the range of his knowledge; it would be a matter of no surprise to me, if, before his death, the world should see him at the head of the American administration.

Wirt's assessment serves as an appropriate starting point for any consideration of Monroe as president, for it addresses two important issues that brought him to the "head of the American administration": his extensive experience in public affairs and his early recognition as contender for the presidency.

## A CAREER IN PUBLIC SERVICE

A major asset that Monroe brought to the presidency was the knowledge, wisdom, and experience gained from over forty years of military, legislative, diplomatic, and administrative service. Monroe's public career began in 1775 when, at age 17, he joined the revolutionary forces in Williamsburg. He served with the Continental Army and at war's end held the rank of colonel in the Virginia militia. He was elected to the Virginia assembly in 1782, elevated to the governor's executive council, and then elected to three consecutive terms in the Continental Congress, serving from 1783 to 1786. He was delegate to the Virginia constitutional ratifying convention in 1788 and was elected to the U.S. Senate in 1790, where he became a prominent member of the Republican faction. He resigned from the Senate in 1794 to accept an appointment as minister to France, a post he held until he was recalled in 1797. In 1799 he was elected governor of Virginia.

In 1803, shortly after Monroe's retirement from the governor's chair, President Jefferson appointed him special envoy to France. Following the signing of the treaty for the acquisition of Louisiana, Monroe remained in Europe as minister to Great Britain and special envoy to Spain. He,

along with special envoy William Pinkney, negotiated a treaty with Great Britain in 1806, but President Jefferson rejected it and Monroe was recalled in 1807. Deeply resentful of what he considered a rejection of his diplomatic expertise, he allowed his name to be offered as a candidate for president in opposition to his longtime friend James Madison, whom he blamed for the rejection of the treaty. A brief hiatus in their friendship and in Monroe's political career followed.

Monroe returned to the political arena in 1810, when he was again elected to the Virginia assembly and then, once again, elected governor. Reconciliation with Madison and an appointment as secretary of state followed in early 1811. Monroe remained at the head of the State Department throughout the remainder of Madison's presidency, serving coterminously as secretary of war in 1812 to 1813 and again in 1814 to 1815.

## AIMING FOR THE PRESIDENCY

When exactly Monroe began to harbor presidential ambitions is not certain. It is probably safe to say that he began to think about it seriously during his first stint as governor, for by that time his fellow Virginians began to think of him as presidential material. Wirt predicted in 1803 that Monroe would become president, and in December 1804, just after Jefferson had been elected to his second term, one of Monroe's correspondents in Virginia suggested that Madison engineered Monroe's diplomatic appointment so that he would be out of the country and not a rival to succeed Jefferson in 1809.

Although this suggestion came from one of Madison's enemies, it was not an absurd notion that Monroe might be considered as a rival to Madison; indeed, political malcontents in Virginia chose Monroe as an opponent to Madison in 1808. Monroe, along with everyone else involved, recognized that his candidacy was merely symbolic and posed no real challenge to Madison's election. At the same time, there was little doubt that Monroe would, sooner or later, be a prime contender for the presidency.

His campaign for the presidency took concrete form in the spring of 1815 when Monroe and George Hay, his son-in-law and chief adviser, began to lay plans to ensure his election in 1816. Both Jefferson and Madison had been nominated for the presidency by a caucus of the Republican members of Congress. By 1816, the caucus nomination was falling out of favor as state legislatures began to take a more assertive role in making nominations for the presidency. This development worked to Monroe's advantage because many members of Congress favored the candidacy of William H. Crawford, the charismatic and popular member of Madison's cabinet and a former senator. Despite his large following in Congress, Crawford was not well known outside of Washington and his home state of Georgia. In contrast, Monroe was known throughout the country and had a strong base of support in the states, with several state legislatures endorsing his candidacy before the caucus met. Although support for Crawford remained firm, abetted by a smoldering sentiment against electing another president from Virginia, the caucus could not ignore Monroe's national constituency and nominated him for the presidency. The nomination assured Monroe's election. Rufus King, the candidate for the all-but-defunct Federalist party, offered little opposition. Monroe received 183 electoral votes and King thirty-four. Governor Daniel D. Tompkins of New York, who had been a staunch supporter of the Madison administration during the War of 1812, was elected vice president.

## CHOOSING A CABINET

Monroe entered the presidency committed to the amelioration of the partisan spirit still lingering from the sharp divisions caused by the War of 1812. And yet, despite his desire for reconciliation, Monroe could not entirely shed his longstanding distrust of the Federalists. He rejected suggestions that he appoint Federalists and former Federalists to top offices, arguing that the reins of power should be entrusted to those who had proven their attachment to the Union and

to the Republican cause. In choosing his cabinet, Monroe sought to master this dilemma by giving careful consideration not only to the appointee's ability but also to the political implications of the appointment.

For the position of secretary of state he chose John Quincy Adams, a longtime diplomat whose experience in foreign affairs and whose views on foreign policy matched the president's. Moreover, the appointment of a New Englander (and the son of a Federalist president) who had proven himself to be a loyal Republican was an important step in the reconciliation of the northeastern states with the rest of the nation. This appointment likewise eased concerns of those alarmed by Virginia's control of the presidency, for the State Department was seen as a stepping-stone to the presidency, with Jefferson, Madison, and Monroe having served as secretary of state prior to becoming president.

The appointment of secretary of the treasury went to William H. Crawford. Although the two men had been rivals for the presidency, Monroe considered Crawford a friend and had great respect for his political and administrative ability. They had served together in Madison's administration, and Monroe was eager for Crawford to remain in the cabinet. The office of secretary of war was initially offered to a westerner, Governor Isaac Shelby of Kentucky. Shelby declined, and after considering several other westerners, Monroe offered the position to William Lowndes, a South Carolina congressman who likewise declined. The appointment finally went to John C. Calhoun, also a congressman from South Carolina. Monroe chose his friend William Wirt, a native of Maryland, as attorney general. Benjamin Crowninshield of Massachusetts, who served as secretary of the navy under Madison, continued in that position under Monroe. Crowninshield resigned in 1816 and was succeeded by Smith Thompson of New York; Thompson resigned in 1823 to accept an appointment to the Supreme Court and was replaced by Samuel Southard of New Jersey.

Monroe's ability as chief executive was most clearly demonstrated in his management of the cabinet. Rarely has the cabinet comprised a stronger, more able, or more ambitious assembly. Monroe, recognizing their abilities (and indeed, having chosen them for that reason), gave the secretaries full authority to conduct the business of the departments and to advise him on matters of state. He greatly cherished their advice and always gave it careful consideration. And yet the advice was always just that. Monroe frequently deferred to the expertise of the secretaries, but in the end the decisions were always his own. He maintained a close working relationship with his cabinet officers and, for the most part, counted them among his closest friends.

Monroe was a firm believer of adherence to the Constitution, loyalty to the republican ideals of the American Revolution, and maintenance of the Union. He believed that national devotion to republican ideals and institutions overshadowed sectional differences. He likewise believed that the union of the states offered the best security to those institutions and to the rights of U.S. citizens. A supporter of states' rights, Monroe thought that the states could find the greatest protection for their rights in a union of states held together by the Constitution and republican ideals.

**REACHING OUT TO THE PEOPLE**

With these views in mind, Monroe set out in the summer of 1817 on a tour of the northeastern states. Although the trip was intended primarily as an inspection tour of coastal fortifications, Monroe saw it also as an opportunity to ease sectional and partisan tensions. The tour immediately became a triumphal procession as thousands of Americans took advantage of the rare occasion to see the president of the United States. In addition to inspecting military installations along the Atlantic coast and the Canadian border, Monroe spent much of his time attending welcoming ceremonies in the numerous towns through which he passed. The symbolic value of a president from Virginia visiting New England, attending Independence Day celebrations in Boston, and meeting with Federalist leaders was not lost, and one newspaper editor

coined the phrase the "Era of Good Feeling" to describe the apparent feeling of national unity. Two years later, in the spring and summer of 1819, Monroe went on an equally successful tour of the southern and western states.

Monroe's two national tours confirmed a popular impression of the president—that of his accessibility. Throughout his career, but especially when he was in Madison's cabinet, Monroe had been perceived not only as a man of power and influence who could deliver results, but also as man who could be approached with requests for assistance and favors. His willingness to help the many correspondents and petitioners seeking his advice and assistance as well as his authority to grant political appointments contributed to his great popularity and national visibility. This sense of accessibility carried over into his presidency; to an extent far greater than his predecessors, he received a barrage of letters requesting appointments to office, petitions for pardons, requests for assistance, and letters of introduction.

**SECURING THE NATION'S BORDERS**

Although all presidents begin their administrations with hopes of pursuing certain goals, they spend much of their time confronting problems not of their own choosing. Monroe was no exception to this, and yet, in retrospect, we can see that he was able to devote a considerable amount of attention to an issue that was of great importance to him: the securing of the nation's boundaries. In 1817 the borders of the United States—with the exception of the Atlantic coast—were undefined or in dispute. Smugglers, pirates, privateers commissioned by foreign nations, filibusters, revolutionary groups, and assorted adventurers operated out of American ports and territory. And, as the War of 1812 had proven so graphically, coastal areas were highly vulnerable to blockade and invasion. Monroe had become familiar with these problems during his years in the cabinet, and he made a concerted effort during his presidency to define the nation's boundaries and to make the borders less vulnerable.

Much of Monroe's concern on this matter stemmed from the experience of the War of 1812 when British warships sailed at will in American territorial waters (a British squadron operated in Chesapeake Bay throughout the war) and British troops captured the nation's capital. In his first inaugural address he recommended that "our coast and inland frontiers . . . be fortified, our Army and Navy . . . be kept in perfect order, and our militia be placed on the best practicable footing." At his instruction, army engineers began work on an ambitious program for the construction of coastal fortifications. Much of this program was implemented, but one of the great disappointments of his presidency came when Congress, motivated by economy and partisan politics, reduced funding and forced the curtailment of construction at several key installations. Monroe also oversaw the reorganization of the army, the improvement of the military academy at West Point (both of which were begun during Monroe's tenure as secretary of war in 1814 to 1815), and the strengthening of the navy.

The war had also underscored the weakness of the border between the United States and the British provinces in Canada. The first treaty signed by Monroe as president—the Rush-Bagot Treaty (named for Richard Rush, who served as acting secretary of state until Adams arrived from Europe, and Charles Bagot, the British minister to the United States)—provided for arms limitation on the Great Lakes. This treaty was a personal triumph for the president, for although it bore Rush's name Monroe had conducted the major portion of the negotiation during his last months as secretary of state.

The United States and Great Britain also attempted to reach agreement on the boundary stretching from the Great Lakes to the Atlantic. Preliminary discussions and surveys were inconclusive, however, and this portion of the border remained in dispute until the late 1840s. Negotiations regarding the western portion of the boundary were more successful, and in 1818 the two nations signed a treaty defining the boundary between the Great Lakes and the Rocky Mountains and agreeing to joint occupation of the Oregon country. The United States urged subsequent negotiations for an end to the disputed claim to Oregon, but joint occupancy was all that the British were willing to concede at that time. The United States had better success with Russia, which signed a treaty in 1824 renouncing its claim to the Oregon country and northern California.

## GAINING FLORIDA

Of even greater concern was the longstanding dispute with Spain over Florida. The United States viewed foreign possession of Florida as a threat to its security, while Spain considered the province essential to the security of its colonies in the West Indies. The Spanish repeatedly rebuffed U.S. efforts to purchase Florida, including Monroe's mission to Spain in 1805. When Monroe became president he was committed to acquiring Florida without provoking war with Spain and its European allies. This goal was becoming increasingly difficult to reach, for many Americans—particularly in the South—were demanding the immediate occupation of Florida. Twice during his cabinet years Monroe had had to restrain unauthorized expeditions into Florida: in 1811, when General George Mathews marched to the aid of "revolutionaries" in Florida, and in 1814, when General Andrew Jackson captured the Spanish post at Pensacola. This tense situation was exacerbated by Spanish and British support for hostile tribes who used Florida as a haven following raids on U.S. territory.

The crisis came to a head in 1818 when Andrew Jackson, marching in pursuit of hostile Seminoles, captured the Spanish forts at St. Marks and Pensacola. Both the cabinet and Congress debated censuring Jackson for his unauthorized actions. In both bodies, many of the proponents of censure hoped to sully Jackson's reputation and diminish his growing popularity as a potential presidential candidate in 1824. Neither President Monroe nor Secretary of State

Adams were interested in this debate. Intent on acquiring Florida, they used Jackson's incursion as a diplomatic lever to force Spain to cede the province. Furthermore, Monroe, committed as he was to strengthening the nation's defenses, was not going to censure or cashier the army's most able general. In later years Jackson claimed that he had received secret authorization from Monroe to capture Pensacola. Jackson had proposed a clandestine operation in Florida, but there is no evidence to support Jackson's claim that the president had instructed him to proceed. Indeed, in the weeks immediately following the incident Jackson defended his actions by insisting that his regular orders authorized him to act as he did.

Spain, beset with domestic unrest and revolt throughout its American empire, finally gave in to U.S. persistence and pressure, agreeing in February 1819 to the cession of Florida to the United States. In the same treaty, the United States and Spain agreed on a boundary line between the western United States and Spanish Mexico that reached from the Gulf of Mexico to the Pacific Ocean. This was a great triumph for both Monroe, who had pursued the acquisition of Florida for many years, and for Secretary of State Adams, who had negotiated the treaty.

## INDIAN POLICY

The continued presence of the Indian nations residing within the United States added to the boundary problems with Great Britain and Spain and the general question of national security. Indian relations were a perennial problem. The United States recognized the tribes as alien nations who resided within the territory of the United States and who retained tribal control over their land. Jeffersonian Indian policy was based on the premise of anglicizing (or "civilizing," in contemporary parlance) the Indians and teaching them to become land-owning farmers. While many Indians accepted this fate as inevitable, others refused to abandon their native culture or to give in to pressure to sell their tribal lands. Monroe

adhered to the Jeffersonian policy, but by 1820 he had become an advocate of a policy of removal, in which the tribes were encouraged to exchange their land in the East for land west of the Mississippi. The president argued that removal would open up millions of valuable acres to settlement and would, by removing the tribes beyond the limits of westward expansion, protect them from depredations by rapacious Americans.

But he was also concerned about security. During the War of 1812 Indians in both the North and the South had sided with the British; removal of the tribes to the West would eliminate this internal threat. Efforts to purchase Indian land in the East and arrange the removal of the tribes to the West were increased, and during the Monroe administration the national government purchased millions of acres of such land. Even so, Monroe held to the principle that Indian land could be acquired only with the consent of the tribes. Georgia was particularly adamant that Indians be removed forcibly from within the boundaries of the state—a demand Monroe rebuffed, stating that to remove them by force "would be revolting to humanity and utterly unjustifiable"—and it was during this period that the conflict between Georgia and the national government over Indian removal began.

## RESPONDING TO LATIN AMERICAN INDEPENDENCE

Monroe's efforts to strengthen the country's borders were further complicated by the independence movement in the Spanish-American empire. The United States had been bedeviled since its inception by adventurers who hatched a variety of schemes for incursions into Spanish territory bordering the United States. This problem was exacerbated by the outbreak of revolution in the Spanish empire in 1810. Between 1810 and 1820, American and European adventurers joined forces with agents from the revolutionary governments to the south. These filibusters comprised a mixed group of patriots who were committed to the cause of independence and freebooters who hoped to reap personal gain from the confusion of war and revolution. Most of this activity centered on the Louisiana-Texas border and in the ports of the Atlantic coast. These adventurers posed a serious dilemma for the U.S. government.

Both the Madison and Monroe administrations united with the vast majority of the American people in their sympathy with the Spanish-American revolutionaries. At the same time, the government did not want to take any action that would alienate the Spanish or jeopardize negotiations for the acquisition of Florida. Nor did the government approve of the open violation of U.S. neutrality by persons making war against Spain from U.S. territory. Monroe had faced this problem during his years as secretary of state, and when he became president he sought to suppress such activity. He cracked down on the illegal outfitting of privateers in U.S. ports. He sent expeditions to destroy pirate and privateering bases in Florida, Louisiana, and Texas. And he ordered the suppression of filibustering expeditions moving against Texas.

These efforts were only partially successful, for it was frequently difficult to differentiate between legal and illegal activities. Furthermore, Monroe had to walk a fine line between domestic politics and diplomatic considerations. Support for the Spanish-American independence movement was widespread throughout the United States, and Monroe's political opponents regularly attacked him for being lukewarm in his support of the cause. Monroe countered these arguments by claiming that a policy of neutrality benefited the United States by keeping it out of a war with Spain and aided the revolutionaries by recognizing them as belligerents with a status equal to that of Spain. Monroe resisted calls for the recognition of the independence of the Spanish-American provinces until he was sure they had truly established themselves as independent nations. In early 1822 he recommended that Congress appropriate money for diplomatic missions to those countries and in June of that year he officially received a minister from Colombia, making the United States the first nation to recognize the independence of a new Spanish American nation.

In a move closely related to the definition and security of the nation's borders, Monroe ordered the navy to undertake a concerted effort to suppress piracy. The European nations and the United States had commissioned a large number of privateers during the Napoleonic wars and the War of 1812 to prey on enemy commerce. When those wars ended in 1815, many of these privateers continued their lucrative attacks on commercial shipping. While some enlisted in the service of the revolutionary governments in Spanish America, others simply became pirates. The United States found these attacks on its commerce intolerable. Pirate bases were destroyed, a special naval squadron cruised the waters of the pirate-infested Caribbean Sea, and captured pirates were condemned to death.

## THE MONROE DOCTRINE

The definition of the boundaries of the United States received a philosophical dimension in 1823 with the enunciation of the Monroe Doctrine. In the summer of that year, British Prime Minister George Canning suggested that Great Britain and the United States issue a joint statement warning the European powers against any attempt to assist Spain in the reconquest of its now-independent former colonies in America. After much thought and consultation with his friends and advisers, Monroe decided to issue a unilateral statement, and he decided to issue it in his annual message to Congress.

The portion of the message that became known as the Monroe Doctrine had three components. The first was a reaffirmation of the traditional U.S. policy of neutrality and noninvolvement in European affairs. The second component, directed toward Spain and its allies, stated that the United States acknowledged the legitimacy of existing colonies, but that it would consider "any interposition for oppressing [the newly independent nations to the south], or in controlling in any other manner their destiny" or any attempt by the Europeans "to extend their system to any portion of this hemisphere" as "dangerous to our peace and safety" and as the "manifestation of an unfriendly disposition toward the United States." A third component, addressed to Russia (which had territorial ambitions in the Pacific northwest), proclaimed that the Western Hemisphere was no longer open to new colonization by European nations.

The declaration was ineffectual as a deterrent to the anticipated invasion, for that threat had already been defused by the British, who had extracted a promise from France that it would not assist Spain in the recovery of its colonies. But it did not matter to Monroe that his pronouncement had no immediate diplomatic effect. The president did not intend his message to be merely a diplomatic missive. (He rejected Adams's suggestion that the policy be enunciated in messages delivered to various foreign governments.) Rather, he perceived it as a statement of the place that the United States envisioned for itself in the world. According to Monroe, the United States was an exceptional place, a nation in which government and society were based on the republican ideals of the American Revolution, ideals that flourished in the Americas but not in Europe. The European monarchies had recently suppressed several liberalization movements, and it was the suppression of a constitutional movement in Spain by a French army that led to fears of a European invasion of the former Spanish colonies.

Monroe argued that any attempt to reconquer those provinces—which were imitating the United States and adopting republican forms of government—or any effort to establish monarchy in the Spanish empire or to establish new colonies in the Western Hemisphere would be viewed not only as an attack on independent nations but as an attack on republicanism and, by inference, on the United States. The Monroe Doctrine defined a hemispheric boundary for American republicanism just as the treaties with Spain, Great Britain, and Russia defined the geographic boundaries of the continental nation.

Monroe's success in securing the nation's boundaries was an impressive feat, but it was not an easy one. The treaty negotiations—especially those with Spain—were long and difficult. Jackson's foray into Florida, the relations with the Spanish-American revolutionaries, the reorganization of the army, and Indian policy were all highly charged political issues. These, along with the other controversies he faced as president, tested Monroe's mettle as a politician and chief executive.

## ECONOMIC TROUBLES

In 1819 the United States witnessed the beginning of the first major economic depression since the 1780s. Although Monroe sympathized with those who were injured by declining exports, curtailed credit, and a shortage of currency, he continued to believe that the national economy was basically healthy and would soon right itself. Furthermore, he—along with most other Americans—believed there was little that the national government could or should do about the crisis. He believed that responsibility for dealing with the problems of the depression lay with the Bank of the United States, which could regulate currency and credit, and with the states, which had the authority to enact debtor-relief laws and—through their chartering of state banks—to regulate currency.

The remedies available to the national government were much more proscribed and heavily influenced by political considerations. Congress passed several laws providing relief to those indebted to the United States for the purchase of public land—a popular and noncontroversial measure—but it refused to undertake the politically dangerous task of revising the tariff. Although it was a small gesture, Monroe showed his sympathy for those experiencing difficulties by readily granting pardons to the many petitioners who had been convicted of defaulting on debts owed to the national government.

Monroe exhibited his constitutional scruples in 1822 when he vetoed the Cumberland Road bill. Although favoring the construction of a national transportation system, he believed that the national government lacked the constitutional authority necessary to undertake such a project. In his first annual message to Congress—and on many subsequent occasions—Monroe recommended that a constitutional amendment granting that power be submitted to the states. When Congress passed a bill in 1822 for the repair of the existing portion of the Cumberland Road and for the collection of tolls, Monroe vetoed it, explaining his views in a long essay and once again calling for a constitutional amendment.

## THE MISSOURI COMPROMISE

Monroe faced the greatest crisis of his presidency in 1819 during the debate over the admittance of Missouri to the Union. Sympathetic to the states' rights position of the South, Monroe supported the unrestricted admission of Missouri as a slave state, blaming the controversy on New England Federalists who, he claimed, were using the slavery issue as a rallying point in an attempt to revive their party. Nevertheless, he realized that the bitter debate over the volatile issue of slavery had the potential to destroy the Union, and his greater loyalty was to the Union. Monroe accepted the proposed compromise that would allow Missouri to enter the Union as a slave state while forbidding slavery in the northern portion of the western territory as a viable solution to the problem. Aware that his open espousal of the plan would jeopardize its success by alienating southerners or those who opposed executive interference in legislative matters, Monroe quietly but effectively helped the proponents of the compromise to marshal the votes necessary for passage of the bill.

Characteristically, Monroe based his support for the Missouri compromise on the preservation of the Union. And also characteristically, he said little about slavery itself, beyond affirming that slavery was a state institution and that Congress had no right to legislate on the matter. Throughout his life, Monroe was generally quiet on the issue of slavery. His few remarks on the subject indicate he believed that slavery was evil, that the United States would be a better place without it, and that he would have supported a practical plan of emancipation if one had been presented.

He had long been an advocate of the abolition of the international slave trade, and in 1820 he signed a law declaring the African slave trade to be an act of piracy. American warships were sent to the coast of Africa and ordered to intercept any American vessels suspected of carrying slaves. Agents were also sent to Africa to assist in the resettlement of Africans released from captured slave ships. Sympathetic with the goals of the American Colonization Society, Monroe allowed it to select these agents and instructed them to cooperate with the society in the establishment of a colony in Africa for freed American blacks. In 1823 he took the even more drastic step of approving a treaty with Great Britain that included provisions allowing the warships of either country to stop and inspect ships of both countries suspected of carrying slaves. (The Senate rejected the treaty.)

## ELECTION OF 1820

Monroe's fears about a revival of the Federalist party proved to be unnecessary, for the demise of the Federalists as a national party was complete—there was no Federalist candidate to oppose Monroe in the 1820 election. The Republicans, assuming that Monroe would easily win reelection, met in caucus but adjourned without making a nomination. Although there was no doubt of Monroe being reelected, there were signs of opposition, mostly stemming from discontent over the Missouri compromise. The Virginia assembly threatened to withhold its endorsement of Monroe and was mollified only when the president gave assurance that he would veto any bill that did not allow Missouri to enter the Union on equal footing with the existing states (that is, with slavery). In other states, including New York, Pennsylvania, and South Carolina, dissatisfaction over Monroe's signing of the compromise bill led to the fielding of alternate candidates. This was merely token opposition, however, and Monroe received every electoral vote except the one cast by the disgruntled William Plumer, Jr., of New Hampshire.

## MANEUVERING FOR 1824

If the election of 1820 was a lackluster affair, the election of 1824 was anything but that. Monroe was the last member of the revolutionary generation to serve as president, and everyone knew that his successor would be from the generation that came of political age during the War of 1812. There was a mad scramble among the many potential candidates, with John Quincy Adams, John C. Calhoun, William H. Crawford, Henry Clay, and Andrew Jackson being the most notable of the presidential aspirants. At one point, Monroe joked with Attorney General William Wirt that Wirt was the only member of the cabinet not running for president. This mirthful remark was a rare one, for the intense rivalry to succeed him—a rivalry that began in 1817—was a source of unending trouble for the president. Monroe got along well with each of the five main candidates, but their mutual distrust and constant maneuvering to discredit their rivals and promote their candidacies frequently undermined Monroe's programs. The treaty with Great Britain that contained provisions for the suppression of the slave trade, for example, was defeated by supporters of Crawford who wanted to discredit Adams.

This rivalry and distrust became particularly intense during Monroe's second term. Monroe tried to remain aloof from the campaign and tried to avoid any action or remark that could be interpreted as favoring any one of the candidates. Despite his efforts, he was nevertheless dragged into the campaign, for the jostling to undermine rival candidates easily became attacks on the president himself. Although Monroe bristled under these attacks, he resisted the urge to respond publicly. He remained on friendly terms with all the candidates except Crawford, whose efforts to sabotage the initiatives of his rivals became too blatant to be ignored. Monroe reprimanded Crawford and would have dismissed him—Crawford had suffered a stroke in 1823 and his continued ill-health, to say nothing of his insubordination, would have justified his removal—had not Monroe feared that dismissal would have enhanced Crawford's candidacy. Monroe probably favored Adams over the other candidates and was pleased by his election.

## ACHIEVEMENTS AND EVALUATION

Monroe left the presidency satisfied that his administration had been a success. His years as president had certainly been filled with controversy and difficulties, most notably the depression of 1819, the acrimonious debate of the admission of Missouri, and the long and bitter contest over the election of his successor as president. There were disappointments as well, the curtailment of the program for construction of coastal fortifications being probably the greatest. And Monroe certainly had his opponents and detractors—the Old Republicans of his native Virginia who believed that in his nationalism he had strayed from the true path of republicanism, politicians North and South who saw his support of the Missouri compromise as a betrayal, advocates of the Spanish-American independence movement who thought he had acted too slowly in support of the revolutionaries, and a host of political rivals.

Monroe, always protective of his reputation and honor, resented the opposition and rankled at the personal attacks. But the years of experience in public office and the driving ambition that carried him to the presidency had also honed him into an expert politician who knew when to remain silent and when to respond. He knew how to promise just enough to keep his supporters in line, and he could judiciously use political patronage to ensure support at crucial moments. He also knew how to tailor his letters for their intended readers. During the Missouri controversy, for example, letters to political associates in Virginia—letters Monroe knew would be read by many in Richmond—emphasized his attachment to states' rights and the Constitution, while his confidential correspondence revealed his avid support for a compromise. He did not lie, but he did carefully compose his remarks to convey a desired impression.

He also knew when to remain silent and aloof from controversy, as in the presidential contest of 1824 when he knew there was nothing to gain from engaging in a public dispute with the partisans of the various candidates. Later in the 1820s, when the supporters of Andrew Jackson attacked the Monroe administration as a way of attacking John Quincy Adams, Monroe continued to maintain his semblance of neutrality by remaining silent himself but allowing his friends to defend his administration and advising them on how to respond to his critics.

For all the tumult, Monroe was justified in his satisfaction with his years as president. His efforts to strengthen the boundaries and defense of the country were immensely successful, and his decision to delay the recognition of the independence of the Spanish American republics to a date later than his critics demanded was vindicated. The country recovered from the economic reverses of 1819 and weathered the sectional crisis of Missouri controversy—at least for a while. He was highly gratified by the many letters he received in praise of his service as president and by the resolutions passed by many of the state legislatures expressing approbation of his conduct. But most important and most satisfactory to Monroe, the United States and its people continued to prosper and flourish under the republican institutions engendered by the American Revolution. Monroe frequently commented on the blessings and prosperity enjoyed by the United States, and he characteristically closed his last annual message to Congress by stating,

I cannot conclude this communication . . . without recollecting with great sensibility and heartfelt gratitude the many instances of the public confidence and the generous support with which I have been honored. Having commenced my service in early youth, and continued it since with few and short intervals, I have witnessed the great difficulties to which our Union has been exposed, and admired the virtue and intelligence with which they have been sur-

mounted. From the present prosperous and happy state I derive a gratification which I cannot express. That these blessings may be preserved and perpetuated will be the object of my fervent and unceasing prayers to the Supreme Ruler of the Universe.

James Monroe will never be remembered as one of our greatest presidents, for he did not possess the traits we admire in those we deem to be our great presidents. He was not a philosopher. By his own admission he was not well educated, and his several attempts at expressing his views on political philosophy were ineffective. He was not charismatic. Those who knew him commented not on his charm or his brilliance but on his kindness and urbanity. And he did not, by the force of his character, lead the nation through a dire crisis. He was, however, a good and competent president, an able administrator, a seasoned diplomat, and a skilled politician who presided over the United States at a difficult period in its history and who conducted the affairs of state in a manner that was honorable both to himself and to the nation.

## BIBLIOGRAPHY

Ammon, Harry. *James Monroe: The Quest for National Identity* (McGraw-Hill, 1971).

Bemis, Samuel Flagg. *John Quincy Adams and the Formation of American Foreign Policy* (Knopf, 1949).

Birkner, Michael J. *Samuel L. Southard: Jeffersonian Whig* (Fairleigh-Dickinson University Press, 1984).

Cunningham, Noble E., Jr. *The Presidency of James Monroe* (University Press of Kansas, 1996).

Dangerfield, George. *The Awakening of American Nationalism, 1815–1828* (Harper & Row, 1965).

May, Ernest R. *The Making of the Monroe Doctrine* (Harvard University Press, 1975).

Mooney, Chase C. *William H. Crawford, 1772–1834* (University Press of Kentucky, 1974).

Perkins, Dexter. *The Monroe Doctrine, 1823–1826* (Harvard University Press, 1927).

Wiltse, Charles M. *John C. Calhoun: Nationalist, 1782–1828* (Bobbs-Merrill, 1944).

# JOHN QUINCY ADAMS
## 1825–1829

*Greg Russell*

*Born 11 July 1767 in Braintree (now Quincy), Massachusetts, to John Adams and Abigail Smith Adams; educated at Harvard College, Cambridge, Massachusetts (B.A. 1787); married Louisa Catherine Johnson, 26 July 1797, London, England; four children; elected president in 1824 in an unusual race in which no candidate received a majority of the electoral college ballots: Andrew Jackson of Tennessee received 153,544 popular votes and 99 electoral ballots; Adams received 108,740 votes and 84 ballots; William Harris Crawford of Georgia had 47,136 votes and 41 ballots; and Henry Clay of Kentucky had 46,618 votes and 37 ballots; the House of Representatives, voting by states, elected Adams as president; the electoral college chose John Caldwell Calhoun of South Carolina as vice president; died 23 February 1848 in Washington, D.C.; buried at First Unitarian Church, Quincy, Massachusetts.*

For John Quincy Adams, the moral component of character in politics could not be detached from the integrity—or lack thereof—exhibited by citizens preoccupied with family life and in community with others. The very fabric of the American Union, according to Adams, was preserved by the obligation of statesmen to work "towards the moral purification of their country from besetting sins." This could be accomplished, in the first instance, only "by setting the example of private morality" and in the second, "by promoting the cause in every way that they can lawfully act on others."

## MORALITY AND POLITICS

The long career of John Quincy Adams offers a vivid profile of a moral man compromised by the political necessities of an immoral society and uncertain world. As one who earnestly believed that moral principle should be the alpha and omega of all political discourse, Adams spent his life at the center of national and international developments that called into question the power and principles of the young American republic. Following his graduation from Harvard (1787), Adams served as minister to the Netherlands (1794–1796), minister to Prussia (1797–1798), member of the Massachusetts senate (1802), member of the U.S. Senate (1803–1808), minister to Russia (1809–1814), minister to Great Britain (1815–1817), secretary of state (1817–1825), president of the United States (1825–1829), and member of the House of Representatives (1831–48). Whether serving at home or abroad, Adams treated even the most mundane political duty as an invitation to reflect on the norms of democratic and republican rule. One seminal principle—"the discharge of some duty to God or man"—was the anchor for Adams as citizen and statesman.

John Quincy Adams was born in the North Parish of Braintree, Massachusetts, on 11 July 1767. His youthful memories encompassed the stirring and portentous events of America's revolutionary struggle against Britain. John Adams was often away at the Continental Congress, and the burden of the young boy's education fell upon Abigail, the "school mistress," and on the young law clerks in his father's employ. Both parents—emphasizing the indissoluble link between morality and liberty—nurtured habits of civic virtue and patriotic resolve. Father reminded son that human nature, in all its infirmities, is still capable of great things. At Harvard, John Quincy's commencement address saluted the importance of *public* faith to the well-being of a community. He spoke against the dangerous proposition that "nations are not subject to those laws which regulate the conduct of individuals."

## A SHAPER OF FOREIGN POLICY

Few other Americans were better qualified to shape and direct U.S. foreign policy during the era of 1814 to 1828 than was John Quincy Adams. President Washington, speaking of Adams's promise as a diplomat, had no doubt "that he will prove himself the ablest of our diplomatic corps." President Madison appointed Adams to head the U.S. delegation to conclude the Treaty of Ghent in 1814. One year later, as minister to Britain, Adams initiated proceedings that resulted in the Rush-Bagot Agreement of 1817. As secretary of state in the Monroe administration, Adams negotiated the Convention of 1818. In addition to providing joint occupation of the Oregon Territory, this agreement defined the American-Canadian border along the forty-ninth parallel.

Secretary Adams was the only member of the cabinet to defend General Andrew Jackson's 1818 invasion of Spanish territory in Florida and seizure of Pensacola. Adams conceded that Jackson's conduct was questionable, that defending it forced him to stretch his principles to the breaking point. Yet the political challenge (avoiding "truckling to Spain") persuaded Adams that it was better to err on the side of vigor than on that of weakness. American honor and prestige would suffer by surrendering to a pusillanimous policy in relations with other nations. No less a moralist than Jefferson himself spoke of Secretary Adams's pivotal state paper defending Jackson's actions as "among the ablest compositions [he had] ever seen;" in fact, the former president recommended that it be circulated widely in Europe as a benchmark of American statecraft. The Adams-Onís Treaty of 1819, regarded by Adams as the crowning achievement of his diplomatic service, ceded Florida to the United States and established the western boundaries of Louisiana. The treaty set the stage for the nation's longest-lived foreign policy—the Monroe Doctrine.

Adams, next to the president himself, took the lead in defining the broad contours of U.S. diplomacy at a time when the national interest was challenged by several developments: British and Russian claims to the Pacific northwest, independence movements by Spain's colonies in South America, and rumors of intervention by the Holy Alliance in the Western Hemisphere. Adams was the architect behind the noninterference clause of Monroe's Doctrine, which stipulated that the "American continents . . . are henceforth not to be considered as subjects for future colonization by any European power."

Adams also drew a sharp line between intervention and sympathy on behalf of those fighting for freedom: America's prayers would be forthcoming wherever "the standard of freedom . . . shall be unfurled"; however, prudence required that the nation abstain "from interference in the concerns of others, even when the conflict has been for principles to which she clings." Moral principles alone did not entitle the United States to venture "abroad in search of monsters to destroy." Adams made room for political realism by recognizing that universal norms cannot be applied to the actions of states in their abstract formulation. He reminded his countrymen that duties to others cannot be separated from duties to oneself.

## THE ELECTION OF 1824 AND THE "CORRUPT BARGAIN"

During Monroe's second administration, presidential ambitions and political networking absorbed the energies of promi-

nent leaders in the cabinet: John Quincy Adams (state), John C. Calhoun (war), and William H. Crawford (treasury). Other candidates in the 1824 election included Henry Clay of Kentucky, the powerful Speaker of the House, as well as the increasingly popular Andrew Jackson, then senator from Tennessee. Family history, no less than his record as secretary of state, convinced Adams that he had "more at stake upon the result [of the election] than any other individual in the Union." He fortified himself with the admonition that an ability to accept success must be tempered by the equanimity to endure defeat.

Such reassurance was difficult to come by during the Era of Good Feelings, a clever slogan that could not conceal the divisiveness associated with the decline of political parties and the virtual eclipse of the congressional nominating caucus. Members of Congress realized over a period of several months that no candidate was likely to win a majority of electoral votes and that, according to the Twelfth Amendment to the Constitution, the election would be decided by the House of Representatives. The expectation of a stalemate was confirmed in December by the final tally of electoral votes: Jackson, 99; Adams, 84; Crawford, 41; and Clay, 37.

The election in the House—on 9 February 1825—took place amid loud cries of "bargain and sale." Clay, being fourth and excluded from the final vote, emerged as the king maker. An entry in Adams's diary on 9 January mentions a conversation with Clay in which the latter wanted Adams "to satisfy him with regard to some principles of great public importance but without any personal considerations for himself." Adams provided few additional clues to their exchange, beyond noting that Clay "had no hesitation in saying that his preference would be for me." Gossip was quick to follow that Clay's support had been bought by a position in the cabinet. The election in the House awarded Adams 13 votes, Jackson 7, and Crawford 4. Clay's subsequent elevation to the State Department confirmed, in the excited mind of John Randolph, that "the coalition of Blifil and Black George" amounted to a swindle of patriotism for patronage.

## TROUBLES FROM THE BEGINNING

John Quincy Adams began his presidency, as he did almost each day of his life, with a prayerful supplication "to Heaven, first, for my country," second, for himself and his supporters so that the "result of . . . events may be auspicious and blessed." Considering the political setbacks Adams experienced over the course of his administration, one could almost conclude that the Puritan fell slowly but surely from divine favor following four years of martyrdom. There is no small irony in the fact that the career of Adams the diplomat, America's most accomplished secretary of state in the nineteenth century, was followed by a presidency seldom remembered for important domestic or foreign policy issues. The president's wife, Louisa Catherine Adams, was not slow to acknowledge that a private station for her husband was "in comparison perfect freedom to the prison house of state."

From the beginning of his presidency, Quincy Adams confronted numerous political and institutional obstacles, some of his own creation. The transition from the Monroe to the Adams administration, concomitant with the disarray of the National Republicans, was a chaotic free-for-all. Adams brought a rigid and austere attitude to his policy of appointments and removals from office. He was as unmoved by Clay's frank appeal to "clear the deck" of his enemies as he was by the pleas of congressional supporters seeking political rewards for their own favorite nominees. To endorse the principle of rotation in office, Adams believed, "would make the government a perpetual and unremitting scramble for office." The counsels of realism could not have been close at hand when Adams "decided to renominate all against whom there was no complaint." With all the vast patronage at his disposal, Adams removed just twelve office holders in four years, and then only for

gross negligence. Potential allies found few advantages—in the way of perquisites—by rallying to Adams's side. Opponents discovered that little was to be lost in working against him.

The desire to retain Monroe's cabinet virtually intact led to President Adams's stunning willingness to consider offering the War Department post to General Jackson, as well as to retaining Postmaster General John McLean, an accomplished trickster who secretly supported Jackson. Adams's goal in putting together his cabinet, as Robert Remini has pointed out, was to form a true coalition of all the Republican factions (headed by Adams, Clay, Crawford, Jackson, and Calhoun). Jackson registered his opposition to such a "monstrous union," retired for a short period to the Hermitage, and left proxy forces behind to declaim the corruption between Adams and Clay.

Crawford resigned his position the day before Adams's inauguration. Richard Rush, former minister to England, became head of the treasury. James Barbour, an avowed Crawford supporter, took over at the War Department, and William Wirt agreed to remain as attorney general. Not a single member of the new cabinet had supported Adams in the 1824 election.

Other disturbing political omens welcomed the new administration. Just two days after the election, Adams was informed by friends that his vice president, John C. Calhoun, had threatened—in the event that Clay was appointed secretary of state—to mastermind the election of Jackson in 1828. Much to Clay's own surprise, 14 out of 41 senators voted against his nomination. In his diary, Adams recorded the vote as "the first act of . . . opposition from the stump which is to be carried on against the Administration from the banners of General Jackson." Neither Clay nor Adams were easily agitated by momentary political furies. Yet consciousness of rectitude, as Carl Schurz pointed out, could not save either statesman from the consequences of neglecting to consider the costs of their alliance. Little time elapsed in Congress before the Jackson, Crawford, and Calhoun factions—under the powerful sway of Senator Martin Van Buren—coordinated their efforts to demolish the legislative fruits of the "corrupt bargain."

## THE DAILY ROUTINE

Adams's daily regimen as president and scholar politician often deprived him of the few opportunities available to expand his narrow base of political support. His day began between four-thirty and five o'clock, at which time he usually read two chapters of the Bible along with related works in either philosophy or theology. During this period of his life, Adams was much concerned about the state of his health and the need for vigorous exercise. He was in the habit of taking long walks and, spring or summer weather permitting, he would startle onlookers by swimming from one side of the Potomac to the other. Always complaining about the absence of time to pursue his own literary interests, Adams spent most mornings poring over newspapers and various public papers from departments of the cabinet. Breakfast occupied the hour from nine until ten. A steady stream of official visitors kept him busy until four or five in the afternoon. According to his custom, the president refused all invitations and declined to appear at social engagements. Dinner was taken between five-thirty and seven; thereafter, until about eleven o'clock, he spent time alone signing land grants or blank patents.

## THE PRESIDENTIAL AGENDA AND ITS CONSEQUENCES

The president's first annual message to Congress on the state of the union, delivered 6 December 1825, was a remarkable document in several respects. First, it laid out all the seminal themes and goals Adams would set before the nation during the course of his presidency. Second, it contended for principles as liberal and far-reaching as its author's political methods were conservative and restrained. Third, it was written with a warmth and enthusiasm not always typical in Adams's state papers. Fourth, it enabled the president to reflect

on the conditions of peace and prosperity then before the nation. Fifth, it succeeded in alienating virtually every organized political interest throughout the Union. New and vital forces in the country—industrialism, the expansion of the West, a constantly widening electorate, and the rise of democracy—would shatter the new president's beliefs about his society and the role of government in defense of the public interest.

The very purpose of government, Adams suggested, was to improve the condition of the people. Indeed, "moral, political, and intellectual improvement are duties assigned by the Author of our Existence to social, no less than to individual man." Members of Congress grew even more restless when Adams called upon them to support the following endeavors: exploration of the northwest coast of the continent; establishment of a uniform system of weights and measures; creation of a national university; provision for astronomical observatories (derided as "lighthouses of the skies"); and appropriation of funds for an extensive system of federally sponsored internal improvements. Even the president's closest friends realized that he had driven yet another nail in his own political coffin. The last line of Adams's address—instructing his fellow citizens on their ironclad obligation to promote "the highest welfare of our country"—offered a standard few would be inclined to follow.

Virtually all the antagonism Adams encountered from Congress over the next four years followed from one or another objection to the broad proposals he laid out in his address. His vision of an activist national government, particularly from a constitutional standpoint, surpassed even the most latitudinarian Federalist doctrines of the past. In addition, his assertion that "liberty is power" was at odds with the current climate of opinion that more often held that the defense of liberty required restraints on governmental power.

More conservative politicians, who gravitated toward a Jeffersonian or Republican creed, thought Adams had clearly trespassed on the reserved rights of states. Jefferson himself questioned the constitutionality of some of the proposals. The champions of strict construction in the South saw in the president's message a harbinger of anti-slavery legislation. Congress, as well as the public at large, took exception with his condescending (though not inaccurate) remark that European monarchies had accomplished more in promoting science and the arts than had the young, virtuous republic. Should Americans, Adams asked, "fold up our arms and proclaim to the world that we are palsied by the will of our constituents?"

## THE PANAMA CONFERENCE

The first actual collision between the administration and its congressional critics occurred in the field of foreign policy. In his presidential address, Adams announced that the United States had accepted an invitation from several independent Latin American countries to attend a congress in Panama. The intrahemispheric conference was the culmination of Simón Bolívar's idea for a Pan-American summit first broached in 1821. In the spring of 1825, ministers from Mexico and Colombia approached Henry Clay hoping to solicit U.S. participation in the summit. The enthusiastic Clay won the less-than-wholehearted approval of the president, who, as secretary of state, had taken exception to Clay's desire to establish a league of republics—a counterpoise to the Holy Alliance—that would make North America the ark of human liberty.

Certainly Adams did not share many of the ambitious goals of his southern neighbors, including proposals for military cooperation against external foes, diplomatic recognition of Haiti, and the liberation of Cuba and Puerto Rico. The president believed the conference might move beyond general agreement on the promotion of religious liberty and liberalization of commerce and take up specific issues related to the prohibition of piracy and the slave trade. Such an agenda, contrary to the allegations of administration critics, had little to do with exporting democracy or interfering in the domestic affairs of foreign regimes.

Opposition to the Panama meeting was orchestrated by Van Buren and Calhoun, in conjunction with the four southern members of the Senate Foreign Relations Committee. For weeks, antiadministration forces in the Senate delayed final confirmation of the president's nominees to head up the U.S. delegation. The president's intricate report on the Panama mission was sensationalized further by Van Buren's successful strategy to bring the president's confidential message before open deliberations in the Senate. "I should leave to themselves," Adams said, "the determination of a question upon the motives for which, not being informed of them, I was not competent to decide." While the president's nominees were finally confirmed, the good faith of the U.S. negotiators was all but undermined by slave-owning representatives in their derisive comments about Latin Americans.

The House of Representatives grudgingly appropriated $40,000 for the Panamanian mission, as the president had requested. Southern legislators—led by Thomas Hart Benton, Robert Hayne, and John Holmes—complained about entangling alliances, the folly of ending the slave trade, and the "insurrectionary" spirit that would infect the slave population of the United States if Cuba and Puerto Rico were revolutionized. John Randolph, still fuming in the Senate, used the Panamanian issue to launch a venomous attack on Adams and Clay, borrowing a wild analogy from Henry Fielding's *Tom Jones* to dramatize the unseemly combination of "the puritan and the blackleg." The latter aspersion, variously defined as a swindler or dishonest gambler, led to an inconclusive duel between Randolph and Clay on 8 April 1826. Adams would never forgive his own vice president for permitting such an outrageous harangue to continue, over the space of six hours, without interruption on the Senate floor.

The outcome of the Panamanian conference was an anticlimax compared with the turbulence and political violence it left behind in the United States. The two U.S. delegates never did attend the meeting: One died en route to the conference and the other arrived after the congress adjourned. Clay's momentous instructions for the diplomats—proposing in essence a Good Neighbor Policy more than a century before the famous statement of Franklin D. Roosevelt—were not published (owing, at the time, to the opposition of Jacksonians) until the opening of the first International American Conference that met in Washington in 1889. The disappointment for Clay and Adams was compounded by Britain's efforts to strengthen its trading position in Latin America.

## GEORGIA AND THE INDIAN LANDS

The Adams administration confronted in 1826 a growing rebellion stemming from the land claims of the Creek Indians in Georgia. At stake was not only the interest of cotton farmers in the rich bottom land inhabited by the Creeks but also the status of tribes (and their land holdings) within states and territories of the United States. Following their defeat in 1814 by General Jackson at the Battle of Horseshoe Bend, the Creeks were left with some 23 million acres in Alabama and Georgia. Central to the controversy was the questionable status of the Treaty of Indian Springs, which had been negotiated late in the Monroe administration and had received a largely pro forma signature by President Adams. The treaty, fraudulently signed only by a minority of the tribe's representatives, obligated the Creeks to surrender almost 5 million acres of land in Georgia in exchange for $400,000 and equal acreage west of the Mississippi. Governor George Troup of Georgia, seizing the banner of states' rights, tried to hasten the process by commissioning a survey of Creek lands. Following an investigation, Adams called a halt to the survey and demanded renegotiation of the treaty.

Efforts to resolve the impasse were affected by the larger debate concerning the acquisition of tribal lands. Historically, the U.S. government had relied on the treaty-making clause of the Constitution for such landed transactions. Secretary of War Bar-

bour suggested, much as Jackson and Calhoun had during the Monroe administration, a new course that would deny tribal sovereignty and subject tribes to the will of Congress. This could be achieved either by relocating Indians, as individuals rather than as tribal members, to a designated territory west of established states or simply by incorporating tribes within the states. Secretary of State Clay, alternating between anger and resignation at a meeting of the cabinet in December 1825, claimed that little good could come from this "inferior" race save their inevitable extinction. The president himself knew of "no practicable plan by which they can be organized into one civilized or half-civilized government." If Clay's position represented administration sentiment, then why not defer to the machinations of Governor Troup in Georgia?

Adams at least insisted on legal means for capitulating to what had become Georgia's fait accompli. The vehicle for this purpose was the Treaty of Washington, by which the Creeks were pressured into surrendering most of the lands claimed by Georgia. The president placed it before the Senate from "a conviction that between it and a resort to the forcible expulsion of the Creeks from their . . . lands within the State of Georgia there was no middle term." When Governor Troup and the state legislature, unwilling to tolerate further federal intervention, renounced the new treaty and pledged that the Georgia militia stood ready to defy U.S. troops, the administration had to yield for lack of political support. By 1837, following the removal legislation enacted under the Jackson administration, Adams confided in his diary: "We have done more harm to the Indians since our Revolution than had ever been done to them by the French and English nations before. . . . These are crying sins."

## TRADE WITH GREAT BRITAIN

A foreign policy stalemate accompanied efforts by the administration to reopen the lucrative trade with the British West Indies.

U.S. diplomacy with England already had been politicized by ongoing negotiations regarding Maine's boundary, navigation of the St. Lawrence, and the northwest boundary between Canada and the United States. Aside from very restricted commercial opportunities allowed by Britain during the Napoleonic wars, U.S. carriers had for decades confronted in the West Indies a system of colonial monopoly and exclusion.

Lord Castlereagh's offer to resume a very limited trade was answered in 1818 by retaliatory legislation shutting U.S. ports to any British ship arriving from a port closed to U.S. vessels. Only minor revisions of the trade law enacted by Parliament in 1822 led Congress, following the example of Secretary Adams, to insist that U.S. ships be allowed into colonial ports on a basis equal with those of Britain. President Adams would find himself in the unenviable position of wanting to advance liberal commercial principles but impeded in negotiations by British arguments alleging that compromise on trade preferences was tantamount to surrendering sovereignty.

By the time Albert Gallatin, the new American minister, arrived in London in 1826, the British had withdrawn all offers for trade liberalization. Adams's vigorous defense of U.S. interests could not be translated into a workable strategy that could win support in Congress and, at the same time, overcome the intransigence of the British Foreign Office. The secretary of state urged the president to compromise on various British claims while striving to uphold, however imperfectly, principles of free trade. Speaking with congressional leaders, Secretary Clay thought it would be a mistake to claim "too much in insisting upon the introduction into the W. Indies of our produce on the same terms with that of Canada."

Many members of Congress, concerned about the long-term importance of this trade, called on the president to scale back his demands for commercial reciprocity. By the time Adams yielded ground in 1827—Clay having informed Gallatin of the president's willingness to lift U.S. trade restrictions—the British Board of Trade had ruled out further negotiations. Facing the alternatives of either resistance or capitulation, though with a clear preference for the former, Adams had to surrender the decision to Congress.

The president's opponents in the legislative branch were interested less in conciliating Britain and more in embarrassing the administration for the purpose of ensuring Jackson's election in 1828. Administration forces in the House and Senate tried to stave off complete failure by proposing retaliatory, nonintercourse legislation—though with the proviso that trade would resume if the president received reassurance that West Indian ports would be open to U.S. ships. The Jacksonians defeated the measure in the Senate, leading Van Buren to celebrate an alliance between the "planters of the South and the plain Republicans of the north." The president, hoisted by his own petard, had no recourse but to close U.S. ports to trade with British colonies, based on restrictions he had helped to implement in 1818.

What few happy moments Adams spent at the White House were eclipsed not only by self-inflicted political wounds but by a philosophical despair about his nation and himself. His father's death in 1826, depriving the son of the one friend who might understand his loneliness, compelled John Quincy Adams to ponder his own escape from the burdens of life: "I shall within two or three years . . . need a place of retirement. . . . This [Quincy, Massachusetts] will be a safe and pleasant retreat, where I may pursue literary occupations as long . . . as I can take pleasure in them."

## THE TARIFF OF ABOMINATIONS

For the first time in the nation's history, both houses of Congress—convened in December 1827—were controlled by a majority party opposed to the administration. If this was a Congress "unexampled in factious violence and fury," as Adams asserted, then no other issue better typified the meteoric collapse of his presidency than did the 1828 Tariff of Abominations.

The tariff legislation, crafted by Van Buren and the Democrats, aimed to secure electoral advantages for Andrew Jackson in those states where he needed to consolidate his support. Protectionist forces in the middle and western states—Kentucky, Pennsylvania, Ohio, and New York—were rewarded with a schedule for increased tariff duties. The lopsided tariff, however, discriminated against the products of New England, especially the manufacturers of woolens, whose rates were raised only slightly. Senator Daniel Webster, a reluctant supporter of the bill, had to decide "whether the good it contained so far preponderated over its acknowledged evil, as to justify the . . . support of the whole together."

Adams could sign the bill and alienate the South or veto it and incur the wrath of the protectionist Middle and New England states. He knew his decision to accept the will of Congress was ill-fated, having to accede to an act that "added appendages to burden New England" and that also foreshadowed a constitutional crisis leading the nation into a civil war. Amid cries of nullification, the radical southerner Thomas Cooper sounded the alarm: "Is it worth our while to continue this Union of States, where the North demands to be our masters and we are required to be their tributaries?"

## EVALUATION

John Quincy Adams was the second president in American history to serve only one term; his father had been the first. The election of 1828 confirmed that Jackson's political practices were more popular than Adams's moral ideals, and Adams was the last genuine intellectual to serve in the White House in the nineteenth century. Historical accounts of his failure in the presidency have, more often than not, emphasized institutional factors: his inability to come to grips with the realignment of political parties; his disinclination to use presidential power for partisan purposes; his unwillingness to compromise with opponents on internal improvements; and his reluctance to veto measures that were properly passed and otherwise constitutional.

Equally important, however, for understanding Adams's presidential legacy is recognizing the tragic dimensions of leadership when principles and power collide in the political arena. Relevant in this connection—at the intersection of ethics and politics—is Goethe's admonition to the statesman: "While trying to improve evils in men and circumstances which cannot be improved, one loses time and makes things worse; instead, one ought to accept the evils . . . as raw materials and then seek to counterbalance them." One cannot help but discern in this president's melancholy resignation to his fate a painful confirmation that "conscience does make cowards of us all." Adams the moralist met in the world of politics the transformation of his good intentions into evil results, often brought about by the very means intended to avert them. His failure as a great leader is typical of the perennial self-destruction of man caused not so much by others but by his overreaching himself.

Presidential character is strengthened only when a president fully appreciates the tension between the viability of righteousness and the viability of the person's own moral base. Although Adams as thinker was never a thoroughgoing moral absolutist, he never fully reconciled the two impulses that dominated his thoughts after a losing battle in 1828. In defeat, he wrote: "The sun of my political life sets in the deepest gloom." He then added, "But that of my country shines unclouded." Little did he know at that time that he would have one more opportunity, as a member of the House of Representatives, to speak moral truth to his countrymen.

## BIBLIOGRAPHY

Adams, James Truslow. *The Adams Family* (Little, Brown, 1930).

Adams, John Quincy. *An Address Delivered at the Request of a Committee of the Citizens of Washington, on the Occasion of Reading the Declaration of Independence, on the Fourth of July, 1821* (Davis & Force, 1821).

——. *Memoirs.* Edited by Charles Francis Adams, 12 vols. (Lippincott, 1874–1877).

Bailey, Thomas A. *A Diplomatic History of the American People* (Crofts, 1946).

Bemis, Samuel Flagg. *John Quincy Adams and the Union* (Knopf, 1956).

Cunningham, Noble E., Jr. *The Presidency of James Monroe* (University Press of Kansas, 1996).

Hecht, Marie B. *John Quincy Adams* (Macmillan, 1972).

Remini, Robert V. *Henry Clay, Statesman for the Union* (Norton, 1991).

Russell, Greg. *John Quincy Adams and the Public Virtues of Diplomacy* (University of Missouri Press, 1995).

★★★ 7 ★★★

# ANDREW JACKSON
## 1829–1837

*Russell L. Riley*

---

*Born 15 March 1767 in Waxhaw, South Carolina, to Andrew Jackson and Elizabeth Hutchinson Jackson; read law in Salisbury, North Carolina, and was admitted to the bar; married Rachel Donelson Robards, August 1791 in Natchez, Mississippi, and then a second time 17 January 1794 in Nashville, Tennessee; no children; ran for president in 1824, with 153,544 popular votes over John Quincy Adams's 108,740 but fell short of a majority of electoral college votes; House of Representatives, voting by states, awarded the presidency to Adams; ran in 1828 with John Caldwell Calhoun of South Carolina as the "Democratic" faction, and defeated John Quincy Adams of Massachusetts and Richard Rush of Pennsylvania, 647,286 popular votes to 508,064, and 178 electoral college votes to 83; reelected in 1832 on the Democratic party ticket with Martin Van Buren of New York over the National Republican (Whig) ticket of Henry Clay of Kentucky and John Sergeant of Pennsylvania, 687,502 popular votes to 530,189, and 219 electoral college ballots to 49; died 8 June 1845 in Nashville, Tennessee; buried at the Hermitage in Nashville.*

---

Andrew Jackson ranks as probably the most controversial of all U.S. presidents, a figure who inspired violent passions among political friends and enemies during his lifetime, and whose place in the nation's history since his death has been subjected to vigorous dispute among the students of his legacy. He was so esteemed by his fellow Americans that he finished first in three consecutive presidential contests, yet his behavior in office brought formal censure from the U.S. Senate and precipitated the development of a mass-based opposition party. Shortly after World War II, a panel of prominent historians judged Jackson to be among the few "great" presidents ever to have served; a panel convened a quarter century later for the same purpose dropped him alone from the individuals occupying that uppermost tier. He has been called both savior and tyrant, the Old Hero and the chief architect of genocide.

At the root of these incongruities is an unresolved conflict among Americans about the nation's commitment to one of its most deeply held principles of governance: the ideal of democracy. Jackson's disputed place in the nation's life arises precisely because he committed himself without reservation to majoritarianism within a nation that tends to prefer popular government in alloy—as a liberal democracy or a constitutional democracy or a democratic republic. In his first annual message, Jackson proclaimed that "the first principle of our system [is] *that the majority is to govern*" (emphasis in the original). The high esteem Andrew Jackson enjoyed among Americans of his time and thereafter grew from his uncompromising fidelity to the wishes of that majority. Yet much of the discontent he stirred during his presidency, and most of the criticism his work subsequently provoked, derives from that same commitment and from its consequences. Thus, in assessing Jackson's legacy, one encounters a nation's democratic impulses at war with its inclinations toward liberalism, republicanism, and constitutionalism. When the former are ascendant, so is Jackson's star; when the latter rise to prominence, that star is eclipsed.

## FROM POVERTY TO HERO

Andrew Jackson's personal history contains early elements of a democratic departure from the more aristocratic standards of the nation's founding generation. Jackson was born on 15 March 1767, not into a family of New England merchants or to the old landed gentry of Virginia but to a poor widow in the backwoods of South Carolina. The young Jackson showed more of a proclivity for horses, guns, and gaming than for books, and he made a name for himself locally by serving with distinction, as a mere adolescent, in the American Revolution. Andrew and his brother Robert were taken captive by the British but were released to their mother, who died from an illness contracted while nursing infirm soldiers back to health. Robert also died of that illness, and Andrew Jackson was, as he later said, "utterly alone" at the age of 14.

Despite Jackson's apparent satisfaction with out-of-doors pursuits, in 1784 he began study of the law. Several years later he moved to the wild frontier country of Tennessee, where in 1791 he was appointed district attorney by President Washington. Thus, Jackson first became schooled in the practical aspects of politics and the law in a place where the duly constituted legal authority was often at odds with the popular will and the realities of squatter's rights and frontier life. In January of 1796, Jackson attended the convention that drafted the state's proposed constitution, and, when it was accepted by Congress, went to Washington as Tennessee's first representative. After just four months in that seat, he was appointed by the state legislature to a term in the U.S. Senate, where he served a year before resigning and returning home to Tennessee. His sole distinguishing act in the nation's capital came when he voted against having the House receive Washington's Farewell Address, at least in part as a protest against Alexander Hamilton's influence in that administration.

On returning to Tennessee, Jackson tried life as a judge and as a planter and merchant, but without a great deal of satisfaction. The trajectory of Jackson's professional life, and of his popular image, however, skyrocketed in the eleven months spanning March 1814 to January 1815. He had returned to military responsibilities, and during those months he successively routed the Creeks from a final stronghold in Alabama and turned away the British at the Battle of New Orleans. Three years later, in 1818, he led a controversial military raid into Florida and effectively grabbed the panhandle area for the United States. Jackson emerged from these military successes a national hero—tough as "Old Hickory"—and a political force to be reckoned with on the national level.

Accordingly, one of the central questions confronting Washington policymakers at this time was, "What shall we do with Jackson?" Jackson's popularity could not be ignored, but his unpolished ways and his militaristic inclinations made courting him a dangerous proposition, akin to inviting Caesar across the Rubicon. The perfect solution seemed to be bureaucratic exile. President Monroe briefly considered sending him to the U.S. embassy in St. Petersburg, Russia, only to have Thomas Jefferson object: "Why, good God, he would breed you a quarrel before he had been there a month!" Jackson was subsequently named governor of Florida, where Jefferson's prophecy was realized. He almost immediately began arguing with Spanish officials, taking advantage of a confused jurisdictional situation to assert his own authority.

In 1823 the Tennessee legislature returned Jackson to the U.S. Senate. He served in that seat only until October 1825, when he retired from it to pursue aggressively the presidency in 1828. That action was prompted by his personal wrath over the results of the 1824 election.

## ELECTION OF 1824

In 1824, Jackson was one of four major candidates for the presidency. The Tennessee legislature nominated him, and he subsequently finished first, surpassing even congressional caucus nominee William Harris Crawford in the general election. Jackson did not, however, win a majority of the electoral vote, as the Constitution requires, sending the ultimate decision to the House of Representatives. There, third-place finisher Henry Clay of Kentucky threw his support to Massachusetts's John Quincy Adams, who had finished a distant second to Jackson in the popular vote and decisively behind him in the electoral count. With Clay's backing, Adams was elected the nation's sixth president.

The loss was a bitter disappointment for Jackson and his followers. Moreover, Adams's subsequent appointment of Clay as secretary of state bore the signs of a "corrupt bargain" and violated Jackson's delicate sense of honor. Consequently, in a pattern to be repeated frequently in later years, Jackson saw his own fate as deeply intertwined with the wishes of the American "People." He pledged to spare no effort in having the people's will prevail over that of a privileged few, including "King Caucus." Four years later, he routed the opposition and won the presidency with nearly 70 percent of the electoral vote and over 55 percent of the popular vote.

## JACKSON AND POPULAR DEMOCRACY

Jackson's success in 1828 coincided with an explosion in popular participation in the presidential selection process, as more and more states had moved toward the practice of universal suffrage for white men. In 1824, 366,000 popular votes were recorded nationwide; by 1828, that figure exceeded 1.1 million. Virginia counted 15,000 voters in the 1824 election and nearly 39,000 four years later. In Pennsylvania the numbers went from 47,000 to 152,000. Thus, Andrew Jackson came to the presidency not just as the first person from outside Massachusetts or Virginia to take that office, and not just as the offspring of a rough-and-tumble western social environment vastly different from the studious milieu of Harvard College or William and Mary, but also the product of an electoral process in which political and economic elites had been supplanted by urban mechanics and dirt farmers and frontiersmen.

The influence of these forces on American political life in the 1820s and 1830s is commonly noted, but their effect on Jackson himself was no less remarkable. His record as a public figure before advancing to the White House indicates that Jackson usually sided against those who sought to turn the laws or the legal processes decidedly to the advantage of society's least favored. His early work as a lawyer in Tennessee was almost always on behalf of creditors rather than debtors, and he had long opposed debt-relief measures advocated by various democratic legislatures in the South. Jackson became the nation's most prominent democrat, but by the standards of the day he was neither the most radical nor the earliest advocate for aggressive democratic reform. The term "Jacksonian Revolution" is a misnomer to the extent that it is used to imply that Jackson was its prime mover. He was as much a product of revolutionary change as a contributor to it.

The impact of all these changes on Washington registered quickly, beginning in March 1829. The capital was overrun at Jackson's inaugural festivities by a phalanx of democrats, putting a human face on the imposing electoral victory returned just months before. The President's Mansion filled with celebrants whose muddy boots and indecorous drinking left much of the interior in a state of wreckage. Eventually the crowd was coaxed outside by the removal of tubs of punch to the lawn. This scene was hardly reassuring to those, now on their way out of power, who had long questioned the suitability of "the People" to govern themselves so directly.

## "TO THE VICTOR BELONG THE SPOILS"

Two matters occupied most of Jackson's attention during his first year in office as he settled on a course for his administration: staffing the government through presidential appointments, and settling a prickly social problem that threatened to shatter his cabinet.

Conventional wisdom holds that Jackson introduced into American politics the practice of putting presidential partisans into appointive positions. "To the victor belong the spoils" was the famous phrase coined to describe the Jacksonian program. Jackson did enter the presidency with a commitment to shaking up what had come to seem a "permanent" Washington establishment. He believed in rotation in administrative as well as elective offices, claiming that extensive tenure in administration led to unresponsive and corrupt—in short, antidemocratic—behavior.

His position was not without merit. During the three decades of the extended era of Jeffersonian presidents, a growing corps of administrators—many of whom had relied on political connections to attain their positions in the first place—had been insulated from any electoral shocks to the system, with the good and the bad that that entails. Further, Jackson and his followers were able in some instances to document corruption among existing officeholders and thereby to justify directly their removal.

The speed with which Jackson acted, announcing many prominent replacements during the opening weeks of his presidency, created within the intimate family of the Washington bureaucracy a sense of dread that their lifetime tenure was at end. Panic-stricken administrators consequently exaggerated the extent to which the newcomers actually purged executive officialdom. One contemporary report, issued by a political opponent, held that Jackson had removed nearly 20 percent of the nation's federal officials in his first year, though later studies indicate that the actual number was around half that. Regardless, Jackson did dramatically escalate the number of removals, especially among those subject to direct presidential appointment.

What Jackson did not do was to depart from his predecessors in using primarily political criteria in filling the administrative slots available to him. He expressed an intention to "grant offices to none but such as was honest and capable," but he tended to favor those with personal, political, or military connections. Critics who charged him, then, with working to create a publicly funded machine for the purpose of advancing his partisan interests did so with some justification, although they commonly overstated their case. In the final analysis, Jackson's appointments record helped remedy one problem—bureaucratic ossification—while opening the door to another one—raw favoritism. The patronage excesses that subsequently occurred later in the nineteenth century and that led to the development of federal civil service reforms can be traced to Jackson's disruptions of the status quo in 1829.

## THE PEGGY EATON AFFAIR

Jackson's second preoccupation during his transitional year was a matter of etiquette, one that reveals much about the president's psychology and the extent to which, for him, the personal became political.

In piecing together his cabinet, the president named as secretary of war Senator John H. Eaton, of Tennessee, who had been very close to Jackson and his family. During Eaton's previous time in Washington, he had conducted an affair with a married woman, Margaret (Peggy) O'Neal Timberlake, who bore the reputation of being of easy virtue. When her husband died at sea—rumors held that he had committed suicide in despondence over his wife's indiscretions—Peggy Timberlake became Mrs. John Eaton. That union scandalized Washington.

Jackson was quite aware of the gossip surrounding Peggy O'Neal Eaton. In quintessential Jacksonian form, however, the president made up his mind that the rumors about her past were baseless, and he expected others to adopt the same position. He was not, in this case, a clear-minded judge. At the time these events were unfolding, Jackson was still deeply grieving the loss of his wife Rachel, who had died less than three months before the inauguration. The Jacksons had lived their entire lives together under a cloud of innuendo surrounding Rachel's past. She, too, had been married when she met her future husband, and that earlier union had also ended under unusual circumstances. Indeed, the Jacksons initially wed under the impression that Rachel's first husband had divorced her, only to discover later that the proceedings had not become final until several years thereafter. Those circumstances—wedded to two men at once—made of Rachel a surrogate target for Andrew Jackson's political enemies, who could impugn his character by attacking hers. The Eatons' plight recapitulated his own.

In supporting Eaton in his cabinet—and Peggy O'Neal Eaton in the capital's social circuit—Jackson found much of Washington unwilling to follow his lead. Almost immediately factions developed within the president's official family. The matter became a preoccupation within the capital, with important consequences for the nation's political life. Vice President John C. Calhoun's influence within the administration suffered irreparably because neither he nor his wife would treat Mrs. Eaton as a social equal. Secretary of State Martin Van Buren, a widower, adopted Jackson's posture as his own, and in the process gained the president's ear on policy matters and patronage. To Jackson's great relief, the Eatons eventually left Washington, but the patterns of interaction established during those early days—and Jackson's tendency to equate the personal with the political—endured. The question of who would be the rightful heir to Jackson's political fortune was framed by this episode.

## DEFINING JACKSONIAN VIEWS

On most matters of policy, Andrew Jackson entered the presidency as an unknown. His heroic stature had made policy pronouncements superfluous, and his campaign team sowed confusion by developing regional appeals throughout the country, sacrificing consistency in the search for marketable messages in each state. Yet the American people knew to expect a major change in tone and emphasis after the 1828 elections. However confusing the details, Jackson brought to the presidency a recognized and consistent mistrust of political and financial elites, an unreserved commitment to the concept of majority rule, and an unshakable confidence in his own capacity for divining and carrying out the popular will of the American people. Martin Van Buren once wrote that the president believed that "to labor for the good of the masses was a special mission assigned to him by his Creator." These inclinations are evident in the two matters that most defined the Jackson presidency to his contemporaries: the fight over the national bank, and the nullification crisis. These controversies extended over both of Jackson's terms.

## THE BANK OF THE
## UNITED STATES

The Second Bank of the United States had been chartered by Congress for a twenty-year period in April of 1816. Although the Second Bank had endured controversy throughout its lifetime, the president surprised some of his confidants when, in preparation for his first annual message, he raised with them the question of its suitability as an instrument of public finance. They knew that the Second Bank's charter was not scheduled for reconsideration for another eight years.

Jackson saw the Second Bank's existence as more of a political than an economic matter. The U.S. Treasury used the Bank as its own primary repository, usually keeping a monthly balance of between $6 million and $10 million there, on which it received no interest. In return for these massive deposits—which afforded interest-free funds that were available for loans on which interest would be paid (thus generating private profits)—the Bank and its branches executed the government's widely diffused financial transactions and served as a unifying force in the pursuit of a stable currency system for the young country. These advantages, Jackson believed, were purchased at too high a price. Private interest had superseded public welfare, with an independent money power threatening to corrupt the nation's political processes.

When his first annual message was delivered, in December of 1829, Jackson sparked controversy, noting

> The charter of the Bank of the United States expires in 1836, and its stockholders will most probably apply for a renewal of

their privileges. In order to avoid the evils resulting from precipitancy in a measure involving such important principles and such deep pecuniary interests, I feel that I can not, in justice to the parties interested, too soon present it to the deliberate consideration of the Legislature and the people. Both the constitutionality and the expediency of the law creating this bank are well questioned by a large portion of our fellow-citizens, and it must be admitted by all that it has failed in the great end of establishing a uniform and sound currency.

He then suggested that Congress should provide for greater public control of the Second Bank's affairs.

The attack was characteristically Jacksonian. Sensing a battle to be waged and won, he sought immediately the offensive against "stockholders['] . . . privileges," despite the fact that the bank charter was not scheduled for review until what would be the final year of his *second* term—if he were to have a second term. He disregarded the weight of expert opinion, which held that the Bank had been reasonably successful in stabilizing the U.S. currency situation, as it often reined in the wildly inflationary tendencies of the state banks. Finally, he turned to the sentiments of his "fellow-citizens" for judging the constitutionality of the Bank's charter, electing at once to emphasize his personal connection with the populace and to ignore the U.S. Supreme Court's landmark ruling, *McCulloch v. Maryland* (1819), decided in the Bank's favor.

Bank President Nicholas Biddle, of Philadelphia, responded to Jackson's charges with an energetic counteroffensive. He used the Bank's economic power to win friends both in Washington and in statehouses across the country. Branch banks were established in the home districts of key politicians, and directorships were offered to those who could influence votes. The Bank's funds became a political weapon in the form of loosely secured loans or retainers for powerful lawmakers, including Daniel Webster. Jackson took these methods as confirmation that his most deeply held suspicions were true: The people's money was being used by commercial elites to advance their selfish interests.

Both houses of Congress reacted to Jackson's initial overture by resolving in the Bank's favor. Jackson's December 1830 message raised the issue again, proposing a vague plan establishing a national bank wholly within the Treasury Department. This, too, Congress rejected, with little active consideration. The president appeared to sound a retreat on the matter in his Third Annual Message. Referring to his earlier failed attempts to stir congressional action, he wrote, "I deem it proper on this occasion, without a more particular reference to the views of the subject then expressed, to leave it for the present to the investigation of an enlightened people and their representatives." The issue did not, however, lay dormant.

Detecting signs of weakness in the president's announced withdrawal from the issue, Jackson's political enemies introduced on 9 January 1832 a memorial from the Second Bank petitioning for a renewal of the charter. Biddle himself moved to Washington to make sure congressional deliberations went according to plan. Moreover, Biddle and the Bank's advocates, doubting that Jackson would long remain content to drop the matter, sought to put a permanent end to executive branch antagonism by rallying around the presidential candidacy of Kentucky's Henry Clay. Clay had long advanced nationalistic policies he generally captioned as the "American System," by which central institutions were to take an activist role in shaping and advancing the nation's economic development. A strong national bank fitted neatly into the Clay program. More important, it was a polarizing issue that held the promise of drawing to Clay's standard those who found Jackson's attacks on the Bank both unwarranted and reckless.

In June, with Clay's influence, a rechartering bill passed the Senate by a vote of 28 to 20. In July, the House adopted it by a 107 to 85 margin. The bill was sent to Jackson on Independence Day, with the Senate voting to adjourn on July 16, thereby denying the president the opportunity for a pocket veto. The bill's advocates sought a formal rejection, which would draw starkly the lines between the two contenders for the presidency that autumn.

Jackson returned the bill on July 10, taking the offensive again with a strongly worded veto message aimed at putting his own spin on the matter. Added to a host of technical objections—based in economic and constitutional rationales—Jackson delivered a scathing political attack on the Second Bank's defenders. He charged that the Bank's managers had engaged in "gross abuse and violation of its charter," and, ignoring his own part in bringing the issue up before its time, he suggested ill intent on the part of those rushing renewal legislation through almost four years before existing authority expired. He concluded by asserting the centrality of the bank battle for preserving popular rule in the United States:

It is to be regretted that the rich and powerful too often bend the acts of government to their selfish purposes. Distinctions in society will always exist under every just government. Equality of talents, of education, or of wealth can not be produced by human institutions. In the full enjoyment of the gifts of Heaven and the fruits of superior industry, economy, and virtue, every man is equally entitled to protection by law; but when the laws undertake to add to these natural and just advantages artificial distinctions, to grant titles, gratuities, and exclusive privileges, to make the rich richer and the potent more powerful, the humble members of society—the farmers, mechanics, and laborers—who have neither the time nor the means of securing like favors to themselves, have a right to complain of the injustice of their Government. There are no necessary evils in government. Its evils exist only in its abuses. If it would confine itself to equal protection, and, as Heaven does its rains, shower its favors alike on the high and the low, the rich and the poor, it would be an unqualified blessing. In the act before me there seems to be a wide and unnecessary departure from these just principles.

A drained but undaunted president privately declared, "The bank . . . is trying to kill me, *but I will kill it.*"

## THE BANK WAR

This he did. He began by successfully joining the strength of his democratic rhetoric (which his opponents charged with fomenting class warfare) with the pragmatic support of state banking interests (which stood to benefit from the dismantling of the national bank), and consequently hoisted Clay by his own petard. The National Republican candidate won only 17 percent of the electoral vote. To Biddle's dismay, Clay's mishandling of the issue allowed Jackson reasonably to claim a popular mandate for the Second Bank's destruction.

The president did not wait long to complete that unfinished business. In his 1832 annual message—delivered just weeks after the election results were returned—Jackson questioned whether the public deposits in the Bank were safe, and he asked for a congressional investigation of the matter. He may have anticipated that his public expressions of doubt about its solvency would bring about the Bank's ruin, but depositor confidence remained largely unaffected and Congress again issued a clean bill of health.

Undeterred, Jackson contemplated crushing the Bank by executive action alone, removing from it all federal deposits. Secretary of the Treasury Louis McLane—who was by statute responsible to the House, not the president, on disposition of deposits—objected. Jackson then fired both McLane and his successor, who also refused to act, and ultimately settled on one of his intimates, Roger B. Taney, for the post. Secretary Taney eagerly met the challenge. In a subsequent report to Congress, he explained the administration's actions in unflinching terms: "It is a fixed principle of our political institutions to guard against the unnecessary accumulation of power over persons and property in any hands. And no hands are less worthy to be trusted with it than those of a moneyed corporation." On 1 October 1833, the removals commenced.

Federal deposits were withdrawn from the national bank and distributed by the administration to a series of state-chartered institutions. Although the president had been highly critical of Biddle for using political factors in making banking decisions, the administration did not appreciably differ from his practices. Those whose directors had been friends of the administration were the preferred recipients of federal accounts. Jackson's opponents took to calling these favored institutions "pet banks."

Political and institutional jealousies immediately erupted over Jackson's decision to act unilaterally. Henry Clay, back in the Senate, took his revenge. He introduced two resolutions critical of the administration, one assailing the logic of Taney's report, the other censuring Jackson directly for usurping legislative powers. The Senate adopted both. A bitter war of words broke out between the president's friends and enemies, making this one of the most bilious quarrels in the long history of Washington partisanship. "With an 'old hero' to support and the 'money power' to assail," noted William Graham Sumner years later, "the politicians and orators of the emphatic school had a grand opportunity."

The president's friends in the upper chamber immediately organized to expunge the censure from the public record. That effort eventually did succeed (in January of 1837), only after the intervening election, during which Jackson's partisans used the censure issue as a rallying cry for the Old Hero's followers.

The economic consequences of Jackson's political victory over the national bank unexpectedly haunted the administration during Jackson's final years in office. A panic arose in 1833–1834, in part the product of a vindictive conspiracy, vigorously executed, on the part of the national bank to manufacture a contraction. "Nothing but the evidence of suffering abroad," Biddle reasoned, "will produce any effect in Congress. . . . A steady course of firm restriction will ultimately lead to . . . the recharter of the bank." Eventually protests from commercial elites strangled by tight credit caused Biddle to relent.

Yet the president's own policies greatly contributed to further paroxysms. His plan to kill the national bank had opened the way for an extensive proliferation of smaller banks, many of which were poorly managed or run by people who sought access to large sums of money for speculative purposes to alleviate their own personal financial problems. Moreover, the administration's fiscal policies were beginning to result in budget surpluses, creating stocks of otherwise idle capital that were given over to the very institutions fueling the speculation. Biddle's panic was accordingly followed by a rampant inflation.

## THE SPECIE CIRCULAR
The president, unwilling to change his mind on banking, turned increasingly to currency reform to arrest the inflationary expansion. According to this logic, the speculative tendencies of a newly created mass of decentralized banking interests could be held in check if the nation moved more heavily toward a bullionist standard; specie was a more naturally conservative instrument than was paper.

In July of 1836, the secretary of the treasury issued, at Jackson's request, what came to be called the Specie Circular, ordering that all sales of federal lands be conducted with gold, silver, or land scrip. Bank notes would no longer be acceptable. The contracting effects on the economy registered almost immediately, and they contributed to a decline that bottomed out in 1837, on Martin Van Buren's watch. Late in Jackson's term, Congress sent the president a bill rescinding the Treasury order; one of his last official acts as president was to pocket-veto that bill.

Jackson's posture on the currency question was a natural outgrowth of the democratic impulses that had motivated his attack on the national bank. Although some Democrats sought to advance the welfare of the nation's "farmers, mechanics, and laborers" through more readily available currency and credit, Jackson's experience taught him that such policies were destructive of democratic interests. He had spent a good portion of his life rescuing friends and adopted members of his family from the consequences of their having borrowed easy money from liberal lenders. Accordingly, Jackson saw loose money not as a boon to average Americans but as a trap into which privileged elites lured the unsuspecting, eventually to lay claim to their homes and farms when the inevitable hard times hit. In his last annual message he explained the point:

> The progress of an expansion, or rather a depreciation, of the currency by excessive bank issues is always attended by a loss to the laboring classes. This portion of the community have neither time nor opportunity to watch the ebbs and flows of the money market. Engaged from day to day in their useful toils, they do not perceive that although their wages are nominally the same, or even somewhat higher, they are greatly reduced in fact by the rapid increase of a spurious currency, which, as it appears to make money abound, they are at first inclined to consider a blessing. It is not so with the speculator, by whom this operation is better understood, and is made to contribute to his advantage.

In Jackson's mind, inflation inevitably led to the "ruin of debtors, and the accumulation of property in the hands of creditors and cautious capitalists." These, in the final analysis, were the undemocratic ends he sought to avoid by killing the Second Bank of the United States and establishing a more stable currency.

Jackson's enemies during his pursuit of a more democratic political economy had been the bankers, the "creditors and the cautious capitalists." During the other signature battle of his administration—the fight over nullification—Jackson's foes were those who sought to elevate the rights of individual states over the prerogatives of the Union.

## SOUTH CAROLINA, THE TARIFF, AND NULLIFICATION

To Jackson, nullification was another assault on democratic principles. The U.S. Constitution was the product of a democratic process in which a popular majority of the American people had formed a "more perfect Union." The will of that majority, Jackson believed, should not be frustrated by a dissenting minority aggregated in a single state or region, regardless of the validity of their grievances. His duty as president was to preserve that popularly conceived Union against those who would threaten its viability through what he perceived to be antidemocratic means.

The roots of the nullification crisis were located in federal tariff policies. In 1816, Congress had adopted a peacetime protective tariff, intended to give emerging native industries shelter from the kind of established international competition that might smother them in their infancy. Tariff rates had occasionally risen in the intervening years, culminating in a massive increase in 1828. The tariff became a divisive issue politically because it burdened some groups more heavily than others. Southern agrarians were especially opposed to the prevailing system as they found themselves marketing their crops abroad at one level of exchange but having to buy finished goods at home—those subjected to tariff constraints—at elevated prices.

The heart of the southern opposition to the 1828 law—which passed before Jackson's election and came to be known as the Tariff of Abominations—was South Carolina. In December 1828, that state's legislature issued a formal protest against the terms of the tariff and provided for the circulation of an "Exposition," drafted by John C. Calhoun, arguing for the right of a state assembled in convention to nullify an act of Congress if it deemed it unconstitutional.

Calhoun's authorship was hidden, for the simple reason that he had been elected to serve as vice president with Jackson, and it was unclear at that time how the president intended to respond to the protests. Many held hope—recognizing Jackson's southern roots and his evident belief in the sanctity of states' rights—that Jackson would use his presidency to combat the nationalizing tendencies promoted by the tariff.

During the first congressional session after Jackson's inauguration, the nullification controversy became a central item on the congressional agenda. Senators Robert Y. Hayne of South Carolina and Daniel Webster of Massachusetts debated the matter extensively, producing some of the most theoretically rich discourse ever to echo in those chambers. Hayne contended that the Union was nothing more than a compact of the states, wherein the states themselves retained ultimate sovereignty. Given this foundation, nullification was an inevitable extension. Webster, conversely, argued that the Constitution was the product of agreement by the American people, acting beyond the confines of the individual states. Given this logic, nullification could not be sustained. It was tantamount to disunion.

Tension mounted in Washington as the disputants waited to hear what Old Hickory would do. His response came in dramatic fashion on 13 April 1830, at a Jefferson Day banquet. The event had been orchestrated by Calhoun's partisans to solidify support for the South Carolinians' position on nullification; they hoped that the power of the event itself might help Jackson resolve any indecision he had about nullification in their favor. With one simply worded toast, however, Jackson dashed their hopes: "Our Union; It must be preserved." All understood this to be a refutation of the South Carolina protest. Jackson later elaborated that his posture was based on the notion that "in all Republics the voice of a Majority must prevail."

Although Jackson elsewhere pronounced the nullifiers' ideas as "absurd," he did take action that he believed might help to alleviate their grievances. As early as 1829 he advocated a reexamination of federal tariff policy, with an eye toward possible reductions in the rate structure, and in his 1831 message, he formally asked Congress to begin taking steps to modify the tariff system. Jackson was motivated primarily by the favorable effect high tariff receipts had already exercised on the federal debt, which was approaching liquidation as he wrote. He was not unmindful, however, that any reduced rates would have the collateral effect of benefiting the southern planters whom the nullifiers claimed to represent. In July 1832 he signed into law a revised tariff bill that significantly reduced rates in a number of areas of interest to the South Carolinians. The overall terms, Jackson claimed, "killed the ultras." His judgment was premature.

The nullifiers were not satisfied with the extent of the reductions, a point that angered Jackson and fueled a growing suspicion that Calhoun was using the issue merely to win political points. In October, the nullifiers claimed a two-thirds majority in the state legislature. South Carolina's governor convened a special legislative session just weeks after the election for purposes of calling a state convention, which met and resolved that the tariffs of 1828 and 1832 were null and void. Collection of those tariffs in South Carolina, by either the state or national government, was to become illegal after 1 February 1833, and the legislature was instructed to create the necessary legal apparatus to enforce the declaration.

Finally, the convention ordinance held that any attempt by the federal government to use force to maintain the tariff statutes or to close the state's ports would be sufficient cause for secession:

> The people of this State will thenceforth hold themselves absolved from all further obligation to maintain or preserve their political connection with the people of the other States, and will forthwith proceed to organize a separate government and to do all other acts and things which sovereign and independent states may of right do.

## PROTECTING THE UNION

Jackson initially sought to undermine the South Carolina threat by making further adjustments in the tariff. In his fourth annual message, the president admitted that the advantages of the tariff system were "counterbalanced by many evils," which "beget in the minds of a large portion of our countrymen a spirit of discontent and jealousy dangerous to the stability of the Union." Thus, the protective system ought to be done away with. However, having held out a carrot to the nullifiers, Jackson quickly moved to make certain that they did not mistake his offer as a sign of weakness.

Less than a week later, the newly reelected Jackson issued what came to be called his Nullification Proclamation, in which he vigorously asserted the unacceptability of the South Carolina convention's acts. Indeed, his expressions of nationalism in that document confused many contemporary observers, who saw it as inconsistent with his long-held views about the desirability of a limited central government. Yet the president wished to leave no room for doubt as to which interpretation of the nation's constitutional arrangements would govern his action in the instant case. He would not brook rebellion.

The force of his rhetoric was punctuated soon thereafter with arrangements for the deployment of arms. He requested unionists in the state to organize volunteers to support the federal marshal in the area, and he pledged to have available 50,000 troops in the event the South Carolinians moved to carry out their threats. Jackson intended, as he claimed in one letter, to "crush the monster in its cradle before it mature[d] to manhood."

Unionists of all political persuasions applauded the president's firm attitude, although some of his friends worried that he seemed to be spoiling for a fight. Van Buren saw danger in alienating moderate southern states' rights advocates, who did not accept nullification as a valid doctrine but might be moved to rally to South Carolina's cause if the president acted precipitously, or if he justified his actions in language insufficiently sensitive to legitimate states rights' concerns. Van Buren's case was buttressed when four southern states refused to back the president's proclamation and instead expressed support for the Virginia Resolutions of 1798. The South Carolinians had cited those resolutions as a precedent for their claims to nullification.

On Capitol Hill, anxious legislators moved to disarm an increasingly explosive situation. The chair of the House Ways and Means Committee, Gulian C. Verplanck, sent to the House floor a bill cutting existing tariff rates to 1816 levels. The bill immediately met opposition from industrial interests, and Jackson did little to come to its defense. He had become increasingly convinced that the tariff question was merely a pretext the nullifiers used to pursue their political aims against the Union and his presidency.

On 16 January 1833, Jackson sent an extensive special message to Congress, laying before the assembled legislators a detailed account of recent events and proposing a series of measures that would help him uphold federal law. He insisted that South Carolina's actions "are to be regarded as revolutionary in their character and tendency, and subversive of the supremacy of the laws and of the integrity of the Union." He then highlighted the antidemocratic nature of the nullifiers' case, asserting that when "any body of men have voluntarily associated themselves under a particular form of government, no portion of them can dissolve the association without acknowledging the correlative right in the remainder to decide whether that dissolution can be permitted consistently with the general happiness."

Jackson recommended a series of steps, including establishing shipboard customs houses at South Carolina harbors where there were no forts and authorizing the transfer of customs cases from state to federal courts; he also stated his intent to use federal troops and call up the militia in the event that South Carolina moved to "the actual employment of military force" against the laws of the United States. The president's opposition quickly labeled the legislation spawned by this message the "Force Bill."

Jackson's proposal encountered difficulty in both the House and the Senate, with delays and extended debate illustrating the limited influence he exercised in those chambers. Further, his efforts to put down the challengers received a major blow when the Virginia legislature refused to endorse his actions. Moreover, the New York legislature, to Jackson's great dismay, remained silent on the issue as the crisis deepened, despite Van Buren's reputed influence in Albany.

## COMPROMISE AND RESOLUTION

While the administration labored to gather support for the Force Bill before the crucial date of 1 February, two related developments emerged that formed the outlines of a resolution. First, Henry Clay, sensing that bloodshed could be avoided with the right mix of compromise measures, offered an extensive tariff reduction proposal (similar to the Verplanck bill, which had already died in the Senate) and was able to gain John Calhoun's assent to it. Both men recognized political advantage for themselves in crafting a solution where Old Hickory was failing. Second, when the nullifiers in South Carolina heard of the Clay-Calhoun development, their hopes were raised; they reassembled and decided to postpone execution of their previously adopted ordinances until they could determine how Congress would resolve the tariff question.

After a series of delicate negotiations, Congress enacted the tariff and enforcement bills (constituting the central trade-off of the compromise) and an internal improvements bill Clay had long promoted. Jackson signed the first two and vetoed the latter. On 11 March 1833, the South Carolinians rescinded their nullification ordinance. Jackson's firmness in opposing the rebellion had set the stage for the final resolution, although others had been more influential in crafting the specific contours of the eventual compromise, and the concessions on the tariff meant that South Carolina could claim a considerable measure of victory from their defiance. At bottom, however, the "general happiness" of the nation's democratic majority had been preserved as Jackson intended.

## INTERNAL IMPROVEMENTS

Jackson's veto of Clay's improvements bill was another manifestation of the president's majoritarian logic at work. In the more famous Maysville Road veto (issued in 1830), Jackson had announced that the project in question failed a crucial test: "Is it national and conducive to the benefit of the whole, or local and operating only to the advantage of a portion of the Union?" His adherence to democratic principles not only in the Maysville Road veto but also in relation to other improvements bills prevented him from spending the majority's money on improvements that benefited a lesser (geographic or class-based) interest. As a general matter, he accepted federal spending on such projects only when he could justify them on grounds of military necessity, something which clearly benefited the whole populace.

Despite Andrew Jackson's many political successes, his fastidious commitment to majoritarianism left him vulnerable to charges by critics of his own day (and of later periods) that other American values were unsafe in his hands. The Jackson presidency revealed with rare clarity the tensions between an unrestrained pursuit of democracy and the preservation of constitutional, republican, and liberal principles.

## DEMOCRACY AND PRESIDENTIAL POWER

The central indictment of Jackson on constitutional grounds—issued despite his Constitution-preserving labors in the nullification crisis—was that he aggrandized presidential powers. His critics accused Jackson of usurping authority not expressly granted by the nation's fundamental law, and thus of destroying the delicate institutional balance the Framers had posed among the three branches in Washington and between the national government and the governments of the various states. Some

had projected this result when Jackson first cast his eye on the executive office, with one southern newspaper warning that although he was an able man in times of crisis, "in times of tranquility and with brisk and favorable gales we should greatly fear he would carry too much sail."

Clay's censure resolution formally held that, in withdrawing federal deposits and in refusing to inform Congress fully, Jackson had "assumed upon himself authority and power not conferred by the Constitution and the laws, but in derogation of both." In private correspondence, Justice Joseph Story of the U.S. Supreme Court wrote that "we are in fact under the absolute rule of a single man." One respected biographer later likened him to Napoleon, and his contemporary opposition dubbed him "King Andrew." Indeed, an opposition party emerged to contend with the Jacksonians, adopting for themselves the name given the enemies of an overreaching monarchy in England: the Whigs.

In part, Jackson's assertiveness in the presidency flowed from his personal temperament. Before becoming president, Andrew Jackson had established a solid public reputation as a man of action who did not easily allow formalities to stand between him and what he wanted. As president, he reacted similarly to what he viewed as vague constraints obstructing him from pursuing policies that were in the public interest, and to surmount them he would avail himself of even the narrowest constitutional ledge from which he could gain purchase. But this was not the sole explanation for his actions. His creativity in departing from the usually restrained standards of his presidential predecessors can also be tied directly to his democratic sensibilities.

The presidency that Andrew Jackson received in 1829 was a different institution from that which had existed even ten years earlier. The Founders had rejected the direct popular election of the president because they anticipated that such a connection would empower the office in unhealthy ways. Yet in the years leading up to Jackson's election, the presidential selection process had become vastly more popularized.

Jackson subsequently proceeded as the Framers had expected, using his more direct connection with the American people as a tool to bend the will of Washington. Claims to be the "people's representative" gave the president a powerful advantage in dealing with other public policymakers, throwing the Framers' system of compromise and consensus into imbalance. Daniel Webster once claimed that half of Jackson's appointments would have been rejected had the Senate not so feared Jackson's popularity outside Washington. The president, however, found that his connection to the American people was not a perfect implement. That he often claimed to represent the people's will did not make it so in the minds of many in Congress, who represented a share of those same people and who could point to constitutional forms that gave them a right to help shape the nation's policies. Jackson lacked the technological advances that would enable his successors in the next century to convince Congress that the president's will and the people's were one. Jackson could justify his activism as philosophically sound but could not fully execute it, unconstrained by others' views. Although Jackson's more direct popular connection provided him some marginal advantages, the designation "King Andrew" did not denote the emergence of an imperial presidency. Despite Jackson's best efforts to convert the president's new-found democratic standing into political primacy, too many other American policymakers were committed to the constitutional forms of the founding generation to permit Jackson the full freedom of movement he sought. There were, in this light, far more Whigs in spirit than in party affiliation.

The critique of Jackson from the perspective of republicanism is more complex. His critics charged him with violating two basic republican principles. First, Jackson adhered to a simple arithmetic in which democratic policies followed the wishes of the majority. In the case of nullification, Jackson asserted that the general welfare of the more numerous American people superseded the interests of the South Carolinians on the tariff question. Consequently, Jackson had to depart from a crucial republican standard, which holds that those representatives closest to the people are best suited to governing for them. That Jackson felt it necessary to proceed as he did indicates the fundamental tension between the unionist standard he reached and upheld (through democratic logic) and the nearer-is-better criterion.

The second basic republican principle he violated was that of republican trusteeship in affairs of state which was dwarfed by his commitment to democratic policymaking. The president's critics contended that his slavish devotion to popular opinion led him into demagoguery. On issues such as the Second Bank question Jackson moved to the attack, they said, less because of rational arguments about the Bank's worth as an instrument of public policy than because he knew it to be a rich target of public discontent. Further, other Washington policymakers, who might have wished to take a longer term view of the bank question, found that the purity of the president's espousal of popular government made it difficult for their views to be heard. Acting as the people's instructed delegate in the capital, Jackson effectively neutralized any attempts by others to assume a role as Burkean trustee, acting momentarily against the popular will because of the special knowledge their talents and positions gave them. With this celebrated democrat in the White House, taking action against the popular will became a perilous course.

Finally, these same tendencies provide the basis for the critique of Jackson from the standpoint of liberalism. Jackson's record of acting to advance majority interests against individual liberties—especially those of specific minorities—drew vigorous criticism in his day from civil libertarians. This critique of his administration has become even more prominent as the nation's political culture has become increasingly sensitive to minority rights.

## JACKSON AND THE INDIANS

One of the primary sources of Andrew Jackson's popularity in seeking the White House was his record as a successful Indian fighter. Although his adoption of a Native American child, orphaned by combat, indicates an absence of the kind of unforgiving personal prejudices characteristic of many Americans in his day, Jackson's policies as a military officer and political figure were draconian.

The administration's removal of five Indian nations from the southeastern states proceeded under clouds of deceit, betrayal, and corruption. The government attempted to negotiate favorable treaties with the leaders of these nations, bearing threats of military force and loss of tribal autonomy. When existing tribal leaders refused to bargain, Jackson's emissaries helped establish rivals who would. When some tribal members decided to remain behind on land provided for under the treaties, the administration pressured them further to move and did little to protect them from white squatters who settled illegally on their lands. Reimbursements promised for abandoned land often went unpaid, and the tribal peoples frequently found the lands set aside for them in the West unacceptable. The removal process itself was conducted under the president's scrutiny, with great attention given to limiting the overall cost. Provisions for food, medicine, and other support were scarce, exacerbating illness and starvation.

## GEORGIA AND THE CHEROKEES

Probably the best sign of Jackson's invidious discrimination against Native Americans arose in relation to Georgia's treatment of the Cherokees. Shortly after Congress adopted an Indian removal bill in 1830, authorizing executive efforts to arrange for relocation, Georgians moved to establish white possession and control of lands that remained officially under Cherokee jurisdiction; neither state officers nor private citizens awaited formal conclusion of the removal process. Whites friendly to the Cherokees worked through the federal courts to stay the intrusions, but Georgia's governor and legislature refused to respect federal authority, formally denouncing the federal courts for meddling in the state's affairs. The governor ignored a subpoena in one suit, and defied a court order in another case, hanging one Cherokee man who had been illegally tried under Georgia state law.

Although the U.S. Supreme Court decided one case in the state's favor, in a second case heard quickly thereafter it decisively ruled that the federal government retained exclusive jurisdiction within tribal lands. The state had required missionaries working within Cherokee territory to be licensed, in order to monitor their activities. Two who had refused were jailed. The Court, in *Worcester v. Georgia* (1832), held that the state statute was unconstitutional and that the convictions should be overturned.

Given the state's previously expressed contempt for the federal judiciary's proceedings, all eyes turned to the president. Would he execute the Court's decision and uphold the supremacy of federal law over Georgia's objections? The answer was no. According to a story reported years later, Jackson responded, "John Marshall has made his decision, now let him enforce it." That account is probably apocryphal, but its durability in Jacksonian lore suggests a ring of truth about the president's disposition. Rather than following the legal forms the Court prescribed, Jackson and Georgia authorities worked together out of public view to have the two prisoners released quietly. This settled the matter in an oblique fashion, depriving the pro-Indian forces of a mobilizing issue at a time when the administration wished to conclude the removal process without complications.

The president's unwillingness to have the missionaries legally vindicated, thereby asserting federal authority in this matter, contrasts starkly with his bold activism in the South Carolina nullification crisis, which was boiling over at the same time and where the issue was effectively the same. Not wishing to alienate Georgia and create an alliance between two southern states on the sovereignty question, Jackson sacrificed the rights of Native Americans on an issue for which he would risk the viability of his presidency in South Carolina. One North Carolina congressman noted that Jackson "could by a nod of the head or a crook of the finger [have] induce[d] Georgia to submit to the law." This he did not do. The people's president—committed to majority rule (and thus the sanctity of federal law)—looked very different to the nullifiers in Charleston, where the threat of armed force to secure federal law attended every presidential move.

## JACKSON AND AFRICAN AMERICANS

Jackson's majoritarian impulses also governed his actions with respect to African Americans, especially on the question of slavery. In the early 1830s, the abolitionist movement was gaining momentum in New England and the northwestern states. Without any direct leverage on southern lawmaking processes, the abolitionists sought to end slavery in the South through a process of "moral suasion"—a grand public relations campaign, relying on mailed publications, to convince individual slaveholders of the sinfulness of their ways. A spate of laws formally restricting black freedoms—and the circulation of "incendiary materials"—was enacted in 1831 after Nat Turner's insurrection in Virginia, which many southerners erroneously attributed to abolitionist direction.

## ABOLITIONISTS AND THE MAILS

In 1835, a mob broke into the Charleston post office to seize a shipment of abolitionist literature that had been mailed through New York. The local postmaster, anticipating trouble with future shipments, requested instructions from Washington. He enquired as to whether he was obliged, as a part of his sworn duties, to protect the materials he received through the U.S. mail. Postmaster General Amos Kendall informed him that he was not. Although the authorizing act for the postal service clearly compelled delivery, Kendall argued that he and the Charleston postmaster were constrained by a higher law to protect the tranquility of that community by avoiding agitation. Kendall, one of Jackson's most trusted associates, received the president's support.

Jackson did acknowledge that the terms of existing federal law required the post office to deliver material entrusted to it. However, he claimed that that obligation could be met by delivering only those papers that had been requested by a specific addressee. (The abolitionists' tracts were usually unsolicited.) Moreover, to discourage further agitation on the slavery issue, Jackson made two specific recommendations.

In his first recommendation, Jackson, recognizing the enormous power of public opinion on the issue of slavery, ordered postmasters to publish the names of anyone ordering abolitionist literature. They could then be subjected to public censure: "when they are known, every moral and good citizen will unite to put them in coventry, and avoid their society." Continued agitation merited death, he claimed. Second, he asked Congress for the formal authority to withhold abolitionist literature from the mails. He was denied that power. Although most legislators clearly agreed with Jackson about the dangers of antislavery agitation—both chambers soon took up "gag rules" refusing to receive antislavery petitions—a majority feared investing the president with censorship authority. The same end could be achieved by leaving the matter to local officials.

The resulting selective enforcement of the nation's postal laws subsequently impaired the abolitionists' exercise of their First Amendment rights to a free press, inasmuch as they were unable to rely on the conventional method of distributing their newspapers. President Jackson's complicity in this enterprise, without explicit legal authority, brought accusations from some that he was engaged in a piece of nullification himself.

## ATTACKING THE ABOLITIONISTS

Jackson also made extensive use of presidential rhetoric to undermine abolitionism. In formal addresses to Congress, in published correspondence, and through his network of administration newspapers, Jackson adopted an aggressive posture to bring public shame on the agitators. Most notably, in his seventh annual message, he charged that those publishing antislavery literature were interested in nothing more than manufacturing bloody revolution. All abolitionist materials sent to the South were, as the southern line had it, "addressed to the passions of the slaves, . . . calculated to stimulate them to insurrection and to produce all the horrors of a servile war."

The executive committee of the American Antislavery Society strenuously objected to Jackson's characterization of their intent and, further, to the extraordinary way he stirred opposition to their cause:

> [I]s it nothing, sir, that we are officially charged by the President of the United States, with wicked and unconstitutional efforts, and with harboring the most execrable intentions? and this, too, in a document spread upon the Journals of both Houses of Congress, published to the nation and to the world, made part of our enduring archives, and incorporated in the history of the age? It is true, that although you have given judgment against us, you cannot award execution. We are not indeed, subjected to the penalty of murder; but need we to ask you, sir, what must be the *moral influence* of your declaration . . . ?

The "moral influence" was to legitimize popular attacks on all who sought to advance the interests of a disfavored minority in an already hostile majority environment. This was as the president intended. Constrained by the formalities of his office, he used the informal weight of his personal and institutional reputation to encourage the American people to do what he could not.

## CONSTRAINTS AND POWER

The power of those constraints merits attention, as one of the great but often unrecognized virtues of the office of the presidency. The mutual empowerment of institution and person are easily seen in Jackson's case. His accession to that office undoubtedly helped to invest popular confidence in an institution that had been discredited after the "corrupt bargain" of 1824. As George Washington had done four decades earlier, Jackson built up the office of the presidency through the strength of his own popular standing. Jackson consequently inherited the considerable powers of the office Washington had formed, and he restored and deployed them to reshape the character of U.S. politics in a more democratic direction.

Yet the office also burdened Jackson with a set of distinctive presidential roles and responsibilities. His entrance into the presidency had the effect of channeling into that office a political force with the potential to be as destructive of constitutional forms outside the system as it ultimately was protective of them inside. Although most of the signs in Jackson's career indicate that he was a nationalist, the full impact of the presidency on his behavior cannot be wholly reckoned without asking how he might have responded to South Carolina's claims for independence had he been at the time governor of Tennessee, or yet again a spurned presidential candidate in the mold of 1824. The nation was spared those possibly divisive contingencies because the most popular political figure of the era was, by virtue of electoral practices and constitutional forms, sworn to "preserve, protect, and defend the Constitution of the United States." His informal powers were channeled toward that end. Although the paths not taken are merely subjects for speculation, their consideration reveals how important the presidential institution can be for converting the raw power of democracy into a force for preserving constitutional and republican forms and, ultimately—given what Lincoln later did from the office Jackson restored—for advancing liberal ends.

**BIBLIOGRAPHY:**

Bassett, John Spencer, and John Franklin Jameson, eds. *Correspondence of Andrew Jackson*, 7 vols., 1926–1935 (Kraus Reprint Company, 1969).

Cole, Donald B. *The Presidency of Andrew Jackson* (University Press of Kansas, 1993).

de Tocqueville, Alexis. *Democracy in America.* Edited by J. P. Mayer; translated by George P. Lawrence (Anchor Books, 1969).

Ellis, Richard E. *The Union at Risk: Jacksonian Democracy, States' Rights, and the Nullification Crisis* (Oxford University Press, 1987).

Hofstadter, Richard. "Andrew Jackson and the Rise of Liberal Capitalism," in *The American Political Tradition and the Men Who Made It* (Knopf, 1948).

Latner, Richard B. *The Presidency of Andrew Jackson: White House Politics, 1829–1837* (University of Georgia Press, 1979).

McFaul, John M. *The Politics of Jacksonian Finance* (Cornell University Press, 1972).

Remini, Robert V. *Andrew Jackson*, 3 vols. (Harper & Row, 1977–1984).

———. *Andrew Jackson and the Bank War: A Study in the Growth of Presidential Power* (Norton, 1967).

Remini, Robert V., and Robert O. Rupp, *Andrew Jackson: A Bibliography* (Meekler, 1991).

Riley, Russell L. *The Presidency and the Politics of Racial Inequality: Nation-Keeping from 1831 to 1965* (Columbia University Press, 1999).

Satz, Ronald N. *American Indian Policy in the Jacksonian Era* (University of Nebraska Press, 1975).

Schlesinger, Arthur M., Jr. *The Age of Jackson* (Little, Brown, 1945).

★★★ 8 ★★★

# MARTIN VAN BUREN
## 1837–1841

*David J. Bodenhamer*

*Born 5 December 1782 in Kinderhook, New York, to Abraham Van Buren and Maria Goes Hoes Van Alen Van Buren; did not attend college; studied law in New York and was admitted to the bar; married Hannah Hoes 21 February 1807, Catskill, New York; four children; ran for president in 1836 on the Democratic ticket with Richard Mentor Johnson of Kentucky, against three separate Whig candidates. Van Buren received 764,198 popular votes and 170 electoral college votes; the Whig candidates received almost as many popular votes; of electoral college votes, William Henry Harrison received 73, Hugh White 26, and Daniel Webster 14. Willie P. Mangum of South Carolina received his state's 11 electoral ballots. Died 24 July 1862 in Kinderhook, New York; buried in Kinderhook Cemetary.*

The third of six children born to a farmer–tavern keeper in the small Dutch village of Kinderhook, New York, Martin Van Buren learned the law at age 15 as an apprentice to a village lawyer. Within two years, he had secured the pa-tronage of fellow townsmen John Van Ness and William Van Ness—Van Buren played an important role in electing John, a Jeffersonian Republican, to Congress in 1800—and soon followed them to New York City. There, he participated at the margins in the fierce political struggle between the Burr and Clinton factions of New York's Republican party. From the experience, Van Buren learned how to remain uncommitted while gauging the strengths of various interests and assessing their potential for success. This skill became a political trademark.

## POLITICAL APPRENTICESHIP

On returning to Kinderhook in 1804, Van Buren established himself as a lawyer and politician. Three years later, he married and moved to Hudson, New York, where his legal practice and family flourished. He misguidedly backed Vice President George Clinton's vain attempt to succeed Jefferson as president, despite Clinton's inability to win the state party's support. From this setback, Van Buren gained an appreciation both for the power of the caucus and for the need for strict party discipline.

Van Buren moved quickly to the first rank of state Republican leaders after winning a seat in the New York senate in 1812, an election he attributed to his strict adherence to correct principles. By 1815, he had gained appointment as state attorney general. Then, in 1816, Van Buren lost his mentor when New York governor Daniel D. Tompkins, an anti-Clintonian, won election to the U.S. vice presidency. Tompkins's departure weakened Van Buren, and the subsequent election of his chief rival, De Witt Clinton, as governor in 1817 marked the low point in Van Buren's political career. The lessons he drew from this experience reinforced his tendency to avoid involvement when factions were too nearly balanced.

## BUILDING THE ALBANY REGENCY

The years from 1817 to 1821 were the most innovative in Van Buren's public life and revealed him a master of politics, gaining him the sobriquets Red Fox from Kinderhook and Little Magician for his craftiness. During this period, he created the modern political machine known as the Albany Regency. To avoid splitting the party, Clinton had kept Van Buren in the council as attorney general. From this position Van Buren

recognized the depth of opposition to the governor and his pet Erie Canal project. He saw an opportunity to use this dislike and distrust of Clinton as a powerful adhesive to bind together otherwise competing factions. His goal was to instill a logical pattern of political behavior based on adherence to Jeffersonian principles, party identity, and unswerving loyalty to majority rule in party affairs. Patronage, a partisan press, and control of local party machinery would be the means of discipline, the way to ensure political regularity. None of these ideas were original. Van Buren's seminal contribution was to meld all the parts into a political structure that, over time, supplied its own momentum and its own ideology.

Van Buren used his new machine cautiously at first, making sure to consolidate its power before challenging Clinton. The Erie Canal proved instrumental in his plans. He persuaded anti-Clinton Republicans and former Federalists, known as Bucktails, to support the project and wrest from the governor's control the vast patronage that went with it. This tactic cost Van Buren his lucrative post as attorney general, but it also freed him to support the candidacy of former Vice President Tompkins in his challenge to Clinton's bid for reelection as governor. Although Clinton won another term in a close vote, the Bucktails gained control of both houses of the legislature, effectively crippling him. Paradoxically, Van Buren, the architect of this triumph, was without government office, having declined to run again for the senate.

## ONTO THE NATIONAL STAGE

Van Buren's absence from public life was short-lived. In 1821, the New York senate elected him to a six-year term as U.S. senator. After attending to the business of a new state constitutional convention, he moved to Washington, intent on making New York the pivotal state in the Union. From this base, he could promote the principles of Old Republicanism and revive its planter-farmer alliance. Strongly opposed to the politics of class and personality, Van Buren sought the steady advancement of a democratic social order that promoted equal opportunity, especially economic opportunity. His challenge always was to control an inherently unstable base in his home state while extending his influence and his bent for party discipline to the more unruly world of the nation's capital.

Convinced that National Republicanism was destructive of Jeffersonian principles, Van Buren sought to create a democratic majority by reviving old party distinctions, the tactic that had worked in New York. The presidential election of 1824 was key to this strategy. When judging the prospects, Van Buren held a central objective, the union of Virginia, Pennsylvania, and New York on one candidate. This alliance, he believed, best promoted Jeffersonian principles—and, not coincidentally, the interests of his state. *Conservative, states rightist, agrarian, party regular:* these terms defined Van Buren's politics. So did *New Yorker, northerner,* and *pragmatic politician.*

Van Buren cast his support to William Henry Crawford, a strict Jeffersonian who posed no threat to the Little Magician's control of party machinery in New York. But securing New York's electoral votes for Crawford proved unexpectedly difficult. Van Buren's absence from the state had weakened his control of the Albany Regency and left the machine in disrepair. Lacking leadership, the Bucktails found themselves opposing a sudden clamor for popular election. Sensing Clinton behind this movement for reform, the Bucktails clumsily attempted to punish him, but instead they created a popular hero. One blunder after another resulted in a Regency loss in the October elections and a subsequent shift of the state's electoral votes to Adams.

Van Buren belatedly recognized that popular attitudes had begun to shift. The Missouri debates over slavery, the economic potential of the Erie Canal, the surge of new immigration to the state, the demand for democratic control over society—all signaled a growing dissatisfaction with politics as usual, including the Virginia–New York alliance and the resulting southern dominance of the presidency. Above all, the de-bacle taught Van Buren that the mechanisms of party must respond more smoothly to changes in public attitudes. The caucus system was waning; to retain power, the Red Fox had to find its replacement.

## JOINING WITH JACKSON

After securing his base in New York, Van Buren reached boldly for national leadership. His primary objective was the restoration of the party system based on principled political behavior. Only party, he believed, offered protection for a democratic citizenry in a rapidly changing social and economic environment dominated by capitalist elites. By combining Andrew Jackson's popularity with the appeal of Jeffersonian republicanism, Van Buren sought to make party identification the talisman of national politics. He associated himself more closely with attacks on the Adams administration. He also cemented his relationship with John C. Calhoun, whom Van Buren saw as necessary to bring southern radicals into the Jacksonian coalition, even as he sought ultimately to displace Calhoun as their leader. Most important, Van Buren made a number of trips, especially to the South, to nurture the budding organization of Jackson supporters from which he would restore the party system.

More was at stake than ensuring Jackson's election. Van Buren already aspired to succeed Old Hickory, and to do so meant that in New York he had to preserve his political strength, in the national arena he had to block Clinton (whom Jackson favored) from advancing his cause, and in the Senate he had to adopt balanced positions that accommodated his state's diverse population and mixed economy. His triumphant delivery of over fifty New York papers in support of Jackson in 1827 marked the success of his strategy. The tariff debate of 1828, which resulted in the so-called Tariff of Abominations, also proved important to Van Buren's political future. Although he tried to cultivate Calhoun, the different economic interests of New York and South Carolina inevitably placed the two men on opposing sides. This separation allowed Van Buren to curry favor with Jackson, who disliked Calhoun, and shielded him from the bitter recriminations that followed the tariff debate.

Thanks in large measure to Van Buren's innovative use of his political organization, Jackson carried New York and the nation in an election that marked the advent of U.S. majoritarian democracy. The strain on the Regency, however, persuaded Van Buren to run for governor in order to retain control over his political base. He won, secure in the knowledge that he had a place in the new Jackson administration. In February he accepted an invitation to become secretary of state. He was the most commanding figure in an undistinguished cabinet.

## IN THE JACKSON INNER CIRCLE

Events early in his first term led Jackson to recognize his affinity with the Little Magician. Van Buren gained the president's personal gratitude by his defense of Peggy O'Neal Eaton, wife of Secretary of War John Eaton, a Jackson friend, who was snubbed by the anti-Jackson social set. Mrs. Eaton's virtue soon became an article of democratic faith—and a test of loyalty—with the president. Equally consequential was Van Buren's shared distress with Jackson over the intemperance of the South Carolina *Exposition and Protest*, the virulent response to the Tariff of 1828 secretly written by Vice President John C. Calhoun. Both Jackson and Van Buren were neo-Jeffersonians who reluctantly opposed tariff reduction for different reasons: for Jackson, it would alienate his important Pennsylvania supporters and delay his desire to eliminate the national debt; for Van Buren, it would disrupt his dreams of a revived alliance between southern planters and northern farmers.

Van Buren's primary role in Jackson's administration had less to do with diplomacy than with politics, his title notwithstanding. He became the president's strategist, advancing both his own and his chief's interests simultaneously. He isolated Calhoun further by leaking William Henry Crawford's statement that Calhoun, then secretary of war, had wanted Jackson disciplined

in 1818 for seizing Florida. He encouraged Jackson's Maysville Road veto, killing the long-held hope of National Republicans for a federal transportation system. He orchestrated calls from Democratic papers in 1830 for Old Hickory's reelection and launched a new pro-Jackson (and Van Buren) administration organ, the Washington *Globe*, to replace the less reliable (and pro-Calhoun) *United States Telegraph*. With the Eaton "malaria" and nullification controversy continuing to divide the administration, Van Buren resigned from the cabinet and persuaded Eaton to do the same, enabling Jackson to announce a cabinet reorganization that removed the dissidents. Then he sailed to England as minister-nominee to the Court of St. James, but not before placing his allies in the new cabinet.

To embarrass the president, Calhoun's supporters in the Senate engineered the defeat of Van Buren's appointment. The slight was meaningless since Jackson had already invited the Little Magician to serve as his vice president during a second administration. There, Van Buren attempted to moderate Jackson's views, especially on the response to nullification and the removal of deposits following the veto of the Second Bank recharter. He initially underestimated the gravity of the nullification crisis and misread the depth of Jackson's opposition to banks. For Van Buren, these matters were primarily political: Differing sectional interests were straining the bonds of the Jacksonian coalition. All his instincts called for a middle course to hold the wings of the party together. Ever cautious, he preferred to wait until public and political opinion could be tested, especially with removal. Van Buren feared the economic consequences of removal and the danger it posed for the coalition he had nurtured. He aspired to the presidency and, in truth, he had more to lose politically than did Jackson. Still, Van Buren did not break with the president—loyalty was a cornerstone of party discipline—even when Jackson's stance worked against his interests. He did absent himself from Washington, however, during the height of each crisis.

## SEEKING THE PRESIDENCY

As Van Buren prepared to seek the presidency, he had to contend with the legacy of Jackson's policies, the emergence of rivals for power, doubts about his sympathy to southern and western interests, and the emergence of slavery as a powerful political issue. The Bank War and removal policy had lessened the moderating influence of the Second Bank, which in turn had freed undercapitalized banks, especially in the West and South, to overextend credit, infecting the economy with an inflationary fever. The administration's restrictive stance on internal improvements and its insistence on hard money in the Specie Circular of 1836 had alienated speculators and others who favored rapid development. The states' rights and executive-centered program of Democrats sparked opposition around which the nascent Whig party coalesced. And slavery emerged as an increasingly volatile issue in the nation's political calculus.

Van Buren shared Jackson's positions on most issues. He believed the federal government lacked the power to build roads and canals or subsidize such projects. He opposed a national bank and supported a hard-money policy. But he expressed these views more cautiously than did Jackson. It was his nature, and his strategy required it. He sought to claim Jackson's legacy through the agency of the Virginia–New York alliance, the coalition that had long been central to his politics. But the South and West viewed Van Buren skeptically; as a northerner, his sympathies and interests were suspect, especially on slavery.

Opposition to antislavery was critical for candidates, like Van Buren, who wanted southern support. Whigs sought to link the Little Magician with antislavery advocates in the North, a position that would undermine the Virginia–New York alliance. Their strategy also would further consolidate anti-Jackson forces. For this reason, Van Buren judged slavery to be the most important issue of the campaign, one that required a carefully nuanced position. He understood how fundamentally slavery threatened the

foundation of the Union, and he believed it unjust and immoral. But he considered it a local matter and constitutionally beyond the authority of Congress. Unable to make the same argument on slavery in the District of Columbia, he remained silent.

In May 1836, the Democrats unanimously chose Van Buren as their nominee for president, with Richard M. Johnson from Kentucky as his vice-presidential running mate. Opposing Van Buren were three sectional candidates running as Whigs— William Henry Harrison, Hugh Lawson White, and Daniel Webster. Jackson had thrown his prestige behind Van Buren, an action that masked the divisions in the party. The Alabama and Tennessee legislatures had already repudiated the nominee, and many convention delegates were unenthusiastic about the choice. In truth, the Democrats were riddled with factionalism in 1836. Southerners distrusted Van Buren, associating him with Jackson's stand on nullification. Division was also rife in the North, where Van Buren found it impossible to appease all interests.

Van Buren gained a clear but narrow victory in an election that was, above all, a referendum on Andrew Jackson. The Red Fox from Kinderhook had a majority of over 25,000 popular votes out of 1.5 million, and an electoral college margin of 170 to the 124 accorded his combined opponents. Democrats maintained a comfortable control of the Senate, but the House was less manageable, with conservative Democrats and radical Whigs holding the balance of power. These totals were not a solid endorsement of the previous eight years, especially its attacks on privilege, wealth, and class. Rather, the election revealed a fairly evenly balanced two-party system in nearly every state in the Union. This circumstance would call forth Van Buren's caution, even as it tested his political skills.

By experience and temperament, Van Buren appeared well-suited for the presidency. He was a master politician, with a deserved reputation for building consensus and maintaining coalitions. He liked people, was suave and tactful by reputation, and relished being on good terms with his political opponents. He had years of experience at the highest levels of both federal and state government. He was honest, knew the value of counsel, made decisions deliberately, and held firm to principles that guided his entire career.

His weaknesses would prove his undoing. Van Buren was often stubborn, a surprising trait in one who learned early how to maneuver successfully in turbulent political waters. He was perhaps overly cautious, born of a need to master a situation completely before acting. At times, he failed to control his subordinates. But ultimately it was a vision he could not sustain—his dream of a union of planters and plain republicans in the Jacksonian democracy—that betrayed him. It did not fit the times, and he could not find the way to make it do so.

Van Buren early signaled his desire to extend the policies of his predecessor. After several prominent men refused his offer of a post, he reappointed Jackson's cabinet, save one. That exception was Joel Poinsett as secretary of war. The other members—John Forsyth (state), Levi Woodbury (treasury), Mahlon Dickerson (navy), Amos Kendall (postmaster general), and Benjamin Butler (attorney general)—were undistinguished. The inaugural message also echoed Jacksonian themes: the sanctity of Union, states' rights, limited government, attention to domestic concerns. One new issue, slavery, brought a reiteration of his preelection promise—opposition to its abolition in the District of Columbia without the consent of the southern states and a determination to resist any attempt to interfere with slavery where it existed. Antislavery advocates bristled at the new president's moral slackness. To Van Buren, however, noninterference was necessary to hold southern planters and republican farmers in concert and to keep at bay an issue that, once it became political, would shake the nation to its foundations.

## THE PANIC OF 1837

It was the economy, not slavery, that soon consumed Van Buren's attention, for the most severe depression in the nation's young history began shortly after his inauguration in 1837. The financial crisis stemmed from a variety of factors. Democrats blamed overexpansion, and "overbanking and overtrading," as they called it, was undoubtedly a cause. With the Second Bank no longer acting to regulate credit, banks had multiplied and loans and notes had expanded without regard to reserves, especially in the South and West. Manic speculation in land and hundreds of millions of dollars in risky loans to state internal improvement schemes had created a mountain of bad debt and bad currency. The Specie Circular of 1836, which required payment in gold or silver for the purchase of government lands, drained reserves from the East to the West, making credit tight on the commercial eastern seaboard and raising doubts about the soundness of the nation's banking structure. Compounding the problem was a depression in England and a sudden drop in the world price for cotton, which drained specie and curtailed foreign investment.

A financial panic, which had been building for months in the West and South, hit the nation full force in April 1837. Thousands of business failures, suspension of specie payments by the nation's largest banks, and many factory closings signaled the start of a depression that lasted fully seven years. Even the optimistic Van Buren, whose inaugural speech had promised prosperity, could not deny the severity of the crisis.

The worsening depression also sowed political disaster for the president. It invigorated the Whigs, who blurred their internal differences by blaming the debacle on Jackson's economic policies, and it fragmented the Democrats into soft-money conservatives and hard-money Locofocos. Whig victories in state and local elections in 1837 were stunning in their scope. Even as the depression provided Whigs with a veneer of unity, it brought into sharp focus long-standing differences among Democrats over hard money, banks, and other parts of the Jacksonian program. State parties in New York, Pennsylvania, New Jersey, and

South Carolina—all states with important commercial interests—split wide open, with key leaders pushing policies and forming alliances that bucked the national administration.

As soon as Van Buren took office he faced demands for repeal of the Specie Circular from Democrats and Whigs alike. By 1 April the president had made his decision: The Circular would remain in effect. This action was as symbolic as it was significant. The Circular had undoubtedly checked the orgy of speculation, but even some of its original supporters questioned its continued usefulness. Clearly, the policy initially had contributed to the deflationary spiral; it is less certain whether repeal would have had any measurable impact, given the depression's other causes. But Van Buren's decision signaled his commitment to Jackson's legacy. In the face of great pressure, he remained true to the general's most unpopular act. He would cling doggedly to a hard-money policy and a limited role for government.

Within weeks, Van Buren called a special session of Congress that would meet in September to resolve a problem resulting from suspension of specie payment by the nation's banks. Suspension made banks ineligible to serve as custodians of the government's funds, since by law they were required to return these deposits in specie upon demand. When combined with the depression's dampening effect on tax revenues, this fact could leave the Treasury without sufficient funds for the ordinary expenses of government.

Van Buren's message to the special session addressed only this need of the government, not the problems of the country. Attributing the causes of depression to overbanking and overtrading, he proposed several measures to safeguard government funds: postponement of the distribution of surplus funds to the states, issuance of Treasury notes to meet the immediate obligations of government, and the establishment of an independent treasury, among others. Adoption of this latter step would allow government to keep its receipts in its own vaults, thus completely divorcing its fiscal operations from the nation's banks.

The proposal made clear Van Buren's narrow view of governmental responsibility. Its role and its authority ran only to its actual needs, and its revenues to its expenses. The central government, unlike the states, had no obligation to provide relief or promote the general welfare. This stance kept faith with the tenets of Jeffersonian republicanism, notably its agrarianism and strict constructionism, to which Van Buren was heir. Ironically, at the state level such laissez-faire attitudes held less truck with Democrats, who vied with Whigs to expand the role of government.

### INDEPENDENT TREASURY

Congress readily supported most of the president's suggestions, except the independent treasury. The proposal, as amended in the Senate, met several administration needs. It satisfied the hard-money, antibank core of the Democratic party, including labor, and offered an effective response to the doctrine that Congress could regulate all the currency, not just coinage. Led by Henry Clay, Whigs countered that the measure would stifle recovery by drawing specie from circulation and by curtailing loans and credit. They also argued that the government should attack the depression more directly by reestablishing a national bank.

On its first attempt, the independent treasury proposal was defeated in the House by Whigs, western Democrats, and Conservatives, alienated southern Democrats who believed a Treasury bank was only a national bank in disguise. Van Buren then sought to curry favor with westerners by supporting the land policy advocated by their spokesperson, Senator Thomas Hart Benton. Built on a theme of "cheap land, easily obtained," Benton's program contained a number of features, two of which the president endorsed—preemption and graduation. Preemption, or securing squatters' rights, passed in 1838, during the session that saw the Specie Circular rescinded and the independent treasury fail again.

Whigs blocked the graduation of land sales—the proposal that the longer lands remained unsold, the cheaper they would become—because they desired to use land revenues to finance a national scheme for internal improvements.

Van Buren's persistence paid off in 1840 when the independent treasury passed narrowly. The depression aided his cause. In May 1838, banks had resumed specie payment as the economy improved, only to suspend them again when conditions worsened toward the end of 1839. Their instability and the collapse of Nicholas Biddle's United States Bank of Pennsylvania (formerly the Second Bank) was a powerful demonstration of the need for an alternative system. Yet for all the struggle surrounding its birth, the independent treasury made no fundamental contribution to financial stability or a uniform currency. The function of regulating the money supply passed entirely to the states.

## INCREASING TENSION OVER SLAVERY

Both the administration's response to the depression and its land policies stirred sectional interests, but nowhere was sectionalism more apparent than in the increasing agitation over slavery. The aggressive tactics of abolitionists continually thrust the question of slavery before the Congress. Gag rules earlier adopted by both houses had not squelched debate, as antislavery advocates repeatedly advanced their petitions. The excitement over slavery also flared when the new Republic of Texas signaled its interest in annexation. Seizing the opportunity, John C. Calhoun presented a series of state-sovereignty resolutions in the Senate in December 1837 regarding slavery and annexation of slaveholding territory. The resolutions, which marked the firm union of proslavery and state-sovereignty arguments, passed the Senate with large majorities. This clamor over slavery vexed the president, who still clung to his hope of building his party's strength through an alliance of southern planters and northern plain re-

publicans. For Van Buren, keeping slavery out of politics remained a primary objective.

The administration's desire to preserve the support of southerners by keeping antislavery at bay was symbolized by the case of *L'Amistad*. This Spanish ship was transporting fifty-three Africans bound for slavery in Cuba when, in June 1839, the Africans seized the ship and steered it toward U.S. waters, where it was picked up by a federal revenue cutter. Although Van Buren had condemned the slave trade earlier, he instructed that, if the U.S. District Court found for the Spanish "owners," the Africans were to be hurried back to Cuba without an opportunity for an appeal. Despite the president's instructions, the Supreme Court ultimately declared the Africans free men.

## THE THREAT OF WAR WITH CANADA

Foreign and domestic affairs merged in a more inflammatory way in the wholesale violence and threat of war that developed in the late 1830s along the U.S.-Canadian border. In the winter of 1837–1838, separate attempts to seek Canadian independence failed and the rebel leaders sought refuge in the United States. There, the insurgents found it easy to recruit men and supplies in places along the northeastern frontier border. They also established a base on Navy Island, a Canadian possession on the Niagara River.

The Canadian government reacted with alarm, fearing a revival of U.S. designs on the provinces. Its troops crossed the Niagara in late December 1837 and seized the *Caroline*, a steamer used to transport supplies from the American side. After a brief skirmish in which one American was killed, the Canadians burned the ship. To calm the excitement Van Buren sent General Winfield Scott to patrol the border. Relations became more tense when a Canadian deputy sheriff, Alexander McLeod, was arrested in New York for the murder of the U.S. citizen killed in the *Caroline* affair. The president refused to become involved in a case under state jurisdiction, and the trial was still pending when he left office.

As tensions mounted, the United States and Great Britain tangled over the northeast boundary between the United States and Canada. This line had been in dispute since the Peace of Paris in 1783. At issue was 12,000 square miles of land, much of it in prime timber. The King of The Netherlands, whom both sides chose as arbitrator in 1826, fixed a line that gave the United States the bulk of the land under contention. Maine protested the award, and the United States refused it, even though Great Britain had accepted. In 1836 Great Britain withdrew her acceptance, and Canadian loggers entered the disputed territory around the Aroostook River valley. Maine called out the militia and in the "Aroostook War" took forcible possession of the land.

Congress immediately authorized Van Buren to call up 50,000 volunteers and voted $10 million for defense. But the president took a calmer approach. He sent Scott to the region, with instructions to secure "peace with honor." The general persuaded the reluctant Maine governor to withdraw his troops, although not without price to Van Buren, whose neutrality cost his party votes in the New York state elections in 1838.

## ELECTION OF 1840

As the election of 1840 approached, no one doubted Van Buren's renomination. Any other alternative would have meant repudiation of Jackson and an admission of defeat. But few Democrats were enthusiastic about their standard bearer as they met in convention in May 1840. Unwilling to renominate Richard M. Johnson, the delegates left selection of a vice-presidential candidate to the states. The platform emphasized traditional Democratic themes, including limited governmental power, states rights, no national program of internal improvements, no national bank, and no congressional interference with slavery.

Whigs faced the opposite problem. They were optimistic about their prospects and divided over their nominee. Henry Clay, William Henry Harrison, and Winfield Scott vied for their party's endorsement. The December 1839 convention turned to Harrison, the Whig who had made the strongest showing four years earlier, with John Tyler of Virginia as his running mate. Unlike the Democrats, Whigs adopted no platform, although Harrison later announced that he was for a strong Union, for a protective tariff and national bank if the public interest required it, and for a limited chief executive.

The Whigs swept the election in the electoral college, in large measure because they did not allow Democrats to monopolize credit as friends of the people. Harrison carried nineteen of twenty-six states, including every northern state but two, and seven from the South, although the figure is misleading. The Democrats had done remarkably well, given the state of the economy and an uncharismatic candidate. A shift of some 8,000 votes in four states would have tilted the electoral vote to Van Buren. The president had suffered from the electorate's tendency to blame economic hard times on the party in power. His failure to advance a constructive economic program had a debilitating effect on his party and his chances for reelection. Complicating his chances was the emergence of slavery—thus sectionalism—as a staple of U.S. politics. Van Buren had long feared that an open discussion of slavery would destroy the Virginia–New York alliance on which he had constructed his vision of national unity. The election of 1840 marked the emergence of a political culture that would confirm his fears.

## AFTER THE PRESIDENCY

Van Buren returned to Kinderhook, intent on enjoying life as the patriarch of a large family. Friends and local Democratic committees urged him to consider another run at the presidency. A 7,000-mile trip through the South and a Democratic victory in the New York state elections convinced him of his renewed popularity. He spent much time keeping the national party together for the 1844 election, when he once again might be the Democratic nominee. The question of

Texas annexation spoiled his plans. Van Buren counseled a diplomatic solution when the national mood ran to annexation. Despite leading the first ballot of the Democratic convention in 1844, the Red Fox could not muster the required two-thirds vote, and he withdrew his name on the ninth ballot.

Repudiated by the convention and ignored by the new Polk administration, Van Buren was content to keep his eye on state politics and to assist the political ambitions of his sons. He did not retreat from national affairs, however. In 1848, he released through his son John the first comprehensive statement of the Free-Soil position. He worked with the Barnburners, radical Democrats in New York, to oppose the renomination of James K. Polk and found himself the nominee of the Free-Soil party, which formed in protest of southern positions on slavery in the territories. This nomination pained Van Buren, always the party regular, although he ultimately accepted it when the New York wing styled itself the Free Soil-Democratic party. He received not one electoral vote.

His third-party candidacy left him with no standing in the national Democratic organization. He spent his remaining years writing his autobiography, corresponding on the momentous events of the 1850s, and tending his dying son, Martin. He witnessed the dissolution of the Union, strongly supporting Lincoln's call for troops to suppress the rebellion. This ringing endorsement of the war effort, his final public pronouncement, helped restore his reputation, which had suffered when he sacrificed his fundamental principles in a vain effort to save the Union.

## BIBLIOGRAPHY

Cole, Donald B. *Martin Van Buren and the American Political System* (Princeton University Press, 1984).

Curtis, James C. *The Fox at Bay: Martin Van Buren and the American Presidency* (University Press of Kentucky, 1970).

Fitzpatrick, John C., ed. *The Autobiography of Martin Van Buren*, 2 vols. (American Historical Association, 1920).

Niven, John. *Martin Van Buren: The Romantic Age of American Politics* (Oxford University Press, 1983).

Remini, Robert V. *Martin Van Buren and the Making of the Democratic Party* (Columbia University Press, 1959).

★★★ **9** ★★★

# WILLIAM HENRY HARRISON
## 1841

*Leonard L. Richards*

---

*Born 9 February 1773 in Berkeley, Charles County, Virginia, to Benjamin Harrison and Elizabeth Bassett Harrison; attended Hampden-Sydney College in Virginia (1787–1790) but left to fight Indians; married Anna Tuthill Symmes, 25 November 1795, North Bend, Ohio; ten children; elected, with John Tyler of Virginia, on the Whig ticket in 1840, gathering 1,275,016 popular votes and 234 electoral college votes over the Democratic ticket of Martin Van Buren of New York and Richard Mentor Johnson of Kentucky, which received 1,129,102 popular votes and 60 electoral college votes; died 4 April 1841 in Washington, D.C., from pneumonia developed from cold caught at his inauguration one month before; buried in William Henry Harrison Memorial State Park, North Bend, Ohio.*

---

What can be said about a president who died one month after taking office? Obviously, William Henry Harrison's time in the White House was a small matter in his long career. And, in reality, nothing earth-shattering happened in his one-month presidency during the spring of 1841.

## THE NEW POLITICS
What makes Harrison important to the annals of the presidency is *how* he got elected.

His campaigns for the presidency marked the coming of age of a new political system, one that would be with the nation for the rest of the nineteenth century and well into the early twentieth century. When political commentators talk about presidential "image" and how image makers manipulate the public, they are describing a process that became well-established in the nineteenth century. The creation of Harrison as a "presidential candidate" was one of the high—or low—points in that process.

But political manipulators in Harrison's day had a talent that their modern counterparts lack: They could get out the vote. They could get millions of people to come out of the hills, down the streams, and to the ballot box on election day. Only about half the electorate now turns out to vote in presidential contests. In 1840, when Harrison won the presidency, 78 percent of the eligible males turned out to vote. That was a new high, but for the rest of the century political operators repeatedly got four out of five eligible voters to the polls on election day. And they did so not only for the great presidents, but also for such second-raters as Franklin Pierce, Rutherford B. Hayes, and James Garfield.

No one has ever claimed that William Henry Harrison was a great president. But he was a very popular candidate, far more popular than most of the men who have been deemed "great presidents." How did that come to pass?

## EARLY CAREER

Harrison was hardly a likely candidate when he was "discovered" in the early 1830s; in fact, his career seemed to be over. Born in Virginia in 1772, the son of a signer of the Declaration of Independence, Harrison attended Hampden-Sidney College at age fourteen. He dropped out of college to join the army when he was eighteen. Rising to the rank of captain, he became at age twenty-five the secretary of the Northwest Territory, and the following year was the Territory's first delegate to Congress. There, he drafted the Land Act of 1800, which provided for the sale of land in tracts of 320 acres or more at a minimum price of $2 an acre. His rapid rise continued and within one more year he was appointed governor of the Indiana Territory, an office that he would hold until the War of 1812. As governor he negotiated several boundary treaties with local tribes and opened more land to white settlers. But as white settlement spread, the Shawnee chief Tecumseh and his brother the Prophet tried to unite the various tribes east of the Mississippi to stop further encroachment.

## INDIAN FIGHTER

At the battle of Tippecanoe in 1811, Harrison achieved what would later be his main claim to fame, when he led an army of almost a thousand men and destroyed a small band of warriors in Prophet's Town. Although Harrison undoubtedly lost more men than did the Prophet, he proclaimed a great victory, telling the secretary of war that "the Indians have never sustained such a defeat since their acquaintance with the white people." His exaggerated version of the minor victory took on mythical proportions until many western settlers came to believe that Harrison had defeated the great Tecumseh himself. Subsequently, during the War of 1812, Harrison led 3,500 troops at the Battle of Thames against 700 British soldiers and 1,000 of Tecumseh's men. His army overwhelmed both, killed Tecumseh and scattered his warriors, and forever ended tribal resistance in the Old Northwest.

## DECLINE AND REVIVAL

After the war, Harrison represented the people of southern Ohio as a congressman from 1816 to 1819, then as a state senator from 1819 to 1821, and then as U.S. senator from 1825 to 1826. As an elected official he opposed the Second Bank of the United States and supported the protective tariff, but he was identified mainly with his anti-Indian views. In 1826 John Quincy Adams appointed him U.S. minister to Colombia, but when Andrew Jackson became president in 1829, he recalled Harrison. By the early 1830s, Harrison's political star had dimmed and he had been reduced to taking the post of county clerk in North Bend, Ohio. That was hardly a high-level job, hardly one with high visibility, and hardly one from which to launch a presidential career. On top of that, Harrison, who had achieved so much in his youth, was now in his early sixties.

What brought Harrison back into the limelight was a letter he wrote protesting the undue attention given to Colonel Richard M. Johnson's military exploits. Johnson, a Kentucky congressman who had commanded a regiment under Harrison at the Battle of Thames, had styled himself as Tecumseh Johnson and had taken credit for killing Tecumseh and opening the Northwest to white settlement. In challenging Johnson's account, Harrison gained wide attention in the press in late 1834. He also caught the eye of a number of political leaders who were looking for a suitable candidate to offset Andrew Jackson's popularity as an Indian fighter and spokesman for the common man. Harrison was soon nominated for president, at a public meeting in Harrisburg, Pennsylvania. Harrison began taking his candidacy seriously when, over the next few months, he was endorsed by similar meetings in Cincinnati, New York, Indiana, and Kentucky. With the backing of Ohio friends, he wrote numerous letters for publication and toured Indiana soliciting support. In December 1835, he won the endorsement of both the Pennsylvania Whig party and the Pennsylvania Anti-Masonic party.

## THE 1836 ELECTION STRATEGY

At the time, Jackson's opponents had neither a national strategy for the upcoming 1836 presidential election nor a national party. Instead, they comprised an inchoate collection of National Republicans, Whigs, Anti-Masons, states' rights advocates, Calhounites, and anti–Van Buren Democrats. In the absence of any sort of unity, there was no possibility of holding a national nominating convention to settle on one candidate and eliminate the rest.

This loose amalgam of anti-Jackson forces finally settled on a strategy of running several men, each supposedly strong in one section of the country, against Jackson's hand-picked successor, Martin Van Buren. Although none of these candidates could possibly get a majority in the Electoral College, they might prevent Van Buren from getting a majority. If successful, this strategy would send the election, as in 1825, to the House of Representatives, where the anti-Jackson forces might rally around one of the anti-Jackson candidates.

Which of the candidates might unite the North and West against Van Buren? Henry Clay, who had run against Jackson in 1832, grudgingly decided that Harrison would be the best choice. Others agreed, and Harrison became one of three anti-Jackson contenders for the presidency in 1836. The anti-Jackson strategy failed, however, because in a close popular election Van Buren won a 23-vote majority in the electoral college. At the same time, the election proved that Harrison was by far the most popular of the three anti-Jackson candidates: Daniel Webster took only Massachusetts; Hugh Lawson White won Tennessee and Georgia; but Harrison showed broad support by carrying Vermont, New Jersey, Delaware, Maryland, Ohio, Indiana, and Kentucky.

## THE WHIGS COALESCE

In the next four years, the anti-Jackson forces, who by this time had agreed to call themselves Whigs, went to work to produce a winner in 1840. Their disunity in the 1836 election had actually worked to their advantage. Scores of political activists had rallied around the party's regional candidates in 1836, generating close elections where heretofore the Jacksonians had won easily. Now they were ready to capture the White House.

Events also worked to the Whigs' advantage. The nation's banks went into a tailspin in the late 1830s, and hard times discredited not only bankers but also political incumbents. A rising Whig vote swept Jacksonians out of office in Tennessee, New

York, Mississippi, Maine, and North Carolina. Partial economic recovery in 1838 briefly stopped the Whig surge, but a second and deeper economic tailspin in 1839 gave it new life, just in time for the 1840 presidential election.

## GETTING THE NOMINATION

Under the guidance of Thurlow Weed, the Whig boss of New York, hard-boiled Whig professionals agreed to hold a national nominating convention to make certain that their party had only one candidate in 1840. Their immediate problem was Henry Clay, the party's most eloquent spokesman in Congress and in the press. Weed bluntly told Clay that Clay would be "unavailable" for three reasons: He was a Mason, he was a slaveholder, and he was too tied to the national bank. Much more "available" in Weed's mind was General Winfield Scott, but the pragmatic New Yorker indicated he was willing to settle for Harrison. Weed wanted a winner, and that meant someone who could carry New York and Pennsylvania. Harrison met those specifications. By a close vote, the "Democratic-Whig" nominating convention at Harrisburg, Pennsylvania, chose Harrison in December 1839.

Harrison was not passive in all this. He had defied convention and actually campaigned in the 1836 election. He made a well-publicized speaking tour of Ohio and Indiana in 1836, depicting himself as an older statesman who had always been "the ardent supporter of the rights of the people, in the councils of the nation, and in the field their faithful and devoted soldier." In November 1839 he secured the nomination of the national Anti-Masonic convention and provided his backers with a seven-point platform in which he pledged he would not so freely use the veto as had that usurper, "King Andrew Jackson." Harrison worked hard to get the party's nomination, and once nominated he worked hard to get elected. He made twenty-three campaign speeches to crowds of fifty thousand or more. He was the first presidential candidate to stump the country in his own behalf.

## CAMPAIGN OF 1840

But all this would be lost in the mindless pageantry and hoopla that has made the 1840 election famous. Whig organizers put together a three-mile-long parade of young Whigs with bands, banners, and campaign songs to capture the limelight and drown out the Democratic nominating convention in Baltimore. When a Democratic newspaper sneered that Harrison would be content with a log cabin and a barrel of hard cider, Whig strategists turned Harrison, who was something of a Virginia-born aristocrat, into a cider-drinking man of the people. In contrast, Van Buren was portrayed as an aristocrat who walked on Royal Wilton carpets, slept on a French bedstead, drank costly wines, ate off a gold plate, and traveled around in a huge, gilded coach made in England.

Log cabins and cider barrels soon appeared on town squares everywhere to celebrate "Old Tip," "the hero of the battle of Tippecanoe," "the plain farmer of North Bend." Sober argument soon got lost in a mighty outpouring of songs, torchlight parades, monster rallies, and log-cabin symbolism. Especially memorable were the songs and jingles. A whole generation of school children learned them, passed them on to their children, and to their great-great grandchildren:

> *Farewell, dear Van,*
> *You're not our man;*
> *To guide the ship,*
> *We'll try old Tip.*

> *Van, Van, Van.*
> *Van is a used-up man.*
> *Tippecanoe and Tyler too.*
> *Tippecanoe and Tyler too!*

Yet Whig humbug did not determine the outcome. By 1840 a new two-party system had come of age. Real contests were being fought in every state of the Union. Both parties had scores of strident newspapers and dozens of spellbinding orators, trying to win supporters in virtually every town and village across the country. Both parties offered candidates for every office from sheriff to president. They were evenly matched, not only on the national level but also in every section, most states, and a majority of towns and villages. For the first time in its history, the nation had a truly national two-party system.

## THE ELECTION

The Harrison campaign thus brought out the largest number of votes yet seen. In 1824, no more than 27 percent of the eligible males had bothered to vote; in the Jackson campaigns of 1828 and 1832, that number had risen to 56 percent; in 1840, a whopping 78 percent went to the polls. The most striking feature was the number of new voters, for nearly one voter in three was casting his first ballot in 1840. No election before or since has brought out so great a portion of new voters.

Many of the state contests were close. Harrison beat Van Buren by a mere 411 votes in Maine and 350 votes in Pennsylvania, while he lost Virginia by 1,120 votes. Overall, however, Old Tip scored a smashing victory over Little Van in the electoral college, and the Whigs carried both houses of Congress for the first time.

Thus crystallized a new system of presidential politics—highly organized, professionally managed, and in which the party apparatus worked not only at the national level, but at the local and state levels to support the presidential candidate. Ironically, Harrison died one month after taking office, the first president to do so, and the image makers were left with a vice president, John Tyler, whom they soon read out of the Whig party. Yet the great Harrison campaign set lasting precedents: Henceforth, presidential candidates were to be plucked out of nowhere and turned into great men, and professional organization and mass participation were to be the hallmarks of presidential elections for decades to come.

## BIBLIOGRAPHY

Cleaves, Freeman. *Old Tippecanoe: William Henry Harrison and His Times* (Scribner's, 1939).

Gunderson, Robert G. *The Log Cabin Campaign* (University of Kentucky Press, 1957).

Holt, Michael F. "The Election of 1840, Voter Mobilization, and the Emergence of the Second American Party System: A Reappraisal of Jacksonian Voting Behavior." In *A Master's Due: Essays in Honor of David Herbert Donald*, edited by William J. Cooper, Jr., Michael F. Holt, and John McCardell (Louisiana State University Press, 1985), 16–56.

★★★ 10 ★★★

# JOHN TYLER
## 1841–1845

*Leonard L. Richards*

*Born 29 March 1790 in Charles City County, Virginia, to John Tyler and Mary Marot Armistead Tyler; educated at College of William and Mary (B.A. 1807); married Letitia Christian 29 March 1813, New Kent County, Virginia; eight children; married Julia Gardiner 26 June 1844, New York, New York; seven children; succeeded to presidency after William Henry Harrison died in office; died 18 January 1862 in Richmond, Virginia; buried at Hollywood Cemetery, Richmond, Virginia.*

John Tyler, the second name in the Whig campaign jingle "Tippecanoe and Tyler Too," was used to get out the vote in 1840. No incumbent president had as yet died in office, and the Whig party bosses who managed the 1840 election never dreamed that Tyler might actually become president. Hardly a true party member, he was a "States Rights Whig," which in the eyes of most northern Whigs was a contradiction in terms—a rare breed found only in Tyler's Virginia and a few odd places in the Deep South. He had been given second place on the Whig presidential ticket only because his presence might win the support of Virginians, states' righters, and Democratic malcontents like himself.

In the past, political manipulators had gotten away with such tactics. For over twenty years the Jeffersonian Republicans had selected one political has-been after another to balance the ticket, including men who were either hopeless drunks or too old and feeble to take over the duties of president. Although the Jeffersonians never had to pay for putting such men a heartbeat from the presidency, the Whigs would pay dearly. When William Henry Harrison died within a month of taking office, they suddenly had to cope with a man who not only disagreed with them on most issues but refused to bend to their wishes.

## A VIRGINIA WHIG

Born into a Virginia aristocratic family in 1790, Tyler was one of the many political men of his generation who achieved success at a young age. He graduated from the College of William and Mary before he was 18 years old and passed the Virginia bar before he was 20. Elected to the Virginia legislature at age 21, he won a seat in the United States House of Representatives at age 26, the governorship of Virginia at age 34, and a seat in the U.S. Senate at age 36. When Harrison died in the spring of 1841, Tyler had just turned 51, thus becoming the nation's youngest president up to that time.

By any ordinary standard, Tyler had been a most successful politician. But he brought to the presidency an unbending and total committment to states' rights and slavery. His views reflected the old Virginian faith in strict construction of the Constitution, legislative dominance, a limited presidential veto, and the primacy of plantation agriculture. He had opposed the Missouri Compromise in 1820, arguing that Congress had no right to bar slavery from the northern half of the Louisiana Purchase. Confining slavery, he had told Congress, would encourage slave rebellions and discourage reform. The "dark cloud" of slavery would become blacker and blacker in the Old South until "its horrors burst." Congress therefore ought to "disperse" the blackness and "reduce it to a summer's cloud." By the same token, when northern abolitionists raised the cry for "immediate abolition" in the 1830s, Tyler saw them as

fomenters of slave rebellions. Those views remained central to his presidency.

Tyler's staunch devotion to states' rights was evident in the early Jackson years, when he had been a States' Rights Democrat. He opposed high protective tariffs to protect northern industry from British competition and, like Jackson, he thought the Second Bank of the United States was unconstitutional. But in the early 1830s, when South Carolina nullified the federal tariff within its borders and Jackson called for the use of force against the nullifiers, Tyler broke with the president. In Tyler's mind, the proposed Force Act endangered both states' rights and slavery.

Yet Tyler did not join the opposition party until three years later, in 1836, when the Jacksonian majority in the Virginia legislature instructed him to support a resolution deleting from the U.S. Senate's official record the previous censure of Jackson for removing government deposits from the Second Bank of the United States and distributing them among selected state banks. Tyler agreed with Jackson that the federal government had no legal right to charter a national bank. Nevertheless, he thought Jackson's claim that the Second Bank was an unsafe federal depository was nonsense, and he believed Jackson had exceeded his constitutional authority in removing federal deposits from the Second Bank. Tyler refused to follow the Virginia legislature's instructions, and they in turn forced him to resign his Senate seat. At that point, he took on the hopeless task of trying to make the Whig party into an uncompromising states' rights party.

A stubborn man with old-fashioned Virginia principles, Tyler had no use for the nationalistic and probusiness policies championed by Henry Clay, the leader of the congressional Whigs. After switching parties, however, Tyler had envisioned a change in the Kentucky legislator, a "new Clay" whom even a genuine States Rights Whig could support. Clay had always agreed with Tyler on the need to "disperse" the slave population and had made a number of speeches in the late 1830s denouncing northern abolitionists as meddling incendiaries. These were comforting words to Tyler, and for a season he thought he could remake the South's most nationalistic Whig into a genuine states' righter. He even became the leader of a movement to gather support among States Rights Whigs for Clay.

## BREAKING WITH CLAY

Tyler's fantasy came to a quick end after the Whigs obtained power in the election of 1840. Clay talked President Harrison into calling a special session of Congress in 1841 to enact a program of higher tariffs, distribution of land revenues to the states for transportation projects, voluntary bankruptcy laws, and a new national bank. The Whigs, who for the first time controlled both houses of Congress, passed Clay's whole program. Then, with Harrison's death, Clay had to cope with Tyler's old-fashioned Virginia principles.

Tyler approved the Preemption Act of 1841, which gave squatters on federal land the right to buy 160 acres at $1.25 an acre whenever the land went on the market. He also approved the Tariff of 1842, which raised duties to the 1832 level. But he vetoed three different bank bills on constitutional grounds. In disgust, Clay's congressional followers read Tyler out of the party, denouncing him publicly as a traitor to Whig principles, and contemptuously referring to him as "His Accidency" and to his few Whig followers as "the Corporal's Guard." Following suit, all but one of Tyler's cabinet members resigned. Secretary of State Daniel Webster was busy negotiating the Maine-Canadian boundary with Great Britain, but after completing those negotiations, he, too, joined the protest.

Thus, within months of taking office, Tyler was a president without a party. But he was still an ambitious man, and hence he embarked on a desperate effort to win reelection in 1844 as either a third-party candidate or—better yet—the Democratic nominee. He lavished patronage on the followers of John C. Calhoun and on the opponents of the Democratic front-runner, Martin Van Buren, hoping to win them to his cause. Most of those he courted turned out to be bootlicking opportunists. Some used their presidential connections to further the presidential hopes of Calhoun or some other anti–Van Buren Democrat. Only a handful even considered joining Tyler's crusade.

## THE TEXAS ISSUE

Above all, Tyler pushed territorial expansion. First, he offered the British concessions on the Oregon boundary if they would coerce Mexico into ceding California to the United States. When that gambit failed, he then launched a huge propaganda campaign for annexing Texas. That was playing with fire. Every political leader in the country knew that annexing the Lone Star Republic might trigger a political crisis. That had been proven in the mid-1830s, when John Quincy Adams and other northern Whigs had labeled the Texas revolution "a Slave Power conspiracy"—not a battle for freedom, as the Texans wanted Americans to believe, but a plot executed by Andrew Jackson and other slavemasters to further southern interests. Since then, northern Whigs had been dead-set against the expansion of slavery, and Whigs in general opposed expansion. Jackson's successor, Martin Van Buren, had decided not to touch the Texas issue, viewing it as too explosive and certain to disrupt the Democrats' agenda.

Not all Democrats were as cautious as Van Buren, and in the early 1840s the penny press and a new school of Democratic politicians calling themselves Young America preached the glories of expansionism. They wanted more land for the United States. They claimed that a democracy of state's rights and limited federal powers could be extended indefinitely. They insisted that the young republic's "manifest destiny" would not be fulfilled until "the whole boundless continent is ours."

Added to this mix was a propaganda campaign devised by the president of Texas,

General Sam Houston. He had his ministers to the United States and England nourish the rumor that the British government would provide Texas with gold and military protection if the Texans would give up slavery. British politicians had been making antislavery statements for home consumption for years, and by 1843 several high English officials were on record as favoring not only an independent Texas without slavery but also the elimination of slavery throughout the Atlantic world. In addition, antislavery men and women in the United States clearly regarded the British as a potential ally.

Houston's emissaries made much of such facts, embellishing them and adding falsehoods. Duff Green, a proslavery zealot and the Tyler administration's confidential agent in London, soon reported that Texas officials were busy negotiating with the British—indeed, trying to float a loan to finance the compensated emancipation of the 12,000 to 15,000 slaves in Texas—and that the British government had agreed to guarantee interest payments. The official dispatches from London contained no hint of such negotiations, but rumors and unofficial accounts added credence to Green's reports.

Having replaced Webster at the State Department with Abel P. Upshur, a fellow Virginia slaveholder and intense admirer of Calhoun, Tyler had at his side a man who strongly supported the cause of slavery. But Upshur, who was clearly Tyler's intellectual superior, had mixed views on the potential consequences of annexing Texas. On the one hand, he rejected Tyler's argument that dispersing the slave population benefited the Old South. Indeed, he wanted the "black belt" to become even blacker so that more white Virginians could become slaveholders and thus supporters of the slave system. He feared that Texas would drain so many slaves out of Virginia and the Old South that it would render Virginia slavemasters like himself powerless.

On the other hand, he warmed to the idea that Texas would boost the price of Virginia slaves in the interstate slave trade. He also believed that the addition of new slave territory in the West would enhance the security of slavery in Louisiana and Arkansas. Having Texas become free, however, would be a real danger to slavery on the southwestern frontier. No slave system, as he saw it, could survive if it were surrounded by free states.

Thus, weighing the options, Upshur agreed with Tyler that the administration had to act swiftly before the British eliminated slavery in Texas. Indeed, Upshur took the lead. Writing anonymously in the administration's newspaper, *The Madisonian*, he threw down the gauntlet to John Quincy Adams and other antislavery Whigs and appealed to the South, Young America, and the widespread hatred of the British. He harped on the dangers of a British takeover of Texas. British monarchists, he claimed, hated and dreaded republicanism; their ultimate goal was to destroy the American Republic. Thus, they had to be stopped before it was too late.

Why, then, were Adams and others standing in the way? The old man, Upshur argued, had once been a patriot; he had played a leading role in the acquisition of Florida and as president had worked hard to acquire Texas; but since losing to Jackson, Adams's patriotism had given way to extreme partisanship. Indeed, "treasonable practices" had become his "chief amusement and solace."

Upshur's arguments, however, failed to win over the hesitant. Many northern Democrats were still convinced that annexation would benefit only the South. For help, the Tyler men turned to Robert J. Walker of Mississippi, the most active Democrat in Tyler's coterie of pro-Texas zealots. Although Walker had made his career in Deep South politics, he had been born and raised in Pennsylvania. He knew the North well and was imaginative, to say the least. Any hope of annexation, Walker realized, depended on northern Democrats. But how could he win their support? They generally hated both blacks and Englishmen, and some saw great riches in

Texas acres and securities. But they dared not support annexation as long as it was identified with the growth of slavery and southern power.

In February 1844, Walker came up with an ingenious public letter, which—thanks to a fund established by Texas land speculators and rich southerners—circulated widely in the North and created a sensation in the press. In the letter, Walker appealed to the old dream of ridding American society of both slavery and blacks. Slavery, he argued, was self-destructive because it ruined the soil. The harsh dictates of economics would eventually force slaveowners to free their slaves, and when that happened, hundreds of thousands of freed blacks would flood northern cities. If Texas were annexed, however, millions of slaves would be diverted from the worn-out lands of the Old South to the rich cotton lands of Texas. Slavery would then be contained in Texas until Texas lands were depleted. At that point, the freed blacks would disappear over the border into Mexico, where the climate better suited them, and live happily among other "colored" people.

**THE TREATY OF ANNEXATION**
Throughout the propaganda campaign, Upshur negotiated secretly with Texas authorities for a treaty of annexation. In late February 1844, he had all but concluded the secret negotiations when a cannon on the warship *Princeton* blew up and killed him. To replace Upshur and complete the negotiations, Tyler turned to slavery's foremost spokesman, John C. Calhoun of South Carolina. That sealed the link between slavery and Texas. After completing negotiations in April 1844, Calhoun sent the treaty to the Senate, along with a copy of a letter he had written to Richard Pakenham, the British minister to Washington.

Calhoun's letter was a bombshell. Besides denouncing Pakenham's government for interfering in Texas and supporting abolition throughout the Atlantic world, Calhoun sang the praises of slavery and cited statistics to prove that blacks were better off as slaves

than as freedmen—and that southern slaves were better off than white workers in industrial England. He went on to justify annexation as a defense measure in behalf of slavery, thereby officially labeling the annexation treaty a proslavery measure.

Calhoun's letter to Pakenham cost Tyler dearly. Whig senators by an overwhelming margin voted down the Texas treaty. Of 22 Democrats who voted, 15 supported annexation; of 28 Whigs who voted, all but one voted against it. Thus, annexation failed by a 2-to-1 margin. Within five days, both leading presidential hopefuls, Clay and Van Buren, went on record against annexation "at this time."

**THE ELECTION OF 1844**
The Texas treaty failed to create a political bandwagon that would carry Tyler into office as the Democratic nominee in 1844. Van Buren's Texas statement, to be sure, had raised a storm of protest among Democrats, especially in the southern and western states, and even Jackson had turned on his hand-picked successor. And at the Democratic convention held in Baltimore, pro-Texas strategists blocked Van Buren's attempt to regain office when they rammed through a measure requiring a two-thirds majority for the presidential nomination. The party did not turn to Tyler, the renegade Democrat, however. Instead, after a long deadlock, Democrats nominated James K. Polk, a Tennessee slaveholder whose hard-money views satisfied the Van Burenites and whose zeal for expansion satisfied annexationists.

In the fall election, Polk edged out Clay in a close contest. In 15 of the 26 states, the election was extremely close; overall, Polk's margin of victory was a mere 1.4 percent. But throughout the campaign, politicians of both parties had assumed that a vote for Polk was a vote for Texas. So once the election was over, Tyler and Calhoun insisted that the election amounted to a popular endorsement of their defeated treaty. They called on both houses of Congress to vindicate their handiwork by passing a joint resolution that embodied the treaty's precise language. There was no need, they maintained, for Congress to deal with "collateral issues" such as the number of states to be carved out of Texas. Such matters could best be decided by future legislatures.

## ADMISSION OF TEXAS

That was too much for northern Democrats, who wanted no association with the renegade president or with Calhoun's Pakenham letter. A host of bills—nine in the House, six in the Senate—appeared in a flurry of counterproposals. Some called for the admission of Texas as a state; others wanted it given territorial status first. Some proposed dividing Texas into two states— or three or four or five or even six; some annexationists obviously hoped all these states would be slave states. Other legislators wanted Texas divided in two parts, half slave, and half free. Most who supported this proposal called for only a token limit on slavery, barring it only in the northernmost tip, the small area lying above the Missouri Compromise line. Views were similarly split on what should be done with Texas's debt. Some wanted no part of it; others insisted that it be charged to the United States.

For a while, it looked as though the differences would produce endless squabbling. But then a group of southern Whigs offered a resolution calling for admission of Texas as a state, with the right to subdivide into four additional states, with slavery being excluded only in the small area above the Missouri Compromise line, and with the debt remaining with Texas. Annexationists, eager to acquire the votes of this group of southerners, quickly embraced their proposal and rammed through both houses of Congress a joint resolution annexing Texas to the United States.

The resolution was hardly the one Tyler had asked for, but he wanted the credit for adding Texas to the United States. So on the next day, 1 March 1845, he signed the document. Three days later, he left office. The problems he left behind were immense. Northern Whigs were furious. How many slave states, they wondered, had Tyler just admitted to the union? Texas was too big to be just one state. Four or five seemed more likely to most northern Whigs. Thus, noted John Quincy Adams, the Texas bill amounted to the "signal triumph" of proslavery forces, and "the heaviest calamity that ever befell myself and my country." Earlier, once Texas annexation had become certain, a Washington slave trader flew a victory banner over his slave pen. On seeing it, one Vermont Whig put the problem bluntly: "That flag means *Texas*, and Texas means *civil war* before we have done with it."

Tyler lived to see the nation split into two warring camps. Hoping to allay sectional tensions, he even presided over a Washington "Peace Convention" in 1861. When that and other peace efforts failed, he supported secession from the Union and was elected to the Confederate Congress. In 1862, nine months after the war began, he died. Although not the only president whose actions helped bring on the nation's bloodiest war, he certainly was one of them.

## BIBLIOGRAPHY

Chitwood, Oliver Perry. *John Tyler, Champion of the Old South* (Appleton-Century, 1939).

Freehling, William W. *The Reintegration of American History: Slavery and the Civil War* (Oxford University Press, 1994), Chapter 6.

Merk, Frederick. *Fruits of Propaganda in the Tyler Administration* (Harvard University Press, 1971).

Seager, Robert, II. *And Tyler Too: A Biography of John and Julia Tyler* (McGraw-Hill, 1963).

★★★ 11 ★★★

# JAMES KNOX POLK
## 1845–1849

*Wayne Cutler*

*Born 2 November 1795, near Pineville, Mecklenburg County, North Carolina, to Samuel Polk and Jane Knox Polk; educated at the University of North Carolina (B.A. 1818); married Sarah Childress, 1 January 1824, Murfreesboro, Tennessee; no children; elected president in 1844 on the Democratic ticket with George Mifflin Dallas of Pennsylvania, with 1,337,243 popular votes and 170 electoral college votes over the Whig ticket of Henry Clay of Kentucky and Theodore Frelinghuysen of New Jersey, who received 1,299,062 popular votes and 105 electoral college ballots; died 15 June 1849 in Nashville, Tennessee; buried at Polk Place, Nashville, but remains were removed in 1893 to the State Capitol grounds.*

President James K. Polk, like three of his southern predecessors—James Monroe, Andrew Jackson, and John Tyler—traveled to New England to pay his respects to her citizens and to solicit their continued regard for the Union. The symbolism of his presidential journey in the summer of 1847 might be easily misread or quickly dismissed without careful examination of the young republic's conflicting concepts of the Union. In the election of 1844, the American people had confronted for the first time in their history an explicit and unequivocal choice between expansion and consolidation. Would Americans think of their Union in terms of an agrarian frontier or a trading commonwealth, each of which was securely grounded in a mindset from the nation's colonial past? The electorate divided almost evenly.

## FRONTIER, SOCIETY, AND TRADITION

Over 150 years of colonial experience had proven how difficult it was for civil and military governance to break down the psychological barriers of frontier isolation and its attendant rule of local self-interest. The English plantations in North America had begun literally at the water's edge, with inadequate capitalizations, inexperienced leadership, and indeterminate development strategies. American colonization had progressed not as a national program of expansion but as sundry localized efforts to achieve limited financial and sectarian goals. In the process of locating and settling the tidewater frontiers, hardship and religion had made a virtue of isolation. Self-rule thus had become all the more consequential to those having known no other choice of individual and collective identities. As colonists had moved inland and established new farms and communities, they had duplicated those patterns of local government taught by experience and had modified those practices unsuitable to new circumstances. For its part, the crown had chosen to allow the colonists exceptional measures of civil and religious self-determination, largely because any alternative course would have proven too costly to sustain. On the frontier, local community thought and action had become normative, for reasons of both preference and necessity.

Unlike the frontier colonials, who formed the bulk of the producing farmers and artisans, substantial numbers of British subjects in the American colonies had gained sufficient status, or expectation thereof, to cross over the physical, mental, and emotional barriers of their locality. These Atlantic colonials had not lived as western pioneers, but they had looked eastward from their port cities and had found release from their new world isolation. They had wanted to recreate in the New World the mores of the land they had left behind. In seeking that more cosmopolitan outlook, they had conserved an English culture more exaggerated and fixed than that found in the England of their day. Their local center of authority and respectability had become that of the colonial governor's court, for that court—however minor its standing in the ranks of the old aristocracy—had provided an otherwise unavailable measure of social and economic stability. Those who feared frontier anarchy more than imperial tyranny had sought their place and protection within government's consolidating powers, despite the limitations of its provincial reach. Both the frontier and the Atlantic perspectives would survive the course of republican revolution and political division within the new republic.

Early in their development, the New World's first thirteen republics had faced a common struggle to define the objectives of their revolutions and the bases of their associated war for independence. Each of the disaffected British colonies had experienced like dangers—economic, civil, and military—on the obscure edges of a global commonwealth; but each of the American outposts also had linked itself more closely to the empire's center than to the nearest sister colony. No two settlements had shared like historical and legal relationships to crown, parliament, and proprietary interest. Ministerial efforts in the 1760s to consolidate imperial rule had met with varying measures of colonial resistance, and after a decade of uneven legislative decisions the King's ministers had yet persisted in underestimating the difficulty and costs of reversing the crown's long-standing policy of salutary neglect. In fighting their common war for political separation, leaders of the thirteen colonial revolutions had learned in great depth and with no little frustration their own limited capacities for united action.

## A REPUBLICAN HERITAGE

Polk claimed a proud republican heritage, for he was a grandson of both the revolution and the frontier. In his view of history, the framers of the constitution had established the greatest of all political experiments in the modern era, a frontier Union, "an empire of liberty," as Thomas Jefferson had phrased it. This republican attempt at self-government had thrust upon the minds of subjected peoples on three continents the new and revolutionary vision of limited government. By treaty, thirteen sovereign states had agreed to create a general government and had assigned to it a small number of specific and exclusive powers to exercise in their behalf. The terms of this compact and its first ten amendments had promised, among other things, that the general government would not be used to create a privileged class, to control the market place, or to establish a state religion. Considering the number of dynastic, trade, and religious wars that had been fought to establish and maintain such important prerogatives, those with more skeptical minds in 1789 had thought that government so restrained and weakened must soon fall prey to anarchy or foreign domination. Those with more sensitive scruples had judged it a peculiar republic wherein the majority race extolled the virtues of freedom and yet accepted and protected the institution of slave labor.

Among the counsels of frontier republicans such practical and idealistic reservations had not proven persuasive; indeed, no experiment in limited union could have been launched without taking great risks and making many compromises. In the public debates over the Constitution's ratification, frontier republicans had objected that the general government's powers would be too great; the newly washed Atlantic republicans had argued that the plan would just barely correct the basic defects of the original Articles of Confederation. Between those two polarities of thought had developed a minimal consensus in favor of the compact and its prospective amendments. Thomas Jefferson's election to the presidency in 1801 and the subsequent embarrassment of Atlantic republicans meeting at Hartford in 1814 had seemed to enlarge the constitutional consensus and tilt its interpretation in favor of frontier republicanism. Yet the tilting had been more of a seeming shift than a fundamental one.

## DISCIPLE OF JEFFERSON AND JACKSON

Family tradition dictated that Polk become a political disciple of Jefferson's Democratic-Republican party. Reared on the frontiers of North Carolina and Tennessee, Polk experienced the isolation of rural life and had learned the common wisdoms of agrarian expansion. Both by necessity and choice American frontiersmen pressed the boundaries of land cultivation as their principal margin of economic opportunity. To sons of the soil, territorial expansion did not mean conquering settled productive populations, but rather overcoming nature's harsh and unrelenting rule of caprice and scarcity. Polk's father, Samuel, had made his fortune in the great American migration, and he had formed close and lasting friendships with Andrew Jackson and other leading land surveyors with whom he had worked the western district of Tennessee. For family business reasons, Sam Polk wanted his eldest son to have a proper education.

Young James attended the University of North Carolina and won first honors in Latin and mathematics, class of 1818. At Chapel Hill he also acquired considerable distinction for his literary club debates; as president of the Dialectic Society he led his fellow debaters into weekly argumentation of the day's current issues. On one occasion the young debaters considered whether further westward expansion would be expedient. Although no notes on the points of this debate have survived, the affirmative line of argument probably followed traditional tenets of the Jeffersonian dogma. Continued westward expansion would ensure diffusion of both wealth and power; without this distribution of agrarian opportunity, the forces of consolidated wealth would gain control of the general government and turn its taxing powers to the greater advantage of the monied few. Once the general government had become a great power to be greatly prized, state and regional jealousies would so intensify and divide the states as to render voluntary or free union both unworkable and undesirable. Further expansion would prove essential to free union, for each new generation doubled both the number of farmers and the demand for first-quality lands. The farming poor could not afford to invest their labor in marginally productive lands, however abundant and cheap the acreage.

Polk took the frontier vision as fundamental to his political and economic thinking, and after college returned home to study law under Felix Grundy of Nashville, one of Tennessee's most able lawyers and prominent Democrats. Within seven years of his graduation from Chapel Hill, Polk had begun the practice of law, served in Tennessee's General Assembly, and won election to Congress. Family traditions, collegiate experiences, and professional connections had led him to choose the Jeffersonian dogma popular among frontier republicans of his day.

Polk won his first election to Congress in 1825, the year after Henry Clay of Kentucky had proposed plans for a market revolution, a new American System of centralized banking, internal improvements, and protective tariffs. Polk had supported Andrew Jackson's presidential bid in 1824 and without reservation had judged John Quincy Adams guilty of having bargained his way into the presidency, thus corrupting public trust in the highest office awarded by a free electorate. On what moral basis could a republic claim its fundamental authority if its lawmakers themselves debased the selection process and thus, indirectly, the will of the people to rule themselves justly, if at all? In his fourteen years of congressional service, Polk would oppose consolidating measures of every description, first as Jackson's floor leader in the House and then as Speaker of that body. As gover-

nor (1839–1841) and party leader in Tennessee, Polk supported the North-South alliance of the Old Democracy, even though those attachments meant loss of his gubernatorial races in 1841 and 1843.

## THE ELECTION OF 1844

In nominating Polk for president in 1844, the Democracy reaffirmed its fundamental creed that America's ongoing agrarian migration westward was not just an appendage of the 1789 constitutional consensus, but its very animus for a voluntary Union. All four of Polk's presidential goals—to establish a republican government in Oregon, to acquire California, to set up an independent Treasury system, and to lower tariffs—had bespoken the frontier agenda of an expanding republic dedicated to the principle of limited government, an "empire of liberty" as it had become and must remain. Polk's Whig opponent, Henry Clay, argued that further expansion might lead the republic into war with Britain or Mexico or both and thus place in grave jeopardy the wealth, unity, and safety of the nation. Clay noted that the republic's true interests might be better served by binding the nation together with a new central bank and continued protection for domestic manufactures. Although Whigs North and South could agree on their probusiness agenda, their economic interests diverged on the question of allowing slave labor to be used in the West.

Northern antislavery elements of the Whig party demanded the prohibition of slavery in the western territories and supported nativist proposals to place naturalization beyond the reach of most immigrants, who more often than not worked for cheap wages and voted Democratic. In an effort to attract dissident Democrats in the large urban centers of the North, Whigs agreed to back local American party (nativist) candidates in exchange for votes for the Whig presidential ticket. In Pennsylvania and New York the Whigs kept their bargain, voted for Clay, and rejected the moral plenitude of the Liberty party's abolitionist candidate, James G. Birney. In Philadelphia and New York City, however, the Whig-American compact failed to realize its designers' hope of carrying the day for Clay. Rationalizing their electoral defeat, Whig partisans claimed the high moral ground and blamed their defeat on Whig defections to Birney, ignoring the fact that in New York, for example, some four thousand more Democrats voted for their gubernatorial candidate, Silas Wright, Jr., than for their presidential ticket. Polk carried the electoral college with 170 out of 275 votes, but by a small margin he failed to win a majority of the popular vote.

In choosing between Polk and Clay, the American electorate had split almost equally over the meaning of the republic's history and its concept of union. Future historians would debate the significance of the frontier's closing in the 1890s, but the lack of virgin soil was not the cause that brought the second republic to its violent end in the 1860s. By 1844, the Union's margin of constitutional consensus had shrunk beyond the point of safety, with or without further expansion, free of slavery or not. Had Clay won the presidency and blocked further western migrations, the secession crisis of 1861 probably would have come a decade earlier. Polk's defense of Texas and his acquisition of Oregon, New Mexico, and California would mask those deeply rooted splits in the body politic. In due course, President Abraham Lincoln would fight and win the war for consolidation that the British had lost and the constitutional fathers had avoided.

## TAKING OVER A TROUBLED NATION

President Polk formed an able though not very clever cabinet, the membership of which represented the party's many divisions. Secretary of State James Buchanan of Pennsylvania was a northerner with southern principles and strong presidential ambitions. Treasury Secretary Robert J. Walker of Mississippi was a confirmed advocate of the subtreasury system with a sense of balance on the tariff question. Secretary of War William L. Marcy of New York was an ex-

pansionist with ties to the anti–Van Buren wing of his state party. Attorney General John Y. Mason of Virginia was a former member of John Tyler's cabinet with several years of prior experience as a U.S. district judge. Postmaster General Cave Johnson of Tennessee was a devoted friend of the president's, with many close connections among Van Buren's friends in Congress. Navy Secretary George Bancroft of Massachusetts was a published historian with a known bias for writing the way he voted. In matters great and small, Polk regularly consulted his cabinet, but in most decisions he followed judgments largely of his own making.

In the first eighteen months of his administration, the president accomplished the domestic side of his program. Equipped with nominal Democratic majorities in both houses of Congress and experienced in legislative management, Polk lobbied his tariff reductions and Treasury reforms through their third readings, despite strong Whig resistance and tricky Democratic infighting. Almost all of the old party wounds, which friends of Van Buren and Calhoun had inflicted on one another before and during the 1844 Democratic convention, remained unhealed. Polk's preelection pledge to serve but a single term did even greater injury to the cause of party harmony. Those with lingering presidential ambitions had taken their new party leader at his word and had begun their 1848 campaigns well in advance of Polk's inaugural.

Yet divisions within the Democratic party had developed for reasons more substantial than mere personal preferences and clan loyalties. Many northern Democrats had shifted ground on the tariff question because of increased local manufacturing and public sensitivity to cheaper foreign products. Resolute southern opposition to protection had provided fertile ground for the growth of antislavery sentiment in the North. Conservative or soft-money Democrats had worried that Polk's Treasury reforms would force their state banks out of business. Whig internal improvement projects had undercut popular support of the Old Democracy in state elections, and thus younger Democrats also found themselves cut off from the local rungs of the political ladder. Domestic issues had ripped gaping holes in the fabric of Jackson's mantle. Had Polk's disputes with Britain and Mexico gone poorly, the republic's youngest president to date might have been its last.

In his inaugural address the new president answered his critics, domestic and foreign, who had accused him of planning an expansionist war of aggression on his neighbors. Foreign powers had not understood the true character of the U.S. government, he said.

> Our Union is a confederation of independent States, whose policy is peace with each other and all the world. To enlarge its limits is to extend the dominions of peace over additional territories and increasing millions. The world has nothing to fear from military ambition in our Government. While the Chief Magistrate and the popular branch of Congress are elected for short terms by the suffrages of those millions who must in their own persons bear all the burdens and miseries of war, our Government can not be otherwise than pacific.

To be certain, he gave no ground on the right of the Republic of Texas "to merge her sovereignty as a separate and independent state in ours."

Nor did he back down on the Oregon issue, for he held that the U.S. claim to that territory was "clear and unquestionable" and that said title was now being perfected by the settlement of immigrants with wives and children in their company. He based his argument on the assumption that governmental claims to unoccupied territory were nominal until validated by the sovereignty of the land's occupants, for the Creator had made the Earth for man, and not otherwise. Like generations of frontier republicans before him, Polk began with the premise that human kind's right to rule nature included the right of self-government. He did not question the extent or timing of the westward migration, for in the oldest tradition of the republic its manifest destiny had

been in the hands of its plowmen, not its government.

The Republic of Mexico had opened its doors to immigration without pressure from the U.S. government; unwilling to accept the overthrow of republican principles, the Texans had established their independence and won the right of self-determination. They could join the Union or not; the choice would be theirs, not that of the military dictatorship in Mexico.

Americans—on their own and without governmental management—took their rights of popular sovereignty to Oregon as well. In the Convention of 1818, the United States and Great Britain had agreed to joint occupational rights in Oregon; by 1845, the tide of American settlement in that territory had carried with it the perfecting powers of occupants' rule. Polk would not leave the Oregon settlers without republican government, however convenient it might be to avoid a collision with Great Britain. He would exercise the Convention's escape clause and give the requisite one-year notice for its termination. Thus expansion into the Northwest, as into the Southwest, would further diffuse the political and economic power of the eastern states and would, to that extent, retard the use of governmental power to develop new schemes of monopoly and corporate financial privilege.

## THE BREAK WITH MEXICO

Within weeks of Polk's taking office, Mexico broke diplomatic relations with the United States. On 15 June 1845, Polk ordered Zachary Taylor to move from his base at Fort Jessup, Louisiana, to the western frontier of Texas. By July 31, Taylor had set up camp on the west bank of the Nueces River, from which position he would move against any Mexican force crossing the Rio Grande into Texas. From the Mexican point of view, the United States had sent an army of invasion into Mexico to make good on its illegal annexation of Texas; the point of Taylor's invasion had begun not at the Nueces or the Rio Grande but at the Sabine River, Mexico's eastern border. In September, Polk dispatched John Slidell to Mexico, hoping that Mexico would resume full diplomatic relations and agree to the U.S. annexation of Texas, the sale of upper California and New Mexico, and the settlement of Mexico's debts to U.S. claimants. Mexico, which had not agreed officially to receive a U.S. minister, in December rejected his credentials.

On the last day of 1845, General Mariano Paredes, who was then in the secret employ of the Spanish crown, overthrew Mexican President José J. Herrera. Spain had hoped that if Paredes could provoke a war crisis, the Mexican army would turn to the monarchist party for the restoration of the Bourbon throne. In January, Paredes pledged to defend Mexico's territorial claims, and Polk countered by ordering Taylor to the Rio Grande. On 8 May 1846, Polk learned of the outbreak of hostilities. Three days later, he asked Congress for a declaration of war; on 13 May he received that authorization. In the winter and spring of his first year in office, Polk had faced difficult decisions on the Texas question and at the same time had risked the dangers of war with Great Britain over Oregon.

## SETTLING THE OREGON QUESTION

On 27 December 1845, Richard Pakenham, British minister to the United States, proposed that the question of a partition of Oregon at the 49th parallel be submitted to arbitration. Polk rejected Pakenham's overture and sent to Congress a request for a resolution terminating joint Anglo-American occupation of Oregon, which Congress approved on 27 April 1845. Within a week after news of the Rio Grande engagement reached London, the British cabinet revisited the Oregon question and authorized Pakenham's direct settlement of the boundary at the 49th parallel. Whether by accident or design, Polk's hard line on the Texas and Oregon disputes had demonstrated to the British government that the president was prepared to fight a two-front war. Pakenham lost no time in arranging productive discussions, and on 15 June the U.S. Senate gave its approval to the British partition proposals. Polk had compromised his campaign pledge to fight for the whole of Oregon, but he had given up no territory then occupied by his fellow citizens. In resolving the Oregon question, Polk discharged a third campaign promise, but he also dampened a substantial part of the expansionist fervor in the northern states.

## THE WAR WITH MEXICO

Taylor's early victories (at Palo Alto, Resaca de la Palma, and Monterrey), Robert F. Stockton's successful naval operations on the California coast, and Stephen W. Kearney's occupation of New Mexico sustained popular support for the Mexican War through September of 1846. By late fall of that year, however, it had become evident that Mexico could and would make it an expensive war of no short duration. Taylor's call for an eight-week truce on 25 September angered his commander-in-chief and handed Whig congressional candidates a timely argument that the president's mismanagement of the war had left the troops in the field exposed to unnecessary dangers and had given supply vendors undue profits.

Second thoughts about Polk's domestic and military measures helped elect a narrow Whig majority in the House, although its control would not pass into opposition hands until the meeting of the next Congress. Buoyed by their electoral victories, Whig politicians heightened the level of their antiwar dissent in the winter of 1847 and demanded an end to "Mr. Polk's" unjust war for the expansion of slavery. For his part, the president became increasingly distrustful of his Whig generals and sought unsuccessfully to place men of his own political persuasion in command of the armies. Political extremism gripped the counsels of both parties, and America's winter of discontent deepened those divisions so clearly evident in the presidential election of 1844.

In the spring of 1847, Taylor's army won a most difficult battle at Buena Vista, and Winfield S. Scott's invasion force landed at Vera Cruz and on 18 April moved inland with success at Cerro Gordo. News of those fresh victories in Mexico encouraged Polk to send Nicholas P. Trist, chief clerk of the

State Department, to Mexico in search of a resolution to the conflict. Taylor's control of northern Mexico and Scott's movements toward Mexico City had dispelled all hopes among Mexican elites of an outright military victory. Given the intensity and depth of political divisions in the United States, however, they viewed further delay as a possible tool for Mexico's winning the peace, if not the war.

## THE NEW ENGLAND TOUR

Polk regained the political advantage at home with news of victories at Buena Vista, Vera Cruz, and Cerro Gordo. Nevertheless, he had learned from experience how little he could do on his own initiative to deflect the criticism of his policies and to unite public opinion, particularly in the Northeast where Whigs controlled almost every statehouse and major city hall. Perhaps he stayed at his desk beyond the limits of his endurance. Perhaps he longed to know what the American people really thought of the War. Perhaps he thought that a presidential tour through the North would show the Mexicans that his domestic opponents could not settle on any less favorable terms than those he proposed.

Polk did not put the motives for his travel plans down on paper, but he must have understood how risky it would be to visit the centers of his Whig opposition and chance the public's merely polite or even hostile response. The president went north for the sake of the Union and risked the sum of his political career because the frontier consensus had to be revived and expanded. Otherwise, the states could not remain at peace with one another; thus might be lost "the only free asylum for the oppressed" left on Earth.

President Monroe had toured New England during his first term in office. That trip had signaled an end to the exile of Federalist political and military leaders, whose opposition to the War of 1812 had divided the Union, as had no prior issue since passage of the Alien and Sedition Acts. In his 1847 trip to New England, Polk similarly wanted and needed to reduce the level of domestic political conflict, just as he also desired and required a settlement in Mexico. He was not successful.

Polk could win peace abroad but not at home. The strident political struggles between parties and sections did not diminish, largely because the fragility of the Union turned on social and economic conflicts for which there were no democratic solutions then or later. Religious strife went unresolved as pious Protestant evangelicals damned Deists, Catholics, and Jews in the flames of revival enthusiasm. Economic competition mixed with social as waged immigrants threatened to undercut native artisans. And both fanatical abolitionists and fire-eating slaveholders pushed far beyond the limits of civil discourse. Even had those social conflicts found resolution, the Union divided sectionally over tariff protection, territorial expansion, and the growth of large-scale market capitalism, which if left unregulated would undermine the foundations of economic democracy, both North and South.

## RESOLVED AND UNRESOLVED ISSUES

Yet the second half of Polk's presidency would see the resolution of the war with Mexico and the expansion of the farmers' republic from Texas to the Pacific Ocean. With the use of the presidential veto, he would block internal improvements at the expense of the general government. Minor achievements came in reforming the postal system, establishing consular ties with the Vatican, and returning the Union to its prewar economic footing. The discovery of gold in California took its own course without immediate reference to the administration in Washington, although the acquisition of that territory did come at a most convenient time for U.S. economic development. To be certain, Polk fought his foreign and domestic enemies with grave intensity and won almost all of his battles; yet he could not make of the Union more than its divergent and conflicting materials allowed. Nor did he try.

At the conclusion of his term, Polk returned to Tennessee and fell victim to a virulent cholera epidemic. He died at home in Nashville on 15 June 1849. Sarah Childress Polk, his spouse and partner in all things political and social, survived him and died at Polk Place forty-two years later.

## BIBLIOGRAPHY

Bergeron, Paul H. *The Presidency of James K. Polk* (University Press of Kansas, 1987).

Johannsen, Robert W. *To the Halls of Montezuma: The Mexican War in the American Imagination* (Oxford University Press, 1985).

McCoy, Charles A. *Polk and the Presidency* (University of Texas Press, 1960).

Merk, Frederick. *The Oregon Question: Essays in Anglo-American Diplomacy and Politics* (Harvard University Press, 1967).

Pletcher, David M. *The Diplomacy of Annexation: Texas, Oregon, and the Mexican War* (University of Missouri Press, 1973).

Quaife, Milo M., ed. *The Diary of James K. Polk*, 4 vols. (A. C. McClurg, 1910).

Sellers, Charles G. *James K. Polk*, 2 vols. (Princeton University Press, 1957–1966).

———. *The Market Revolution: Jacksonian America, 1815–1846* (Oxford University Press, 1991).

Smith, Justin H. *The War with Mexico*, 2 vols. (Macmillan, 1919).

Watson, Harry L. *Liberty and Power: The Politics of Jacksonian America* (Noonday Press, 1990).

Weaver, Herbert, and Wayne Cutler, eds. *Correspondence of James K. Polk*, 9 vols. (University of Tennessee Press, 1969– ).

★★★ **12** ★★★

# ZACHARY TAYLOR
## 1849–1850

*Paul Finkelman*

---

*Born 24 November 1784, Montebello, Orange County, Virginia, to Richard Taylor and Sarah Dabney Strother Taylor; career soldier, did not attend college; married Margaret Mackall Smith, 21 June 1810, near Louisville, Kentucky; six children; elected president in 1848 on the Whig ticket, with Millard Fillmore of New York, with 1,360,099 popular votes and 163 electoral college ballots over the Democratic ticket of Lewis Cass of Michigan and William Orlando Butler of Kentucky (1,220,544 popular votes and 127 electoral votes); died 9 July 1850 in Washington, D.C.; buried in Louisville, Kentucky.*

---

Zachary Taylor was one of a string of usually forgotten presidents who served in the two decades preceding the Civil War. Unlike the trio of lilliputians who followed him, Taylor was competent, judicious, and generally effective. He managed to avoid international conflict, kept conflict with native peoples to a minimum, and worked hard to defuse the national crisis over slavery in the territories. As a war hero, Taylor had enormous personal popularity, and this popularity was enhanced by his unassuming personality and reputation as a "soldier's general." Although a wealthy slaveowner from an aristocratic family elected as a Whig, Taylor adopted a simple lifestyle that made him seem much more like a common man than had any other Jacksonian era president.

Taylor's untimely death, less than a year and a half after taking office, has obscured the promise of his administration. Even had he lived, his personal prestige would probably not have been enough to rescue the nation from the sectional animosity emerging in the 1850s, although he doubtless would have been more effective than his successors. Indeed, the very quality that made Taylor attractive—his total lack of political experience and his sense that as president he should be a national leader above politics—also severely undermined his administration. In office, Taylor managed to alienate most of the Whigs in Congress, including Henry Clay, the most important leader of that party, who complained in 1850 that he had "never before seen such an Administration. There is very little cooperation or concord between the two ends of the avenue. There is not, I believe, a prominent Whig in either House who has any confidential intercourse with the Executive." In fact, Taylor had little contact with John Bell, Daniel Webster, or any other senior party members, except Kentucky's John J. Crittenden.

Taylor was the second and last Whig candidate elected president. Like the first, William Henry Harrison, Taylor was a southerner by birth, a slaveholder, and a general. Like Harrison, Taylor also died in office, only the second president to do so. Although a slaveowner, Taylor tried to balance sectional interests, always looking to the needs of the nation first. He believed slavery was a legitimate institution that should be preserved where it existed. He told Jefferson Davis, "We of the south must throw ourselves on the constitution & defend our rights under [it] to the last, & when arguments will no longer suffice, we will appeal to the sword, if necessary to do so." But, at the same time, he saw no need to extend slavery to the West, and as an uncompromising Unionist he had little tolerance for proslavery extremism or secessionist arguments.

Born in Virginia, Taylor was raised in Kentucky, the son of a well-to-do planter who held minor elected and appointive offices. Colonel Taylor, as his father was known, was collector of the Port of Louisville until the Louisiana Purchase made that position unnecessary.

Unlike every previous president, Taylor came to the position without any experience as an officeholder. He had gained his fame, and his qualifications for office, on the battlefield, not in the statehouses or courthouses of the nation. He joined the army in 1807 and remained a soldier for most of the rest of his life until he ran for president. By then he was a full major general, the highest rank in the army. His long military career did, however, prepare him for the presidency in a number of ways. He had firsthand knowledge of the West, of Indian policy, and of the problem of territorial expansion.

## PREPRESIDENTIAL CAREER

In 1807, Taylor asked his second cousin James Madison to help him obtain a commission in the army. In May 1808, Taylor became a first lieutenant. He was a captain by 1811, served in the War of 1812, became a major in 1814, and was discharged in 1815. Within a year, his kinsman President Madison recommissioned him as a major; he made lieutenant colonel in 1820 but remained at that rank until 1832, when he was finally promoted to full colonel. Taylor saw combat in the Old Northwest during the Black Hawk War, where Abraham Lincoln briefly served under him. Taylor later served in Wisconsin and Louisiana. During this period, Taylor's daughter, over her father's objections, married a young army lieutenant named Jefferson Davis. Taylor led troops in Florida during the Second Seminole War, and after his victory at the battle of Lake Okeechobee he was promoted to brevet brigadier general. In that battle he also gained his nickname "Old Rough and Ready." In 1838 he was briefly commander of all troops in Florida, but he requested reassignment, declaring that Florida was a "miserable country" and that, as a result of U.S. policy toward the Seminoles, "an officer who has any regard for honesty, truth, or humanity, has but little to gain, and everything to lose." He briefly served as the Indian agent in Florida before taking a six-month leave.

Taylor traveled to Washington, Philadelphia, Boston, and western New York and Pennsylvania before heading to Baton Rouge for his new assignment. In 1844, he went to Fort Jessup, Louisiana, where he became commander of all U.S. troops in the Southwest. While in Louisiana, he also spent time in Arkansas and the Indian Territory. Immediately after the annexation of Texas in 1845, Taylor was ordered to occupy a position "on or near the Rio Grande." On 31 July 1845, Taylor reached Corpus Christi, where he remained until March 1846, when he moved to disputed territory along the Rio Grande. Mexico claimed that its northern boundary extended to the Nueces River, whereas the United States claimed the land south of the Nueces all the way to the Rio Grande. This provocative deployment led to a battle between Mexican and U.S. soldiers on 24 April. Even before he heard about this battle, President Polk had decided to ask Congress for a declaration of war against Mexico; the battle simply made it easier for Polk to get congressional support for his military plans.

While Winfield Scott dallied in Washington, Taylor won stunning victories over much larger Mexican forces at Palo Alto and Rescara de Palma. He was an instant hero and by May was promoted to brevet major general. He attacked the well-fortified city of Monterrey with only six thousand troops and accepted a surrender of the city in return for a short-term armistice. Fearful of Taylor's rising popularity, Polk reassigned most of Taylor's troops to Winfield Scott, and Scott ordered Taylor to return to Monterrey. Instead, Taylor boldly marched toward General Santa Anna. With only 6,000 soldiers, most of them inexperienced volunteers, Taylor defeated Santa Anna's army of 20,000 at Buena Vista. Taylor's fearless leadership at the battlefront was largely responsible for the dramatic victory over a much larger force.

## PRESIDENTIAL NOMINATION AND ELECTION

Polk correctly saw that Taylor's popularity might threaten Democratic control of the White House. Similarly, Scott had presidential ambitions of his own, which Taylor also threatened. Thus, after Buena Vista, Polk and Scott kept Taylor out of further combat, and Democrats in Congress denounced him. To the public, however, Taylor was a hero who had defeated much larger Mexican armies not once, but four times. He was soon the favorite among Whigs who hoped to win the White House for only the second time in two decades.

At one level, Taylor was the least qualified of all the candidates who had run for the presidency to that time. He had never before run for an elected office, had never held a civilian political office, and had never even voted in a presidential election. Yet, to many voters, this apolitical past made him attractive, as did his status as a bona fide war hero. And at another level, Taylor brought important experience to the office. He had lived in a greater number of states than had any other president, and he had visited even more. He had been raised in the border state of Kentucky, lived much of his adult life in the North, and at the time of his candidacy owned a sugar plantation and 145 slaves in Louisiana. Although not a politician, he was related to many, and he surely understood the nature of political compromise. He was skillful at maneuvering, as he had demonstrated during the Mexican War, when he adroitly defeated Polk's attempts to undermine his command and popularity.

Most Whigs wanted to nominate Henry Clay, the party's "Grand Old Man." But, as a two-time loser, Clay offered little prospect of taking the party to victory in 1848. On the first ballot at the party convention in Philadelphia, Taylor had 111 votes, Clay 97, Winfield Scott 43, and Daniel Webster 22. Antislavery Whigs, led by William H. Seward of New York, reluctantly accepted the slaveholding general because they sensed he could bring the party a much-needed victory. Moreover, the only viable alternative was the slaveholding Clay.

The Democrats nominated Lewis Cass, an uninspiring political hack from Michigan. Cass managed to offend the antislavery wing of his party by opposing any federal interference with slavery in the territories, and at the same time, to offend the extreme proslavery forces by not promising to guarantee slavery in the new land acquired from Mexico. The Democrats were unable to finesse the issue, as the antislavery Democrats from New York supported former president Martin Van Buren, then running on the Free-Soil ticket. Meanwhile, southern extremist followers of John C. Calhoun endorsed Taylor. Democratic divisions led to Taylor's victory. Taylor won 163 electoral votes and 1,360,099 popular votes, while Cass won 127 electoral votes and 1,220,544. The key to Taylor's victory was Van Buren, who won 291,263 popular votes and prevented Cass from carrying New York and the election.

## THE PRESIDENCY IN A TIME OF CRISIS

The Whigs chose Taylor in part because he could overcome sectional tensions and win votes in the North and the South. Taylor chose his cabinet with the same goal in mind. He appointed three southern slaveowners (Reverdy Johnson of Maryland as attorney general; George W. Crawford of Georgia as secretary of war; and William Ballard Preston of Virginia as secretary of the navy). He also appointed three northerners (William M. Meredith of Pennsylvania as secretary of the treasury; Thomas Ewing of Ohio as secretary of the interior; and Jacob Collamer of Vermont as postmaster general). For the seventh spot, secretary of state, he chose Senator John M. Clayton of Delaware, the least southern of the slave states. None of his cabinet officers was an extremist on issues surrounding slavery.

In this area, Taylor contrasts sharply with other administrations of this period in which fanatical proslavery and southern ideologues like Abel Upshur, Robert J. Walker, John C. Calhoun, and Jefferson Davis held cabinet posts. Similarly, in his personal and political life Taylor maintained cordial and even friendly relations with opponents and supporters of slavery. Although a southerner and slaveowner, Taylor became a close personal and political ally of the antislavery William Henry Seward of New York. Taylor did not believe that slavery should be imposed on the new territories, but he also believed in protecting the institution, with "the sword" if necessary, as he told his son-in-law, Jefferson Davis, with whom he was also on excellent terms.

## INDIAN POLICY AND FOREIGN AFFAIRS

The most important "foreign policy" issues for most nineteenth-century presidents were the policies towards Indians. Although Taylor had waged military campaigns against Indians most of his life, he was never enthusiastic about those wars. As president he urged restraint, often resisting local demands for all-out war against native peoples. After a few Seminoles killed a few whites, General David Twiggs in Florida asked for permission to conduct a full-scale war against the Seminoles. Taylor, who knew Florida well, rejected this demand. In the end, the Seminoles turned over the five culprits to the U.S. military, thus averting war.

Taylor similarly resisted demands by whites to wage war against tribal groups in Texas and New Mexico, although he did authorize limited campaigns with specific objectives. In New Mexico, this approach led to a major treaty with the Navajos. Democrats, who had aggressively supported attacks on Indians in the past, accused Taylor of unnecessarily causing wars. In fact, as historian Elbert B. Smith correctly concluded, "Taylor's sense of justice and his policy of trying to keep the peace even at the risk of infuriating the local citizenry probably prevented Indian wars of a far more serious nature."

Taylor followed a similarly nonaggressive, moderate policy in foreign affairs. His policies led to treaties in Central America, including one giving the United States rights to build a canal across Nicaragua. He resisted Americans who wanted to invade Canada, and he refused to support those who wanted to intervene in Cuba on behalf of Narciso Lopez. When a small army of southern filibusters invaded Cuba, Taylor did nothing to help them and initially ignored their pleas for aid when Spanish authorities arrested them. Instead, the president had their leaders in the United States prosecuted for violating federal law. Although the prosecutions failed, Taylor's position earned him the respect of Spain, which eventually released the captured Americans.

**THE COMPROMISE OF 1850**
The possibility of domestic war and disharmony within the Union, rather than foreign affairs, was the most important issue in Taylor's administration. Taylor became president at a time of great national crisis. Since the end of the war with Mexico, the nation had been arguing over the status of the newly acquired territories. During the war, the House had passed the Wilmot Proviso, which would have prohibited slavery in all the territories. The Senate, however, rejected it. In 1848 the Senate, with a southern majority, passed the Clayton Compromise, which would have allowed slavery in some of the territories. The House refused to act on that measure. Thus, at the time of Taylor's inauguration, the new territories lacked any formal government. Southern extremists wanted all the territories acquired from Mexico, as well as Oregon, opened up to slavery. Meanwhile, Texas was claiming much of New Mexico, and appeared to be willing to use military force to get its way.

In January 1849, two months before President-Elect Taylor took office, a slim majority of the southern members of Congress endorsed John C. Calhoun's "Address of the Southern Delegates in Congress to Their Constituents." The address was a one-sided and bizarre history of the nation, arguing that since the adoption of the Northwest Ordinance in 1787 the national government had been aggressively attacking slavery. Throughout the South almost all Democrats supported the address, as did

southern intellectuals. By the end of the year, impassioned disunion sentiments were common throughout the South.

When Congress met in December 1849, the Union was in crisis. California was filled with gold prospectors and had more residents than many existing states. Despite the lack of a congressionally approved territorial government, Californians had written an antislavery constitution and were demanding immediate statehood. Texas had declared that it owned the western portion of New Mexico and was preparing to send troops to enforce that claim. Southerners were demanding a new fugitive slave law to counteract northern refusal to aid in the return of fugitive slaves and to offset the Supreme Court's decision in *Prigg v. Pennsylvania* (1842), which undermined enforcement of the existing Fugitive Slave Law of 1793. On top of all this, Calhoun and his followers were talking about secession if Congress threatened their right to bring slaves into the territories. At no time since the adoption of the Constitution had the Union been so imperiled.

In his annual message to Congress, sent to that body on Christmas Eve 1849, Taylor endorsed California statehood under its already written, antislavery, constitution. He argued for quick admission of New Mexico as well, implying that he would not support the claims of Texas against its western neighbor. He ended by proclaiming his strong attachment to the Union and his intention to "stand by it and maintain its integrity to the full extent of the obligations imposed and the powers conferred upon me by the Constitution." In the weeks following this message, southern extremists accused the president of endorsing the Wilmot Proviso, which he had not done. In reality, he had endorsed popular sovereignty for California and New Mexico; the population in both places wanted statehood without slavery.

Taylor in fact opposed the Wilmot Proviso with his typically practical outlook. He thought the Proviso was "a mere bugbear, & amounts to nothing." He was certain it would "soon fade and be looked upon as a seven day wonder." As a Kentuckian who owned a sugar plantation in Louisiana, Taylor viewed slavery as tied to the staple agriculture of the South. Unlike almost everyone in Congress, the president had been to the regions won from Mexico, and he fully believed slavery was unsuitable to them. He considered the Proviso provocative, insulting, and unnecessary to prevent slavery. For similar reasons, he condemned southern demands for opening the West to slavery, where he was certain it could not survive. Taylor's thoroughly practical analysis of the situation ignored the political implications of the fight over slavery and the symbolic importance of the Wilmot Proviso. Moreover, Taylor underestimated the possibility of growing cotton with irrigation in the Southwest or of using slaves in mining or even in cattle ranching, as they had been used in colonial South Carolina.

For the next six months, the Senate debated a series of compromise measures proposed by Senator Henry Clay of Kentucky, measures that, with the support of Senator Daniel Webster of Massachusetts, would eventually take shape as the Compromise of 1850. Taylor's support for the compromise was ambiguous. He refused to comment on it, but on 13 February sent the Congress California's new constitution prohibiting slavery. Taylor did condemn William H. Seward's "higher law" speech in March, but this was consistent with Taylor's hostility to extremism on both sides. Only a few weeks earlier, Taylor had told Senator Hannibal Hamlin of Maine that he would personally lead troops into Georgia to hang Alexander Stephens and Robert Toombs if they tried to lead the South out of the Union.

In May 1850, with the compromise still being debated, the Texas legislature attempted to organize counties in eastern New Mexico. When New Mexican leaders and the U.S. Army rebuffed these attempts, calls echoed throughout the South for armed intervention to help Texas enforce its grandiose claims. Southern senators, led by Jefferson Davis, argued that the issue was not about land but about slavery. If New Mexico continued to be governed by local authorities, slavery would be prohibited; if Texas took over the region, slavery would be allowed. Taylor stood firm, personally ordering the army in New Mexico to protect the integrity of the territory. By 3 July a crisis was at hand. Taylor was demanding statehood for California and New Mexico, both without slavery; southerners asserted that admission of New Mexico as a free state could lead to secession.

## THE DEATH OF A PRESIDENT

On 4 July 1850, Taylor attended public speeches, ate large quantities of raw fruits and vegetables, drank a prodigious amount of milk, and sat outdoors for much for the day. He suffered from sunstroke, and by evening he had acute gastroenteritis. The medical attention he received—including doses of calomel (which is made from mercury) and opium, as well as induced bleeding—doubtless exacerbated his condition. He died on the evening of 9 July.

Most of Taylor's enemies spoke no ill of the dead president. His pall bearers included Lewis Cass, whom he had defeated for the presidency in 1848; prominent at his funeral was General Winfield Scott, who had tried to undermine his military career in Mexico. Even the fanatically democratic *Washington Union*, which had demanded his impeachment two days before he died, now praised the late "hero" and "patriot." Of the major national papers, only the *Charleston Mercury* would not join in honoring him. That voice of proslavery and secessionist fanaticism continued to carp that Taylor had not acted to guarantee that the newly acquired western territories would be open to slavery.

The *Mercury* was of course right. Taylor's position was one of moderation and support of the status quo. He wanted California to enter the Union as a free state because that was what the people living in California wanted and because it was the only practical choice for California. For similar reasons, Taylor defended the integrity of New Mexico against claims by Texas and defended that territory's free-soil status. But he refused to insult the South with the Wilmot

Proviso, and he was prepared to protect slavery where it existed. He was a southerner who had no problems with slavery itself. In June 1850, in the midst of the compromise debates, Taylor invested $115,000 in the purchase of more slaves and land in Louisiana.

Taylor's evenhanded approach to slavery makes him stand out in an era when all other presidents acted to expand and protect slavery. Perhaps because he was an active owner and user of slaves, Taylor felt able to resist the arguments of southern extremists. This would fit his generally moderate, nonideological, and apolitical approach to his office.

Had he lived, Taylor might have been able to use his prestige and personal popularity to shape a stronger, more lasting compromise. It is doubtful that any compromise between slavery and freedom would have worked in the long run. But the strong Unionism of the slaveholding southern general might have strengthened support for the Constitution in the South and could possibly have undermined the emerging secessionists. Unfortunately, the death of the twelfth president left a leadership vacuum that would not be filled until the sixteenth took office in 1861.

## BIBLIOGRAPHY

Bauer, K. Jack. *Zachary Taylor: Soldier, Planter, Statesman of the Old Southwest* (Louisiana State University Press, 1985).

Hamilton, Holman. *Zachary Taylor: Soldier of the Republic* (Bobbs-Merrill, 1941).

———. *Zachary Taylor: Soldier in the White House* (Bobbs-Merrill, 1951).

———. *Prologue to Conflict* (University Press of Kentucky, 1964).

Rayback, Robert G. *Free Soil: The Election of 1848* (University Press of Kentucky, 1970).

Smith, Elbert B. *The Presidencies of Zachary Taylor and Millard Fillmore* (University of Kansas Press, 1988).

★★★ 13 ★★★

# MILLARD FILLMORE
## 1850–1853

*Paul Finkelman*

*Born 7 January 1800, Summerhill, Cayuga County, New York, to Nathaniel Fillmore and Phoebe Millard Fillmore; attended rural schools and was self-instructed; after teaching school, admitted to the bar and practiced law; married Abigail Powers 5 February 1826, Moravia, New York; two children; married Caroline Carmichael McIntosh, 10 February 1858, Albany, New York; no children; succeeded to presidency upon death of Zachary Taylor; died 8 March 1874 in Buffalo, New York; buried at Forest Lawn Cemetery, Buffalo, New York.*

Fillmore was born to extreme poverty in Cayuga County in upstate New York. Virtually illiterate, he was apprenticed to a cloth dresser and then a textile mill. While at the mill he began a program of self-education, which culminated in his attending the private Academy of Good Hope during a brief layoff. He then became a teacher (1818–1819) in Scott, New York, and began reading law. In 1823, Fillmore won admission to the Erie County bar and began practicing just outside of Buffalo. Two years later, he married Abigail Powers, whom he had met at the Academy of Good Hope.

## EARLY CAREER

Tall, handsome, dignified, and always dressed in the height of fashion, Fillmore rose rapidly in the legal and political community around Buffalo, New York. Remembering his own struggle to gain an education, Fillmore was an active supporter of public schools, lyceums, and universities. In 1842, he became the honorary chancellor of the University of Buffalo, a position he held until his death.

In 1828, Fillmore won a seat in the New York State assembly. He subsequently served one term in Congress in 1832 but refused to run for reelection in 1834. He reversed that decision in the next election, and from 1837 to 1842 he again served in Congress. In his third congressional term, he came in second in balloting for the position of Speaker of the House, and he served as chairman of the Ways and Means Committee. After three terms, Fillmore again refused to run for reelection, in part because his family disliked Washington. In 1844, he was offered up as the vice-presidential candidate on the Whig ticket, with 53 votes on the first ballot, he became a distant third with 40 votes on the third. Later that year he lost a bid for the governorship of New York, as the Whig nominee. In 1847, he was elected comptroller of New York, a position he held until the 1848 National Whig Convention gave him the vice-presidential nomination on the second ballot, with a total of 173 votes. Curiously, Zachary Taylor, the presidential nominee, won his nomination only on the fourth ballot and with only 171 votes.

## VICE-PRESIDENTIAL YEARS

As vice president, Fillmore felt humiliated and excluded. President Taylor relied heavily on the advice of Senator William Henry Seward of New York, who was Fillmore's rival and enemy within the New York Whig Party. Taylor ignored Fillmore's patronage suggestions, refusing even to appoint Fillmore's law partner to his administration. Fillmore's only joy as vice president was his position as ex-officio chairman of the Smithsonian Institution. Otherwise, he was unhappy in the office and often at odds with the president.

The main issue of Fillmore's vice-presidential years was the debate over the Compromise of 1850. Since the end of the Mexican-American War in 1847, the nation had been paralyzed by the conflict over slavery in the new territories. In January 1850, Senator Henry Clay introduced compromise legislation, a series of bills collectively known as the "omnibus bill," to resolve the sectional tensions of the nation. To placate the South, the proposed legislature included a new and harsh fugitive slave law, allowed slavery in most of the land conquered in the Mexican War, and provided that the United States would pay off debts accumulated by the Texas Republic. The free states also were promised satisfaction on specific issues: the immediate admission of California as a free state, a ban on the public sale of slaves in the District of Columbia, and the settlement of a border dispute between New Mexico and Texas in favor of New Mexico.

President Taylor opposed the compromise package, although he supported the immediate admission of California as a free state and the speedy admission of New Mexico as a free state. In early July 1850, Fillmore did something that would be inconceivable in the modern era: He informed President Taylor that he would probably oppose the administration on the compromise legislation if he had to cast a tie-breaking vote. Fillmore told the president his support for the bill would not be "out of any hostility to him or his Administration, but the vote would be given, because I deemed it for the interests of the country." Taylor's death on 9 July 1850 eliminated the possibility of Fillmore's breaking with the president. Suddenly Fillmore *was* the president, and he took the oath of office on 10 July.

## THE NEW PRESIDENT
## AND THE COMPROMISE OF 1850

Scholars debate the extent to which Fillmore reversed the policies of his predecessor. Fillmore's ultimate support for the Compromise of 1850 was a significant rejection of Taylor's policies: immediate admission of California; accelerated statehood for New Mexico, which would also enter as a free state; and protection for New Mexico from territorial claims made by Texas. In the end, Fillmore supported none of these goals. He did sign the bill making California a state, but that was part of the final version of the Compromise of 1850. Fillmore did not push for immediate statehood for California or for New Mexico statehood, and in the end he did not stop Texas's encroachment into New Mexico.

In addition to policy differences, Fillmore differed from Taylor in his style and approach to political crises. Taylor, the lifelong military officer, appeared rigid and uncompromising (although in fact he was not). Fillmore, the lifelong politician, appeared willing to sacrifice any principle for political success: He had favored the Wilmot Proviso and opposed slavery before running for vice president; yet as president he abandoned any attempt to prevent slavery in the territories and signed and enforced a new fugitive slave law that seemed to mock due process and fair jurisprudence.

The other major difference between the two presidents was in their attitude toward southern radicals. Taylor, like Andrew Jackson, was prepared to confront secessionists with force and to stare them down while standing at the head of his army. He would not support the compromise legislation because he understood that in the end there was no compromising with the southern extremists. In contrast, Fillmore willingly made any compromises that would placate the deep South, a tendency that may in the end have only encouraged southern nationalists and secessionists to believe that they could coerce concessions out of the national administration whenever they wanted them.

Fillmore's first act as president in 1850 was unique in U.S. history. He became the first—and so far the only—vice president to take office after the death of a president and immediately ask for the resignation of the entire cabinet. Nothing could better illustrate his estrangement from Taylor and his administration than this request. Fillmore

then indicated his full support for the compromise legislation by making Daniel Webster his secretary of state. In this famous "Seventh of March" speech, Webster had endorsed the compromise legislation, much to the shock of his Massachusetts constituents, who felt betrayed by Webster's willingness to allow slavery in the new territories and by his support for a new fugitive slave law. Although a pariah in his own state, Webster was a hero to supporters of the Compromise of 1850. As secretary of state, Webster would prove unrelenting in his support for the new fugitive slave law after the compromise legislation passed. However, due to his declining health and presidential ambitions Webster proved to be an ineffective secretary of state.

## TEXAS AND NEW MEXICO

Following his endorsement of the compromise legislation, Fillmore turned to the dangerous situation on the Texas–New Mexico border. Taylor had promised to use force to protect the integrity of the New Mexico Territory while at the same time pushing for immediate statehood for New Mexico as a free state, which would have conformed to the wishes of the residents. The South viewed a free New Mexico as symbolically blocking the movement of slavery west. Furthermore, a free New Mexico would have meant that the Wilmot Proviso had been partially implemented.

Like Taylor, Fillmore promised to guarantee New Mexico's border. But, unlike Taylor, Fillmore was more interested in conciliating Texas than in protecting New Mexico. Thus, Fillmore said that he would ask for congressional support for any action he took and would also seek "the consent of the State of Texas" or "some appropriate mode of legal adjudication." Significantly, Fillmore did not ask Congress to grant New Mexico statehood, nor, when the final settlement was made, did he defend the integrity of the New Mexico territory. Rather, he supported and signed legislation that gave to Texas 33,333 square miles of territory that had previously been part of New Mexico.

What had been developing as a major confrontation—perhaps armed conflict—between the United States and the state of Texas simply disappeared. But it disappeared only because Fillmore appeased southern radicals by giving them huge concessions. Under Taylor, Texas would have been smaller and New Mexico would first have been a free territory and soon thereafter a free state; under Fillmore, Texas grew larger and New Mexico remained a territory, open to slavery. This final resolution of New Mexico happened in September of 1850, after Fillmore had supported the compromise legislation, and Stephen A. Douglas had rewritten it.

After Taylor's death, the compromise measures collapsed in Congress. Henry Clay had wanted to solve a series of problems with one overriding bill. However, the issues surrounding slavery in the territories, the boundary question in New Mexico, the slave trade in the District of Columbia, and the southern demand for a new fugitive slave bill were too divisive. Instead of getting bipartisan and sectional support for compromise, Clay found that senators voted against the bill because of the portions they did not like, rather than for it for the portions they did like. On 31 July Clay's bill collapsed in a chaotic session of the Senate.

## PASSAGE OF THE COMPROMISE

At this point, Senator Stephen A. Douglas of Illinois took up the compromise measures, one by one. On 6 September the Senate passed a bill finally resolving the Texas–New Mexico boundary and provided a territorial government for New Mexico without any mention of slavery. California statehood, the organization of the Utah Territory, and the new Fugitive Slave Law soon followed. By mid-September, the last piece of the compromise, the abolition of the slave trade in the District of Columbia, had passed. Douglas, a Democrat, adroitly put together coalitions of a few members from one section, and virtually all members from the other section, to get each bill through the House and the Senate. Unlike Taylor, who had indicated he might veto the whole compromise, Fillmore signed each piece of legislation as it came to his desk.

Elbert B. Smith, a historian of the Fillmore administration, has argued that "the only part of the compromise that gave the south anything was the Fugitive Slave Act." But the reality is that the compromise mostly favored the South. The compromise, as rewritten by Senator Douglas and signed by President Fillmore, gave Texas 33,333 square miles of territory that had previously been part of New Mexico. In addition, the United States agreed to pay off $10,000,000 worth of Republic of Texas bonds. Fillmore, once an advocate of the Wilmot Proviso, had now signed legislation allowing slavery in all of the Southwest, except the new state of California.

The new Fugitive Slave Law was harsh and draconian. It denied alleged fugitives any due-process rights, set the stage for kidnapping free black Americans, and created a mechanism for national enforcement, thus placing the military and financial might in the hands of a master chasing a runaway slave. The abolition of the slave trade in the District of Columbia was at best a moral victory for the North. Private sales were still legal under this law and public sales were still permitted in Maryland and Virginia, right next door to the national capital.

## POLITICAL CONSEQUENCES

Fillmore's overriding goal was to placate the South, where noisy protosecessionists had been talking about disunion since the end of the Mexican War. Fillmore ignored northern opponents of slavery while doing everything to court southern support. Part of this strategy was based on his belief that secession was a real threat to the nation that could be headed off only by appeasing southern radicals. But electoral politics were also an issue.

Fillmore, much like Taylor, was a president without a political base. Taylor had gained his office because he was a war hero untainted by political intrigue or apparent political ambition. He could plausibly, and in part successfully, portray himself as an authentic American patriot, above politics and parties. But Fillmore had no such advantages. He was a lifelong politician, but he was one without a base. Even in his home state of New York, Fillmore was politically weak. Senator Seward and the editor Thurlow Weed controlled the Whig Party in that state. Thus, shortly after Fillmore signed the last of the compromise bills, the president suffered a huge defeat in the New York Whig convention. By a vote of 70 to 40 the convention urged Congress to prohibit slavery in the newly created New Mexico and Utah territories. By the same vote, the convention thanked Senator Seward for his opposition to the proslavery parts of the compromise.

In response to these resolutions, Fillmore's supporters walked out of the convention. Leading the walkout was Fillmore's ally and chief lieutenant Francis Granger, a former congressman and postmaster general, distinctive for his flowing silver-gray hair. Thereafter the conservative Whigs in New York and elsewhere were known as the "silver grays." The resolutions that precipitated this walkout showed that Fillmore could not control his party even in his home state.

## FILLMORE'S
## SOUTHERN STRATEGY

In other parts of the North, especially in New England, revulsion over the new Fugitive Slave Law and the opening of the southwest to slavery undermined Whig support for the administration. In Massachusetts, Fillmore played to the "Cotton Whigs," conservatives who had declining power and influence. When Supreme Court Justice Levi Woodbury died, leaving the "New England seat" empty, Fillmore appointed Benjamin Robbins Curtis, a deeply conservative lawyer who had once represented a slaveowner trying to keep a slave in the Bay State. Curtis was personally tied to the strongest supporters of the enforcement of the Fugitive Slave Law.

Similarly, Fillmore appointed the aging and increasingly ill Daniel Webster as secretary of state. Such an appointment would have made sense a decade earlier, when

Webster was popular throughout much of the North. But, after supporting the Fugitive Slave Law, Webster had become a pariah in his own state. Massachusetts chose Robert Rantoul, an opponent of the Compromise of 1850, to finish Webster's term in the Senate, and in 1851 Charles Sumner succeeded to Webster's seat. Sumner was an eloquent and unflinching foe of slavery, a tireless advocate of racial equality, and an unrelenting opponent of the Fugitive Slave Law.

Given the hostility to the compromise in much of the North, Fillmore's southern strategy made sense. Emphatic enforcement of the Fugitive Slave Law strengthened southern Whigs and undermined radical southern fire-eaters. Initially this strategy seemed to pay off. In 1850, moderate Whigs and Constitutional Unionists swept almost all the congressional seats in Georgia and Mississippi; gained substantially in Alabama and Missouri; and made some gains in Kentucky, Virginia, and Louisiana. In 1851, Whigs and Unionists won statewide elections in South Carolina, Georgia, Alabama, and Mississippi. But Whigs also lost congressional seats in 1850 in New York, Pennsylvania, New Jersey, and most of New England.

## RESISTANCE TO THE
## FUGITIVE SLAVE LAW

After 1850 Fillmore pursued his southern strategy by vigorously enforcing the Fugitive Slave Law. He authorized the use of the military to enforce the law, even though he was uncertain about his authority for doing so. He also sent Daniel Webster on a speaking tour throughout the North to gain support for the new law. In Syracuse, New York—an abolitionist stronghold—Webster predicted that the Fugitive Slave Law would be enforced there within the year. This bravado failed to cow the opponents of slavery. When a U.S. marshal arranged for the arrest of the fugitive slave Jerry McHenry in Syracuse the following fall, a riot broke out, leading to McHenry's rescue, the indictment of the federal marshal for kidnapping, and eventually a series of trials of some of the rescuers. A few weeks before the Jerry

Rescue, as the Syracuse events became known, a bloodier incident had taken place in Christiana, Pennsylvania, where armed black Americans threatened violence against a Maryland man attempting to regain his fugitive slave. The federal marshal called on white bystanders to help, but they refused and urged the slave catchers to withdraw peacefully. They did not, and after a brief fire-fight the slaveowner, Edward Gorsuch, lay dead.

The Fillmore administration responded by arranging for the indictment of forty-one men—thirty-six blacks and five whites—not for violation of the Fugitive Slave Law but on the more serious charge of treason. This was the largest treason indictment in U.S. history. This prosecutorial overkill doubtless helped Fillmore's allies in the 1851 elections, but it failed to convict the defendants. Only one, Castner Hanway, actually went to trial. Supreme Court Justice Robert C. Grier heard the case while attending to his circuit duties. The trial collapsed when Grier ruled that violation of the Fugitive Slave Law, even resistance to its enforcement, did not constitute treason.

Not content with one treason trial, Fillmore urged the federal prosecutor in upstate New York to bring treason indictments against the Jerry Rescuers. The prosecutor refused and instead pursued indictments under the 1850 Fugitive Slave Law. The Jerry Rescue trials also went nowhere. All but one ended in an acquittal or hung jury. The one conviction was on appeal when the defendant, an elderly free black, died.

## ELECTION OF 1852

By early 1852, Fillmore appeared to many free-state residents as a "doughface," a northern man with southern principles. Fillmore was uncertain about his future and intimated to friends that he would not seek a full term on his own. However, southern Whigs and his supporters in parts of the North, urged him to accept the nomination for the 1852 campaign. Followers of Seward, adamant in their opposition to Fillmore, backed General Winfield Scott, the other hero of the Mexican War. Scott's sup-

porters argued that the only Whigs elected to the White House—Harrison and Taylor—had been military heroes, and that Scott fit that image. Secretary of State Daniel Webster, although in poor health, was also in the race.

Balloting at the national Whig convention began on Friday evening, 18 June. On the first ballot Fillmore had 133 votes, Scott 131, and Webster 29. By the tenth ballot Scott was at 135 and Fillmore was down to 130. All but one of the Southern delegates voted for Fillmore, and Webster's support came from New England. Scott dominated the rest of the country. Balloting seemed endless and went nowhere, as the convention voted and revoted all day Saturday. After casting forty-six ballots over two days, the delegates adjourned until Monday. Over the weekend Whig leaders pleaded with Webster to throw his votes to Fillmore, but the stubborn, aging politician refused. Indicative of Fillmore's political weakness was his inability to win renomination because his own secretary of state blocked him.

Fillmore even considered withdrawing in favor of Webster, but his mostly southern supporters would not support Webster. Meanwhile, supporters of Scott reminded the southern delegates that the general was one of them—a Virginian and a military hero. In the end, Webster indicated he would support Fillmore but his decision came too late. Two southerners switched from Fillmore to Scott on the forty-eighth ballot, but Webster still did not release his delegates. On the fifty-third ballot Scott won the nomination. In the election Scott carried only four states, as the Democrats swept into office behind the little-known and easily forgettable Franklin Pierce.

Fillmore's presidency had been superficially successful. In foreign policy he had helped secure greater trading rights for the United States in China, dispatched Commodore Matthew Perry to open Japan to U.S. trade, and faced down an attempt by France to secure influence in Hawaii. Fillmore followed Taylor's policy of refusing to support American filibusters who wanted to overthrow Spanish rule in Cuba. In domestic affairs, the compromise had headed off secessionist notions in the South, although at greater costs than Fillmore ever understood.

## POSTPRESIDENTIAL YEARS

Fillmore happily left office. He had never liked Washington, and he professed to being content with serving as president for even a short time. He had come a long way from the poverty and illiteracy of his youth, and he was ready to return home a success. His retirement, however, was marred by the death of his wife in March 1853 and of his daughter in July 1854. In 1855 he took the Grand Tour of Europe, meeting Queen Victoria, having an audience with the Pope, and declining an honorary degree from Oxford University, declaring, "I had not the advantage of a classical education, and no man should, in my judgment, accept a degree he cannot read."

Before leaving for Europe, Fillmore informed leaders of the nativist Know-Nothing party that he would accept its 1856 nomination for the presidency, an act that suggests his assertions of disinterest in the presidency in 1852 may not have been entirely honest. The conservative Silver Grays of the now-defunct Whig party followed Fillmore into the Know-Nothing movement. Campaigning on a weird platform of anti-immigration, anti-Catholicism, support for the Union, and noninterference with slavery in the territories, Fillmore carried only Maryland. Nationally he won almost 29 percent of the popular vote but, like everyone else in the 1856 election, his support was sectional. In the North he ran a distant third, with only 13 percent of the popular vote. In the South, he carried 43 percent of the vote. It was a humiliating last hurrah for the ex-president.

By 1860, most former Whigs had joined the Republican party. Fillmore refused to do so and probably supported the last remnants of Whig conservatism, in the form of the Bell-Everett ticket on the Constitutional Union party. After Lincoln's victory, Fillmore professed his loyalty to the Union and criticized President James Buchanan for not fortifying military installations in the South, particularly at Fort Sumter in Charleston harbor.

## FILLMORE AND THE CIVIL WAR

Fillmore initially supported the war effort to maintain the Union. He was the first person in Buffalo to pledge money for the cause, and he then organized a military unit of older, retired former militia officers to serve as an honor guard for public functions. The former commander-in-chief became the commander of the Union Continentals, leading the "large portly grandfathers with gray heads" as they marched to pro-Union rallies. Fillmore's support for the war, however, was tempered by his belief that the Republicans and antislavery northerners had caused the crisis. In a public speech in 1864, Fillmore denounced the administration and the handling of the war. The former Whig now campaigned for the Democratic candidate, George B. McClellan. Fillmore, who had always claimed his goal was to preserve the Union, was now willing to allow the South to leave the United States and become an independent nation.

Fillmore's response to the Civil War characterized his political career. He had become, by the end of his presidency, a doughface—a northern man with southern principles. He supported the Union but could not support emancipation, civil rights for African Americans, or the destruction of the slave South. As president he supported slavery and the South, but never disunionists. Although a northerner, he never fully understood his neighbors' hostility to slavery and to the aggressive slave South. Nor did he ever grasp the fundamental immorality of the Fugitive Slave Law of 1850 or its threat to the rule of law in the nation.

## BIBLIOGRAPHY

Hamilton, Holman. *Prologue to Conflict: The Crisis and Compromise of 1850* (University of Kentucky Press, 1964).

Rayback, Robert J. *Millard Fillmore: Biography of a President* (Buffalo Historical Society, 1959).

Smith, Elbert B. *The Presidencies of Zachary Taylor and Millard Fillmore* (University of Kansas Press, 1988).

★★★ 14 ★★★

# FRANKLIN PIERCE
## 1853–1857

*Melvin I. Urofsky*

*Born 23 November 1804 in Hillsborough, New Hampshire, to Benjamin Pierce and Anna Kendrick Pierce; educated at Bowdoin College, Brunswick, Maine (B.A. 1824); admitted to the bar and practiced law; married Jane Means Appleton, 10 November 1834, Amherst, Massachusetts; three children; elected president in 1852 on the Democratic ticket with William Rufus De Vane King of Alabama, with 1,601,274 popular votes and 254 electoral college ballots over the Whig ticket of Winfield Scott of New Jersey and William Alexander Graham of North Carolina (1,386,580 votes and 42 electoral ballots); died 8 October 1869 in Concord, New Hampshire; buried in Old North Cemetery, Concord, New Hampshire.*

Looking back, one can see that in 1852 as in 1856 only a "doughface," a northerner supportive of southern aspirations, could have won either the Democratic nomination or the presidency itself. Historians disagree, however, on whether the alleged ineptitude of the 1850s presidents—lilliputians, in the words of one scholar—hastened the dissolution of the Union or postponed it until circumstances allowed for a stronger leader to come to the fore.

It would be hard to make a case that Franklin Pierce pursued policies that had been carefully thought through. At best, he was a man of good intentions and strong beliefs who proved unable to resolve the overwhelming issue of slavery in the territories, an issue that in the end led to the secession of the southern states. As a sympathetic biographer put it, Pierce "was a politician of limited ability, and instead of growing in his job, he was overwhelmed by it."

## NEW HAMPSHIRE AND NATIONAL BEGINNINGS

Franklin Pierce was born in 1804 in Hillsborough, New Hampshire, then still considered quasi-frontier territory. He had the advantages of not only a good education at Bowdoin College but also strong political connections through his father, General Benjamin Pierce, a fierce nationalist and an important political figure in the state. After his son had read law under Levi Woodbury, General Pierce helped him get started in both his law practice and politics. Admitted to the state bar in 1827, young Pierce immediately joined the Democratic party and two years later won his first election, becoming a member of the New Hampshire General Assembly at the same time that his father was elected to his second term as governor.

Franklin Pierce proved an adept student of politics and, despite his youth, he had been elected speaker of the lower chamber by 1831. In 1833 he won the first of two terms in the U.S. House of Representatives, and then in 1836 a seat in the Senate. In his ten years in Congress Pierce spoke little but earned a reputation as a diligent and conscientious committee member, and even more important, as a loyal Jacksonian Democrat. Pierce hewed to the party line on all issues save that of internal improvements, where he stuck to the classic Jeffersonian view that federal monies should not be spent for state projects. He also developed a strong sympathy for the southern philosophy and shared its antipathy to abolitionists, whom he considered nothing more than troublemakers.

Pierce chose not to take a second term in the Senate for a variety of reasons. His wife,

who suffered from tuberculosis, disliked Washington society, and it reciprocated that feeling for her. She also disapproved of her husband's enjoyment of the parties and the extent to which his convivial nature had earned him the liking of many politicians and society leaders. Pierce had his own reasons for leaving the capital: He did not have independent means, and he found the congressional salary inadequate for his family's needs. He returned to Concord and soon established a thriving law practice, but despite his wife's frowns, he continued to engage in social events more than she thought proper.

Pierce did not abandon politics when he left Washington; instead, he became an important figure in New Hampshire Democratic affairs. He managed most of the statewide campaigns in the 1840s and accepted an appointment from President Polk as district (federal) attorney for the state. But although the president invited Pierce to join his cabinet in 1846 as attorney general, Pierce refused, much to his wife's relief. When the war with Mexico broke out, Pierce volunteered as a private, but he actually entered service as a colonel and wound up as a brigadier general. He led an army from Vera Cruz to join up with Winfield Scott, but accidents and illness prevented him from seeing much combat. As soon as the war ended, he resigned his commission and returned to New Hampshire.

## "WHO IS FRANK PIERCE?"

New Hampshire had hoped to field Justice Levi Woodbury of the U.S. Supreme Court as a favorite son candidate at the 1852 Democratic convention. Woodbury, like Pierce an ardent Jacksonian, had gone onto the bench still planning to become president. He had been seriously considered by the Democrats in 1848, and had he not suddenly died in September 1851, he might have won the party's nomination the following year.

Pierce's friends immediately began talking him up for the nomination, although he himself initially thought he had little chance of winning. Despite the fact that the Democrats smelled victory in the air, there were too many candidates vying for the nomination, and none of them could claim even a majority of the delegates, much less the necessary two-thirds. The factionalism that had split the party for more than a decade made it difficult for the various groups to agree on any of the leading candidates, all of whom, including James Buchanan, Stephen A. Douglas, William Marcy, and Lewis Cass, had long records of public service and positions on issues that alienated one faction or another. When the Democrats met in convention on 1 June in hot, stifling Baltimore, it seemed clear that none of the leading candidates could win the 197 votes needed for nomination.

The balloting droned on for three days, with Pierce's managers reminding southern delegates of their man's sympathies for their views. Finally, on the forty-ninth ballot, North Carolina delegate James C. Dobbin gave an impassioned speech for Pierce and cast his state's vote for the New Hampshire man. The stampede began, and at the end of the count, the convention chair announced the results: "Cass 2, Douglas 2, Butler 1, Franklin Pierce of New Hampshire (God bless him!) 282 votes." To further strengthen southern support, and to make peace with the Buchanan forces, the convention chose William R. King of Alabama, a close friend of Buchanan, as the vice-presidential candidate. (King died on 18 April 1853 before the Thirty-third Congress met and thus served only 45 days as vice president.)

While the Democrats had, at least temporarily, buried their differences and stood united, one question arose—"Who is Frank Pierce?" While well-known in New Hampshire and within the leadership of the Democratic party, Pierce, and what he stood for, were unknown to the common people, the ones who would cast their votes for or against him. Within a short time, a half-dozen campaign biographies appeared, including one by Pierce's old college friend Nathaniel Hawthorne. Hawthorne noted that ever since his terms in Congress, Pierce had recognized "the rights pledged to the South by the Constitution," and that he had not departed from that stance even after

antislavery agitators had made it difficult. An honorable man, Pierce shunned "the obloquy that sometimes threatened to pursue the northern man who dared to love that great and sacred reality—his whole, united, native country—better than the mistiness of a philanthropic theory."

The Whigs hoped to repeat their earlier triumphs of 1840 and 1848 by nominating a war hero named Winfield Scott, a man whose muddled record alienated many in the party. Horace Greeley told Schuyler Colfax as the Whig convention opened that "I suppose we must run Scott for president, and I hate it." There proved to be no crucial issues that the two sides wanted to debate, and the campaign generated little excitement outside of the frequent mutual mudslinging. The united Democrats distributed thousands of pieces of literature in several languages trumpeting the virtues of Frank Pierce to both native- and foreign-born voters, and their better organization got the votes out on election day. Although Pierce had a margin of only 50,000 votes out of more than 3 million cast, he won a landslide victory in the electoral college, carrying all but four states. It was, as many Whigs recognized, the death knell of their party. In 1856, it would be the new Republican party that would challenge the Democrats.

## TRAGEDY STRIKES

Like many Americans, Pierce hoped that the Compromise of 1850 would put an end to agitation over slavery in the territories, much as the Missouri Compromise had done a generation earlier. As they would all eventually recognize, the issue of slavery could not be resolved either legislatively or judicially. In the end, it would take a bloody fratricidal war to do away with the South's "peculiar institution."

Pierce entered the White House with the specter of slavery temporarily hidden, but with a much more personal tragedy still horribly fresh in his mind. Of the three children born to the Pierces, the first had died three days after birth and the second at the age of four. On 6 January 1853, Pierce, his wife and their remaining son, eleven-year-old Benjamin, boarded a train to return to Concord after visiting friends in Boston. Within minutes after leaving the station there was an accident, and the passenger car in which they were traveling rolled off the tracks and down an embankment. Neither Pierce nor his wife was injured, but they saw their son crushed to death in the wreckage. According to Roy Nichols, the experience "completely unnerved" Pierce, and Larry Gara believes the tragedy cast a pall over all four years of the Pierce administration, leaving a man formerly known for the strength of his administration and decision making now haunted by guilt and indecisiveness.

## REACHING FOR HARMONY

Pierce hoped, rather naively, that if he could bring all the different factions in the Democratic party into his administration, he could not only secure national unity but also strengthen his chances for a successful tenure as well as reelection in 1856. His cabinet had the virtue of representing every segment of the party—William L. Marcy of New York as secretary of state; Jefferson Davis of Mississippi, secretary of war; Caleb Cushing of Massachusetts, attorney general; James Guthrie of Kentucky, secretary of treasury; James Campbell of Pennsylvania, postmaster general; James C. Dobbin of North Carolina, secretary of the navy; and Robert McClelland of Michigan, secretary of the interior. Pierce believed that with all factions represented, he could then use his cabinet to distribute patronage on a more or less equal basis. In theory, it made a great deal of sense but, like most theories in those times, it fell apart on the rocks of sectionalism.

To begin with, Pierce chose these men, who had nothing in common save loyalty to the Democratic party, without consulting party leaders. Francis Preston Blair, one of Andrew Jackson's trusted advisers, told Pierce that he had put his enemies in the cabinet, men who viewed his nomination and election as blows to their own ambitions and who would welcome his failure. Banker and politician August Belmont saw the gathering of Marcy and Cushing of the North alongside Jefferson Davis of the South as sure to breed disharmony.

On 4 March 1853, Franklin Pierce affirmed rather than swore the required oath and then, despite the falling snow, took off his overcoat and astonished those gathered in front of the capitol by delivering his inaugural speech without either a manuscript or notes. He pledged an active foreign policy and preservation of the Compromise of 1850, and he expressed his hope that the divisive issue of slavery in the territories could finally be laid to rest. It was no doubt a sincere wish, one around which he hoped the entire country could rally, but it completely ignored the reality of the situation—the rigid belief of slaveholders that they must be allowed to take their property anywhere within territory owned by the United States, and the equally rigid opposition of the so-called Free-Soilers that slavery must not be allowed to spread from the South into the western territories.

## AN AMBITIOUS FOREIGN PROGRAM

Pierce recognized that a number of issues facing the United States needed to be resolved, and he believed he could do so not only within the parameters of traditional Democratic doctrine but also without alienating any sizable portion of the electorate. In foreign policy he would defend the Monroe Doctrine, yet also vigorously pursue U.S. interests. Both France and Great Britain had given signs that their ambitions in the New World had not been quenched, and Pierce intended to force England to live up to the terms of the Clayton-Bulwar treaty by withdrawing from Nicaragua and Honduras. He also wanted to eliminate tensions in the Newfoundland fishing banks, where armed naval vessels were required to protect U.S. interests and a misstep on either side might easily involve both countries in an unwanted war. He sent James Buchanan to England to try to settle the issues in Central America, while Secretary of State William Marcy negotiated a treaty in Washington in which Canada granted U.S. fishing ships rights in the Grand Banks in return for commercial reciprocity.

He also turned his attention to U.S. interests south of the nation's borders. The war with Mexico had added a great deal of territory to the United States, but Mexico still retained one relatively small piece of land which lay athwart the most desirable right of way for a southern transcontinental railroad. Pierce dispatched James Gadsden to Mexico to negotiate the purchase of some 250,000 square miles. The Mexicans agreed to sell only 54,000, and northern senators cut out another 9,000 before agreeing to ratify the treaty in early 1854. The United States then took title to what is now the southern parts of Arizona and New Mexico, thus completing its territorial expansion on the North American continent.

Pierce and other Americans throughout the nineteenth century had their eyes on Cuba, the "pearl of the Antilles" lying ninety miles off the coast of Florida. Southerners especially wanted the island, seeing it as a natural venue for the expansion of slavery. The so-called Young America faction of the Democratic party, which favored aggressive foreign policy to expand U.S. territory and international prestige, had Cuba high on its list of priorities. Pierce sent August Belmont as minister to The Hague with instructions to try to buy Cuba from Spain, in the hope that the nearly bankrupt Spanish government would be eager to raise cash. Secretary of War Jefferson Davis pushed for an outright invasion either by the federal army or by a government-backed filibustering expedition. Pierre Soulé wanted to get Cuba anyway he could, and he had accepted Pierce's offer of the ministry to Spain for no other reason.

A crisis arose on 7 March 1854 when Cuban officials seized a U.S. vessel, the *Black Warrior*, and arrested its captain for technical violations of harbor regulations. The Young Americans, led by Jefferson Davis, pushed for war against Spain in response to this insult to both U.S. honor and shipping interests, and at first Pierce seemed willing to follow their lead. In response to a House request for information on the event, Pierce sent a message in which he declared that it was "vain to expect that a series of unfriendly acts . . . can long be consistent with peaceful relations." Should negotiations with Spain fail to resolve the issue, Pierce said, he would "not hesitate to use the authority and means which Congress may grant to insure the observance of our just rights, to obtain redress for injuries received, and to vindicate the honor of our flag."

Pierce hoped that the threat of war might force Spain to agree to selling Cuba, but the overt desire of southern states for the island produced a backlash in the North. Aside from Cuba, there had been several efforts to expand into Latin America through filibustering expeditions, nearly all financed and manned by southerners. Northerners objected not only to the expansion of slavery into the western territories but also to the acquisition of more lands that might become slave states. In Congress, one northerner after another blasted the efforts to go to war for Cuba, while in Spain Pierre Soulé overplayed his hand, making extravagant demands on the Spanish government until it lost all patience with him. When the Pierce administration did nothing to back Soulé, he lost all face with the officials in Madrid. The *Black Warrior* incident brought the United States and Spain close to war, and it is likely that had the nations fought, the United States could easily have grabbed Cuba.

Even with war averted, however, various efforts, some with Pierce's blessing, were made to get the island, although nothing came of them. Some scholars have suggested that Pierce wanted to divert attention from domestic difficulties by fanning up nationalistic fervor to expand. If so, the Cuban venture proved a dismal failure.

## KANSAS-NEBRASKA

Slavery was the bad apple that soured everything in the Pierce administration. It generated such bitter feelings in the nation and in Congress that even the treaties negotiated with Great Britain to withdraw from Latin America failed in the Senate due to sectional bickering. At the heart of the slaery debate during Pierce's tenure lay the fate of the Nebraska territory, a huge bloc of land that lay within the Louisiana Purchase and needed to be organized as hundreds of settlers began streaming into it.

The first effort to establish a territorial government for Nebraska was a bill introduced in February 1853, a month before Pierce took office. Since Nebraska was north of 36°30', the Missouri Compromise of 1820 banned slavery there. Southern senators killed that bill, and in essence demanded the repeal of the Missouri Compromise. If Nebraska were made a free territory, a St. Louis newspaper explained, then Nebraska would be surrounded on three sides by free territory "where there will always be men and means to assist in the escape of our slaves."

Stephen Douglas of Illinois, the chair of the Senate committee on the territories, at first resisted southern demands but eventually agreed to them. In early January 1854, Douglas introduced the Kansas-Nebraska bill, which divided the territory into two parts, Kansas to the west of Missouri (which could then become a slave state) and Nebraska to the north, which would most likely be free. To satisfy southern demands, Douglas revived his idea of popular sovereignty, by which the inhabitants of a territory would choose whether it would be free or slave. Southerners insisted that this decision had to be made before statehood was granted, because under the terms of the Missouri Compromise there could be no slaves in those territories. Popular sovereignty both in name and in fact repealed the Missouri Compromise. Douglas and a delegation of leading southern senators went to the White House, and Pierce agreed to the plan. This made it an official Democratic plan that could be enforced by party discipline and patronage.

Douglas sponsored the bill for several reasons—his desire to make Chicago the eastern terminus of a transcontinental railroad that would run through the territories, his ambitions for the 1856 Democratic nomination, and his sympathy for, or at least indifference to, slavery. Pierce's reasons are not as clear. Despite his acknowledged sympathies for the South, he had been born and bred in New England, the very heart of antislavery agitation. He must have known, as did Douglas, that repeal of the Missouri agreement would unleash a firestorm of criticism in the North. James McPherson describes Pierce's role in this whole transaction as "reluctant but weak-willed." Pierce apparently believed that the Missouri Compromise had always been unconstitutional (a position that a bare majority of the Supreme Court would declare in the 1857 *Dred Scott* decision), and under strong pressure from southern senators and Douglas, he finally agreed to their plan.

Douglas had predicted that the bill would "raise a hell of a storm," but it is doubtful if even he anticipated the depths of opposition to the nullification of the Missouri Compromise. Douglas managed to get the Senate to approve the bill 37 to 14, with most northern senators going along under the lash of party discipline. In the House, however, northern Democrats split 44 to 44, and the final vote was only 113 to 100. Pierce and the Democratic leaders may have thought the issue now resolved, but in fact the problems had just begun. Throughout the North, newspapers and politicians damned the bill as "a triumph of Slavery and Aristocracy over Liberty and Republicanism." Horace Greeley later declared that the bill had created more abolitionists in two months than William Lloyd Garrison and Wendell Phillips had been able to do in twenty years. The bill tarred the Democratic party with the odor of slavery, a charge not completely false since the southern Democrats provided the bulk of the party's support and leadership. The Whigs had no position on the bill and in any event were already dead as a party. The opposition, whether by the name of Free-Soilers, Independents, or Fusioners, gradually coalesced around a new party dedicated in general to opposition to slavery and in particular to the expansion of slavery in the territories. In Ripon, Wisconsin, a meeting of opponents to the bill adopted the name Republican, and within a short time that name had become the umbrella under which all the different antislavery groups would converge.

That fall the Democrats reaped the first fruits of the Kansas-Nebraska Act when they suffered staggering defeats throughout the North. The Democratic party became an even more sectional organization, as about one in four northern Democrats deserted the party. Of the 91 free-state Democratic congressional incumbents, 66 went down to defeat. Neither Democrats nor Republicans had a majority in the House of Representatives, which left a variety of splinter groups holding the balance of power; it took 133 ballots to elect a speaker of the House, Republican Nathaniel P. Banks of Massachusetts. The results boded ill for an administration that could no longer rely on party discipline to ensure passage of its proposals.

## BLEEDING KANSAS

If Franklin Pierce is remembered for anything in history texts, it is for his fumbling over the Kansas issue in the latter part of his administration. Even southerners recognized that Nebraska would be free, but for one reason or another they believed Kansas should be a slave state. The result was that southerners rushed into Kansas taking their slaves with them, while Northern antislavery groups organized expeditions of settlers to counter the southern migrations. By the time the first governor of Kansas—Andrew Reeder, a Pennsylvania Democrat—arrived in October 1854, he found several thousand settlers already taking up residence. He ordered a census and then scheduled elections for a territorial legislature in March 1855. That election, and all subsequent ones in the next few years, were marred by blatant irregularities, as the so-called Border Ruffians crossed over from Missouri to elect proslavery delegates. Reeder denounced the fraud but did nothing about it. The legislature met, expelled the few antislavery members, adopted a drastic slave code, and made it a capital offense to aid a fugitive slave. In addition, it passed a law making it a felony

even to question the legality of slavery in the territory!

The free-state faction denounced the "elected" government. In October it held its own constitutional convention, adopting a plan that excluded both slaves and free Negroes; and then applied for admission to the Union. By March 1856 Kansas had two governments, and violence plagued the territory. This reached a climax in May 1856 when a proslavery mob entered the free-state town of Lawrence, stole everything that was not nailed down, and burned the rest. Although only one person lost his life, the "sack of Lawrence" infuriated northerners. John Brown, a fanatical free-soiler, believed God had called him to avenge this atrocity. Brown led his followers to the proslavery settlement at Pottawatomie Creek, where on 24 and 25 May they killed five men in cold blood. Altogether, by the end of 1856 the death toll in bleeding Kansas stood at 200, with about $2 million worth of property destroyed. The violence even spilled over into the hallowed chamber of the U.S. Senate, where on 22 May Representative Preston S. Brooks of South Carolina attacked and seriously injured Senator Charles S. Sumner of Massachusetts for alleged insults against a fellow South Carolinian, Senator A. P. Butler.

Where was Franklin Pierce during all this commotion? Trying not only to carry out what he saw as the spirit of the Kansas-Nebraska Act but also to rally the Democratic party around him. To achieve these goals, he sent a southerner as governor to the Nebraska territory, a northerner into Kansas, and he tried to divide up all the government positions fairly evenly. Andrew Reeder of Pennsylvania proved a disaster in Kansas, failing to keep order. When Pierce finally removed him in the summer of 1855, however, it was not for incompetence but for greed—Reeder and others had been lining their pockets by running illegal land operations in the Indian reserves.

To replace Reeder, Pierce named Wilson Shannon, a proslavery lawyer from Cincinnati, who upon arrival in Kansas immediately made known his support of the proslavery government. Pierce offered army troops to Shannon to help enforce the peace, but Shannon turned out to be completely incompetent. In September 1856, Pierce finally removed him, replacing him with John Geary, a tough and fair-minded man who had learned about fighting as a captain in the Mexican war and about politics as mayor of San Francisco. Geary managed to calm passions and with the use of federal troops—which Shannon had not deployed—finally brought peace and order into the territory.

Franklin Pierce for some reason thought that he deserved a second term in office, and in 1856 he took several steps to show the American people that they should return him to the White House. In addition to sending Geary to Kansas, he "stood up" to Great Britain, publicly condemning the British minister to Washington for allegedly recruiting U.S. citizens illegally for the war in Crimea. The Democrats, unsure of just how strong the Republican challenge would be, knew that Pierce, the compromise candidate of 1852, had little popular support. They turned instead to another old Jacksonian warhorse, James Buchanan of Pennsylvania. Pierce left office comforted by the fact that not only did Buchanan win but that the Democratic party had regained control of Congress in the 1856 elections.

## EVALUATION OF PIERCE'S PRESIDENCY

Franklin Pierce was an honest man who had strong beliefs, but by the time he became president a good part of the country no longer shared his views. He did not become a pawn of southerners—in truth, he had always been sympathetic to southern views on constitutional interpretation and slavery. In the late 1820s and even into the 1830s, most northerners had also shared this outlook; by the 1850s even those northerners who were not abolitionists opposed the expansion of slavery into the territories. The country had changed, and Pierce found himself in the position of trying to justify the spread of sla-

very which, aside from its moral ambiguity, no longer had any political support outside the South.

If we measure presidents by the way in which they lead the country in response to crises, then Franklin Pierce is a failure. He agreed to the Kansas-Nebraska bill, knowing not only that it had little support outside the South but also that it would deeply offend the sensibilities of those who believed that the issue of slave expansion had been settled in the Missouri Compromise. The depth of this feeling can be gleaned from the fact that over a century later, when an Ohio historian visited the Pierce home in Concord and asked the guide why New Hampshire did not do more to publicize the home of its only president, the guide responded: "Folks here don't think much of Mr. Pierce. The Kansas-Nebraska Act, you know."

When a civil war broke out in Kansas, the ineffectiveness of the men Pierce sent to the territory was overshadowed by the moral and political ineffectiveness of the president. It was his responsibility to ensure that the question of whether Kansas should be free or slave would take second place to whether Kansas was safe from violence while that question was resolved.

After Pierce left the White House he took an extended tour of Europe before returning to Concord. In 1860 he deplored the "folly" of the Republicans but also opposed what he considered the hasty action of the southern states. He initially supported Lincoln's efforts to save the Union, but before long his constitutional beliefs about the limited powers of the federal government led him to denounce what he considered Lincoln's "usurpations" of power. What little popularity Franklin Pierce may have had at home soon dissipated, and he died in 1869 in political obscurity.

## BIBLIOGRAPHY

Craven, Avery. *The Coming of the Civil War*, rev. ed. (University of Chicago Press, 1957).

Gara, Larry. *The Presidency of Franklin Pierce* (University Press of Kansas, 1991).

Gienapp, William E. *The Origins of the Republican Party, 1852–1856* (Oxford University Press, 1987).

Johannsen, Robert W. *Stephen A. Douglas* (Oxford University Press, 1973).

Nichols, Alice. *Bleeding Kansas* (Oxford University Press, 1954).

Nichols, Roy F. *Franklin Pierce: Young Hickory of the Granite Hills,* rev. ed. (University of Pennsylvania Press, 1958).

Wolff, Gerald W. *The Kansas Nebraska Bill: Party, Section, and the Coming of the Civil War* (Revisionist Press, 1977).

★★★ 15 ★★★

# JAMES BUCHANAN
## 1857–1861

*Paul Finkelman*

*Born 23 April 1791 in Cove Gap, Pennsylvania, to James Buchanan and Elizabeth Speer Buchanan; educated at Dickinson College, Carlisle, Pennsylvania (two-year course); admitted to the bar and practiced law; elected president in 1856 on the Democratic ticket, with John Cabell Breckinridge of Kentucky, receiving 1,838,169 votes and 174 electoral college ballots, over the Republican ticket of John Charles Frémont of California and William Lewis Dayton of New Jersey (1,341,264 popular votes and 114 electoral ballots), and the American party ticket of Millard Fillmore of New York and Andrew Jackson Donelson of Tennessee (874,534 votes and 8 electoral ballots); died 1 June 1868 in Lancaster, Pennsylvania; buried in Woodward Hill Cemetery, Lancaster, Pennsylvania.*

Few presidents have entered office with greater experience or preparation than did James Buchanan; no other president ever left office in such a dire situation. Buchanan is the only president to have seen the size of the nation diminish during his tenure. Two states—Minnesota and Oregon—entered the Union during his term, but seven others—South Carolina, Georgia, Florida, Alabama, Mississippi, Louisiana, and Texas—had declared themselves no longer in the Union by the time

Buchanan left office. Although professing to regret secession, Buchanan did virtually nothing to stop it. Moreover, his policies throughout his administration, but especially during the election of 1860 and during the winter of 1860 to 1861, directly and indirectly encouraged and aided secession. If the measure of executive competence is the condition of the nation when the president leaves office, then Buchanan was unquestionably the least successful president in U.S. history.

Buchanan gained his presidential nomination in 1856 in part because he had been out of the country for more than three years as an ambassador and had been out of politics for eight years; thus, he was the only nationally recognized Democrat who had not made any new enemies in the past few years. His contemporary nickname, the "Old Public Functionary," illustrates that even in his own time Buchanan was seen as a political cipher of very limited merit or skill.

There is a sense that no one really trusted Buchanan, and few liked him. Andrew Jackson once explained that he had appointed Buchanan ambassador to Russia because "it was as far as I could send him out of my sight; and where he could do the least harm. I would have sent him to the North Pole if we had kept a minister there." Buchanan lacked candor. According to the political journalist Murat Halstead, who knew and wrote about him, Buchanan was "the personification of evasion, the embodiment of an inducement to dodge." Senator Henry S. Foote of Mississippi, a friend of Buchanan, noted that "even among close friends, he very rarely expressed his opinions at all on disputed questions, except in language especially marked with a cautious circumspection almost amounting to timidity."

Buchanan in fact did have a few principles. He supported basic Democratic policies, opposing internal improvements, homesteads, tariffs, and even land grants for schools. He was unalterably opposed to antislavery and black rights. Some scholars argue he was the ultimate doughface—a northern man with southern principles—and in practice was one of the most proslavery politicians in the North. Other scholars

claim he was not proslavery but merely antiabolitionist. The evidence suggests he was both proslavery and antiabolitionist. Throughout his career, Buchanan defended the interests of slavery, saw nothing immoral about it, and was uncompromisingly opposed to free blacks. In 1864 he urged that the southern states be allowed to reenter the Union "just as they were before they left it, leaving the slavery question to settle itself." In his autobiography written in 1866 Buchanan still insisted that emancipation had been wrong, that the North had no right to complain about slavery in the South, and that abolitionists and northerners were to blame for the Civil War.

## POLITICAL BACKGROUND
Buchanan was born near Mercersburg, Pennsylvania, and grew up in moderate circumstances. In 1809 he graduated from Dickinson College in Carlisle, Pennsylvania, and then read law in Lancaster. Through his law practice and shrewd investments Buchanan acquired a large fortune. He entered politics in 1813 as an assistant prosecutor in Lebanon, Pennsylvania. He then served as a Federalist member of the Pennsylvania House of Representatives (1814–1816) and as a U.S. congressman (1821–1831). In 1828 he left what remained of the Federalist party to support Andrew Jackson for the presidency, remaining an ardent Democrat the rest of his life. After serving as ambassador to Russia for three years, he returned to the United States to serve in the Senate from 1834 to 1845. During this period, he declined appointments as attorney general (1839) and associate justice of the Supreme Court (1844). He next served as secretary of state in the Polk administration (1845–1849). After Zachary Taylor's victory, Buchanan retired to his estate near Lancaster, Pennsylvania, and briefly served as president of the board of trustees of Franklin and Marshall College. With the Democrats back in power, he returned to politics in 1853, this time serving as ambassador to Great Britain (1853–1856).

A life-long bachelor, Buchanan usually shared lodgings with southern senators. His relationship with his longtime roommate Senator William R. King of Alabama was so close that one Washington observer referred to the two men as "Buchanan & *his wife.*" His close relationship with southerners helps explain his lifelong support for slavery. In the 1830s he endorsed the censorship of the mail to prevent the dissemination of abolitionist literature. He later supported Texas annexation on the grounds that slavery needed room to expand. While ambassador to England he joined two southern politicians in issuing the Ostend Manifesto, calling for U.S. purchase or annexation of Cuba. This had been a longtime goal of southern filibusters, who wanted the island for its slaves and for its potential as another slave state. The manifesto stressed that the abolition of slavery in Cuba would threaten the South.

## PRESIDENTIAL CANDIDACY

In 1844, 1848, and 1852, Buchanan was a candidate for the Democratic presidential nomination, always running second or third in the balloting. In 1856 he took an early lead at the Democratic convention, ultimately winning on the seventeenth ballot when Stephen A. Douglas of Illinois threw his support to Buchanan, who was then unanimously nominated.

The election featured two new political parties, the Republicans and the Know-Nothings. The Republicans, who had emerged out of opposition in the free states to the Kansas-Nebraska Act, were running John C. Frémont, a hero of western exploration. The Know-Nothings, a strange coalition of conservative former Whigs and rabid opponents of Catholics and immigration, ran former Whig president Millard Fillmore.

The election was essentially two separate contests. In the South, Buchanan's only opposition was Fillmore; in the North, Fillmore was on the ballot but the real contest was between Buchanan and Frémont. Buchanan swept the slave states, losing only Maryland to Fillmore. Frémont carried eleven free states, but Buchanan held on to his home state of Pennsylvania, plus New

Jersey, Indiana, Illinois, and California, winning 174 electoral votes to Frémont's 114 and Fillmore's 8. Buchanan's apparently substantial victory was clearly sectional. He was the first president since John Quincy Adams not to carry a majority of both the North and the South. Furthermore, although winning 19 of 31 states, he carried only 1,838,000 popular votes, 45 percent of the total vote, while his two opponents won 2,215,000 votes.

The sectionalism of Buchanan's election underscored the problems he faced. The Democrats were the only "national" party, and they controlled Congress and the White House. But the party itself was increasingly controlled by the South, and Buchanan was a classic doughface.

## CREATING AN ADMINISTRATION

Although Buchanan had been on the political scene for a long time, his election came after eight years of being out of office and three years out of the country. He was sixty-five at the time of his election and clearly out of touch with his party and his nation. Buchanan had no recent enemies, but he also had no understanding of the depth of northern opposition to slavery in the territories. His cabinet appointments illustrated his myopic approach to the sectional issues facing the nation. Four members of the cabinet, Howell Cobb of Georgia (secretary of the treasury), John B. Floyd of Virginia (secretary of war), Aaron Brown of Tennessee (postmaster general), and Jacob Thompson of Mississippi (secretary of the interior) were slaveholding southerners. Secretary of the Navy Isaac Toucey of Connecticut was so tied to the South that his own state legislature accused him of treason for his behavior during the secession crisis. Secretary of State Lewis Cass of Michigan was a doughface Democrat who never opposed the expansion of slavery into the West. Only Attorney General Jeremiah Black of Pennsylvania was not intimately tied to the South, but he was intensely hostile to the antislavery movement and the Republican party.

In choosing a cabinet, Buchanan placed great stress on personal friendship rather than on skills or competence. Two cabinet choices, Black and Cobb, were in fact quite talented. Floyd was incompetent, Cass was lazy and verging on senility, and the rest were mediocre at best. Most important, Buchanan snubbed Stephen A. Douglas and his wing of the party in choosing his cabinet, even though Douglas was the most popular Democrat in the North, if not the whole nation.

In seeking advice outside the cabinet Buchanan turned to only one northerner, Jesse Bright, an enemy of Douglas. Bright, although a senator from Indiana, owned a plantation and a large number of slaves in Kentucky. (Indeed, he was so much a doughface that during the Civil War he would be expelled from the Senate for disloyalty.) In addition to Bright, Buchanan listened to Henry Wise of Virginia, John Slidell of Louisiana, and his friend and cabinet member Howell Cobb. Not surprisingly, these four slaveholders gave him advice that was sectional and in the end not helpful.

Thus, Buchanan began on the wrong foot. He had been elected by southern votes, but to govern he had to gain the confidence of the North. His cabinet appointments did little to accomplish that, and his policies once in office did not improve matters.

## SLAVERY IN THE TERRITORIES AND THE DRED SCOTT DECISION

The most important issue facing Buchanan was the conflict over slavery in the western territories. The Missouri Compromise, passed in 1820, prohibited slavery in almost all of the then-existing territories. The annexation of Texas (1845) added a huge new slave state to the nation. The Mexican-American War (1846–1847) added vast new territory to the nation and reopened the debate over slavery in the territories. Northerners wanted to prohibit slavery in the new territories; southerners demanded access to them. The Compromise of 1850 opened up the new territories to slavery while admitting California as a free state. Then, in the Kansas-Nebraska Act (1854), Congress par-

tially repealed the Missouri Compromise by allowing slavery in the western territories comprising all or part of the present-day states of Kansas, Nebraska, the Dakotas, Montana, Colorado, and Wyoming. This law, although guided through Congress by Senator Stephen A. Douglas, horrified much of the North and led to the creation of the Republican party, which was dedicated to prohibiting slavery in the territories.

The 1856 election had to a great extent centered on the issue of slavery in the territories and the on-going civil war in Kansas between free-state and slave-state settlers. Buchanan, lacking any sense of the depth of northern hostility to slavery in the territories, saw his main role as protecting the interests of the South in the contest.

In the early winter of 1856, before the presidential campaign began, the Supreme Court heard oral arguments in *Dred Scott v. Sandford*. Scott, a Missouri slave, had lived in what is today Minnesota—a territory that had been made free by the Missouri Compromise—and had then been taken back to Missouri as a slave. Scott initially won his freedom in a trial court in St. Louis, but the Missouri Supreme Court reversed this outcome. He subsequently appealed to the U.S. Supreme Court, arguing that under the Missouri Compromise he was free. The Court failed to decide the case before the election, and instead had a second round of arguments in December 1856.

In his inaugural address, Buchanan declared the issue of slavery in the territories to be "a judicial question, which legitimately belongs to the Supreme Court of the United States" and which, he noted, would "be speedily and finally settled." Buchanan pledged his support for the decision. Two days later Chief Justice Roger Taney delivered his opinion in the case, declaring that Congress did not have the power to prohibit slavery in any of the federal territories.

Buchanan hoped that the *Dred Scott* decision would settle the issue of slavery in the territories and relegate free blacks to permanent inferiority. His endorsement of the decision, before it was announced, might have been seen as an act of statesmanship, supporting the outcome, whatever it might be. But it was not viewed that way. As he walked to the podium to take the oath of office and give his inaugural address, Buchanan stopped briefly to chat with Chief Justice Taney. The inauguration crowd witnessed this conversation, and Americans later read about it in their newspapers.

Senator William Henry Seward of New York and other Republicans, including Abraham Lincoln, would later speculate that in this conversation Taney had told Buchanan what the Court was about to decide. Seward claimed that the "whisperings" between Taney and Buchanan were part of a conspiracy to hang "the millstone of slavery" on the western territories. We will never know what Taney said to Buchanan, but we do now know that even before that conversation Buchanan *already* knew what the Court was going to decide. In a major breach of Court etiquette, Justice Robert Grier (who, like Buchanan, was from Pennsylvania) had kept the president-elect fully informed about the progress of the case and the internal debates within the Court. So when Buchanan urged the nation to support the decision, he already knew what Taney would say. Republican suspicions of impropriety turn out to be fully justified. There may have been no ongoing conspiracy, but collusion abounded. The Court and the president-elect worked closely to get the decision Buchanan and Taney wanted and to get the nation to accept it.

Thus, Buchanan's endorsement of *Dred Scott* before it was announced did not help his cause at all. Rather, it furthered the belief among many, probably a majority, of northerners, that the president was untrustworthy and that the Supreme Court and the president were part of a Slave Power conspiracy.

## KANSAS

In his inaugural address, Buchanan also declared that the settlers in the territories would be "perfectly free to form and regulate their domestic institutions in their own way, subject only to the Constitution." He promised that his administration would "se-cure to every resident" of the territories "the free and independent expression of his opinion by his vote." The mini–civil war in the West, known as Bleeding Kansas, would test this pledge, and in the end Buchanan would fail the test miserably.

Buchanan's first move was probably his best. To restore order in Kansas Buchanan appointed Robert J. Walker as territorial governor. Although a former slave owner and a southerner by choice, Walker also believed in a fair administration of the law and was probably personally in favor of making Kansas a free state.

The Kansas territory had two governments—the official one, which was proslavery and met in Lecompton, and an unofficial free-state government in Topeka. Although supporters of slavery dominated the territorial legislature through gerrymandering and vote fraud, free-staters in the territory outnumbered their southern opponents by approximately 5 to 2. Governor Walker reported this ratio to Buchanan, stating that about 17,000 voters opposed slavery and only 7,000 supported it.

In February 1857—a month before Buchanan's inauguration—the proslavery legislature called for a convention to write a state constitution for Kansas. In his inaugural address as governor, Walker indicated that he did not believe slavery could ever be successfully introduced into Kansas. He also declared that Kansas would never become a "slave state or a free state, unless a majority of the people shall first have fairly and freely decided this question for themselves by direct vote on the adoption of the Constitution, excluding all fraud or violence."

Almost from the moment he arrived in Kansas, Governor Walker was under attack from proslavery extremists. The *Charleston Mercury*, never known for its rational or honest appraisal of any situation regarding slavery, called Walker the "greatest Abolitionist in Kansas," while a Mississippi editor declared he was "cunning and treacherous." Almost all northern Democrats applauded Walker's attempts to administer the law honestly and to move fairly toward popular sovereignty. Many southern moderates agreed. The *Richmond Enquirer*, the *New Orleans Picayune*, and the *Memphis Appeal* all urged support for Walker, who was trying to bring Kansas into the Union as a state committed to supporting Buchanan and the Democratic party. These papers fully realized that slavery would never work in Kansas, and that if popular sovereignty was to work it would have to be fairly implemented.

It was on the issue of Kansas and Governor Walker that Buchanan probably made his greatest mistakes. With virtually all northern Democrats and a good number of important southern Democrats supporting Walker, Buchanan could easily have backed his appointee. Initially he did, and in doing so Buchanan undermined the Republican critiques of the *Dred Scott* decision, the Kansas-Nebraska Act, and the concept of popular sovereignty. In the summer and early fall of 1857, Democrats won in a number of northern state elections. Buchanan had the clout within his party to face down the southern fire-eaters, bring Kansas into the Union as a free state that would support the Democrats, and perhaps begin to end the debate over slavery in the territories.

Ironically, it was the elections in Kansas that undermined Walker and led Buchanan to abandon him. In October, Kansas held elections for the territorial legislature and for its delegate to Congress. Marcus J. Parrott, the Free-Soil candidate for Congress and a former Democrat, won a huge victory with a majority of more than 4,000 votes. Republicans joined northern Democrats in sending this opponent of slavery to represent the territory in Washington.

However, to the shock of everyone, a majority of proslavery men were elected to the territorial legislature as a result of massive fraud in a number of districts. In Johnson County for example, Oxford precinct provided more than 3,200 votes for proslavery candidates, even though that precinct had fewer than 200 voters.

Governor Walker, going technically beyond his powers, issued a proclamation rejecting these fraudulent votes and declaring victory for a number of antislavery candidates. Southern fire-eaters were outraged; the Alabama legislature demanded his removal. However, Walker's actions probably prevented a civil war in the territory. Most Kansans appreciated his decisive action, as did most northern Democrats. At this juncture, firm leadership from the president and praise for Walker's success would have made a huge difference in the politics of Kansas and the nation. However, despite the territorial secretary's requests for such support, Buchanan remained noncommittal on Walker's performance.

After the October territorial election the Kansas convention met in Lecompton to write a constitution for statehood. The delegates to that convention had been chosen the previous spring in an election gerrymandered to produce an unrepresentative, proslavery convention: 6 proslavery counties got 37 of the delegates, while the 30 Free-Soil counties were awarded only 23 seats. Initially the leader of the proslavery forces in Kansas, John Calhoun—who was, ironically, a Douglas Democrat from Illinois—promised that the constitution would be submitted to the voters for their approval. Calhoun backed away from this promise after the Free-Soilers carried the election for the territorial legislature.

The delegates to the Lecompton convention wrote a constitution that went to great lengths to protect existing slave property in the territory. The convention then refused to allow the people of the territory the opportunity to vote the constitution up or down. Instead, voters were given only the option of banning the further importation of slaves. However they voted, there would be slaves in the state and there would be no provision preventing masters from smuggling new slaves into Kansas.

The refusal to allow for a yes-or-no vote on the whole constitution went directly against Walker's promise of a fair election. Had Buchanan intervened, he might have persuaded the delegates to put the issue to a fair vote. He might even have persuaded the convention to go back into session to change the terms of the referendum. But he did not, and in December 1857, even before the vote on the constitution, Governor Walker resigned.

Meanwhile, on December 17, the recently elected territorial legislature, dominated by opponents of slavery, had passed a resolution sending the constitution to the residents of Kansas for an up or down vote. This was Buchanan's last chance; had he endorsed *this* election, he would have salvaged Kansas and his party. But Buchanan had already endorsed the Lecompton convention with its refusal to submit the constitution to the voters for a fair vote.

On December 21, the Lecompton convention's constitutional referendum took place. To no one's surprise, most Free-Soilers in the state refused to participate since they were not allowed to vote against the entire constitution. The convention officials who ran the referendum declared there were 6,226 votes for the constitution with full slavery, and 569 for banning the further importation of slaves. Everyone who knew Kansas politics realized that once again there had been massive vote fraud, as hundreds of Missourians crossed into the territory to vote. On January 4 the referendum sponsored by the legislature recorded 10,226 votes against the constitution, 138 in favor of it with full slavery, and only 24 in favor of it with partial slavery. Clearly, an overwhelming majority of the settlers in Kansas did not want anything to do with the Lecompton constitution. Buchanan was nevertheless determined by this time to bring Kansas into the Union as a slave state.

Buchanan submitted the Lecompton constitution and Kansas statehood to a Congress with large Democratic majorities in both houses. But, as David Potter noted, his "basic mistake—part of the basic dilemma—was his failure to see how badly the northern wing of the Democracy would be damaged, even by a victory, and his failure to appreciate what a fearful handicap his northern followers would incur if they supported him on this issue." Even before the issue came before the Congress the mood of the North was clear. In Indiana and Pennsylvania, conservative strongholds that Buchanan had carried in 1856, Democrats were in open revolt against the administration's Kansas policy. Ignoring the fact that there had never been a democratic vote on the Lecompton constitution, Buchanan insisted that the free soilers in Kansas were in open rebellion and needed to be crushed. Northerners knew better.

Stephen Douglas fought Buchanan with all his considerable political skills. Antislavery Republicans voted side by side with Douglas and his Democratic allies. Some eastern Republicans got so carried away by this alliance that they urged their colleagues in Illinois to support Douglas in the 1858 senatorial race. But Illinois Republicans also knew better. Douglas opposed the Lecompton constitution because the process violated popular sovereignty and because he would lose the 1858 election if he did not oppose that constitution. Republicans opposed Lecompton because they did not want slavery in Kansas or in any other territory. Buchanan tried to coerce support by firing patronage officeholders, like postmasters, if their congressional patrons did not support Lecompton. Throughout the North, papers denounced Buchanan and Lecompton.

In the end, the House defeated the Lecompton constitution and Kansas statehood by a vote of 120 to 112. For Buchanan this was not simply the loss of a bill in Congress, it was the loss of his party and his presidency. Buchanan had essentially gone to war against northern Democrats in order to make Kansas a slave state and to satisfy southern fire-eaters.

After the loss Buchanan made one final, face-saving attempt to gain approval for Kansas statehood, but this, too, backfired and appeared simply another clumsy attempt to use patronage, bribes, and threats to make Kansas a slave state. Buchanan persuaded a slim majority in Congress to pass the English Bill—named for Congressman William English of Indiana—offering Kansas immediate statehood and 19 million acres of public lands if the people of the territory would endorse the Lecompton constitution. If they did not do so, the bill prohibited Kansas from applying for statehood until the territory had 90,000 settlers. For the South it was a no-lose vote. If the people accepted the offer, Kansas would be a slave state; if they rejected it, Kansas could not enter as a free state for many years. In the only fair vote on the Lecompton constitution, the people of Kansas defeated it 11,300 to 1,788.

## BEYOND KANSAS

The fallout from Kansas was disastrous for Buchanan, the Democratic party, and the nation. In Illinois Buchanan tried to unseat Douglas and failed miserably. In a heated and famous campaign, Douglas barely defeated Abraham Lincoln for the Senate seat. The campaign made Lincoln a national political figure and made Douglas the most popular Democrat in the North. It was a huge slap at President Buchanan, who had once again clumsily used patronage and threats to punish Douglas. Republicans did well throughout the North, winning 109 seats in the House of Representatives. In addition, 13 anti-Lecompton Douglas Democrats also won. The new Congress also had 88 administration Democrats and 27 Whigs and Know-Nothings, mostly from the South. The Democrats might have been able to elect a speaker, but the fire-eaters from the South would not support a Northerner. After two months, the Republicans managed to elect William Pennington of New Jersey, a conservative ex-Whig who had recently joined their party.

The contest to nominate a speaker took place in the wake of two events that shook the South: John Brown's raid at Harpers Ferry and the publication of Hinton Rowan Helper's *The Impending Crisis*. Southerners were shocked by Helper's book because it was the first sustained attack on slavery by a white southerner. In the debate over the speakership, southerners attacked Republicans who had endorsed Helper's book.

Southerners in Congress, along with northern Democrats loyal to Buchanan, tried to blame Republicans for John Brown's raid at Harpers Ferry. Hearings led by Senator James Mason of Virginia and Jefferson Davis of Mississippi could establish no connection between Brown and any Republicans. Instead, they exposed the fearful—almost paranoid—state of mind of many southern leaders.

In Congress, Republicans combined with free-state Democrats to pass a homestead bill, offering 160 acres of free public land to anyone who would settle on it. Almost all opposition came from southerners, who feared the offer of free land would encourage settlers who were not slaveowners. Buchanan, appearing as always the pliant tool of the South, vetoed the bill. Southerners and a few Buchanan supporters from the North defeated a transcontinental railroad bill and a new tariff to protect northern industries. Buchanan increasingly stood for slavery and against economic progress or support for the small farmers of both sections who would benefit from free land and a railroad to take them to it. Meanwhile, Republicans exposed corruption in the War Department and in the issuing of government printing contracts. The postmaster general also discovered that the postmaster in New York City had fled the nation after stealing $160,000 from the government.

With Buchanan opposed to a homestead act, his allies in the Senate proposed a slave code to protect human property in the federal territories. Although it had no chance of passing, this proposal introduced by Jefferson Davis created a litmus test for Democrats—one that very few northern members of the Party could support. The slave-code debate laid the groundwork for the collapse of the Democratic party at its national convention in 1860.

## ECONOMICS, FOREIGN POLICY, AND THE DOUGHFACE ADMINISTRATION

By 1860 the nation was recovering from the Panic of 1857, which had put the nation's economy in a tailspin for two years. The panic began in August 1857, when the Ohio Life Insurance and Trust Company—which, despite its name, was actually a bank—

collapsed. Banks throughout the nation began to fail in the weeks that followed. By the end of October, banks in New York, New England, and Pennsylvania had suspended payment in specie. By the end of the year, only a few banks in Indiana, Kentucky, and New Orleans still redeemed their notes for specie. The nation was in a recession of major proportions.

Following traditional Jacksonian economic policies, Buchanan tried to tighten the money supply, just as the weakening economy needed an infusion of cash and capital. Northerners blamed the panic on a low tariff, which had been passed because of southern demands. In the Northwest many people blamed the panic on Buchanan's failure to move on a transcontinental railroad and on his opposition to internal improvements and a homestead bill. It is unclear whether these policies in fact caused the panic. Certainly they hurt a system already undermined by twenty years of foolish Democratic party hostility to a national bank. More important, Buchanan's policies—on tariffs, western improvements, and banking—once again appeared to favor the South at the expense of the North and the West. His policies of tight money and blind support for traditional Jacksonian hostility to a national banking system illustrated Buchanan's lack of imagination and leadership in the face of a painful economic crisis.

In foreign policy Buchanan's imagination was apparent only in its proslavery bias. Like his predecessors, he refused to live up to treaty obligations to enforce the ban on the African slave trade. He also threatened to use military force to prevent the British government from searching suspected slave traders if they were flying the U.S. flag. As a result, the U.S. flag became increasingly a banner of protection for illegal traders. Buchanan ordered the navy into the Gulf of Mexico to protect all ships flying the nation's flag, and in so doing he gave further U.S. protection to illegal slave traders. Meanwhile, he asked Congress for an appropriation of $30 million to buy Cuba, to create yet another slave state.

Buchanan refused to crack down on American filibusters, who sought to seize territory in Latin America. The most notorious of these was William Walker, who briefly and illegally seized Nicaragua. Walker was jailed in New Orleans, but he escaped after the Buchanan administration asked that bail be set at only a $2,000. Walker then went back to Nicaragua with a small army, but that foray ended when Commodore Hiram Pauling captured Walker near Nicaragua and brought him back to the United States, Buchanan ordered Walker released and, according to Elbert Smith's account, "reprimanded Pauling personally for exceeding his authority in leading an armed force into the territory of a friendly nation." Walker claimed Buchanan secretly encouraged his activities in Nicaragua, and there is substantial evidence to support his claim.

## THE ELECTION OF 1860

One measure of presidential leadership is the ability of a president to keep his party in power. Here, as in virtually all other areas of his administration, Buchanan was an abject failure. By 1860 only one Democrat—Stephen A. Douglas of Illinois—had any chance to win a national election: But from the moment Buchanan took office he insulted Douglas, ignored his supporters within the party, and denied him access to the patronage he deserved. Since the debate over the Lecompton constitution, Buchanan had even been trying to expel Douglas from the party and destroy his career.

Buchanan had always disliked—indeed hated—Douglas. By 1860 he considered him a threat to the nation because Douglas refused to placate the South on all issues. Buchanan expected Douglas to support every southern demand, even at the cost of his political career. Had Douglas supported Kansas statehood under the Lecompton constitution he would probably have lost his Senate seat and Republicans might have done even better in the 1858 elections. Buchanan could never comprehend either the intensity of northern opposition to the spread of slavery or the necessity of occasionally placating northern opinion on the question of slavery. This in part stemmed from his odd career. Since his reelection to the Senate in 1840, Buchanan had not been personally involved in politics in the North. His last position before winning the nomination had been overseas. He was truly out of touch with his own section, which by 1860 held the overwhelming majority of the nation's population.

At the 1860 Democratic conventions the party fractured, and its northern wing nominated Stephen A. Douglas. Although many in the party pleaded with Buchanan to endorse Douglas, as Douglas had done for him four years earlier, the president refused. Southern delegates held their own rump convention and nominated Buchanan's friend and vice president, John C. Breckinridge. Meanwhile, in Chicago the Republicans had already nominated Abraham Lincoln after only four ballots. Even before any of these nominations had occurred, the remnants of the Whigs and Know-Nothings had joined a few disaffected Democrats to create the Constitutional-Union party, nominating John Bell of Tennessee, who ran with Edward Everett of Massachusetts.

Buchanan doubtless hoped that the election would produce no victor. If Breckinridge carried the South, and Douglas, Lincoln, and Bell split the North, then there would be no majority in the electoral college. The names of the two candidates with the most electoral votes would then go to the House of Representatives, where each state would have one vote. Buchanan was confident that all the slave states and at least two free states—Oregon and California—would support Breckinridge and his runningmate, Senator Joseph Lane of Oregon. Thus, Buchanan used all of his patronage powers to gain support for Breckinridge.

Like other strategies Buchanan embraced during his presidency, this strategy was misguided. Lincoln carried all of the North and a majority of the electoral college. Buchanan's lifelong allies and friends from the deep South now openly moved to leave the Union. By the time he left office, seven southern states had announced their withdrawal from the United States and the creation of a new nation, dedicated to the proposition that slavery was a positive good to be perpetuated forever.

## THE SECESSION WINTER

Buchanan blamed secession on northerners, abolitionists, Abraham Lincoln, and Stephen A. Douglas. Buchanan thought secession was wrong, and he certainly did not want to see the Union destroyed. He also doubtless felt betrayed by the South's leaving the Union while he was still president. As Elbert Smith wrote, "The Southerners knew that he had long been their faithful ally, and their unwillingness to wait for Lincoln was most ungrateful."

In the weeks after Lincoln's election Buchanan was paralyzed; he knew secession was coming but he did not know what to do about it. He said nothing until his annual address in early December. Then he proposed a constitutional convention to solve the problems of the nation. He simultaneously denied the right of the southern states to secede and also denied that he as president could stop them. He blamed only the North, complaining that the crisis had been caused by the "incessant and violent agitation of the slavery question throughout the North for the last quarter of a century."

As always, Buchanan failed to see the threats that southern demands posed to civil liberties and civil rights in the North and the territories, and he failed to grasp the moral problem of slavery itself. Once again, he misunderstood his own section. In calling for a convention to resolve the problems of the nation, Buchanan essentially asked the North to surrender to the South on all issues concerning slavery. Buchanan would have nullified the 1860 election by constitutional convention.

In the end, the president did nothing, as his government and his nation collapsed around him. All his career he had supported the South, and he was perhaps the most proslavery president since the passage of the Missouri Compromise. But while he stood by the South, the South left him. Throughout November southern states began to call for secession conventions. To no one's surprise, the South Carolina legislature led the way, voting on 9 November to hold an election for a state convention on 6 December and setting a date for that convention to meet on 17 December. Mississippi, Alabama, Florida, Georgia, and Louisiana soon followed South Carolina. On 8 December Buchanan's longtime friend, Treasury Secretary Howell Cobb of Georgia, left the cabinet.

Fearful he might offend southerners, who were rapidly leaving the Union, Buchanan refused to reinforce U.S. forts in South Carolina and Florida. On 12 December General Winfield Scott asked that reinforcements be sent to Fort Sumter, in Charleston Harbor. When Buchanan refused, Secretary of State Lewis Cass resigned in protest. Buchanan then moved Attorney General Jeremiah S. Black to State and replaced him with Edwin B. Stanton, the first openly antislavery member of a cabinet in anyone's memory.

The most pronounced evidence of Buchanan's failure of leadership was who he kept in his cabinet. On 22 December Buchanan discovered that John B. Floyd of Virginia was involved in a massive embezzlement, or at least misappropriation of funds, perpetrated in the War Department by a relative of Floyd's wife. Instead of firing Floyd, Buchanan allowed him to remain in office, hindering any possible defense of Sumter and other forts in the South. Floyd had previously told Assistant Secretary of State William H. Trescot, a South Carolinian, that he would cut off his right arm rather than approve any reinforcements for the southern forts. Two days before the embezzlement scandal broke, Floyd had ordered that a heavy cannon, which had been cast in Pittsburgh, be sent to a Texas fort at a time when Texas was taking steps to leave the Union. With secessionists everywhere, Buchanan did almost nothing.

Buchanan's only positive act in this period was to approve the appointment of Major Robert Anderson as commander of the U.S. forces in the Charleston area. Buchanan hoped that Anderson's Kentucky background would placate the South. On December 27, Anderson spiked all the cannon at Fort Moultrie, in Charleston, and moved all his troops to Fort Sumter, the most defensible position on Charleston harbor. Only when Floyd denounced this action did Buchanan finally remove him from office. At the same time, Buchanan reversed Floyd's attempt to send the newly produced cannon to Texas.

However, Buchanan also indicated that he was prepared to give up Sumter in exchange for a promise of peace from South Carolina. On hearing that proposal, Black, Stanton, and Joseph Holt, the Unionist postmaster general from Kentucky, all threatened to resign, and Buchanan backed down. He had no southern friends he could count on any longer; he could ill afford to lose those from the North he trusted most. Instead, he sent a ship, the *Star of the West*, to reinforce and resupply Fort Sumter. He had failed, however, to warn Major Anderson of this plan, and when the South Carolina shore batteries fired on the *Star of the West*, Anderson did not fire back in its defense. The ship retreated, and Sumter remained under siege. Buchanan looked weak and ineffective to the North, and the South branded him as an enemy.

Only a few weeks earlier, General Scott had reminded the president of Andrew Jackson's success in stopping the South Carolina nullifiers with a show of force and strong backbone. But, Buchanan could not muster the first and lacked the second. As the nation drifted into dissolution, Buchanan remained weak. On 18 February, even before Buchanan was out of office, the Confederate States of America inaugurated Jefferson Davis and Alexander Hamilton Stephens as president and vice president of the new nation.

Finally, on 4 March Buchanan left office. His outgoing secretary of war, Joseph Holt, informed President Lincoln that Fort Sumter was in dire straights, nearly out of food, and that relief of the fort was probably impossible. Holt claimed this surprised him, but in fact he had known the situation for weeks. The entire outgoing administration had watched as the authority of the U.S.

government disappeared throughout the South while Buchanan did nothing.

## CONCLUSION

Buchanan's retirement was neither peaceful nor satisfying. War broke out within a month after he left office. The public blamed, not inappropriately, the Old Public Functionary for the condition of the nation when Lincoln took office. The failure of the Buchanan presidency was monumental. He left a shattered nation to his successor. He had developed no policy for keeping the nation together, made no plans to uphold the Constitution, and made no preparations for the coming war.

Newspapers and politicians alike accused him of arming the South in the last year of his presidency, supporting secession in office, and working for the Confederacy after he left office. Most of these accusations were overblown, and the last was clearly false. Many northerners, including some of his neighbors, considered him a traitor. This was probably unfair, but Buchanan opposed virtually all of the Lincoln administration's policies, and even in the midst of the war wanted to make peace and bring the South back into the Union with slavery protected.

In his 1866 memoir, *Mr. Buchanan's Administration on the Eve of the Rebellion*, the ex-president attacked Republicans, abolitionists, and all opponents of slavery for causing the war. Buchanan opposed emancipation, civil rights for blacks, racial equality, and of course black suffrage. The book, like much of his career, was a proslavery apologia.

In the 1920s and 1930s, scholars approached the coming of the Civil War from the perspective of national leadership. The cause of the war, these scholars argued, was a blundering generation of incompetent leaders. This analysis is out of fashion today. Most scholars agree with Buchanan's successor, who noted in his second inaugural, that "All knew that" the southern interest in slavery "was somehow the cause of the war. To strengthen, perpetuate, and extend this institution was the object for which the insurgents would rend the Union even by war."

But, to understand that slavery caused the war—and even to believe that slavery made the war inevitable—is not to believe that its timing was inevitable. Certainly the blundering generation of presidents from Fillmore to Buchanan set the stage for the war. In the end, Buchanan was the most blundering of them all. He left a legacy of a failed presidency and a nation nearly destroyed. If he left anything of value to the nation, it was that he had set the stage for his successor, who turned out to be the greatest of presidents, ironically following the nation's worst president.

## BIBLIOGRAPHY

Birkner, Michael J. *James Buchanan and the Political Crisis of the 1850s* (Susquehanna University Press, 1996).

Buchanan, James. *Mr. Buchanan's Administration on the Eve of the Rebellion* (Appleton, 1866).

Finkelman, Paul. *Dred Scott v. Sandford: A Brief History, with Documents* (Bedford Books, 1997).

———, ed. *His Soul Goes Marching On: Responses to John Brown and the Harpers Ferry Raid* (University Press of Virginia, 1995).

Klein, Philip S. *President James Buchanan* (Pennsylvania State University Press, 1962).

Potter, David. *The Impending Crisis: 1848–1861* (Harper & Row, 1976).

Smith, Elbert B. *The Presidency of James Buchanan* (University Press of Kansas, 1975).

Stampp, Kenneth. *America in 1857* (Oxford University Press, 1990).

———. *And the War Came* (Louisiana State University Press, 1950).

★★★ 16 ★★★

# ABRAHAM LINCOLN
## 1861–1865

*Richard J. Ellis*

*Born 12 February 1809 in Hodgenville, Hardin County (now Larue County), Kentucky, to Thomas Lincoln and Nancy Hanks Lincoln; read law and admitted to the bar; married Mary Todd, 4 November 1842, Springfield, Illinois; four children; elected president in 1860 on the Republican ticket with Hannibal Hamlin of Maine, receiving 1,866,452 popular votes and 180 electoral college votes, over the regular Democratic party ticket of Stephen A. Douglas of Illinois and Herschel V. Johnson of Georgia (1,375,157 and 12 electoral ballots), the southern Democratic party ticket of John Breckinridge of Kentucky and Joseph Lane of Oregon (847,953 and 72 electoral votes), and the Constitutional Union ticket of John Bell of Tennessee and Edward Everett of Massachusetts (590,631 and 39 electoral votes); reelected in 1864 on the Republican/Union Party ticket with Andrew Johnson of Tennessee, receiving 2,213,635 popular votes and 212 electoral college ballots over the Democratic ticket of George B. McClellan of New York and George H. Pendleton of Ohio (1,805,237 popular votes and 21 electoral ballots—11 Confederate states with 80 electoral ballots did not vote); died 15 April 1865, Washington, D.C., the first president to be assassinated; buried in Oak Ridge Cemetery, Springfield, Illinois.*

We remember Abraham Lincoln as a great statesman; we forget he was a gifted politician. We remember him as a symbol of national unity, yet too often forget that he was thoroughly partisan. We cherish him as our most beloved president, but forget how hated he was, not only by the South but also by abolitionists and antislavery Republicans who felt Lincoln was inept and spineless. We remember Lincoln as an exemplar of humane understanding and compassion, ignoring his burning political ambition and his frequent bouts of depression. We wish our contemporary presidents could be as forceful and strong as Lincoln was, yet we overlook that it was the extraordinary circumstances of the war that gave Lincoln the warrant to act as he did. How we have chosen to remember Lincoln tells us a great deal about American political culture, especially our deep suspicion of politics, politicians, and political parties, but it obscures Lincoln himself, specifically his political talents and the historical circumstances that made him a successful president.

## LINCOLN THE WHIG

From early manhood Lincoln identified with and actively participated in party politics. The trouble for Lincoln was that his chosen party, the Whig party, was a vehicle ill suited to his national political ambitions. Henry Clay, the Whig standard-bearer and Lincoln's political idol, lost all three presidential elections in which he participated. The only Whig successes in presidential contests, General William Henry Harrison in 1840 and General Zachary Taylor in 1848, had depended on submerging party principles and policies. From the sobering experience of Clay's defeats in 1836 and 1844, as well as from the victories of the apolitical generals in 1840 and 1848, Lincoln learned that his own personal advancement would depend on creating a party that could elevate not only famous military heroes but an Illinois party politician to the presidential office. To make the Whig party a majority party required transforming the party's political culture, specifically subor-

dinating its marked paternalism and even elitism to a democratic individualism more in tune with the aspirations of the young American nation.

In presidential politics in the 1830s and 1840s, the Whigs' most popular cause had been the cry of executive usurpation. In the Whig mind, "King Andrew [Jackson]" signified the degeneration of egalitarianism into the charismatic leader who would replace the law with his personal wishes. In an 1837 address before the Young Men's Lyceum of Springfield, Illinois, Abraham Lincoln delivered a typical Whig warning against the charismatic leader. Firmly grounded in the legal tradition of conservative Whig jurisprudence, with its respect for law and belief in strong government, Lincoln admonished his young audience not to be seduced by the "towering genius" who "disdains a beaten path." Such a demagogue, warned Lincoln, would disregard precedent and convention, trample on established laws, and tear down the careful work of the founders. Lincoln pleaded for the American people to make "reverence for the laws . . . the political religion of the nation."

The Whigs were torn between their hierarchical inclination to support central authority and their fear of the disruptive potential of presidential power. The result was that they wanted an anomalous executive, one who stood for, but did not actually exercise, authority. The chief executive was to enforce the laws of the land but otherwise was to be confined within narrowly circumscribed limits: no veto power, no congressional influence. As president, Lincoln had to reconcile the Whig doctrine of presidential power with his own will to power and the achievement of his political goals of restoring the Union, building up the fledgling Republican party, and eventually ridding the country of slavery.

What was the relationship between the Whiggish Lincoln of the Lyceum speech and Lincoln the Republican president? Was he, as David Donald maintains, essentially a Whig in the White House or, as Stephen Oates contends, had Lincoln jettisoned his

Whig past in becoming a Republican in the White House? How did Lincoln reconcile his career as an orthodox Whig in the 1830s and 1840s with his subsequent identity as a Republican proponent of "free soil, free labor, free men"? Lincoln struggled with the question of what it meant to be a Republican. "I think I am a whig," he mused in an 1855 letter to a friend, "but others say there are no whigs, and that I am an abolitionist." During the latter half of the 1850s Lincoln would be instrumental in creating a new Republican party identity that by synthesizing Whiggery with aspects of Jacksonian political culture would dominate U.S. politics for the next half century.

## LINCOLN THE REPUBLICAN

The Republican party of Lincoln, as Daniel Walker Howe has brilliantly shown, left the old Whig paternalism behind. In place of Whiggish condescension, Lincoln glorified upward social mobility, making himself the cultural archetype. "The old hierarchical idea of a harmony of interests between classes," Howe explains, "was not encouraged by the Republicans. Instead they argued that America ought to become a classless society, in which individual initiative and hard work received their just reward when the laborer became a capitalist in his own right."

The Republican move away from hierarchy and toward competitive individualism manifested itself in a number of specific policy areas. Where the Whigs had promoted mixed public-private corporations, the Republicans opted for a system of free enterprise aided by subsidies. The Republican party also overcame the Whig fear of western expansion, and many—like Lincoln—reversed their previous opposition to free land for homesteaders. Such policy changes were both cause and consequence of the migration of a sizable segment of former Democrats into the Republican party. With hierarchical Whiggery clearly subordinated to a democratic individualism, the Republican party could attract and hold the support of antislavery Democrats. As president, Lincoln helped foster the Republican synthesis

of Democratic and Whig political cultures by selecting a cabinet that included four ex-Democrats: Montgomery Blair, Salmon Chase, Simon Cameron, and Gideon Wells.

The political isolation and confusion of the more hierarchical Whigs during the 1850s is further evidence of the extent to which the Republican party had transformed its political culture. Rufus Choate, who had so much in common with the Lincoln of the Lyceum address, now turned to the Democratic party of James Buchanan. Other leading spokesmen for conservative New England Whiggery, such as Josiah Quincy and Edward Everett, felt they had been left without a party with which they could identify.

Still, Lincoln did retain some important elements of hierarchical Whiggery. The hierarch's sense of a "duty to posterity" to preserve and transmit the work of past generations, expressed so vividly by Lincoln in the Lyceum speech, remained with him as president. "Fellow citizens, we cannot escape history," he declared in his annual message to Congress in 1862. "The fiery trial through which we pass will light us down, in honor or dishonor, to the latest generation." Two years later Lincoln told the nation, "We are striving to maintain the government and institutions of our fathers, to enjoy them ourselves, and transmit them to our children and our children's children forever."

Lincoln's rhetoric during the Civil War also drew upon the hierarchical conception of the need for the parts to sacrifice for the whole. Lincoln, as Howe points out, "fulfilled the hopes of Whig conservatives like Daniel Webster and Choate, who had wanted to endow American nationality with a sacrosanct aura." Having elevated the Union "to the sublimity of a religious mysticism," in Alexander Stephens's words, "Father Abraham" was able to call on individuals and states to sacrifice life and limb for the good of the collectivity.

Moreover, it is important to remember, as historian George Fredrickson reminds us, that when Lincoln confronted the secession crisis as president-elect "he presented himself primarily as defender of law and order, a champion of the procedural community against those who refused to abide by a public decision constitutionally arrived at." There appears here a recognizable continuity with the prescription of the Lyceum speech "never to violate in the least particular, the laws of the country; and never to tolerate their violation by others." Yet, as Fredrickson also points out, "the Lincoln of the 1850s was not purely and simply what he had been in the late 1830s—a conservative of the rational-legalistic persuasion." In the hierarchical view of conservative Whigs, the true object of war with the South, as James Russell Lowell put it, was "maintenance of the idea of Government." By contrast, Lincoln explicitly defined the Civil War as a struggle "to elevate the condition of men—to lift artificial weights from all shoulders—to clear the paths of laudable pursuit for all—to afford all an unfettered start, and a fair chance, in the race of life." For Lincoln, the purpose of the war was not only to reaffirm national authority but also to vindicate the northern system of free labor and democracy, both a competitive economic system and a competitive political system.

## LEADERSHIP IN AN ANTILEADERSHIP SYSTEM

Downplaying the paternalism of Whiggery while stressing the individualism of the Republican party helped make Lincoln the sixteenth president of the United States. But shackled with the Whig antiexecutive tradition, the slavery issue, and an antileadership system, the prospects for presidential leadership looked bleak. The presidencies of James Buchanan, Franklin Pierce, and Millard Fillmore were grim reminders of the extraordinary impediments to effective leadership during this period.

Although we will never know whether Lincoln desired the onset of war to resolve the dilemmas handcuffing his party, there is no doubt that a Lincoln presidency apart from the Civil War is inconceivable. The firing on Fort Sumter provided Lincoln with an opportunity to avoid his predeces-

sors' fate, for now the slavery issue, which had split parties and shackled presidents in the previous decade, actually served as a means for expanding presidential power. A widespread perception of crisis empowered the presidency, permitting Lincoln to reconcile personal ambition and Whig theory.

Support for authority, however, even during war, was far from automatic. Lincoln's behavior as president reflected his acute awareness that support for leadership in the United States was meager at best. Lincoln understood (as John Adams and John Quincy Adams had not) that given the weakness of a hierarchical political culture in the United States, a leader could not rely on the formal authority of office alone. Although Lincoln occupied an office of great formal power, it was, as J. G. Randall observes, "a power that had to be exercised with deference. He could govern, but only if his governing voice was not too bluntly audible." To counteract the political system's inherent tendency to dissipate power, Lincoln had to act "with the tact of a moderator instead of the scowl of a dictator."

The willingness of a predominantly individualist population to trust in government, even during wartime, was sharply limited. Military setbacks were blamed not on the North's lack of military preparedness but on the "fixed belief that the managers . . . at Washington are incompetent." The government's demands for additional material sacrifices were met with skepticism from individualists who wanted some indication that their sacrifices would not again be wasted. The weakness of hierarchy in the North was underlined by the utterly inadequate method of raising troops. It took two years to set up a system of national conscription, and even then a drafted man could gain exemption from service by either raising $300 or furnishing an acceptable substitute. "Bounty brokers" flourished as a result of the elaborate system of bounties designed to encourage volunteering. The individualist's preferred way of life, bidding and bargaining, proved to be a very expensive and inefficient way to fight a total war.

Given the enormous human and material costs of the Civil War, together with the entrenched antiauthority and anti-Washington sentiments of the population, popular wrath was bound to strike the national government and the president. One of Lincoln's tasks, therefore, was to set up lightning rods that could deflect the full brunt of popular anger when the Union army suffered reverses. To shield himself from the torrent of abuse, Lincoln skillfully used the old Whig executive doctrine. Lincoln's need to exert leadership in an antileadership system explains that "peculiar paradox" of his presidency first pointed out by David Donald in his seminal essay, "Whig in the White House."

## THE WHIG IN THE WHITE HOUSE

Donald contrasts Lincoln's vigorous extralegal use of executive authority in regard to his war power with the timid, obsequious, virtual nonuse of presidential resources to influence domestic policy. "Were I president," Lincoln had written in 1848, "I should desire the legislation of the country to rest with Congress, uninfluenced by the executive in its origin or progress, and undisturbed by the veto unless in very special and clear cases." Donald contends that Lincoln, as president, showed little interest over a wide range of domestic policies, including tariffs and banking, the introduction of the first income tax, creation of the Department of Agriculture, and land-grant colleges. "Less than any other major American President," concludes Donald, "did Lincoln control or even influence the Congress." Indeed, when his proposed appointees were turned down by the Senate, Lincoln thought it improper even to resubmit their names.

What explains the paradox of a chief executive simultaneously strong and weak? Donald argues that Lincoln's puzzling behavior in the presidency stemmed not from lack of time for domestic policy but rather from an inability to "rid himself of the political ideas with which he had been raised." And Donald continues, "Both in strongly

asserting his war powers and in weakly deferring to Congress, he was following the Whig creed in which he was raised."

Though not explicitly taking issue with Donald's thesis, Gabor Boritt's interpretation of Lincoln's behavior in the White House undercuts Donald's contention that Lincoln's Whig "political education" explains the paradox of his presidency. Lincoln, points out Boritt, faced a Congress dominated by a Republican party that was in essential agreement with Lincoln's preferred economic policies. Therefore, "there was little call for Lincoln to pressure Senators and Congressmen, to use those 'certain indirect influences' on behalf of 'sound' economics." Lincoln did not have to work so hard because Congress was already disposed to do much of what he liked with regard to tariffs, internal improvements, finance, and homestead legislation. "Lincoln thus had the pleasure of signing into law much of the program he had worked for through the better part of his political life," legislation that amounted to what one historian has called a "blueprint for modern America."

Boritt also shows that Lincoln was much more active in domestic policy than he appeared to either Donald or to his own contemporaries. When it came to establishing a national banking system, for instance, Lincoln did attempt to influence Congress. He sent one of his private secretaries to sway wavering senators, persuaded influential senators to go to bat for him, talked the matter up in the cabinet, and even seems to have cashed in on patronage, all the while exclaiming to New York financiers, "Money, I don't know anything about money."

Lincoln, Boritt explains, "took up a Whiggishly circumspect championship of almost the full range of his old economic policies. He felt free to follow such a . . . course because to the country it could appear as part of the war effort." Put another way, the sharp distinction that Donald draws between domestic and war measures was in fact quite blurred. A sound and stable financial system, in the view of Lincoln and his fellow Republicans, was essential to the Northern war effort.

"The Whig in the White House," Boritt shows, "knew when to apply his theory of the executive, and also when to discard it." One area in which Lincoln completely disregarded Whig theory was southern Reconstruction. His pocket veto of the Wade-Davis bill, a radical Reconstruction measure endorsed by virtually the entire Republican party, violated the most hallowed Whig precept. Lincoln's Whig political education, which taught him of the "despotism" of the veto power, proved to be much less restraining than Donald assumed. Reconstruction did not come prelabeled as a war issue or a domestic issue. Here as elsewhere, this ambiguity gave Lincoln discretion to decide what he would consider within his purview while still nominally adhering to Whig doctrine.

Given the lack of support for presidential leadership among political elites as well as the public at large, Lincoln knew he had to rest content with the fewest possible priorities: unity to win the war, and achieving whatever national economic policy was possible without making a target of himself. When Lincoln overstepped the bounds of "the light-handed Whig executive," Congress often subjected him to contemptuous treatment. A Whiggish deference toward Congress, Boritt rightly observes, "helped cultivate the goodwill of Capitol Hill." Lincoln's Whiggish behavior as president, then, was not simply dictated by early political education but rather was a conscious political strategy, an adaptive response to a systemic suspicion of presidential leadership.

What about Lincoln's "curious failure" to control his cabinet, which Donald sees as compelling evidence of the grip the Whig view of the presidency had on Lincoln. This interpretation neglects the advantages Lincoln reaped by distancing himself from cabinet members. "When Congress showed unhappiness with executive direction," Boritt points out, "the separation between the President and his official family often diverted the legislators to attacking the latter. With the Cabinet absorbing much of

the fire, the White House could often escape unscorched." When Lincoln decided not to enforce congressional acts confiscating the property of slave owners, for example, Attorney General Edward Bates took most of the heat from the radicals.

Likewise, the relatively free hand given to Salmon Chase as secretary of the treasury was well suited to deflecting criticism away from the president. Lincoln knew full well that raising the financial resources necessary to support a war was not likely to be easy—getting individualists to fight was often easier than getting them to pay. By leaving the obligation of raising taxes to the treasury secretary and Congress, Lincoln was able, as Boritt puts it, to take "refuge in his Whiggishness," letting public displeasure at higher taxes fall on other heads.

We may be excused for believing that this man, whose intellect was as formidable as any this nation has produced, was fooling his fellow Americans by his avowals of naiveté or disinterest about such matters as banking, finance, and foreign affairs—"You understand these things. I do not," Lincoln told Chase. Allowing his cabinet members to think themselves superior may have given Lincoln protection against what would otherwise have been a crescendo cry of usurpation. His humble stance, the log cabin stories, and similar postures served as a shield against the nation's pervasive antiauthority bias.

## SPEAKING FOR THE PEOPLE
Just how decisively Republican President Lincoln broke with his Whiggish past can be seen by focusing on the transformation in Lincoln's conception of the relationship between the president and the people. As a young Whig congressman from Illinois, Lincoln had vigorously defended presidential candidate Zachary Taylor against Democratic charges that Taylor had failed to articulate his opinions on the leading issues of the day. Taylor's insistence that leading questions should be decided by "the will of the people, as expressed through their representatives in congress," was not evidence that Taylor lacked principles, Lincoln said,

but rather a demonstration of the general's firm adherence to "the true republican position, . . . the principle of allowing the people to . . . have their own way, regardless of [the president's] private opinions." Executive deference to Congress was in reality deference to the people.

To those Democrats who argued that "the president is as much the representative of the people as Congress," Lincoln conceded that the president was "in a certain sense, and to a certain extent . . . the representative of the people" because the president and the Congress were both elected by the people. But the president, Lincoln insisted, "in the nature [of] things, [could not] know the wants of the people, as well as three hundred other men, coming from all the various localities of the nation." The Whig party and their standard bearer, Lincoln continued, were committed to not transferring legislative responsibilities away "from those who understand, with minuteness, the interests of the people, and giv[ing] it to one who does not, and cannot so well understand it." Taylor's deference to Congress was thus entirely appropriate and reflected his own and his party's trust in the people.

Lincoln's speech, however, did more than echo the standard Whig attack on the Jacksonian doctrine of presidential power. Lincoln went deeper still, raising profound objections to the practice of presidents' claiming popular mandates for specific policies. The Jacksonian idea, as Lincoln understood it, was that "if a presidential candidate avow his opinion upon a given question, or rather, upon all questions, and the people, with full knowledge of this, elect him, they thereby distinctly approve all those opinions." Although admitting that this idea might initially seem plausible, Lincoln condemned it as "a most pernicious deception." For by means of it, "measures are adopted or rejected, contrary to the wishes of the whole of one party, and often nearly half of the other." This was because a candidate's positions "are strung together; and [voters] must take all, or reject all. They cannot take what they like, and leave the rest." There were many issues, Lincoln was saying, but only one vote.

This was particularly a problem, Lincoln suggested, given the strong ties of party. If a presidential candidate took a position that was opposed by a majority within his party, there was tremendous pressure for partisans to "shut their eyes, and gulp the whole." The party is then forced to sustain the president's position, as during Jackson's bank war, and that position becomes a permanent part of the party platform. Lincoln believed that "almost, if not quite all the articles of the present Democratic [party] creed, have been at first forced upon the party in this very way." And he worried that in the coming election, opposition to internal improvements would be established in the same way if Democrat Lewis Cass was elected, even though a clear majority of the nation favored supporting improvements.

Like Henry Clay and Daniel Webster, Lincoln was better as a critic of the mandate concept than at creating a satisfying alternative interpretation of the meaning of presidential elections or a persuasive account of the president's relationship to the people. Lincoln's Whiggish preference for "making Presidential elections, and the legislation of the country, distinct matters; so that the people can elect whom they please, and afterwards, legislate just as they please, without any hindrance" hardly seemed satisfactory. For as Lincoln himself conceded, the president was elected by the people, just as Congress was. And presidents were widely asked and expected, just as members of Congress were, to give their views on leading issues of the day. It was no longer plausible to describe a presidential candidate's political opinions as merely "private opinions," particularly since partisan conflict was increasingly centered on the presidential contest. Why should a popularly elected, not to mention independent, branch of government simply carry out the legislature's bidding? Lincoln's answer—that the legislature was only doing the people's bidding—begged too many hard questions.

## RECONSTRUCTING PRESIDENTIAL POWER

Upon assuming the presidency, Lincoln quickly found that the Whig conception of the president as only an instrument of the legislative will was both unduly restrictive and impractical. After the firing on Fort Sumter, Lincoln delayed calling the legislature into session for several months so that he could act without congressional interference. Upon meeting Congress on 4 July 1861, Lincoln explained that the measures he had adopted, "whether strictly legal or not, were ventured upon, under what appeared to be a popular demand, and a public necessity; trusting, then as now, that Congress would readily ratify them." So much for the president as merely an executor of the legislative will.

Though Lincoln's expansive use of presidential power clearly imperiled Whig doctrine and worried many Whigs-turned-Republicans, it is significant that throughout most of his first term Lincoln tried to justify his power on grounds that many ex-Whigs could accept. First, Lincoln emphasized that his oath to preserve the Constitution imposed upon him the duty to take extraordinary actions that he deemed necessary to national self-preservation. Lincoln eased concerns about expanding presidential power by emphasizing the extraordinary if not unique character of the emergency. Second, Lincoln cloaked his power in the president's role as commander-in-chief of the armed forces. Lincoln's Emancipation Proclamation, for instance, began by invoking "the power in me vested as Commander-in-Chief of the Army and Navy." Congressional Republicans who defended Lincoln also stressed the commander-in-chief clause as the warrant for presidential actions.

As the end of the war grew near, and as attention increasingly focused on the question of how to reconstruct a defeated South, Lincoln faced the prospect of governing without the two constitutional warrants—preserving the Constitution and acting as commander-in-chief—that had sustained him during the war. Throughout his first term, Lincoln had skillfully distributed patronage and discreetly used his powers of persuasion to build support for his objectives, but by themselves these powers could not possibly be adequate if Lincoln wanted Reconstruction to bear a strong presidential imprint. Reconstruction thus impelled Lincoln to repudiate explicitly and decisively the Whig doctrine of presidential power that he had expounded as a congressman.

Throughout the war, even with one of their own in the White House, prominent ex-Whigs in the Republican party continued to insist that the president was an agent of the legislative will. According to Charles Sumner, the president was "only the instrument of Congress, under the Constitution." Massachusetts's other senator, Henry Wilson, agreed that "it is our duty as the Representatives of the States and of the people to indicate to those who administer the laws of the country what we think the policy of this Government should be." Even a Democrat turned Republican like Illinois Senator Lyman Trumbull insisted that the president "is just as much subject to our control as if we appointed him, except that we cannot remove him and substitute another in his place."

The Wade-Davis bill, passed on 2 July 1864 with near-unanimous Republican support in Congress, laid down conditions under which southern states would be readmitted to the Union, and it asserted that the task of Reconstruction was a congressional rather than an executive responsibility. Lincoln promptly pocket-vetoed the bill and then issued a short proclamation explaining his position to the public. He noted that the plan contained in the bill "expresses the sense of Congress" but that he felt it was now proper "to lay [that plan] before the people for their consideration." The legislative will, Lincoln was suggesting, could not be assumed necessarily to reflect the popular will.

Even moderate Republicans were angry with Lincoln for vetoing the legislation; the bill's authors, Henry Wade Davis and Benjamin Wade, both former Whigs, were apoplectic. In the infamous Wade-Davis Manifesto, they blasted Lincoln for "dictatorial usurpation," and vigorously reaffirmed the Whig conception of a limited executive. The authority of Congress, they insisted, was "paramount and must be respected." Never had "a more studied outrage on the legislative authority of the people . . . been perpetrated." Davis and Wade warned that "if [the president] wishes our support, he must confine himself to his Executive duties—to obey and execute, not make the laws—to suppress by arms armed rebellion, and leave political reorganization to Congress."

The Wade-Davis Manifesto was a reminder of the intensity with which many former Whigs held to their old antiexecutive bias; but Republicans' strong negative reaction to the Wade-Davis Manifesto shows even more starkly how the party system undercut Whig doctrine. Even the most outspoken Republican radicals, aware that both their own fate and the cause of emancipation were tied to Lincoln's electoral fortunes, were sharply critical of the manifesto's scathing denunciation of the Republican nominee. So powerful were the ties of party that within six weeks even Wade and Davis were campaigning for Lincoln.

If, as Charles Sumner said during the midterm election campaign of 1862, the Republican party went to the country "with the President for its head, and Emancipation its glorious watchword," then where did that leave the old Whig view of the president as merely an instrument of Congress? And if Lincoln and the Republican party stood for the abolition of slavery through constitutional amendment, as affirmed in the Republican party platform adopted in June 1864, then what was left of the old Whig view of elections as judgments on character rather than as mandates on policies? The short answer is that very little was left. In the 1864 presidential election, the old Whig view would be thoroughly transformed by the Republicans' need and de-

sire to claim popular approbation for their party's policies.

## THE ELECTION OF 1864 AS A MANDATE TO END SLAVERY

From the outset of the 1864 campaign, Lincoln had determined to make the presidential election a referendum on slavery. Working behind the scenes, Lincoln insisted that a proposal to amend the Constitution to abolish slavery be included in the Republican platform. He then publicly affirmed his support for such a constitutional amendment in his proclamation explaining his pocket-veto of the Wade-Davis bill, and at several junctures during the fall campaign he reiterated his support for the abolition of slavery.

Immediately after Lincoln's reelection, Republicans claimed that the president's triumph represented a popular mandate for the abolition of slavery. At least one Republican senator even used the word itself. Lincoln's triumph, Sumner argued,

> is kindred to that famous jubilee in sacred history, when the mandate went forth, "Proclaim Liberty throughout all the land, unto all the inhabitants thereof: it shall be a jubilee unto you; and ye shall return every man unto his possession, and ye shall return every man unto his family." And now this same mandate has gone forth, assuring the return of patriot Unionists to their possessions, and the return of patriot soldiers to their families, and crowning all with Universal Emancipation, the sign and seal of union and peace. Such is the mandate of the American people in the reelection of Abraham Lincoln. I pray that it may all be executed promptly and triumphantly.

Sumner, who just two years earlier had called the president "an instrument of Congress," now loudly trumpeted the Jacksonian notion that the people expressed their policy preferences directly through the president.

In 1860, any inclination Lincoln might have had to claim a popular mandate was undermined by the fact that he had won only about half the states and polled slightly under 40 percent of the popular vote. In contrast, Lincoln's decisive victory in 1864—he lost only three states and won 55 percent of the popular vote—placed him in good position to parlay his electoral victory into a warrant for power. Moreover, the initial reactions to his victory suggested widespread support among Republican elites for interpreting his election as an expression of popular opinions. Lincoln's incentive to use the election results in this way was increased by the impending end of the war, which meant that Republicans and Democrats alike would be less inclined to let Lincoln rely so heavily on the commander-in-chief clause. Lincoln, then, had both the opportunity and motive to exploit the mandate; but would this lifelong Whig do so?

An unambiguous affirmative answer came in Lincoln's last State of the Union address, delivered on 6 December 1864. Lincoln recommended to Congress "the reconsideration and passage" of the proposed constitutional amendment abolishing slavery, a measure the House had considered and defeated less than six months before. Lincoln conceded that "of course the abstract question is not changed," but he pointed to the recently concluded election as definitive evidence that the people favored such a constitutional amendment. While careful to deny "that the election has imposed a duty on members to change their views or their votes," Lincoln insisted that through the election,

> the voice of the people [is] now for the first time heard upon the question. In a great national crisis, like ours, unanimity of action among those seeking a common end is very desirable—almost indispensable. And yet no approach to such unanimity is attainable, unless some deference shall be paid to the will of the majority, simply because it is the will of the majority. In this case the common end is the maintenance of the Union; and, among the means to secure that end, such will, through the election, is most clearly declared in favor of such a constitutional amendment.

Lincoln's switch from Whig to Republican was complete, and the idea of a presidential mandate from the people, once a fiercely contested partisan issue, had become something that presidents of either party could claim.

At the time Lincoln delivered his message, the fate of the proposed Thirteenth Amendment was still very much in doubt. The Senate had already approved the proposed amendment, but when it came before the House in June it fell well short of the two-thirds vote required. To gain the needed Democratic votes, Lincoln invited a number of lame duck Democrats for informal interviews at the White House, and various administration proxies aggressively lobbied wavering Democrats. Lincoln's willingness to use his powers of persuasion and patronage were critical to the eventual passage of the proposal on 31 January 1865, but perhaps equally vital was Lincoln's Jacksonian willingness to claim that through him the people had spoken and expressed their preference to abolish slavery.

## CRISIS LEADERSHIP

War creates a severe dilemma for political cultures not predisposed to support centralized political authority. The heavy emphasis on individual rights in an individualist culture is ill-suited to wartime demands of sacrifice for the collectivity. And crises requiring extensive mobilization and coordination of people and resources jeopardize individualist principles of self-regulation.

Adherents of an individualistic culture hope that temporary but extraordinary grants of power to the leader will enable society to survive the crisis without creating a permanently strengthened authority structure. Power granted to leaders in emergencies, individualists fear, may subsequently be used as a precedent for more centralized authority in future noncrisis situations. An individualist leader must therefore repeatedly reassure followers that this power is justified only by the exceptional nature of the situation. For fear of establishing precedents and alienating wary followers, individualist leaders may resist attempts to have their powers codified or systematized. The paradigmatic formulation of individualist leadership in crisis situations is John Locke's understanding of the executive's emergency powers as an undefined extraconstitutional weapon that the law of necessity and self-preservation periodically forces upon the nation.

Faced with a crisis of similar proportions, a hierarchically inclined leader will try to squeeze maximum mileage from existing roles and functions. Such a leader would perceive expansion of the office's authority not as a threat but as an opportunity permanently to strengthen hierarchical relations. Adherents of a hierarchical culture may even welcome wars they think they can win in the hope that a successful collective effort will reflect positively on those in leadership positions and thus increase support for authority in peacetime.

Lincoln's behavior in office reflected both hierarchical and individualist impulses. He appealed to the situation and to the role, stressing the exceptional nature of the circumstance as well as the enduring institutional prerogatives of the executive office. He voiced the hierarchical hope that the Civil War would strengthen and ennoble the collectivity, but he also expressed the individualist concern that war would set precedents that would endanger American liberties in the future.

At the outset of the war, Lincoln articulated the individualist definition of the nation's dilemma: "Must a Government, of necessity, be too strong for the liberties of its own people, or too weak to maintain its own existence?" He explained to Congress at the 1861 special session that his sweeping actions of the previous three months had been thrust upon him by "public necessity." Lincoln appealed to Congress to ratify presidential actions taken in the name of national self-preservation. He elaborated on his individualistic justification of emergency leadership in a letter to A. G. Hodges, dated 4 April 1864, in which, using words that directly echoed Jefferson's justification of the Louisiana Purchase, he explained that just as "often a limb must be amputated to save

a life," so "measures, otherwise unconstitutional, might become lawful by becoming indispensable to the preservation of the Constitution through the preservation of the nation." Because the life of the nation was at stake, Lincoln argued, he had no choice but to assume the powers he did.

Although Lincoln's individualist propensities led him to accent the extraordinary nature of the situation, his hierarchical background inclined him to turn also to established roles and offices for sanction of his authority. As the war continued, Lincoln increasingly relied on the role of commander-in-chief to justify his unprecedented exercise of presidential power: He did so in large part because invoking the law of self-preservation did not address the question of why decisions about public safety should rest with the president rather than with Congress. "When rebellion or invasion comes," he reasoned, "the people have, under the Constitution, made the commander-in-chief of their army and navy . . . the man who holds the power and bears the responsibility of . . . [deciding what] the public safety requires." And, as noted earlier, he began his Emancipation Proclamation by invoking "the power in me vested as Commander-in-Chief of the Army and Navy."

Whereas for Locke and Jefferson the executive's emergency power had been, as Arthur Schlesinger, Jr., explained, "a weapon outside and beyond the Constitution," Lincoln's innovation was "constitutionalizing the law of necessity." He wrung authority from the commander-in-chief role, from the presidential oath to "preserve, protect, and defend the Constitution of the United States," and from the constitutional injunction that the president "shall take Care that the Laws be faithfully executed."

In Whig thought, presidential power had been suspect because of its association with the subversion of law. By presenting the president as upholding the supreme law in the face of lawless southern secession, Lincoln managed to attract political support from legal-minded former Whigs. Despite his own frequent disregard for the legal limits on presidential authority, Lincoln was able to place himself on the side of law and order by sustaining the assertion that "the Constitution invests its commander-in-chief clause with the law of war, in time of war." On the basis of power invested in him through the role of commander-in-chief, Lincoln distinguished his Emancipation Proclamation—which he termed "a fit and necessary war measure"—from General John C. Frémont's Declaration of Emancipation, which Lincoln condemned as "simply dictatorship."

If the adherents of a hierarchical culture feared that a charismatic president would substitute his personal will for the law, the primary concern of the individualists was that Lincoln's personal power would become institutionalized. A central authority thus strengthened might permanently restrict individual autonomy. To assuage such individualist fears, Lincoln justified the Emancipation Proclamation—which would result in what proponents of slavery viewed as the confiscation of millions of dollars' worth of private property—as an act of military necessity. The implication was that such an act was warranted only because emancipation was necessary to defeat the South and that it therefore could not constitute a precedent for the central government's powers in peacetime. Lincoln's disregard for formality, system, and ceremony perhaps served as further reassurance to individualists concerned that his wartime leadership would establish precedents for peacetime governing.

From the individualist perspective, Lincoln's greatness lies in showing that an individualist regime could cope with large-scale crises without undermining individualist institutions, specifically competitive elections and competitive markets. Lincoln's example offered hope that individualist regimes were not subject to an "inherent and fatal weakness"—such a regime could be strong enough to function successfully in an emergency without permanently altering social and political relations in a hierarchical direction. Temporary emergency leadership in times of total war, individualists now

knew, did not lead inexorably to permanent dictatorship in peacetime.

Lincoln's leadership is equally exemplary from a hierarchical standpoint, but for very different reasons. In Woodrow Wilson's view, Lincoln's greatness lay in moving the United States "from a divided, self-interested contractual association to a unified, spiritual, organic state." Also, his presidency had rebuilt the alliance of strong government with a strong executive that had been rent asunder by the party battles of the 1830s and 1840s. By elevating the prestige and expanding the prerogatives of the presidential office Lincoln had left a permanent legacy on which future presidents could try to build.

## THE ABOLITIONIST CHALLENGE TO THE GREAT EMANCIPATOR

Today Americans are likely to recall Lincoln as the Great Emancipator, but abolitionists of the 1860s, who had for decades called for the immediate emancipation of slaves, had far more ambivalent feelings about Lincoln. The Civil War had elevated abolitionists from a despised, fringe minority to a respected and influential group at the center of the political process, and under the pressures of war, immediate emancipation became an increasingly popular policy option. As the idea of abolition grew in popularity, so, too, did the prestige of abolitionists. Their newfound popularity greatly complicated Lincoln's leadership task, for he had to resist the abolitionists' desire to invest him with charismatic qualities, making him purely good and the South purely evil. Framing the struggle in this way, Lincoln feared, would weaken the northern war effort by alienating the border states and northern Democrats and would dash hopes of eventual national reconciliation. Balancing the zeal of the abolitionists against the caution of the establishment cultures constituted perhaps the central dilemma of Lincoln's leadership.

To win abolitionist support for the war effort Lincoln had to show that the war was aimed at the abolition of slavery. Only such a lofty goal could justify jettisoning abolitionists' pacifist and antimilitarist principles. The prospect of emancipation enabled even those who believed "all war to be wicked and unchristian" to "delight that this conflict is upon us." After all, reasoned Wendell Phillips, "the bloodiest war ever waged is infinitely better than the happiest slavery which ever fattened men into obedience." In a speech announcing his support for the war, Phillips justified his decision by drawing attention to the glorious ends that would be served. Following the bloodletting and atonement, "the world will see under our banner all tongues, all creeds, all races,—one brotherhood." Yesterday, reasoned Phillips, the government had been an agreement with Hell; today it was "the Thermopylae of Liberty and Justice." Phillips's speech made it clear that abolitionist support depended on the government's transforming the war into a crusade against slavery.

In the early days of the war, William Lloyd Garrison advised his fellow abolitionists to mute their criticisms of the government. This was no time, he explained, "for minute criticism of Lincoln, Republicanism, or even the other parties, now that they are fusing for a death-grapple with the Southern slave-oligarchy." But the abolitionist press made it clear that if the government demonstrated a lack of moral purpose, then "the time of criticism and censure will have come again."

Abolitionists remained divided over whether to support the war. The most radical, like Parker Pillsbury and Stephen Foster, were, in the words of historian James McPherson, "incapable of supporting any government." They vehemently opposed Garrison's call for a temporary cessation of criticism of the government. At a July Fourth gathering of Garrisonian abolitionists, Foster proposed a resolution stating that until the administration proclaimed emancipation to be the aim of the war, abolitionists would "give it no support or countenance in its effort to maintain its authority over the seceded States." And on 1 August, Pillsbury introduced another resolution denouncing the Lincoln administration. "I

have no higher opinion of Abraham Lincoln, and his Cabinet . . . than I have of the President and Cabinet . . . of the Confederate States," declared Pillsbury. "Abraham Lincoln is as truly a slaveholder as Jefferson Davis."

These extreme resolutions were defeated; most abolitionists preferred to follow the lead of Garrison and Phillips, supporting the war while pressing the North to embrace emancipation. But having overridden their firmly held objections to coercion in any form, abolitionists engaged in a desperate search for signs that "the Cause of the North will become the Cause of Truth." The trouble was that Lincoln was giving few visible signs of such inner grace. More and more it was beginning to seem that the Lincoln administration had no intention of declaring a holy war on slavery. "If there is one point of honor upon which more than another this administration will stick," the Illinois *Springfield Republican* assured the nation, "it is the pledge not to interfere with slavery in the states." Lincoln's July Fourth message to Congress reaffirmed the administration's pledge not to interfere with slavery in the southern states. At the end of July 1861, the House and Senate passed near-unanimous resolutions stating that "this war is not waged upon our part . . . for any purpose . . . of overthrowing or interfering with the rights or established institutions of . . . southern States." Restoration of the Union, not emancipation of slaves, clearly and unmistakably was being proclaimed as administration policy. Such a policy was consistent with the establishment cultures—for whom maintenance of national institutions and concern for property rights, order, and liberty were high priorities—but not with the abolitionist culture for whom equality and purity were the guiding norms.

In view of the abolitionists' enthusiastic embrace of the war, Lincoln's refusal to make it a war for emancipation left abolitionists feeling betrayed and even defiled. Their early hope for a war to redeem a guilty nation redoubled their sense of betrayal. By September 1861, haunted by the unbearable thought that they were supporting a bloody war that might leave slavery untouched, egalitarians began to retreat from their tenuous truce with Lincoln.

Fearing that a speedy end to the war would leave slavery in place in the South, abolitionists now prayed for defeat of the impure Union forces. "God grant us so many reverses," Phillips prayed, "that the government may learn its duty." Because only a prolonged war seemed capable of converting the North to emancipation, abolitionists were in the awkward position of simultaneously demanding a more vigorous prosecution of the war while withholding full support until the administration adopted its antislavery cause. But to the abolitionists there was no contradiction between effective prosecution of the war and morality. They were convinced that emancipation was necessary to inspire the North. The knowledge that they were fighting on the side of justice, they believed, would impart "superhuman strength" to Union soldiers. "The strongest battalions," they insisted, "are those on the side of God."

On 30 August 1861, General John C. Frémont issued a proclamation freeing the slaves of every rebel in the state of Missouri. Here, finally, was a leader willing to give to the war a great moral purpose that could justify the carnage. Lincoln's modification of Frémont's order, to conform to the Confiscation Act of 6 August, left the abolitionists aghast. Garrison charged Lincoln with a "serious dereliction of duty" and said revoking Frémont's order was "timid, depressing, suicidal." Privately, Garrison fumed that Lincoln was "only a dwarf in mind." Edmund Quincy believed it to be "one of those blunders which are worse than crimes." Another abolitionist lamented the president's "pigheaded stupidity." The limited armistice between the abolitionists and the administration seemed to be over.

The president's annual message in December 1861, warning against degeneration of the war "into a violent and remorseless revolutionary struggle," met with widespread abolitionist condemnation. In the *Liberator*,

Garrison characterized Lincoln's message as "feeble and rambling." Garrison privately confided his belief that Lincoln "has evidently not a drop of anti-slavery blood in his veins" and concluded by lamenting that Lincoln was "a man of very small calibre." Gerrit Smith publicly assailed the president's address as "twattle and trash." An even more hostile critic called it a "timid, timeserving, commonplace sort of an abortion of a message, cold enough . . . to freeze h–ll over." In the fight against evil, moderation was no virtue.

Throughout 1862 the abolitionists rode a roller coaster of hope and despair. A wave of optimism swept over them in the early spring of 1862 after Lincoln signed legislation abolishing slavery in the District of Columbia. The *National Anti-Slavery Standard* heralded this as "the Beginning of the End of Slavery." With Edwin Stanton installed as the new secretary of war and with growing popular support for ending slavery, abolitionists now seemed more confident of Lincoln's intentions and capacity.

But events of late May 1862 led abolitionists to despair once again of the Lincoln administration, and their criticism of the government mounted. Within the span of a few weeks, Lincoln had revoked General David Hunter's military order proclaiming emancipation in Georgia, South Carolina, and Florida; the House had defeated a bill to emancipate all slaves of rebel masters; and the administration was firmly enforcing the Fugitive Slave Law in the District of Columbia. In the pages of the *Liberator* Garrison again scolded Lincoln: "Shame and confusion to the President for his halting, shuffling, backward policy." Anna Dickinson pronounced the president as "not so far from . . . a slave-catcher after all."

More abolitionist criticism was prompted by Lincoln's appointment of General Henry Halleck (who, while in command of the Western Department, had tried to exclude fugitive slaves from the area under his jurisdiction) as general-in-chief of the U.S. Army and by the president's refusal to issue a proclamation ordering his generals to enforce the second Confiscation Act. The administration, Garrison despaired, "is blind as a bat to its true line of policy." And he noted that the only words he could find to describe Lincoln's policy were "stumbling, halting, prevaricating, irresolute, weak, besotted." To demonstrate that the cause of the North was just, abolitionists wanted a ringing declaration of immediate freedom for all slaves.

Lincoln's preliminary Emancipation Proclamation, issued on 22 September, won fervent applause from abolitionists. In a letter to Garrison, Theodore Tilton confessed himself to be "half crazy with enthusiasm." Frederick Douglass, who only two weeks before had expressed his "ineffable disgust" with Lincoln's behavior, declared, "We shout for joy that we live to record this righteous decree." "Joy, gratitude, thanksgiving, renewed hope and courage fill my soul," echoed Samuel May, Jr. "God bless President Lincoln," declared another abolitionist. "He may yet be the Moses to deliver the oppressed." Seeking deliverance from oppression, abolitionists earnestly sought the inspired, charismatic leadership necessary to reach the promised land.

The leadership dilemma the abolitionists posed for Lincoln can be seen most starkly in the career of Wendell Phillips. Across the nation and throughout the war, Phillips preached that the country needed decisive and bold national leadership; in speech after speech he told his audiences that the country was suffering from a crisis of leadership. But while demanding stronger leadership, Phillips was simultaneously engaging in sustained, ruthless criticism—at one point damning Lincoln as an "unlimited despot"—that sought to undermine the president's leadership.

During the election of 1860 Phillips had refused to support Lincoln or any other candidate. He denounced Lincoln as the "Slave-Hound of Illinois." After the nomination Phillips asked, "Who is this huckster in politics? . . . Who is this who does not know whether he has got any opinions?" Over the next four years Phillips vigorously criticized the Lincoln administration for its failure to give wholehearted support to the

ideals of egalitarian democracy. In a letter to Charles Sumner, Phillips expressed his belief that Lincoln "is doing twice as much today to break this Union as [Jefferson] Davis is." Labeling Lincoln "a timid and ignorant President," Phillips urged the radicals in Congress to withhold money and supplies until Lincoln redefined the war aims. On 1 August 1862, Phillips publicly expressed the view that if Lincoln had been a "traitor," he could not have been of more aid to the South.

Phillips oscillated between periods of scathing denunciation and guarded approval. After Lincoln's preliminary Emancipation Proclamation in September 1862 and the dismissal of McClellan a few weeks later, Phillips publicly announced that he would no longer criticize the president. "I trust the President," he informed a Boston gathering in November. But only three days after Lincoln issued the Emancipation Proclamation, Phillips was calling it a "reluctant gift," and once again stepped up his attacks on the administration. He refused to support Lincoln in the 1864 election and he persisted in his attacks to the point where, by the end of the war, Garrison was accusing his fellow abolitionist of being "a bayoneter of presidents."

Only those willing to take decisive, dramatic action against slavery earned Phillips's praise. Like many other abolitionists, Phillips idolized General Frémont, who, after declaring martial law in Missouri, had issued a proclamation freeing the slaves of every rebel in the state of Missouri. Another of Phillips's heroes was Benjamin F. Butler, who declared all fugitive slaves who came into his lines to be "contraband" and put them to work for the Union cause. As military governor of New Orleans, writes Irving Bartlett, Butler acted "almost as a law unto himself. . . . Butler assumed the entire financial control of the city, [and] hanged a man for hauling down the American flag." Though long an opponent of capital punishment, Phillips was so enamored with Butler's decisive leadership that he told a crowd that if "I were he and were to die soon, I would have a tombstone inscribed 'I was the only Major General of the United States that ever hung a traitor; that ever, by the boldness of my action, and the method of the death, told the world it was a Government struggling with rebels, with the right and purpose to put them beneath its laws, at any cost.'"

For Phillips, attention to legality was timidity; he desired a leader who would substitute his will for the law in order to achieve an exalted objective. Phillips demanded men with "wills hot enough to fuse the purpose of nineteen millions of people into one decisive blow for safety and union." No leader who needed to hold the support of a national constituency, encompassing a wide array of interests, was going to find it easy to meet Phillips's standards.

The conflict between Lincoln and Phillips can be conceived as a conflict between what political scientist James Mac-Gregor Burns has called transactional and transforming leadership styles. Phillips desired a thoroughgoing social revolution: "The whole social system of the Gulf states is to be taken to pieces; every bit of it." A revolutionary transformation of southern society required leadership willing to disregard convention, law, and precedent. The compromises and half measures that Lincoln engaged in to keep his party together could not satisfy Phillips's demand for charismatic, transformative leadership. Their different goals—revolutionary transformation of the southern social structure versus reconciliation with the South—required different modes of leadership.

Perhaps because of Lincoln's establishment vision—the attempt to find a meeting ground between self-regulation and collective authority—Lincoln would neither replace nor abandon the law. More than any other president before or since, Lincoln tried to distinguish between a president with emergency powers and a charismatic leader. Much is sometimes made of Lincoln's suspension of *habeas corpus*, but those observations often lose sight of the lengths to which Lincoln went to avoid substituting his personal preferences regarding slavery for the written law.

Lincoln admitted on occasion that he considered slavery to be morally wrong. Given this admission, abolitionists believed Lincoln was obligated to do everything in his power to abolish slavery. They could not understand the president's hesitancy to act publicly on his private conviction. "If all earthly power were given me," Lincoln had stated in 1854, "I should not know what to do [about slavery]." During the war years the abolitionists prayed Lincoln would assume such earthly powers and abolish slavery at a single stroke. But Lincoln's comment, in the last months of his presidency, indicated that he never came around to the abolitionist conception of leadership. "I am naturally anti-slavery. If slavery is not wrong, nothing is wrong. . . . And yet I have never understood that the Presidency conferred upon me an unrestricted right to act officially upon this judgement and feeling." There was something of the old Whig left in Lincoln after all.

## LINCOLN AS POLITICIAN

During the 1860 election, abolitionist Wendell Phillips had ridiculed those who "rejoice that [Lincoln] can ride on two horses," but the ability to ride horses that are charging in divergent directions is no small feat. How did Lincoln as a political leader hold his followers together? As president, Lincoln had to appeal to several distinct political cultures, each making contradictory demands. Abolitionists pressured him to convert the war into a moral crusade against slavery, but any signs of administration hostility toward slavery could alienate critical border states and swing the balance of military power to the South. Support from the abolitionists was premised on the war's being a morally just war against slavery; establishment support entailed limiting the war aims to restoration of the Union with a minimum of tampering with southern property rights. Lincoln's dilemma was to reconcile the competing cultural claims of order, liberty, and justice.

Emancipation coupled with confiscation created a thorny problem for an individualist culture. Did the war make it legitimate for the government to take actions that all

Republicans agreed government could not do in time of peace—namely, take away southern property? Lincoln's proclamation calling for 75,000 troops to suppress the rebellion explicitly promised "to avoid any destruction, or interference, with [southern] property." In 1863 Lincoln told a Baptist delegation, "When brought to my final reckoning, may I have to answer for robbing no man of his goods." But this is precisely what abolitionists were demanding. Only one month after the firing on Fort Sumter, the abolitionist William Goodell called for confiscation of rebel land and redistributing it among freed slaves. Abolitionists, in the words of historian James McPherson, pressed for "full-scale expropriation." After emancipation had been adopted as the official war aim, abolitionists stepped up these demands for redistribution of southern land.

The debate that still persists about Lincoln's intentions vis-à-vis slavery testifies to his skill in bridging the competing cultural visions of the Civil War. If modern historians, well versed in Lincoln's private correspondence, have been unable to decide whether Lincoln was a cautious conservative or a stalwart champion of racial justice, the confusion of Lincoln's contemporaries is understandable. And, just as scholars today seem to see in Lincoln a reflection of their own preferences, so during the Civil War Lincoln managed to be different things to different people.

Historian Richard Hofstadter has written that the Emancipation Proclamation "had all the moral grandeur of a bill of lading." Hofstadter cites the *London Spectator*'s jibe that "the principle is not that a human being cannot justly own another, but that he cannot own him unless he is loyal to the United States." Yet McPherson dismisses this "old cliché" that the proclamation did not free a single slave because it applied only to those states where the government had no power, as completely missing the point. "From the time the Emancipation Proclamation went into effect at the beginning of 1863," McPherson argues, "the North fought for the revolutionary goal of a new

Union without slavery." Scholars' continued debate over the true meaning of the proclamation serves to highlight the vexing ambiguity that enabled groups with widely divergent goals to support the proclamation.

If, as Hofstadter claims, Lincoln's message contained no indictment of slavery, it is all the more remarkable to find some of the most morally exacting abolitionists enthusiastically hailing it. "All . . . trials . . . are swallowed up in the great deep joy of this emancipation," wrote a correspondent of Garrison's. Another abolitionist rejoiced, "This is a great Era! A sublime period in history! The Proclamation is grand. The President has done nobly." Garrison himself publicly hailed it as "a great historic event, sublime in its magnitude, momentous and beneficent in its far-reaching consequences."

Perhaps the most impressive aspect of Lincoln's leadership was the way in which he persuaded many antislavery people that his heart was with them when his public behavior told a different story. Even after Lincoln revoked General Hunter's order, Carl Schurz remained confident of Lincoln's good intentions. After meeting with Lincoln, Schurz wrote to the president, "After you had explained your policy to me the other day I left you perfectly happy and contented, fully convinced that, in spite of appearances to the contrary, you were determined to use all your constitutional power to deliver this country of the great curse, and so I would receive all your acts and manifestations with the utmost confidence."

A striking example of Lincoln's ability to persuade antislavery advocates of his good intentions in the face of contrary or ambiguous public evidence is Sydney Gay's reaction to Lincoln's famous public letter to Horace Greeley in which the president announced that "my paramount object in this struggle is to save the Union, and is not either to save or to destroy slavery." A Garrisonian abolitionist and editor of the *Anti-Slavery Standard* for fourteen years, Gay had become managing editor of Horace Greeley's New York *Tribune* in the spring of 1862. Gay met with Lincoln in the summer of 1862 and argued for emancipation; although Lincoln made no promises, Gay was favorably impressed by Lincoln's antislavery convictions. A few weeks later, when Greeley's "Prayer of Twenty Million" demanding emancipation was published, Lincoln's prompt reply to Greeley apparently disavowed emancipation as a war aim. Yet, clinging to Lincoln's promise that "if I could save it [the Union] by freeing all the slaves I would do it," Gay wrote Lincoln that "your letter to Mr. Greeley has infused new hope among us . . . I think that the general impression is that . . . you mean presently to announce that the destruction of Slavery is the price of our salvation."

Lincoln also persuaded the highly influential and vain chairman of the Senate Foreign Relations Committee, Charles Sumner, that they both had the same goals. In December 1861 Sumner confidently reported that "the Presdt. tells me that the question between him & me is one of 4 weeks or at most 6 weeks, when we shall all be together." A frequent visitor at the White House, Sumner came to have not only a "profound pity" for Lincoln but also a belief that the president wanted "to do right & to save the country." Sumner's trust in Lincoln's intentions enabled Lincoln to act in ways that otherwise Lincoln might have found difficult to sustain politically.

Despite moments of doubt and despair, Garrison supported Lincoln's reelection in 1864. At the annual meeting of the Massachusetts Anti-Slavery Society in January 1864, Garrison, although willing to criticize certain features of Lincoln's policy, refused to question the president's good intentions. He defended Lincoln by arguing that the president had moved as fast as public opinion had allowed. After meeting with Lincoln in June, Garrison pronounced the interview "very satisfactory": "There is no mistake about it in regard to Mr. Lincoln's desire to do all that he can . . . to uproot slavery, and give fair-play to the emancipated. I was much pleased with his spirit." Indeed, to Garrison, something in their struggle had

seemed to rub off on the president. Most abolitionists would now have agreed with Owen Lovejoy that although Lincoln "does not drive as fast as I would, he is on the right road, and it is only a question of time."

Although Garrisonian abolitionists were evenly divided over the question of Lincoln's renomination, it was an impressive achievement to have won over about half of the most radical of the abolitionists. In the general election, all but a few abolitionists followed Garrison in supporting Lincoln. It is not surprising, as McPherson writes, that "the very nature of the presidency compelled Lincoln to proceed more cautiously than radicals desired." What is impressive is that Lincoln convinced ardent abolitionists that this necessary deference to public opinion, rather than his personal motives, explained why his actions diverged from their desires.

The extent to which Lincoln was able to gain the support of radical abolitionists is particularly striking in view of the fact that many "conservative" and border-state Republicans counted the Kentucky-born Lincoln on their side. Up until late 1863 even the archconservative New York *Herald* was calling on all "the conservative Union men of Congress and the country" to support Lincoln. The attorney general from Missouri, Edward Bates, considered Lincoln "an excellent man," although Bates sensed and feared a lack of "will and purpose." Joshua Speed, a longtime friend of Lincoln, worried that a "large and powerful party of . . . ultra men" was "being formed to make war upon the President and upon his conservative policy." While the moderate and conservative elements of the Republican party periodically doubted Lincoln's ability, they rarely questioned his motives.

Lincoln was able to keep the support of such radically divergent groups by conveying, shrewdly and calculatingly, different intentions to the different sides. "My policy," Lincoln was fond of telling people, "is to have no policy." Just as he used the political pressure of conservatives to temper or thwart radical demands, Lincoln skillfully manipulated and even fabricated abolitionist pressures to move the border states and conservatives from their seemingly intransigent position (thereby converting abolitionists' moral pressure into a chip comprehensible to those accustomed to the language of political bargains). In effect, Lincoln argued that his actions were resultants, a product of external pressures, rather than a reflection of his intentions, which, he assured both sides, were fully in sympathy with their own. Both sides could thus believe they had a sympathetic friend in the White House.

Aimed at maintaining a governing coalition, Lincoln's strategy risked courting a reputation for vacillation and weakness. Repeatedly charging him with indecision and with lacking control of men or events, many critics disparaged Lincoln's policy as "muddy." Another typical criticism of Lincoln began by admitting that "Mr. Lincoln may mean well," but went on to condemn the president for being "vacillating in policy, undecided in action, weak in intellectual grasp."

To the extent that Lincoln's leadership style contributed to an appearance of not being in control, it sometimes drew into question his ability to lead and therefore encouraged those looking for strong leaders to condemn the president. But, given the often disastrous northern war effort, the substantial criticism and unpopularity of Lincoln is not remarkable. Rather, what is noteworthy is his ability to maintain sufficient popular support to become the first president since Andrew Jackson to gain re-election. More often than not, his strategy helped him by diverting attention from his actions (which inevitably had to alienate one faction) to his intentions (which could be different things to different people). This rainbow strategy enabled him to avoid becoming identified exclusively with any one political faction or political culture. Lincoln's political success was made possible by his ability to appeal to diverse constituencies. His everlasting fame, fittingly, is owed at least in part to a political persona that still allows people of diverse ideological predis-

positions to infuse Lincoln with their own cause, whether it be egalitarian justice, hierachical order, or individualistic liberty.

## BIBLIOGRAPHY

Boritt, Gabor S. *Lincoln and the Economics of the American Dream* (Memphis State University Press, 1978).

———, ed. *The Historian's Lincoln: Pseudohistory, Psychohistory, and History* (University of Illinois Press, 1988).

———, ed. *Lincoln, the War President* (Oxford University Press, 1992).

Burlingame, Michael. *The Inner World of Abraham Lincoln* (University of Illinois Press, 1994).

Current, Richard N. *The Lincoln Nobody Knows* (Hill & Wang, 1958).

Davis, Cullom, et al., eds. *The Public and Private Lincoln* (Carbondale: Southern Illinois University Press, 1979).

Donald, David. *Lincoln Reconsidered: Essays on the Civil War Era* (Vintage, 1961).

Donald, David Herbert. *Lincoln* (Simon & Schuster, 1995).

Fehrenbacher, Don E. *Lincoln in Text and Context: Collected Essays* (Stanford University Press, 1987).

Howe, Daniel Walker. *The Political Culture of the American Whigs* (University of Chicago Press, 1979).

McPherson, James M. *Abraham Lincoln and the Second American Revolution* (Oxford University Press, 1991).

Miers, Earl Schenck, ed. *Lincoln Day by Day: A Chronology, 1809–1865*, 3 vols. (Lincoln Sesquicentennial Commission, 1960).

Neely, Mark E., Jr. *The Fate of Liberty: Abraham Lincoln and Civil Liberties* (Oxford University Press, 1991).

———. *The Last Best Hope on Earth: Abraham Lincoln and the Promise of America* (Harvard University Press, 1993).

———, ed. *Abraham Lincoln Encyclopedia* (McGraw-Hill, 1992).

Oates, Stephen B. *With Malice Toward None: The Life of Abraham Lincoln* (Harper & Row, 1977).

Paludan, Philip Shaw. *The Presidency of Abraham Lincoln* (University Press of Kansas, 1994).

Peterson, Merrill D. *Lincoln in American Memory* (Oxford University Press, 1994).

Randall, J. G., and Richard N. Current. *Lincoln the President*, 4 vols. (Dodd, Mead, 1945–1955).

Thomas, Benjamin. *Abraham Lincoln: A Biography* (Knopf, 1952).

Thomas, John L., ed. *Abraham Lincoln and the American Political Tradition* (University of Massachusetts Press, 1986).

Wills, Garry. *Lincoln at Gettysburg: The Words That Remade America* (Simon & Schuster, 1992).

★★★ 17 ★★★

# ANDREW JOHNSON
## 1865–1869

*Edgar A. Toppin*

---

*Born 29 December 1808 in Raleigh, North Carolina, to Jacob Johnson and Mary McDonough Johnson; did not attend college; married Eliza McCardle, 17 May 1827, in Greeneville, Tennessee; five children; succeeded to presidency upon the death of Abraham Lincoln, 15 April 1865; died 31 July 1875 at Carter's Station, Tennessee; buried in Andrew Johnson National Cemetery, Greeneville, Tennessee.*

---

Andrew Johnson served during one of the most controversial periods in U.S. history, the Reconstruction after the Civil War. The strong traits—especially stubborn conviction of his own righteousness—that propelled his rise from poverty to the White House left him unsuited for the delicate task of binding up the nation's wounds after the bitter fratricidal war. Johnson fought hard to uphold his view of the Constitution, to protect presidential power from congressional encroachment, to preserve the integrity of southern states against an overbearing central government, and to maintain white supremacy. His stubborn adherence to his points, usually oblivious to compromise or conciliation, led to divisiveness, chaos, and racial bitterness—in short, to a disastrous three years, ten months and two weeks in office for the man who succeeded the assassinated Abraham Lincoln. Johnson's obstructionism finally impelled a wrathful Congress to impeach him on rather flimsy charges. Until 1998, he was the only president ever impeached. (Richard Nixon surely would have been the second had he not resigned in 1974. Bill Clinton was impeached in 1998 and tried and acquitted by the Senate in 1999. Johnson missed conviction by only one vote.)

Lincoln owned no slaves, hated slavery, was a Republican and, though southern-born, had made his home in the northern state of Illinois. Johnson was a slave-owning southern Democrat. His elevation to the post of vice president for Lincoln's second term was a result of one of those calamitous gambles made too often by American political parties. Seeking to broaden their appeal to the voters, parties sometimes nominate for vice president a person unfit by view or temperament to carry on the president's work in the event of the chief executive's death.

### THE RISE FROM POVERTY
Andrew Johnson was born on 29 December 1808 (42 days before Lincoln) into a hard-working family in Raleigh, North Carolina. He was the younger of two children, both boys, born to Jacob Johnson, a laborer/handyman in a local tavern, and Mary McDonough Johnson, a maid in the tavern. When Andrew was only three, his father died as an aftermath of his courageous rescue of people from a boat that capsized as he was walking nearby. His widow took in sewing and washing to support her two young sons. When Andrew was 13, she apprenticed him to a tailor where, besides the craft, he began to learn to read. Throughout his life, Johnson would never attend classes in conventional schools. After serving two years of his six-year apprenticeship, Johnson ran away and tailored in various places, and eventually settled in 1826 in Greeneville in eastern Tennessee, a small isolated mountain community that was his hometown thereafter. He eventually brought his poverty-stricken mother and stepfather to live there with him.

From these humble origins, of which he was always conscious and sensitive, Johnson began to rise. His tailor shop in Greeneville prospered through his hard work and thrift, and he invested shrewdly in property in the town. In 1827 he married Eliza McCardle, daughter of a shoemaker. She added to his education, teaching him to write, to do simple calculations, and to read extensively to broaden himself. Her steadfast support helped him immensely, even though she was an invalid during much of their life in high posts. They had five children (two girls and three boys) to whom he was a devoted father, but alcoholism afflicted two of his sons. One of those two was also hampered with tuberculosis and the other was killed in a fall from a horse.

Johnson ventured into politics, attracting support through his strong voice, wit, and prowess as a debater. All his life he chose Andrew Jackson (also born in the Carolinas and settled in Tennessee) as his model. Johnson championed the working classes, taking the side of mechanics, craftsmen, tradesmen, and laborers against the great landowners, especially the cotton planters of west Tennessee, whom Johnson seemed both to envy and to hate. He wanted their acceptance but often felt himself sneered at and shunned as the pants-mender, even after he rose to high positions in the state. The snobbery of these plantation aristocrats irked him and reinforced his deep beliefs that they were to blame for bringing on secession and the Civil War.

Johnson rose steadily in politics. He became a town alderman in 1829, then mayor, and then state legislator. Fearing corruption, he opposed state aid to railroad building even though railroads were needed in eastern Tennessee. This early stance of courageous opposition became a hallmark of his career and led to the loss of his seat in the 1837 election (the first of only two defeats during his forty-five years in politics). He regained his assembly seat two years later and after serving one more term was elevated to the state senate. From there he moved to the national level, serving five terms in the U.S. House of Representatives before returning to state government, where he was governor of Tennessee for two terms (1853 to 1857). In 1857, he was elected to represent Tennessee in the U.S. Senate. Here he continued to champion free land for farmers, pushing his homestead bill. He crusaded for homesteading for sixteen years, from 1846 to 1862, even though the South was increasingly opposed to the measure. Johnson left the Senate two months before the Homestead Act was passed in May 1862.

## THE WAR DEMOCRAT

A strong Unionist, Andrew Johnson opposed secession from the start, calling secessionists traitors. He stood firmly opposed when the seven deep South states seceded, formed a new nation, and attacked Fort Sumter in April 1865, launching a civil war. When Tennessee and three others of the eight upper South slave states seceded to join the Confederate States of America, Johnson refused to join them. He alone of the twenty-two senators from the eleven Confederate states remained at his desk in the U.S. Senate. His courageous refusal drew increasing national attention, but being in the opposition was a familiar stance for Johnson. His term in the Senate was cut short because President Lincoln needed his services elsewhere. Union forces had captured enough of Tennessee to create a need to administer the state, and Lincoln wanted Johnson to fill that office. To accept the president's request took courage because secessionist sentiment was strong in the state, but Johnson, who never backed down from a challenge, agreed to serve as military governor, holding that post from March 1862 to March 1865.

Always ambitious, Johnson had maneuvered to try to gain the Democratic nomination for president in 1856 and 1860. Subsequently, he considered positioning himself either to become a future nominee of the Union Party (the name chosen by the combination of Republicans and War Democrats) or to form his own Union Democratic party, appealing to moderates nationwide, and run for president on its ticket. As he considered these options, another path to the top opened for him when Lincoln and his party (called the Union Party in the crisis) decided to seek a War Democrat to run for vice president on the ticket in 1864. Several persons, including General Benjamin Butler, were considered, but Andrew Johnson became the favorite. Consequently, Lincoln's first-term vice president, Hannibal Hamlin of Maine, was shunted aside. On the convention's second ballot, Hamlin received 17 votes to Johnson's 494, whereupon the choice was made unanimous. Lincoln and Johnson became the team in the bid for a second term.

The two won the election of November 1864, easily defeating the Democratic ticket of General George McClellan and George Pendleton. The inauguration of Lincoln and Johnson was set for 4 March 1865. Meanwhile, Johnson had been working furiously in Tennessee to finish his task as military governor. He used harsh measures against secessionists while seeking to strengthen Unionists in the state. He was not altogether successful, alienating many people and increasing polarization rather than bringing about unity and conciliation. He pushed a stricter loyalty oath than Lincoln required, and he insisted on emancipation of slaves but coupled that with white domination in government and/or shipping African Americans out of the nation.

As inauguration day loomed, Johnson was recovering from the discomfort and difficulties of a mild bout of typhoid fever, and he also had not yet completed his work in Tennessee. He sought permission to miss the inauguration, but Lincoln insisted that, healthy or not, he should be there. Johnson fortified himself with alcohol, and the unfortunate combination of a fever that weakened him and the alcohol that unsteadied him caused Vice President Andrew Johnson to appear inebriated at the inaugural ceremony. People noted that he could not walk or stand as a sober man would, and that he slurred his speech as if drunk. That reputation haunted him long afterward even though Johnson was only a moderate drinker. He may not have had a drinking problem, but many found it easy to believe that he did.

Only 42 days after the inauguration, Johnson became the seventeenth president of the United States. An assassination plot had been hatched by an embittered southern zealot, John Wilkes Booth, a member of the famous acting family. Booth and his fellow plotters, seeking revenge for the humiliation of the Confederacy, planned to kill some high federal officials, including President Lincoln, Vice President Johnson, and Secretary of State William Seward. Most of the clumsy plot fell apart. Seward was stabbed in his home but was able to save his life by warding off a fatal blow with the help of an arm cast he wore from a riding accident. The plotter sent to kill Johnson lost nerve and did not go through with his attack. Only Booth was successful, shooting Lincoln in the back of his head while the president was at Ford's Theater on the evening of Good Friday, 14 April. The president was carried to a house across the street where Johnson came to see him. Lincoln never regained consciousness and died about 7:20 A.M. on Easter Saturday morning, 15 April. Johnson was sworn in as president at his hotel at about 10:00 A.M. that same morning by Chief Justice Salmon Chase. He kindly refused to move into the White House for six weeks until Mrs. Lincoln could get composed and get her affairs in order.

**LINCOLN AND RECONSTRUCTION**
Some of the Radical Republicans, a relatively small but powerful extremist faction in Lincoln's party, welcomed the advent of Johnson as president. His harsh denunciation of secessionists and of the planters and other southern aristocrats misled the Radicals into thinking Johnson would cooperate with the rigorous measures they planned to take against the South. They had clashed with Lincoln during his first term over the proper way to reconstruct the nation.

President Lincoln and the Congress had been operating from different premises.

Lincoln's primary position was that the eleven Confederate states had not actually left the Union because secession was illegal—there was no basis in the Constitution for a state to withdraw from the Union. Lincoln refused to recognize the Confederacy as an actual nation, and he instead insisted that a state of insurrection existed in the eleven states. Hence, as chief executive sworn to enforce the nation's laws everywhere, and as commander-in-chief in charge of the army and navy, the president had the responsibility to put down the insurrection, to declare the states free from control of those seeking to disrupt the Union, and to restore states to their rightful place in the Union. The executive—not Congress—would have the central role in this process.

Although this was his primary position, Lincoln at times acted as if the states had left the Union. The key was that Lincoln was flexible, fluid, pragmatic, and not tied to a rigid doctrine. Long before formally announcing his plan to Congress in his State of the Union address in December 1863, Lincoln experimented with reconstruction. Lincoln put his plan in effect in three states—Arkansas, Louisiana, and Tennessee—that had come substantially under the control of Union forces. He had, for example, made Johnson military governor of Tennessee nearly two years before informing Congress of his thoughts on how to restore the eleven states to the Union.

Lincoln's plan came to be known as the "10 percent plan": When as many as 10 percent of those who had voted in 1860 in a state took a simple oath of loyalty to the Union, the president would permit them to form a loyal government and the state would be restored to the Union. Led by the Radical Republicans, Congress insisted that Lincoln's plan was far too lenient, and offered instead the Wade-Davis bill, also known as the "50 percent plan." According to that plan, 50 percent of all voting-age males would have to take a loyalty oath. To vote for, or serve as, delegates to a state constitutional convention, they would have to take a much more stringent oath, the ironclad oath, swearing that they had not been disloyal, borne arms, or served in the Confederate government.

## THEORIES OF DISUNION

The Radical Republicans—led by Representative Thaddeus Stevens of Pennsylvania and Senator Charles Sumner of Massachusetts—operated from a different premise than did Lincoln. They contended that the eleven Confederate states had left the Union and could be restored only by applying to Congress, as had every territory that became a state. The Constitution gave Congress the power to admit states. The Radical Republicans advanced several theories as to how the states had lost their proper relationship to the Union. Representative Stevens suggested the "conquered provinces" theory, namely that these states by seceding had removed themselves from the protection of the Constitution and were to be treated as foreign territory captured in war and subject to whatever terms Congress would set for restoring them to the Union. Senator Sumner's "state suicide" theory argued that the eleven Confederate states had committed suicide as states and would thus be ruled as territories while Congress imposed terms for restoring them to the Union.

Both the "conquered provinces" and "state suicide" theories posed difficulties, leaving Representative Samuel Shellabarger of Ohio as the proponent of the most satisfactory theory, the "forfeited rights" theory, which was eventually accepted by the majority of Congress. That theory argued that the states remained states, but by their action in seceding they had forfeited their rights as states. Since Congress, under the Constitution, was to guarantee each state a republican government, it was up to Congress to set the terms for readmitting these states to the Union. Lincoln and Congress stymied each other. Lincoln in July 1864 used the pocket veto (used only once before—by President Andrew Jackson in 1832 to kill the Maysville Road bill) to block the Wade-Davis bill of 1864. But Congress retaliated by refusing to seat the representatives and senators from the states restored by Lincoln.

## JOHNSON AND EARLY RECONSTRUCTION

Johnson's supporters claim that Johnson was simply following in Lincoln's path, carrying out the president's 10 percent plan. But Andy Johnson was no Abe Lincoln. Johnson was rigid, dogmatic, combative, and doctrinaire. Lincoln was the very model of fluidity, flexibility, and conciliation. This can be seen in Lincoln's response to the Wade-Davis bill. True, he vetoed it, but he did not denounce it as an unconstitutional measure, as Johnson surely would have. Instead, Lincoln said that although the Wade-Davis bill was a satisfactory mode of restoration, he did not wish to be tied to it—he wanted to continue to experiment. He suggested, perhaps tongue in cheek, that Wade-Davis was "a proper plan for the loyal people of any State choosing to adopt it." Patently, people would not opt for the more stringent 50 percent plan when his 10 percent plan was an alternative.

Johnson felt sincerely that he was following in Lincoln's footsteps, but his plan differed from Lincoln's in at least four major ways. First, Lincoln's plan, a wartime measure, sought to undermine Confederate control. If only 10 percent of the people in a state signed loyalty oaths, up to 90 percent would still be Confederate supporters. A loyal government based on 10 percent of the electorate would offer, however, an alternative loyal flag around which more and more people could rally. Hence, 10 percent constituted only an opening wedge. As Eric McKitrick pointed out, Lincoln offered this as a wartime president in an effort to sap Confederate control. Johnson, by contrast, became president six days after Lee's surrender to Grant at Appomattox on 9 April 1865. The war basically had ended, and the main reason for the 10 percent plan no longer existed. Yet Johnson continued to pursue it, not even insisting on loyalty oaths from as many as one-tenth of the 1860 voters.

Second, Congress, as in every major American war, had surrendered considerable power to the president. Lincoln, Woodrow Wilson, and Franklin Roosevelt exercised in the exigency of wartime extraordinary powers that would never be allowed in a time of peace (unless in a crisis like the Great Depression). Inevitably, the pendulum swings back after a major war as Congress moves to reassert itself and reclaim powers surrendered to the president in the war emergency. It seems to have escaped Johnson and his supporters that the president was trying to exercise in peacetime powers that Congress, understandably, would be seeking to regain in the postwar world. This was not a case of villains in Congress hell-bent on revenge and maliciously and evilly ignoring the Constitution.

Third, although Lincoln's premise was that he as president could put down the insurrection and restore the states, he did not take a combative stance vis-à-vis Congress. He accepted the Wade-Davis bill as a worthy alternative, but he did not wish to have his hands tied. Had he lived, he probably would have worked out his differences with Congress in pragmatic fashion. Johnson, on the other hand, made a big constitutional issue of his differences with Congress, acting as though the congressional plan was flagrantly unconstitutional whereas the presidential plan was the only logical, constitutional, and sound approach. Oddly enough, as military governor in Tennessee from March 1862 until he became vice president in March 1865, Johnson had followed a program almost as harsh as the Wade-Davis strictures.

Fourth, as McKitrick explains, there was not one sole constitutional theory of Reconstruction. Instead, the theories advanced by Congress—conquered provinces, state suicide, and above all forfeited rights—were just as sound, valid, and constitutional as the presidential plan. Lincoln would have recognized that and would have acted accordingly. The Stevens and Sumner theories were developed well before Lincoln's death, but Shellabarger's theory on forfeited rights was not enunciated until January 1866, nearly ten months after Lincoln died.

## MISLEADING THE SOUTH

Lincoln's assassination made him enormously popular, whereas before he had often been under bitter attack. Leaders and people in the Confederate states feared northern vengeance after the president's death, and they were willing in April 1865 to do almost anything to avert a harsh retribution. That was the strategic point at which to impose terms to remake the South in a more democratic mold. That was the time to make the United States solidly one nation and to take positive steps toward securing a new birth of freedom for the freedmen. But Andrew Johnson clouded the issue. In conferences with varying delegations from the South, he gave the impression that he had the sole power to carry out Reconstruction and that southerners need not worry about the views of Congress or northerners. Hence, he laid the groundwork for a foolhardy defiance of northern opinion. That defiance would be manifested in three areas: (1) the individuals who would be elected to high state and national office by the former Confederate states; (2) the hostility that would be displayed toward southern Unionists, northern Unionists, and freedmen; and (3) the laws that would be passed by former Confederate states that seemed virtually to restore slavery.

Johnson had been warned about what could lie ahead; Congressional leaders approached him in April 1865 and begged that any actions he planned to take in regard to the secessionist states would be taken in concert with Congress, not by him alone. Johnson told them that "treason must be made infamous and traitors punished," leaving the impression that he would cooperate with the Radicals. Instead of calling a special session of Congress or waiting until Congress reconvened in December, however, Johnson pushed ahead, issuing proclamations restoring these states to the Union.

His plan was similar to Lincoln's 10 percent plan, except that Johnson did not require 10 percent of the 1860 voters to take an oath of loyalty. He also added some features of his own. First, the states would have to ratify the Thirteenth Amendment, ending slavery everywhere. (Lincoln's Emancipation Proclamation had applied only to areas still in rebellion as of 1 January 1863.) Second, persons owning property worth $20,000 or more could not simply take an oath of loyalty but would have to make a special appeal to the president in order to be pardoned and be eligible for restoration of any property seized by Union forces. Third, the states would have to repudiate the Confederate debt. Fourth, they had to repeal or make void their ordinances of secession.

With the $20,000 property clause, the tables were turned. Confederate aristocrats had to beg the president's pardon to have their civil rights and property restored. Having the planters and other aristocrats humbling themselves before him must have been an exhilarating experience for Johnson. He tied up a lot of time listening to the personal appeals of the high and mighty, although a pardons clerk (a former Confederate colonel) handled most of the other cases. How sweet it must have been to have aristocrats coming to Johnson, clogging his anteroom, humbly awaiting their turns to plead with him. The world was indeed turned upside down.

Johnson's first proclamation setting a state on the path to restoration was issued to North Carolina on 29 May 1865 while Congress was out of session. Over the next six weeks, he proceeded to restore the other states with similar proclamations. By the time Congress convened in December 1865, the president had restored every state but Texas. Johnson had done just the opposite of what the congressional leaders thought he had agreed to do—namely, to wait and work with the leadership in carrying out Reconstruction. Instead, he plowed ahead on his own, presenting Congress with a fait accompli.

Congress in its turn retaliated. It refused to admit to their seats the representatives and senators from the states Johnson had restored. Congress also set up a Joint Committee of Fifteen on Reconstruction to determine if the former Confederate states were ready to be restored to the Union. This joint committee was to recommend measures to ensure the states were ready for restoration. Those measures would include steps to ensure that the Unionists (southern and northern) and the former slaves were treated fairly and respectfully in these states.

## SOUTHERN DEFIANCE

Under the Constitution, Congress has the right to decide its membership and to set aside for good reason any representative or senator chosen by a state. But what would prompt the wholesale action of blocking all representatives and senators from the eleven states that had formed the Confederacy? Some understanding can be gleaned from looking at the individuals the southern states had chosen to represent them: These were the same leaders who had taken the South down the path of secession, formed a Confederacy, and waged a bloody four-year war against the Union. When Congress met in December 1865, the Confederate vice president (Alexander Stephens of Georgia) came to serve as one of the two senators from Georgia. Others sent to Congress included six members of President Jefferson Davis's cabinet, 58 Confederate congressmen, four generals, and five colonels. Moreover, former Confederate leaders, military and civilian, were predominant in the governance of the states restored by Johnson. It was almost as if the war had never happened. Such defiance resulted in part from Johnson's misleading the states about the limits that would be placed on their actions.

Another source of strife was the great hostility the former Confederate states showed toward southern Unionists and those northern Unionists who settled in the South after the war. Residents of those states acted with even greater bitterness toward the former slaves, especially those who had deserted their masters and served in the Union army and navy. During the first year after Appomattox, some five thousand African Americans were murdered, almost as if an open season had been declared on them. The Joint Committee on Reconstruction held hearings documenting this rash of violence and other abuses. Admittedly, the committee was controlled by the Radical Republicans: Senator William Pitt Fessenden of Maine (one of six senators on the committee) was chairman, but Representative Thaddeus Stevens of Pennsylvania (one of nine representatives) dominated the committee by the sheer force of his caustic tongue, acerbic wit, and domineering personality.

Nonetheless, the states Johnson restored gave ample ammunition by their own actions. Black Codes were passed giving the freedmen some rights (to marry legally, own property, sue, and testify) but withholding major rights (voting, holding office, serving on juries). President Johnson, sensing the northern reaction, tried to persuade these states to let a few freedmen vote (especially those who were literate or propertied), but the South rebuffed him. Not a single state offered the ballot, even though northern sentiment increasingly called for it as a means of protecting the freedmen. The great leader, Frederick Douglass, said repeatedly that black Americans could defend themselves if given three boxes—ballot, cartridge, and jury. Furthermore, the South passed apprenticeship and vagrancy clauses that seemed a means of restoring slavery in a disguised form. Northern revulsion to these clauses was epitomized by a *Chicago Tribune* editorial that declared the North would invade Mississippi again and convert it into a frog pond rather than permit such laws to sully the memory of the northern soldiers who had died to free the slaves.

## REPUBLICAN CONCERNS

The Radical Republicans had mixed motives in their opposition to President Johnson's policies. Partly, they feared a loss of political power because emancipation ended the three-fifths clause of the Constitution, which established that five slaves counted as three persons in the census. In the absence of that clause, the South—the most heavily Democratic part of the nation—would be counted as having more people because former slaves who had counted as 3,000 persons would now count as a full 5,000. When the war began, nearly 4 million slaves lived in the South, but they had been counted as only 2.4 million people. With slavery ended, these Americans would be fully counted and the South would gain between twelve to twenty representatives in Congress. If only the prewar voters (white men) cast ballots, these additional representatives would probably all be Democrats. As the Union party, the Republicans had won the war but could lose the peace, as the more numerous Democrats took control.

Republicans also feared that the economic gains and benefits for industry enacted in the war (tariffs, subsidies, and general support) would be eroded and that the Confederate war debt might be paid and the Union war debt repudiated. But above all, the Republicans were actuated by humanitarian concerns. They genuinely sought means to enable the freedmen to gain the political rights that would enable them to protect themselves. If at the same time these new black voters were Republicans, as was likely, they would serve as a counterbalance to the increased southern Democratic vote. Thus, humanitarian, political, and economic considerations were intermingled in Republican policies.

With Andrew Johnson in the White House, these issues became increasingly bitter controversies rather than reconcilable points, and a titanic struggle ensued between the president and Congress. Early in 1866, Congress passed measures to protect the freedmen. It extended for another year the Freedmen's Bureau, which had originally been intended to last only one year; it also passed a temporary civil rights measure recommended by the Joint Committee to protect the freedmen. President Johnson vetoed each bill, declaring that since the slaves were now freed, they needed no special legislation and were to be treated exactly as all other Americans, with no special aid and benefit designed exclusively for them. Theoretically, that made sense, but given the reality of nearly two and a half centuries of the cruelties of slavery in America, the postwar violence, and the Black

Code clauses that seemed to be renewing slavery, African Americans did need help.

Speaking at a George Washington Birthday Celebration, Johnson exulted after his vetoes, referring to some Republicans as lame ducks and to others as traitors. He had begun with widespread popular support, but by his own contentiousness he drove away moderate Republicans who might have backed him. Instead, Republicans of all persuasions pulled together in the face of his onslaughts. Thus united, they quickly revived and passed both measures. Predictably, Johnson vetoed them again, with ringing declarations against special-interest legislation; Congress promptly pushed through both measures over his vetoes.

## THE FOURTEENTH AMENDMENT AND THE 1866 ELECTION

When the Joint Committee reported in June 1866, it recommended a fourteenth amendment to the Constitution. The Thirteenth Amendment, ratified in December 1865, had ended slavery. The proposed new amendment would provide citizenship and civil rights for all persons native born or naturalized, including equal protection under the law; would put civil disabilities on Confederate supporters who had held state or national office before the war (but give Congress the power to remove such disabilities); would permit Congress to reduce proportionately the representation in Congress of states denying voting rights to a sizeable portion of their inhabitants; and would ensure that the Union debt would never be questioned and that the Confederate debt would never be paid.

President Johnson denounced the proposed amendment as a violation of state sovereignty and urged the South not to ratify it. Tennessee nevertheless ratified it in July 1866 and reentered the Union, ending the anomaly of having the president's home state not in the Union. The other ten former Confederate states refused to ratify. The stage was set for the voters to register their approval or disapproval either of the president or of Congress in the upcoming election of 1866. In this midterm election all

members of the House and one-third of the Senate would, as usual, be up for reelection. Johnson decided to make a direct appeal to the electorate by traveling via train to key cities to make his pitch.

The trip was a disaster for Johnson. Eric McKitrick explains what happened in terms of Johnson's political roots. In his campaigning for office in eastern Tennessee, where communications were poor, Johnson had used a basic stump speech, with variations to suit each locality he visited. These communities were so isolated and communications were so poor that the speech had seemed fresh and new in each community he visited. But as president of the entire nation, Johnson's speech in Boston or Philadelphia or Cleveland or Chicago would be printed word for word in newspapers throughout the nation. When he attempted to deliver his basic stump speech with suitable local variations in one city after another, people soon became bored, for the speech was old news. The bored audiences gave free rein to the squads of Republican hecklers sent to annoy him, and Johnson then made a fatal mistake. Instead of ignoring or humoring the hecklers and gaining sympathy from the audience, he descended from the lofty perch of his position as president to debate the hecklers in a scene reminiscent of brawling in a fish market.

Race riots in Memphis and New Orleans during the spring and summer of 1866 formed a background to the president's feeble show and seriously undercut his claim that freedmen did not need special protection. Hundreds of African Americans were killed or injured in those two riots. The outcome of the 1866 election was a severe blow to Johnson and his policies. Republicans increased their control of the Congress with huge margins of 44 to 12 in the Senate and 143 to 49 in the House.

## CONGRESSIONAL RECONSTRUCTION

Republicans, led by the Radicals, could now enact their own program of Reconstruction with majorities large enough to override any presidential veto. These laws—since labeled

Congressional Reconstruction or Radical Reconstruction or Military Reconstruction—were not enacted until the new Congress convened in March of 1867. The South had had nearly two full years of home rule (April 1865 to March 1867) before military occupation began. The four major reconstruction acts passed by the new Congress (two in March 1867, one in July 1867, and one in March 1868) remade the South.

The ten Confederate states still out of the Union were divided into five military districts: Virginia; the Carolinas; Georgia, Florida, and Alabama; Mississippi and Arkansas; and Louisiana and Texas. Each district was headed by a Union general. A total of twenty thousand soldiers backed all five generals, an average of four thousand per district. The state governments recognized by President Johnson were removed from power and replaced by military occupation. State lines were not blurred, however, and the provisions applied to each state within its own boundaries. The five generals registered voters in each of the ten states, including not only white males but also black males, while at the same time excluding those leaders (perhaps fifty thousand in all) who would have been barred under the proposed fourteenth amendment. The voters, supervised by the military, then chose delegates to state constitutional conventions. Each convention had to write a new state constitution providing for, among other things, voting rights for black men. Each constitution then had to be ratified by the voters. Finally a new state government had to be chosen under the constitution, and the new state legislature had to ratify the proposed fourteenth amendment. When all this was done, and not until then, the state would be eligible for readmission to the Union.

## DEFYING CONGRESS
Johnson opposed the whole program and labeled it unconstitutional. He contended that the program violated state sovereignty, that Congress had usurped presidential power, and that illiterate, ignorant, and inexperienced blacks were voting and holding office. John Hope Franklin, however, documents that many of those blacks elected to high offices were as well educated as their white conterparts. Many had lived in the North, were college trained, and had degrees. The president fought back by using his veto power, only to be overridden, and by doing his utmost to obstruct the smooth operation of the program. Instead of accepting the reality of a congressionally mandated reconstruction, Johnson remained defiant, feeling that his fights for states' rights and white supremacy were vital. This belief led him to try to subvert Radical Reconstruction in his role as chief executive. His secretary of war controlled the War Department (the army) but the president as commander-in-chief was empowered to give orders to the general-in-chief and all other generals and officers. In this capacity, Johnson tried to remove those generals who commanded the five military Reconstruction districts and who were faithfully carrying out congressional wishes. He tried especially hard to remove Philip Sheridan.

Meanwhile, Congress tried to tie down Johnson, especially with two measures: a chain-of-command provision in an Army Appropriations Act and a Tenure of Office Act. The former pushed Johnson out of the loop so that he could not interfere with the generals heading the five military reconstruction districts. Orders were to go from the secretary of war through the general-in-chief to other generals and officers. Johnson, though commander-in-chief, was bypassed. The Tenure of Office Act barred the president from removing from office without permission of Congress any official whose appointment had been confirmed with the advice and consent of the Senate.

If this act was a deliberate trap, President Johnson certainly bit the bait. The key figure involved in the act was the secretary of war, Edwin B. Stanton. In an effort to minimize disruption at the onset of his administration, Johnson had retained Lincoln's cabinet intact. Most served Johnson well, but Stanton collaborated with and spied for the Radical Republican element. In August 1867, Johnson asked Stanton to resign, but he refused. A week later, the president suspended Stanton and named the popular war hero, General Ulysses Grant, to replace him on an interim basis. Grant was hesitant but complied. Johnson also removed two of the five generals commanding military reconstruction districts—Philip Sheridan and Daniel Sickles—replacing them with more conservative generals.

## IMPEACHMENT

The removal of the generals and Stanton hastened efforts, long brewing, to impeach President Johnson. In compliance with the Tenure of Office Act, the president sent a message to Congress stating why he had suspended Stanton. Congress considered the president's reasoning when it convened in December. In January 1868, the Senate rejected the president's explanation and reinstated Stanton, who returned to the War Department, where Grant surrendered the office to him. Grant's action disappointed Johnson, who thought he had an understanding that Grant would not let Stanton return but would turn the office over to the president. On 21 February, the president fired Stanton, naming Adjutant General Lorenzo Thomas as his replacement. Republicans, including Grant, rallied around Stanton, supporting him in his refusal to leave the premises.

Three days later, the House of Representatives voted overwhelmingly to impeach the president and set up a committee to prepare charges. Early in March the House adopted eleven articles of impeachment, nine of them revolving around the removal of Stanton. On 30 March 1868, the trial of the president began in the Senate, with Chief Justice Salmon Chase presiding. The president wanted to go to the Senate and make an impassioned speech on his behalf, but his defense managers persuaded him not to appear in person and to let them handle the matter. In May, the Senate voted on three articles. Although senators deemed the president guilty by a vote of 35 to 19, they were one vote short of the two-thirds (36 to 18) majority required to convict Johnson. Seven Republicans joined the 12

Democrats in the Senate to provide the 19 votes to acquit, while the other 35 Republicans voted to convict. By a margin of one vote, the president was saved from being convicted and removed from office. Removal would have severely strained the delicate constitutional balance of powers between the branches, but Johnson certainly provoked the Congress into this reckless act.

## FOREIGN AFFAIRS

Johnson's Reconstruction policies and the consequent impeachment and trial so dominate his administration that they overshadow some fine things that happened while Johnson was at the helm. This was truer in foreign affairs than in any other area. For the most part, the president allowed Secretary of State William H. Seward a free hand. Johnson backed Seward in the highly controversial purchase of Alaska from Russia in 1867 for $7.5 million; derided as "Seward's Folly" at the time, the purchase has come to be recognized as a great bargain and diplomatic coup. Johnson also backed Seward in pressuring the French to leave Mexico. France had taken advantage of U.S. preoccupation with the Civil War to enter Mexico and install Archduke Maximilian of Austria as Emperor. The emperor should have left with the last French soldiers protecting him but he remained (deluded that Mexicans accepted him), only to be arrested, tried, and executed.

## JOHNSON AFTER THE TRIAL

Contrary to popular thought, Johnson was not a broken man after his close escape from conviction and removal. Although he refrained from obstructing congressional reconstruction as before, he remained active in politics. The Republican party had repudiated him, but he sought the nomination of the Democratic party for the presidential campaign of 1868. He stood second on the first ballot, garnering 65 votes to the 105 for the front-runner, George Pendleton. Former governor Horatio Seymour of New York eventually won the Democratic nomination on the twenty-first ballot.

After his term ended in March 1869, Johnson returned to Tennessee and again became involved in state politics. He actively sought election to the U.S. Senate in 1869, but the Tennessee legislature chose another man by a vote of 55 to 51. Johnson tried again, this time for congressman-at-large from Tennessee, but he placed third in the election, only his second defeat in a popular vote in his long career. He made a final bid for office, winning election to the U.S. Senate in January 1875. That March he took his seat in the Senate, a body that had narrowly missed convicting him and removing him from office seven years earlier. Only two presidents have ever served in Congress after being president: John Quincy Adams in the House and Andrew Johnson in the Senate. Johnson's term was short-lived. Four months after taking his Senate seat, he suffered two strokes after a trip home to Greeneville, where he died on 31 July 1875 at the age of 66.

## EVALUATION OF ANDREW JOHNSON'S PRESIDENCY

Despite some achievements in such areas as foreign affairs, Andrew Johnson must be judged by his handling of Reconstruction. The period following the Civil War was one of the most crucial in U.S. history. The times cried for a skilled, sensitive, conciliatory hand at the helm, and Andrew Johnson's clumsy, bull-headed approach had disastrous consequences for the freedmen, the South, and the nation. He fought a backward-looking fight, determined to preserve the world as he knew it. True, the prejudices he displayed were in tune with the thinking of most Americans, North and South. Greatness like Lincoln's, however, lay not in pandering to prejudice but in having a vision to help a nation rise above it, to see the world as it should be. The energy Johnson expended on fighting the Radicals would have been better spent in working to harmonize his views with theirs in a forward-looking manner. That did not happen because Johnson was too narrow to rise above the partisanship and prejudice of his time.

Oddly enough, he thought of himself as a friend of black people, especially because of his push to emancipate slaves. That drive, however, was as much a result of his dislike of the planter class as it was of his concern for the welfare of African Americans. When Johnson had a chance to really help them, he reneged. He fought a bitter fight against efforts, supported by many Americans, to provide protection and assistance to the men and women so recently freed from slavery. He set a tone that increased, rather than diminished, racial hatred in America. Unfortunately, that undercurrent of racism persists and seems destined to continue to be a major problem in the twenty-first century.

## BIBLIOGRAPHY

Benedict, Michael Les. *The Impeachment Trial of Andrew Johnson* (Norton, 1973).

Bowen, David Warren. *Andrew Johnson and the Negro* (University of Tennessee Press, 1989).

Castel, Albert E. *The Presidency of Andrew Johnson* (University Press of Kansas, 1979).

Cox, LaWanda, and John H. Cox. *Politics, Principle, and Prejudice, 1865–1866: Dilemma of Reconstruction America* (Free Press, 1963).

Foner, Eric. *A Short History of Reconstruction, 1863–1877* (Harper & Row, 1990).

Franklin, John Hope. *Reconstruction After the Civil War*, rev. ed. (University of Chicago Press, 1994).

McKitrick, Eric L. *Andrew Johsnon and Reconstruction* (University of Chicago Press, 1960).

Riddleberger, Patrick W. *1866: The Critical Year Revisited* (Southern Illinois University Press, 1979).

Sefton, James E. *Andrew Johnson and the Uses of Constitutional Power* (Little, Brown, 1980).

Stryker Lloyd Paul. *Andrew Johnson: A Profile in Courage* (Macmillan, 1929).

Trefousse, Hans L. *Andrew Johnson: A Biography* (Norton, 1989).

———. *The Impeachment of a President: Andrew Johnson, the Blacks, and Reconstruction* (University of Tennessee Press, 1975).

## ★★★ 18 ★★★

# (HIRAM) ULYSSES SIMPSON GRANT
## 1869–1877

*Edgar A. Toppin*

*Born Hiram Ulysses Grant 27 April 1822 in Point Pleasant, Ohio, to Jesse Root Grant and Hannah Simpson Grant; educated at the U.S. Military Academy at West Point (B.S. 1843); married Julia Boggs Dent, 22 August 1848, St. Louis, Missouri; four children; elected president in 1868 on the Republican ticket with Schuyler Colfax of Indiana, receiving 3,012,833 votes and 214 electoral college ballots, over the Democratic slate of Horatio Seymour of New York and Francis Preston Blair, Jr., of Missouri (2,703,249 popular votes and 80 electoral ballots); reelected in 1872 with Henry Wilson of Massachusetts, receiving 3,597,132 votes and 286 electoral ballots, over the Democratic party and Liberal Republican party candidates, Horace Greeley of New York and Benjamin Gratz Brown of Missouri, with 2,834,079 popular votes (Greeley died three weeks after election and the electoral votes of the six states he carried were split among other candidates); died 23 July 1885 in Mount McGregor, New York; buried in Grant's Tomb, New York City.*

Ulysses Simpson Grant, eighteenth president of the United States, presided over one of the most corrupt administrations in U.S. history, matched only by the scandals of the Harding years. Both Grant and Harding were ill prepared for the White House. Harding's main interests were newspaper publishing and his buddies, Grant's main interest was military service. Harding had served briefly in office in Ohio (in the state legislature and as lieutenant governor) and in the U.S. Senate, but he showed little interest in carefully supervising the cronies he put in office, who dishonored him and caused him to lose his will to live. Grant had little interest in politics, having voted in only one presidential election before running for the office himself. He, too, failed to exercise tight control over friends and relatives who saw national office as a way to line their pockets.

Abraham Lincoln, the first Republican president, had won in 1860 when the Democratic party split over the slavery issue; he achieved a second term in the euphoria of the Union victory in taking Atlanta. Grant's easy victories in 1868 and 1872 were propelled by his status as a great war hero. Americans have a penchant for electing war heroes, usually generals, to the highest office in the land. This love of the man on horseback began with George Washington and continued with Andrew Jackson, William Henry Harrison, and Zachary Taylor. Following Grant, the nation selected Theodore Roosevelt and Dwight Eisenhower.

**THIRTY-NINE YEARS OF FAILURE**
Grant was born on 27 April 1822 in southwestern Ohio, at Point Pleasant, along the Ohio River near Cincinnati. He was the eldest of six children (three boys and three girls) born to Hannah Simpson Grant and Jesse Root Grant, who was both a farmer and the owner of a prosperous tannery. A year and a half after the future president was born, the family moved to Georgetown, Ohio, a nearby town farther back from the Ohio River; there the five younger children were born. Grant's original name was

Hiram Ulysses Grant, but he did not like or use his first name and everyone knew him as Ulysses or Lyss. He acquired the middle name Simpson when a congressman commissioned him to attend the military academy at West Point, New York. He listed his name as Ulysses Simpson Grant and assumed the young man followed the practice common in those days of using his mother's maiden name as his own middle name. At West Point, Grant planned to enroll as Ulysses Hiram Grant but found that he was stuck with a new middle name. In the end, U. S. ("unconditional surrender") Grant fitted in much better with his future military prowess.

As a youngster, Grant was quiet, introspective, and shy, talking little and keeping pretty much to himself. He did not fathom people, but he loved animals, especially horses, and seemed to understand and be at his best with them. He was an excellent horseman, and in later life, he found some of his greatest moments of bliss in getting away for long rides on horses or in horse-drawn vehicles. He derived at least part of his strong will, quiet resolve, determination, self-reliance, and sturdy character from his mother, who was somewhat strange and reclusive.

Other than his skill with horses and his bravery in action in the Mexican War, Grant's first thirty-nine years were an almost unrelieved record of failure and mediocrity. Realizing that his eldest son had no interest in or aptitude for the farm or the tannery, his father zealously sought a good education for him. In his early years, Grant was an indifferent scholar who made little headway in schools in Georgetown or academies at Maysville in Kentucky or Ripley in Ohio. Mathematics was the only subject that sparked his interest and in which he received decent grades. Jesse Grant despaired of his son's future. Grant knew this, and part of his drive for military and political success was to refute his father's low estimate of him. In Grant's four years at West Point (1839 to 1843), he proved to be only an average student but an exceptional horseman, one of the best in the academy's history. On graduating, he yearned to join the cavalry, but no slots were available. He had no intention of making the military his career, however; he hoped to serve the requisite term and then become a teacher, or a professor, of mathematics. Barred from the cavalry, he joined an infantry regiment and was stationed near St. Louis, where he met his future wife, Julia Dent, a Missouri belle and sister of Grant's West Point roommate, Frederick Dent, who also served in the infantry regiment. She was the only woman in Grant's life and was a source of strength for him.

Grant served in the Mexican war and was praised for his skill, bravery, and administrative abilities as quartermaster of his regiment. He married Julia Dent in August 1848, and they had four children. The family lived together when Grant was stationed at Detroit and upstate New York, but when he was transferred out West, especially on the Pacific Coast, Grant's pay was too low to relocate and support his family, even when he was promoted to captain. Compounding his loneliness during this period was a commanding officer at Fort Humboldt, California, who was a tyrant. Grant apparently became depressed and began drinking at this time, but his biographers disagree on whether or how much he drank. After a blow-up with his colonel, Grant resigned his commission in 1854, after eleven years of active duty. While on duty, he had lost some $1,500—years of his army salary—that he had given to an apparent con artist to invest in a business in San Francisco. This pattern of gullibility would follow Grant throughout his life.

For the next seven years (1854 to 1861), Grant had a rough time of it. He failed at farming on several plots in Missouri provided by his in-laws; he built a house there, naming it appropriately Hardscrabble. At one point, he was reduced to peddling firewood door-to-door in St. Louis, and later he was a rent collector for his wife's cousin in that city, but he proved ill-suited for the work. Finally, in 1860, he became a clerk in his father's leather goods store in Galena, Illinois, a store managed by his two younger

brothers. No one would have predicted that this clerk who turned 39 two weeks after the Civil War began would four years later become the nation's general-in-chief and go on to be elected president.

## GRANT IN THE CIVIL WAR

Grant's rise in the military was slow, steady, and well deserved. He was easily the best general in all the Civil War, and his reputation for being simply a butcher who used attrition to overwhelm undermanned Confederate forces was without merit. He had a brilliant military mind, especially his strategic grasp, and he applied it better than any general on either side. He was decisive, unafraid to face challenges and make decisions, clear and precise in his commands, dogged, and a good student of military minds, both friends and foes. War, along with horsemanship, was the one thing he did superbly. If he had had an equal grasp on business or governmental affairs, his success would have been greater, but in those areas he remained a lamb, ready to be fleeced.

When war came at Fort Sumter on 12 April 1861, Grant, as a West Pointer, had a chance to prove himself and to erase his painful memories of years of failure. He helped Illinois recruit and train troops, eventually becoming colonel of a state regiment. Soon he was made a federal brigadier general of volunteers. Grant had found his milieu. Not very studious in most areas, he was an intense student of military affairs, both of tactics and men. He had learned and grown in the Mexican War, and he continued to do so in the Civil War. He made mistakes but never repeated them, always learning, growing, and advancing. In his early Civil War years, he served under General Henry Halleck, a West Pointer who lacked the vision and imagination that drove Grant.

In February 1862, Grant took Fort Henry on the Tennessee River and Fort Donelson on the Cumberland, the former barely with Halleck's sanction, the latter over his vehement objections. These twin triumphs aroused a victory-starved nation and made Grant a hero, especially because of his response to the Fort Donelson commander, Simon Buckner. This Confederate general was an old friend and West Point schoolmate of Grant's who had gone hiking with him and had lent him money to rejoin Julia and the children at a time when Grant was scraping bottom. Based on this old friendship, General Buckner expected leniency when he asked for terms. Instead, Grant replied, "No terms except an immediate and unconditional surrender can be accepted," and he stated further that if Buckner did not give up at once, Grant would attack. Buckner and his nearly 12,000 men surrendered, the first such result in the war. The phrase "unconditional surrender" caught on, making Grant a national hero.

That was a high point, but there were also low points and lessons to be learned. As Grant's army moved southward, it was taken by surprise at Shiloh in Tennessee in April 1862, when General Albert Sidney Johnston's Confederate forces attacked. The Union forces, who had not yet dug in, were nearly overwhelmed; Grant rallied them and won but at a heavy loss of life. Rumors of Grant's drinking and incompetence surfaced in the wake of that near disaster. Nothing could be done to dispel the gossip about his drinking, but Grant dug in whenever his men stopped overnight thereafter. Many urged the president to remove Grant because of the heavy losses at Shiloh, but Lincoln replied, "I can't spare this man—he fights." With the president's strong backing, Grant would go on to lead the Union to victory in the war. Like Grant, Lincoln had a strong grasp of strategic needs, though in his case it was more from intuition than from study. Both realized the need to crush enemy armies rather than merely to seize places.

Grant's supreme victory came at Vicksburg, Mississippi, on 4 July 1863. In a daring move, he led an army of twenty thousand men across the Mississippi River on 10 April into enemy country. There, with no supply line or provisions but living off the land, he faced Confederate forces (under such generals as Joseph Johnston and John Pemberton) that totaled more than

three times his number. In a lightning series of strikes, Grant battled these forces separately, kept them from linking, and laid siege to Vicksburg. Pemberton surrendered an army of nearly 30,000 on July Fourth, a fitting birthday gift for the Union. Port Hudson, Louisiana, fell a few days later, giving the Union control of the entire Mississippi River and severing the southwest (Arkansas, Louisiana, and Texas) from the other eight states of the Confederacy. Vicksburg showed how Grant could operate without overwhelming superiority on his side; he was not a "butcher" there.

Eventually, Lincoln gave Grant control of Union armies, first in the West and then in the entire nation. As overall commander, Grant conceived a grand strategy to win the war: The main Union forces would advance simultaneously, pinning down General Robert E. Lee in Virginia while engaging the other main Confederate forces. As the plan ultimately unfolded, Sherman was to take Atlanta, cut loose as at Vicksburg, march to the sea at Savannah, and then head north through the Carolinas to join Grant in crushing Lee. To deprive the Confederates of the advantage of interior lines and of moving forces back and forth to reinforce points under attack, the Union troops would have to ensure that the Confederate armies, especially Lee's, were continually engaged. Union troops would abandon the old pattern of advance, fight, retreat to lick wounds, rebuild for some months, and then come forth to advance again. The new watchword was continual fighting. If, in the process, Grant's superior forces wore down Lee's irreplaceable manpower, that would be a side benefit, but the key point was to keep Lee engaged. Even the most astute Grant biographer, William McFeely (*Grant: A Biography*), seemed to miss that point, putting his main emphasis on attrition and the resultant slaughter of men on both sides, especially the Union. That approach mistakenly paints Grant as a callous butcher. Moreover, rifles had generally replaced the old smooth-bore guns by 1864, making assaults much more costly. Fortunately, President Lincoln recognized the strategic picture and backed Grant despite the howls of protest.

The strategy worked, and Lee surrendered at Appomattox on 9 April 1865, basically ending the Civil War. If newspapers had taken polls in those days, Grant's popularity would have gone off the charts, for his victory enhanced his popularity in the North while his generous terms to Lee gave him new stature in the South. One biographer suggests that if Grant had captured Richmond in spring 1864, without the frightful losses at Wilderness, Spotsylvania, and Cold Harbor, he might have been nominated and elected in 1864. The nation was so grateful for his victories that Congress created a new four-star rank of general for Grant, simultaneously awarding it to George Washington posthumously.

### TRYING TO LIVE WITH JOHNSON
As with Dwight Eisenhower in 1952, no one was certain of Grant's political allegiance. The only time he had voted for president had been in 1856 when he cast his ballot for the Democrat, James Buchanan. Grant knew the first Republican presidential nominee, General John C. Frémont, and later described his ballot as more a vote against Frémont than for Buchanan. Andrew Johnson, the Democrat who succeeded the slain Lincoln, vied with the Radical Republicans to gain Grant's allegiance. Nonetheless, Grant increasingly sided with moderates and the Radical Republicans because he believed Johnson's policies were detrimental to freedmen. Grant himself had owned only one slave, William Jones. (Grant's wife owned four through her family.) Grant had set Jones free in 1859, refusing to sell him even though Grant was desperately in need of money.

Grant accompanied Johnson on his political swing around the circle in the off-year elections of 1866 but very reluctantly, because he was increasingly leery of the president's policies. Grant was caught in the middle when Johnson, defying Congress by testing the Tenure of Office Act, replaced Secretary of War Edwin Stanton with Grant on an interim basis. Grant served for five months but, much to Johnson's anger, he surrendered the office to Stanton when Congress rejected Johnson's rationale for suspending Stanton. President Johnson had expected Grant to remain in place and turn the office over to him or to his representative. The rupture was completed when Johnson rebuked Grant severely at a cabinet meeting.

### BECOMING PRESIDENT
After the confrontation between Johnson and Congress, it was only a matter of time until Grant would move into the White House. The Republicans needed him, with his enormous popularity, to head the ticket in 1868. Grant was nominated at the convention in Chicago on the first ballot, with Schuyler Colfax of Indiana as his running mate. They defeated the Democratic nominees, former governor Horatio Seymour of New York and Francis Blair, Jr., of Missouri, by an electoral margin of 214 to 80 and a popular vote of 3 million to 2.7 million. Considering that Democrats had strength throughout the United States and that Republicans had very little support among southern white voters, this was a huge margin. Newly enfranchised black voters in the former Confederate states were a key to Grant's victory.

Accustomed to making decisions all on his own in the military, President Grant made the mistake of selecting his cabinet without consulting anyone. Mostly he chose friends, especially old mates from the military or people to whom he felt obligated for their support in his career. As a result, he was surrounded by weak men who succumbed to temptation, and the postwar atmosphere provided temptations galore. The sacrifice and idealism of wartime had given way to a general let-down in America. Corruption was rampant at the state and municipal levels, such as the notorious Tweed Ring in New York City, and it infested the federal government as well. Moreover, the get-rich-quick atmosphere of the new and developing business and finance capitalism as the nation underwent its industrial revolution reinforced the unfettered greed and selfishness sweeping the nation. All these factors combined into scandals under Grant, who was generally gullible except in military matters.

Not only did Grant appoint weak men to high office in government, he compounded the error by not supervising them closely. As a military man, he did not micromanage—he was accustomed to issuing precise orders and relying on able subordinates to carry them out. Applied to government, this proved a recipe for disaster. Although he could size up men accurately in military affairs, he was not the best judge of character in governmental matters. He proved an easy mark for hustlers who sought to enrich themselves at the government's expense. Grant did favor reform of the spoils system to lessen corruption in the civil service, but he lacked the political skills to get such reform through Congress. Eventually it took the shock of President James Garfield's assassination by a disappointed office seeker in 1881 to open the door to enactment of civil service reform.

## THE GOLD CORNER
The first big scandal broke during Grant's first year in office, when two charming, bold, and unscrupulous financiers—Jay Gould and Jim Fisk—tried to make a killing by cornering the gold market. The only possible impediment was that the Treasury Department might release some of its large supply of gold into the market. Gould and Fisk used Grant's brother-in-law, Abel Corbin of New York City, to ensure that the Treasury would not ruin their scheme by releasing its gold. Early in 1869, Corbin, a 61-year-old financier, had wooed and married Virginia (Jennie) Grant, the president's 37-year-old sister, whose stock had shot up when Grant took office. At the urging of Gould and Fisk, Corbin tried to keep Grant from letting the secretary of the treasury release gold, and for months, the Treasury Department was inactive in that sphere. Abel and Jennie Corbin were given accounts with which to speculate and enrich themselves as the price of gold, manipulated by Gould and Fisk, climbed higher and higher.

They tried to have one of Corbin's relatives appointed as assistant secretary of the treasury to keep an eye on things from the inside. Failing that, Corbin and the schemers urged Grant to appoint a fund raiser, General Daniel Butterfield, who joined the plot and opened a speculative account in an area where he was supposed to be a watchdog for the public.

When the price rose too high, President Grant and Secretary of the Treasury George Boutwell contemplated selling government gold. Corbin's desperate pleas not to do so alerted Grant that something was fishy. He finally moved to thwart the scheme, conferring with Boutwell and releasing gold when the price reached $160 an ounce. On Black Friday, 24 September 1869, the price fell to $140 within half an hour, ruining many speculators and causing severe losses for a great many more. Gould got word early and sold out, leaving Fisk holding the bag. The Corbins took a beating also, and General Butterfield was forced out of office. Two of Grant's closest White House aides—Generals Orville Babcock and Horace Porter—who had been on his military staff during the war, were also apparently involved in this scandal, with gold-speculating accounts of their own. Some persons then even questioned whether Grant's wife, Julia, might be involved, but that seems unlikely.

Although rumors of other misdeeds were swirling by the time of the election of 1872, they were not enough to ruin Grant's chance of reelection. The Liberal Republicans, a reform wing of his party, broke with Grant and nominated Horace Greeley, editor of the *New York Tribune*. So as not to split the anti-Grant vote, Democrats accepted Greeley as their nominee also. Grant was nominated for a second term on the first ballot at the Republican convention in Philadelphia. Vice President Colfax, however, had been tainted by the Credit Mobilier scandal, in which many members of Congress had accepted bribes of stock in a phony construction company that siphoned off federal aid in the building of the Union Pacific Railroad. In place of Colfax, the convention chose Senator Henry Wilson of

Massachusetts as Grant's running mate. Grant and Wilson won the popular vote by 3,598,000 to 2,835,000. Greeley's death, three weeks before the electoral college met, resulted in Grant winning the electoral count by 286 to 3, with most of Greeley's 63 electors casting their ballots for other men in view of his death.

## WHISKEY AND OTHER SCANDALS

Still more scandals came to light during Grant's second term, especially after Democrats took control of the House in the off-year congressional elections in 1874 and zealously investigated wrongdoing. The Whiskey Ring Fraud involved distillers routinely bribing federal tax agents so as to avert paying the required excise tax. Tax agents had been bribed during earlier administrations, but not at such very high levels as in the Grant administration. Grant's third secretary of the treasury, Benjamin Bristow, worked vigorously to expose the fraud in 1875. His investigation showed that top officials in the Internal Revenue Service in St. Louis and Chicago were heavily involved and that General John McDonald, head of the St. Louis district (covering seven states), was the boss of the ring. McDonald was a Grant appointee and a friend of Julia Dent's family.

Grant at first cooperated with the investigation, but when it began to touch men very close to him, such as his personal secretary, General Orville Babcock, Grant became very angry with Bristow, feeling that his zealous pursuit of corruption was playing into the hands of the president's enemies, both the Democrats and the Liberal Republicans. Not only General Babcock, but General Horace Porter (likewise a close friend and a member of Grant's wartime staff) was also part of the Whiskey Ring, a shattering revelation to Grant. Increasingly, Grant came to feel that he was the real target and that Babcock and Porter were being used to get at him.

Other scandals, exposed in 1875 and 1876, reached all the way to Grant's cabinet and to another of his siblings. One cabinet member was Secretary of War William

Belknap, yet another general whose ethics in postwar government service were questionable. Belknap had served under William Tecumseh Sherman and had succeeded John Rawlins at the War Department upon the latter's death in September 1869. Belknap took bribes from men to whom he gave lucrative trading posts out West, in places like Fort Sill, Oklahoma, where huge profits were made by cheating the Native Americans.

Under siege and on the verge of impeachment, Belknap tearfully confessed the bribes to Grant, who calmly let him resign on the spot on 2 March 1875. House members, furious at Grant for letting Belknap go, impeached the former secretary of war later that same day. The impeachment trial was held in the Senate despite his resignation, and when that body voted in early August, Belknap was acquitted only because the Senate fell short of the required two-thirds vote to convict. Some 23 senators deemed the former secretary guilty but— since the only penalty for impeachment is removal from office—saw no need to convict a man who had already resigned. If Grant had not let him slip away, Belknap would have been convicted and removed from office, even though Republicans controlled the Senate 54 to 19.

Both a cabinet and a family member were involved in another scandal. Secretary of the Interior Columbus Delano and one of his administrators, Surveyor-General Silas Reed, were implicated in a scheme whereby surveying contracts were awarded in return for kickbacks; the group receiving the contracts included Delano's son John and Grant's brother Orville Grant. When this clear defrauding of the government was exposed, Reed and Delano resigned.

Almost all of Grant's departments were touched by scandal. In addition to those already discussed, the Navy Department also caused Grant embarrassment. George Robeson, a Philadelphia lawyer, made $8,000 per year as Secretary of the Navy, but he deposited $300,000 in his bank account. A Philadelphia grain merchant firm, Cattell & Company, apparently advanced

Robeson's fortunes in exchange for his awarding the firm lucrative contracts to supply the U.S. fleet. The president's diplomatic representative to Great Britain, General Robert Schenck of Ohio, pushed the British to invest in American enterprises, including a silver-mining company in which he was involved personally. While in his diplomatic post, Schenck also looked out for interests of the Jay Cooke Banking firm, apparently with retainers from that company.

## FOREIGN POLICY

Despite the rampant corruption, the Grant administration did have some successes, especially in foreign relations, thanks in large measure to Secretary of State Hamilton Fish. Grant's initial secretary of state was his local congressman, Elihu Washburne of Galena, who had applied political pressure to help Grant advance in the military early in the Civil War. Washburne, crude, countrified, and almost unlettered, was poorly suited for the post. Grant got him to resign after six days and to accept instead the post of American minister to France. Hamilton Fish of New York then became secretary of state and served throughout Grant's two terms. Fish was an aristocrat, a patrician figure of courtly manner and bearing who was quite comfortable in the world of diplomacy.

The most notable fruit of the Grant-Fish diplomatic thrust was the settlement of the *Alabama* claims, which involved various matters, including fishing rights and the naturalization of former British subjects as U.S. citizens. The principal focus, however, was on Confederate raiders built in England during the war. These ships—especially the *Alabama* under Raphael Semmes, but also the *Florida, Georgia, Rappahannock,* and *Shenandoah*—dealt devastating blows to Union shipping. The *Alabama* pursued American merchant ships all over the globe, forcing much of the merchant marine to stay home. The Chairman of the Senate Foreign Relations Committee, Charles Sumner of Massachusetts, demanded that

Great Britain pay indirect damages that amounted to several billion dollars and included the cost of U.S. ships kept off the seas by the Confederate raiders. Hamilton Fish sought, more realistically, direct damages of less than $50 million. Grant sided with Fish and against Sumner.

The president and the senator differed on other issues as well. Sumner blocked Grant's efforts to acquire Santo Domingo. Grant retaliated, first by removing Sumner's friend, John Motley, from the post of minister to Great Britain, and second, by getting Senate Republicans to strip Sumner of his chairmanship of the Foreign Relations Committee. With Sumner out of the way, Fish easily secured approval of the Washington Treaty and its provision for arbitration of the disputed *Alabama* claims. Arbitrators awarded the United States $15 million in direct damages, which Britain paid, averting a threat to peace.

Grant's ill-fated efforts to annex Santo Domingo nevertheless failed. Sumner bitterly resented the attempt to annex one of the few independent black republics in the world. He also despised Grant's failure to aid freedmen and carpetbaggers against hostile southerners.

## GRANT AND MINORITIES

If judged by intent, Grant might be given high marks for his relations with the two leading minorities of the time—his heart generally was in the right place when it came to African Americans and Native Americans. But his record is rather dismal when one considers his achievements in regard to these two groups. Grant had a deep-seated sense of fair play, and he had opposed James Polk's action in provoking the war with Mexico. Although Grant sided with the Mexicans, he had honored his obligation to his country and fought against them. Similarly, Grant had kindly feelings toward African Americans and Native Americans, well ahead of the normal sentiments of his time. He had opposed Andrew Johnson because he saw Johnson as a racist who supported white supremacy. Yet Grant, fearful of reigniting the Civil War, was reluctant to use the army or black militia to stop the white supremacists who terrorized and murdered African Americans and drove carpetbag governments out of power in the South.

The Fifteenth Amendment granting the right to vote to black men was ratified under Grant. Moreover, he tried his best to acquire Santo Domingo as a place to which African Americans could go and control their own lives instead of trying to live with their racist white neighbors. But Grant turned a blind eye when his son, Frederick, actively harassed and helped drive out James Webster Smith, the first black cadet to enter West Point. Grant could have used his enormous prestige as a West Pointer and president to integrate West Point, but he did not choose to do so.

Nor could Grant bring himself to use federal power to stop land-hungry and gold-seeking Americans from running roughshod over the treaty rights of Native Americans. This failure provoked bitter retaliation, such as occurred at the Battle of Little Big Horn where Custer's force was wiped out in 1876. Grant did, however, appoint the first Native American to hold the post of commissioner of Indian affairs—Ely Parker, a full-blooded Seneca who had served on Grant's military staff.

## WORLD TOUR AND THIRD-TERM HOPES

Grant's supporters sought a third-term nomination in 1876, but he was willing, albeit reluctantly, to step aside. He was only 54 years old when his party nominated Rutherford B. Hayes of Ohio to face Samuel Tilden of New York. Grant's solid strength of leadership kept the nation together through the disputed Hayes-Tilden election, a situation that could have sparked another civil war. Instead, the nation accepted the verdict of an electoral commission that by an 8-to-7 vote gave Hayes the presidency.

After leaving the White House, Ulysses and Julia Grant set out from Philadelphia on a world tour that lasted two and a half years (May 1877 to December 1879). Grant had enormous popularity worldwide as the general who had won the Civil War, and their trip began to take on dimensions of a preliminary campaign for a third term. Returning home, the Grants landed in San Francisco and traveled across the United States. But if a third term was his goal, Grant peaked too soon, returning to the United States nine months before the Republican convention opened in June 1880. Had he returned on the eve of the convention, a third term might have been his. Even so, Grant led on the first ballot with 304 votes, 66 short of the 370 needed for nomination. His chief rival, James Blaine, had 284. President Hayes was not a factor and Grant's 300 delegates stuck with him. In the end, a coalition of the other candidates gave the victory to a compromise nominee, James Garfield, who went on to win the election.

## THE LAST BATTLE

Grant's last fight was his most valiant. He had almost the opposite of the Midas touch, losing money in every investment to which he put his hand. He simply lacked good business sense. If he had remained a general, he would have had a good pension for life, but there was no provision in those days for former presidents. Admirers raised a trust fund of $250,000, hoping the income would support Grant. Homes were provided for him in Galena, Illinois, and in Philadelphia and New York. His trust fund investments went bad, and in 1881, he entered a brokerage firm, Grant and Ward, along with his son Ulysses, Jr., known as Buck Grant. Ferdinand Ward turned out to be another scoundrel and the business failed, forcing Grant into bankruptcy.

Grant was destitute but had to support his wife and himself. He wrote a few magazine articles on several Civil War battles. They proved so successful that he was offered a chance to make money writing his memoirs. When it became clear that the publishing company he had originally signed with was not going to give him a fair share, Samuel Clemens (Mark Twain) took over and gave him a much fairer deal. It soon became a race between the book and death because Grant developed a fatal throat cancer, caused no doubt by his habit of smoking about a score of cigars a day throughout his adult life. He moved to a home at Mount McGregor, New York, to complete his manuscript. Painfully, day-by-day he kept toiling on, knowing this was the only way to leave his family an income. He won his last race and completed the manuscript shortly before he died on 23 July 1885. The book was a great success, providing nearly $500,000 to sustain his wife comfortably the rest of her days, till her death in 1902.

Grant was temporarily buried in Riverside Park until Grant's Tomb, a magnificent structure, was completed in 1897, in Morningside Heights in New York City, overlooking the Hudson River. Julia Grant was later buried there alongside her husband.

## BIBLIOGRAPHY

Catton, Bruce. *U. S. Grant and the American Military Tradition* (Little, Brown, 1954).

Grant, U. S. *Personal Memoirs of U. S. Grant* (C.L. Webster, 1885–1886; reissued, University of Nebraska Press, 1996).

Hesseltine, William. *Ulysses S. Grant, Politician* (Ungar, 1957).

McFeely, William. *Grant: A Biography* (Norton, 1981).

Pitkin, Thomas M. *The Captain Departs: Ulysses S. Grant's Last Campaign* (Southern Illinois University Press, 1973).

Simon, John Y., ed. *The Personal Memoirs of Julia Dent Grant* (Putnam's, 1975).

Simpson, Brooks. *Let Us Have Peace: Ulysses S. Grant and the Politics of War and Reconstruction, 1861–1868* (University of North Carolina Press, 1991).

Williams, T. Harry. *Lincoln and His Generals* (Knopf, 1952).

★★★ 19 ★★★

# RUTHERFORD BIRCHARD HAYES
## 1877–1881

*Ari Hoogenboom*

*Born 4 October 1822 in Delaware, Ohio, to Rutherford Hayes and Sophia Birchard Hayes; educated at Kenyon College, Gambier, Ohio (B.A. 1842); attended Harvard Law School (LL.B. 1845); married Lucy Ware Webb, 30 December 1852, Cincinnati, Ohio; eight children; ran for president in 1876 on the Republican ticket with William Almon Wheeler of New York and received 4,036,298 popular votes and 165 electoral college ballots; the Democratic ticket of Samuel Jones Tilden of New York and Thomas Andrews Hendricks of Indiana received 4,300,590 popular votes and 184 electoral ballots, one shy of the needed 185; a special electoral commission gave all three disputed states, with 21 electoral votes, to Hayes; died 17 January 1893 in Fremont, Ohio; buried in Spiegel Grove, Fremont, Ohio.*

Although a puny baby, Rutherford Birchard Hayes survived the vicissitudes of childhood (including his mother's sheltering) and as an adolescent loved sports and hunting. He was diligent in school but had difficulty studying on his own. Fortunately his uncle, Sardis Birchard, sent him to preparatory school, and Hayes entered Kenyon College in 1838. Four years later, he was surprised to be named the valedictorian of his graduating class, since he had not accepted Jesus Christ as his personal savior. Hayes spent an unrewarding year reading law in Columbus, Ohio, before attending Harvard Law School, from which he graduated in 1845.

## THE WAR AND OHIO POLITICS

After practicing in Uncle Sardis's town of Lower Sandusky (later named Fremont), Hayes moved to Cincinnati in 1850, where he built a reputation as a competent lawyer and married Lucy Ware Webb on 30 December 1852. Lucy, a Methodist, a total abstainer, and an abolitionist, tolerated Hayes's unorthodox Christianity, his temperate drinking, and his moderate antislavery views. In time, she influenced him to attend and support (but not join) a church, to become a teetotaler, and to be more committed to antislavery. He defended runaway slaves, joined the Republican party, and fought four years and was wounded five times in the Civil War, which he quickly came to regard as a crusade against slavery.

As a war hero Hayes attracted voters. He was easily elected and reelected to Congress (serving from 1865 to 1867), where he supported Radical Reconstruction measures. He next served two terms as governor of Ohio from 1868 to 1872. As governor he was primarily responsible for the state's ratification of the Fifteenth Amendment and for the establishment of Ohio State University. He also earned a reputation as a civil service reformer and as a humane administrator because of his concern for society's less fortunate members and his generous use of the pardoning power. Refusing a minor office from the Grant administration, Hayes retired from politics and moved to Fremont.

Hayes had scarcely escaped from the "bother" of politics when the Republican party fell into disarray. The Panic of 1873 marked the beginning of a severe depression with widespread unemployment and falling prices for farmers. Coincidentally, Grant's administration ended with major scandals involving his secretary of war and his private secretary. In Ohio the Democrats

in 1873 elected as governor William Allen, an advocate of inflation, and appeared ready to sweep into the presidency in the election of 1876.

Ohio Republicans persuaded Hayes, their strongest candidate, to come out of retirement in 1875 to challenge Allen, who was up for reelection as governor. Hayes won that election by a narrow margin and was immediately spoken of as a candidate for the 1876 Republican nomination for president. Although other candidates had loyal followers and were more prominent on the national scene, Hayes, Ohio's favorite son, was almost everybody's second choice. When neither the charismatic but corrupt James G. Blaine, nor the reformers' favorite Benjamin H. Bristow (whom Grant hated), nor the quintessential spoilsman Roscoe Conkling (whom the reformers despised), nor the radical's favorite Oliver H. P. Morton (who was in poor health) could muster a majority, the convention turned to Hayes. He was a war hero who as a congressman and governor had been a radical on Reconstruction issues, and he was a reformer who had remained loyal to Grant in 1872, when many of that persuasion strayed to support the Liberal Republican party. Hayes, it was hoped, would unite Republicans and stanch desertions to the Democrats.

## THE ELECTION OF 1876

The campaign of 1876 was an uphill struggle for the Republicans, especially since the Democrats nominated Governor Samuel J. Tilden of New York, a formidable political organizer with a reform reputation. Charged with corruption and blamed for hard times, Republicans found that their standard tactic of identifying the Democrats with wartime treason and peacetime persecution of black Republicans had lost some of its appeal. On the evening of election day the Democrats claimed victory for Tilden. Hayes (and Republican National Chairman Zachariah Chandler) believed they were defeated, but Daniel Sickles (an incompetent Civil War general known for the corruption, seduction, and murder that were ancillary to his political career) dropped by the nearly deserted Republican headquarters in New York. Sifting through late returns, Sickles concluded that if Hayes could carry South Carolina, Louisiana, and Florida—southern states the Republicans still controlled—he would win the election by one electoral vote. Accordingly, Sickles dispatched telegrams urging Republican authorities to "hold" those states for Hayes. Encouraging responses to Sickles's telegrams led Republicans to dispute the Democrats and claim those states and victory for Hayes.

The tallies available immediately after election day were unofficial. Returning (or canvassing) boards in the disputed states would make the official count. They were empowered to throw out votes in areas where fraud or intimidation occurred, and in the three disputed states these boards were controlled by Republicans. With Democratic and Republican "visiting statesmen" converging on the disputed states, the returning boards set to work. Unofficial returns had Hayes narrowly carrying South Carolina, losing Florida by only 94 votes, but failing in Louisiana by a substantial 6,300 votes. Because black Republican voters were intimidated in all three states, the returning boards threw out enough Democratic ballots to ensure Republican victories on both national and state levels, but the Democrats claimed (with reason) that many of their ballots were thrown out fraudulently. The votes of Republican electors for Hayes were officially certified and sent to Washington to be counted by the president of the Senate (a Republican) in the presence of a joint session of both houses of Congress (in which the Democrats had a majority). Rival votes of Democratic electors for Tilden in those three disputed states were certified by the highest ranking Democrat available and were also sent to Washington.

The Republicans and Democrats could not agree on whether the president of the Senate or the majority of the joint session should decide which set of disputed returns should be counted. A bipartisan majority in Congress—realizing that a mechanism was needed that would decide which votes to count and that would confer as much legitimacy as possible upon the victor—devised the Electoral Commission Act of 1877. That act set up a commission of five representatives, five senators, and five Supreme Court justices; seven were Republicans, seven were Democrats, and the fifteenth member, it was presumed, would be politically independent Supreme Court Justice David Davis. But Illinois Democrats miscalculated woefully when, to buy his vote for Tilden, they elected Davis to the Senate. Instead of supporting Tilden's claims on the commission, Davis disqualified himself, and his place was taken by Justice Joseph P. Bradley, a Republican. The count got under way, and when disputed returns were reached they were referred to the commission. By an 8-to-7 majority, the commission decided not to question the official returns from the Florida, Louisiana, and South Carolina canvassing boards and awarded the disputed votes to Hayes.

When it became obvious that the commission would decide the election for Hayes, the Democratic majority in the House of Representatives delayed the count with frequent adjournments. They hoped that the threat of chaos, if no president were sworn in by 4 March, would force the Republicans (who were anxious to complete the count) to agree to their demands for withdrawing the federal support that propped up Republican state governments in the South and, to a lesser extent, for providing railroad subsidies for the South. Despite negotiations, nothing was conceded beyond the terms Hayes had publicly promised during the recent campaign. If southern Democrats would respect the civil and voting rights of black and white Republicans, he would order federal troops to return to their barracks. Indeed, the negotiations had little to do with ending the filibuster effort in the House. It was the rulings of Speaker of the House Samuel J. Randall, not the statements of negotiators, that completed the count early in the morning of 2 March 1877.

## THE HAYES PROGRAM

Hayes was privately sworn in on 3 March to avoid an interregnum, since the formal inauguration took place on Monday, 5 March 1877. His inaugural address discussed the South, civil service reform, currency, foreign relations, and the recent disputed election. He reiterated his support of local self-government as long as the Fourteenth and Fifteenth Amendments were obeyed, and he recognized the federal government's obligation to secure the civil rights of those who had been recently emancipated. He did not call for railroad subsidies for the South; instead, insisting that universal suffrage had to rest on universal education, he requested generous state support of free schools supplemented by federal aid to education where needed.

Calling for a "thorough, radical, and complete" reform of the civil service, Hayes wished to return to the less partisan practices of the founders, to retain capable civil servants in office rather than rotate them out, and to eliminate congressional dictation of appointments. Although fully aware that he was elected by political partisans, Hayes reminded himself "that he serves his party best who serves his country best." And to avoid the temptation to distribute patronage to secure reelection, Hayes pledged to serve only one term.

Hayes ardently favored a return to the gold standard. He believed that the fluctuating value of greenbacks (paper money that was issued during the Civil War and that was not backed by gold) accentuated the severe depression that began in 1873. He therefore called for legislation implementing the return to specie payments—that is the redemption in gold of greenbacks.

Hayes stressed arbitration. He wished to follow that policy, which Grant had inaugurated with the Treaty of Washington (1871), and also follow the traditional American policy of noninterference with other nations. He congratulated the American people for arbitrating the recent disputed election and called on them to build a union based not on force but on "the loving devotion of a free people."

## THE CABINET BATTLE

Hayes had spent only one night in the White House before he was attacked by members of his own party. His inaugural address had pleased reformers but had angered some congressional party leaders whom Hayes had already offended by ignoring their candidates for the cabinet. Senators James G. Blaine and Roscoe Conkling (although mortal enemies) had made the appointment of their lieutenants William P. Frye and Thomas C. Platt, respectively, to the cabinet "as a condition for good relations." When neither was appointed, Blaine immediately attacked the president and Conkling never again spoke to Hayes.

Although congressional Republicans found Hayes's selection of Senator John Sherman as secretary of the treasury very acceptable and approved of three others—George W. McCrary of Iowa for secretary of war, Richard W. Thompson of Indiana as secretary of the navy, and Charles Devens of Massachusetts as attorney general—they were outraged by the appointment of William M. Evarts as secretary of state, David M. Key as postmaster general, and above all by Carl Schurz as secretary of the interior. Evarts was the leader of New York reform-minded Republicans who were in opposition to Roscoe Conkling. Key was a Tennessee Democrat whose appointment (and dispensation of patronage) was designed to entice prewar Whigs to join postwar Republicans. And Schurz was unacceptable since he had led the Liberal Republican revolt and had joined the Democrats in an attempt to defeat Grant in 1872. Consequently, the Senate took the then-unprecedented step of referring all of Hayes's cabinet nominees to committee and roundly denounced Evarts, Key, and Schurz. Hayes, however, stood firm, and a flood of letters, telegrams, and editorials caused the Senate to back down and confirm the cabinet. Relying on the politics of reform and the force of public opinion, Hayes won this first skirmish with senators, who relied on the politics of organization.

Hayes still faced a huge task and a great problem. About one thousand civil servants, requiring senatorial confirmation, had to be either reappointed or replaced and, of greater import, Republican governments in South Carolina and Louisiana had to be either restored to power or abandoned. Through a Florida Supreme Court decision, that state had already been captured by the Democrats. With a minuscule staff designed to help with correspondence but not to evaluate policies, Hayes had to rely on his cabinet and on congressional representatives and friends for advice. The presidency in 1877 was an individual, not an institution. After chatting with Representative James A. Garfield, Hayes decided to fill only the vacant offices and to allow incumbents to remain on the job while he deliberated on their replacements. Hayes's appointments were good and less partisan than those of any president since John Quincy Adams, but none was better than that of John Marshall Harlan, a champion of civil rights and a foe of monopoly, whom he named to the Supreme Court.

## WITHDRAWAL OF FEDERAL TROOPS FROM THE SOUTH

When Hayes took office, rival Democratic and Republican governments existed in South Carolina and Louisiana. The Republican regimes, made victors by the same returning boards that declared Hayes victorious, held sway only in the vicinity of state capital buildings, where small detachments of federal troops upheld their authority. The extralegal Democratic challengers, supported ardently and violently by the white minority, controlled both states. If Hayes were legally elected, consistency and legitimacy demanded that federal power uphold the beleaguered Republican governments. But even if he were so inclined, the high-handed use of federal power was not open to Hayes. With the shakiest title to the presidency of any of his predecessors, with half of the country convinced he had reached the White House by fraud, Hayes had the poorest mandate imaginable. Furthermore, he believed, as had Grant before him, that northern public opinion would not sustain the use of an army of occupation to restore the authority of the Republican governments throughout South Carolina and Louisiana. And the House of Representatives—controlled by the Democrats—refused to appropriate money for the army as long as it propped up Republican regimes in the South.

The question was not whether the troops should be withdrawn, but when the troops would have to be withdrawn. Occupying an eroding bargaining position, Hayes extracted from the Democratic governments of South Carolina and Louisiana pledges that the civil rights of black and white Republicans would be respected before he withdrew the troops. By simultaneously distributing patronage through Key, Hayes tried to attract prewar southern Whigs to the Republican party in an effort to erase the color line in southern politics. He was not optimistic that the color line could be obliterated, but he had hopes that the pledges respecting civil rights would be kept.

Hayes's last-ditch effort to salvage something from Reconstruction for the Republican party and for African Americans failed. The prewar Whigs remained in the Democratic party, race divided the parties more sharply than ever, and the pledges by South Carolina and Louisiana Democrats to uphold the Fourteenth and Fifteenth Amendments were quickly broken. Although Hayes gained nothing, he gave up nothing beyond what in a short time he would have been forced to yield.

## CIVIL SERVICE REFORM

With his new southern policy in place, Hayes exclaimed, "Now for Civil Service Reform." He believed that congressional control of patronage had politicized the public service and was the source of its shortcomings. Only Carl Schurz in the cabinet wholeheartedly supported Hayes in his efforts to end the spoils system, and Hayes encountered virulent opposition among his own party members in Congress. On 22 June 1877, Hayes prohibited political assessments (forced contributions) by civil servants and forbade their "management of political organizations, caucuses, conventions, or election campaigns." When naval officer Alonzo B. Cornell of the New York customhouse defied that order, and his superior, Collector Chester A. Arthur, gave Hayes the impression that he would not reform his office, Hayes tried to replace them both. Senator Roscoe Conkling of New York regarded that customhouse as his fief and, invoking "senatorial courtesy" (the notion that senators could control appointments to federal offices in their states), he blocked confirmation of the Hayes appointees.

Undeterred by this defeat and biding his time, Hayes suspended Arthur and Cornell in July 1878. He then triumphed over Conkling and senatorial courtesy on 3 February 1879, when his nominees Edwin A. Merritt for collector and Silas W. Burt for naval officer were confirmed by the Senate. Hayes ordered Merritt and Burt to make the New York customhouse a showcase for civil service reform, and the widely publicized open-competitive examinations under Burt's supervision did just that. Their success in that large office demonstrated that civil service reform was not an impractical scheme of visionaries, but a workable efficient system. The passage of the Pendleton Civil Service Reform Act in 1883 owed much to Hayes's insistence on reform in the New York customhouse. During Hayes's presidency, members of the House and Senate could suggest but could not dictate appointees. Given the partisan attitudes prevalent in the civil service, Hayes was wise not to go beyond his modest efforts at reform. And although his moves anguished spoilsmen, Republican party organizations functioned well in the 1880 campaign. A moderate advocate of reform, Hayes accurately judged how much of it the nation could sustain at that time.

## RECLAIMING THE GOLD STANDARD

The nation's currency problems troubled Hayes more than the need for civil service reform. Taking office during the severe depression following the Panic of 1873, Hayes was convinced that it was prolonged by fears of inflation. His commitment to the gold standard, to hard, "sound," or "honest" currency, was not pragmatic but moral. Since he was heavily in debt as a result of real estate investments, inflation would have been advantageous to him personally. But he opposed the expansion of the greenbacks in circulation and the coinage of silver at the inflationary ratio of sixteen parts of silver to one part of gold, and he favored the resumption of specie payments. A two-thirds majority in Congress, however, reflecting their constituents attitudes, thought the economy needed inflation, and in 1878, over Hayes's veto, they passed the Bland Allison Act, calling for a limited coinage of silver at the 16-to-1 ratio. Although troubled by the infusion of these inflationary dollars, Hayes limited their effect by coining the minimum required and redeeming them in gold at face value, not intrinsic value. Specie resumption in January 1879 (required by act of Congress in 1875) was accomplished without a hitch thanks to careful preparation by Sherman and Hayes. Whatever the validity of Hayes's monetary theories, this return to the gold standard was accompanied by a stunning business revival.

## LABOR UNREST

The depression with its wage cuts and layoffs provoked labor unrest from the East coast to the West. The Great Strike of 1877 began on the Baltimore & Ohio Railroad and soon spread to other railroads and industries. It involved numerous unemployed men and boys and resulted in unprecedented riots, violence, and destruction of property, especially in Baltimore and Pittsburgh. Although fearful of labor unrest, Hayes did not break the strike, although historians have frequently accused him of doing so. He dispatched federal troops (who did not fire a shot), but only when local and state officials had requested those troops when they believed they could no longer control the situation. Hayes refused to allow troops (as Thomas Scott of the Pennsylvania Railroad urged) to run the railroads to halt interference with interstate commerce in general and the mails in particular. Sympathetic to individual laborers (Hayes believed in the eight-hour work day), he cared for neither labor agitators nor railroad moguls and favored the federal regulation of railroads.

Labor agitation in California reflected racial rather than class animosities. "Sandlotters"—Caucasian laborers unemployed because of the depression, the influx of eastern goods with the completion of the transcontinental railroad, and the increased competition from Asian laborers no longer needed by the railroad—attacked Chinese workers and, joined by most other Californians, tried to prevent Chinese immigration to the United States.

**FOREIGN AFFAIRS**
Congress aided the Sandlotters' cause in 1879, passing a Chinese Exclusion bill. Hayes vetoed it. Not only did the bill contradict and therefore denounce the 1868 Burlingame Treaty, which permitted Chinese emigration to the United States, but its action was unnecessary since Chinese migration was already tapering off. Yet Hayes, aware of political reality, sent envoys to China to negotiate a new treaty that permitted the United States to curb the influx of Chinese workers but that did not interfere with the ongoing operations of U.S. merchants and missionaries in China. Maintaining the Open Door in China was already an objective of U.S. foreign policy. The treaty was ratified in 1881 after Hayes left office, and in 1882 Congress suspended the immigration of Chinese workers for ten years.

With two other exceptions foreign policy was unimportant during Hayes's term in office. The Mexican government, while the dictatorship of President Porfirio Díaz was emerging, was unable to stop incursions by outlaws into the United States. Over Mexican protests, Hayes permitted U.S. troops to pursue marauders across the border. This action raised fears that Hayes had imperialistic designs on Mexico, but he opposed the acquisition of territory by conquest. In due time, Mexico secured its border and U.S. troops no longer crossed the Rio Grande.

The supposedly impractical project of Ferdinand de Lesseps to build a water level interoceanic canal across the Isthmus of Panama excited Hayes far more than did Chinese or Mexican problems. Foreshadowing the Theodore Roosevelt corollary to the Monroe Doctrine, Hayes feared that the presence of a French company might stimulate French imperialism. After all, Napoleon III had invaded Mexico during the American Civil War. Despite assurances that the Third French Republic harbored no designs on Panama, Hayes declared that strategic and commercial considerations made it imperative that any canal connecting the Atlantic and Pacific Oceans be under U.S. control.

The first two years of Hayes's presidency were difficult. Although most Republicans accepted his southern policy, old abolitionists like William Lloyd Garrison, committed Radicals like Benjamin F. Wade, and some partisan Republicans like James G. Blaine denounced Hayes. His civil service reform policy infuriated machine politicians like Roscoe Conkling, but they failed to satisfy idealistic reformers like Edwin L. Godkin. Hayes's temperate response to the most severe strike the nation has experienced endeared him to neither labor nor capital, and his adamant rejection of the strident demands for inflation angered its numerous proponents in the West and South. He was even hanged in effigy in the far West for his veto of the Chinese exclusion bill. With Republican dissension and the persistence of hard times, the Democrats in the 1878 campaign gained control of both the Senate and the House of Representatives.

**THE "RIDERS" BATTLE**
Ironically the hostile Democratic Congress inadvertently enabled Hayes to unite Republicans and bring about their defeat in 1880. The Democrats wished to repeal the election laws that Republicans had passed during Reconstruction to enforce the Fourteenth and Fifteenth Amendments guaranteeing civil and voting rights for black Americans. Hayes defended these laws, which enabled federal officials to ensure

that ballot boxes were not stuffed by Democratic machines in northern cities (especially New York City) and that black voters were not prevented from voting (especially in the South). To force Hayes to agree to repeal the Enforcement Acts, the Democrats in 1879 added the repeal legislation as "riders" to appropriations bills that were essential to operate the government. A warrior at heart, Hayes entered the battle of the riders with relish, vetoing the appropriations bills on constitutional and political grounds.

Hayes argued the bills were unconstitutional because Congress was trying to destroy the founder's design of separated powers by enhancing congressional power through the elimination of the executive's veto power. He charged that the bills also should be rejected on political grounds because the Democrats were reviving the recently vanquished doctrine of states' rights by insisting that the federal government had no right to supervise elections for members of the U.S. Congress. It was obvious to Hayes, and it became obvious to all Republicans, that the Democrats wanted Tammany Hall corruptionists to steal elections in New York and white supremacist "red shirts" rather than federal "bluecoats" to be present at polls in the South. In their defense of executive power and the sanctity of the ballot, Hayes's vetoes reunited and aroused Republicans who rallied around him. In defeat, the Democrats succeeded only in shutting off money for the employment of federal marshals to supervise elections, but the election laws remained on the books and a future Republican Congress and president, if committed, could supervise elections.

## A MODERN PRESIDENT

In the battle of the riders, Hayes played the role of a modern twentieth-century president. He recognized that public opinion governed the nation, and to rally that opinion Hayes exploited issues in his vetoes—which he knew newspapers would disseminate—to defeat Congress and to gather the support of the rank and file of his party, many of whom were disaffected.

Hayes used not only the veto as a bridge to the people but also his travels, which were more extensive than those of any previous chief executive. "Rutherford the Rover" was the first president to visit the West Coast while in office, and he made short speeches (which the press would pick up) hammering home one point at every whistle-stop from coast to coast. In rallying public opinion to his administration, Hayes was helped in his last two years in office by an obtuse Democratic Congress and by the business boom that accompanied the resumption of specie payments and the return to the gold standard. At every opportunity Hayes insisted that the return of prosperity was directly tied to his sound money policy. Even if it were possible that prosperity resulted from an inevitable swing of the business cycle, no one could deny that the implementation of Hayes's hard-money policy was accompanied by good times.

In his exploitation of issues, enhancement of executive power, and introduction of modern bureaucratic procedures, Hayes demonstrated that he was a master of the politics of reform (presidential politics) as distinct from the politics of organization (congressional politics). Ironically, historians, misled by the sneers of Conkling—that spoilsman master of organization politics whom Hayes demolished—have inaccurately regarded Hayes as an inept politician, which he surely was not. For example, he banned liquor from the White House both to support temperance and as a shrewd political calculation. He and Lucy opposed prohibition and wished to advance temperance by example and argument, but not by coercion. Hayes especially opposed the fast-growing Prohibition party since virtually all of its members had belonged to the Republican party and threatened that party's chances of carrying close states like New York. He realized that his highly visible embrace of teetotalism in the White House would keep most dry Republicans in the party and alienate virtually no wets. Hayes's analysis was borne out four years later: His successors restored liquor to the White House, the Prohibition party multiplied, and as a result the Republicans lost New York and the 1884 election.

Thanks to Hayes the Republicans entered the presidential campaign of 1880 united, with its organization intact, and with high morale. By his own choice Hayes was not a candidate to succeed himself. He believed consistently, as his ardent supporters discovered, that presidents prostituted themselves to secure reelection and that they should therefore serve only one term— ideally of six or seven years—but in any event only one term. Hayes regarded the nomination of Garfield, a friend and supporter from Ohio, rather than of Grant or Blaine, as an endorsement of his administration by the Republican party, and Garfield's election was widely perceived as the ratification of that endorsement by the people.

## ENJOYING LAME-DUCK STATUS

Having returned from his delightful West Coast trip on the eve of Garfield's election, Hayes was ready to enjoy his last four months in office as a "lame duck." Departing from their earlier practice, he and Lucy began to accept invitations to dinner parties. They continued to entertain lavishly in the White House (whatever money they saved on liquor they spent on food), which they loved dearly. Accompanied by friends, their three older boys frequently visited, joining their younger sister and brother to complete the family circle. The First Family proudly dispensed informal western hospitality, with young relatives and friends often crowding the White House. To help her entertain and put White House guests at ease, Lucy Hayes usually surrounded herself with a bevy of young women. Gossips accused her of trying to marry off these young women, and in fact she did match Lizzie Mills, the daughter of a wealthy California banker, with Whitelaw Reid of the *New York Tribune*, and Hayes's niece with one of his army buddies.

Even as the end of his term approached, Hayes continued to be very busy. He prepared his fourth annual message, which stressed his usual concerns: the virtues of civil service reform, the threat of the French in Panama, the evils of inflation, the antidemocratic Mormon theocracy in the Utah territory, and the happy state of relations with the land's indigenous people, the Native Americans, or as Hayes and his contemporaries called them, the Indians.

## INDIAN RELATIONS

The Hayes administration had made significant progress in Indian relations. On taking office, Hayes and Secretary of the Interior Schurz had built upon the beginnings of a more humane Indian policy adopted by Grant. Nevertheless, serious mistakes were made. One was carrying out an earlier decision to remove the Nez Perces from their ancestral home in the Wallowa Valley in Oregon to a nearby reservation in Idaho. In the tragic war that followed, the heroic Nez Perces under Chief Joseph, though encumbered with noncombatants (women, old men, and children), outwitted the pursuing federal army. When they were finally trapped near the Canadian border, the surviving Nez Perces were removed to the Indian Territory (present day Oklahoma), where they had difficulty acclimating to the Southwest. Learning from this experience, the Hayes administration soon abandoned the removal policy and worked to prevent subsequent Indian wars.

No sooner had Hayes written so optimistically about Indian relations in 1881 than a poignant reminder of the cruel policy of removal to the Indian Territory surfaced. Like the Nez Perce decision, the decision to remove the Poncas from their ancestral lands in Nebraska and the Dakota Territory to the Indian Territory was made before Hayes took office and was carried out while Schurz was learning his new job. The Poncas' plight would not have been noticed were it not for Standing Bear, a Ponca chief, and Bright Eyes, the daughter of a chief of the related Omahas.

Upon the death of his grandchild in the winter of 1879, Standing Bear set off with thirty-four followers and the child's remains, which they planned to bury in ground hallowed by their ancestors. After suffering great hardships he and his people were arrested by the army in Nebraska but freed by a federal judge on a writ of habeas corpus. Having attracted attention, Standing Bear, accompanied by Bright Eyes, embarked on a speaking tour of the East. Her eloquence, his story, and their dignity captivated audiences, led to the establishment of a Ponca Relief Committee in Boston, and aroused Congress. Senator Henry L. Dawes of Massachusetts was especially moved. He bitterly attacked Schurz for not allowing the Poncas to return to their home.

Wanting to be just, Hayes reviewed the relevant documents. He appointed a commission to investigate and he followed its advice: to allow all Poncas who wished to return to their ancestral lands to do so, and to allow those who were content in their new surroundings (about half) to remain in the Indian Territory. Since the Poncas were uprooted during his presidency, Hayes assumed responsibility and did his best to make amends. In his dealings with all Native Americans he reflected the best reform thought of his day and worked to integrate them into the larger society as productive citizens. Several of Hayes's ideas came to fruition in the Dawes Severalty Act of 1887.

Hayes eased Garfield's transition into the presidency. He assured Garfield, who was not wealthy, that his $50,000 salary would more than cover expenses and he left his equipage for Garfield's use until he could acquire his own. More significantly, Hayes saved Garfield heat by making some controversial appointments that he desired. When president, Garfield reciprocated by naming Hayes's friend Stanley Matthews to the Supreme Court.

## A CHAMPION OF EDUCATION

Retiring to Spiegel Grove, his home in Fremont, Ohio, Hayes resolved to "promote the welfare of his family, his town, his State, and his country." For the remaining twelve years of his life he worked tirelessly for causes he embraced. Even before leaving the White House Hayes had decided to make education his "hobby." An optimist and an egalitarian, he had faith that an educated people would reform inequities and progress toward an ideal society. He was also realistic and perceived that progress would be slow for disadvantaged groups like African Americans and that education would be their key to economic improvement and civil rights.

Hayes served on the boards of trustees of Ohio State, Western Reserve, and Ohio Wesleyan Universities, but he was especially committed to the education of disadvantaged children in the South and West. When president he was appointed to the board of the Peabody Fund, which was devoted to the education of southern children. Shortly after leaving the White House, he became president and guiding spirit of the Slater Fund, which concentrated its resources on educating black southerners. Hayes not only conscientiously attended meetings of these organizations, but also went on inspection tours and played a major role in distributing grants. He was, for example, primarily responsible for the ultimate decision to concentrate Peabody money in the George Peabody College for Teachers in Nashville, Tennessee, and W. E. B. Du Bois was deeply grateful to Hayes for support he received from the Slater Fund, which enabled him to study in Berlin.

Hayes realized that the support these funds could give toward educating poor children was paltry in comparison to the resources of the federal government. Accordingly, as president and as a private citizen, he urged Congress to pass the Blair bill, which would funnel federal funds into poverty-stricken school districts, which were often located in the South and West. Southern Democrats, agreeing with Hayes that educated black Americans would ultimately secure civil rights, tried to stave off that day by defeating the Blair bill. Some Republicans especially disappointed Hayes by objecting to the extension of federal power and by doubting the capacity of black Americans to take advantage of educational opportunities. On these grounds, Whitelaw Reid would not back in the *Tribune* Hayes's scheme of distributing the tariff surplus to poor school districts.

Hayes also advocated industrial education for all young people. He believed that everyone, no matter what their race or station in life, should have a skilled trade to fall back on. In keeping with his faith in education as the panacea for society's ills, Hayes thought that if capitalists and politicians knew what it is like to work with their hands they would be more understanding of labor. Hayes was disturbed in the last decade of his life by the proliferation of millionaires and of monopolies. He believed that the pristine republican values of early America were threatened by railroad kings, and he declared that "the Standard Oil monopoly . . . is a menace to the people." The "government of the people, by the people, and for the people" had become "a government of corporations, by corporations, and for corporations." To counteract the development of a plutocracy, Hayes suggested redistributing wealth through confiscatory inheritance taxes.

Hayes also believed that education, especially industrial education, could rehabilitate criminals. Until his death he served as president of the National Prison Reform Association. In his presidential address in Atlanta he attacked the Georgia chain gang system, and in the one in Boston he charged that the greed and extravagance of the wealthy deprived an underclass of a decent income and caused crime. Hayes came to oppose the death penalty and both as governor and as president was accused of overusing his pardoning power.

Hayes, who enjoyed sharing memories with comrades in arms, was active in veterans' organizations. Feeling that the country could never repay its debt to the soldiers of the Union army, he was a consistent advocate of generous pensions for Union veterans. He never regretted signing the Pension Arrears Act (1879), which aided needy disabled veterans. If the government paid its bondholders in gold, he argued, it surely could afford pensions for the men whose health had been broken defending the Union.

Even after his wife died in 1889, Hayes continued his extensive travels to veterans meetings, for prison reform, and for education. He was in Cleveland on Ohio State University business when he suffered an attack of angina pectoris. Saying that "I would rather die in Spiegel Grove than live anywhere else," he insisted on returning home, where three days later, on 17 January 1893, he died.

## EVALUATION OF HAYES'S PRESIDENCY

During his White House years Hayes anticipated the modern twentieth-century presidency, and in retirement he was a precursor of the Progressive movement. He arrested the decline of executive power by successfully combating the Senate's domination of appointments (senatorial courtesy) and by vetoing House attempts to force on the president unwanted legislation as riders on necessary appropriation bills. In these struggles to preserve and enhance presidential power, Hayes rallied public opinion to his side. He realized the power of the press, traveled more widely in office than his predecessors had, and in frequent short talks hammered home his opinion on pertinent issues. Although his civil service reform and sound currency stands engendered opposition, he did not sacrifice his convictions, and with the success of reform in the New York customhouse and a rebounding economy, he exploited these issues in the last two years of his presidency. Unlike spoils-minded congressional representatives of his day who stressed the politics of organization, Hayes embraced the issue-oriented politics of reform that modern presidents with their capacity to generate public opinion use so effectively. Hayes was a shrewd politician who defeated his enemies both within and outside his party. He unified the divided party he inherited and enabled it to triumph handily in 1880. A moderate reformer, a principled politician, and a committed Republican, Hayes proved his belief that "he serves his party best who serves his country best."

## BIBLIOGRAPHY

Barnard, Harry. *Rutherford B. Hayes and His America* (Bobbs-Merrill, 1954).

Davison, Kenneth E. *The Presidency of Rutherford B. Hayes* (Greenwood Press, 1972).

Geer, Emily Apt. *First Lady: The Life of Lucy Webb Hayes* (Kent State University Press and Rutherford B. Hayes Presidential Center, 1984).

Hoogenboom, Ari. *The Presidency of Rutherford B. Hayes* (University Press of Kansas, 1988).

———. *Rutherford B. Hayes: Warrior and President* (University Press of Kansas, 1995).

Polakoff, Keith Ian. *The Politics of Inertia: The Election of 1876 and the End of Reconstruction* (Louisiana State University Press, 1973).

Rubin, Louis D. *Teach the Freeman: The Correspondence of Rutherford B. Hayes and the Slater Fund for Negro Education, 1881–1893,* 2 vols. (Louisiana State University Press, 1959).

Williams, Charles Richard, ed. *The Diary and Letters of Rutherford Birchard Hayes: Nineteenth President of the United States,* 5 vols. (Ohio State Archaeological and Historical Society, 1922–1926).

———. *The Life of Rutherford Birchard Hayes: Nineteenth President of the United States,* 2 vols. (Ohio State Archaeological and Historical Society, 1914).

Williams, T. Harry. *Hayes of the Twenty-Third: The Civil War Volunteer Officer* (Knopf, 1965).

———, ed. *Hayes: The Diary of a President, 1875–1881* (David McKay, 1964).

# JAMES ABRAM GARFIELD
## 1881

### R. Hal Williams

*Born 19 November 1831 in Orange, Ohio, to Abram Garfield and Eliza Ballou Garfield; educated at Williams College, Williamstown, Mass. (B.A. 1856); married Lucretia Rudolph, 11 November 1858, Hiram, Ohio; seven children; ran for president in 1880 on the Republican ticket with Chester Alan Arthur of New York, and received 4,454,415 popular votes and 214 electoral college ballots over the Democratic ticket of Winfield Scott Hancock of Pennsylvania and William Hayden English of Indiana (4,444,952 popular votes and 155 electoral ballots); died 19 September 1881 in Elberon, New Jersey, from the effects of a gunshot wound received eighty days earlier; buried in Lake View Cemetery, Cleveland, Ohio.*

In office only 120 days before he was shot, James A. Garfield, one of the "martyr presidents," has faded into obscurity. Many modern surveys that ask historians to rank the presidents do not even include him (nor, for that matter, do they include William Henry Harrison, the only president in U.S. history to serve a shorter term), and in a well-known passage, the author Thomas Wolfe called him one of "the lost Americans," vacant, bewhiskered, forgotten. "[W]ho was Garfield, martyred man, and who had seen him in the streets of life? Who could believe his footfalls ever sounded on a lonely pavement?" Contemporaries heard those footfalls, however, and to them Garfield seemed an important president: important in promise, in accomplishments during his brief tenure in office, and, most significant, for the imagery of his painful suffering and death.

To a large degree, they were right. Garfield's presidency did have promise and some worthy achievements, all cut short by an assassin's bullet. Like other presidencies, his turned in part on chance and fate—in his case, death. For it is a plain fact that if Garfield had somehow survived the bullet, his influence would have been immense, his presidency very likely one of the most important in the last half of the nineteenth century.

## THE DARK HORSE PRESIDENT

A political dark horse, Garfield was nominated for the office in the longest convention in the history of the Republican party to that time. Through six days and thirty-four ballots, the forces of the two major Republican factions held firm. The Half-Breeds, a wing of the party that urged more focus on the newer issues of urban and industrial America, backed James G. Blaine of Maine, one of the era's most popular political figures. Their opponents, the Stalwarts, stressed factional loyalty and the older issues of the Civil War and Reconstruction, issues that had given birth to the Republican party. Led at the convention by the influential Senator Roscoe Conkling of New York, the Stalwarts supported former president Ulysses S. Grant for the nomination. As the convention deadlock deepened into its sixth day, Blaine's Half-Breeds suddenly shifted to Garfield of Ohio, who captured the nomination on the thirty-sixth ballot.

Trying to make peace with Conkling and the Stalwarts, Garfield's friends first offered the vice-presidential nomination to Levi P. Morton of New York. When Conkling persuaded Morton to decline the honor, they turned to Chester A. Arthur, another New York Stalwart and Conkling ally. Garfield had not authorized the offer, and he turned pale when he learned of it, but he was young and healthy, and to most observers the choice seemed unimportant. According to the influential journal, *The Nation*, there was "no place in which [Arthur's] powers of -mischief will be so small as in the Vice-Presidency. . . . It is true General Garfield, if elected, may die during his term of office, but this is too unlikely a contingency to be worth making extraordinary provisions for."

## A STRONG CANDIDATE

Garfield's death seemed unlikely, indeed. Forty-nine years old in 1880, he was tall and strongly built, smart, vigorous, well educated, a talented speaker, and an imposing presence. The last president born in a log cabin, he was also born to poverty—his father died when Garfield was two—a fact that enabled him to run for the presidency as a self-made man whose hard work and honest virtues had brought success. His job at the age of sixteen on a canal boat in Cleveland formed the image of his 1880 presidential campaign—"From the Towpath to the White House"—although campaign biographies usually failed to mention that the candidate, prone to daydreaming, had often fallen into the canal. An avid student, Garfield went on to study at Hiram College in northern Ohio and at Williams College in Massachusetts, from which he graduated in 1856. Study gave him a lifelong belief in the value of education, a philosophy he later wanted to apply to help African Americans in the South.

As the Republican candidate for the presidency, Garfield offered solid Republican credentials, stretching back to the party's initial presidential campaign in 1856. In 1859 he had won his first race for public office, an election to the Ohio state senate. When the Civil War broke out, he quickly enlisted and saw duty at Shiloh, Corinth, and Chickamauga, ending up as a major general. When he returned home to Ohio, Republican leaders, alert to the young man's growing reputation, nominated him for Congress in 1862. Serving from 1863 to 1880, he became one of the most influential Republicans in the House, studious and diligent, interested in issues, feared in debate.

He urged stern measures to reconstruct the South, made himself an expert on the currency and tariff, and though briefly brushed with the Credit Mobilier scandal, was held in widespread esteem.

In 1880, combining older issues and new, Garfield campaigned on tariff protection for U.S. industry and on distrust of the South, a section, he said, still "steeped to the lips with treason and disloyalty." In a razor-thin election, he won 214 electoral votes to 155 for Winfield S. Hancock, the Democratic nominee, but his popular margin amounted to fewer than 10,000 votes out of a total of 9.2 million votes cast. Margins of that sort did not make mandates. Though Rutherford B. Hayes had tried to build a Republican party in the South, Hancock carried the entire section, confirming the existence of a solid South that Republicans after Garfield would spend nearly a century trying to break.

Moody and subject to occasional fits of self-pity and depression, Garfield had an unusual sense of foreboding about the presidency. "[T]here is a tone of sadness running through this triumph which I can hardly explain," he told his diary, and on New Year's Eve 1880, two months from the inauguration, he reflected on "a sad conviction that I am bidding good-by to the freedom of private life, and to a long series of happy years, which I fear terminate with 1880." Party leaders reinforced his doubts. "Your real troubles will now begin," Carl Schurz, a prominent Republican, told him.

Schurz was right, but there seemed at the outset plenty of reasons to expect success. Few new presidents could match Garfield in experience with the inner workings of government. He had served seventeen years in the House of Representatives, four of them at the head of the crucial Appropriations Committee. He was thoughtful, dedicated, and unafraid of hard work. He was such a persuasive speaker from both stump and pulpit that he could, if he chose, make his policies known around the land. He took a limited view of the presidency, reflecting his own service in Congress and the opinions of most of his contemporaries. Government, he once said, should merely "keep the peace and stand out of the sunshine of the people."

## FORMING A CABINET

The troubles Schurz envisioned began immediately. Even forming a cabinet turned out to be a tricky business, not a good sign for Garfield's success. The slate changed often, sometimes daily, and several leading candidates accepted posts and then declined them, occasionally when Conkling, who held grudges, instructed them to do so. Cabinet-making continued to the morning after the inauguration. Blaine, brilliant and mercurial, assumed command of the State Department. Other good appointments included William Windom of Minnesota as secretary of the treasury, Wayne MacVeagh of Pennsylvania as attorney general, and Thomas L. James of New York as postmaster general.

Once settled in the White House, the Garfield family soon enchanted the country with their homespun ways, though temperance leaders protested when the president and his wife Lucretia reversed the Hayes's policy of not serving wine to guests. In a charming fashion, Garfield's younger children turned the executive mansion into a playroom, romping through the corridors, pounding on the grand piano, and riding bicycles down the staircase. Young at heart, the president joined freely in the fun. He also worked hard, beginning his day at seven A.M. and ending late in the evening.

Most of the work he did himself. In the 1880s, the White House staff was small, reflecting the president's limited powers. Garfield had one private secretary, whom he paid out of his own pocket, and a half-dozen clerks. Like other presidents of the era, he stood in endless receiving lines and shook hand after hand, a symbol of the openness of the presidency and the relationship between the office and the people. In Garfield's case, some of the hands belonged to office seekers, looking for one of the 100,000 jobs that the federal government could dispense. There were so many of them that they reminded one observer of "the sound of beasts at feeding time." Those who missed Garfield in his office stopped him on the street, and the new president, who had never liked the business of handing out offices, quickly grew tired of it. "These people would take my very brain, flesh and blood if they could," he said.

## THE PATRONAGE WAR
## WITH LORD ROSCOE

Aware that the patronage had important symbolic purposes—recognition of this faction or that—Garfield early decided to reward all wings of the Republican party to bind them together into a unified organization. It was a sensible idea, but a difficult policy, and he soon collided head on with the conflicting ambitions of Half-Breeds and Stalwarts, of Blaine and Conkling and their numerous allies. Blaine was the period's most talented politician, far-sighted and temperamental, though when it came to temperament, Roscoe Conkling—Lord Roscoe, the newspapers called him—put everyone to shame. Never lacking in flair, he wrote his letters in lavender ink and wore bright canary waistcoats; a blond spitcurl dangled over his forehead. He liked to rule. Garfield himself had once called Conkling "a great fighter, inspired more by his hates than his loves," characteristics the new president was about to experience first hand.

On 22 March 1881, two weeks after taking office, Garfield sent to the Senate a number of nominations for offices in New York State, most of them Conkling's allies. When Blaine protested, Garfield the next day added to the list several Conkling opponents, most notably William H. Robertson, who had opposed Conkling and Grant at the 1880 Republican national convention. He named Robertson to the key post of collector of customs of the Port of New York. "[P]erfidy without parallel," Conkling promptly said and began to organize opposition to the appointment. Fighting back, Garfield shrewdly cast the contest in terms of a constitutional battle over presidential power. "I wanted it known soon," he told one senator, "whether I was the registering Clerk of the Senate or the Executive of the government."

Even close friends had doubts about Garfield's backbone—"At critical moments he wavers when firmness is indispensable," fellow Ohio Republican John Sherman once observed—and Conkling hoped to exploit the trait. "He has no sand," Conkling believed; but Lord Roscoe miscalculated, and Garfield, conscious of the struggle's importance, held firm. On 5 May, in a stunning stroke that Blaine had devised, Garfield withdrew all nominations from the Senate except Robertson's. The Senate now had no choice except to act one way or another on the nomination. "Gen. Garfield," a Chicago newspaper said, "has determined to be President of the United States." Garfield was pleased. It was not, he wrote a friend a few days later, a mere "difference between two individuals" but an issue that involved "the independence of the executive."

Facing defeat, Conkling and Thomas C. Platt, his fellow senator from New York, abruptly resigned their seats in the Senate, an action Garfield predicted would "be received with guffaws of laughter." It was. Within two days of the event the Senate confirmed Robertson's nomination, and soon thereafter both Conkling and Platt lost their bids for reelection in the New York state legislature. Garfield had won; his popularity in the country soared.

The struggle, as he had sensed, had involved far more than the question of who collected customs in New York. It had involved the powers of the president and Senate, mastery of the Republican party, and, above all, the future direction of the party itself. Conkling and the Stalwarts, in the end, spoke for a local and factional view; Garfield and Blaine thought more broadly, in terms that looked decades ahead. They had in mind a future in which both nation and party would turn to the challenges of social and economic growth.

## THE UNFINISHED AGENDA

Scarcely a month after his triumph Garfield was shot, and it is difficult to tell the precise uses to which he would have put his new authority. He would certainly have moved ahead on civil service reform, for he had already instructed Postmaster General James, whose office alone accounted for nearly half the government jobs, to institute promotion by competitive examination and removal from office only for cause. He probably would have turned attention to the currency and tariff, two of his favorite subjects from his congressional days. In April and May, with his approval, Secretary of the Treasury Windom refunded, at substantially lower rates, some $200 million worth of Treasury bonds from the Civil War, cutting interest on the public debt almost in half.

There were serious troubles in the "Star Route" mail service, a special mail delivery for lightly populated areas of the West and South that had given rise to padded contracts and fraud. Alerted to the problem, Garfield a few days after his inauguration instructed James to investigate. In mid-April he ordered an overhaul of the department, and in early June, learning that high Republican party officials might be involved, he told investigators to proceed. "Go ahead regardless of where or whom you hit," he ordered. "I direct you not only to probe this ulcer to the bottom, but to cut it out."

Finally, it was clear that Garfield also had in mind a new policy toward the South, a constant preoccupation of Republican presidents in the late nineteenth century. Rejecting Hayes's policy of using patronage to woo southern Democrats into the Republican fold—a strategy he called a "dreary failure"—Garfield wanted instead to emphasize economic issues, "the saving influence of universal education," and measures to protect the voting rights of African Americans. Signaling his commitment, Garfield named several prominent African Americans to high federal offices, including Frederick Douglass as recorder of deeds in Washington, D.C., and Blanche K. Bruce as registrar of the Treasury, the highest position an African American had yet occupied. In the fall, Garfield planned to deliver a major speech in Atlanta outlining his new southern policies, a speech he was discussing with Blaine at the moment he was shot.

## BLAINE AND FOREIGN POLICY

The outlines of Garfield's foreign policies are much clearer, in part because Secretary of State Blaine had to carry them out a month or two after Garfield's death. Like others who watched events abroad, both Garfield and Blaine had grown concerned about Europe's intentions in the Western Hemisphere. The British seemed more and more involved on the west coast of South America, the French had started digging a canal across the Isthmus, and there were reports of German designs on Hawaii and other parts of the Pacific. Although U.S. fears turned out to be exaggerated, Great Britain did dominate trade throughout much of Latin America, an area Blaine in particular wanted to tap.

Hoping to restrain British influence, Blaine tried to mediate the bitter War of the Pacific between Chile and Peru, but his efforts succumbed to partisan infighting and his own miscalculations. He also started to pressure Britain to renegotiate the Clayton-Bulwer Treaty of 1850 to allow an American-dominated Isthmian canal, but he did not have the time before Garfield died. In the most important of the administration's initiatives, Garfield and Blaine planned to issue invitations to a Pan-American conference in Washington that would promote peace in the hemisphere and increase inter-American trade. After Garfield's death, President Arthur authorized Blaine to issue the invitations to the conference, but he soon withdrew them. Not until the administration of Benjamin Harrison, with Blaine again as secretary of state, did the United States host Garfield's Pan-American conference, which gave rise to the Bureau of American Republics and, in time, to the Organization of American States.

## THE SHOOTING

With the beginning of July 1881, Garfield had been in office almost four months. As the summer's heat settled over Washington, he planned a welcome trip to Williams College to celebrate his twenty-fifth reunion and enroll two of his sons in the college's freshman class. Garfield was in good spirits, pleased with recent successes. As he and Blaine walked to the train the morning of 2 July, Charles J. Guiteau, a deranged lawyer and party hack, stepped up behind the president and shot him in the back. Crying, "My God! What is that?" Garfield threw up his hands and fell to the floor. As policemen led Guiteau away, he told them, "I am a Stalwart, and Arthur will be President."

Doctors probed the wound but could not find the bullet. As infection set in, Garfield literally wasted away. Departing from traditional presidential privacy, daily news bulletins detailed his decline. "I should think the people would be tired of having me dished up to them in this way," he remarked. After eighty days of suffering, Garfield died at 10:35 P.M. on 19 September 1881, the anniversary of the Battle of Chickamauga, just a few weeks short of his fiftieth birthday. Cabinet members wired Arthur in New York to take the oath of office as president of the United States. Honoring Garfield's congressional career, the president's body lay in state in the Rotunda of the Capitol instead of in the White House, the first president to do so. Thousands came to pay their respects.

In his struggle against death, Garfield had achieved a degree of public devotion he never quite acquired in life. Had he lived he could have tapped that devotion to accomplish much. As it was, he died, and Americans everywhere admired his courage, steadfastness, and good humor. They made of his life an American fable. A later generation would best remember his most famous presidential plea: "My God!" he once shouted. "What is there in this place that a man should ever want to get into it?" In standing up for presidential authority, in beginning to point the Republican party in the directions that soon gave it dominance, he helped make the place, in the end, worth getting into.

## BIBLIOGRAPHY

Brown, Harry James, and Frederick D. Williams, eds. *The Diary of James A. Garfield*, 4 vols. (Michigan State University Press, 1967–1981).

Doenecke, Justus D. *The Presidencies of James A. Garfield and Chester A. Arthur* (University Press of Kansas, 1981).

Norris, James D., and Arthur H. Shaffer, eds. *Politics and Patronage in the Gilded Age: The Correspondence of James A. Garfield and Charles E. Henry* (State Historical Society of Wisconsin, 1970).

Peskin, Allan. *Garfield* (Kent State University Press, 1978).

Pletcher, David M. *The Awkward Years: American Foreign Relations Under Garfield and Arthur* (University of Missouri Press, 1962).

Shaw, John, ed. *Crete and James: Personal Letters of Lucretia and James Garfield* (Michigan State University Press, 1994).

Smith, Theodore Clarke. *The Life and Letters of James Abram Garfield*, 2 vols. (Yale University Press, 1925).

★★★ 21 ★★★

# CHESTER ALAN ARTHUR
## 1881–1885

*R. Hal Williams*

---

*Born 5 October 1830 in Fairfield, Vermont, to William Arthur and Malvina Stone Arthur; educated at Union College, Schenectady, New York (B.A. 1848); admitted to the bar and practiced law; married Ellen Lewis Herndon, 25 October 1859, New York, New York; three children; succeeded to presidency upon the death of James Abram Garfield; died 18 November 1886 in New York, New York; buried in Rural Cemetery, Albany, New York.*

---

Chester A. Arthur first heard the news from a reporter who called at his New York townhouse the evening President Garfield died. "I hope—my God, I do hope it is a mistake," Arthur said, his voice shaking with emotion. A moment later the official message arrived, confirming the news, along with advice from Garfield's cabinet that Arthur take the oath of office at once. Reporters rushed to the house and asked the doorkeeper if the vice president would say anything about his plans. "I daren't ask him," the doorkeeper replied, "he is sitting alone in his room sobbing like a child, with his head on his desk and his face buried in his hands. I dare not disturb him."

**TRANSITION**

Two hours later, a member of the New York State Supreme Court administered the oath, making Arthur the nation's twenty-first president. People near him warned of a possible constitutional crisis. There was now no vice president, president of the Senate, or speaker of the House. To deal with the problem, Arthur drafted a proclamation calling the U.S. Senate into immediate special session to fix the succession—by electing its own president pro tem—should he die on his way to Washington. He mailed it to himself at the White House and once safely there, he destroyed it.

On 22 September 1881, Arthur repeated the oath of office before the chief justice of the United States and, with an audience of about forty guests, including former presidents Grant and Hayes, read a brief and elegant inaugural address that praised the policies of "my lamented predecessor." "[I]t will be my earnest endeavor," the new president said, "to profit, and to see that the nation shall profit, by his example and experience."

Around the country, people breathed with relief, Garfield's long struggle over at last. The relief, however, had little to do with Arthur, for many in fact doubted his capacity for his new office. He was, in their view, a well-known spoilsman, a loyal follower of the controversial New York Stalwart Roscoe Conkling, and a member of a repudiated faction of the Republican party. Immediately after Garfield's shooting, some had even suspected him of complicity in it. "I did it and will go to jail for it," the assassin, Charles J. Guiteau, had said as the police led him away. "I am a Stalwart, and Arthur will be President." On trial for Garfield's murder, Guiteau went on to claim a friendship with Arthur, telling the court, among other things, that during the 1880 campaign he "used to go to General Arthur and talk just as freely with him as I would with anybody."

Suspicions of Arthur's complicity faded quickly, but even in the brighter glow of his first days in the White House, people still expected little of their new president. They "look upon this Administration as a sort of summer holiday," a prominent Republican said, "a kind of lapse between one man who was elected and another who is going to be elected." Arthur, who was intelligent enough to be chosen for Phi Beta Kappa on his graduation from Union College in Schenectady, New York, knew very well what people were thinking. In a rare private moment, he described his feelings to a trusted reporter, who remembered him saying that "the American people would never have chosen him if it had been thought that he would reach the presidency, and so it was for him to show that he was worthy. The only way was for him to be the president of the whole people and nobody's servant."

## RISING THROUGH THE RANKS

To show he was worthy, with a divided party and a worried country, was no easy task, but Arthur had some of the skills to do it. Fifty-one years old in 1881, he was experienced and ambitious, a successful politician who had made his way shrewdly up the ladder of political and professional advancement. After graduating from Union College, he had taught school for a time and then practiced law in New York City. Although his was a lackluster practice, in the course of it he had taken on several difficult cases. He participated in one important suit that freed eight slaves who had stopped off with their owner in New York on their way to the South. In 1854, he had helped integrate New York City's streetcar system, successfully representing a black woman who had been told to get off a segregated streetcar.

Named to the key posts of engineer-in-chief and then quartermaster general of New York State during the crucial first two years of the Civil War, Arthur displayed valuable managerial skills, a capacity to take charge of men, and measures that could be helpful in the White House. With "great executive ability and unbending integrity," as the governor who appointed him said, he worked night and day to organize, house, and equip the thousands of Union troops headed south. Following the war, Arthur attached himself to New York's imperious representative and senator, Roscoe Conkling, and as Conkling rose in power, so did "Chet," becoming the dutiful party functionary, the high-level subordinate who carried out the instructions of those at the top. Preferring politics to policy, he "expressed less interest in the principles then agitating parties," an associate later said, "than in the machinery and maneuvers of the managers."

In 1871, the machinery paid off. President Grant, a friend of Conkling, named Arthur to the post of collector of customs for the Port of New York, the highest paying position in the federal government—at over $50,000 a year, higher even than the president, vice president, members of the House and Senate, and justices of the Supreme Court. With some one thousand jobs at its disposal, the office also offered a ready source of patronage for the Conkling machine, and Arthur dispensed it freely and effectively. He held the collectorship until 1878, when a special investigating panel, finding waste, corruption, and excessive partisanship in the customhouse, persuaded Rutherford B. Hayes to relieve Arthur of it. Offered the vice-presidential nomination as a sop to the Stalwarts after Garfield's victory at the 1880 Republican national convention, Arthur took the offer to his leader Conkling who told him to "drop it as you would a red hot shoe from the forge." Arthur winced but held firm in accepting the offer. "The office of the Vice President is a greater honor than I ever dreamed of attaining," he said to Conkling, adding that "in a calmer moment you will look at this differently."

The incident spoke well for Arthur's independence, but the public did not know of it, and what they had seen of Arthur during Garfield's brief presidency had not won their praise. Though vice president, he had openly sided with Conkling in efforts to defeat Garfield's nomination of William H. Robertson—who had broken with Conkling to support Garfield at the 1880 national convention—to the New York collectorship Arthur himself had once held. The vice president had continued to share rooms with Conkling, frequently consulted with him over strategy, and even signed a petition against Robertson's appointment. After Conkling resigned in a huff from the Sen-

ate, Arthur went with him to Albany to work for his reelection; he was at Conkling's side the very moment he learned Garfield had been shot. Upset by his behavior, newspapers cautioned the vice president to stop "before his inexcusable indiscretion becomes a National scandal," and Thomas Nast, the country's most prominent cartoonist, sketched biting pictures of Arthur polishing Conkling's shoes.

Fortunately for Arthur, Garfield's sad summer of suffering enabled the vice president to grow in the public eye. Earnest and dignified, he remained in quiet seclusion in his New York home, saying little, going about his normal routines, declining invitations to visit Washington in order not to appear eager to assume the presidency. Sounded out on the idea of taking the office temporarily while Garfield recovered, he refused. Once Garfield died, a nationwide swell of sympathy eased Arthur's entry into the White House. The *New York Times*, which had attacked the vice president again and again, called for a period of goodwill toward the new president. "No man," it said, "ever assumed the Presidency under more trying circumstances, no President has needed more the generous appreciation, the indulgent forbearance of his fellow-citizens."

## REDECORATING THE WHITE HOUSE

For a time, Arthur got the needed forbearance. In his first important presidential decision, he set out to renovate the White House, an action that said something about his presidency itself. Taking personal charge, he ordered furnishings, measured floors, and stood on ladders. Twenty-four wagonloads of clothing and furniture were hauled away, including a birdcage from the Grant administration and a pair of Abraham Lincoln's pants. Arthur purchased an expensive glass screen from Tiffany's to set off the main corridor and installed an elegant billiard room in the basement. The work complete, he hired a French chef for the kitchen, restocked the wine cellar, and laid on the food. Arthur enjoyed entertaining, and during his three years in office he gave some fifty state dinners. He savored nothing more than postmidnight suppers with friends. At one dinner for fifty-five people, the table held 378 glasses to allow for the different bottles of wine. Critics raised eyebrows, questioning the way Arthur's attention centered upon "[f]lowers and wine and food, and slow pacing with a lady on his arm," but the entertaining served a purpose in a nation so recently in grief.

## GRACIOUS AND LAZY

A gracious and congenial host, Arthur was actually timid and anxious, weighed down with the heavy burdens of the presidency, which he found filled with work, worry, and fatigue. Someone who knew him well thought him during the early days in the White House "in a measure stunned, uncertain, and in any event, moody, possibly unhappy." He was also lazy. On one occasion it took him a month simply to copy a letter of condolence to a European government, a letter the State Department had already drafted. Members of the small White House staff often found it necessary to turn his attention to business. "President Arthur never did today what he could put off until tomorrow," a clerk later recalled.

A late riser, Arthur commonly arrived at the office about 10 A.M. and received congressional visitors until noon. After lunch he spent two or three hours in his office, seeing callers by appointment. The cabinet met on Tuesdays and Fridays, and on Wednesdays, Thursdays, and Saturdays Arthur shook hands with the public for an hour. After 5 P.M. he rested or rode horseback, entertained over dinner, and rarely retired before 2 A.M. He took Sunday and Monday off. To keep people at bay, he often carried a set of fake documents to rustle impatiently if the conversation lagged. Valuing his privacy, Arthur detested the sort of scrutiny that Garfield had received while dying, and in a famous phrase, he once snapped at a nosy visitor: "Madam, I may be President of the United States, but my private life is nobody's damned business."

## POOR-QUALITY APPOINTMENTS

Taking office in late 1881, Arthur had the advantage that almost a full term stretched ahead, ample time to develop and carry out his policies. To ensure continuity he initially invited Garfield's cabinet to remain in their posts. One by one, most of them soon resigned, and as Arthur chose their replacements, the quality of the group visibly declined. In December 1881, former New Jersey senator Frederick T. Frelinghuysen, orthodox and undistinguished—"a figurehead of mush," one onlooker said—replaced the energetic Blaine, which had some advantages for caution but few for vision. Lesser figures also replaced Garfield's appointees at the Treasury and Justice Department and at the Post Office. Only Secretary of the Navy William E. Chandler of New Hampshire, energetic and farsighted, a master of detail and organization, improved on Garfield's original choices.

In filling the other offices, Arthur chose mainly Republican Stalwarts, though not enough even of them to satisfy the clamorous demands of his former allies. Recognizing the political dangers of removing Robertson, Arthur retained him in the New York collectorship, surprising many, including leading Stalwarts who had expected the new president to wipe the Half-Breed slate clean. Arthur could not have expected much praise from the Half-Breeds, but he was no doubt surprised by the chorus of complaints that soon rose from the Stalwart camp. "He has done less for us than Garfield, or even Hayes," one Stalwart said. Conkling himself, the president's longtime mentor and ally, soon railed in private against Arthur's "cowardice," and he icily told a reporter that the Hayes administration, which he had detested, was "respectable, if not heroic" compared with Arthur's.

In an ill-considered move, Arthur did offer Conkling a seat on the Supreme Court, but Conkling curtly declined it. He practiced corporate law in New York City and became, in the words of a former Senate colleague, "a gorgeous reminiscence." Plainly a mistake, the lonely offer won

Arthur no praise from Half-Breeds, Stalwarts, or even "Lord Roscoe" himself.

Luckier than many presidents, Arthur had two seats on the U.S. Supreme Court to fill during his term, giving him a welcome chance to shape judicial policy. To one seat, he named Horace Gray, a well-known legal scholar and member of the Massachusetts Supreme Court; to the other, Samuel M. Blatchford, a New York jurist who had sat for fifteen years on the federal bench. While neither appointment was outstanding, both were reasonable, though Gray in particular joined the Court's majorities in the late nineteenth century that overturned the Civil Rights Act of 1875, struck down the nation's first income tax in the 1890s, and upheld the segregation of races in the unfortunate decision of *Plessy v. Ferguson* in 1896.

## CHINESE IMMIGRATION

Holding (like most of his countrymen) a narrow view of the presidency, Arthur largely confined his own activities to annual messages and vetoes. Brandishing the veto, he sent back to Congress in 1882 a bill that suspended the importation of laborers from China for twenty years, denied citizenship to the Chinese, and required all Chinese to register before leaving the country if they wished to return. But Arthur, as his veto message made clear, had no objection to the anti-Chinese nature of the bill, only to the length of the ban it imposed—"nearly a generation," he complained—and soon thereafter, when Congress shortened the ban to ten years, he promptly signed the Chinese Exclusion bill into law.

## TARIFF AND REVENUES

In dealing with another problem, too much money in the federal treasury, Arthur and Congress took the fairly novel step of appointing a tariff commission that recommended substantial cuts in tariffs, added to the products admitted free of duties, and proposed the creation of a customs court to rule on conflicting interpretations of the tariff laws. With its emphasis on expert commissions and courts, the action smacked a bit of later Progressive reforms, but it made little headway in the climate of the early 1880s. As Congress dealt with the commission's report, it bent to protectionist arguments and passed a tariff law so full of awkward compromises that critics labeled it the Mongrel Tariff. On average, the new law lowered duties 1.47 percent. Sloppily written, on one type of steel it imposed three different tariff rates in three different places.

## BLAINE, FRELINGHUYSEN, AND FOREIGN POLICY

The popular and dynamic Blaine also posed problems for Arthur. On becoming president, he had asked the secretary of state to stay on for a time, recognizing Blaine's stature and hoping to narrow the breach with the Half-Breeds. Blaine stayed for three months and launched a number of dramatic initiatives. In a series of notes to Great Britain, he defended the U.S. right to control a canal across the isthmus and sought to modify or abrogate the Clayton-Bulwer Treaty of 1850 that shared control with Britain. He warned European powers to stay away from Hawaii in language that came close to announcing a U.S. protectorate over the islands. And on 29 November 1881, following through on an imaginative policy he and Garfield had devised, he sent invitations to most of the nations of Latin America to attend a peace congress in Washington aimed at strengthening the bonds of friendship in the Western Hemisphere and finding ways to avert for all time "the horrors of cruel and bloody combat between countries."

Controversial in any event, Blaine's initiatives became more so when Frelinghuysen, who took over the State Department at the end of 1881, quickly reversed them, countermanding Blaine's instructions to envoys attempting to settle a bitter war between Chile and Peru, backing away from his efforts to expand U.S. influence in Central America, and raising doubts about the need for an inter-American peace congress. In an unpleasant public squabble,

Frelinghuysen tried to undercut Blaine by leaking official State Department documents to Congress and the press. Blaine retaliated, and Americans looked on as the two secretaries of state exchanged ugly charges.

Worse, Frelinghuysen even saw to the publication of confidential instructions to several U.S. envoys abroad, who wound up finding foreign governments more informed about current administration policy than they were. In a particularly unfortunate case, a special envoy to Chile called on the Chilean foreign minister in Santiago and started (as instructed) to offer an invitation to the peace congress, only to hear his host say, "It is useless. Your government has withdrawn the invitation." The envoy was stunned. His new instructions were making their way to him on board a slow ship to Chile, and in the meantime Frelinghuysen had given them to the press. Similar incidents followed. "Get me home at the earliest practicable moment," the envoy soon begged Washington. "I can't stand this much longer."

## THE MIDTERM ELECTIONS OF 1882

Nor could the public stand much more, and they showed their impatience at the polls. Beset with troubles, the Republicans lost badly in the midterm elections of 1882, their worst defeat since the party was formed nearly thirty years earlier. Stalwarts were listless; Half-Breeds like Blaine stayed home. Democrats won 200 seats in the House of Representatives to the Republicans' 119, and they swept the key states of New York, Ohio, Pennsylvania, and Indiana. Embarrassing Arthur, Grover Cleveland, a newcomer to the national scene, crushed his Republican opponent in the race for governor in Arthur's home state of New York, pointing the way for a Cleveland presidential bid in 1884. A good deal of the blame for the losses fell on the president— "A Crushing Administration Defeat," a Half-Breed newspaper called it—though the results in truth owed as much to Republican factionalism, problems in the economy, and a long-term strengthening in

the Democratic vote. Whatever the causes, the defeat damaged Arthur's prospects for renomination in 1884.

So did the bad news that followed the election. Inheriting the Star Route mail fraud case from the Garfield administration, Arthur continued the investigation his predecessor had begun, instructing the attorney general to move ahead "earnestly and thoroughly." In March 1882, after a lengthy inquiry, a grand jury indicted nine men for involvement in the frauds, including several who were prominent in the Republican party. Following two closely watched trials in 1882 and 1883, all nine won acquittal. The verdicts, stemming in part from government incompetence in prosecuting the cases, embarrassed Arthur, as did evidence in the trials that showed his friendship with some of the most well-known defendants.

## MODERNIZING THE NAVY

As the administration lurched toward 1884, even its successes often eluded the public eye. In the Navy Department, Secretary Chandler started a rebuilding program that would take years to bear fruit. A powerful fleet during the Civil War, the U.S. Navy had since fallen into disrepair. By 1881, it had no up-to-date warships, and most of its ships could not safely fire a gun. All but four were made of wood; all carried sails. In an age of rifled artillery, the U.S. Navy mounted ineffective smooth-bore, muzzle-loading guns. Leadership was lacking. The secretary of the navy under Hayes, a Republican politician from the heartland of Indiana, was said to have expressed surprise that ships were hollow. "We have not six ships that would be kept at sea in war by any maritime power," a naval strategist reported in 1882.

As other nations expanded their fleets— and with them, their trade—agitation began at home for a new navy, especially after experts warned that Chile, China, Brazil, and Turkey all had navies that could humiliate the United States at will. Garfield's secretary of the navy picked up the theme, establishing a planning board that studied the problem and recommended the creation of a modern steel navy. Once in office, Chandler argued the need for "invincible squadrons." He streamlined the officer corps, opened the Naval War College in Newport, Rhode Island, and established the Office of Naval Intelligence. With Arthur's urging, Congress in early 1883 authorized the construction of three steel cruisers, an important start. Much remained to be done—the new cruisers, for example, still carried sails as well as steam engines—but Arthur and Chandler had begun to build the U.S. fleet that overwhelmed Spain in 1898.

## THE SPOILSMAN
## AND THE PENDLETON ACT

One visible achievement remained: In a ceremony that carried some irony, "Chet" Arthur, the notorious spoilsman, in 1883 signed into law the nation's first significant step toward reform of the civil service. Beginning with his annual message the year before, Arthur had voiced warm support for the Pendleton bill (named after an Ohio Democratic Senator) that had quickly won favor in the wake of Garfield's tragic shooting. "[A]ction," Arthur had said firmly, "should no longer be postponed." Influential portions of the public agreed, and in January 1883, with the passage of the Pendleton bill, Congress created a permanent civil service commission with power to prescribe rules for hiring. It also called for competitive examinations for the filling of about ten thousand positions, authorized the president to expand the list of classified jobs, and provided for promotions based on merit and competition.

While Arthur's signature on the law surprised some, the efficient manner in which he went on to administer it pleased many. Responding to the advice of reformers, he named Dorman B. Eaton of New York, a respected leader of the reform cause, to chair the new Civil Service Commission, and he heeded most of the recommendations it made. Under Arthur, the commission expanded the civil service list and tried to curtail the collection of campaign funds from officeholders. Lasting to the present day, the Pendleton law brought a welcome and important change in the way the nation

filled its offices. "The good results . . . foreshadowed have been more than realized," Arthur reported in 1884. As he left office in March 1885, the Civil Service Commission itself acknowledged with gratitude his "constant, firm, and friendly support."

## FRELINGHUYSEN, ARTHUR,
## AND A FAILED FOREIGN POLICY

At the State Department, Frelinghuysen meanwhile had surprised the country by pursuing an expansionist foreign policy that went well beyond Blaine's, remarkable in light of his bitter criticism of his predecessor's so-called jingoism. In May 1882, Frelinghuysen officially informed London of the U.S. desire to abrogate the Clayton-Bulwer Treaty, a proposal the British promptly rejected. In August he and Arthur quietly withdrew Blaine's invitations to the inter-American peace congress, and he focused instead on negotiating a series of specific agreements with countries in Central America and the Caribbean. The most important of the agreements, the Frelinghuysen-Zavala Treaty with Nicaragua, provided for a canal across the isthmus, to be built by the United States and owned jointly with Nicaragua. Signed in December 1884, the treaty promised the United States a protectorate of sorts over a strip of territory through Nicaragua.

In other moves, Frelinghuysen also pressed to expand U.S. trade south of the border. Working toward the same end, Blaine had urged aggressive marketing and an expansion in the U.S. Merchant Marine, but Frelinghuysen favored commercial reciprocity, the negotiation of treaties to encourage trade by lowering tariffs on selected goods. Carrying out his idea, he negotiated major agreements between 1882 and 1885 with Mexico, the Dominican Republic, and Hawaii and arranged a treaty with Spain covering Cuba and Puerto Rico. The treaties went far in extending U.S. influence abroad. The Cuban treaty, for example, offered "the almost complete commercial monopoly of the commerce of Cuba . . . ," as the envoy who negotiated it said. "It will be annexing Cuba in the most desirable way."

But treaties need to be ratified, and in that vital task the Arthur administration suffered failure after failure. Despite strong pressure from the president, the Senate refused to ratify the Frelinghuysen-Zavala Treaty, arguing that it violated the Constitution and could involve the United States in military adventures abroad. In similar fashion, the reciprocity treaties with Spain, Hawaii, and the Dominican Republic went down to defeat in the Senate. After lengthy debate, the Senate did ratify Frelinghuysen's reciprocity agreement with Mexico, but the House of Representatives proceeded to cripple the measure by refusing to pass the legislation necessary to put it into effect.

## A PRESIDENT WORN-OUT AND ILL

Coming one after another, the defeats hurt Arthur, who had tired visibly as his term wore on. More and more he tried to get away on vacation, and he complained to friends of his growing inability to keep his mind on business. Those close to him reported that he looked forward "with intense longing to the day of his release from his irksome responsibilities."

And no wonder. The fact was, Arthur was ill, seriously ill, though few people even in the White House knew it. "The President sick in body and soul," his physician wrote in his diary in August 1882. Doctors that year diagnosed him with Bright's disease, a severe kidney ailment, whose symptoms of mental depression and fatigue might help explain Arthur's languid approach to his office. Adding to his woes, Arthur caught malaria during an 1883 vacation trip to Florida, and afterward he cut back even more on his working hours. Unaware of the president's illnesses, newspapers complained of "the shadow of repose that has come over the Government business."

Even so, Arthur hoped to win his party's renomination for the presidency in 1884, though in light of his sickness it is difficult to say why. It may be that once again he simply wanted to show he was "worthy," to demonstrate he had been a more effective president than most people had predicted in

September 1881. But conducting his campaign with the usual lethargy, he failed to muster enough support, and the Republican national convention turned instead to his old opponent Blaine. To the party's nominee Arthur pledged "earnest and cordial support," but still angry at Blaine's refusal to campaign in 1882, he did nothing to help the Republican's difficult canvass.

Worn out, Arthur spent his last weeks as president lobbying unsuccessfully for the ratification of his treaties and presiding at various White House ceremonies. In February 1885, he dedicated the Washington Monument, finished at last after thirty-six years. On his final day in office, he placed his old friend Ulysses S. Grant, who was bankrupt and dying, on the Army retired list at the rank and pay of general. On that day, too, he signed into law a bill authorizing the construction of two more steel cruisers, a measure that must have pleased him. He had few thoughts for the future. "Well," he replied to someone who asked about his plans, "there doesn't seem anything else for an ex-President to do but to go into the country and raise big pumpkins."

Leaving the White House, Arthur moved back to New York City and rejoined his old law firm, but declining health often kept him at home. When a group of New York Stalwarts sounded him out on running for the U.S. Senate, he refused. Bitter, he told his son to stay out of politics, that the personal cost was too high. Arthur died of a massive cerebral hemorrhage on 18 November 1886 at age 57. "He was a brave, strong man to the last," his physician said, "and few men deserved better to live."

## EVALUATION OF ARTHUR'S PRESIDENCY

At his death, the New York *Sun*, a Democratic paper, called Chester Alan Arthur "one of the most successful and meritorious in our whole list of Presidents." The judgment was kind but generous, and it enlarged the mark on both success and merit. In the sense that Arthur's central task had been to restore calm and confidence after Garfield's assassination, he had done it well. He had also put together some laudable achievements: reform in the civil service and the rebuilding of the U.S. Navy, most significantly. To a limited degree, Frelinghuysen's work for an interoceanic canal and reciprocity in trade foreshadowed later policies pursued under Presidents McKinley, Roosevelt, and Wilson.

But in the end, indolence and lack of action (even if accounted for in part by illness), a failure to heal the divisions in the Republican party, and, above all, an inability to assess and master the newer forces at work in the country were the essential hallmarks of the Arthur administration. Fortunately for the Republican party, Arthur's successor, Grover Cleveland, managed no better. Scarcely ten years after Arthur's death, the Republican party of McKinley and then Roosevelt achieved mastery of the country. Though an honest and decent man, Arthur had neither the capacity to foresee such mastery, nor the vision to work toward it.

As a consequence, his administration became simply a transition between Reconstruction and the crucial years at the end of the century. When it was over, aside from a civil service law that would likely have passed in any event and a small start toward a new navy, the nation under Arthur had only the transition—and a newly decorated White House—to show for it.

## BIBLIOGRAPHY

Doenecke, Justus D. *The Presidencies of James A. Garfield and Chester A. Arthur* (University Press of Kansas, 1981).

Howe, George F. *Chester A. Arthur: A Quarter-Century of Machine Politics* (Dodd, Mead, 1934).

Pletcher, David M. *The Awkward Years: American Foreign Relations Under Garfield and Arthur* (University of Missouri Press, 1962).

Reeves, Thomas C. *Gentleman Boss: The Life of Chester Alan Arthur* (Knopf, 1975).

# ★★★ 22 and 24 ★★★

# STEPHEN GROVER CLEVELAND
## 1885–1889 and 1893–1897

*Robert M. Goldman*

*Born 18 March 1837 in Caldwell, New Jersey, to Richard Falley Cleveland and Anne Neal Cleveland; did not attend college; admitted to the bar and practiced law; married Frances Folsom, 2 June 1886, Washington, D.C.; five children; elected president in 1884 on the Democratic ticket with Thomas Andrews Hendricks of Indiana, receiving 4,874,986 popular votes and 219 electoral college ballots over the Republican party ticket of James Gillespie Blaine of Maine and John Alexander Logan of Illinois, which received 4,851,981 popular votes and 182 electoral ballots; ran for reelection in 1888 with Allen Granberry Thurman of Ohio, and received 5,537,857 popular votes but only 168 electoral college ballots, and thus was defeated by the Republican ticket of Benjamin Harrison of Indiana and Levi Parsons Morton of New York, who received 5,447,129 popular votes but 233 electoral college ballots; ran again in 1892 and was elected, along with Adlai Ewing Stevenson of Illinois, receiving 5,556,918 votes and 277 electoral college ballots, over the Republican ticket of Benjamin Harrison of Indiana and Whitlaw Reid of New York, which received 5,176,108 popular votes and 145 electoral ballots; died 24 June 1908 in Princeton, New Jersey; buried in Princeton, New Jersey.*

During his first term as president, Grover Cleveland exclaimed to a friend, "My God, what is there in this office that any man should ever want to get into it?" A strange remark, perhaps, considering it came from a man who would run for the office twice more, including once after he had already been defeated for re-election. Yet because of that persistence, Cleveland has the unique distinction of being both the twenty-second and twenty-fourth president of the United States.

If Cleveland's persistence in running for the presidency is evident, the quality of his performance in that office during a most critical period in U.S. history is less clear. Few presidents can boast such enormous variation in historical evaluation—he has been described as everything from a dull failure to a heroic giant of true courage. Historians talk about the Cleveland era, yet no great initiatives or policies were associated with the man. Even those who praise him often do so in spite of themselves. Richard Hofstadter called Cleveland "the sole reasonable facsimile of a major President between Lincoln and Theodore Roosevelt," while admitting that he was "dogmatic, obtuse, and insensitive" with a "far from nimble mind." In the popular imagination, he often stands in the company of those presidents who are often remembered for not being remembered. Few tangible reminders of his career exist, unless one counts the still popular Baby Ruth™ candy bar named for Cleveland's first-born daughter.

**EARLY CAREER**

Grover Cleveland's nomination by the Democratic party in 1884 as their presidential standard bearer was as surprising and meteoric as his life and career had been unremarkable up to that point. He was born on 13 March 1837 in Caldwell, New Jersey, to Richard and Ann Neal Cleveland. His father was a Congregational-Presbyterian minister who died in poverty in 1853, leaving Grover and his older brother William financially responsible for their mother and seven other siblings. Having had little formal education, Grover worked at a series of jobs before moving to Buffalo, New York, in 1855. There, through the help of an uncle, he obtained an apprenticeship in a local law firm, and four years later he was admitted to the state bar.

While building up what would become a successful and lucrative legal practice, Cleveland became associated with the Democratic party machine in Buffalo. He served as a ward supervisor and an assistant district attorney, and in 1870 was elected sheriff of Erie County. As sheriff he demonstrated both his integrity and an obsessive commitment to duty by refusing to delegate the unpleasant task of serving as hangman in the execution of two convicted felons. Cleveland's reputation for honesty and efficiency eventually led him to be nominated and elected as mayor of Buffalo in 1881 and, based on those same qualities, he was elected governor of New York the following year. His brief record of clean government and his independence of any of the various factions of the Democratic party, particularly the notorious Tammany Hall machine, earned him the Democratic nomination for president in 1884.

Despite having paid for a replacement to fight for him in the Civil War and allegations (in fact true) that he had fathered an illegitimate child, Cleveland defeated Republican candidate James G. Blaine. Cleveland's electoral victory was substantial, but his popular vote plurality of 20,000 votes out of some 9 million votes cast was one of the smallest in U.S. history. In large part, he was the beneficiary of the public's disgust with the fraud and corruption that had marked Republican administrations since Lincoln. He was also aided by a series of Republican mistakes, including a Blaine supporter's unfortunate, though perhaps valid, reference to the Democratic party as the home of "Rum, Romanism, and Rebellion."

**LACK OF A CONSISTENT POLITICAL PHILOSOPHY**

If Cleveland had a systematic or coherent philosophy of government and the presidency, no one has yet been able to uncover it. He did seem to hold to a set of beliefs with a tenacity that his supporters saw as the very "symbol of civic staunchness," and that his detractors viewed as the height of stubbornness and parochialism. He set great store with tradition, and his models were Washington and Jackson, or at least his own perspective on them. His conception of the presidency was largely negative. While he confidently believed that he had been placed in the White House to promote the national good, he saw his primary role as preventing others from doing bad.

More than once he proclaimed that "the office of the President is essentially executive in its nature," and he was a passionate adherent of the idea of separation of powers. He proposed no legislation for congressional action during either of his two terms. But when Congress acted in ways he thought inimicable to his principles and the nation's, he felt no hesitation in acting. During his first term alone he vetoed over 300 bills, more than the total vetoes of all his predecessors. And while his cabinet appointments during his two terms were generally men of recognized ability and experience, he made it clear that he considered them more a privy council than heads of independent executive departments and that they would be answerable for their agencies' actions only to him, not to Congress.

Yet it is also fair to say that at the end of his two nonconsecutive terms he left the presidency stronger on balance than he had found it. In part, this strength was a reflection of the string of weak presidents following Lincoln. But it was also in part directly attributable to Cleveland's actions; on a number of occasions, he successfully asserted and expanded executive authority and influence. During his first year in office he rebuffed attempts by Senate Republicans to use the Tenure of Office Act, although much modified from the one used by Republicans in their impeachment of Andrew Johnson in 1868, to block the president's appointments. Indeed, the act was eventually repealed. For the new president, the repeal was a clear defeat of "an encroachment upon constitutional Executive prerogatives"

and "thus was a time-honored interpretation of the Constitution restored to us."

## CIVIL SERVICE

The Tenure of Office Act struggle was part of a broader conflict over civil service reform that occupied a good portion of Cleveland's first administration. The new president took office after the Democrats had been out of power for more than two decades, and it was inevitable that he would be under intense pressure to replace Republican federal office-holders with loyal supporters of the Democratic ticket. Cleveland's first weeks as president were literally filled with consideration of patronage requests. The task was made more difficult by Cleveland's refusal to delegate any part of it to others; he routinely stayed up into the small hours of the morning carefully scrutinizing applicants' request. Adding to the difficulty of the task was Cleveland's record of honesty and good government prior to his coming to the White House, which had created high expectations of a true reform of the spoils system. Those expectations were especially prominent among Mugwumps, independent Republican reformers who believed the new president would retain honest, effective Republicans currently holding appointive positions. As it turned out, Cleveland pleased neither the Mugwumps nor the more partisan members of his own party. By the end of his first term, Republicans had watched more and more of their number replaced by Cleveland "with good men of our own party," but those good men were never sufficient in number to satisfy everyone who had requested patronage.

What Cleveland did accomplish, with reluctance, was the significant expansion of the percentage of federal employees, from 12 to 40 percent, subject to nonpartisan appointment under the provisions of the Pendleton Civil Service Act of 1883. He also managed to maintain two scandal-free administrations and a deserved reputation for personal honesty. Indeed, his concern for setting the highest standards was such that he even paid for all of his own and his family's vacations.

## FOREIGN AFFAIRS

Cleveland's expansion of executive prerogatives found some expression in his handling of foreign affairs, although here, too, the impetus was largely negative. By the 1880s, many Americans had become supporters of greater overseas expansion and involvement. Whether for economic, religious, or political reasons, the new "manifest destiny" appealed to those who saw a greater role in world affairs for the United States commensurate with the nation's industrial development at home. As in other areas, Cleveland had no particular or systematic conception about America's relations with the world. His experience in this area was virtually nil; he himself would never travel west of the Mississippi or venture beyond America's borders farther than a brief visit to the Caribbean.

Cleveland was to some extent an anti-imperialist. In foreign affairs as in other areas, he tended to be guided by his sense of U.S. traditions, which in this instance meant an uncritical acceptance of the principles of conduct first set forth in George Washington's Farewell Address. In that statement, Washington had called for American isolationism and the rejection of any "entangling political alliances" with other countries. Cleveland was also guided by his vague but somewhat more activist understanding of the Monroe Doctrine and the nation's role in the Western Hemisphere. It is perhaps not surprising that he resolved this conflict during his first term by displaying little if any interest in foreign affairs, leaving them to his capable, if inexperienced, secretary of state, Thomas F. Bayard. During his second term, with Republican Walter Q. Gresham as secretary of state, Cleveland had to confront issues from abroad.

## HAWAII

In January 1893, during President Benjamin Harrison's watch and just before Cleveland's second term began, a revolution overthrew the monarchy of the Hawaiian Islands. American expansionists had focused on the islands for a number of years, and a commercial treaty with the monarch Queen Lil-iuokalani was already in place. Cleveland himself had supported this treaty, admitting that the islands were "an outpost of American commerce and a stepping-stone to the growing trade of the Pacific." The 1893 uprising was in fact less a revolution than a coup led by wealthy American planters such as Sanford B. Dole. The planters believed that to protect their economic interests the United States would be forced to annex the islands, and President Harrison had given every indication that he would do so.

What the planters did not count on was the new president's principles. Shortly after taking office in March, Cleveland quietly had the annexation bill withdrawn from Senate consideration. For the rest of his administration he unsuccessfully attempted to find some way to avoid annexation. Annexing the islands went against Cleveland's moral principles but was the popular choice; returning the islands to their people by restoring the monarchy may have appealed to the president but it was neither popular nor any longer feasible. Ultimately, the islands were annexed in the wake of the Spanish-American War, but the president continued to claim a moral victory of sorts by having frustrated the annexationists.

## LATIN AMERICA

Cleveland was more successful in his attempts to enforce the Monroe Doctrine. That opportunity grew out of a long-running dispute between Great Britain and Venezuela over the boundary between the latter country and British Guiana. In response to Venezuela's request for help in 1895, Cleveland sent what was even for him a sternly worded message to the British government of Lord Balfour to resolve the situation. The message, drafted by Richard Olney, who had become secretary of state on the death of Gresham, implied U.S. willingness to use force to support Venezuela against British actions that might be taken as a violation of the Monroe Doctrine. England refused the bait but agreed to the creation of a special arbitration commission to settle the matter, which, as it turned out, settled the dispute almost entirely in England's favor. Nonetheless, Cleveland garnered tremendous popular support for his efforts, discovering—as many future presidents would—that a seeming foreign policy success can work wonders for taking the public's mind off of domestic failures.

## RACIAL ATTITUDES

Cleveland's views on foreign affairs were in most regards the mirror image of his attitudes and actions toward racial and ethnic minorities at home. As the head of the party responsible for "redemption" of the South through disfranchisement and segregation, Cleveland had little sympathy for, and much less interest in, the condition of African Americans. There is no evidence that he was any more racist than most northerners during that time, but he certainly was willing to continue the implicit arrangements first worked out in the Compromise of 1877. According to that agreement, the former Confederate states would be left more or less on their own to determine the future course of race relations.

By Cleveland's first term, this agreement had informally sanctioned a variety of methods that prevented African Americans from voting and state laws establishing racial separation via Jim Crow segregation laws. However, the Democratic platform of 1884 did pledge the president to protect what was called "the free ballot and a fair count." Cleveland's choice of a moderate southerner, Augustus Garland, as his attorney general reflected some desire to calm the fears of black voters. Indeed, Garland did attempt to enforce the federal voting-protection laws that were on the books, and in one instance he instituted a number of prosecutions against Democrats in Washington County, Texas, under the Enforcement Acts of 1870 and 1871.

By Cleveland's second term, the various laws protecting black voters in the South had virtually been repealed and state disfranchisement had begun to take hold. By then, the president, like many Americans, was convinced that government, especially the national government, bore no responsibility for the future of African Americans.

Adopting a sort of passive paternalism, he believed their future well-being was in education and economic self-improvement and he supported efforts by private northern philanthropies to set up schools for blacks in the South. When Booker T. Washington made his famous 1896 "Atlanta Compromise" speech, calling for African Americans to focus on self-improvement and acceptance of racial separation, Cleveland sent the president of Tuskeegee Institute a letter of praise, noting that "your words cannot fail to delight and encourage all who wish well for the race."

## INDIAN POLICY

Cleveland's attitudes toward Native Americans were actively paternalistic. Despite his usual abhorrence of government action that might help a particular segment of society, Cleveland did encourage federal legislation intended to protect the western Indian tribes. He believed that Native Americans were wards of the nation who needed to be looked after and educated or "civilized," so that ultimately they could be assimilated into American society. In 1887 he signed into law the Dawes Severalty Act, also known as the Indian Emancipation Act, which provided for the division of reservation land into private allotments of from 40 to 160 acres. Those responsible for the legislation maintained that individual ownership of land, plus improved educational facilities provided through the sale of such lands, would enable Indians to escape "pauperism" and ultimately to achieve the "habits of civilized life." The Dawes Act, although certainly well-intentioned, proved to be as much of a failure as the earlier policy of setting aside tribal reservations to "protect" Native Americans. The misguided educational attempts not only were ineffective but also contributed to a further breakdown of tribal culture and traditions. And the severalty provisions opened up tribal lands to further exploitation by white Americans.

Cleveland's views on race may appear contradictory, but they were guided by a fairly simplistic criterion: whether a particular group seemed capable of "assimilation" into American society. Indians were capable; African Americans, probably not. He extended this test into the area of immigration. When riots broke out against Chinese laborers in the West in 1885, Cleveland began a campaign to limit Chinese immigration on the grounds that, since the attacks were racially motivated, the only way to prevent future persecution was to remove the victims—especially since the Chinese were not capable of assimilation. But Cleveland had no patience with growing nativist calls for limits on Southern and Eastern Europeans, since these groups were capable—they could become "real" Americans.

Ultimately, any evaluation of Cleveland as president must focus on the three principal issues which confronted his two administrations. Although civil service reform, foreign policy, and minorities were significant, Cleveland's views during both his administrations were consistent and there was little change in the circumstances involving these issues between his split terms. However, in the cases of the currency question, tariff reform, and labor-management relations, the consistency of Cleveland's beliefs were significantly challenged by changing circumstances and conditions between his terms. And all three issues were a reflection of the fact that the Cleveland presidencies coincided with fundamental changes in the American economy such as the rise of business trusts and monopolies, massive immigration, urbanization, and labor unrest.

## ECONOMIC VIEWS

In concert with his social and political views, Cleveland's economic views were largely traditional, simple, and unwavering. He supported the idea of *laissez faire* to the extent that he believed government should play no role in economic affairs if that meant showing any kind of favoritism to a particular segment of society. This seemingly could and would produce yet further contradictions. While he supported government paternalism towards Native Americans, he opposed any similar program for farmers or workers. He made this quite

clear, for example, in his 1887 veto of a bill that would have appropriated $10,000 to purchase seeds for farmers in several Texas counties that had been experiencing severe drought conditions for several years. The amount was trivial, but the principle was not, and Cleveland had as little trouble justifying this as he did rejecting attempts to increase government pensions to veterans or extend them to their dependents.

At the same time, Cleveland was instrumental in expanding the amount of western land protected from "appropriation" by the railroads, timber companies, and cattle interests, which he viewed as favoritism. By the end of his second term, Cleveland had doubled the size of the National Forest Reserve. One recent historian has accurately concluded that "but for Theodore Roosevelt's vastly more skillful flair for self-advertisement, Cleveland might be remembered as our presidential pioneer in imposing sanity on federal land use policy." Neither charity nor favoritism was one of the functions of his kind of government.

## TARIFF REFORM

Cleveland's tight purse strings were all the more interesting given the fact that by 1888 the federal government had accumulated a surplus of almost $125 million, largely through excise taxes and tariffs. The problem was what to do with this money. Like most Americans at the time, Cleveland knew almost nothing about tariffs. Shortly after taking office in 1884 he admitted as much to Carl Schurz, asking Schurz to "tell me how to go about it to learn." Cleveland then held a series of meetings with party and congressional leaders at his home, Oak View, in suburban Washington, and became convinced that tariff reform was the answer to the federal surplus. In December 1887 the president took the unusual step of devoting his entire State of the Union message to that topic. He attempted to avoid supporting what he viewed as either extreme of free trade or high-tariff protectionism and he argued that "it is a *condition* that confronts us, not a theory." However, it was evident that, when forced to choose,

Cleveland spurned protectionism. He felt that high tariffs raised prices for ordinary citizens and provided excess profits for a few industries or businesses; they were therefore an unwise and dangerous example of government paternalism and favoritism. The president called for a reduction of import taxes on both the "necessities of life" and the raw materials necessary for manufactures. He did stand firm on no reductions of duties on tobacco or liquor or other "luxury" items.

The legislation that grew out of Cleveland's message, the Mills bill, reflected few of his beliefs. It contained some small cuts on sugar, rice, and cotton textile duties, which clearly favored the South, and some deep cuts on iron products and glass tariffs, which angered midwesterners. The bill never made it out of Congress. Cleveland had committed himself and the Democrats to doing something about the tariff and had then accomplished nothing; the tariff issue probably hurt the Democrats in 1888 and helped Harrison defeat Cleveland's reelection bid.

When he recovered the presidency in 1894, Cleveland was quick to remind congressional Democrats of their duty, as he saw it, finally to reform the tariff. But Cleveland was out of step—while his views had not changed, conditions had. By 1894 the country was suffering one of the worst economic depressions since the founding of the Republic, and the federal government was running a deficit. The McKinley Tariff of 1890, which represented the protectionist views of the incumbent Republicans, had increased duties on many items but had also helped to lower revenues. The Wilson-Gorman tariff bill of 1894, supported by Cleveland, was a modest reform that passed the House but mushroomed in the Senate, where more than 600 amendments were added, most raising tariffs on specific items. Forced between signing a bill that embodied the very favoritism he so opposed and vetoing reform legislation that he had promised to make, Cleveland allowed the Wilson-Gorman Tariff to become law without his signature. Disregarding his own lack of leadership in seeing the legislation

through, the president blamed what he labeled a "mongrel tariff" on the "party perfidy" of his own Democratic colleagues.

Cleveland's failure to reform the tariff by the standards he himself set out suggest his success and limitations as president. Throughout his two terms he committed himself to the reform of the tariff. No one could fault him for flip-flopping. However, having committed himself to this issue he likewise refused to accept a number of very important factors. For one thing, he gave but token recognition to the changed circumstances between conditions that were prevalent when he gave his 1887 message to Congress and those in place in 1894. In 1887 he could defend reduced tariffs because they held no threat of producing a deficit; by 1894, there already was a deficit, and a nationwide depression as well. Moreover, Cleveland's argument in 1894 that tariff reform would expand foreign trade and thus help the nation move out of the depression was not the best argument in appealing for public support. Indeed, throughout the fight for reform Cleveland made little or no attempt to "educate" the public on the effects of tariffs, which is, after all, an exceedingly complex and difficult issue.

## CURRENCY

Grover Cleveland tackled the currency issue, like the tariff question, with unyielding principle in the face of changing circumstances. The currency issue alone was complex enough to discourage politicians and citizens from engaging in any truly substantive discourse, but it was also symbolically significant enough to become a critical issue by the last decade of the nineteenth century. Here, too, Cleveland's views were clear and unencumbered by any sophisticated knowledge. He opposed any and all attempts to change the gold standard used for American currency. He accepted as gospel Gresham's Law, the idea that in the long run cheap money drives dear money out of circulation. It follows from that view that any attempt to dilute the currency by including silver in addition to, or in place of, gold as the monetary standard would inevitably bring about the great evils of inflation, damaged credit, and lower foreign trade. For Cleveland this threat was more than demonstrated by the 1878 Bland-Allison Silver Coinage Act, which required the government to purchase $2 to $4 million of silver each month. This silver would then be turned into coins at the ratio of 16 to 1. In effect, this meant that every silver dollar was worth only 80 cents, or 80 percent of the gold in a gold dollar.

In his first inaugural address Cleveland pledged to repeal the Bland-Allison Act. He argued that the gold reserves in the Treasury were being seriously depleted under the measure and that the inevitable result would be the complete displacement of gold by silver. However, the new president quickly discovered that by this time a growing segment of the Democratic party, especially in the Midwest and South, were not only opposed to a return to the gold standard but were calling for the complete and unlimited coinage of silver. Farmers especially were coming to see "free silver" as the answer to their growing problems. They were, after all, largely debtors, and inflation brought about by silver currency meant they could repay their debts in cheaper dollars and, hopefully, receive higher prices for their produce. With congressional opposition from his own party, Cleveland's first administration passed having done nothing: no repeal, no free silver.

Cleveland was not given another chance to preserve the gold standard for another four years. In 1888, in another close election, Cleveland lost to Ohio Republican Benjamin Harrison even though Cleveland's share of the popular vote was slightly higher than his opponent's. Four years after that, the Democrats turned once again to Cleveland and he was able to defeat for re-election the same man who had displaced him in 1888. But no sooner had Cleveland returned as the twenty-fourth president than the nation underwent a financial panic that quickly developed into a nationwide depression. By the winter of 1893–1894 thousands of banks and other businesses had failed and unemployment was estimated at

over 20 percent. The effects of the depression were spread fairly evenly throughout the nation, but farm regions were hit particularly hard since farm prices had already been in steady decline before the depression struck. The widespread financial disaster of 1893 was merely the last straw, and from the wreckage of the camel's back would emerge the Populist or People's party as a new competition for Cleveland's Democrats.

For Cleveland, the explanation and remedy for the depression were the same: silver. For businessmen, the possibility of silver as the only currency standard—monometallism—had been enough to close the banks and factories. Silver monometallism would inevitably debase the currency and erode the American consumer's purchasing power. Worse yet, during the Republican interregnum, Congress had seen fit to pass the Sherman Silver Purchase Act, which actually increased the amount of silver to be purchased by the government. In Cleveland's view this act (and the McKinley Tariff) had seriously depleted the gold reserves of the government, helped contribute to the financial panic and depression, and most important, hurt America's credit overseas.

Economic historians agree that Cleveland was not entirely wrong in his understanding of the causes of the depression of 1893. It was his solution that did him in. In June 1893 Cleveland called for a special session of Congress to be held that August for the sole purpose of repealing the Sherman Silver Purchase Act. The repeal measure passed the House despite opposition from western and southern Democrats, including a young congressman from Nebraska, William Jennings Bryan. Senate opposition was fiercer as moderate Democrats attempted to make the repeal less draconian, but after almost two months of consideration, the measure passed in the upper chamber, too.

In securing the repeal of the Sherman Act, and shortly thereafter vetoing a bill that would have committed the government to using the silver already in its possession for coinage, Cleveland demonstrated his ability to refuse compromise when his principles were at stake. But predictions of an immediate upturn of the economy following the repeal proved wrong. As fall turned to winter, wages and prices declined as bank failures and unemployment again rose. And despite the repeal, the gold reserves in the federal treasury continued to fall, forcing the president to offer a series of government bond issues. One of these was a private bond sale to an investment syndicate owned by the most infamous symbol of Wall Street financial power, J. P. Morgan. Although the sale was perhaps justified by the dire condition of the government's finances at the moment, the deal dealt a fatal blow to Cleveland's hopes for renomination by the Democratic party. The contrast between the millions of dollars in profit that would flow to Morgan and his Wall Street cronies, while ordinary Americans still struggled for a job and a meal, was just too great. Cleveland's crusade to preserve the gold standard at all costs opened the way in 1896 for the Democratic party to take a 180-degree turn, supporting the free-silverites and William J. Bryan.

## BUSINESS AND LABOR

Cleveland's stands on the tariff and currency issues were straightforward and consistent and his failures were at least to some extent the result of an unwillingness to bend to political expediency. More ambiguous, however, were his views and actions with respect to business, businessmen, and their relations with labor. Here the paradoxes of Cleveland as president truly mount up. As previously discussed, he certainly believed in free enterprise, and from his first inaugural promised Americans an administration guided by the same principles of economy and efficiency that were the hallmark of corporate success. Yet he also genuinely saw himself as the friend of the average working American, and he was willing to allow government involvement in regulating the worst excesses of American business in the late nineteenth century. Two often-cited examples of this role are his signing into law

the Interstate Commerce Act of 1887, which created the Interstate Commerce Commission (ICC), and his grudging acceptance of the 1890 Sherman Antitrust Act. However, from its inception the ICC had limited powers with respect to regulating railroad rates, and even these were further eroded through a series of hostile Supreme Court rulings during the 1890s.

Cleveland did not oppose passage of the Sherman Act (he was not in office at that time), but he did have doubts about its constitutionality. It was Cleveland's attorney general, Richard Olney, who brought one of the first major cases prosecuted under the act, the E. C. Knight Company Sugar Trust, before the Supreme Court. And it was a Supreme Court whose chief justice, Melville Fuller, was a Cleveland appointee, that would fatally weaken enforcement of the Sherman Act in its 1895 *U.S. v. E.C. Knight* decision. Indeed, all four of Cleveland's appointments to the Supreme Court—Fuller, Lucius Q. C. Lamar, Edward White, and Rufus Peckham—would distinguish themselves by their fairly unanimous and consistent support for the preservation of property rights and the use of judicial review to block regulatory and social legislation.

The most publicized examples of Cleveland's attitudes toward business and workers were his responses to two events. The first was the quixotic march to Washington by Jacob Coxey and his "army" of unemployed workers in the spring of 1894. Jacob Coxey, an unemployed Civil War veteran from Ohio, believed he, too, had the answer to getting the country out of the depression, and he called for the federal government to allocate $500 million for road construction. When Congress refused to act on his written petitions, Coxey, his family, and several hundred supporters headed off from Massilon, Ohio, to make a "living petition" to Washington. By the time the "army" reached Washington there were more spectators than soldiers, and a number were eventually arrested for trespassing on the government's grass. While Cleveland made no open expression of opposition to the march, he did approve the use of Secret Service agents to track the marchers across the country.

The second event that clearly revealed the president's attitude toward business and labor was the strike at the Pullman Car Company outside Chicago in the summer of that year.

## THE PULLMAN STRIKE

During the depression winter of 1893–1894 George Pullman decided to reduce expenses by cutting his employees' wages by a quarter. This produced a serious problem for many of his workers who lived in the owner's model community, Pullman, where no corresponding decrease was made in rent and utility costs. As a result, many workers suddenly found themselves penniless on payday. Their attempt to send a delegation to Pullman himself ended in three of the delegates being fired, and at that point, almost all the workers went on strike. With support from the American Railway Union, led by Eugene V. Debs, the strike expanded rapidly, eventually affecting most of the country. Debs called for strikers and the Pullman managers to resolve the dispute by means of an impartial arbitration panel. Pullman refused. Ironically, the idea of using arbitration panels to mediate labor disputes had been championed by Cleveland during his first term in office.

By July rail traffic through Chicago, the hub of the nationwide system, was seriously curtailed. With the threat of a complete shutdown of mail delivery, Cleveland took action. Attorney General Richard Olney obtained a federal court injunction forbidding the unions from interfering with rail traffic to and from Chicago. Over the protests of Illinois governor John P. Altgeld, himself a Democrat, the president sent a contingent of federal troops to Chicago. Not surprisingly, violence quickly erupted and deaths occurred. Within a week Debs and other strike leaders had been arrested for violating the injunction, and the troops had restored rail service and mail deliveries. Sympathy strikes in other states, mostly in the West, were ended in similar fashion.

The U.S. Supreme Court upheld the use of a court injunction to stop the strike in its 1895 *In re Debs* ruling. A commission appointed by the president to investigate the events during and leading up to the Pullman strike also, for the most part, supported the government's actions. But even Cleveland's most admiring biographer conceded that sending the troops was "precipitate" and that it was done under the "undue influence" of his attorney general. The use of federal troops to quell domestic unrest was not unique. After all, southern Reconstruction was carried out largely by using at least the threat of federal troops, and troops had been used in earlier labor unrest. But the price for this victory of national sovereignty and executive activism was considerable. Cleveland's actions in quelling the Pullman strike earned him the immediate and deep scorn not only of labor unions and workers but also of leaders in his own party, particularly Governor Altgeld. Thus Cleveland—the man who saw himself as the friend of working people and the ordinary citizen—found himself by the last year of his administration as the enemy of industrial workers and farmers, two of the primary groups that make up the working people of America. More important, he was hated, as he himself admitted, by a good portion of his own party. At the 1896 Democratic party convention he watched as the nomination went to his own sworn enemy, the silverite William Jennings Bryan.

## ELECTION OF 1896

The presidential election of 1896 was not a pleasant ending for Cleveland's political career. With the president's tacit support Democrats who could not tolerate Bryan's silverite views, or the radical platform of the Populist party that also nominated Bryan, formed their own national Democratic party and nominated the elderly Illinois senator John M. Palmer. The campaign—the battle of the standards, as it came to be called—was one of the most bitter in U.S. history. Although he voted for Palmer, Cleveland probably was satisfied that in the end William McKinley and the Republican party emerged victorious. McKinley, thanks to his campaign manager Mark Hanna, had become a convert to the gold standard. Following McKinley's inauguration, Cleveland and his family moved to Princeton, New Jersey. He spent the remainder of his life quietly, doing occasional consulting, writing brief articles, and serving as a trustee of Princeton University.

## EVALUATION

Cleveland believed that the Democratic party, although no longer the party of Jefferson and Jackson, would be able to regain national power. He was more wrong in this than in anything else. Whatever his own responsibility was for its loss of power, the Democratic party that Cleveland led for over a decade was undergoing a transformation. With the exception of Wilson's two terms, the Democrats would not win the White House for another generation. And when they finally did return, the victory would be achieved by a coalition of farmers, workers, and ethnic and racial minorities—the very groups Cleveland had managed either to ignore or to antagonize.

Any evaluation of Grover Cleveland's significance and greatness must take into account his character and personality. Even at his most popular, Grover Cleveland was not a popular fellow. *Provincial, stubborn, dull, rude,* and *obtuse* were all terms that his contemporaries would have recognized as applicable to the man. He had few really close friends and, unlike most prior presidents, had no close advisers or "kitchen cabinet" with whom he could freely test his views and actions. In modern terminology, Cleveland was a perfect example of a workaholic, and during his eight years in the White House he successfully resisted attempts to increase his personal staff beyond a single secretary. Even with that addition he spent much time reading and answering his own correspondence. Samuel Tilden aptly remarked that Cleveland would rather do something badly than have someone else do it. He distrusted and despised reporters and newspaper editors, and they generally were only too happy to return the compliment.

Aside from politics, Cleveland's sole outside interest appeared to be a night of poker or heading out to the country for a hunting or fishing expedition. Even his White House marriage in 1886 to Frances Folsom, the much younger daughter of his former law partner, never quite erased the public's image of Cleveland's bachelor days—and nights—as a saloon habitué who drank, swore, ate to excess (he weighed almost 300 pounds at the time of his first term), and, given the illegitimacy charges, womanized.

Yet historians by and large have been far kinder and more respectful to Cleveland than were his contemporaries. The most comprehensive academic biography, that by Allan Nevins in 1932, portrayed Cleveland's life as a "study in courage" matched only by that of George Washington. In the modern mania for surveys and rankings Cleveland has also not fared badly. In both the 1948 and 1952 polls conducted by historian Arthur Schlesinger, Sr., Cleveland placed in the "near great" category (although in the second survey he dropped from seventh to eleventh). In 1968 he appeared in a collection of essays as one of *America's Ten Greatest Presidents*. By the 1980s his reputation had begun to slide somewhat, and a poll taken among historians placed him as "above average." This decrease was due in part to the revisionist writings of Horace Samuel Merrill, who characterized Cleveland as the spokesman for the conservative "Bourbon Democrats" of the late nineteenth century. Those Democrats were blatantly intent on preventing any kind of meaningful social and economic response to the tremendous changes that were taking place during these years. According to Merrill, Cleveland's only achievement was therefore his successful "preservation of the *status quo.*"

When historians have not been trying to rank Cleveland, they have often been engaged in lesser or greater attempts to somehow find the key to understanding and explaining the man, as if hidden among the mass of successes, contradictions, and failures was a simple message or code that would illuminate and reveal the essence of this president. Some have focused on his early life, emphasizing either his father's strict Calvinist religious values or Cleveland's early poverty and his devotion to his family. Others have fixed on his psychological insecurities stemming from the charges surrounding the widow Maria Halperin and the illegitimate child she had with Cleveland. The chapter title in one recent study of the history of the Democratic party is particularly succinct, stating merely: "Grover Cleveland: Honest and Lucky."

The search for some key to understanding Cleveland or the quest to fit Cleveland into some sort of competitive ranking seems to speak mainly about our own times and our own standards of what constitutes presidential greatness or success. At least since the Watergate scandals, presidential attributes such as character, honesty, and trustworthiness have become more valued. By those standards, Cleveland was a qualified success. However, the United States in the last quarter of the nineteenth century was undergoing momentous changes: the rise of giant corporations, urbanization, massive immigration, and political realignment, to name but a few. It was a nation that, in the words of one historian, was engaged in its own "search for order." Grover Cleveland's real failure was that he consistently missed just about every opportunity to creatively assist that search by means of his position as leader of both the nation and his political party. His statement to Congress in his 1887 message on the tariff that "it is a condition that confronts us, not a theory" is perhaps a fitting, if ironic, summation on his own

presidencies. Too often he responded to changing conditions with the same old theories. His achievements, such as they were, like the "restoration" of honesty in government and the expansion of presidential authority, seemed to come when he did respond to changing conditions with new or different approaches. Even here he did so in spite of, rather than because of, his own inclinations. That is not the standard for a successful president, and the final irony is that Cleveland himself would probably have agreed.

## BIBLIOGRAPHY

LaFaber, Walter. *The New Empire: An Interpretation of American Expansion, 1860–1898* (Cornell University Press, 1963).

McElroy, Robert. *Grover Cleveland: The Man and the Statesman* (Harper & Bros., 1923).

Merrill, Samuel Horace. *Bourbon Leader: Grover Cleveland and the Democratic Party* (Little, Brown, 1957).

Morgan, H. Wayne. *From Hayes to McKinley: National Party Politics, 1877–1896* (Syracuse University Press, 1969).

Nevins, Allan. *Grover Cleveland: A Study in Courage* (Dodd, Mead, 1932).

———, ed. *Letters of Grover Cleveland, 1850–1908* (Houghton Mifflin, 1933).

Summers, Mark Wahlgren. *The Gilded Age: Or, the Hazard of New Fortunes* (Prentice-Hall, 1997).

Welch, Richard E., Jr. *The Presidencies of Grover Cleveland* (University Press of Kansas, 1988).

Wiebe, Robert H. *The Search for Order, 1877–1920* (Hill & Wang, 1967).

★★★ 23 ★★★

# BENJAMIN HARRISON
## 1889–1893

*Lewis L. Gould*

*Born 20 August 1833 in North Bend, Ohio, to John Scott Harrison and Elizabeth Ramsey Irwin Harrison; educated at Miami University, Oxford, Ohio (B.A. 1852); married Caroline Lavinia Scott, 20 October 1853; two children; married Mary Scott Lord Dimmick, 6 April 1896, New York, New York; one child; elected president in 1888 on the Republican ticket with Levi Parsons Morton of New York, with 5,447,129 popular votes but with 233 electoral college ballots over Grover Cleveland of New York, and Allen Granberry Thurman of Ohio, who had 5,537,857 popular votes but only 168 electoral college ballots; died 13 March 1901 in Indianapolis, Indiana; buried in Crown Hill Cemetery, Indianapolis, Indiana.*

Benjamin Harrison's administration is generally regarded as one of the "failed presidencies" that marked the late nineteenth century. Although Harrison brought distinctive talents and impressive abilities as an administrator and executive to the White House between 1889 and 1893, his years in office were troubled and he did not win reelection. William McKinley and Theodore Roosevelt, his more activist and charismatic Republican successors, eclipsed the innovations that Harrison brought to the presidency. Although a fresh look at Harrison cannot turn him into a dynamic president or the architect of a productive term, he does deserve a reappraisal as a chief executive who anticipated many of the techniques and changes of the twentieth-century White House. His presidency illustrates why the evolution of the modern chief executive came slowly in a period of partisan stalemate and suspicion about an activist national government.

## THE ROAD TO THE
## WHITE HOUSE

Born in Ohio on 20 August 1833, Benjamin Harrison was the grandson of President William Henry Harrison. A lawyer and staunch Republican during the 1850s, the younger Harrison practiced law in Indianapolis, Indiana. He married Caroline Lavinia Scott in 1855. During the Civil War, Harrison rose to the rank of brigadier general. In 1876, he ran unsuccessfully for governor of Indiana; five years later he was elected to the U.S. Senate, where he served a single term.

As the election of 1888 approached, Harrison's name began to be mentioned for the Republican presidential nomination. He came from a midwestern state whose support the Republicans needed to win the White House, and he was identified with the protective tariff, an economic policy the Republicans supported and incumbent president Grover Cleveland opposed. Had James G. Blaine, the Republican standard bearer of 1884, made another run at the nomination in 1888, Harrison would not have had a strong chance. When Blaine withdrew from the race early in 1888, Harrison became a dark-horse contender, and he emerged on the eighth ballot as the nominee of the Republican national convention in Chicago. To run with Harrison, the delegates selected Levi Parsons Morton of New York for the vice-presidential slot, thereby balancing the ticket with an easterner.

Harrison proved to be a very effective campaigner. He drew praise for his crisp, lucid speeches on behalf of the protective tariff and Republican economic nationalism, which he delivered from his front porch in Indianapolis. With a united party

behind him, Harrison emerged as a credible national politician. His rival, President Grover Cleveland, did not campaign, as befitted an incumbent chief executive in those days. The Democrats were as divided over the protective tariff as the Republicans were unified. Harrison and the Republican ran slightly behind the Democrats in the popular vote, but his ticket won 233 electoral votes to Cleveland's 168. The Republicans also secured narrow control of both houses of Congress, an unusual accomplishment in that period. The political situation seemed propitious for the Grand Old Party in March 1889 when Harrison was inaugurated in a driving rainstorm. He told his audience, "No other people have a government more worthy of their respect and love, or a land so magnificent in extent, so pleasant to look upon, and so full of generous suggestion to enterprise and labor."

## AN ORDERLY EXECUTIVE

The new president brought efficiency and order to the executive mansion. He instituted procedures for following the flow of mail that came to the president, and he worked hard in his daily routine. With only a small White House staff of a secretary and some clerks, Harrison faced the onslaught of correspondence and visitors without the aides who assist modern presidents. The White House had telephones by 1889, but they were not yet systematically used. The president was also expected to hold regular public receptions, which Harrison did three times a week until the pressure of government affairs caused the public events to cease. Harrison's secretary, Elijah W. Halford, handled most of the routine work of the office. He had a reliable method of judging the president's mood from day to day. "When I see him in the morning and he greets me with, 'Halford, how are you today?' I sit down by his desk for a pleasant talk about matters. When he greets me with 'Good Morning, Mr. Halford,' I bolt the door and wait until after lunch for the talk." Harrison was a conscientious chief executive whose orderly habits and dedicated schedule attested to a lawyer's self-discipline.

His papers are evidence of his efficiency and desire to proceed in a businesslike fashion.

Despite his strengths as an administrator, Harrison had very little sense of effective public relations. He ignored the press and did little to humanize his administration. In his dealings with politicians and the public, he became legendary for his cold, aloof manner. Visitors might find themselves dismissed after only a brief, unrewarding conversation. Only five feet six, "Little Ben" could, it was said, charm an audience of twenty thousand with his prepared remarks and then alienate each one when he shook hands with them.

Caroline Scott Harrison, the First Lady, endeavored to renovate the White House as well as to enlarge it with an art gallery and a botanical conservatory. Her plans were embodied in a Senate bill that died in the last weeks of the Fifty-first Congress, and her impact was limited to a thorough cleaning of the executive mansion. She also served as president-general of the Daughters of the American Revolution. As with her husband, her tenure in the White House was most notable for an inability to translate good intentions into substantial achievement.

## IRRITATING THE FAITHFUL

For his cabinet, Benjamin Harrison selected the leading figure in his party, James G. Blaine, to be his main adviser and the secretary of state. Harrison knew he had no choice but to name Blaine to the State Department, but he took enough time with the appointment to make Blaine uneasy. The two men drifted apart later in the administration, but at the outset they worked together productively. Harrison made sure that the other seven cabinet members were the kind of men he wanted—all were Presbyterians, five had studied law, and several had been officers during the Civil War.

Putting the cabinet together, however, revealed the patronage problems that plagued Harrison. His selection of William Windom of Minnesota for secretary of the treasury left Republicans in New York and Pennsylvania unhappy. His choices of Benjamin Franklin Tracy (Navy), Redfield Proctor (War), and William Henry Harrison Miller (Justice) were made from a desire for competent officials, but the selections generated hard feelings among organization Republicans around the country who believed the new president had slighted their claims.

Since Congress did not hold its regular session until December 1889, more than a year after the election, President Harrison's first task was dealing with his fellow Republicans' hunger for government positions. He rejected Blaine's suggestion of a special session during 1889 and thus ensured that the political burden of what Congress did would fall on the 1890 elections. The first months of the new administration saw the president grapple with an endless array of office seekers, many of whom came away angry at Harrison's icy demeanor. As Senator Shelby Cullom of Illinois put it, Harrison "treated me about as well in the way of patronage as he did any other senator, but whenever he did anything for me it was done so ungraciously that the concession tended to anger rather than please." The remarks of other GOP stalwarts were unprintable.

Two appointments came to symbolize the difficulties of Harrison's patronage policy. First, he named Corporal James R. Tanner, a member of the Grand Army of the Republic from Illinois, as commissioner of pensions. The large number of Civil War veterans within the GOP expected a liberal policy toward their claims, and Tanner obliged them in a very public way. His free-spending tactics, loose tongue, and careless administrative style produced a popular uproar that led to his resignation within six months. Unhappy veterans voted Democratic in the 1889 off-year elections.

The other controversial patronage choice was James S. Clarkson of Iowa, who served as first assistant postmaster general. The allocation of fourth-class postmasters represented the most important government jobs that a president could dispense during the late nineteenth century. Clarkson, a dedicated Republican partisan who had performed important organizational work with the Republican National Committee, set to work to replace Democratic postmasters with Republican successors. He did so with great relish amid extensive publicity that embarrassed the administration.

Apart from the postal service, Harrison's record on the issue of civil service reform was good. He named Theodore Roosevelt to the Civil Service Commission, and he resisted efforts of disgruntled Republicans to rein in the reform-minded commissioner, who repeatedly showed his capacity to draw attention to himself in public controversies. In the Indian service, Harrison extended civil service protection to those who taught and worked in Native American schools. His selection of Thomas J. Morgan as commissioner of Indian affairs drew criticism because Morgan disliked the contract schools that Roman Catholics operated on the reservations. In many respects, the Harrison presidency became bogged down in patronage battles during its important initial phase.

## ORGANIZING THE
## NEW CONGRESS

At the end of 1889, senators and representatives assembled for the first session of the Fifty-first Congress. The Republicans hoped to use their majorities in both houses to enact a program of legislation that would solidify their status as the nation's majority party. In his inaugural address President Harrison had spoken of the need to revise the tariff, the obligations of large corporations to obey the law, and the issue of election frauds in the South against African American citizens. These issues, along with the question of the currency, claimed the attention of the victorious GOP as the lawmakers opened their deliberations.

With a narrow Republican majority (168 to 161) in the House of Representatives, the GOP's first task was establishing that it could carry its program through the lower house. For years the Democrats had practiced "the disappearing quorum" and other tactics that limited the number of members on the floor and thereby prevented the House from conducting business. When the Republicans elected Thomas B. Reed of Maine as Speaker of the House in December 1889, observers wondered what the stocky, sarcastic Reed would do to push legislation through over Democrats' objections. Late in January, Reed stunned the House when he announced that members refusing to vote were present for the purposes of making up a quorum. The Democrats protested loudly, but within a few weeks the Republicans had made their point. They now had the parliamentary muscle to put through their program.

## TARIFFS AND RECIPROCITY

The protective tariff represented the first priority for the GOP lawmakers. Faced with a federal surplus of more than $100 million, the Republicans proposed using it to stimulate the economy, but they disagreed about whether tariff rates should move upward and how far. Some in the party, most notably Secretary of State Blaine, envisioned using the tariff as a bargaining chip in trade negotiations with other countries through reciprocal tariff treaties. Writing the new legislation became the task of William McKinley of Ohio, the chairman of the House Ways and Means Committee, and he included increased duties on wool, tin plate, and some industrial products. As a benefit to consumers, the tariff on sugar would be removed and payments would be made to domestic sugar producers.

Secretary of State Blaine sought to persuade Congress to give the president the power to negotiate trade treaties; he also urged retaining duties on sugar to induce Latin American countries to make concessions for U.S. products they imported. During the maneuvering that ensued during the summer of 1890, Harrison worked behind the scenes to rally Congress behind reciprocity. His techniques included private meetings and dinners at the White House where he underlined his support for a more liberal trade policy. Harrison proved quite adept at this kind of presidential persuasion, and in his own presidency William McKinley later applied some of the tactics he had learned while watching Harrison.

The president's backstage lobbying brought McKinley around to an endorsement of Blaine's idea, and the reciprocity provisions became part of the McKinley tariff bill, which cleared Congress just before the start of the congressional election campaign. It raised tariff rates, split the Republicans, and gave the Democrats a campaign issue that they exploited to the fullest.

## SHERMAN ANTITRUST LAW

The issue of trust regulation proved less controversial in 1890. All parties agreed that some form of antitrust legislation should be passed. In that climate, a bill written by Senator George F. Edmunds of Vermont and introduced by John Sherman of Ohio moved rapidly through the Congress. Harrison signed what became known as the Sherman Antitrust Law on 2 July 1890. Once passed, the law did not receive vigorous enforcement from the Justice Department. Congress had not provided money for the department to pursue monopolies, and the government filed only seven cases during the last two years of the Harrison presidency. Despite this lackluster record, the Sherman Antitrust Law remained one of the enduring legacies of the Harrison years.

## THE CURRENCY ISSUE

More controversial was the issue of the currency. A growing movement in the South and West advocated the free and unlimited coinage of silver into money at a fixed ratio with gold. Harrison did not believe in a rigid adherence to the gold standard, but neither did he want to endanger the soundness of the nation's currency. The president found himself with few attractive options. In the end he accepted a compromise worked out by John Sherman, providing for the purchase of 4.5 million ounces of silver each month. The bill satisfied neither the adherents of the gold standard nor the passionate advocates of free silver. To Harrison it represented the best middle ground on the issue, and he signed the Sherman Silver Purchase Act on 14 July 1890. The outcome postponed the showdown over monetary policy until after Harrison left office in March 1893.

## THE "FORCE" BILL

Benjamin Harrison made his strongest moral commitment as president to the future of African Americans and their right to take part in politics at the ballot box. His service in the Civil War and his own experience in Congress convinced him that the Fifteenth Amendment, giving former slaves the right to vote, was correct and should be enforced. He mentioned the issue during the campaign of 1888, and he returned to it in his inaugural address, posing the issue this way: "Shall the prejudices and paralysis of slavery continue to hang upon the skirts of progress?"

Many northern Republicans agreed with Harrison that election frauds in the South blocked the progress of their party in Dixie. They also thought that Republicans had a moral duty to preserve the voting rights of all citizens. During 1889 GOP lawmakers worked to devise legislation that would safeguard the free ballot. A leader of this effort was Congressman Henry Cabot Lodge of Massachusetts, and he drafted a measure that would have provided for the federal government to supervise congressional elections throughout the country. Harrison gave the campaign his endorsement in his annual message of December 1889. He wanted to know when "the black man" would "have those full civil rights which have so long been his in law?"

The introduction of the federal elections bill set off the most bitter legislative battle of Harrison's administration. Southerners in Congress called it the Force Bill and said that it would bring back the evils they associated with the Reconstruction era. Republicans countered that the measure would simply ensure a fair opportunity for African Americans in the South to have their ballots counted. The Republican leadership in the House pushed the bill through to a narrow victory in early July. When it got to the Senate, however, it ran up against the opposition of southern Democrats, the pressure to enact other legislation before the election, and the desire of western Republicans to make deals in exchange for free silver. In September the Republican Senate decided to put off action on the elections bill until after the voters had made their choices in 1890.

## MIDTERM DEBACLE

The Harrison administration and the Republicans believed that the GOP majorities had shown their ability to govern in a constructive manner and that their record in the Fifty-first Congress deserved the approval of the electorate. To their disappointment, the 1890 elections produced a Democratic landslide as the voters registered an emphatic disapproval of the recent congressional record. The Democrats won 235 seats to the Republicans' 88. Another 10 seats went to members associated with the Farmers' Alliance, an agrarian protest group in the South and West.

A number of causes contributed to the Republican debacle. In several key midwestern states, party members had irritated Irish, German, Catholic, and Lutheran voters by pushing an array of religious and ethnocultural issues, such as prohibition, Sunday-closing laws, and measures requiring state-supported schools to teach in English. The Democrats also charged that the McKinley Tariff would raise prices, and they sent out campaign workers to pose as salesmen with high-priced goods. Many Americans simply believed Congress had gone too far in the direction of governmental activism and intrusion in private affairs. It was the first Congress to appropriate more than $1 billion—the resulting term, "Billion Dollar Congress," was not a compliment in 1890.

In the wake of the election defeat, the federal elections bill became a political casualty. Early in 1891, under pressure from western free-silver Republicans, the lame-duck Republican Senate decided to defer further consideration of the measure. With a Democratic Congress taking over, the proposed law was dead. It represented the last chance to preserve some of the political gains of Reconstruction for black Americans. With its demise Congress abandoned efforts to help mitigate even some of the effects of racism for African Americans. President Harrison made the case for further action throughout the remainder of his presidency, but to no avail.

## PROSPECTS FOR REELECTION

The political repudiation of the 1890 elections did not ensure that Harrison would be a one-term president, but it did indicate that his prospects for reelection were limited. Within the Republican party, the president's relations with leading figures were strained. He and House Speaker Thomas B. Reed had quarreled over patronage. In New York State, the party leadership was restive. Throughout the nation, Republican stalwarts questioned whether Harrison could or should be renominated in 1892. As one of them put it, running Harrison again would mean spending four more years "in a dripping cave."

As he contemplated his reelection prospects, Harrison hoped that his creditable record in foreign policy and military affairs might win him another term in the White House. Harrison and Secretary of the Navy Benjamin F. Tracy had revived the U.S. Navy from its post-Civil War doldrums and begun the process of creating a modern fleet. The administration started the construction of seven modern warships—three cruisers and four battleships. Tracy also improved the organizational structure of the navy and the overall quality of the service. The secretaries of war, first Redfield Proctor and then Stephen B. Elkins, sought to make similar improvements in the army. They achieved some reforms in the status of the ordinary soldier, but the real changes toward a modern army would occur in the aftermath of the war with Spain, eight years after the Harrison administration had left office.

## FOREIGN POLICY

Under Harrison, the nation followed a more assertive foreign policy that anticipated the imperialism at the end of the 1890s. Modern scholarship assigns the president, rather than Secretary of State Blaine, most of the credit for the new energy in diplomacy. Blaine sponsored the Pan-American Conference in

1889 and fought hard for trade reciprocity in the McKinley Tariff in 1890. In other respects, Blaine's frequent illnesses and erratic mental state meant that Harrison had to oversee foreign affairs by himself, especially during the later years of his presidency.

In the field of foreign trade, the administration pursued with energy the reciprocity policy of the McKinley Tariff. They negotiated eight treaties, the most notable of which was with Brazil in 1891. Despite the hard work that Harrison put into this endeavor, the treaties did not have much time to prove their effectiveness before the Democratic Congress of 1893–1894 rendered them moot.

On another exports issue, Harrison sought to end longstanding bans on the admission of U.S. pork products to Europe. The rationale for the European action was that the pork produced medical problems, but critics charged that protection for domestic pork producers in Germany and France was the real motive for the ban. Lengthy negotiations that Harrison oversaw led to removal of pork restrictions before the president left office.

Other diplomatic problems also claimed Harrison's attention. He negotiated with Great Britain about the fate of fur seals in the Bering Sea off Alaska. In 1891 he helped resolve a dispute about the conduct of American sailors that precipitated a foreign policy crisis with Chile and seemed for a time to threaten war between the two countries. His attentions were also required that same year over a crisis that was triggered when several Italian immigrants in New Orleans were lynched. Relations between Italy and the United States broke down until cooler thoughts brought about an acceptable resolution.

During his presidency, Harrison traveled extensively in a manner that would become familiar for his twentieth-century successors. He was at his best in the brief, effective speeches he delivered to generally enthusiastic audiences. In 1890, he traveled during the weeks preceding the election campaign but did not make an explicit appeal for Republican votes. Harrison sometimes used his appearances to build support for his policies, but he did not do that in a systematic fashion. In that sense, Harrison's frequent travels represented both a precedent for future executives such as William McKinley and Theodore Roosevelt as well as a missed opportunity for Harrison himself.

## ELECTION OF 1892

The 1890 congressional election results convinced the Democrats that they could regain the White House in 1892. The presidential election also promised to have a third political party in the race. Angry farmers in the South and West, upset about falling prices for wheat and cotton as well as their burden of debt, formed the People's party in 1892, an outgrowth of the Farmers' Alliances that had appeared during the late 1880s. Members of the People's party—the Populists—capitalized on the growing sentiment for the free coinage of silver as a means of addressing the nation's agrarian problems. The Republicans would face a stiff challenge to reelect Harrison.

Many in the GOP did not wish to support the president, and they looked instead to the perennial Republican frontrunner, Secretary of State Blaine. It was an improbable scenario. Although Blaine retained great popularity within the party, he was a very sick man who had been unable to discharge the duties of his office for several years. Any good feelings that had existed between Harrison and Blaine had long since disappeared by the early days of 1892. The president believed Blaine was incapable of carrying out the work of the State Department, and their correspondence became increasingly formal and distant as the months passed.

Outside the White House, sentiment for Blaine as the best alternative to Harrison increased as the Republican national convention drew nearer. Blaine seemed to take himself out of the race in February 1892 but, under pressure from his wife and family, he flirted with the nomination once again. Early in June, just days before the Republicans gathered in Minneapolis, Blaine resigned as secretary of state and his friends pushed his candidacy at the convention.

Harrison and his allies had no real difficulty in turning back a challenge from the Blaine forces. An incumbent president enjoyed decisive advantages over a challenger within his own party by this time. Nonetheless, the large vote for Blaine in the convention and the substantial support given to Governor William McKinley of Ohio attested to the lingering discontent with Harrison inside his own party. To run with the president, the delegates chose Whitelaw Reid, a New York newspaper publisher. Most of the Republican leaders expected to lose the presidential contest.

The Democrats chose Grover Cleveland to run again. He ran an effective, well-financed campaign that exploited public discontent with Republican spending and governmental activism. Harrison also faced the challenge of James B. Weaver, the People's party's presidential candidate. Although the campaign season was relatively quiet, with few of the rallies and parades that marked elections in that era, the events of 1892 indicated the volatility of popular attitudes. In July, labor violence broke out in Idaho at the Coeur d'Alene silver mines. In Pennsylvania, there was a bloody confrontation between strikers and Pinkerton detectives at the Homestead steel mills of Andrew Carnegie. Since Carnegie was a well-known Republican, Harrison's campaign suffered from the incident.

Tradition held that an incumbent president should not campaign for reelection, and Harrison observed the unwritten custom. He issued a letter of acceptance that served as the main Republican document for the election. Mrs. Harrison's lingering illness, which culminated in her death on 25 October, made it impossible for the president to campaign, even had he wanted to do so. The election of 1892 wound its way to November and was remembered as one of the dullest and least inspiring of the Gilded Age.

Cleveland won a decisive victory. He ran almost 400,000 votes ahead of Harrison and won by a large margin—277 to 145—in the electoral college. The Democrats gained control of both houses of Congress, although they had lost some seats in the House after their landslide victory in 1890. Meanwhile, the Populists gathered 1 million popular votes and 22 electoral votes in the West. Commentators wondered whether the Democrats might now be in power for a generation and the Republicans in danger of disappearing.

## HAWAII

Although Harrison's presidency had only a few months to run, his foreign policy initiatives had not ended. The issue of Hawaii arose in the final days of the administration when the president endeavored to secure the annexation of the Pacific islands. By the end of the 1880s, Hawaii had become a virtual American protectorate. A reciprocity treaty linked the two countries economically, and the United States had received the right to use exclusively the superb strategic asset of Pearl Harbor.

Within Hawaii, the white settlers and the native rulers clashed over the islands' future. When King Kaluka died in 1891, his sister, Queen Liliuokalani, came to power. Her dislike of Americans and the worsening trade relations produced by the McKinley Tariff's removal of duty-free status on Hawaiian sugar spurred sentiment for annexation among the white settlers. James G. Blaine told Harrison in 1891 that "Hawaii may come up for decision at any unexpected hour, and I hope we shall be prepared to decide it in the affirmative."

The hour came early in 1893. At the end of 1892, Queen Liliuokalani dismissed the Hawaiian legislature and took away many of the powers the white settlers had exercised under the existing constitution. Those favoring annexation began a revolt and called on the U.S. minister and the U.S. Navy for assistance. The coup was successful, largely because of the presence of 150 U.S. Marines, and a provisional government was set up. "The Hawaiian pear is now fully ripe," said the American minister, "and this is the golden hour for the United States to pluck it." The Harrison administration agreed to a treaty of annexation with the rebels on 14 February 1893. Harrison immediately sent the treaty to the Senate with a message announcing his full support. With the Democrats in control of the Senate, there was no chance of getting the two-thirds vote needed for approval. The incoming Cleveland administration indicated that it did not want the treaty decided until it took office. Once in power, President Cleveland withdrew the treaty and annexation did not occur until 1898 under William McKinley.

## POSTPRESIDENTIAL YEARS

After leaving office, Harrison also left active Republican politics. There was some talk that he might run for president again in 1896, but he never seriously threatened William McKinley's grip on the Republican nomination. In 1896, he married his first wife's niece, Mary Lord Dimmick. The move split the Harrison family since Caroline Scott Harrison had told relatives before her death that her husband had been too fond of Mrs. Dimmick. The First Lady had even threatened to move out of the White House before the 1892 election in protest against her husband's philandering. The second Mrs. Harrison gave birth to a daughter in 1897.

## EVALUATION OF BENJAMIN HARRISON'S PRESIDENCY

Although the Fifty-first Congress was very constructive and important, the Republicans' political repudiation in 1890 and 1892 doomed any chance for Harrison's reelection. Sandwiched between the two terms of Grover Cleveland, Harrison's presidency has faded into historical obscurity, leaving little to attract historians' attention. His administration lacked the controversy that accompanied the presidency of Rutherford B. Hayes in the disputed election of 1876 or the excitement of the war with Spain that gave McKinley's terms historical importance at the end of the 1890s.

In many respects, Harrison's administration is a record of false starts and incomplete initiatives. His work with Congress behind the scenes taught much to his successor William McKinley about the management of Capitol Hill. Harrison's travels were a model for McKinley, Roosevelt, and subsequent presidents. Harrison deserves credit for organizational work within the White House on which others built in managing the day-to-day operation of the presidency. His initiatives in foreign affairs kept in motion currents of expansionism that would crest ten years later. Harrison will never be seen as more than an average president during the era of change from an agrarian to an industrial nation. He did not grow in office, nor did he overcome great challenges. Yet in their shortcomings and missed opportunities, his years in the White House offer a manageable case study of how the presidency operated in a time and place far removed from the imperial chief executives and expanded federal government that Americans know as the twenty-first century begins.

## BIBLIOGRAPHY

Calhoun, Charles W. "Caroline Scott Harrison." In *American First Ladies: Their Lives and Their Legacy*, edited by Lewis L. Gould (Garland Publishing, 1996), pp. 260–276.

Harrison, Benjamin. *Public Papers and Addresses of Benjamin Harrison, Twenty-Third President of the United States, March 4, 1889, to March 4, 1893* (Government Printing Office, 1893; Kraus Reprint, 1969).

Morgan, H. Wayne. *From Hayes to McKinley: National Party Politics, 1877–1896* (Syracuse University Press, 1969).

Sievers, Harry J. *Benjamin Harrison, Hoosier President: The White House and After* (Bobbs-Merrill, 1969).

Socolofsky, Homer E., and Allan B. Spetter. *The Presidency of Benjamin Harrison* (University Press of Kansas, 1987).

Volwiler, Albert T., ed. *The Correspondence Between Benjamin Harrison and James G. Blaine, 1882–1893* (American Philosophical Society, 1940).

Williams, R. Hal. *Years of Decision: American Politics in the 1890s* (Waveland Press, 1993).

★★★ 25 ★★★

# WILLIAM McKINLEY
## 1897–1901

*Lewis L. Gould*

*Born 29 January 1843 in Niles, Ohio, to William McKinley and Nancy Campbell Allison McKinley; attended Allegheny College, Meadville, Pennsylvania, but left before graduation; married Ida Saxton, 25 January 1871, Canton, Ohio; two children; elected president in 1896 on Republican ticket with Garret Augustus Hobart of New Jersey, with 7,104,779 popular votes and 271 electoral college ballots, over Democratic/Populist slate of William Jennings Bryan of Nebraska and Arthur Sewall of Maine, with 6,502,925 popular votes and 176 electoral ballots; reelected in 1900 with Theodore Roosevelt of New York, garnering 7,207,923 popular votes and 292 electoral ballots, over Democratic ticket of William Jennings Bryan of Nebraska and Adlai Ewing Stevenson of Illinois, with 6,358,138 popular votes and 155 electoral ballots; shot by an assassin on 6 September 1901; died 14 September, Buffalo, New York; buried adjacent to Westlawn Cemetery in Canton, Ohio.*

The administration of William McKinley has usually been interpreted as either a mere forerunner to the more important presidency of Theodore Roosevelt or as a foreign policy embarrassment because of the involvement of the United States in the Spanish-American War and its imperial aftermath. In fact, McKinley is one of the most underrated presidents in the nation's history. He set the pattern for the modern evolution of the office, and he was a forceful chief executive in domestic and foreign affairs. A century after his service in the White House, McKinley is coming into clearer focus as one of the presidents whose impact on the nation's highest office was permanent and decisive. Even though a generation of historians have done much to rehabilitate McKinley's reputation, he remains an overshadowed figure who deserves more attention for his notable accomplishments.

## POLITICAL CAREER

A native of Niles, Ohio, William McKinley spent a brief time at Allegheny College before the Civil War erupted. He rose to the rank of major, and he became known by that title throughout his years in public life. He practiced law in Canton, Ohio, after the war was over, and married Ida Saxton in 1871. Both of their daughters died in infancy, and Mrs. McKinley's resulting poor health required that her husband serve as a kind of psychiatric nurse to his ailing spouse throughout their life together.

McKinley ran for Congress in 1876 as a Republican. He spent fourteen years in Washington, where he became an expert on the protective tariff, a policy that separated the Republicans from their Democratic rivals in the Gilded Age. As chairman of the House Ways and Means Committee, he crafted the McKinley Tariff of 1890. He lost his congressional seat in the Democratic landslide of 1890.

In 1891 McKinley won the governorship of Ohio and was reelected in 1893. As the 1896 election approached, his popularity with the Republican voters and his strength as a candidate in the Middle West made him a frontrunner for the presidential nomination. The friendship and financial support of Cleveland industrialist Marcus A. Hanna helped McKinley win a first ballot victory at the Republican National Convention. Although historians still write as though Hanna was the driving force behind McKinley's selection, it was McKinley's own standing within his party that produced his nomination. The party chose Garret A. Hobart of New Jersey as his running mate.

In the 1896 campaign, McKinley faced the youthful standard bearer of the Democrats, William Jennings Bryan, who ran as the champion of free silver. Rather than emulate Bryan's whistlestop style of campaigning, McKinley adopted a "front-porch strategy" that kept him at home in Canton where he addressed some three-quarters of a million people in a series of speeches that emphasized the tariff and the dangers of inflation. Meanwhile, the Republicans launched what Hanna called a "campaign of education," sending voters more than 250 million pamphlets. The result was a decisive success for the Republican candidate, who gathered 271 electoral votes against Bryan's 176. McKinley had demonstrated impressive vote-getting ability as the architect of his party's return to national power.

## REVIVING THE PRESIDENCY

McKinley came to the presidency in March 1897 after a difficult second term for President Grover Cleveland. The Panic of 1893 and the resulting depression had discredited the Democratic party, and Cleveland's inept leadership had wounded the office of the presidency. McKinley promptly took a number of steps to revive the authority and influence of his position. He made the White House more accessible to the public through a series of official receptions. He became a frequent traveler, using his junkets to shape popular attitudes. Most important, he reestablished good relations with the press after the tensions of the Cleveland years. His press secretary arranged for journalists to use a table on the second floor of the White House, with seats for reporters who covered the president.

This innovation, often credited to Theodore Roosevelt, actually began with McKinley. In his personal dealings with reporters, McKinley proved a master of the timely leak, and journalists found him an excellent source.

The increasingly efficient workings of the White House can be attributed in part to George B. Cortelyou. Originally an assistant secretary, Cortelyou took over many of the duties of the president's secretary, John Addison Porter, and evolved into a forerunner of the modern White House Chief of Staff. He conducted the frequent tours and developed a system of news releases and official texts of speeches that facilitated coverage of the president's administration. By 1901, Cortelyou and McKinley had laid the foundation for many of the now-routine processes for handling press inquiries and supplying the public with information.

### CHOOSING A CABINET

The shaping of McKinley's cabinet was done in more traditional fashion, with the usual attention given to politics and geography. McKinley chose Senator John Sherman of Ohio as his secretary of state. Unfortunately for the president, the aged and ailing Sherman could not perform the duties of his office competently, and McKinley had to name an old friend, William R. Day of Canton, as assistant secretary of state to handle the duties of the post. The senator's selection became an embarrassment to the administration, and Sherman was replaced when the war with Spain occurred.

Another difficult selection was Russell A. Alger as secretary of war. A longtime Republican stalwart, Alger was popular with veterans, but his failing as an administrator and leader became evident once war began. The other choices for the cabinet included John D. Long as secretary of the navy, Joseph McKenna as attorney general, Joseph Gary as postmaster general, Lyman Gage as secretary of the treasury, and Cornelius N. Bliss as secretary of the interior. Over the course of his presidency, McKinley strengthened the Cabinet with appointments that improved the quality of his official family.

### TARIFF REVISION

During his first year in office, McKinley moved forward with the Republican agenda. A special session of Congress considered the tariff, and after several months of parliamentary maneuvering, the Dingley Act—raising tariff rates and expanding reciprocity provisions—was adopted in late July. Protectionist in character, the measure did allow the president to negotiate reciprocal trade treaties with other nations, a strategy McKinley pursued vigorously during the ensuing four years. After an initial and unsuccessful endeavor to broaden the use of silver through an international bimetallic agreement, the administration committed itself to monetary orthodoxy and supported the Gold Standard Act of 1900.

### FOREIGN POLICY PROBLEMS: HAWAII AND CUBA

A major foreign policy problem of the first year of McKinley's presidency was Hawaii. A treaty of annexation was drafted during 1897 in response to, among other things, growing Japanese immigration into the islands, and McKinley sent the pact to the Senate in July. When the regular session of Congress met in December, the White House could not muster the two-thirds vote needed for approval of the treaty. Sugar-producing states led the opposition. McKinley and his advisers looked to the idea of a joint resolution of annexation during the early months of 1898.

McKinley's most worrying diplomatic problem after he took office was the war in Cuba between the Spanish and the rebellious inhabitants of what Madrid regarded as the "Ever Faithful Isle." The rebellion had begun in 1895, and a bitter struggle had ensued since that time between the two sides, whose war aims were irreconcilable. The Cubans wanted nothing less than a complete break from Spain and would not accept a negotiated settlement that fell short of that goal. Spain believed Cuba was part of its sovereign nation and found Cuban independence intolerable. Madrid sent the flower of its armed power to Cuba in an effort to suppress the rebellion. No government that agreed to relinquish Cuba without a fight could retain power in Spain.

McKinley's predecessor, Grover Cleveland, believed that Spain deserved the opportunity to conquer the rebels and remain in control of Cuba. As a result, the Spanish concluded that the United States would not insist on withdrawal from Cuba and that a policy of delay could work in Madrid's interest. This judgment proved to be a basic miscalculation when McKinley took over the presidency.

McKinley, like Cleveland, believed that Spain deserved the opportunity to put down the rebellion, but he did not think Spain should have an open-ended period to accomplish that goal. In addition, he firmly believed that the Spanish must pursue humane policies in dealing with the rebels, and, most important, that the rebels themselves must agree to any negotiated settlement. The difficulty was that Spain would never accept Cuban independence; the rebels would not settle for less. No peaceful solution seemed likely unless one of the parties altered its position This point is often overlooked when McKinley's diplomacy is assessed.

The United States sought to change Spanish behavior through a gradual intensifying of diplomatic pressure on Madrid, and the policy seemed to be working during the second half of 1897. Spain ceased the practice of housing Cubans in "reconcentration camps" and proclaimed that Cuba would receive autonomy. While this meant more home rule for the Cubans, the Spanish retained their sovereignty. Nonetheless, the White House was reasonably optimistic as 1898 opened.

## THE U.S.S. *MAINE* AND IMPENDING WAR OVER CUBA

Matters worsened dramatically during the first three months of 1898. Pro-Spanish Cubans rioted in early January in opposition to Madrid's autonomy proclamation, an event the McKinley administration viewed as a bad omen for Spain's ability to keep its word. The uproar led the White House to dispatch the battleship U.S.S *Maine* to Havana in late January. A week later, Spain responded in a diplomatic note and stated it intended to preserve its sovereignty over Cuba and would not tolerate foreign intervention. During February 1898, a series of events plunged McKinley's presidency into prolonged crisis. On 9 February newspapers published a private letter written by the Spanish minister in Washington, Enrique Dupuy de Lôme, and intercepted by the Cubans; in it, the minister had criticized McKinley, calling him "weak and a bidder for the admiration of the crowd." More important, statements in the letter revealed that Spain was pursuing delay in its talks with the State Department. The minister was recalled, but the damage had been done.

The most devastating event on the road to war came on 15 February 1898, when the *Maine* exploded in Havana harbor and took the lives of 260 officers and crew. At the time, the public believed that the explosion was caused by a mine, and that Spain had either directly caused the disaster or had allowed it to take place. (Modern historians now believe that a coal bunker exploded.) President McKinley had to exercise leadership while a naval court of inquiry pursued its investigation into the cause of what had happened. The court was scheduled to make its report during the middle of March.

Tensions escalated further. A speech by Senator Redfield Proctor of Vermont on 17 March graphically described horrible conditions in Cuba. Forty-eight hours later, McKinley received the conclusions of the naval board, which had decided that an external explosion brought about the destruction of the *Maine*. As soon as Congress received the report, pressure for a declaration of war would intensify.

To forestall the expected crisis in Congress, McKinley urged Madrid either to agree to an armistice with the rebels or to look toward U.S. mediation of the conflict, which would mean Cuban independence. To all these initiatives from Washington, the Spanish replied in March 1898 with firm refusals. McKinley began to prepare a message to Congress in which the lawmakers would be asked to deal with the Cuban issue.

The president sent his message in on 11 April. Some historians believe that by the time Congress got the message the Spanish had accepted U.S. demands, which would have made war unnecessary. In fact, what Spain agreed to on 9 April was a suspension of hostilities in Cuba. For Madrid, the key point was that such a break in the fighting would not carry with it a political recognition of their enemies. Once again, the Spanish were playing for time. As for the central issue of Cuban independence, to that the Spanish would not agree. So no Spanish capitulation ever occurred. The main elements of the friction between Madrid and Washington remained as unresolved as they had been in 1897 and early 1898.

The message that McKinley sent to Congress sought legislative authority not to commence hostilities with Spain, but to end the fighting in Cuba through the use of armed force if required. As McKinley put it, "The war in Cuba must stop." For that reason, he did no more than mention the suspension of hostilities that Spain had offered at the last minute.

During the week that followed, Congress passed the Teller Amendment disavowing any U.S. intention to control the island of Cuba and authorizing McKinley to intervene on 19 April. Within days the Spanish broke off diplomatic relations and declared war. The United States responded with its own declaration of war on 25 April. As president, McKinley had tenaciously pursued a diplomatic solution throughout the early months of 1898. Ultimately, the crisis became a war because of the belief on the part of both Spain and the United States that they were fighting for a just cause and to protect their national honor and self-interest.

## WAR AND THE SHAPING
## OF THE PRESIDENCY
Although the war with Spain that followed was over in a little more than three months,

it represented a crucial episode in McKinley's emergence as a strong and effective president. He used the war power to shape strategy and to manage the way in which the United States acquired a colonial empire. In pursuing ratification of the peace treaty, he also wielded the weapons of presidential influence with great skill.

From the outset, the fortunes of war favored the United States. On 1 May 1898 Commodore George Dewey and a naval squadron won a decisive victory over Spain at the Battle of Manila Bay. That triumph posed the issue of what role the United States should play in the Philippines if Spain relinquished the islands. Although the president believed that a port in the islands might be all that the United States would need, he acted in a way to preserve his options as the fighting continued. This approach conflicted with the aspirations of the Filipinos and their leader Emilio Aguinaldo, who wanted to see their country become independent of Spain. The administration ordered that the U.S. military avoid contacts of an official character with the Filipinos. The president also pressed ahead with the annexation of Hawaii to ensure that the United States had a secure supply route to a possible Philippine installation.

The war in Cuba occupied most of the nation's attention during the spring and summer of 1898. McKinley played a very active role as a war leader. His staff set up a War Room in the White House that contained a telegraph switchboard with twenty lines, war maps, and continuous monitoring of the situation that enabled the president to contact his commander in Cuba within twenty minutes and to function as a strong president in managing the war. Newspaper reporters called him "the Man at the Helm" in 1898.

## CONDITIONS OF WAR,
## TERMS OF PEACE
The prosecution of the war presented the administration with political problems that plagued it during the year that followed. Mobilization of the massive volunteer force did not go smoothly, and the record of

Secretary of War Russell A. Alger came under intense criticism for the slowdowns and mixups that ensued. These problems eased as the war proceeded, but the issue lingered on into the fall of 1898.

After the invasion of Cuba in late June 1898, the fortunes of the U.S. war effort improved. By the first week of July, the U.S. Navy had won a decisive battle off the coast of Cuba, and the U.S. Army had beaten the Spanish defenders of Santiago de Cuba in a fight that made Theodore Roosevelt a national hero. During the two weeks that followed, the administration pressed for the capitulation of the Spanish garrison, which took place on 17 July. The fall of Puerto Rico also came as the fighting wound down. By this time the White House was realizing that the greatest enemy confronting the American military might be the threat of disease and yellow fever.

By the middle of July, the Spanish had decided that negotiations must begin. Through the French ambassador in Washington, talks commenced on 26 July, and it soon became clear that President McKinley expected major concessions to the victors. He demanded that Spain relinquish possession of Puerto Rico and Cuba and delegate the fate of the Philippines to the peace conference. Spain had no alternative but to agree to an armistice in mid-August.

The major issue that faced the president at this time was the fate of the Philippines in the peace talks. Secretary of State Sherman had by this time been replaced by McKinley's close friend William R. Day, who in turn was succeeded by John Hay. To conduct the negotiations in Paris, McKinley placed three senators on the peace commission. In that innovative use of presidential influence, he ensured that the resulting treaty would have support from those who had to vote on the pact. McKinley also expanded the prerogatives of his office when he made a series of speeches across the Midwest during October in which he prepared the nation for the ultimate acquisition of the Philippines. In the process he aided Republican candidates for the fall congressional elections.

McKinley was now convinced that the United States would have to acquire the Philippines. The victors could not sail away and leave the archipelago to the Filipinos who would then fall prey to either Japanese or German intervention. A protectorate would not safeguard U.S. interests as would outright acquisition. In instructions to the peace commissioners on 28 October 1898, McKinley insisted that the Philippines had to be ceded to the United States. The peace treaty signed on 10 December 1898 in Paris accorded the Philippines, Guam, and Puerto Rico to the United States. Spain received $20 million and gave up Cuba.

The president's next political goal was Senate ratification of the treaty. Once again, he behaved in the manner of a strong chief executive. He made speeches in the South to attract Democratic senators. He used patronage and favors to gather more votes. The willingness of William Jennings Bryan to back the treaty and the splits within the anti-imperialist opposition led to a favorable vote on 6 February 1899. The margin was close, 57 to 27, just one vote more than the necessary two-thirds.

## LINGERING CONCERNS: THE PHILIPPINES, CUBA, CHINA

Even as the vote was taking place, Americans learned that hostilities had begun between the Filipinos and the U.S. soldiers in the islands. Although McKinley insisted that his country had no imperialistic goals for the Philippines, the rebels began a protracted war that aroused political opposition for McKinley at home and military problems on the ground.

To deal with the insurrection, the United States deployed troops who established military command over the islands by the spring of 1899. The president then endeavored to get a civil government in place through the Philippine Commission. This use of expert private citizens as an advisory commission would be one of McKinley's favorite presidential devices. Despite protests from the anti-imperialists about news censorship from the Philippines, the president's policy worked well enough that he sent a second commission to the archipelago in early 1900, led by William Howard Taft, to install a more permanent civilian government.

Another legacy of the war with Spain was the unsettled situation in Cuba. The Teller Amendment prevented the United States from annexing Cuba, but the president also sought to ensure that the island remained free from the influence of European nations such as Germany. McKinley used the war powers of his office to establish a military government, restore the country's economy, and disband the rebel forces. The mechanism for tying the political destiny of Cuba to that of the United States was written into the Platt Amendment of 1901. McKinley played a large role in devising the language that Congress adopted, which gave the United States the authority to intervene in Cuba to maintain a stable government there. U.S. bases in Cuba served as a guarantee of this relationship.

Other foreign policy issues also lingered from the conflict with Spain. The difficulty of moving ships from the Atlantic to the Pacific in wartime increased the nation's interest in a canal across Central America. Obtaining such a route meant negotiations with Great Britain to change the Clayton-Bulwer Treaty of 1850. Smooth relations with London were impossible, however, without easing the tensions over the boundary between Canada and Alaska. A joint commission failed to resolve the boundary problem, but the commission did work out a treaty with Britain giving the United States the right to build an undefended canal that would be open to all nations during a war. When the Senate resisted those terms, the pact had to be renegotiated.

The acquisition of the Philippines heightened U.S. interest in China and its potential markets. As European nations vied for influence there, the administration worried about the maintenance of China's territorial integrity. Those concerns led the president and Secretary Hay to propose what became known as the Open Door Notes, sent out in September 1899. In these diplomatic statements, the United States urged nations involved with China to protect trading rights and other concessions that allowed the United States to compete economically. Although they had relatively little effect at the time, the Open Door Notes became an important statement of U.S. policy toward China.

## DOMESTIC CAUTIONS

While he was an activist and a strong president in the foreign policy sphere, McKinley was more cautious on domestic issues. At a time of racial tension in the nation, he emphasized sectional reconciliation between northern and southern whites, often at the expense of black Americans. McKinley also failed to take the lead in the area of civil service reform. In 1899, he broadened the number of government positions for which competitive examinations were not required. He moved slowly on the issue of the trusts, which were becoming a source of greater controversy at the end of the 1890s, and did not expand the government's role in regulating corporations. By 1900, McKinley was giving signs that he intended to be more forceful in dealing with the trusts, but they were not a priority in his first term.

In the year before he faced the voters for a second term, McKinley moved to reshape his government in response to public criticism. The War Department and Secretary Alger were a popular target because of their performance during the war. A commission that McKinley appointed to look into the record of the War Department in 1898 concluded that the military needed to be reformed to make it more efficient. As a result, the president eased out Alger during the summer of 1899. His replacement was Elihu Root of New York, a corporation attorney who brought a good sense of organization and efficiency to the task of managing the colonial possessions and revitalizing the army itself.

## GOOD AND BAD
## POLITICAL SIGNS

By the autumn of 1899 the likelihood of McKinley's reelection seemed promising. His speaking tours during the summer and fall attracted friendly crowds, and he continued his strategy of rallying public opinion to his policies with frequent travels. The Republicans did well in the off-year elections, too. The only political problem for the president arose when Vice President Garret A. Hobart died in November 1899. Calls came from within the party for the selection of Theodore Roosevelt, a war hero and the popular governor of New York State.

Good signs turned to bad during the early months of 1900, when McKinley's relations with Congress encountered several rough spots. When the administration tried to make some tariff concessions for the newly acquired island of Puerto Rico, Republicans balked at these modifications in the doctrine of protection. McKinley compromised with his congressional critics. The Hay-Pauncefote Treaty, allowing the United States to build an isthmian canal, also encountered Senate resistance that compelled the secretary of state to renegotiate the pact. Finally, Republican protectionists balked at the reciprocity treaties that the administration had worked out with countries such as Argentina and France. None of these controversies seriously damaged the president's prestige on the eve of his reelection campaign.

## THEODORE ROOSEVELT JOINS THE TICKET

With his own renomination a certainty, McKinley had to resolve the issue of his vice-presidential candidate. Enthusiasm within the Republican party for Theodore Roosevelt ran strongly during the spring of 1900. McKinley recognized that Roosevelt's eastern background, war record, and popularity with western Republicans made him a good balance for the ticket. Conservatives wondered, however, about Roosevelt's reliability and devotion to traditional party doctrine. Their problem was the absence of a good alternative to Roosevelt. McKinley frowned on efforts to block Roosevelt at the Republican national convention, and the New Yorker went on the ticket. To oppose McKinley, the Democrats again chose William Jennings Bryan.

Even before the campaign began, the president faced a foreign policy crisis in China, where the Boxer Rebellion had threatened westerners with destruction. McKinley sent several thousand U.S. soldiers and marines with the China Relief Expedition to Peking. He did so even though the United States was not at war with China and at a time when Congress was in recess. The president's justification rested on the war powers of his office, and his action represented an important broadening of executive authority.

## THE ELECTION OF 1900

McKinley did not campaign for reelection in 1900; political custom at that time precluded incumbents from actively seeking votes. Roosevelt made the energetic Republican campaign. With economic good times once again in evidence and the United States in a strong position in the world, McKinley's victory over Bryan was assured. The president added to his popular vote margin and achieved 292 electoral votes to Bryan's 155.

During the session of Congress following the election, McKinley demonstrated his skill with Capitol Hill in the adoption of the Spooner Amendment and the Platt Amendment. The Spooner Amendment provided him with the authority to deal with the Philippines after the insurrection ended, and the seizure of Aguinaldo in March 1901 signaled that the rebellion was winding down. At the same time, the Platt Amendment gave the United States the leverage it needed with the newly independent Cubans.

## PLANS END IN ASSASSINATION

McKinley had an ambitious agenda for a second term. He told the French ambassador that he planned to travel to Cuba or Puerto Rico and thus end the tradition that kept the president inside the continental United States during his term of office. He warned his secretary that the trust issue would also have to be dealt with. His first priority, however, was to secure ratification of the tariff treaties that the State Department had been negotiating for several years.

While he remained committed to the protective system, McKinley knew that gradual, phased reductions in tariff rates had become politically necessary. He believed that using reciprocity would enable the process to go forward in a controlled manner that would not undermine the Republican doctrine, as an effort to lower tariffs through legislation would have done. The president now intended to make the case for reciprocity in a series of speeches during 1901. When the First Lady became ill, McKinley postponed the speaking tour until autumn.

The first step in the president's tour was scheduled for the Pan-American Exposition in Buffalo, New York, in early September. There, on 5 September, McKinley argued that "the period of exclusiveness is past," and he called for action on the trade pacts. He never lived to see his program become a reality. On 6 September, standing in a receiving line to meet his constituents as part of the openness and accessibility that had marked his presidency, McKinley became the victim of an assassin's bullets. Leon Czolgosz, a professed anarchist, shot the president. Despite popular hopes that he would recover, McKinley died on the morning of 14 September 1901.

## EVALUATION OF McKINLEY'S PRESIDENCY

For much of the twentieth century, McKinley's historical reputation went into an eclipse. The disenchantment about the war with Spain and the perception that he represented a mindless Republican conservatism made McKinley seem colorless and ineffectual. With Theodore Roosevelt as his successor, McKinley had the misfortune to

seem only a prelude to an activist and modern chief executive. By the 1960s, however, reappraisals of McKinley's performance began, and his standing among presidents rose.

McKinley was the first of the modern presidents. He wielded the war power in a manner that anticipated other twentieth-century presidents. His relations with Congress were fruitful and productive. He and Cortelyou laid the foundation for how presidents have handled the press ever since, and McKinley used the "bully pulpit" of his office before Theodore Roosevelt ever coined the term. While he will never be regarded as a great president, William McKinley was one of the most important chief executives in the nation's history, and his presidency will retain its fascination both for what he accomplished and the ways in which he transformed the office.

## BIBLIOGRAPHY

Gould, Lewis L. *The Presidency of William McKinley* (The University Press of Kansas, 1980).
——— (with Craig H. Roell). *William McKinley: A Bibliography* (Meckler Publishing, 1988).
Leech, Margaret. *In the Days of McKinley* (Harper & Bros., 1959).
McKinley, William. *Speeches and Addresses of William McKinley from March 1, 1897 to May 30, 1900* (Doubleday and McClure, 1900).
Morgan, H. Wayne. *William McKinley and His America* (Syracuse University Press, 1993).
Offner, John L. *An Unwanted War: The Diplomacy of the United States and Spain over Cuba* (University of North Carolina Press, 1992).
Williams, R. Hal. *Years of Decision: American Politics in the 1890s* (Waveland Press, 1993).

★★★ 26 ★★★

# THEODORE ROOSEVELT
## 1901–1909

*Jonathan Lurie*

*Born 27 October 1858 in New York, New York, to Theodore Roosevelt and Martha Bulloch Roosevelt; educated at Harvard College, Cambridge, Massachusetts (B.A. 1880); and Columbia University Law School in New York (did not take a degree); married Alice Hathaway Lee, 27 October 1880, Brookline, Massachusetts; one child; married Edith Kermit Carow, 2 December 1886, London, England; five children; succeeded to presidency upon death of William McKinley, 14 September 1901; reelected on the Republican ticket with Charles Warren Fairbanks of Indiana in 1904, receiving 7,623,486 popular votes and 336 electoral college ballots, over the Democratic ticket of Alton Brooks Parker of New York and Henry Gassaway Davis of West Virginia, which received 5,077,911 popular votes and 140 electoral ballots; died 6 January 1919 in Oyster Bay, New York; buried in Young's Memorial Cemetery, Oyster Bay, New York.*

Theodore Roosevelt's life appears full of stark contradictions. Although frail and sickly as a youth, he made himself into a model and proponent of physical fitness. Devoted to the rule of law, he exhibited a continuing impatience with the legal process and never completed law school. Denouncing politics and politicians in terms typical of the patrician class from which he came, he nonetheless loved the quest for office and exercise of political power. Indeed, for Theodore Roosevelt such activity was the sine qua non of his career. He often succeeded by relying on his keen awareness of political reality, but when that skill counted most it eluded him. A political figure who extolled devotion to the Republican party and the absolute necessity for working within it, Roosevelt in 1912 deliberately violated his own precepts—ensuring both the defeat of its nominee and himself and control (albeit temporary) of Congress by the Democrats. Although in his last years Roosevelt advocated unity, as a political malcontent he in fact nurtured a crude jingoistic nationalism, disagreement, and disunity.

## A UNIQUE PREPARATION AND PERSONALITY

Theodore Roosevelt's "preparation" for the presidency was similarly varied. His previous careers included a half-hearted attempt to study law at Columbia University Law School, election as a New York state legislator, a brief career as a Dakota cowboy, the presidency of a western stockman's association, U.S. civil service commissioner, police commissioner of New York City, assistant secretary of the navy, a ranking officer in the most famous volunteer regiment to serve in the Spanish-American War of 1898 (an event he described as "the splendid little war"), governor of New York, and vice president.

But there was much more to this man who gloried in the varied life he led. Fluent in several languages and habitually reading one to three books a day, Roosevelt also possessed a remarkably urbane mind. Before he turned 43, he had written extensively, including multivolume histories of the American West and the War of 1812, several biographies, and fourteen additional volumes of natural history, history, literary criticism, and political philosophy—to say nothing of about 75,000 letters. And all this, as biographer Edmund Morris emphasizes, took place *before* Roosevelt became the youngest president in U.S. history. By the time of his death in 1919, ten years after leaving the White House, Roosevelt's published book total had reached thirty-eight.

Indeed, many "firsts" applied to this president. He was the first to be elected with such a varied background, the first to be reelected in his own right upon succeeding to the office due to the death of the incumbent, the first to use the presidency as a platform from which to articulate his views and values, the first U.S. president to receive the Nobel Prize for Peace, the first to state in a moment of triumph in 1904 that "under no circumstances will I be a candidate for or accept another nomination," and the first to break such a pledge, with unfortunate results for both him and his party.

Theodore Roosevelt not only possessed the broadest intellect of any president but—with the possible exception of his cousin Franklin—he was also this nation's most popular chief executive. In him, much of the nation saw themselves, and his unique ability to sense their aspirations, goals, and values explains his great success as our first "preacher president." What many sought, he seemed to have accomplished. Replete with his expectations, contradictions, and inconsistencies, Theodore Roosevelt, according to John Morton Blum, "contained within him the best and the worst of America, the whole spectrum from practical enlightenment and sound moral judgment to sentimentalism and braggadocio."

Given this amazing range of accomplishments by one possessed both of a mercurial personality and a brash demeanor (although rarely unintentionally so), he both authored and inspired numerous expressions of strong feelings. In 1898, an impatient Roosevelt allegedly called his boss, President McKinley, "a white-livered cur," one with "no more backbone than a chocolate eclair." He apparently referred to Charles Evans Hughes (a future governor of New York and the only person to serve on the U.S. Supreme Court for two separate periods) as a "psalm-singing son of a bitch." Woodrow Wilson was "a Byzantine logothete," his soul "rotten through and through."

Invariably TR had to take as well as give. Henry Adams noted that he was "pure act," a "bore as big as a buffalo." A not-too-friendly British critic described his Oxford lecture as "longitude, latitude, and platitude." A member of Congress complained that Roosevelt has "no more respect for the Constitution than a tomcat has for a marriage license." Even those working closely with him as members of his cabinet were sometimes unable to resist the temptation to voice similar comments. "Ah, Mr. President," said one such official upon hearing a Roosevelt proposal, "why have such a beautiful action marred by the taint of legality?"

Although treated affectionately by his family, Roosevelt as an undergraduate at Harvard gained a sense of self-discipline and determination. He soon needed them both, for early in his career he suffered multiple tragedies. His father died while Roosevelt was still an undergraduate. Happily married when he was only 22 to Alice Lee, whom he had met while at Harvard, the young man had barely three years of companionship with his wife. On 14 February 1884, after giving birth to their first child, she also passed away, to be followed within a matter of hours by Roosevelt's mother, who died in a different part of their New York City residence.

Writing that "when my heart's dearest died, the light went from my life forever," Roosevelt went on with his life. Employing a grim determination from which he apparently never wavered, Roosevelt did not mention Alice again. Remarriage, five additional children, and fame came to him, but there is no evidence in his correspondence or autobiography that Alice Lee had ever existed. Solely in biographies written by others does she appear, and one of them well

noted that "only Alice Lee remains young and does not fade. She is forever fair; a figure on a Grecian urn."

## A DIFFERENT TYPE OF CONSERVATIVE

As a young Republican reacting to controversial events such as the Haymarket riot of 1887, the Pullman strike of 1894, or the 1896 presidential campaign, Roosevelt echoed the standard conservative party viewpoint. Writing from his western ranch about the riot, he wished that he had some of his ranch hands "with me and a fair show at ten times our number of rioters; my men shoot well and fear very little." Those who opposed use of the injunction as a tool against strikers were "cave dwellers," seeking to force "the country into anarchy." William Jennings Bryan would transform the Lincoln ideal of government by and for the people into government "of a mob, by the demagogue, for the shiftless . . . disorderly and . . . criminal."

In 1901 when reacting to the news that McKinley had been shot, Vice President Roosevelt sounded like a thoroughgoing reactionary. Even though he had welcomed the enthusiasm whipped up by William Randolph Hearst for the Spanish-American War—an encounter so important to Roosevelt personally—he now denounced Hearst. The flamboyant publisher had been very critical of McKinley. In Roosevelt's view, Hearst was a "scoundrel . . . who for whatever purpose appeals to and inflames evil human passion . . . [,one who] has made himself accessory . . . to every crime of this nature; and every soft fool who extends a maudlin sympathy to criminals has done like wise."

But this dread of social violence was always accompanied by a contempt for the greedy and avaricious, a sentiment that seems to have grown stronger as Roosevelt matured. While he "detested the lunatic fringe," he also despised "the social rich . . . the hauteur of wealth newly won." More and more, he realized that modern industrialism had created social and political problems "beyond the capacity of local authorities to resolve." If their solution required an abandonment of traditional laissez-faire attitudes accompanied by federal intervention, so be it. Republicans, Roosevelt consistently argued, ought to "set our faces as resolutely against improper corporate influence on the one hand as against demagogy [sic] and mob rule on the other." Governmental power, not passivity, was necessary.

## KICKED UPSTAIRS

These beliefs shaped Roosevelt's conduct as governor of New York from 1898 to 1900. Selected by a political machine that saw him as a probable winner, he accepted its support because he understood that to be exercised, power must first be possessed. Roosevelt, as William Harbaugh notes, realized that "he had to have office or a good chance of getting it before he could act constructively." As governor, he skillfully used "public opinion which he both formed and reflected." This practice, together with his tendency to consult outside experts—often from the academic world—enabled him to succeed more often without surrender to the New York politicians who helped elect him.

After two years in which Governor Roosevelt proved to be colorful, unpredictable, and quite at home with what Republican boss Tom Platt called "visionary reformers," the New York politicos had had enough. One can understand their enthusiasm for moving him out of New York politics into what seemed to be a place of safe isolation—the vice presidency. Roosevelt, however, opposed such a step, and for precisely the same reasons that the bosses welcomed it. "I do not want to be a figure head," he noted. "Now, as Governor, I can achieve something, but as Vice President I should achieve nothing."

For a variety of reasons, various Republican factions agreed to support placing him on the national ticket. When McKinley voiced neither support nor opposition to the proposal, the vice-presidential nomination was offered to the restive Roosevelt despite party leader Mark Hanna's famous query in 1900: "Don't you realize that there's only one life between this madman and the White House?" That life ended with an assassin's bullet, and on 14 September 1901 "this madman" became the youngest president in U.S. history; he was not yet 43.

## CONFRONTING MODERN INDUSTRIAL SOCIETY

President by accident, and titular leader of a party synonymous with industrialism, stability, and wealth, Roosevelt hinted after only three months in office that his views of labor, capital, and their relationship to government differed from those held by most Republicans. He would be the first president to warn *both* labor and capital that "I set my face like flint against violence and lawlessness of any kind on their part, just as much as against arrogant greed by the rich." This dual emphasis stemmed in turn from convictions the young president had long held about exercise of *his* power to govern, and the accompanying desire for outcomes that were possible, practicable, yet at the same time popular.

Again unlike any of his predecessors, Roosevelt insisted that "there inheres in the Presidency more power than in any other office in any great republic or constitutional monarchy of modern times." Moreover, "I believe in a strong executive; I believe in power." In truth, he gloried in its exercise. Having attained it, he proposed to use that power to delineate not only basic order but also the appropriate relationships between labor and capital, government and business, and indeed even between Congress and the president.

Roosevelt realized better than other Republican leaders that the current era, replete with rapid industrial change and technological innovation, caused severe social dislocation. He shared their belief that "Big Business" was inevitable and desirable. But unlike them, he insisted that the new industrial forces should be controlled by the central government—through vigorous executive action. Fully aware of the industrial wealth and power represented in the U.S. Senate, he also realized its potential as a barrier to reform. "I do not much admire the Senate," Roosevelt once observed, "because it is such a helpless body when efficient work for good is to be done." Further, in matters of reform, Congress should not only clear the way, but then keep out of the way as well.

In his initial message to Congress, Roosevelt became the first chief executive ever to acknowledge a "widespread conviction" that trusts "are in certain of their features and tendencies hurtful to the general welfare." Indeed, this conviction assumed that "combination and concentration" should be "not prohibited, but supervised and within reasonable limits controlled; and in my judgement this conviction is right." He emphasized further the good that "has been and will be accomplished by associations or unions of wage-workers," especially "when they combine insistence upon their own rights with law-abiding respect for the rights of others." As for corporations, Roosevelt insisted that "they shall be so handled as to subserve the public good. We draw the line against misconduct, not against wealth."

## THE 1902 COAL STRIKE

These comments should be kept in mind when considering Roosevelt's actions during the 1902 strike of mine workers against the coal-mine owners. This was one of three episodes that offer valuable insights into both Roosevelt's goals and operating methodology as president. His response to the greatest work stoppage thus far in U.S. industrial development was unlike that of any previous chief executive. In 1877 Hayes, and in 1894 Cleveland, had used federal authority to break widespread strikes. Roosevelt, however, saw both his office and the federal function in very different terms. For the first time, an American president employed the prestige and pressure of his office to resolve rather than break a strike.

Although labor conditions in the mines were widely acknowledged to be awful, the mine operators refused to make any compromises whatsoever. Miners "don't suffer," proclaimed the owners' chief spokesman, George Baer. "Why, they can't even speak English." Although it seems difficult to believe, Baer actually topped the stupidity of this observation with another—that the miners would be protected "not by the labor agitators but by the Christian men to whom God in his infinite wisdom has given the control of the property interests of the country."

As the strike continued during the summer of 1902, Roosevelt seriously investigated the possibility of bringing antitrust proceedings against the coal companies, probably the first time in a confrontation between labor and capital that the Sherman Act had been considered as a weapon against corporations instead of against labor unions. Advised that the evidence of conspiracy required under the act was lacking, the president fumed with frustration. Watching the price of coal in New York City rise from less than $2.50 a ton to $6.00, Roosevelt took another step, again without precedent, and brought both sides together to confer with him. The leader of the United Mine Workers assured the president that if the owners accepted creation of a presidential commission to resolve the strike, his members would accept the recommendations put forth by such a group "even if [they] be against our claims."

George Baer not only rejected the creation of a presidential panel out of hand but also lectured the president that "the duty of the hour is not to waste time negotiating with the fomenters of this anarchy." Roosevelt had no business dealing "with a set of outlaws." What he ought to do was what other chief executives had done: send federal troops to break the strike, use the Sherman Act as a weapon against the strikers, and let local courts settle any claims the miners might have *after* they had returned to work. Roosevelt later recalled of Baer that "if it weren't for the high office I hold, I would have taken him by the seat of the breeches and the nape of the neck and chucked him out of that window." The conference ended with nothing resolved. By October, Roosevelt had made secret plans to seize the mines and operate them under government receivership, even going so far as to give preliminary instructions to an army general "who possessed the necessary good sense, judgment, and nerve to act."

At this point Elihu Root, a leading Republican and a member of Roosevelt's cabinet, visited New York City as a private citizen with the president's approval to speak with J. P. Morgan. Although disturbed by what he considered ill-advised intransigence by the owners, the financier was also troubled by Roosevelt's actions to break up a railroad monopoly that Morgan had carefully worked out, a step ultimately endorsed by the U.S. Supreme Court. Morgan was probably even more upset when he learned about the president's intended course of action. Root proposed an alternative course: the creation of an independent presidential arbitration commission, which Morgan would help to sell to the mine owners. Morgan agreed. After several days of intense discussion the owners also acquiesced, but they rejected the presence of any union official on the commission. Continued stalemate again seemed inevitable. The president considered the owners as "still in a condition of wooden-headed obstinacy and stupidity."

The owners hesitated to antagonize the new president—if only because he had been so unpredictable in earlier actions—but they refused as a matter of principle to sit down with a union officer. The administration proposed a final agreement that called for a sociologist to serve as a commission member, and the owners agreed. The president then appointed an "eminent sociologist" who just happened also to be the Grand Chief of the Order of Railroad Conductors. Roosevelt later recalled that "the mighty brains of these captains of industry . . . would rather have anarchy than tweedledum, but if I would use the word tweedledee they would hail it as meaning peace." With the commission established, the strike quickly ended and in due course the panel made a number of findings favorable to the miners.

Roosevelt's reactions to the entire episode are instructive. Using the unheard-of threat of government seizure, he willingly settled for less because it contained what he had deemed so necessary—an end to the strike and some favorable action on the grievances of the minors. Moreover, the president blamed the operators, *not* the strikers for its extended length. Roosevelt had sought, he later recalled, to save these "big propertied men . . . from the dreadful punishment which their own folly would have brought on them." They were "so blinded" that they could not understand the president's desire "to save them from themselves and to avert . . . the excesses which would have been indulged in at their expense if they had longer persisted in their conduct." Furthermore, their property rights "were of the same texture as were the human rights, which they so blindly and hotly denied." Most important, Roosevelt had determined that the interests of both miners and operators had to be subordinated to "the fundamental permanent interests of the whole community."

## PUTTING TEETH INTO THE INTERSTATE COMMERCE COMMISSION

Roosevelt's actions reflected a similar sense of purpose in 1905 and 1906, when he attempted to strengthen the Interstate Commerce Commission's (ICC) ability to regulate the railroads. He regarded the regulatory commission as the best prototype for effective government supervision. Thus, in calling for effective railroad administration, he envisaged a powerful commission that would be established by Congress but staffed by members he himself would select. Such an agency should, for example, be able to regulate issuance of stocks, compel public disclosure of business accounts and procedures, and, if necessary, set maximum rates to deal with the question of monopoly.

Roosevelt preferred a commission rather than a court to monitor business activities. Accurately sensing the innate conservatism inherent in lawyers, especially to organized labor, more and more he distrusted courts. That distrust perhaps blinded him to two difficulties inherent in administrative regulation: capture by the interests subject to regulation and the unwholesome influence of politics on the regulatory process. Roosevelt saw administration by persons *he* had selected as *the* means to govern, to exercise power in the public interest. He was not the first, nor would he be the last, to equate his own appointees with what he considered necessary for effective regulation.

Roosevelt realized that an indirect approach in the area of railroad regulation might bring better results than confrontation between himself and Congress. Deliberately focusing not on the issue of railroad rates but rather on tariff rates, he sent shock waves through the Republican party. Increased railroad regulation would upset some Republicans, but the tariff remained crucial to a great majority of party members. By threatening to push for major tariff reform, the president was in effect offering Republicans a choice—either adopt some sort of meaningful revisions for the ICC or face a serious dispute over an issue that would split the party. Rather than risk internecine strife, Republican House leaders quickly came to an "understanding" with Roosevelt. He would back away from tariff reform, and the House would support strengthening the ICC to deal with railroad rate regulation.

The Senate, however, was not so easily swayed. According to John Morton Blum, no matter how minor the proposed railroad reforms seem in retrospect, in 1906 they "challenged the most hoary tenet of free private enterprise, the ability freely to make prices." Roosevelt had the Senate in mind when he wrote that "there are several eminent statesmen at the other end of Pennsylvania Avenue whom I would gladly lend to the Russian government, if they care to expend them as bodyguards for Grand Dukes wherever there was a likelihood of dynamite bombs being exploded." The conservative tendencies of the upper chamber made compromise a necessity if the House bill was to survive.

Roosevelt adjusted to the gales, sometimes working with, sometimes opposing William Allison—one of the most powerful and conservative Senate Republicans. Although the president agreed with Robert La Follette of Wisconsin that ICC rate-making authority had to be augmented, he warned the aggressive senator that "you can't get any such bill . . . through this Congress. I want to get something through." Roosevelt could have insisted on principle, joined reformers such as La Follette, and attained great public acclaim—all at the cost of the pending legislation. The most important issue concerned the power of the courts to intervene in regulatory matters. Conservatives like Allison called for broad judicial review, including the facts of each case, something that would have given real authority over rates to judges, considered friendly by the railroads, rather than to the commission, which the railroad barons feared. Above all, the president did not want to have a law passed and then have it declared unconstitutional.

Although Roosevelt did not hesitate to use public opinion as a weapon in negotiating with Congress, ultimately he settled—more often than he liked to admit—for what was possible. In this instance, it was an amendment—the Hepburn Act of 1900—that gave circuit courts jurisdiction over cases arising from ICC action but that failed to define the scope of such review. Because the measure allowed for court intervention, conservatives accepted it. But because other parts of the bill gave the ICC expanded powers, a number of Democrats as well as Progressive Republicans also could accept it. Indeed, as Henry Pringle noted, Theodore Roosevelt followed "more or less consistently the policy of recoiling in horror from the radical ideas of the Democrats, then adopting them with slight modifications, and finally condemning as obstructionists, those who opposed his adaptations." An agency that could offer "continuous, disinterested," and effective administrative action was the key to coping with industrial society, and the power it exercised. In the Hepburn Act, Roosevelt believed he had moved as far as practicable towards this goal.

## SECURING PURE FOOD
## AND DRUG LEGISLATION

Effective administrative regulation should also extend to issues concerning wages, hours of work, and other "conditions of labor." Here again, Roosevelt demonstrated his skill in using publicity to enhance his exercise of political power, without endorsing "radical" proposals—acting always, in his view, in the public interest. For a number of years, proponents had sought a federal law that would require accurate labels on food, drink, and drugs. Once or twice bills had even passed in the House, only to expire in the Senate. In December 1905, Roosevelt supported such a measure but with minimal enthusiasm. Nevertheless, a few months later the Senate approved the proposal for a number of reasons having little to do with the merits of the legislation.

As the bill lay pending in the House, the president, along with many others, read *The Jungle*, a novel in which Upton Sinclair described in graphic prose a gruesome picture of conditions in the meat-packing houses. Roosevelt ordered the secretary of agriculture to investigate the matter, but he distanced himself from Sinclair's socialist leanings, as portrayed in the last part of the novel. The president wrote Sinclair that while I "distrust men of hysterical temperament," the "specific evils you point out shall, if their existence be proved, and if I have power, be eradicated." Within a few weeks, his investigators had prepared a report, verifying the basic truth of Sinclair's claims. In May the Senate approved a meat-inspection proposal. This time, the House Committee on Agriculture blocked the bill, its chairman being very solicitous of the packers' interests.

Roosevelt, now caught up in the drive for pure food and drug regulation, informed the committee chair, Representative James Wadsworth, that he would not release the investigators' findings, which were "hideous," *if* the committee approved the Senate's statute. "I should not make the report public with the idea of damaging the packers," he added. He would take that step "only if

it were necessary to secure the remedy." Eventually he deemed that it was necessary, and in June he released part of the report, hinting that more would be forthcoming. Faced with reaction to the report, the fallout from Sinclair's best seller, and a noticeable decline in meat sales, the packers decided they could support "an inspection law . . . strong enough to still public clamor, while not so drastic as to inconvenience them too greatly." Roosevelt insisted on "a thorough and rigid, and not a sham, inspection."

The president broke the stalemate with what was now a well-established pattern— pressure for congressional action, matched by preparation for compromise. He wrote to Wadsworth, denouncing the committee's substitute proposal as "very, very bad." At the same time, he accepted two changes sought by the packers. Costs for the new inspection program would be paid by the government, and the inspection dates would not be listed on the products. The inspectors would, however, be subject to civil service, and the government could decline to inspect and thus withhold its stamp of approval if the packers did not cooperate. When Wadsworth tried to ensure that the packers could easily obtain court review, Roosevelt published his "very, very bad" letter. Ultimately and unwillingly, Wadsworth agreed that packer access to the courts would be restricted. Losing a reelection bid to the seat he had held for twenty five years, Wadsworth later described the president as "unreliable, a faker, and a humbug."

As he had over the issue of railroad regulation, Roosevelt proved himself in the meat inspection matter to be an adept dancer of the accommodation waltz—one step forward, one step backward, and three steps to the side. Moreover, as Roosevelt received acclaim for the Pure Food and Drug Act he declined to acknowledge the help of individuals such as Sinclair, whose work had been so important. Indeed, the president was so concerned about not appearing to be radical in any way, that he later denounced muck raking, of which *The Jungle* was a prime example.

It seems clear that traditional labels such as *conservative* or *liberal* meant little to President Roosevelt. While not eschewing their use, he was perfectly candid when he insisted that a true conservative was in reality a progressive. "The only true conservative is the man who resolutely sets his face towards the future." Some objected to this constant equation of apparent opposites. Robert La Follette recalled that Roosevelt "in this way . . . sought to win approval, both from the radicals and the conservatives. This cannonading, first in one direction and then in another, filled the air with noise and smoke, which confused and obscured the line of action, but when the battle cloud drifted by and quiet was restored, it was always a matter of surprise that so little had been accomplished."

## THE BIG STICK
## IN LATIN AMERICA

Roosevelt's approach to diplomatic activity emphasized the same ordered power that characterized his domestic politics—the tendency "to equate right with order" and to ensure order as the result of "self-restrained power." To a greater extent than any previous president, Roosevelt enjoyed dealing in foreign policy. More than many Americans, he willingly accepted two ideas that in his time were considered controversial: first, that the United States could no longer be isolated from world events, and second, that the United States must participate in and ultimately win the struggle for world power. In his attempts to achieve those ends he sometimes demonstrated sensitivity along with bluster, impetuous belligerence along with accommodation, and—particularly in his dealings with Latin America—an unfortunate arrogance and coarseness.

Such was the case when Colombia vetoed a U.S. treaty favorable to the proposed isthmus canal through Central America. Roosevelt vented his irritation in terms that still seem offensive: Colombian opponents were "contemptible little creatures, and foolish and homicidal corruptionists"—"Dagos" who had acted like bandits, he

raved. "I do not think that the Bogota lot of jack rabbits should be allowed permanently to bar one of the future highways of civilization."

In trying to resolve the indebtedness of several Latin American countries and thus forestall European intervention, Roosevelt modified the Monroe Doctrine—insisting that if any intervention was necessary, it would be American. "It would show these Dagos that they will have to behave decently." Interspersed with the requirement for "reasonable efficiency" [order] from Latin American countries was also the promise [power] that if such a nation "keeps order and pays its obligations, it need fear no interference from the United States." Overall, Roosevelt's actions reflected his assumption that world peace was feasible "upon consciousness by each great nation of counterbalanced power."

## PLAYING A ROLE
## IN THE WORLD

The notion of balancing powers was also evident in Roosevelt's handling of the Russo-Japanese War. Although he could use bluster when necessary as an instrument of international diplomacy, he could also use patience, tact, and his large network of friends in foreign countries. Roosevelt had little sympathy for Russia's desire to expand its influence in Asia, and when Japan in 1904 challenged and then defeated the Russians on both land and sea, the president was delighted. Japan was doing "our work" in China, he said, and it was "bully" the way Japan had started the war with a surprise attack. But it would not do if Japan won too great a victory, and if the United States then had to deal with an Asia dominated by Japan, which would threaten American economic interests in China as well as the newly acquired Hawaiian and Philippine islands.

With such interests in mind, as well as his desire to play a major role in world affairs, Roosevelt agreed to mediate the war. It proved a daunting task, with both sides initially demanding far more than the other would concede, but Roosevelt kept them talking in Portsmouth, New Hampshire, until they finally agreed to a peace treaty in 1905. For his efforts, Roosevelt won the Nobel Peace Prize, the only American President ever to do so.

In order to expand America's influence in the world, Roosevelt made the grand gesture in December 1907 of ordering the American battle fleet to make a fifteen-month cruise around the world. The so-called "Great White Fleet" was the culmination of a building program begun more than two decades earlier which replaced the country's antiquated wooden navy with new state-of-the-art steel battleships. The cruise made a splendid show of force in foreign ports, and it was one of his acts as president for which Roosevelt professed great pride.

## A GROWING RADICALISM

As his second term drew to a close, Roosevelt—always a severe critic of labor violence—became even more critical of capitalistic intransigence that appeared to make violence an attractive alternative. He was well aware of the industrial changes that he assessed as "at least as dangerous to the country's welfare" as had been the slavery conflict of a generation before. From his perspective, the danger lay in how the legal order responded to the awesome industrial power that now dominated American society. Both executive and legislative branches of government had much to offer, but the judiciary had been less than even-handed in resolving disputes between labor and capital. Injunctive power should be promptly employed when dealing with disorder, he observed, but it should not be abused "as is implied in forbidding laboring men to strive for their own betterment in peaceful and lawful ways." Nor should it be used "merely to aid some big corporation in carrying out schemes for its own aggrandizement."

In his private correspondence, Roosevelt was even harsher toward his own class. He especially objected to "the dull, purblind folly of the very rich men; their greed and arrogance, and the way in which they have unduly prospered by the help of the ablest lawyers, and too often through the weak-

ness or shortsightedness of the judges." Here, TR noted the unfortunate use of the injunction as an antilabor weapon: "Where it is [used] recklessly or unnecessarily, the abuse should be censured, above all by the very men who are properly anxious to prevent any effort to shear the courts of this necessary power." The president also supported the relatively new concept of workmen's compensation.

Indeed, as his second term drew to a close, Roosevelt reiterated his point that "we are the true conservatives [who] . . . in the long run . . . give wise guidance to those who are struggling towards the idea of fairer dealings between man and man." Our "worst revolutionaries today are those reactionaries who do not see and will not admit there is need for change." This uneasy tension between stability and change, the need to maintain one even while ensuring the other, became a sort of obsession with Roosevelt during his presidency.

## PARTING FROM THE PARTY

Even before 1908, his last full year as chief executive, Theodore Roosevelt found that his reputation as the enemy of "the malefactors of wealth," the foe of Wall Street, the attacker of railroads, and the opponent of corporate greed had come at a heavy price. Intentionally or not, he had so deepened the gap between himself and the main body of Republican conservatives as to make it virtually unbridgeable. This group formed the vast majority of the Republican party, and they had supported Roosevelt unwillingly while suspecting him unwaveringly. After 1907, if Republican opposition to him was noticeable it did not deter him.

Timber, mining, and cattle interests also resented Roosevelt's enthusiasm for conservation; by 1908, he had more than doubled the national parks that had been created by all his predecessors. Their antagonism merged with the general conservative opposition to his policies. In 1907, for example, without even a role call the Senate passed an amendment to the agricultural appropriations bill, barring the establishment of any forest reserve in six western states.

Roosevelt's response was clever. Within the ten days allowed him to consider the bill, he signed presidential proclamations setting aside more than 16 million acres of forest reserves within the six states. He then approved the appropriations bill.

In January 1908, the president sent a special message to the Republican-controlled Congress insisting that judges had sometimes used the injunctive power "heedlessly and unjustly," inflicting on occasion "irreparable wrong upon those enjoined." He bluntly warned his party that unless some way could be found to prevent such judicial abuses, "the feeling of indignation against them among large numbers of our citizens will grow so extreme as to produce a revolt against the whole use of the process of injunction." As the Republican members of Congress listened in silence, the message further criticized jurists who failed in their duty to the public by improper dealings with lawbreaking corporations and lawbreaking men of wealth. Proposing that 10,000 extra copies of the message be printed, one representative noted that "it was the best Democratic doctrine I ever heard emanating from a Republican source."

By December 1908, Theodore Roosevelt—only 50 years old—had become a lame-duck president. In 1904, Elihu Root, who had served as Roosevelt's secretary of state and of war, had congratulated the president on his forty-sixth birthday on having reached such a "respectable age." Your friends, Root added, "have great hopes for you when you grow up." Four years later, with his chosen successor—William Howard Taft—already elected, much of his party remained restive under Roosevelt's unrelenting suggestions for change, even as they realized that the power so vital to his conception of government was no longer his to exercise. Yet his final annual message to Congress was typical.

He categorized the reactionary as "the worst enemy of order," and noted pointedly that "the men who defend the rights of property have most to fear from the wrongdoers of great wealth." TR insisted once again that "a blind and ignorant resistance

to every effort for the reform of abuses and for the readjustment of society to modern industrial conditions represents not true conservatism, but an incitement to the wildest radicalism; for wise radicalism and wise conservatism go hand in hand." Acknowledging that "in no other nation in the world do the courts wield such vast and far-reaching power as in the United States," Roosevelt urged Congress to "face the fact that there are wise and unwise judges." It was all the more important, then, that "the duty of respectful and truthful criticism, which should be binding when we speak of anybody, should be especially binding when we speak of them."

## IN THE WILDERNESS

So Roosevelt left the White House, still voicing his frenetic calls for power, principle, and progress. In truth, he had never wanted to leave the presidency in 1909, a fact that could only have troubled his chosen successor William Howard Taft. Theodore Roosevelt would have been a very hard act for any politician to follow, but Taft—ponderous, phlegmatic, and uninspiring—found the way exceedingly difficult. "There is no use trying to be . . . Taft with Roosevelt's ways," he conceded. "Our ways are different." Taft managed to deepen the split between conservatives and insurgents within the Republican party—thereby exacerbating tensions between himself and the former president—in three areas.

First, Taft replaced many of Roosevelt's appointments with his own choices, although Roosevelt himself had done the same soon after he became president. Second, Taft, like his predecessor, supported lower tariffs, but he differed from him in lacking the skill to employ the tariff as a bargaining chip with which to win concessions from Congress in other areas he deemed more important, such as railroad regulation. The tariff that finally emerged from the legislature was among the highest in history, but Taft with incredible insensitivity pronounced it to be "the best tariff bill that the Republican Party has ever passed." And third, when insurgent Republicans sought successfully to lessen the authority of House Speaker Joseph Cannon, Taft did nothing to support them.

For more than a year ("Why not for life?" asked one observer), Roosevelt traveled abroad, visiting heads of state and hunting game in Africa. "I trust," added another of his critics, "that some lion will do its duty." Far away, he watched and worried as Taft appeared to bungle. "The right type of aggressive leadership," he wrote in 1910, was lacking in Washington because it was the type that "a lawyer's Administration is totally unfit to give." Indeed, he added, "there is not a greater delusion than the belief that a lawyer is, *per se*, also a statesman." One month later, Roosevelt warned that "the conduct of the bench in failing to move with the times, . . . rather than turning to broad principles of justice and equity, is one of the chief elements in producing the present popular discontent."

Roosevelt returned to the United States in June 1910. He became increasingly unhappy with what he described as the typical judicial mind "which may be perfectly honest, but is absolutely fossilized, which declines to allow us to work for the betterment of conditions." The former president was soon surrounded by political insurgents and Republican malcontents who urged his intervention in party affairs. Yet now he found himself popular but powerless. Restive and resentful, Roosevelt had to learn again "how difficult was politics without power." Moreover, Roosevelt kept harping on the judiciary. As he neared the decision to challenge Taft for renomination, he conceived of a solution to the problem of judicial absolutes and popular rule. Indeed, the fact that he spent so much time and energy on it indicates his great concern with the issue.

## POPULAR OVERRIDE OF JUDICIAL DECISIONS

Thus Roosevelt in 1912 described a Connecticut Supreme Court decision holding workmen's compensation unconstitutional as "an incredible perversion of the Constitution. . . . Every strained construction of the Constitution which declares that the nation is powerless to remedy industrial conditions which cry for law gives aid to these enemies of our American system . . . who wish to furnish in its place some new, vague and foolish substitute." The basis for the decision, a questionable judicial interpretation of the Constitution called "freedom of contract" was, he said, "a relic of barbarism, an empty and imaginary theory." Even worse, "the so called conservatives who work for and applaud such decisions, and deprecate criticism of them, are doing all in their power to make it necessary for the Nation as a whole . . . to go to a far more radical extreme."

But in a democracy, Roosevelt insisted, "the people have the right to rule when we have thought out our problems and come to a definite decision." This applied to judges as well. The people "must have the power to act." This could be done by allowing voters "the right if they so desire, in any given case, to vote finally as to whether or not the decision is to be accepted as binding." And he concluded, "this people must ultimately control its own destinies, and cannot surrender the right of ultimate control to a judge any more than to a legislator or executive." Here again he returned to the theme that had dominated his thinking long before he entered politics.

"What I have advocated," he insisted, "is not revolution. It is not wild radicalism. It is the highest and wisest kind of conservatism." Of course the judges were not corrupt, "But they are absolutely reactionary, and their decisions . . . have been such as almost to bar the path to industrial . . . and social reform. By such decisions they perpetuate misery, they increase unrest and discontent."

One judge who corresponded with Roosevelt concerning his ideas was Learned Hand, who would become one of the truly great American jurists. Hand objected to the basic, although unarticulated, premise behind Roosevelt's plan. He correctly saw the proposal as a way of putting popular pressure on judges in advance, seeking thereby to ensure certain outcomes in key cases. Moreover, Hand might well have asked if judges could function properly in an atmosphere with a sword of censure hanging over their heads, ready to be activated by popular agitation.

Roosevelt reiterated his point that in constitutional cases an important alternative "must be to have the right of appeal from the judges." It was not a matter of legislative supremacy over a court. "I propose merely to allow the people, after ample deliberation to decide whether they will follow the legislature or the court." Far from recalling the judges, Roosevelt's plan would recall the decisions themselves. According to one correspondent, this idea has served "to throw the property owning class and all reverers of our institutions into pink fits."

## ARMAGEDDON AND BEYOND

By 1912, Roosevelt experienced a relapse of presidential fever, having never recovered from presidential fervor. Knowing not only that his course would damage himself, Taft, and the party, but also that victory was virtually impossible, Roosevelt ignored such advice and charged ahead—seeking to wrest renomination from one who had been his hand-picked successor. When Taft supporters exercised their organizational control at the 1912 Republican convention (just as Roosevelt's had done at the 1904 conclave), Roosevelt and his supporters walked out, formed a new party—and standing at Armageddon, battled for the Lord. He merged his discussion of courts and judges into a broader political platform called the New Nationalism, one that essentially recapitulated his long-held views on politics and power. And he insisted anew that "wise progressivism and wise conservatism go hand in hand, and . . . the wise conservative must be a progressive because otherwise he works only for that species of reaction which inevitably in the end produces an explosion."

Forced again to the sidelines after his defeat by Wilson in 1912, shunned by Republican party regulars, Roosevelt watched as Wilson grappled with the onslaught of World War I and the American response. He hoped to be the Republican nominee in

1916, but he had to concede that too many party regulars "are convinced that I am actuated by motives of personal ambition and . . . have not the good of the country at heart." Instead, he gamely campaigned for Charles Evans Hughes and angrily berated Wilson for timidity, indecisiveness, and an apparent fixation on the military status quo. For Theodore Roosevelt, with memories of the triumphant Rough Riders Brigade in the Spanish-American War, the Democratic campaign emphasis that Wilson "kept us out of war" was "yellow . . . plain yellow! . . . I fail," he fulminated, "to see anything but degradation in the appeal . . . to the yellow streak."

With the United States finally at war in 1917, Roosevelt tried in vain to persuade Wilson to let him raise a volunteer regiment and fight in France. But political and personal antagonism aside, Wilson had sound reasons for refusing the former president's request. Trench warfare, poison gas, conscription, and torturous military stalemate represented the new reality. The Rough Rider's version of vigorous participation, to say nothing of his age, forced him to remain once again on the sidelines. In his place he sent his four sons to the front, where his youngest, Quentin, died.

Roosevelt's shrill invective contributed to the wartime hysteria. Denouncing dissent, he preached the worst kind of intolerance and conformity. He saw no middle ground, only patriotism or sedition, and he insisted that Germany should be forced into a peace that was severe and stringent. Wilson's passion for internationalism seemed contrary to Roosevelt's long-held visions of ordered power to be exercised by those who had won the war. And when Republicans took control of Congress in 1918, Roosevelt rejoiced, seeing in it a repudiation of Wilsonian cant.

After the armistice ended the fighting on 11 November 1918, Roosevelt seemed to recover his sense of proportion. In the postwar world, the Republican party must be one "of sane, constructive radicalism," one that would avoid "criticism, delay and reaction." Indeed, "negation and obstruction and attempts to revive the dead past spelled ruin." Although in poor health, the former president looked forward eagerly to 1920, hoping against hope that once again he might lead the Republican party to what he sensed was inevitable victory. Yet he emphasized that "by George, if they take me, they'll take me without a single modification of the things I have always stood for." Instead, early in January 1919, Roosevelt died in his sleep. He did not live to see the utter tragedy that befell Woodrow Wilson, and if the contrast between Wilson's vision and Roosevelt's had been striking, the difference between Roosevelt's vision and Warren Harding's would be even more dramatic.

## EVALUATION OF THEODORE ROOSEVELT'S PRESIDENCY

In so many ways, Theodore Roosevelt left his mark on the United States. During his administration, vigorous presidential leadership reached a new level, augmenting the chief executive's role as a spokesman for American values and goals. In his lifetime, the industrial, social, geographic, and economic contours of American society had been transformed. Roosevelt was very much aware of the need for changes that would render twentieth-century industrial society more acceptable and beneficial to its people. His emphasis on conservation as national policy, and his love of life as a pattern of challenges, goals, and attainments would influence future presidents, especially his cousin, Franklin Delano Roosevelt. But the mark he left was not always a good one. His excessive appeals toward dogmatic patrio-

tism, his denunciation of those with whom he disagreed, his intolerant bullying of those who stood in his way, and his crass political manipulation have also left their footprints in the nation's history. What has been said of other world figures may well be said of Theodore Roosevelt: For better or for worse, "if you seek his monument, look around."

## BIBLIOGRAPHY

Beale, Howard K. *Theodore Roosevelt and the Rise of America to World Power* (Collier Books, 1965).

Blum, John M. *The Republican Roosevelt*, 2nd ed. (Harvard University Press, 1977).

Chessman, G. Wallace. *Theodore Roosevelt and the Politics of Power* (Little, Brown, 1969).

Garraty, John. *Henry Cabot Lodge: A Biography* (Knopf, 1953).

Hagedorn, Hermann. *The Roosevelt Family of Sagamore Hill* (Macmillan, 1954).

Harbaugh, William. *The Life and Times of Theodore Roosevelt*, rev. ed. (Oxford University Press, 1975).

Leopold, Richard. *Elihu Root and the Conservative Tradition* (Little, Brown, 1954).

Link, Arthur. *Woodrow Wilson and the Progressive Era* (Harper & Row, 1958).

Lurie, Jonathan. *Law and the Nation, 1865–1912* (Knopf, 1983).

Morris, Edmund. *The Rise of Theodore Roosevelt* (Ballantine Books, 1979).

Mowry, George E. *The Era of Theodore Roosevelt and the Birth of Modern America, 1900–1912* (Harper & Row, 1958).

Pringle, Henry F. *Theodore Roosevelt: A Biography* (Harcourt, Brace, & World, 1956).

★★★ 27 ★★★

# WILLIAM HOWARD TAFT
## 1909–1913

*David W. Levy*

---

*Born 15 September 1857 in Cincinnati, Ohio, to Alphonso Taft and Louise Maria Torrey Taft; educated at Yale College (B.A. 1878) and Cincinnati Law School; married Helen Herron 19 June 1886, Cincinnati, Ohio; three children; ran for president in 1908 with James Schoolcraft of New York on the Republican ticket; elected by a popular vote of 7,678,908 and 321 electoral college votes over the Democratic ticket of William Jennings Bryan of Nebraska and John Worth Kern of Indiana (6,409,104 popular votes and 162 electoral college votes); died 8 March 1930 in Washington, D.C.; buried in Arlington National Cemetary, Arlington, Virginia.*

---

In the presidential election of 1908, William Howard Taft polled almost 7.7 million votes to Democrat William Jennings Bryan's 6.4 million. In the electoral college, Taft registered a crushing victory, overwhelming his opponent by 321 to 162. Outside of the solidly Democratic South, he lost only three states. A scant four years later, however, it was an entirely different story. In the three-way race of 1912, Taft finished a dismal third, a half-million votes behind Theodore Roosevelt and a full three million behind Woodrow Wilson. Taft got only 8 votes in the electoral college, and for every 100 voters who supported him in 1908, only 44 voted for him in 1912. Rarely in the history of presidential politics has there been so dramatic a fall from popularity. Inevitably, trying to explain Taft's presidency is, to some extent, the attempt to explain his political collapse.

Accounting for Taft's fall is complicated by the fact that he was neither a villain nor an incompetent. His administration could boast significant achievements. His intelligence was of a high order, and to all but his bitterest opponents, his honesty and fundamental decency were beyond reproach. In the end, his failure as president and his loss of the public's confidence stemmed from flaws in his personality, some unfortunate decisions during the first half of his administration, and his particular view of the proper role of the president in the U.S. political system. Most of all, Taft fell victim to a large shift in American politics, a dramatic movement in public opinion that would have been difficult to overcome even for someone with much sharper political skills than his.

## A "WELL-TRAINED OHIO MAN"

William Howard Taft was born in Cincinnati on 15 September 1857. His father was Alphonso Taft, a prominent Republican who served as President Grant's secretary of war and attorney general. Like his father, William graduated from Yale, completing in 1878 a successful undergraduate career as an able student and a popular and trusted student leader. He returned home and enrolled in the Cincinnati Law School; two years later, he graduated and gained admission to the Ohio bar. By the time he was 25, "Big Bill" Taft was 6 feet, 4 inches, and he weighed more than 240 pounds. His personal traits were already established. Affable, easygoing, and good humored, Taft made friends easily and, because of his transparent honesty and personal morality, won the regard, trust, and often the loyalty of those who knew him. He had absorbed from his family's New England heritage a rigorous sense of right and wrong, a belief in personal honor, and a commitment to "duty," particularly as it was expressed in public service. He had a decidedly "judicial"

disposition rather than a "political" one, and even at an early age he believed himself destined to be a judge; his highest ambition, he freely admitted, was to sit some day on the U.S. Supreme Court. He was thoughtful and intelligent, somehow above the battle of everyday politics. This temperament accounted for much that was admirable in him. It was also partly responsible for some of his weaknesses and failures as president.

From the beginning he was a loyal Republican like his father, and from the beginning he also benefited from the combination of undoubted ability and connections to powerful Ohio Republicans. "Like every well trained Ohio man," he said, "I always had my plate right side up when offices were falling." In 1881, he was appointed assistant prosecuting attorney for Hamilton County (Cincinnati), a reward for having campaigned for the man who appointed him. A year later, Taft became collector of internal revenue for Cincinnati, but he found the patronage aspects of the job so distasteful that he resigned and returned to his law practice. After two years, he accepted appointment as assistant county solicitor. His big opportunity arrived in March 1887. Governor Joseph Foraker, whom Taft had supported through failure and success, appointed him, at age 29, to Ohio's superior court. By this time, Taft had married Helen ("Nellie") Herron, a talented and ambitious woman who was to be his closest adviser. If his tastes ran to the judicial and he was happiest on the bench, hers ran to the political and she remained alert for opportunities to advance her husband's career.

Taft was first considered for the Supreme Court in 1889, by President Benjamin Harrison. The appointment went elsewhere, but Harrison compensated Taft the following year by making him solicitor general of the United States. The Tafts moved to Washington and began to mingle with wellplaced national Republicans: Brooks and Henry Adams, John Hay, Henry Cabot Lodge, and, most important for the future, the energetic civil service commissioner, Theodore Roosevelt. In March 1892, after two years as the government's chief lawyer before the high court, Taft earned another judicial position. Harrison appointed him to the sixth district, and Taft returned to Cincinnati as a federal judge. He was overjoyed; his wife was dismayed but resigned. For the next eight years he happily carried out his judicial duties. His decisions revealed a profound philosophic commitment to the sanctity of private property, but the reputation he gained as an antilabor judge (which haunted him once he entered presidential politics) was not entirely just. He would probably have been content to remain where he was until his ambition for a seat on the Supreme Court could be realized.

In early 1900, however, President William McKinley, a fellow Ohio Republican, prevailed upon Taft to resign his judicial office and head the Philippine Commission, a body appointed to move that newly acquired possession from military to civilian rule. McKinley may also have hinted that Taft would not be forgotten if a seat opened on the Supreme Court. In July 1901, Taft's common sense and diplomatic skill earned him the position as the first civil governor of the Philippines, and after McKinley's assassination, Theodore Roosevelt asked his friend to remain in that politically sensitive position for the time being. Taft's performance was superb—marked by efficient administration, good judgment, and a sincere desire to be fair and helpful to the Filipino population. In February 1904, Roosevelt returned Taft to Washington to serve as his secretary of war and, more important, as one of his closest and most trusted advisers. The president sent his friend on sensitive missions to Panama, Cuba, and Japan, and in each case, Taft fulfilled his assignment with competence and skill.

As Taft's stock with Roosevelt rose, so did his prospects as Roosevelt's successor. Urged on by his wife and brothers, gaining personal confidence with each success, he put aside his doubts and agreed to run. With Roosevelt smoothing the way, Taft easily won the Republican nomination. In the campaign, which he regarded as "a nightmare," he promised to continue the Roosevelt policies at home and abroad: "For the past ten years," the candidate proclaimed, "he and I have on every essential point stood in the heartiest agreement, shoulder to shoulder." He entered upon his presidential duties on 4 March 1909.

Taft's rise had been quick and steady—he was only 51 when he reached the White House. But his advance had been accomplished almost entirely without recourse to politics. Taft got to be president because other men recognized his abilities and appointed him to offices of trust. Not counting a perfunctory campaign for reelection to his Ohio judgeship in 1888, Taft had never been elected to anything before winning the White House. If his administrative, diplomatic, and judicial experience was wide and valuable, his knowledge of rough-and-tumble practical politics was narrow indeed.

## CAUGHT BY THE TARIFF AND UNCLE JOE CANNON

Practical politics, however, were destined to be particularly important during Taft's administration. The Republican party was in the midst of a painful and growing split. A powerful and conservative wing of the party, centering primarily in the East, tightly controlled power in both houses of Congress. Meanwhile, a progressive midwestern and western wing was rapidly increasing in strength. The battle cries of progressivism were growing stronger across the nation, and voters kept sending to Washington eloquent and energetic voices for social, political, and economic change. During the first decade of the century, progressive demands filled the air: to control the wealthy, help the poor, regulate the abuses of corporations, enhance democratic processes, conserve natural resources, and enlist government in a host of unprecedented activities to combat the dislocations of an industrial and urban society. Theodore Roosevelt managed to contain the division in the party by virtue of his enormous popularity and his willingness, at least until near the end of his presidency, to shout reform boldly while behaving with studied moderation. Nor was the party's progressive element yet at the height of its strength while Roosevelt was president.

Taft inherited the full brunt of the Republican split but few of his predecessor's gifts for managing it. The Colonel had been colorful, dramatic, energetic, and widely loved. Taft was slow, almost lethargic, giving the impression of laziness—on the day of his inauguration he weighed around 330 pounds. He lacked the knack of winning the hearts of the populace and liked to hide on the golf course. Instead of flare, he had a genial affability that made him effective among acquaintances, but even there his good nature rendered him reluctant to offend people he liked, even if they opposed his views. He entirely lacked Roosevelt's skill in self-publicity, in dramatizing issues, in engaging the nation's attention.

Taft began his administration by declining to join the House progressives, who would soon boldly call themselves "insurgents," in their attempt to unseat the archconservative speaker, Joseph Cannon. Taft personally disliked the uncouth and dictatorial Cannon but was unwilling to endanger his entire legislative program by supporting a probably unsuccessful attempt to remove him from office. If the president's reluctance to join the Republican rebels in the matter of the speakership raised some eyebrows among them, the next thing he did aroused them to fury.

Taft chose to tackle the nettlesome issue of the tariff, an area of legislative activity that had caused nothing but trouble for more than a century. In the Republican platform, in his campaign, and in his inaugural address, Taft had stressed the need to lower tariff rates. On 15 March, eleven days after taking office, Taft summoned a special session of Congress to adjust the rates downward. Unfortunately for him, the powers in Congress were firmly on the side of protectionism, not on the side of freer trade. Nelson Aldrich in the Senate and Speaker Cannon and Sereno Payne in the House were determined to defend the Republican party's tradition of maintaining high rates as protection for domestic industry. By the time the Payne-Aldrich tariff passed, on 5 August, the technical problems of rate fixing had fallen victim to special interests and the usual variety of horse trading.

Taft not only signed the bill, he had the temerity to go around the country praising it: In Minnesota he called it "the best tariff bill the Republican party has ever passed." To progressives, for whom the tariff was a symbol of special privilege, greed, and indifference to consumers, it was the ultimate betrayal. After the tariff fiasco of 1909, it seemed obvious to progressives that Taft had thrown in with the Old Guard, and a breach opened between them that was to grow ever wider.

## THE PINCHOT-BALLINGER AFFAIR

Relations grew even more strained after a bitter battle over conservation. The Pinchot-Ballinger controversy arose at the end of 1909 and captured enormous national attention through the first half of 1910. President Roosevelt and his friend and adviser on conservation matters, chief forester Gifford Pinchot, had withdrawn from entry in the public domain millions of acres in forest reserves and future water-power sites. Taft, who was in general sympathy with conservationist goals, retained Pinchot as chief forester, but dropped James Garfield, Roosevelt's secretary of the interior, in favor of Richard A. Ballinger, a progressive from Washington state. Taft and Ballinger, convinced that Roosevelt and Pinchot had exceeded their legal authority in making their withdrawals from the public lands, moved to restore some of them to public sale and development. This was the beginning of animosity between Pinchot, firmly established in the department of agriculture, and Ballinger, in the department of the interior.

Things finally exploded over the leasing of coal lands in Alaska. Louis Glavis, a minor official of the land office, believed Ballinger to be part of a conspiracy to lease 5,000 acres in Alaska to a man named Cunningham, who would then transfer the land to the powerful Morgan-Guggenheim mining syndicate. As an attorney, Ballinger had once done work for Cunningham. Glavis brought his suspicions to Pinchot, who launched spirited public attacks on those in the capital who would despoil the nation's natural resources. Glavis also laid his findings before Taft. After studying Ballinger's reply to the charges, Taft defended Ballinger and agreed that Glavis should be fired. In November, Glavis took his story to *Collier's* magazine. Pinchot defended Glavis and by January 1910, Taft had no choice but to fire him, too. That action produced two immediate results: Congress held hearings to get to the bottom of a matter that was by now causing considerable public excitement. And the firing of Pinchot drove a serious (and predictable) wedge between Taft and Roosevelt.

By the time the joint congressional committee began its hearings on 26 January, Taft believed the insurgents were allied with Pinchot, and the insurgents believed Taft and Ballinger were anticonservationist allies of the Old Guard. Even though the joint committee eventually exonerated Taft and Ballinger by a narrow and partisan majority, Taft's reputation suffered badly from a revelation made during the hearings. Louis D. Brandeis, a reform attorney from Boston, had been hired to appear before the committee by *Collier's*, which feared a lawsuit if Ballinger should be vindicated. In poring over the voluminous record, the sharp-eyed Brandeis caught Taft, Attorney General George Wickersham, and Wickersham's assistant, Oscar Lawler, in a shabby scheme to predate a document to create the false impression that Taft had reached his conclusion on Glavis only after studying that document. On the basis of that revelation, writes historian Paolo Coletta, "Taft was laid wide open to charges of being a liar and forger in the public press, which thereupon 'convicted' him and 'vindicated' Pinchot and Glavis."

Just as ominous for Taft's future as the beating he took in the press was the second result of the debacle. Both Pinchot and Norman Hapgood, the managing editor of *Collier's*, hurried to Europe, where Roosevelt was touring after his adventure in Africa, and laid their complaints before the former president. By contending that Taft had aligned himself shamelessly with the Old Guard and against the progressives, and that he had betrayed the Roosevelt policies and record, the two men sowed the seeds of animosity and suspicion between the two former friends.

## THE TAFT RECORD

Much of the progressives' criticism against President Taft was far from fair. Any impartial examination of his administration reveals the extent to which he was sincerely committed to progressive goals. Roosevelt had instituted antitrust suits against 44 corporations; Taft initiated 90 such suits. Taft also attempted to gain a "federal incorporation" act and a federal corporation commission, both aimed at better control of corporations; Congress rejected both initiatives. Although it was virtually unnoticed at the time, Taft secured as a part of the Payne-Aldrich tariff bill a tax on corporations earning more than $5,000, a critical move in the direction of investigating the earnings and regulating the activities of corporations. He also recommended what became, after considerable modification by the progressives, the Mann-Elkins Act. That act, passed in June 1910, put telephone, telegraph, cable, and wireless companies under the jurisdiction of the Interstate Commerce Commission. It also created a court of commerce (discontinued in 1913) to hear appeals concerning rates. Taft established two new commissions as well. The first was to investigate corporate stock-issuing practices, the second was to study the cost of production at home and abroad so that tariff rates could be fixed more scientifically. As far as conservation was concerned, Taft secured a law that permitted the president to withdraw lands pending congressional determination of their future, and he promptly withdrew 8.5 million acres from the public domain. He also successfully urged Congress to appropriate $20 million for reclamation.

Other measures initiated, encouraged, or endorsed by Taft should also have served to validate his progressivism. He was an unceasing advocate of governmental efficiency, particularly in the postal system. In 1910 and 1911 his commission on economy and efficiency prepared more than a hundred reports on ways to streamline the federal government and improve the budget-making process. He wanted to limit the use of injunctions in labor disputes and increase the number of federal workers covered under the merit system. He approved a system of postal savings banks that would pay depositors interest. In June 1910 he signed the Mann Act, which prohibited the transportation of women across state lines for immoral purposes—the so-called white slave act to police more effectively the business of prostitution. One could make a strong case that Taft had accomplished more for the cause of progressive reform in four years than Roosevelt had done in seven. But the progressives had decisively turned against him by the summer of 1910 and, given his distaste for political brawling and his ineptitude in the techniques of building public opinion, Taft could never persuade the American people that he was as interested in reform as they seemed to be.

## DOLLAR DIPLOMACY

Taft entered the White House with more experience in international affairs than most American presidents have had. His work in the Philippines, combined with his diplomatic assignments as Roosevelt's secretary of war, made him almost a fully seasoned diplomat. He chose as his secretary of state Philander Chase Knox, a diminutive, wealthy corporation lawyer from Pennsylvania. Knox had served as McKinley's attorney general and remained as an important adviser to Roosevelt. For a while he was mentioned as a rival to Taft for the 1908 Republican nomination. Knox was intelligent, efficient, and devoted to public affairs, but he had little experience in international relations. In the area of foreign policy, Taft is best remembered for his statement about the need to substitute "dollars for bullets." Abbreviated into the catch-phrase "Dollar Diplomacy," the expression had two general meanings. First, it meant furthering and protecting U.S. business interests abroad:

"Today," Secretary Knox remarked, "diplomacy works for trade." Second, Dollar Diplomacy meant using those interests to further large U.S. policy purposes. It would be hard to argue that the dollar-driven foreign policies constructed by Taft and Knox were unqualified successes.

In eastern Asia, Taft departed significantly from the policies of Theodore Roosevelt. His predecessor admired the Japanese and was contemptuous of China. Taft (who, in 1905, echoed Theodore Roosevelt's offhand ethnic insults by blithely asserting that "a Jap is first of all a Jap and would be glad to aggrandize himself at the expense of anybody") reversed these feelings. Taft respected the Chinese and was one of many turn-of-the-century Americans mesmerized by visions of the United States exploiting the limitless Chinese market. His administration therefore committed itself to pursuing, with more enthusiasm than Roosevelt had, the Open Door Policy of John Hay and to preserving the territorial integrity of China. The most obvious threat to the latter was the influence of Japan and Russia in Manchuria. Thinking that the best way to counter Japanese influence was to encourage U.S. capital investment in China, Taft pressured China to accept U.S. bankers on an equal footing with those of the other economic powers.

At the end of 1909, Knox and Taft ineptly attempted to push Japan out of southern Manchuria by having a consortium of bankers buy the Japanese railroad and turn it over to the Chinese government. The administration overestimated both the degree to which the other powers, particularly Britain, would cooperate in this venture and the willingness of Japan and Russia to pull out. The policy had the opposite effect of the one intended. In 1911 Russia and Japan recognized each other's spheres of influence in Manchuria and, contrary to American hopes, drew closer together in the face of U.S. interference. Another result of the Taft policy was to convert Japan from a power friendly to the United States, as it had been under Roosevelt, to one suspicious of American motives and methods.

If Taft and Knox failed in Asia while trying to reverse Roosevelt's policies, they faltered in the Caribbean and Central America while trying to continue them. In December 1904 Roosevelt had announced his "corollary" to the Monroe Doctrine. To forestall European powers from entering the Western Hemisphere to collect debts owed to them by Latin American nations, it might be necessary, Roosevelt said, for the United States to intervene and manage the affairs of the incompetent nation. Roosevelt's corollary (which converted the Monroe Doctrine from a warning against European intervention in the Western Hemisphere to a warning that the United States itself might in fact intervene) was first applied to the Dominican Republic in January 1905. The United States took over the customs collection of that nation and undertook to settle the debts owed to European creditors. The takeover seemed to be working as Taft entered the White House—the Dominican debt was being paid, trade was increasing, and the government was stable. An assassination in 1911 ended the period of Dominican stability, but before that happened, Taft and Knox applied Roosevelt's corollary in other places in the region.

Taft's attempt to apply the policy in Nicaragua had disastrous results. A dictator, Jose Santos Zelaya, whom Americans suspected of harboring designs of conquest on his neighbors and who tried to cancel U.S. concessions, had been forced to resign in 1909 by a combination of local insurrection and pressure from the United States. The need for stability and good relations was greatly increased by the emergence of a momentous U.S. interest in the neighborhood: the Panama canal, now rapidly nearing completion. Taft then did in Nicaragua what Roosevelt had done in the Dominican Republic—he arranged to refinance the country's European debts, provided a loan from U.S. bankers, and took over the customs collection. When, in the summer of 1912, the regime that the state department supported faced an insurrection of its own, Taft sent in 2,700 marines—making it clear

that even if dollars were preferred to bullets, bullets could still serve a purpose. Intervention, particularly of the military variety, naturally aroused in Latin American countries a deep antagonism and suspicion toward the giant to the north. Nevertheless, before leaving office Taft and Knox also attempted to invoke the Roosevelt corollary and the Monroe Doctrine in Guatemala and Honduras.

Taft also had to deal with special problems involving the nation's closest neighbors, north and south. In the summer of 1910 and again in early 1911, he tried to secure an agreement with Canada that would have lowered tariff barriers on a reciprocal basis. Ironically, the same midwestern Republican progressives who had denounced Taft for not lowering tariff rates in the Payne-Aldrich bill, opposed the Canadian agreement because their rural constituents feared a flood of cheap Canadian agricultural produce. The reciprocity arrangement was favored by Democrats, eastern Republicans, and particular economic interests (such as newspapers hoping to acquire cheap Canadian wood pulp), and a special session of Congress eventually passed the necessary legislation. By then, however, a wave of nationalist sentiment had swept over Canadian politics and the Conservative party, capitalizing on fears of U.S. influence and even possible annexation, won power and killed the reciprocity effort.

Finally, when revolutionary disturbances erupted along the U.S.-Mexican border, Taft resisted strident calls for armed retaliation, even after some Americans were killed on U.S. soil. He massed troops along the border, adopted a policy of cautious observation, and bequeathed the Mexican problem to his successor, Woodrow Wilson.

## REPUBLICAN DEBACLE

By midsummer of 1910, the Republican party was in shambles. Roosevelt returned from abroad in June and was immediately besieged by loyal supporters angry at his successor. He maintained a polite distance from Taft, but inevitably, snubs and fancied-snubs occurred. Roosevelt embarked on a well-publicized, sixteen-state speaking tour of the West, and some of his remarks might easily have been interpreted as criticism of the man who had replaced him. Slights, even unintentional ones, festered into deepening resentments. Soon each man was more than ready to think the worst of the other old friend. Roosevelt gravitated steadily to the left; Taft steadily to the right. By autumn Taft had alienated almost every important segment of the party except the stand-pat, largely eastern, conservatives, and the stage was set for a crushing, double humiliation in the off-year elections. First came the Republican primaries. Despite Taft's efforts (sometimes behind the scenes) to purge the party of insurgents, no fewer than forty regular, Taft-supporting Republicans running for House seats had been defeated by Republican rebels by the time the primaries were over. Not a single insurgent who was up for reelection lost. And the primary disaster was merely a prelude to the general election in November. For the first time since 1892, the Democrats took control of the House of Representatives. And although the Republicans had a formal majority in the Senate, they could not count on a majority because progressive Republican senators often voted with the Democrats. Twenty-six of the forty-six states elected Democratic governors in 1910.

Republican progressives were certain, by the middle of 1911, that they could not support Taft in the upcoming presidential election. Some favored Robert M. La Follette, the dynamic progressive senator from Wisconsin; others supported former president Theodore Roosevelt. In mid-February 1912, when La Follette's health collapsed, the progressives turned overwhelmingly to Roosevelt. "He is surrounded by so many sycophants and neurotics who feed his vanity and influence his judgment," wrote Taft, "that his usual good political sense is at fault."

Roosevelt—still young and ambitious, unable by virtue of his restless temperament to stand for very long on the sidelines, urged and fawned over by rank-and-file Republicans from across the nation—announced on 24 February that he would be a candidate for the presidency. He expressed the hope that "so far as possible the people may be given the chance, through direct primaries to express their preference." It was an understandable hope on Roosevelt's part; Taft lacked every trait that made Roosevelt so irresistibly attractive to so many Americans. Thirteen states held Republican primary elections in 1912, and the verdict of everyday Republicans became perfectly clear. Roosevelt received more than 1.5 million votes; Taft, 761,000. In the matter of convention delegates, La Follette, even in poor health, received 36, Taft won 48, and Roosevelt took 278. The magnetic Roosevelt beat Taft even in Ohio, where the Taft family had been prominent for so long; the president made more than one hundred speeches there, but when the primary votes were counted, he had lost 34 out of 42 delegates to his opponent.

By this time, the normally easygoing Taft was mad enough to fight. He might have lost the popularity contest, but he could still control the Chicago convention opening on 18 June. In the days of the solidly Democratic South, a Republican incumbent could always count on a large bloc of southern delegates, and in Taft's case, he had appointed many of them to office. As an incumbent, he also controlled the convention apparatus, including the all-important national committee. Of the 254 seats that were contested when the convention opened, the committee awarded 235 of them to delegates supporting the president. The chairmanship of the convention went to Elihu Root, an influential Taft man. On 22 June the nomination, to no one's surprise, went to Taft on the first ballot.

It was, of course, more than Roosevelt could stomach. Claiming that the very man he himself had made president in 1908 had stolen the convention from the people of the United States, Roosevelt gave the order and his delegates walked out and split the party. On 5 August, also in Chicago, the dissatisfied Republicans formed the Progressive party, and Theodore Roosevelt, claiming he was as fit as a bull moose, became its nominee. Between the two

Chicago conventions, the Democrats, in a dramatic and marathon convention of their own, nominated Governor Woodrow Wilson of New Jersey. The Republican division cleared the way for one of the most dramatic presidential contests in U.S. history—but it was essentially between Wilson and Roosevelt. President Taft, finding the whole process demeaning and distasteful, decided not to make a single speech during the campaign. "I think I might as well give up so far as being a candidate is concerned," he wrote his wife Nellie. "There are so many people in the country who don't like me." Like many others, he could see the result in advance. His one satisfaction was that his mere presence in the race would prevent the "dangerous demagogue" Roosevelt from returning to the presidency.

## TAFT'S PHILOSOPHY OF GOVERNMENT

Taft left the White House with a particular view of executive power in the U.S. system of government, a view forged, in part, under the pressure of his rivalry with Roosevelt, who had a much different opinion. No doubt Taft's book, *Our Chief Magistrate and His Powers* (1916), articulated the so-called literalist position more starkly than was actually manifested during his presidency. But, in contrast to Roosevelt's notions of presidential activism and stewardship, Taft—the constitutional scholar and former (and future) member of the judiciary—took a more cautious and legalistic position. Being elected president, he insisted, did not mean acquiring an unlimited license to exercise powers in the name of the people. Every legitimate use of presidential power had to be directly derived from a particular clause in the Constitution.

Some have tried to explain the failure of Taft's administration in terms of his limited view of executive power, his tendency to see the presidency as an isolated and independent branch of the government with carefully circumscribed duties in the lawmaking process. It is true that his concept of presidential leadership was "weaker"—more reserved, ceremonial, and dignified—than

Roosevelt's; it is also true that a different view might have won him a warmer relationship with the citizenry and spared him some pain. But Taft's frustrations as president stemmed much more directly from the civil war in his party and the steady movement of public opinion in a progressive direction than from a philosophy of restraint. Donald F. Anderson, a close student of Taft's philosophy of executive leadership, reminds us that the views in Taft's book have to be read in conjunction with his judicial opinion, ten years later, in *Myers v. United States*. There, Taft boldly asserted the powers of the presidency, at least in the matter of the removal of federal officeholders.

Taft left the White House with few regrets. They had not been happy years for him, and he would never have undertaken the unpleasantness were it not for his strong sense of public duty and the persistent urging of an ambitious family. When Yale offered him the Kent Professorship in Constitutional Law (at around one-twentieth of his presidential salary), he joyfully returned to his alma mater. With a short interruption to undertake the joint-chairmanship of the War Labor Board, he gladly carried out his teaching duties in New Haven. On 30 June 1921 another Ohio Republican, Warren G. Harding, granted him his fondest and longest-lasting wish by nominating him to be the chief justice of the United States. He was at last in the job he had always desired. He brought to the court a set of conservative principles that he ably defended in his opinions. And he performed his duties with competence, administrative skill, and a conciliatory spirit. The only man in U.S. history to hold both the presidency and the chief justiceship, William Howard Taft remained at his final post for as long as his health permitted, indeed longer than he should have. He reluctantly retired on 3 February 1930; a month later he was dead. One of Taft's best biographers, Henry F. Pringle, has written that "before he died, it is a safe assumption, his quadrennium in the presidency had faded like an evil dream into those mists which memory no longer penetrates."

## BIBLIOGRAPHY

Anderson, Donald F. *William Howard Taft: A Conservative's Conception of the Presidency* (Cornell University Press, 1973).

Broderick, Francis L. *Progressivism at Risk: Electing a President in 1912* (Greenwood Press, 1989).

Burton, David H. *William Howard Taft: In the Public Service* (Krieger, 1986).

Coletta, Paolo. *The Presidency of William Howard Taft* (University Press of Kansas, 1973).

Hicks, Frederick C. *William Howard Taft: Yale Professor and New Haven Citizen* (Yale University Press, 1945).

Manners, William. *T. R. and Will: A Friendship That Split the Republican Party* (Harcourt, Brace, and Jovanovich, 1969).

Mason, Alpheus T. *William Howard Taft: Chief Justice* (Simon & Schuster, 1965).

Mowry, George. "The Election of 1912." In *History of American Presidential Elections, 1789–1968*, edited by Arthur M. Schlesinger, Jr., and Fred Israel, 4 vols. (Chelsea House, 1971).

Pringle, Henry F. *The Life and Times of William Howard Taft* (Farrar and Rinehart, 1939).

Scholes, Walter V., and Marie V. Scholes. *The Foreign Policies of the Taft Administration* (University of Missouri Press, 1970).

★★★ 28 ★★★

# THOMAS WOODROW WILSON
# 1913–1921

*John Milton Cooper, Jr.*

*Born 29 December 1856 in Staunton, Virginia, to Joseph Ruggles Wilson and Jessie Janet Woodrow Wilson; educated at Princeton University, Princeton, New Jersey (B.A. 1879), University of Virginia Law School (did not take a degree), and Johns Hopkins University (Ph.D. 1885); married Ellen Louise Axson, 24 June 1885, in Savannah, Georgia; three children; married Edith Bolling Galt, 18 December 1915, Washington, D.C.; elected president in 1912 on the Democratic ticket with Thomas Riley Marshall of Indiana, receiving 6,293,454 popular votes and 435 electoral college ballots, over the Republican ticket of William Howard Taft of Ohio and James Schoolcraft Sherman of New York (3,484,980 popular votes and 8 electoral ballots) and the Progressive party ticket of Theodore Roosevelt of New York and Hiram Johnson of California (4,119,538 popular votes and 88 electoral ballots); reelected in 1916 with Marshall, receiving 9,129,606 popular votes and 277 electoral ballots, over the Republican ticket of Charles Evans Hughes of New York and Charles Warren Fairbanks of Indiana (8,538,221 popular votes and 254 electoral ballots); died 3 February 1924 in Washington, D.C.; buried in National Cathedral, Washington, D.C.*

Thomas Woodrow Wilson was one of the most unusual figures ever to hold the office of president of the United States. He was the only professional educator and holder of the Ph.D. degree, having served as a professor and university president and written and lectured widely. He was a latecomer to politics; he ran for his first office, successfully, at the age of 53, just two years before becoming president. Moreover, unlike other chief executives with little or no experience running for office, Wilson had held no official appointments, either. Finally, he lacked both strong personal ties to any region of the country and deep ancestral roots in the United States. All of those circumstances, combined with his personality, bred qualities of detachment and reflectiveness in Wilson that have been rare in American political leaders since the 1820s. For the most part, those qualities served him well in his public career and helped to make him one of the strongest and most effective presidents since the Civil War.

## SOUTHERN UPBRINGING AND RELIGION

His birth in Staunton, Virginia, on 29 December 1856 made Wilson the last of the six men who claimed nativity in the state called the Mother of Presidents. Unlike the other five, however, he was only an accidental Virginian and barely that. The son of a Presbyterian minister who had moved to Virginia only a few years earlier, "Tommy" Wilson left his native state when he was less than two years old and spent his boyhood and youth in Georgia and South Carolina, where his father, Joseph Ruggles Wilson, held pastorates and a seminary teaching post. The elder Wilson was a polished orator, pulpit performer, and worldly man of the cloth who had been born and raised in Ohio as the son of Scotch-Irish immigrants. Woodrow, the boy's middle name, which he used exclusively after college, came from the family of his mother, Janet ("Jessie") Woodrow. She was the English-born daughter of a Scottish Presbyterian clergyman who had immigrated to the United States in 1837, settling in Ohio but later moving to South Carolina. His mother's English birth made Wilson the only president with a foreign-born parent since Andrew Jackson and the only one born after 1776 with no American-born grandparents. Likewise, the repeated moves of his father and his mother's family made him one of the few presidents without strong ties to a particular section of the country and the only one who in his own person would straddle the division between North and the South.

That sectional division, which exploded into the Civil War when Wilson was only 4 years old, formed one of the two major influences of his childhood and later played a big role in his political career. His father became an ardent convert to the southern cause. During the war, he served as a chaplain with the Confederate army and turned his church in Augusta, Georgia, into a military hospital. In 1864, 7-year-old Tommy himself witnessed the blue-clad soldiers of Sherman's army occupy his hometown. This upbringing left a deep impression on Wilson, who later remarked, "The South is the only place where things do not have to be explained to me." Although he spent all but three years of his life after the age of 18 outside the South, the South left a permanent mark on his life: He married a woman from Georgia, studied law at the University of Virginia, practiced law briefly in Atlanta, evidently never thought of joining any party except the Democrats, and chose many of his closest political associates from the South. But the North also left its mark: Even during his childhood, Wilson's family maintained their ties to northern relatives, and, after a year at Davidson College in North Carolina, Wilson received his higher education in the North, first at Princeton and later at Johns Hopkins, and he pursued his academic career in Pennsylvania, Connecticut, and New Jersey.

The other, even stronger influence on Wilson's early years was Presbyterianism. He was the son, grandson, nephew, and eventually son-in-law of Presbyterian ministers. As an adult, his strong-jawed face and piercing gray eyes behind pince-nez glasses and his polished, yet fervent, speaking style made him look and sound like a clergyman. His upbringing was in churches and manses and on the campus of a theological seminary, where not only his father, but also his uncle James Woodrow, the family's intellectual star, taught. He was steeped in an atmosphere of learned, liberal Protestantism in general and of Calvinist doctrine in particular, and this deep religious grounding would become one of the most noticed and most misunderstood aspects of Wilson's public career. His appearance and style made him seem much more of an idealistic crusader and "political preacher" than he really was. The young Wilson never considered entering the ministry, and he took little interest in theology. Although he was a cheerful fatalist about his own life and believed himself an instrument of God's will, he, unlike more evangelically influenced politicians of his time, rejected such "moral" reforms as prohibition. He eschewed mixing religion in politics and took a benign though critical view of material self-interest in human affairs.

## A STUDENT OF POLITICS

"The profession I chose was politics," recalled the young Wilson in the early 1880s. Politics had fascinated him from an early age. Family lore recounted his hanging a picture of the British prime minister William Ewart Gladstone in his bedroom and composing a calling card that read, "Thomas Woodrow Wilson, Senator from Virginia." He also developed a high degree of intellectual independence. As a college student, he slighted Princeton's prescribed classical curriculum in favor of independent reading, which included his discovery of the English writer Walter Bagehot, who argued for the study of how politics really worked rather than instruction in formal institutions. Wilson made this his own approach to both the study and the practice of politics, and he expressed his newfound views in his first magazine article, which was published just after his graduation in 1879. The young man also rejected such fashionable notions as blaming the shortcomings of American

democracy on universal suffrage and political parties, both of which he found necessary and beneficent if properly used. More remarkable still for a white southerner growing up so soon after the Civil War, Wilson came to believe that the Confederate defeat had been a blessing in disguise and that African Americans were not inherently inferior to whites. "Ever since I have had independent judgments of my own, I have been a Federalist," Wilson later asserted, by which he meant that he favored strong central authority and rejected the prevalent southern Democratic fealty to states rights and limited government.

As an aspiring politician, "the profession I entered was the law. I entered the one because I thought it would lead to the other." Pressure from his father also played a part in choosing that path for the young Princeton graduate, who had already shown strong inclinations toward writing and scholarship. Wilson spent a year and a half in law school at the University of Virginia before leaving without taking a degree to study on his own and to set up practice with another young man in the bustling city of Atlanta. This legal interlude lasted four years, during which Wilson again devoted much time to his own reading and writing. He found the law intellectually narrow and sterile as a discipline and boring as an occupation, and in 1883, he gladly left both the bar and the South for graduate study at Johns Hopkins. All was not wasted in his years in Atlanta, however, because while on legal business in Georgia he met and fell in love with Ellen Axson, the daughter of a Presbyterian minister. The couple became engaged before Wilson left for Baltimore, and they were married in 1885. A shrewd, strong, warm woman, Ellen shared with Wilson a happy, devoted marriage. They had three daughters, and, since Ellen's mother and father had died by the time they married, they also raised her two younger brothers and younger sister.

Academic life differed from Wilson's expectations of it. Although he believed that he was renouncing office seeking, he hoped to become "an outside force" in politics, by which he meant a commentator, expert adviser, and perhaps appointive officeholder. This parapolitical role never materialized, largely because Wilson grew absorbed in writing and lecturing about politics and government. For the next two decades he took no part in politics except to vote, and, with one exception, he did not pay close attention to the major issues of the 1880s, 1890s, and early 1900s. The exception came at the turn of the century, when he broke with most fellow Democrats to become an ardent imperialist and to regret not having fought in the Spanish-American War. In much of his teaching, Wilson did seek to improve the tone and style of politics by directing better-educated young men toward that career, and in 1901 he briefly collaborated with then Vice President Theodore Roosevelt in a project to interest Harvard, Yale, and Princeton students in public service.

In his early years at John Hopkins, the German-inspired "scientific" ethos championed there had left him cold, but he was allowed to resume his independent work habits. In less than a year, he wrote and got accepted for publication his first book, *Congressional Government*. Wilson almost missed the distinction of becoming the only president with a Ph.D., inasmuch as it took the combined persuasion of his wife, professors, and first employers to get him to submit the book as his dissertation and undergo to the formality of a final examination. *Congressional Government* would remain Wilson's best book, and it both embodied his approach to the study of politics and foreshadowed his approach to the practice of politics. True to Bagehot's influence, Wilson analyzed where power really resided in the American system—mainly in congressional committees, he argued—and he became an early practitioner of comparative government by judging his country's system less efficient and less accountable than the British parliamentary system. As reforms, he advocated bringing serious public business onto the floor of Congress for debate and using parties as bridges between the executive and legislative branches, with the

president acting as a prime minister. (Three decades later, Wilson would get the chance to follow his own advice, and the prime ministerial model would serve him well during most of his two terms in the White House.) His later writings included a political science textbook, two works of American history, and a large number of articles—many of which he delivered first as public lectures—in scholarly journals and intellectually oriented magazines. During the 1890s, Wilson experienced a second great intellectual awakening when he reread Edmund Burke and grasped his vision of organic, nonideological politics. Burke's inspiration was to be the basis for what Wilson planned as his great work, provisionally entitled "Philosophy of Politics." He shelved that project after 1902, first to attend to academic administration and then to politics.

## THE ACADEMIC LIFE

Absorption in the institutional side of academic life came as another surprise to Wilson. As with many who became professors then and later, he was initially attracted to the academic life by the possibility of having free time for research and writing, while teaching and administration seemed incidental. Lecturing offered opportunities for public speaking, at which he excelled both in the classroom and on the public lecture circuit, where he earned fees that often doubled his salary. Small-group and individual instruction suited Wilson less well, and he spawned no coteries of scholarly disciples, although he did influence and act as a mentor to the historian Frederick Jackson Turner. Wilson taught at four institutions, two years each at Bryn Mawr College and Wesleyan University, part time for several years in the 1890s at Johns Hopkins, and full time after 1890 at Princeton.

Although Wilson soon chafed at the somnolence and intellectual conservatism of the Princeton administration, he took little part in the reformist intrigues of younger faculty and trustees, and he devoted scant thought to the vexing educational debate of the time between proponents of German-style specialized research and defenders of

English-inspired liberal arts and classical training. Instead, Wilson worked hard at his writing and public lecturing and remained on good terms with almost everyone in the increasingly divided Princeton community. His unexpected elevation to the presidency of the institution in 1902 came as a tribute to his acceptability to all sides and to his esteem beyond the campus. The Princeton presidency opened unexpected horizons for Wilson, especially in two directions. One was shaping and managing an organization; the other was the high-profile visibility that attracted the press and opened a path into politics.

Wilson's orderly mind and disciplined work habits lent themselves readily to the normal tasks of administration, and he delegated major responsibilities to trusted lieutenants, the most important of whom was the mathematician Henry B. Fine. He appointed Fine to the main deanship, trusted him to oversee the scientific departments, and made him his right-hand man. Wilson showed a real flair for such expected duties as fundraising, faculty recruitment, and relations with the trustees and alumni. New buildings, star professors, and an expanded endowment all adorned his university presidency. Sectarianism and parochialism correspondingly waned, as the student body enrolled young men from all parts of the country and all religious persuasions, although no African Americans would come to Princeton for another four decades. Wilson deliberately broke the lingering grip of Presbyterianism on the faculty, as he drew in men of all Protestant denominations and appointed the first Catholic and the first Jew to the Princeton faculty.

Beyond making such predictable moves of a dynamic, progressive college president, he also set new standards of boldness and vision. An early goal was transforming Princeton from an old, socially prestigious but intellectually undemanding college into a front-rank university, capable of challenging Johns Hopkins and Harvard for primacy. He concocted three projects to serve that end. First, he grasped the nettles of combining liberal arts instruction with spe-cialized research, and small college intimacy with university challenges. His strategy was to create and recruit a separate junior faculty of fifty "preceptors" who would teach small groups of students. This project, which Wilson brought from inception to completion in two years, made him a hero to the Princeton community, the toast of the academic world, and moderately famous to a broader public.

Wilson next sought to enhance intellectual seriousness and excitement through establishing quadrangles in which students would live and study with professors and preceptors. Coincidentally, these quadrangles would also have supplanted the fraternity-style undergraduate clubs, which had come under fire for their exclusiveness and rowdiness. Opposition from wealthy alumni and second thoughts by influential trustees caused this project to fail after an initially promising start. This was Wilson's first setback in his Princeton presidency, but it won him still broader fame as a battler against snobbery and privilege.

Finally, Wilson became embroiled in a battle over where to house the students in Princeton's small but growing graduate school. He wanted these older, more serious students to live among the undergraduates, thereby, in his view, exerting a mature, sobering influence on their younger and less intellectually motivated peers. Pitted against him stood the graduate school's dean and founder, Andrew Fleming West, who had earlier entertained hopes for the presidency and now wanted to have a separate facility for his domain. Like many academic controversies, this one often looked to outsiders like a tempest in a teapot, but it reached a pitch of bitterness unmatched in many other walks of life. (Later, after he entered politics, Wilson often quipped that he found "real" politicians far more decent and easier to work with than academic ones.) The fight boiled down to a fundraising contest, and when West enlisted a succession of rich donors the press again depicted Wilson as a battler against wealth and privilege. Money ultimately talked loudest in West's favor in 1910, by which time faculty, trustees, and alumni had fallen into such envenomed factionalism that Wilson believed he must resign. Yet he had not failed. Dean Fine summed up his leadership best when he stated, "When all is said and in spite of controversies and other difficulties, Wilson *made* Princeton."

## GOVERNOR OF NEW JERSEY

The other unexpected vista that the Princeton University presidency opened to Wilson was politics. The office itself gave him far greater public visibility than his writing and lecturing had done. Once he embarked on his educational reforms, the press took greater notice, and once the controversies over the quadrangle plan and the graduate school erupted, reporters and commentators spread his fame further still, cloaking him with a socially reformist reputation. Even before those latter-day slants were put on Wilson, political kingmakers had spotted him. Within the Democratic party, a conservative faction was looking for a fresh new face to put up against both the agrarian-based reformers in their party and the more moderate but pungent anti–big business fulminations of the Republican president, Theodore Roosevelt. This articulate, highly respectable president of a leading university looked perfect to them. For his part, Wilson could hear opportunity knocking, and he responded with an effort to champion the conservative Democratic viewpoint. That effort fizzled both because Wilson could never bring himself sincerely to espouse this faction's states rights, limited-government ideology and because, like most observers, he saw that the political tide was running in the opposite or "progressive" direction. Still, Wilson stayed friendly enough with his party's conservatives to get their backing for the Democratic nomination for governor of New Jersey in 1910.

This gubernatorial nomination came as a heaven-sent chance to escape an intolerable predicament at Princeton. Deftly switching careers, Wilson reverted to his original ambition without missing a beat. Despite having enjoyed the sponsorship of conservatives and party bosses, he quickly proved himself an ardent progressive and a dynamic campaigner. He specifically advocated new measures of business regulation and taxation and direct primaries for all elective offices and generally promised to make government more open, accountable, and responsive to the people's wishes. Between the fame that had preceded him from Princeton and the dashing figure that he now cut on the campaign trail, Wilson rose to national political stature even before he won a landslide victory in the 1910 election. Nor did he wait for his inauguration as governor to live up to expectations of bold, progressive leadership, as he openly defied his erstwhile patrons and organized his party's legislators behind his program. Once in office, Wilson speedily enacted his campaign agenda and, when opponents balked at his next set of reform measures, he took his case to the people with a dramatic speaking tour. By the middle of 1911, this 54-year-old political neophyte was one of the hottest properties on the national scene, already conceded by many to be the front-runner for the Democratic presidential nomination in 1912.

## THE PRESIDENTIAL NOMINATION

Such a meteoric rise could not help but falter. A modest organization to promote Wilson's presidential candidacy coalesced around a group of people like himself, southern expatriates living in the North. They did not prove to be skilled political managers, and they fumbled until William Gibbs McAdoo, a highly successful New York businessman originally from Georgia, took control. Much of Wilson's backing came from more progressive, better-educated, white southerners, such as the North Carolina newspaper editor Josephus Daniels, who liked the governor's politics and relished the prospect of putting a native son in the White House. But others in Dixie—conservative states rights devotees and agrarian radicals alike—disliked Wilson, viewing him as not a "real" southerner but a turncoat who had adapted too much to northern ways.

Party professionals tolerated the newcomer's rise so long as it looked as though the Republicans were likely to win in 1912, as they had done consistently since 1896. By 1911, however, the Republicans' growing internecine strife had dimmed their prospects. In February 1912, when Roosevelt declared his candidacy for the nomination against his own hand-picked successor, President William Howard Taft, the Democratic nominee—whoever he was—looked like a sure winner. Wilson now faced competition from the party's two highest national officeholders, Speaker of the House Champ Clark of Missouri and the House majority leader, Representative Oscar W. Underwood of Alabama.

Of the two, Clark posed the more serious threat. He enjoyed backing from party organizations outside the South, and he entered the national convention with the largest number of delegates. Underwood mounted a strictly regional candidacy, backed by unreconstructed southerners of varied views, but he undercut Wilson in what should have been his natural base. As matters turned out, only the Democrats' antiquated and unloved two-thirds rule, sectional prejudice, and crass horse trading saved Wilson's political hide. On several ballots Clark won a majority of the delegates, which at a Republican convention would have given him the nomination. Fortunately for Wilson, his managers had made a pact against withdrawal in Clark's favor with Underwood's backers, who still preferred any southerner, even an expatriate. That ironclad agreement, together with McAdoo's tireless persuasion and deals with northern delegations, finally got Wilson the nomination after three days of balloting.

That victory contained a supreme irony. Roosevelt, who had meanwhile bolted the Republicans to run at the head of his new Progressive party, was contending that his former party was hopelessly reactionary and that the Democrats would prove their unfitness by nominating either a machine-picked hack or a southerner. Instead, for the most unprogressive reasons, the Democrats had chosen the candidate best calculated to spike the claim of Roosevelt and his Progressives that they were the only up-to-date, idealistic, and intellectually respectable reformers.

## THE 1912 CAMPAIGN

In the ensuing campaign, Wilson quickly proved how formidable a contender he was by matching Roosevelt, the reigning national political champion, blow for blow, while on a deeper level he engaged his great adversary in the finest philosophical debate ever witnessed in a presidential contest. Freed as he was from normal partisan constraints, the ex-president enunciated his program of the New Nationalism, which was an essentially conservative reform vision of transcending what he deplored as "the greed of the 'haves' versus the envy of the 'have-nots.'" Roosevelt advocated far-reaching measures of government intervention in the economy, coupled with an approach that favored regulating rather than breaking up big businesses, and he preached incessantly against "materialism," by which he meant pursuit of individual and group self-interest. Wilson, who received timely tactical advice from the Boston attorney and economic reformer Louis Brandeis, attacked his opponent's acceptance of bigness in business and advocated breaking up monopolies. More generally, Wilson painted a vision of social and economic renewal through dynamic but carefully superintended pursuit of self-interest. "I am for the man on the make, not the man who is already made," declared Wilson, who called his program the New Freedom.

The 1912 race teemed with color and excitement, including an assassination attempt on Roosevelt, which prompted Wilson to suspend campaigning until his opponent recovered from his wound. Each man struck at the other's vulnerable point. Roosevelt tried to pin the stigma of states rights and limited government on Wilson, who easily refuted the charge. Wilson in turn portrayed Roosevelt as a tool of big business, which forced the ex-president to retreat toward more of an antitrust position. Little difference separated them on specific reform measures, not even nationwide woman suffrage. Although Roosevelt endorsed woman suffrage and Wilson shunned it, neither man really cared much about the issue. (Wilson, two of whose daughters were suffragists, eventually came around and provided critical support in the passage of the Nineteenth Amendment.) Both candidates gave short shrift to African Americans, declining to address their organizations and ignoring their grievances. President Taft also stayed in the race as the Republican nominee. Taft wanted to prevent his supporters from voting for Roosevelt; he was successful, although he finished third, behind the Progressive nominee.

Wilson pulled no more than the normal Democratic vote, about 42 percent, but thanks to the Republican-Progressive split, that margin gave him an electoral college landslide and Democratic majorities in both houses of Congress. The only real surprise in the 1912 result came with the showing for the Socialist candidate Eugene Debs, who doubled his previous total to garner 6 percent of the vote, the biggest share of the electorate that a socialist would ever get.

The distribution of votes in 1912 really set the course of Wilson's domestic presidency. Shrewd politician that he had become, Wilson knew that to be reelected in 1916 and to retain Democratic congressional majorities, he needed to win over a large share of Roosevelt's Progressives. That necessity reinforced the overarching priority Wilson already placed on legislative leadership that relied almost exclusively on control and direction of his own party, with the administrative side of government taking second place. Cabinet appointments went mostly to loyal Democrats, headed by the party's three-time presidential nominee and ideological conscience since 1896, William Jennings Bryan, who became secretary of state. Early Wilson backers McAdoo and Daniels became heads of the Treasury and Navy, respectively. Overall, the new administration had a strong southern and southern expatriate flavor. One unfortunate consequence of this regional tilt was that some of the new cabinet members

attempted to introduce racial segregation into their departments. Although Wilson did not initiate these segregation moves, he permitted them to go forward, in keeping with his practice of delegating authority and giving wide administrative leeway to his lieutenants. Protests spearheaded by the newly founded National Association for the Advancement of Colored People succeeded in halting the effort, but both the number and status of African Americans in federal service fell drastically during Wilson's eight years in office.

## A DARING BEGINNING

In his pursuit of legislative leadership, Wilson executed a number of innovations. First, between the election in November 1912 and his inauguration in March 1913, he drew up a preliminary legislative program in consultation with party leaders; this was the first time an incoming president had ever done such a thing. Next, he called the newly elected Congress into session just one month after his inauguration, and, breaking the precedent begun by Thomas Jefferson, he appeared in person before a joint session. By that act, Wilson symbolically bridged the separation of powers between the executive and legislative branches. Thereafter, he regularly used speeches to Congress to discuss pressing issues and to lay down major policy pronouncements, in addition to delivering an annual State of the Union address. (By the end of his two terms, Wilson would have spoken to Congress more than any other president.) After convening Congress in April 1912, he kept the two houses in session continuously, with just one short recess, for eighteen months. That had never happened before, not even during the Civil War. Finally, and perhaps most important of all, Wilson established close working relations with his party's leaders on Capitol Hill, and he used his secretary, Joseph Tumulty, and key cabinet members, especially Secretary of State Bryan and Postmaster General Albert Burleson, as liaisons with congressional Democrats. The one-time theoretician of prime ministerial leadership was translating his ideas into practice.

## THE NEW FREEDOM

Wilson wrought spectacular feats. During this eighteen-month forced march he got Congress to pass three monumental pieces of legislation. The first was tariff revision, which was coupled with the first permanent and graduated federal income tax. This legislation got the president and his party off to an excellent start, both because they succeeded where Taft and the Republicans had failed four years earlier and because lobbyists' efforts to weaken the tariff reductions gave Wilson a chance to denounce their doings in a blaze of publicity. The income tax measure, made possible by the recently ratified Sixteenth Amendment, was ostensibly intended to offset lost revenue from the reduced tariffs, but its proponents, including Wilson, touted both the tax itself and its modestly graduated rates as ways to force richer people to return a fair share of their gains to the public purse.

The second piece of legislation concerned banking and currency reform. Recurrent financial panics, together with chronic shortages of money and credit in the South and West, had spawned a nationwide consensus in favor of establishing some kind of central bank and reserve system. Behind that consensus for change, however, lay disagreements among the most interested groups, particularly over whether the new system should be controlled by the government or by the banking industry and whether it should be centralized or decentralized into regional operations.

This legislation took the longest time to pass, occasioned the most heated debate, and tested Wilson's leadership most severely. He again sought expert advice from Brandeis and relied on Bryan to bring rebellious southern and western Democrats into line. He also had to practice patience and indulge in a bit of wheeling and dealing. Finally passed in January 1914, the Federal Reserve Act embodied a grand synthesis of public control and centralization through a board of governors, with banker participation and decentralization in naming some of the boards of nine regional banks. Though amended in the 1930s toward more centralized government authority, the Federal Reserve System remains nearly a century later the most powerful single factor in the U.S. economy.

Wilson's third big piece of legislation addressed the subject he and Roosevelt had debated in 1912—control of big business. A detailed law prohibiting practices in restraint of trade emerged as the Clayton Anti-Trust Act of 1914. The Clayton Act fulfilled the demands of southern and western reformers for a stronger legal attack on big business, and it also partially granted organized labor's wishes exempting unions from the act. Again on the advice of Brandeis, Wilson supplemented the antitrust law by getting Congress to create a new regulatory agency, the Federal Trade Commission, which drew upon Roosevelt's approach without embracing his approval of bigness.

This trinity of measures of 1913 and 1914 enacted the core of Wilson's New Freedom program, and they added up to the most impressive demonstration of legislative leadership by any president up to that time. Nor had Wilson finished. In 1916, he pushed through Congress another raft of reform measures. He unfurled his progressive colors, first by nominating Brandeis to the Supreme Court and by battling anti-Semitism and economic and legal conservatism to get him confirmed by the Senate. Then he followed with the first program of federal aid to agriculture; creation of federal agencies to oversee the U.S. Merchant Marine and advise on setting tariff rates; a prohibition of child labor in interstate commerce; higher and more steeply graduated income taxes; and a law establishing an eight-hour workday for interstate railroad workers.

This second display of Wilsonian legislative leadership in some ways surpassed the first. A conservative Republican comeback in the 1914 elections had reduced the Democratic majorities in Congress while also virtually wiping out the Progressives. At the same time, Wilson was dealing with dangerous problems in national defense and foreign affairs, especially regarding World War I. Clashes over foreign policy had impelled Bryan to resign from the cabinet and fight Wilson for control of the Democratic party. To succeed, as Wilson did, in the face of such obstacles and distractions offered the strongest testimony to the president's pursuit of the prime ministerial model.

## MEXICO: THE OPENING ACT IN FOREIGN AFFAIRS

"It would be an irony of fate if my administration had to deal chiefly with foreign affairs," Wilson had remarked to a friend shortly after the 1912 election. That irony began to overtake him almost as soon as he took the oath of office. The revolution in Mexico, which had fallen into internecine violence in February 1913, confronted Wilson with pressures to intervene and found him torn between past imperialist leanings and newfound appreciation for strivings for democracy. The unfortunate incident at Vera Cruz in 1914, involving U.S. sailors and marines in a bloody battle with Mexican troops, strengthened the president's resolve to avoid intervention if at all possible, despite clamoring from Roosevelt and Republican warhawks. Nonintervention proved impossible in 1916, when the Mexican dissident leader Pancho Villa raided U.S. territory, thereby provoking the dispatch of a punitive expedition under General John J. Pershing on an unsuccessful mission to catch and punish the offender. Mexico provided a constant irritant in foreign affairs throughout Wilson's first term, and it offered him his first experiences with the violence and revolutionary upheavals that would dominate world politics for the rest of his presidency and most of the twentieth century.

## THE GUNS OF AUGUST

The greatest violence and upheaval of all erupted in August 1914 with the outbreak of World War I. This was an especially painful time for the president. His wife Ellen died after a lingering illness just as the war started, and he lived through an agony of grief for several months. Fortunately for his happiness and emotional balance, Wilson

met and fell in love with a Washington widow, Edith Bolling Galt, in 1915, and he courted her by making her his closest confidant and adviser. Over the objections of political advisers, Wilson married Edith Galt at the end of 1915. By that time, U.S. relations with the warring nations in Europe had burgeoned into the most pressing problem on the president's policy agenda and a major domestic political issue.

In 1914 the war had seemed remote to most Americans, and the main diplomatic concerns had involved trade, given the British blockade of the Central Powers. Both Wilson and Secretary of State Bryan had moved cautiously to avoid trouble with the belligerents, especially the British, and to keep the door open for possible U.S. mediation of the war. The situation started to change early in 1915, when the Germans commenced submarine warfare, killing a few Americans in their first attacks. Before the Wilson administration could devise a response, a German submarine sank the British liner *Lusitania* on 7 May 1915, killing 128 Americans, causing a diplomatic crisis, and raising the danger that the United States might be dragged into the war.

For the next two years, Wilson trod a difficult, dangerous path, trying to satisfy what he called his people's "double wish" to stay out of the war and yet maintain national honor. Repeated submarine incidents, though none again on the scale of the *Lusitania*, imperiled U.S. neutrality abroad, while Wilson's effort at a middle way drew fire from both sides at home. Roosevelt demanded a firm response to Germany and a big build-up of the army and navy, and he used these issues as a bridge back to the Republicans, ditching the Progressives along the way. Bryan, objecting to Wilson's remonstrance to Germany over the *Lusitania* as too warlike, resigned his cabinet post in protest and attempted to rally Democrats against the president. During the year following the sinking of the *Lusitania*, Wilson had to fight foreign policy battles on several fronts. He dueled with the Germans over the permissible limits of submarine warfare and informally threatened war against them until they backed down and promised to restrict their attacks. Meanwhile, he faced down Bryan's opposition to his defense increases and diplomacy toward Germany. He forced Democrats to choose between Bryan and himself, and he mounted a speaking tour to stir up public opinion in support of his policies. By the end of May 1916, Wilson had won those battles and was ready to run for reelection with the threat of war abated and his party united behind him.

## THE CAMPAIGN OF 1916

In many ways, 1916 marked the peak of Wilson's political life. More achievements and victories followed later, but things never went so consistently right for him again. Wilson's success at temporarily fending off the German submarine threat allowed his party to brandish the campaign slogan "He Kept Us Out of War!" Foreign policy ultimately swayed fewer voters than domestic issues, but the twin spectacles of Bryan returning to the fold behind Wilson and Roosevelt ferociously backing Republican nominee Charles Evans Hughes offered a dramatic contrast in symbolism. More important to Wilson's continued tenure in the White House were the advantages of incumbency, a flawless campaign, and the legislative record that he and the Democratic Congress had compiled. Conversely, despite Roosevelt's reenlistment in the Republican ranks, the opposition party fumbled through much of the campaign and showed that its earlier rift was not completely healed. Even so, Wilson had to buck the normal Republican majorities of the era to eke out a narrow victory with less than a majority of the popular vote and a small margin in the electoral college. Still, it was a remarkable feat. Wilson was the first Democrat since Andrew Jackson to win a second consecutive term and the only one thus far to banish the Republicans from the White House for longer than four years. Furthermore, the coalition he put together, particularly the ardent support from organized labor, foreshadowed Democratic majorities later in the twentieth century.

## IMPENDING WAR

Wilson's troubles commenced as soon as the election had passed. Private word from Germany indicated that submarine warfare might soon be reopened. Wilson met this threat with a bold initiative to end the war. In December 1916 he publicly dispatched a diplomatic note to the belligerent nations offering mediation, asking them to state their peace terms, and pledging U.S. membership in a postwar international organization to maintain peace. (This marked Wilson's first attempt to establish and have the United States join a league of nations.) Although the warring governments replied equivocally, he pressed his peace offensive further with a speech on 22 January 1917, in which he called for "a peace without victory" to be ensured through "a covenant of cooperative peace." In this call for a nonpunitive peace and a league of nations, Wilson sketched the basic design of the new world order he would seek to build during the rest of his presidency. Unfortunately, the Germans has already secretly decided to resume and widen their submarine offensive, which they did on 1 February 1917. The president immediately severed diplomatic relations in protest, but he spent the next two months grasping for some middle way between peace and war.

Wilson did not succeed, even though the public's "double wish" evidently remained as strong as ever. He gradually and painfully reached the conclusion that continued neutrality would entail most of the disadvantages of war without offering the advantage of influencing the outcome and shaping the peace settlement. Without disclosing his decision, Wilson called Congress into session and spoke to the members on 1 April 1917. He delivered the greatest speech of his life when he confessed

> It is a fearful thing to lead this great peaceful people into the most terrible and disastrous of all wars, civilization itself seeming to be in the balance. [But] . . . the right is more precious than the peace, and we shall fight for the things we have always carried nearest our hearts,—for democracy, . . . for

a universal dominion of right by such a concert of free peoples as shall bring peace and safety to all nations and make the world itself at last free. . . . America is privileged to spend her blood and her might for the principles that gave her birth and happiness and the peace which she has treasured. God helping her, she can do no other.

Despite impassioned opposition from such senators as Robert La Follette of Wisconsin and George Norris of Nebraska, the declaration of war passed easily in both houses of Congress, and the United States formally entered World War I on 6 April 1917. Wilson then proceeded to oversee the most efficient and least corrupt U.S. war effort up to that time. As he had done earlier in domestic affairs, he delegated authority in military matters to his civilian secretaries and to professional officers. He also embraced the heretofore controversial idea of filling the ranks through a draft, which was quickly set up and smoothly administered. This delegatory approach paid off handsomely. During the year and a half that the United States was at war, 5 million men and women entered military service; over 1 million of them went overseas, and more than 500,000 went into combat on the Western Front.

Comparable feats of production, transportation, and supply accompanied the raising and dispatch of what was called the American Expeditionary Force (AEF). Wilson enlisted experts from business and universities to manage the home-front effort, which witnessed unprecedented government planning and direction in the economy. Unlike previous presidents, Wilson did not give prominent military and civilian posts to members of his own party. Instead, most of the top jobs went to such nonpolitical figures as General Pershing, who commanded the AEF; Herbert Hoover, who managed food production and distribution, and Bernard Baruch, who headed the main industrial agency. The one exception was McAdoo, who became the nation's transportation czar when the government took over the railroads early in 1918.

## CIVIL LIBERTIES IN PERIL

Those achievements, together with the AEF's combat victories, should have made intervention in World War I a satisfying experience for Americans. But that was not the case. The home front witnessed bitter conflicts. Political rancor boiled over when Roosevelt and other Republicans demanded a clamp-down on all kinds of criticism and dissent. Antiwar sentiment persisted, especially on the left, and after the Bolsheviks took power in Russia and made a separate peace with Germany at the end of 1917, antiradical sentiment took a punitive turn. Wilson attempted to find a middle way here, too. He set up an official propaganda agency, the Committee on Public Information, which used sophisticated psychological and advertising techniques to promote the war effort and toned down more virulent anti-German rhetoric. The president got Congress to pass restrictions on speech and publications that, although stringent, fell far short of the virtual imposition of martial law demanded by his critics. These efforts at moderation fizzled, however, and the country descended into a flurry of crackdowns on the left-wing press and organizations. Conscientious objectors and antiwar speakers, the most famous of whom was Eugene Debs, were imprisoned, and a melee of acts of hysteria and prejudice—and sometimes of violence—broke out against German Americans and radicals. World War I would not be remembered in the United States as a "happy war."

The trampling on civil liberties and the home-front atrocities revealed a less salutary side to Wilson's delegatory approach. By leaving the administration of wartime measures to his postmaster general and to successive attorneys general the president relied on heavy-handed operators who shared many of the popular prejudices and wanted to smash domestic opponents. The worst example of such actions came in 1919 and 1920 when Attorney General A. Mitchell Palmer led the postwar antiradical rampage known as the Red Scare. During much of that later time, Wilson was physically incapacitated and knew almost nothing about Palmer's activities. Before then, however, he had become increasingly absorbed in wartime diplomacy and his strategy for peacemaking and establishment of a postwar world order. This was the one area in which Wilson delegated almost nothing of importance. Since Bryan's departure in 1915, he had kept major foreign policy decisions largely to himself. Wilson served, in effect, as his own secretary of state, relegating Bryan's successor, Robert Lansing, to less important areas and technical work. With the exception of Edith Wilson, the only person whom he allowed to have a hand in the main area of foreign policy was Edward M. House, the shadowy Texas "colonel" and unofficial presidential confidant. And after 1915, Wilson used House more as a negotiator and less as a true adviser.

## A VISION OF A NEW WORLD ORDER

Wilson was playing a delicate diplomatic game, and there was much that he legitimately did have to control himself. As the president openly stated in his war address, he was trying to build the new world order of "peace without victory" through intervention in this horrible conflict. Rather than make a rip-snorting common cause with the Allies, as Roosevelt and other belligerent enthusiasts wanted, Wilson kept his distance from them and enunciated a set of liberal, nonpunitive war aims. He gave his most compelling expression of those aims in a speech to Congress on 5 January 1918, in which he laid down what were instantly dubbed the Fourteen Points. They included territorial adjustments in Europe, more general principles such as ethnic autonomy, "freedom of the seas," and reduction of armaments, a proposal for "a general association of nations . . . under specific covenants" to keep the peace, and an overall promise of a settlement based on fairness and compassion, not on spoils and vengeance. Allied leaders coyly kept their disagreements to themselves and savored the international propaganda triumph that Wilson scored with the speech. Translated into German

and other languages and broadcast in millions of leaflets, the Fourteen Points played a big part in undermining enemy morale, and they furnished the diplomatic basis on which the German government sued for the surrender that came with the armistice on 11 November 1918.

The armistice should have put Wilson on top of the world, and it did, fleetingly. The president soon announced that he would head the U.S. delegation to the peace conference in Paris. At the beginning of December 1918, he sailed for Europe, where he was treated to triumphal receptions in London, Paris, and Rome. This period, which lasted into the beginning of 1919, was what one historian has labeled "America's moment," a time when it really did look as if this mighty nation and its inspired, idealistic leader could reshape the world along lines of freedom, justice, and peace. But that moment passed quickly. Serious weaknesses underlay Wilson's political and diplomatic positions. Many at home, particularly Roosevelt and his closest friend, the Republican leader in the Senate, Henry Cabot Lodge, decried the Fourteen Points and urged an old-fashioned victors' peace that would crush Germany. Despite Wilson's public plea for support of his party, the Republicans, harping on domestic discontents and capitalizing on heated wartime emotions, won majorities in both houses of Congress in November 1918. The election winners gleefully interpreted the result as a repudiation of the man and his policies. Abroad, Allied leaders were breaking their previous silence and advancing territorial, financial, and colonial claims against their defeated foes. And throughout all this, Wilson's health was deteriorating. He had suffered for years from circulatory problems, and he was showing telltale signs of the condition that would lead to a crippling stroke in less than a year.

A more cautious leader might have trimmed sail under these conditions and sought to salvage what little he could from an unpromising situation. But that was not and never had been Wilson's way. Instead, he plunged boldly ahead. His first order of business at the peace conference was a league of nations, and he drove the drafting committee to finish work on the project in just over a month. On 14 February 1919, Wilson presented the Draft Covenant of the League of Nations to the conference. This document initially scored another triumph akin to the Fourteen Points. Wilson immediately sailed for home on a brief trip to attend to business at the end of the congress and to try to forestall opposition to the Draft Covenant. His prospects at first seemed good. Roosevelt had died unexpectedly at the beginning of January, and Taft, the other Republican ex-president, was head of the main organization lobbying for a league of nations, and he warmly supported the draft covenant. But Wilson's effort to win support for the League of Nations quickly fell flat. Lodge and thirty-eight other Republican senators, seven more than the one-third needed to block a treaty, issued a statement known as the Round Robin, which expressed their opposition to the draft covenant "in its present form" and advised the conference to separate the League of Nations from the peace treaty. Wilson defiantly replied that the two were inseparable and left again for the conference.

**THE RUINATION OF A DREAM**

The remaining two years of Wilson's presidency bore witness to a defeat and a political fate that were for him possibly worse than death. Back at the peace conference, Wilson labored under the handicap of his exposed domestic vulnerability. The Allied leaders pushed harder than ever for a harsh peace, and they exacted a price from the president for changes made in the Draft Covenant in an effort to mollify Republican senators. The revised Covenant did not satisfy Lodge and his cohorts, while the hard bargaining over the peace terms created a widespread impression that the final product, the Treaty of Versailles, departed more than it really did from the Fourteen Points. Thus, when Wilson returned to the United States in July 1919, he faced a situation even less promising than before. Not only were his senatorial detractors un-

appeased, but erstwhile supporters who had hoped for a liberal peace fell away, many crossing over into opposition. The domestic scene was also in turmoil. Inflation and unemployment were rising, due to the lifting of wartime controls, shortages of consumer goods, and the flood of returning troops. Strikes in major industries not only vexed the public but also fed the persisting mood of antiradical hysteria, soon to explode into the Red Scare. During the summer of 1919, cities in the North were already exploding into race riots, fueled by white prejudice and resentment against the influx of African Americans who had left the South, particularly during the war.

Slighting domestic concerns, Wilson devoted almost all of his attention to the League of Nations and the peace treaty. He used first the carrot and then the stick on his senatorial adversaries. For two months he patiently negotiated with individual senators, trying to find mutually face-saving grounds for compromise. Lodge, who was also chairman of the Foreign Relations Committee, responded by holding hearings that generated unfavorable publicity about the president's conduct at the peace conference and fed misgivings about U.S. obligations under the treaty. Then Lodge got the committee to adopt a series of amendments that offended other nations and a statement of reservations that severely curtailed the U.S. role in the League.

Exasperated, Wilson took his case to the people with a speaking tour, as he had done earlier in New Jersey and on the national scene. The tour lasted three weeks in September 1919. Wilson traveled more than 8,000 miles and gave more speeches than he had ever given before, even during presidential campaigns. Although he showed the effects of fatigue and ill health, he often glowed with his old eloquence as he warned repeatedly that the nation's failure to join the League and to enforce the peace settlement would doom the next generation to fight "that final war" in which "the very existence of civilization would be in the balance." The glow of eloquence was like the last flare-up of a dying star. Two-thirds of the way through the trip, the president's physician canceled the rest of his engagements and rushed him back to the White House, where he suffered a massive stroke on 6 October 1919.

## AN INCAPACITATED PRESIDENT

That stroke precipitated the worst crisis of presidential disability in U.S. history. It also sealed the doom of both Wilson's presidency and his struggle for a new world order. The stroke itself did not threaten his life, although accompanying infections did for a brief time. Nor did it affect his mental capacity, although it drastically shortened his attention span and upset his emotional balance. It also left him with partial paralysis on his left side, impaired vision, and little energy and stamina. In short, Wilson was a broken man who never really filled his office again. He should have vacated the presidency, either voluntarily or through some arrangement with the vice president. Unfortunately, the Constitution makes only vague reference to presidential "inability," and the strong-willed Edith Wilson regarded retention of his office as essential to her husband's survival. Loyalists in the cabinet smothered all discussion of his being replaced, while the First Lady, with the reluctant complicity of the president's physicians, embargoed all news about his condition except occasional misleading reassurances. The government continued to function mainly through the cabinet officers, and Edith Wilson unwittingly acted as a surrogate chief executive by controlling access to the president and screening the few major matters that reached him for decision.

The stroke occurred at a singularly inopportune moment in the debate over the peace treaty. Almost totally incapacitated and incommunicado for a month, Wilson could take no part in the final bargaining over a package of reservations to U.S. ratification of the treaty that would have permitted circumscribed, conditional membership in the League. By November, when he had recovered enough to be apprised of

the situation in the Senate, Wilson ordered the Democrats to spurn this arrangement, and the treaty went down to defeat in a stalemate between Republican backers of the reservations and the president's followers. Outraged public opinion forced the senators to make a second try at accommodation early in 1920, but this effort met the same fate, thanks to Wilson. He continued to recover sufficiently to attend to a few more affairs of state, but the effect of the stroke on his judgment was unmistakable. Wilson proposed that Democrats turn the 1920 election into "a great and solemn referendum" on the League. Once more, he adamantly refused to consider any thought of compromise, and the treaty suffered a second defeat in March 1920. Wilson also fired Secretary of State Lansing in what looked like a fit of petulance, and he harbored delusions about running for a third term. These events, together with the unabated domestic troubles, finally turned public sentiment massively against the president, and the Democrats suffered a devastating defeat in the 1920 elections.

Wilson left office in March 1921 one of the most decisively repudiated presidents in U.S. history. He lived only three more years and was unable to do much more than function as a semi-invalid. The triumphant Republicans undid most of his handiwork at home and abroad, and conservative probusiness policies held sway domestically for the next decade. The United States never joined the League of Nations, although the new Republican secretary of state, Charles Evans Hughes, did conduct some highly creative diplomacy regarding naval disarmament and financial reconstruction in Europe. Yet, for all his physical and political reverses, Wilson did not descend into bitterness or fade away. Privately, he accepted the refusal to join the League as evidence that the American people were not yet ready to play their required role in world affairs. Publicly, he attracted a collection of believers in his foreign policy who labored for the next twenty years to fulfill his legacy. When Wilson died in February 1924, millions around the world mourned him as a prophet of peace. Within a decade, his domestic political orientation would be back on top, and within two decades his reputation would undergo a spectacular apotheosis during World War II and with the founding of the United Nations. For the last half-century, Woodrow Wilson has always ranked among the top five or six in surveys of presidential "greatness."

## BIBLIOGRAPHY

Baker, Ray Stannard, and Willian E. Dood, eds. *The Public Papers of Woodrow Wilson*, 6 vols. (Harper & Bros., 1925–1927).

Clements, Kendrick A. *The Presidency of Woodrow Wilson* (University Press of Kansas, 1992).

Cooper, John Milton, Jr. *The Warrior and the Priest: Woodrow Wilson and Theodore Roosevelt* (Harvard University Press, 1983).

Davidson, John Wells, ed. *A Crossroads of Freedom: The 1912 Campaign Speeches of Woodrow Wilson* (Yale University Press, 1956).

Heckscher, August. *Woodrow Wilson* (Scribner's, 1991).

Knock, Thomas J. *To End All Wars: Woodrow Wilson and the Quest for a New World Order* (University of Pennsylvania Press, 1992).

Link, Arthur S. *Woodrow Wilson*, 5 vols. (Princeton University Press, 1947–1965).

———. *Woodrow Wilson: Revolution, War, and Peace* (AMH Publishing, 1979).

———, ed. *The Papers of Woodrow Wilson*, 69 vols. (Princeton University Press, 1966–1992).

Mulder, John M. *Woodrow Wilson: The Years of Preparation* (Princeton University Press, 1988).

Weinstein, Edwin A. *Woodrow Wilson: A Medical and Psychological Biography* (Princeton University Press, 1981).

★★★ 29 ★★★

# WARREN GAMALIEL HARDING
## 1921–1923

*Robert F. Martin*

---

*Born 2 November 1865 in Corsica (later Blooming Grove), Ohio, to George Tyron Harding and Phoebe Elizabeth Dickerson Harding; attended Ohio Central College, Iberia, Ohio (A.B. 1882); married Florence Kling De Wolfe, 8 July 1891, Marion, Ohio; no children (she had one child through a previous marriage); elected president in 1920 on the Republican party ticket with Calvin Coolidge of Massachusetts, receiving 16,152,200 popular votes and 404 electoral college ballots, against the Democratic candidates James Middleton Cox of Ohio and Franklin Delano Roosevelt of New York, who received 9,147,353 votes and 127 electoral ballots; died 2 August 1923 in San Francisco, California; buried in Marion Cemetery, Marion, Ohio.*

---

Warren Gamaliel Harding has been the object of more derision and less respect than almost any other occupant of the White House. He lives in popular memory as the chief executive who, unable to read correctly his own speeches, mistook *normality* for *normalcy*, and thereby provided the best-known categorization of his presidential agenda. H. L. Mencken's characterization of him as "simply a third-rate political wheel-horse, with the face of a moving-picture actor, the intelligence of a respectable agricultural implement dealer, and the imagination of a lodge joiner" has become conventional wisdom; while William Allen White's description of a president, painfully aware of his own limitations, lamenting "My God, this is a hell of a place for a man like me to be!" has forever cast him as overwhelmed by the responsibilities of office.

Scholars usually rank Harding at or near the bottom of any continuum reflecting qualitative judgments of the nation's chief executives. His lowly station in the pantheon of presidents is not unwarranted, yet critics have often exaggerated his weaknesses and underestimated his strengths. It is true that he brought to the presidency limited vision, an undisciplined intellect, and little talent or inclination for strong leadership, but he also brought to the office commitment to the nation and to his job, sound political instincts, and fundamental, though flawed, decency.

## MODEST BEGINNINGS

Harding was born into relatively modest circumstances in the little eastern Ohio hamlet of Blooming Grove in November 1865, the oldest child of George Tryon and Phoebe Elizabeth Dickerson Harding. His father, a teacher who abandoned the classroom for a career in medicine, was never more than marginally successful, and the family's middle-class status was sustained in part by his mother's income as a midwife and homeopath. Although they were never poverty stricken, their finances were sometimes precarious.

Despite the family's somewhat unstable economic condition, in 1879 the Hardings' oldest son was able to enter Iberia College, a struggling institution that was little more than a preparatory school. Warren, never predisposed to the life of the mind, found the intellectual atmosphere there satisfactory. According to a contemporary, his main interests were "debating, writing, and making friends," but it was there also that he got his first journalistic experience as cofounder and editor of the college's newspaper.

After graduating in 1882 Harding joined his family, now living in Marion, Ohio. He worked for a year as a rural schoolteacher, which he later described as the hardest job he had ever had, and then read law briefly while supporting himself in very modest fashion as the agent of three insurance companies. In the fall of 1884 Harding and two friends purchased the *Star*, a failing Marion newspaper. He became editor and eventually sole proprietor of the paper and within a few years had established it on a sound financial footing.

While Harding projected a carefree "hail-fellow-well-met" persona, he seems to have experienced considerable stress and anxiety during these early years in Marion. He was chronically insecure. Reasons proposed for that insecurity include self-consciousness about the alleged African-American component of his ancestry; financial or other strains within his family; or some other quirk of personality. In the fall of 1889, suffering from a bout of ill health that he later described as a nervous breakdown, he entered a Seventh Day Adventist sanitorium run by Dr. J. P. Kellogg in Battle Creek, Michigan. The diet and regimen there apparently had a salutary effect, and Harding returned home much improved in early 1890.

Unfortunately, his visit to Battle Creek did not result in a permanent cure. Over the next twelve years he made eleven more such visits in an effort to deal with chronic health problems. Whether physiological or psychological, these illnesses did not seriously disrupt the normal course of events in the young man's personal or professional life. By the early 1890s he had begun to emerge as a successful businessman and respected member of his community.

In 1891 he married Florence Mabel Kling DeWolfe, the daughter of a prosperous local merchant. A divorced woman five years older than Harding and with one son, Florence Kling was strong willed, assertive, sharp-tongued, and intelligent. Though the marriage endured and was marked by mutual respect, Harding, who had a deep-seated need for affection and approval, appears to have found his life with "the Duchess" emotionally and sexually unsatisfying. Although Mrs. Harding was a valued political adviser,

Harding strayed early and often, indulging in numerous extramarital affairs that posthumously marred his reputation.

## ENTERING POLITICS

Harding enjoyed the role of newspaper owner and editor and was proud of the success of the *Star*; but he found the routine, discipline, and detail of the world of business confining and burdensome. He needed and enjoyed the companionship of others and soon became involved in what was to him the more convivial and interesting arena of local and state politics. Throughout the 1890s he attended and often spoke at Republican party meetings and other public functions, becoming increasingly well known and gaining a local reputation as an orator of considerable ability. In 1899 he was elected to the first of two terms in the state senate, and, in 1903, to a term as lieutenant governor.

In the turbulent years of the mid-nineteenth century the Hardings had been proponents of both abolitionism and the Free Soil cause, but there was little of the dissenter or reformer in Warren Harding. As editor of the *Star* he opposed prohibition, was hostile to the Knights of Labor, and expressed suspicion of and antagonism toward individuals and groups outside the mainstream. As a state legislator in the faction-ridden world of Ohio politics he was something of a moderate, although his predisposition toward conservatism was evident. He defended protectionism, expressed misgivings about the "new immigration," mistrusted organized labor, and was equivocal about prohibition. He refrained, however, from taking dogmatic positions. Preferring conciliation and compromise to confrontation and schism, he tried to play the role of mediator and to offend as few people as possible. This tact was as much a matter of temperament as expediency and was to be characteristic of his approach to politics throughout his career.

## SENATOR HARDING

After an unsuccessful bid for the governorship on the Republican ticket in 1910,

Harding rode a GOP landslide in Ohio in 1914 into the U.S. Senate. There, as in the Buckeye State legislature, he sought to avoid controversy and to play the role of mediator and compromiser. He spoke rarely, and such modest influence as he wielded among his colleagues was the product not of oratory, intellect, or commitment to principle but of charm and congeniality. During his first year in the Senate he was absent roughly 40 percent of the time, and he avoided voting on most issues that could alienate his Ohio constituency. During his six-year tenure he introduced 134 bills, most addressing local issues and none dealing with matters of national importance. His voting record on legislation favorable to business was almost universally positive while his stance on measures beneficial to labor was varied but often negative.

On the two most significant domestic issues of the day, women's suffrage and prohibition, he was cautious. He supported women's suffrage only after the direction in which the political tide was flowing became clear; and he voted to submit the Prohibition Amendment to the states not out of sympathy for the dry cause but as a political expedient and means of allowing the people of the states to decide the vexing question for themselves. He approved the nation's entry into World War I, but he was not enthusiastic about the Treaty of Versailles, seeing little of value in it for the United States. Yet, he was not an isolationist and preferred compromise to rejection. Thus, in the fight over the treaty he found himself among the ranks of the "strong reservationists."

## A NOT-SO-RELUCTANT CANDIDATE

As early as 1918 there was some inconsequential talk in Ohio of Harding as a presidential prospect. Most people, however, assumed that the nomination would go to Theodore Roosevelt if he wanted it. The Rough Rider's death in January 1919 was followed by widespread uncertainty within Republican ranks about who would be the party's nominee. Several of Harding's friends urged him to seek the nomination.

He was flattered by this vote of confidence and thought that he might well "make as good a President as a great many men who are talked of for that position" and almost certainly "a more 'commonsensible' President" than Wilson. Yet, he genuinely enjoyed the respected and not terribly arduous life of a U.S. senator, and—believing he would "never have any more fun or any real enjoyment in life" if he won the nomination and election—he was, at first, unenthusiastic about making the race.

The image of Harding as a reluctant presidential candidate is, however, erroneous. By late 1919 he had decided to seek the nomination, a decision probably motivated initially as much by concern to protect his political position in Ohio as by a genuine desire for the nomination. Rather quickly, however, he became enamored of the idea of being a serious contender, and in the winter and spring of 1920 he threw himself actively into the effort to generate support for his candidacy.

After Roosevelt's death the leading contenders for the nomination were General Leonard Wood, Governor Frank O. Lowden of Illinois, and Senator Hiram Johnson of California. Harding ran in only two state primaries, those in Ohio and Indiana. In the former he defeated Wood by only 15,000 votes; in the latter, he finished a disastrous fourth behind Wood, Johnson, and Lowden. So poor was his primary showing that he would have withdrawn from the race had it not been for the objections of his wife and his campaign managers.

Harry Daugherty, chief architect of the Harding campaign, understood that his candidate would not go to the convention with great delegate strength, but he hoped for a deadlocked convention in which he might be able to maneuver the Ohio senator into a position of strength. Daugherty's strategy was to persuade as many delegations as possible to commit themselves to Harding as their second or third choice and to throw their support to him in the event of a stymied convention.

Events in Chicago in July 1920 unfolded almost as if Daugherty had written the script. Roll call after roll call made it apparent that no major contender could muster sufficient support to secure the nomination. Exhausted by heat and fatigue, delegates eventually turned to Harding as a compromise candidate. They did so not because of the alleged machinations of senators and party leaders in the famed smoke-filled room of the Blackstone Hotel, but because the convention was deadlocked and Harding and his managers had carefully positioned the Ohioan to be an available alternative to the front-runners.

## THE CAMPAIGN OF 1920

Historians have sometimes portrayed Harding's campaign in the general election as vacuous and his victory as little more than a rejection of Wilsonianism. Such interpretations underestimate the inherent appeal of Harding, his running mate, Calvin Coolidge of Massachusetts, and the Republican agenda they espoused. With the exception of foreign policy, about which he was undeniably ambiguous, Harding clearly stated his position on most issues, calling for measures such as an emergency tariff for the benefit of beleaguered farmers, more stringent immigration policies, lower taxes, reduced government spending, a national budget system, a large navy and merchant marine, and a federal antilynching bill.

Clearly the nation was tired of reform, war, the problems of postwar readjustment, and Wilsonian idealism, but the election returns of 1920 also suggest that the charming and handsome Harding, who embodied the values and experiences of small-town America and who advocated a return to the normal patterns of American life, struck a chord that resonated in the hearts and minds of millions of voters. Although he did not generate the enthusiasm or personal loyalty of a Theodore Roosevelt, Harding won 60 percent of the popular vote against the Democrat James M. Cox's 34 percent and the imprisoned Socialist Eugene Debs's 5 percent. Harding carried every state outside the South and won 40 percent of the vote there. Although voter turnout was somewhat lower than in previous elections, the decline was less indicative of voter apathy than of the fact that many women, who were for the first time enfranchised, chose not to vote.

## HARDING'S VIEW
## OF THE PRESIDENCY

With the inauguration of Warren G. Harding on 4 March 1921, the bleak and forbidding atmosphere surrounding the White House during the closing months of the Wilson administration were transformed into a much more vital and hospitable one. The quickening pace of life at 1600 Pennsylvania Avenue was symbolic of the changes in the government as a whole. The image of Harding as a poker-playing, cigar-smoking, scarcely competent pawn of Republican politicos, whose role in government was little more than symbolic, is grossly exaggerated. It is true that Harding liked best, and was most comfortable with, the public and symbolic functions of his office, and that his understanding of the presidency was more akin to McKinley's than to that of Roosevelt or Wilson. It is also true that he needed and enjoyed the companionship of old and new friends and often entertained them in the White House. Yet, once in office, he worked very hard to do the best job of which he was capable.

Although he found routine and detail distasteful, he faithfully and perhaps excessively attended to the minutia of the presidency. Aware of his own limitations of understanding and experience, he devoted much of his energy to comprehending issues with which he had never seriously grappled. He did not, however, think it his responsibility to formulate or initiate policy. Harding believed that the chief executive should surround himself with "the best minds" and these advisers in consultation with congressional and party leaders would play the primary role in the formulation of legislation and in decision making. The president's chief function was to coordinate and facilitate this process.

An able cabinet was crucial to the effective functioning of government as Harding understood it, and in several instances he demonstrated superb judgment and consid-

erable political independence in the selection of his cabinet officers. Charles Evans Hughes (secretary of state), Herbert Hoover (secretary of commerce), Henry C. Wallace, (secretary of agriculture), and Andrew Mellon (secretary of the treasury) served their president and their nation faithfully and ably. When, however, Harding abandoned his best-minds principle and made appointments on strictly political or personal grounds he made some grievous mistakes, such as his selection of Harry Daugherty as attorney general and Albert Fall as secretary of the interior.

Once they were in place, the president allowed his department heads considerable autonomy in both policy and personnel decisions. He called on cabinet members frequently for advice, but his cabinet meetings rarely became the forum for collective discussion of policy that he had envisioned—most of the secretaries preferred to deal with him individually. Such coherence as there was to the policies of the Harding administration resulted not from cabinet-level collaboration but from presidential synthesis of the ideas of his cabinet secretaries.

## PRESIDENT AND CONGRESS

Harding had a profound respect for the principle of separation of powers, but he also believed deeply in the interdependence of the three branches of government. His experience in the Senate during the Wilson years, his need to be liked, and his sense that conciliation and cooperation were more constructive than controversy and confrontation persuaded him that dramatic improvements were needed in relations between the president and Congress. His own temperament and legislative background and his party's control of both houses of Congress by wide margins led him to believe that executive-congressional relations would now be more harmonious than they had been in recent years. In an effort to keep lines of communication between the White House and Capitol Hill open, he consulted regularly with congressional leaders concerning administration policies, and they helped to shape and to secure the passage of "normalcy" legislation.

Dealing with the Sixty-seventh Congress was not, however, an easy task; although dominated by the Republican party, the legislative body was seriously factionalized. In addition to traditional partisan divisions, fissures ran along ideological and regional lines as well. There were seemingly irreconcilable differences in foreign policy and deep splits on domestic issues, with progressives advocating additional domestic socioeconomic reforms, old guard Republicans committed to the interest of business, southern Democrats often behaving as obstructionists, and an emerging farm bloc that tenaciously championed the cause of rural America.

## HARDING'S AGENDA

Shortly after taking office, Harding called this contentious body into special session. In an address to the House and Senate he outlined his understanding of the problems facing the nation and his administration's agenda for their resolution. Aware of public dissatisfaction and disillusion with the recent emphasis on questions of foreign policy, the president suggested that Congress should first address domestic concerns. Among the legislative proposals he enumerated were higher tariffs, lower taxes, economy in government, the creation of a national budget system, expansion of the merchant marine, farm credit legislation, tighter immigration controls, creation of a national highway system, the development and regulation of the aviation and radio industries, passage of an antilynching law, and creation of a department of public welfare.

With regard to foreign affairs, Harding expressed hope for world disarmament and for the establishment of an association of nations for the prevention of war, but he reiterated his opposition to U.S. membership in the League of Nations. He called for the immediate negotiation of treaties with our former wartime enemies and an orderly funding of the war debt. While there was nothing extraordinary about the speech, neither was it the work of an incompetent politico overwhelmed by the presidency. Harding demonstrated a rather perceptive grasp of the national mood and with the help of his advisers proposed a plausible and politically astute agenda for alleviating some of the nation's problems.

Although congressional leaders were not always cooperative, Harding, having outlined a plan of action, tried to work with them, giving them as much latitude as possible and respecting the independence of a legislative branch that sometimes seemed in disarray. His attempts to intervene in the lawmaking process were rare; two such examples were his unsuccessful efforts on behalf of subsidies for an expanded merchant marine and his opposition to a bonus bill for veterans of World War I.

By late 1922, Congress had acted on many of the legislative goals Harding had enumerated early in his presidency. On the domestic front, accomplishments the president could point to with satisfaction were lower taxes, higher tariffs, farm credit and other agricultural legislation, a national budget system, and a temporary measure restricting immigration. In foreign policy, an area that had proven most problematic for Woodrow Wilson, Harding had equal, if not greater success. At the president's request, the Sixty-seventh Congress quickly adopted a joint resolution formally ending hostilities, and the Senate subsequently ratified peace treaties with the nation's World War I adversaries. The Senate also finally approved the controversial compensation treaty with Colombia (which Wilson had proposed to indemnify Colombia for the loss of Panama), and accepted Harding's more lenient approach to the question of war debts, giving European countries a chance to refinance the loans.

The Washington Conference of 1921–22 was the zenith of Harding's efforts in the arena of foreign policy. Learning from Wilson's mistakes, Harding allowed Secretary of State Hughes to take the lead in the negotiations, and he appointed Henry Cabot Lodge and Oscar W. Underwood, the ranking members of the Senate Foreign Relations Committee, to the U.S. delegation and gave them the responsibility of piloting through the Senate the treaties arising out of the conference.

## MIDTERM PROBLEMS AND REVERSES

Despite these accomplishments in both domestic and foreign policy, Harding and his party faced serious problems in the autumn of 1922. Part of the difficulty stemmed from a rather negative public perception of the Republican-dominated Sixty-seventh Congress and part was the result of unpopular actions taken by the president.

Harding's stance on veterans' bonuses was one of the most controversial of his presidency. In 1922, recognizing the value of such a measure in an election year, Congress passed a bill authorizing a bonus for World War I veterans. Harding appreciated the service rendered by the doughboys but considered the proposed legislation too costly. He believed that the measure would increase the public debt by one-sixth and would thereby seriously undermine the nation's credit. Consequently, in an action that was widely unpopular, he vetoed the bill. The House voted 258 to 54 to override the veto, but the vote to override in the Senate (44 to 28) fell 4 votes short of the necessary two-thirds majority. The bill was dead and the voting public was angry.

Harding's veto of the bonus bill was by no means the only presidential action that alienated voters. High on that list were his reactions to the problems of labor. Although usually and correctly perceived as primarily sympathetic to the nation's business interests, Harding—early in his administration and desirous of as many friends as possible— had attempted to develop a good rapport with labor. He sponsored an unemployment conference, and he attempted to bring an end to the 12-hour workday in the steel industry. Whatever goodwill these efforts may have generated quickly evaporated during the rail and coal strikes of July and August 1922. Harding initially tried to be impartial and to play the role of mediator; he personally developed several compromise proposals that nonetheless failed to end the strikes.

Finally, when there seemed little alternative, Harding allowed Attorney General Daugherty to secure an injunction against the striking railway workers. The injunction issued by federal district judge James Wilkerson was sweeping and repressive, even abridging many of labor's legal rights, including that of picketing. Harding was surprised and upset by its harshness and subsequently ordered it modified. Nevertheless, it effectively undermined the position of labor. Although the injunction resulted in a settlement of the railway strike and indirectly of the coal strike, it was politically costly. For many workers it confirmed the impression that the president was fundamentally committed to the interests of business and unsympathetic to the problems of the nation's industrial labor force.

Harding's reputation suffered further damage in 1922 as a result of his support for Senator-Elect Truman H. Newberry of Michigan, who had virtually bought his Republican primary nomination over Henry Ford. There seemed little doubt of Newberry's guilt after he and more than one hundred of his friends and supporters were convicted of fraud, corruption, and conspiracy. Although the Supreme Court overturned these convictions, Newberry's reputation was tainted and for more than two years the Senate refrained from allowing him to take his seat. Harding believed that Newberry had been duly elected and was entitled to his seat, despite evidence of unethical and even criminal activities. He even sent a letter of congratulations to the controversial politician after the Senate had accepted him. The president's support for a man of such questionable ethics seemed to many to cast doubt on Harding's own integrity.

The Sixty-seventh Congress's reputation as a strife-ridden and sometimes inept legislative body, along with Harding's stance on the bonus bill, his use of the labor injunction, and his support for Newberry set the stage for a significant Republican setback in the elections of 1922. In the Sixty-eighth Congress the Republican majority in the Senate dropped from 24 to 10, and that in the House was reduced from 172 to 26.

The political reverses of 1922 not with-standing, the Harding administration had actually achieved many of its objectives by 1923. A modest program of legislation reflecting a number of the campaign issues of 1920 was in place. The president's conciliatory approach to problems had helped to noticeably cool political passions. Economic recovery was under way and prospects for the future seemed bright. Indeed, the nation appeared to be returning to "normalcy."

## HARDING TAKES A TRIP

In the summer of 1923 Harding traveled across the United States on his way to Alaska. The trip, intended largely to improve the president's political fortunes, was designed to enable the nation to get a look at its leader and to help him to get a better read on the mood of the people. The president delivered fourteen major addresses and numerous minor ones. Neither profound nor innovative, the speeches were, however, those of a man who was politically astute and had a reasonable grasp of the significant issues of the day. He advocated additional agricultural legislation; a nationally integrated highway system; further development of the nation's aviation, automotive, and radio industries; the wise use of both natural and human resources; the creation of a federal department of welfare; and U.S. membership in the World Court.

He reiterated his administration's commitment to business and to economic progress but warned that if industry failed to act responsibly with regard to the public interest or the rights of workers, it would be subject to additional government regulation. At the same time, he expressed the conviction that unions were beneficial and that workers had a legitimate right to organize and to strike when necessary. He credited his administration's governmental economy, tax decreases, and debt reduction with promoting the recovery now under way and predicted a prolonged period of prosperity.

Although some of what Harding said was self-serving rhetoric that did not align with his policies, the nation seemed impressed with what it saw and heard, and the trip no doubt served its purpose. The president, however, was not to reap its political rewards. Harding had not been well for a number of years, and the stresses of office and of the first inklings of the scandals that would unfold after his death aggravated chronic health problems, including heart trouble, high blood pressure, and insomnia. The trip west afforded little opportunity for rest or relaxation, and his thousands of miles of travel and scores of speeches enervated rather than rejuvenated him. After returning from Alaska, Harding suffered an undiagnosed heart attack on the train trip from Seattle to San Francisco. Doctors in San Francisco recognized the seriousness of his condition, confined him to bed, and began medication, to which he seemed at first to respond. On 2 August, however, he died suddenly.

Harding knew his limitations and had no illusions that he would be remembered as one of the nation's great chief executives. But he had once expressed the hope that he would be one of its best-loved presidents, and for a brief moment in the summer of 1923, he was. The nation genuinely mourned its fallen leader, not for his record of accomplishment nor because he was a strong or innovative president. Rather, the millions of Americans who mourned him saw in him a relatively ordinary person like themselves who had parlayed modest talents into a successful public career and who had qualities of kindness, gentleness, and decency, to which they responded warmly.

## THE SCANDALS EMERGE

The honor and outpouring of affection accorded Harding was all too brief. Soon disclosures of public and private scandals and the post-1920s backlash against the era of Republican ascendancy would cast a pall over his presidency from which his reputation would not recover.

The extent and degree of criminality during the Harding administration was sometimes exaggerated by legislators embroiled in a power struggle with the executive branch of government and by partisan critics, as well as the media, who found the scandals a useful means to their own ends. Harding was never personally guilty of malfeasance in office, but he was a poor judge of character, blindly loyal to his friends and slow to believe the charges of misconduct that began surfacing shortly before his death. There is no question that Harding's administration suffered from the irresponsible and criminal actions of some within its ranks. Though the corruption was never as widespread and systematic as in some state political machines, it did occur, and it occurred on Harding's watch. Among the scandals were graft and profiteering within the Veterans' Bureau; the wheeling and dealing of the loose-knit band of petty criminals known as the "Ohio Gang"; the Elk Hills and Teapot Dome scandals that led to criminal charges against Secretary of Interior Albert Fall; and the apparent obstruction of justice and lax enforcement of the law by Attorney General Harry Daugherty. Harding bears responsibility for the actions of the subordinates he chose to serve in his administration.

## EVALUATION OF HARDING'S PRESIDENCY

The Harding era has become almost synonymous in the popular mind with ineptitude and scandal, but these were not years in which government completely foundered in a morass of incompetence. Harding occasionally exhibited courage, as in his veto of the veterans' bonus bill and his call in Birmingham, Alabama, for greater economic and political equality for African Americans. Furthermore, some scholars believe that by the time of his death Harding was beginning to exercise more independence and strength of will than he had early in his presidency. In any case, these were not years of inactivity. Robert K. Murray, the most thorough student of the Harding presidency, has argued that the achievements of the early 1920s were relatively impressive. They included the peace treaties ending World War I, the Washington disarmament conference, several significant pieces of agricultural legislation, creation of a budget bureau, reduced government spending, enactment of a new tariff, immigration restriction, lower taxes, and reduction of the federal debt.

It is axiomatic that hindsight is more acute than foresight, and in retrospect it is easy to question the wisdom of many of these achievements. Given the course of events in the 1930s and 1940s, the treaties resulting from the disarmament conference seem limited and naive. The agricultural reform measures of the early 1920s failed to address the problem of overproduction. The protectionism of the Fordney-McCumber Tariff was ill-conceived and economically unsound. The temporary legislation restricting immigration was irrational and culturally biased. The reduction in taxes may have had short-term benefits, but it also contributed to the economic debacle of the 1930s. Yet the Republican victory of 1924 and the fact that the economic and social policies put in place during the Harding administration survived throughout the remainder of the decade suggests that millions of Americans did not seriously question the fundamental tenets of the Republican regime inaugurated under Harding.

## BIBLIOGRAPHY

Allen, Frederick Lewis. *Only Yesterday* (Harper & Bros., 1957).

Mencken, H. L. *A Carnival of Buncombe: Writings on Politics* (University of Chicago Press, 1984).

Murray, Robert K. *The Harding Era: Warren G. Harding and His Administration* (University of Minnesota Press, 1969).

———. *The Politics of Normalcy: Governmental Theory and Practice in the Harding-Coolidge Era* (Norton, 1973).

Russell, Francis. *The Shadow of Blooming Grove: Warren G. Harding in His Times* (McGraw-Hill, 1968).

Sinclair, Andrew. *The Available Man: The Life Behind the Masks of Warren Gamaliel Harding* (Macmillan, 1965).

White, William A. *The Autobiography of William Allen White* (Macmillan, 1946).

★★★ 30 ★★★

# JOHN CALVIN COOLIDGE
## 1923–1929

*John W. Johnson*

*Born 4 July 1872 in Plymouth Notch, Vermont, to John Calvin Coolidge and Victoria Josephine Moor; educated at Amherst College, Amherst, Massachusetts (B.A. 1895); admitted to the bar and practiced law; married Grace Anna Goodhue, 4 October 1905, Burlington, Vermont; two children; succeeded to the presidency upon the death of Warren Gamaliel Harding, 2 August 1923; elected in 1924 with Charles Gates Dawes of Illinois with 15,725,016 popular votes and 382 electoral college ballots over the Democratic ticket of John William Davis of New York and Charles Wayland Bryan of Nebraska (8,386,503 popular votes and 136 electoral ballots), and the Progressive party slate of Robert Marion LaFollette of Wisconsin and Burton Kendall Wheeler of Montana (4,822,856 popular votes and 13 electoral ballots); died 5 January 1933 in Northampton, Massachusetts; buried in Notch Cemetery, Plymouth Notch, Plymouth, Vermont.*

Virtually every written account of the life of Calvin Coolidge has relied heavily upon witticisms. The thirtieth president of the United States was indeed a "capital character." However, as one biographer put it, his presidency cannot be explained merely with "apocryphal anecdotes held together by a glue of fact and blather." Coolidge served as president for nearly six years during a remarkable run of prosperity in the 1920s. His administration was perhaps the most trouble-free of any twentieth-century chief executive. When Coolidge left office in 1929, he was regarded as one of the most popular figures ever to inhabit the White House. Some commentators said Coolidge was lucky; others maintained that he sold out to the business leadership and slept through his administration; and more than a few argued that the country did not want or need a strong leader in the 1920s. Nevertheless, to survive—even to thrive—in Washington in the chaos of the post–World War I decade took an adroitness that cannot be explained away by a handful of anecdotes.

## SMALL-TOWN ORIGINS

John Calvin Coolidge—generally called by his middle name or just "Cal"—was born on the Fourth of July in 1872 in the small Vermont community of Plymouth Notch. Partisans of Coolidge later emphasized the patriotic and rural symbolism of his birthdate and birthplace. Coolidge's father, for whom he was named, was a farmer, storekeeper, and part-time Vermont legislator. Calvin's mother, Victoria Josephine Moor Coolidge, was a sickly but sensitive woman. Her death, when Calvin was 12 years old, was one of the great sorrows of his life. As an adult Coolidge carried a picture of his mother and reportedly gazed at it often. Hardly wealthy, the Coolidges were comfortable enough financially to send their young son to Amherst College in nearby Massachusetts. There he was a middling student, although he excelled at public speaking, history, and philosophy.

After college Coolidge apprenticed himself to a Massachusetts lawyer. He was ad-

mitted to the bar in 1895 and began a small practice in Northampton, Massachusetts. During his early years there, Coolidge met his future wife under unusual circumstances. Grace Anna Goodhue, a teacher of the deaf at a local college, was watering flowers one day outside her school and happened to glance through the window of a nearby boarding house. There she saw a young man, clad only in long underwear and a hat, shaving. She burst out laughing at the sight and attracted the attention of the embarrassed shaver. She and young Coolidge were later more properly introduced, and they married in 1905, when she was 26 and he was 33. Throughout Coolidge's public life, Grace Goodhue Coolidge would be a striking, vivacious presence. She was a charming hostess, possessed of a positive outlook on life, and exceedingly clever. From all accounts the Coolidges were a devoted and happily married couple.

## A POLITICAL SUCCESS STORY

About the time of his marriage, Coolidge followed his father's example and plunged into politics as a Republican. Never a reformer or an activist, Coolidge the politician was known for good judgment, hard work, and party loyalty. In short order he completed a remarkable ascent in public office: Northampton City Council, Northampton city solicitor, Massachusetts state legislator, mayor of Northampton, Massachusetts state senator (including a term as senate president), lieutenant governor, and then governor of Massachusetts.

In 1919 Governor Coolidge attracted national attention when a police strike threatened in Boston. Coolidge initially delayed ordering action against the strikers, but after the mayor had called out state troops, Coolidge dispatched additional state forces. In an open letter, he also informed Samuel Gompers, president of the American Federation of Labor, that "there is no right to strike against the public safety by anybody, anywhere, any time." In the midst of the Red Scare following World War I, Coolidge's rhetoric—notwithstanding his slow response to commit state forces—resonated positively with Americans worried about radical challenges to civic order. In fact, the notoriety Coolidge realized from this episode was largely responsible for his securing the Republican party nomination for the vice presidency in the first postwar national election.

On the "Return to Normalcy" ticket in 1920, the Republican duo of Warren Harding and Calvin Coolidge swept to an easy victory. In his two years as vice president Coolidge was essentially a cipher at cabinet meetings and in his presiding role over the Senate. Late in the summer of 1923, Coolidge was vacationing at the family home in Plymouth Notch while President Harding was in the midst of a western campaign swing. About 2:30 A.M. on 3 August 1923, Coolidge was awakened from a sound sleep by a frantic group consisting of a reporter and two of the vice president's aides. They quickly informed him that on the previous afternoon Harding had suffered a heart attack and died and that he, Coolidge, was now president of the United States. Coolidge's first reaction on hearing the news was the thought "I believe I can swing it." He knelt with family members for a brief prayer and then allowed his father, a notary public, to administer the oath of office to him. Finally, in an act that was both characteristic and symbolic, the new president went back upstairs and completed his night's sleep.

## THE CARRY-OVER CABINET

One of Coolidge's first tasks as president was to decide which of Harding's advisers and agency heads to retain. Never one to embark upon a new course without substantial provocation, Coolidge decided to keep in office virtually all of Harding's cabinet. Coolidge, like Harding, listened closely to his cabinet and frequently acceded to their wishes without question—or even comment.

Charles Evans Hughes was the inherited secretary of state. A New York attorney, Hughes had earlier served as an associate justice of the Supreme Court before leaving the bench in 1916 to run for the presidency. Hughes had a distinguished bearing: He looked the part of a senior statesman or judge. After serving for two years, Hughes resigned from the Coolidge cabinet to resume a remunerative private law practice. (In 1930, on the nomination of President Herbert Hoover, Hughes returned to the Supreme Court as chief justice.) His successor at state was Frank B. Kellogg of Minnesota. Kellogg's name will long be identified with the Kellogg-Briand Pact of 1928, which sought to outlaw war as an instrument of national policy.

The secretary of the treasury was Andrew Mellon, a shy but brilliant Pittsburgh banker and industrialist. Mellon had served in this capacity for Harding, and he would continue under Coolidge and Hoover. His philosophy of tax reduction and debt cutting coincided with Coolidge's own fiscal precepts. More than any other cabinet member, Mellon agreed with Coolidge's dictum that "the chief business of the American people is business." Mellon's personally reticent demeanor matched that of the president. After Hughes resigned from the cabinet, Coolidge came to regard Mellon as his "prime minister."

Another holdover from the Harding administration was Herbert Hoover, the secretary of commerce. A mining engineer with extensive international experience in business and humanitarian causes, Hoover was the whiz kid of the Harding and Coolidge administrations. Although personally too brash and too fond of the public stage for Coolidge's taste, Hoover had administrative skills and leadership ability that earned him the president's respect and kept him in place as the head of the Commerce Department until his own run for the presidency in 1928. Other bequeathed cabinet members who stayed on for a long time in the Coolidge administration were Postmaster General Harry S. New and Secretary of Labor James J. Davis.

The Justice Department was a problem for Coolidge. Attorney General Harry Daugherty's role in upholding the legality of the oil leases in the infamous Teapot Dome affair had led to widespread calls for his resignation or termination. Coolidge, who at first resisted bowing to the calls for Daugherty's ouster, finally dismissed him when the attorney general balked at opening his department's files to congressional investigators. Coolidge selected as Daugherty's successor an acquaintance from his college days, Harlan Fiske Stone, who restored integrity to the Justice Department. Among other things, Stone was responsible for appointing J. Edgar Hoover as director of the Federal Bureau of Investigation. When a vacancy on the Supreme Court presented itself in 1925, Coolidge nominated Stone. Some contemporary political observers suggested that Stone was too successful at cleaning up the old-boy system in the Justice Department and was thus "kicked upstairs" to the Supreme Court. Coolidge's final attorney general was John G. Sargent, who faced the increasingly unpopular task of enforcing the widely flouted prohibition laws.

The Teapot Dome oil-leasing scandal affected two other Coolidge cabinet members: Secretary of the Navy Edwin Denby unwittingly accepted the transfer of Wyoming oil leases from the Navy Department to the Department of the Interior. In 1924, in the face of this alleged impropriety and the call from the Senate for his resignation, Denby stepped down from his post in Coolidge's cabinet. Secretary of the Interior Hubert Work, yet another holdover from the Harding administration, stayed on under Coolidge to help repair the integrity of the department in the wake of the Teapot Dome criminal prosecution of the former secretary, Albert Fall.

The holdover Harding appointee who presented the most problems for Coolidge was Henry C. Wallace, the secretary of agriculture. Wallace was a champion of the McNary-Haugen farm relief bill which, if passed, would have provided for government purchase of farm surplus crops at fixed prices for resale in international markets. This bill was not popular with the free enterprise–oriented Coolidge. In spite of disagreements with Wallace over "McNary-Haugenism," Coolidge kept the Iowan in his cabinet position until the latter's death in 1924. The two succeeding secretaries of agriculture, Howard Gore of West Virginia and William M. Jardine of Kansas, shared Coolidge's distaste for government involvement in agriculture.

## THE COOLIDGE STYLE

Although Coolidge's conservative Republican politics were virtually a carbon copy of Harding's, his style as an executive differed markedly. Whereas Harding was garrulous and allowed constituents and politicians to roam the White House, Coolidge was quiet, remote, and—as a devout Congregationalist—much more straight-laced. Harding served liquor at presidential parties; Coolidge scrupulously observed prohibition and did not drink alcohol throughout his two terms as president.

Unlike Harding, who had been a senator before his run for the presidency, Coolidge was not comfortable dealing with legislative bodies. His experience in the Massachusetts legislature did not prepare him to deal with the egos and wheeling and dealing of the U.S. Congress. Harding's "hail-fellow-well-met" style made him a consummate backroom politician, but Coolidge remained aloof and was frequently frustrated by congressional actions (or inactions). Coolidge did inaugurate a custom of inviting members of Congress to breakfast in the White House, but he used that time to eat his breakfast in silence rather than to participate in policy discussions.

As president, Coolidge kept to a relaxed schedule, seldom tending to business for more than a few hours a day. In the summer he took long vacations, mainly to Vermont. That Coolidge took afternoon naps in the White House was not a myth spread by humorists and presidential critics. Coolidge slept about ten hours a night and an hour or two each afternoon. In part, his need for sleep may have stemmed from several chronic health problems. Coolidge suffered from respiratory and digestive disorders, and he relied on nasal sprays and an arsenal of pills to treat his symptoms. Coolidge was also a big eater, particularly of sugary and starchy foods. Thus—given his sleeping habits, his health, and his diet—it is not surprising that the president was lacking in energy.

Coolidge was also extremely shy and undemonstrative. As an adult he had few close friends, the most prominent being Boston businessman Frank W. Stearns. Biographers maintain that Calvin Coolidge probably spent more time in the family quarters in the White House than any president. He was devoted to his wife Grace and to their two sons, and the death of his younger son—from an infected blister during the presidential campaign of 1924—devastated Coolidge more than anything, with the possible exception of his mother's death.

Coolidge deserved his reputation as a man of few words. It was not just shyness, however, that caused his reticence. He was a good listener and strategically waited to hear the advice and the comments of others before speaking himself. Because he could deliver a stinging barb with a straight face, he became known for possessing a sardonic wit. Grace Coolidge contributed to this image of her husband as a capital character by telling Silent Cal anecdotes. Her favorite was the story of the hostess who lamented to the president, "Oh, Mr. Coolidge, you are so silent. But you must talk to me. I made a bet today that I could get more than two words out of you." According to the First Lady, the president flatly replied, "You lose."

During his first term, Coolidge relied almost entirely upon his cabinet for legislative recommendations. He proposed a massive list of spending cuts, making his submitted budget the smallest since before World War I. Following the advice of Treasury Secretary Mellon, Coolidge also proposed a plan for reducing the national debt. However, congressional scrutiny of Mellon's personal tax deductions succeeded in delaying and ultimately derailing most of the administration's program for spending cuts and debt reduction in Coolidge's first term.

## THE TEAPOT DOME SCANDAL

Also frustrating Coolidge during his first term was the continuing Teapot Dome investigation. Because of the investigation and the accompanying public pressure to do something about corruption in Washington, Coolidge accepted the resignations of Attorney General Daugherty and Secretary of the Navy Denby. Thus, the Coolidge administration got off to a stumbling start. Although Coolidge had attended some of the cabinet meetings in which Teapot Dome had been discussed, he was vice president at the time and was not personally in legal difficulties. It was, perhaps, the image of Coolidge's Yankee asceticism, a far sight from the cronyism of Harding and his advisers, that persuaded the public that Coolidge did not line his pockets with bribe money from Teapot Dome. Moreover, when Coolidge stipulated that he had had no conversations on Teapot Dome with any of the guilty parties, his silence was eminently believable.

## IMMIGRATION AND VETERANS' BENEFITS

Herbert Hoover remembered Coolidge once saying that "if you see ten troubles coming down the road, you can be sure that nine will run into the ditch before they reach you and you have to battle with only one of them." One of the ten that persisted to collision in 1924 was immigration legislation. Both major political parties favored immigration legislation that not only would restrict the total number of individuals entering the United States, but also would discourage immigration from specific countries, most notably Japan. Coolidge and Secretary of State Hughes did not favor the total exclusion of Japanese immigrants, which had been proposed by Congress. Instead, they believed that a previous "gentlemen's agreement" (in which the Japanese government promised to discourage emigration of its subjects to the United States) was sufficient "protection" for the nation. Congress, however, insisted on the absolute exclusion of Japanese nationals and put such language into the final bill. Coolidge recognized the damage to American-Japanese relations, but he reluctantly signed the legislation. The Immigration Act of 1924 also changed the census year that would be used to ascertain "national origins" quotas from 1910 to 1890, thereby establishing a baseline that would substantially reduce the number of southern and eastern European immigrants (most of whom had arrived since 1890) allowed to come into the country. Coolidge, Hughes, and the majority of both houses of Congress had no problem with the patent racial discrimination underlying the 1924 law.

Another failure of leadership in Coolidge's first term involved financial concessions to U.S. veterans of World War I. Congress passed a bill in 1924 to award veterans paid-up insurance plans, redeemable in twenty years. Coolidge, who had no military experience himself, felt that the insurance scheme was fiscally irresponsible and, to the consternation of the military and millions of the men who served in Europe, he vetoed the bill. Coolidge's contention, that the veterans' insurance legislation was not good economics, also did not sit well with critics who had characterized the president's earlier tax-reduction bill as tax reform only for the wealthy.

## THE CAMPAIGN AND ELECTION OF 1924

Had Coolidge not chosen to run for a full term as president in his own right, or had he been defeated in the 1924 election, his reputation as a chief executive would have been even lower than it is. His few legislative initiatives in 1923 and 1924 had been rebuffed, and he had sustained a poor record in resisting what he considered to be the inadvisable legislation that Congress sent to his desk. However, Coolidge did choose to run in 1924, was elected easily, and moved on to a relatively successful term of presidential leadership.

Once Coolidge indicated his willingness to stand for the Republican nomination, his choice by the convention was assured. After the usual speeches at the national convention in Cleveland, Coolidge received 1,165 votes on the first ballot—far more than enough to secure the nomination. To no one's surprise, the 1924 Republican platform endorsed tax reduction and the collection of loans to foreign nations. On the great international issue of the day, the Republicans refused to support U.S. membership in the League of Nations but did endorse participation in the World Court. Once again the Republicans took a stand against McNary-Haugenism, which proposed to support farm prices by having the federal government buy up farm surplus commodities, but did support a broadening of the farm export market and the establishment of a national cooperative to market farm products. The party also endorsed stronger enforcement of prohibition. Finally, perhaps bowing to the pull of the progressive wing of the party, the Republican platform supported a constitutional amendment banning child labor, an eight-hour workday, and a federal antilynching bill.

The Democratic party was, as usual in the 1920s, in disarray. The 1924 Democratic convention, held in New York, bogged down into a contest between William Gibbs McAdoo of California, favored by westerners and the South, and Alfred E. Smith of New York, the candidate of the eastern political machines. Finally, after a convention stalemate of historic proportions (a total of 103 ballots), John W. Davis, a New York lawyer originally from West Virginia, prevailed as a compromise choice. The Democratic platform favored a graduated income tax, farm relief on the order of McNary-Haugenism, multilateral disarmament, and a national referendum to allow the American people to decide whether the United States should join the League of Nations.

A resurgent Progressive party selected Senator Robert La Follette to head its national ticket. The Progressive party platform supported congressional legislation to break up monopolies; governmental ownership of water resources and railroads; steeply progressive taxes; abolition of the use of labor injunctions; and a multinational agreement to outlaw war.

The election campaign of 1924 which returned Coolidge to the White House was one of the strangest in U.S. history. The Republican slogans, "Keep Cool with Coolidge" and "Coolidge or Chaos," seemed to have broad appeal to an electorate that did not appear to want many changes. As with William McKinley in 1896 and 1900, the Republican political bosses kept their candidate under raps. For public consumption, the Republican campaign managers not only compared Coolidge to Washington and Lincoln but also cast him as a match for Caesar and Charlemagne. The Teapot Dome scandal of the previous administration did not appear to hurt Coolidge because voters seemed unwilling to blame him for the criminal activity of Harding's underlings. Davis, for the Democrats, however, took strong stands. He favored U.S. membership in the League of Nations, and he issued statements denouncing the Ku Klux Klan. The Progressive party candidates campaigned vigorously and ultimately drew a surprising amount of support.

H. L. Mencken, the brilliant satirist, wrote a number of columns on the 1924 election. On 25 August 1924 he ruminated on what the candidates for each of the three major parties represented in that election, and in so doing he succinctly captured the problem faced by the Democratic ticket: "Dr. Coolidge is for the Haves and Dr. La Follette is for the Have Nots. But whom is Dr. Davis for? . . . I have read all his state papers . . . and yet all I can gather from them is that he is for himself." In the ensuing election Coolidge received 54 percent of the popular vote. La Follette ran strongly for a third party candidate, picking up 17 percent of the vote; and Davis received a mere 29 percent of the votes. In the electoral college, Coolidge was a landslide winner. He clearly had a mandate to continue his nonaggressive leadership for four more years.

## THE SECOND TERM
Coolidge began his second term as he had his first—he stressed the importance of tax reduction. This time he would be more suc-

cessful. The Coolidge-Mellon tax bill that Congress passed in 1926 substantially reduced income and inheritance taxes and completely abolished the gift tax and most of the excise taxes levied during World War I. Subsequent tax legislation proposed by Coolidge and passed later in his administration reduced the corporate rates. All of the tax reductions achieved in the 1920s constituted a financial victory for the millionaire business tycoons whom Coolidge enjoyed entertaining in the White House.

Despite his success with tax legislation, Coolidge continued to butt heads with Congress on other issues. An example of this tension was the sphere of agricultural policy. The McNary-Haugen plan, intended to support farm prices by having the federal government buy farm surplus commodities and sell them abroad, emerged again from Congress. And again Coolidge vetoed it—and then once more in his second term. Coolidge's McNary-Haugen vetoes were probably wise because the legislation would have exacerbated the already serious problem of agricultural overproduction and, by permitting the dumping of surpluses abroad, the bill would have accelerated the international decline in commodity prices. Although Coolidge should be given credit for standing in the way of imprudent agricultural legislation, his administration took very few other positive actions to deal with the problems of the country's farmers.

## FRICTION WITH CONGRESS
In the last Congress of the Coolidge years (1927–1929) the president used his veto twelve times, compared with his total of five vetoes in the previous two Congresses. Experience in the White House, thus, did not improve Coolidge's ability to work with the legislative branch. The problem may have been endemic to the Vermonter's style of presidential leadership. Coolidge, of course, did not believe that a president should have an active legislative agenda. Nevertheless, he acknowledged that there were times that a president needed to set a direction for legislative action. In such instances he preferred to leave the particulars to Congress.

If Congress was in fundamental agreement with the president—as was the case with the Air Commerce Act of 1926, which placed aviation under the authority of the Commerce Department—Coolidge's approach worked well. But where Congress was not already predisposed to the president's position—as on immigration legislation—Coolidge did not possess the will or the political tools to bend the legislators to his wishes. Moreover, when legislation that Coolidge did not favor arrived on his desk—such as the McNary-Haugen farm bills—he did not hesitate to throw it back in the collective face of Congress, packaged in stinging vetoes. Coolidge seldom gave up something to receive something in return—there was little of the wheeler-dealer in him, and he had few friends in the House and Senate.

## FOREIGN AFFAIRS

Coolidge's record in foreign affairs, especially in his second term, was stronger than in domestic matters. This is surprising because, before becoming president, Coolidge had never left North America. One danger for a president in foreign affairs is to try to do too much, to be too aggressively international. By erring on the side of caution, Coolidge avoided problems that handicapped a committed internationalist such as Woodrow Wilson.

For example, Coolidge possessed the good political sense to avoid the volatile issue of membership in the League of Nations, and he and his secretaries of state left Great Britain to deal with the simmering revolution in China. But he did not turn his back entirely on the international scene. He wisely sought to bolster European prosperity by authorizing the renegotiation of the terms on loans owed to the U.S. government and by encouraging private investment in European businesses. He was also willing to allow the country to participate in the World Court.

In addition, the Coolidge administration deserves some credit for its dealings with Latin American nations. Coolidge's appointment of his Amherst classmate, Dwight Morrow, as ambassador to Mexico was a master stroke. Morrow's sympathetic understanding of the Mexican situation may have prevented serious strife in the 1920s between the United States and its southern neighbor. The major setback to relations with Latin America was the invasion of Nicaragua in 1927, but Henry Stimson, Coolidge's emissary to Nicaragua, conducted a successful mission to Managua that smoothed over many of the tensions and laid the basis for the withdrawal of U.S. forces from Nicaragua in the early 1930s.

The Coolidge administration's most notable foray into international affairs was the Kellogg-Briand Pact of 1928. Coolidge gave grudging support to Secretary of State Frank Kellogg in his quest, in consort with French Foreign Minister Aristide Briand, to secure signatures to an international resolution "outlawing war" as an instrument of national policy. The resulting agreement—although it now appears hopelessly naive given the horrors of World War II, the war in Vietnam, and the continuing strife in the Middle East—made sense in the late 1920s. Ultimately sixty-two nations would sign the agreement renouncing war as a means of settling disagreements with other nations. Although the pact's supporters failed to halt the militaristic rise of Germany and Japan in the 1930s, their short-sightedness was shared by the more hard-headed politicians and diplomats of the era. The Kellogg-Briand Pact took a risk for peace, which in itself is noteworthy. That it failed should not be laid completely at the door of Kellogg or Coolidge.

## THE U.S. BUSINESS COMMUNITY

Above all else, the Coolidge presidency has been known for its support of business. As long as Andrew Mellon was the president's principal adviser, the Coolidge administration's probusiness policy was a given. It is interesting that Coolidge, who had been a career politician and had never built a business himself, would have such a strong devotion to big business, but his commitment was a sincere one. The various Coolidge tax packages were consistently probusiness. At no time in his administration did the president or his attorneys general seek to break up conglomerates. In addition, Coolidge enjoyed the company of the captains of industry, whether in the White House or in their palatial homes.

Coolidge sensed that in the 1920s, most Americans wanted business to prosper. The president's style of laissez-faire executive leadership and his visceral commitment to the aims of business dovetailed nicely, as one of his most famous statements reveals: "Do the day's work. . . . If it be to help a powerful corporation better to serve the people, whatever the opposition, do that. . . . Don't expect to build up the weak by pulling down the strong."

Historians will probably never cease debating the degree to which the Coolidge administration's hands-off attitude toward business contributed to the Great Depression. It is true that the president did not heed warnings that the lack of regulation of banks was potentially dangerous. It is also true that several members of Congress expressed to him their apprehensions that stock speculation had gone too far, and that Democrats registered persistent criticisms that workers were not sharing sufficiently in the prosperity of the Roaring Twenties. However, given Coolidge's philosophy of executive leadership, he was a prisoner of the prosperity of his era. Late in his presidency Coolidge asserted that "four-fifths of all our troubles in this life would disappear if we would only sit down and keep still." The looming hard times were part of the problematic one-fifth of Coolidge's problems that could not be avoided by inertia. For that, Coolidge will long bear a measure of the blame for the Depression.

## LEAVING THE "SPLENDID MISERY"

To the surprise of most Americans, Coolidge announced in the summer of 1927 that he would not seek another term as president. Despite attempts to get the president to reconsider or at least amplify upon his brief declination statement, Coolidge provided few clues as to the reasons behind his refusal to run. Health and fatigue were probably concerns, as was his desire to spend more time with his family. Some historians and biographers have speculated that Coolidge saw the Depression on the horizon and wanted to leave with his reputation for presiding over a period of prosperity intact. Coolidge was fond of quoting Thomas Jefferson's statement that the U.S. presidency was a "splendid misery." In March 1929, a scant six months before the stock market crash, Coolidge was finally released from his gilded cage, handing over the presidency to his fellow Republican Herbert Hoover.

The Coolidges retired to the site of their first political triumphs, Northampton, Massachusetts. In retirement Coolidge served on the board of directors of a life insurance company and wrote his autobiography and occasional articles for magazines and newspapers. In some of his writings he addressed the problems posed by the Depression. His proposed solutions were essentially those of stand-pat Republicanism—reduce individual and government spending, pay off debts, and bear the short-term losses without complaint.

By 1932 Coolidge's health, which had never been good, had deteriorated markedly. He even lost his once-prodigious appetite. On 5 January 1933, he came home from his Northampton office after only about an hour spent working on his correspondence. Around midday he died of a coronary thrombosis. The following morning newspapers around the country carried long and generally glowing tributes to Coolidge. The *New York Times* that day printed fully twelve pages of details, reminiscences, and evaluations of the man from Vermont and his presidency.

## EVALUATION OF COOLIDGE'S PRESIDENCY

Polls of historians rating American presidents have consistently placed Calvin Coolidge near the bottom. That is unfortunate because the Coolidge presidency was far from a failure. Taxes were reduced and prosperity reigned, relations abroad improved, and corruption in the high reaches of government was exposed and routed out. Moreover, Coolidge was consistently popular during his years in Washington. As more than one obituary writer pointed out, Coolidge was exactly the kind of president that most voting Americans wanted in the 1920s. Historians of the twenty-first century, however, will probably continue to disparage the Coolidge administration for contributing to the dizzying financial spiral that led to the Great Depression and for turning a blind eye to the threat of totalitarianism in Europe and Asia. President Coolidge, despite his popularity in the 1920s, will continue to be described as a reserved and slightly humorous bumbler. Someday, perhaps, a biographer of Coolidge will apply the so-called hidden-hand analysis of quiet, delegatory leadership to rehabilitate the executive reputation of the man from Vermont. Until that happens, Coolidge will probably remain in the bottom fifth of historians' pantheons of the American presidency.

## BIBLIOGRAPHY

Abels, Jules. *In the Time of Silent Cal* (Putnam's Sons, 1969).

Allen, Frederick Lewis. *Only Yesterday* (Harper & Row, 1931).

Coolidge, Calvin. *The Autobiography of Calvin Coolidge* (Cosmopolitan Book, 1929).

Ferrell, Robert H. *The Presidency of Calvin Coolidge* (University Press of Kansas, 1998).

Fuess, Claude M. *Calvin Coolidge: The Man from Vermont* (Archon Books, 1965).

Leuchtenburg, William E. *The Perils of Prosperity, 1914–1932* (University of Chicago Press, 1959).

McCoy, Donald R. *Calvin Coolidge: The Quiet President* (Macmillan, 1967).

Mencken, H. L. *A Carnival of Buncombe: Writings on Politics.* Edited by Malcolm Moos (Johns Hopkins University Press, 1956).

Murray, Robert K. *The Politics of Normalcy: Governmental Theory and Practice in the Harding-Coolidge Era* (Norton, 1973).

Ross, Ishbel. *Grace Coolidge and Her Era* (Dodd, Mead, 1962).

Schlesinger, Arthur M., Jr. *The Crisis of the Older Order, 1919–1933* (Houghton Mifflin, 1957).

White, William Allen. *A Puritan in Babylon: The Story of Calvin Coolidge* (Macmillan, 1938).

★★★ 31 ★★★

# HERBERT CLARK HOOVER
## 1929–1933

*Paul W. Glad*

*Born 10 August 1874 in West Branch, Iowa, to Jesse Clark Hoover and Hulda Randall Minthorn Hoover; educated at Stanford University, Stanford, California (B.A. 1895); married Lou Henry, 10 February 1899, Monterey, California; two children; elected president in 1928 on the Republican ticket with Charles Curtis of Kansas, receiving 21,391,993 popular votes and 444 electoral college ballots, defeating the Democratic ticket of Alfred Emanuel Smith of New York and Joseph Taylor Robinson of Arkansas (15,016,169 votes and 87 electoral ballots); died 20 October 1964 in New York, New York; buried at West Branch, Iowa.*

No man has ever become president of the United States with qualifications surpassing those that Herbert Hoover presented to voters in the election of 1928. As a spectacularly successful mining engineer, Hoover had gained great respect within his profession during the years before World War I. Participating in international mining operations, he had also made his mark among business leaders of the prewar global economy. Then, turning from private pursuits to public administration, he had served the nation in several influential positions: as a dauntless director of international relief programs during World War I; as a reliable adviser to presidents in both major parties; as a trustworthy associate of political leaders and diplomats representing the great powers; as an effective troubleshooter who seemed to have a solution for every problem that vexed the nation. With those credentials, Hoover easily captured the nomination on the first ballot at the 1928 Republican national convention, and he overwhelmed his Democratic opponent, Al Smith, in the general election. Gaining more than 58 percent of the popular vote nationwide, Hoover won the electoral votes of forty states, including five in the normally Democratic solid south.

## THE "NEW DAY"

Confident of his administrative skills and certain of his ability to meet whatever emergencies might arise, Hoover adopted a felicitous byword for his presidency. He assured Americans that they stood at the dawn of a "New Day." The term suggested more than a continuation of the economic well-being associated with the 1920s; as Hoover used it, he seemed to be forecasting an expansion of prosperity to include Americans of all regions, interests, and classes. Unable to anticipate the irony that historians were to find in his prediction, he asserted that "with the help of God," Republican policies would lead to a happy future "when poverty will be banished from this nation." Unfortunately, Hoover's expectations proved grievously misleading. The New Day that opened with sanguine anticipation of good things to come ended with economic dysfunction during the long twilight of Hoover's final three years in the White House.

What went wrong? Why did Hoover, whose achievements before 1929 provided substance for one of the most celebrated success stories of U.S. history, seem diffident and feckless in meeting the economic calamity that befell the American people during his presidency? Before scholars peeled away layers of his career to probe the workings of his mind, the complexities of his character, and the nature of his administrative style, analysis of his presidency remained fixed in stereotypes formed during

the Great Depression. Franklin D. Roosevelt defeated Hoover in 1932, and more than three decades were to pass before those somber, derogatory representations began to change. Only after Hoover's death in 1964 and the opening of the Hoover Presidential Library in 1966 did scholarly studies of the man and his times appear in increasing number. The new investigations not only revealed strengths that explain Hoover's early achievements culminating in his victorious presidential campaign, but also provided a basis for dispassionately assessing weaknesses and shortcomings, as well as difficulties and obstacles, that help to account for the failures of his presidency.

## A MOST IMPRESSIVE RESUMÉ

At the time Americans elected Hoover to succeed Calvin Coolidge, however, they foresaw neither economic breakdown nor political frustration. Hoover's reputation for accomplishment had reached every corner of the planet, and at home, supporters gloried in his achievements as verification of success myths that held a central place in the nation's folklore. Indeed, Hoover seemed to have come striding into public consciousness directly from the pages of a Horatio Alger novel. Like an archetypal hero of the didactic boys' books that were supposed to instill young readers with manly virtues, he had demonstrated quickness of mind and strength of character in overcoming adversities early in life. He had also experienced the good fortune that according to popular scribblings always descends on the virtuous, and he had risen to prominence in the world of affairs.

Born in 1874 in the pleasant Quaker community of West Branch, Iowa, the son of a blacksmith, Herbert ("Bert") Hoover later recalled an idyllic childhood. The family of five lived in a tiny three-room house on the banks of Wapsinonoc Creek, where Bert developed a fondness for fishing that was to last a lifetime. Securely established in that little Quaker village nestled in the center of some of the world's richest farmland, the Hoovers looked optimistically toward the future. Then calamity struck. Both parents died before Hoover reached the age of 9, and relatives took on the responsibility of caring for the three children. Bert went to live with a maternal uncle in Newberg, Oregon, where he attended the Friends' Pacific Academy and worked as an office boy for a real estate company.

His uncle wanted him to enroll in a Quaker college, but Hoover took the entrance examinations for the new Stanford University, and he became a Pioneer, as members of the university's first class called themselves. In 1895, Hoover graduated with an A.B. degree in geology, and after some months of hardship during the severe depression of the 1890s, he managed to find work with Louis Janin, one of the most influential mining engineers in the American West. Hoover succeeded brilliantly. Within two years, the London-based Bewick, Moreing and Company hired him to manage a gold mine in Australia; by 1901, after conducting mining and other operations in China, he became a partner in the firm. With a residence in London and with global interests in mining, he left Bewick, Moreing in 1908 to work independently as a consultant in mining operations worldwide. Four years later, though not yet 40, Hoover decided he had no further need to increase his fortune, and he resolved to spend the rest of his life in activities serving the broader interests of humanity.

## THE GREAT WAR

Not one to dally when he knew what he wanted, Hoover soon gave full attention to his second career. Included among his first public service activities was the promotion of a world's fair planned by California interests to commemorate Balboa's discovery of the Pacific. Using British connections, Hoover hoped to persuade King George V that a state visit to San Francisco and Vancouver would do wonders for English-speaking peoples. A strong believer in direct contacts, he sailed to London to present his plan for the proposed exposition. Thus he was on hand when the Great War broke out in 1914, and he immediately took the lead in

organizing a safe return for Americans traveling abroad that summer. The task accomplished, Hoover turned his attention to organizing relief programs for war-devastated populations of Europe. Frequently and fearlessly crossing lines of battle, he managed to coordinate relief efforts and at the same time to secure cooperation from the Central Powers. His performance drew general praise, and after the United States entered the war, President Woodrow Wilson asked Hoover to become head of the U.S. Food Administration.

With his success in meeting wartime responsibilities, Hoover emerged as one of Wilson's trusted experts. He gained even greater influence as a member of the Allied Powers' Supreme Economic Council and as an economic adviser to the U.S. delegation at the Paris Peace Conference of 1918. Although Hoover had backed Theodore Roosevelt in the election of 1912, the influence he wielded during and after the war was consistent with his admiration of Wilson. Before going to Paris, he had urged voters to support the president's policies in the elections of 1918; after returning from the conference, he pleaded with the Senate to ratify the treaties that Wilson brought back. Then, during the dark months after the president's physical collapse and the Senate's rejection of the treaties, Hoover confronted the possibility that his own influence might be slipping away.

## PRESIDENTIAL HOPES IN 1920

Hoping to avoid animosities such as those Wilson confronted, Hoover concluded that the time had arrived for reestablishing his professional association with engineers, as well as for reaffirming his political ties to the Republican party. In 1920, he participated in forming the Federated American Engineering Societies, and in June his colleagues chose him as the organization's first president. Convinced that engineering techniques could provide the key to solving problems in postwar American society, Hoover allowed supporters to organize a campaign for the Republican presidential nomination in 1920.

Committed also to principles that Theodore Roosevelt had championed, Hoover thought that the best hope for the future rested in the progressive wing of the Republican party. As a candidate for the Republican nomination, he therefore sought to meld Bull Moose political objectives with engineering methods to ensure economic and technical progress for the American people in the postwar period. At the same time, he intended to remain steadfast to important ideas embodied in Wilson's New Freedom. By using powers of the federal government, he sought to encourage voluntary activities, and in that way he thought he could promote economic well-being without limiting the imagination and the initiative of individual Americans.

Old guard Republicans, who had responded neither to the call of the Bull Moose nor to the reforms of Wilson's New Freedom, remained unimpressed with Hoover's ideas. Hostile to the international program that had led to formation of the League of Nations, they questioned Hoover's commitment to the Republican party. Strongly suspecting him of opportunism, they made common cause with farmers who thought that the price controls of Hoover's wartime Food Administration had discriminated against agricultural interests. The combined opposition of the old guard and the agrarian radicals was enough to block Hoover's nomination, but his following was too strong to be ignored. After Warren Harding's victory in 1920, Hoover agreed to serve as secretary of commerce, and in that position he became indispensable to the success of the Republican party during the new era of the 1920s.

## SECRETARY OF COMMERCE
In both the Harding and the Coolidge administrations, Hoover succeeded in greatly expanding his department's responsibilities and influence. Writing about his energetic activity in many areas of the U.S. political economy, journalists often described him as a human dynamo. Even a partial list of his accomplishments is impressive. He increased the data-gathering capabilities of key bureaus in his department so as to offer business enterprises the information they needed for making intelligent decisions. He used his cabinet position to help establish regulations for the burgeoning aeronautics, radio, and movie industries. He aided in creating imaginative programs for housing a population that was rapidly leaving the countryside to pursue new opportunities in urban settings. He worked at improving inland waterways in order to lower transportation costs. He promoted the construction of dams and levies, especially along the Mississippi and Colorado Rivers, thereby conserving precious water resources, providing facilities for irrigation, meeting the electric power needs of vast areas, and protecting farms and cities from the effects of devastating floods.

Just as important as the variety of problems for which Hoover found solutions as secretary of commerce was the method he used to secure approval of programs he wished to undertake. Isolating an area of concern, he would consult experts or call for a conference of experts to gain a sense of current thinking on the matter. Then, using both the data gathered in specialized bureaus and the focused research of specialists, he would work with private individuals and associations to achieve consensus on an appropriate response to the problem.

Although Hoover seldom spoke about the ways his Quaker upbringing affected his conduct in business and government, the Friends' influence was certainly evident in his approach to administration. His fondness for conferences derived in part from the Quaker practice of using meetings as means of clarifying and guiding day-to-day activities of the faithful. While Hoover's concern for consensus may at times have seemed incompatible with his individualism, his emphasis on the free individual also derived from Quaker convictions. Believing that all human beings are equal in the sight of God, the Friends have consistently held that every person might receive guidance from the Inner Light, or the light of God's spirit that shines in every human soul. In so recognizing the fundamental dignity of every person, Quakers have aided rather than inhibited cooperative efforts of individuals working to improve society. Hoover himself, for all his forcefulness and determination, always stood closer to the benign individualism of the Quakers than to the rugged individualism of nineteenth-century captains of industry.

## HOPES FOR HIS PRESIDENCY

The president-elect's basic convictions remained unchanged after his victory at the polls in 1928, and he obviously expected to continue the administrative methods he had found successful in the Department of Commerce. Yet the election victory brought a significant shift in Hoover's responsibilities, and altered circumstances affected his demeanor as he set to work in anticipation of the New Day. No longer subordinate to Calvin Coolidge, a chief executive whose every instinct was to avoid tinkering with the machinery of government, Hoover felt driven to use his constitutional powers to promote as never before a variety of cooperative activities. Without imposing controls such as he had seen in eastern Europe after the Bolshevik Revolution in Russia in 1917, he hoped to encourage individual creativity among citizens working cooperatively to achieve unprecedented progress in the United States.

Despite Hoover's aspirations, he sometimes worried about earlier successes and a favorable press creating unrealistic expectations among American citizens. He knew that he would encounter obstacles to the achievement of his hopes and was confident that he could overcome them, but the sad truth is that for all his apprehensions he could not anticipate every problem that lay ahead. A major difficulty, one that grew increasingly troublesome during his presidency, was his awkwardness in coping with differences of opinion. His great success in nearly everything he had undertaken tended to make him impatient with those who disagreed with him, but there was more to the problem than that. Convinced that all who held office should serve the public interest without thought of gain for themselves, he

was bound to experience disappointment in his associations with politicians less highminded than he.

Mark Requa, a California oil man who had long served as an adviser, thought Hoover's great weakness as president was his impatience with small talk and petty politics, his inability "to slap people on the back and tell them they have done a good job." Hoover had too many admirers to justify the conclusion that he was always so unresponsive to loyalty, but the evidence of his tendency to focus on the dark side of every question—and sometimes to feel betrayed by his associates—is overwhelming. During 1931, as Hoover worked ceaselessly but vainly to restore prosperity, Secretary of State Henry Stimson wrote of the president that "it was like sitting in a bottle of ink to sit in his room."

Long before economic conditions reached that point, even before the inauguration, Hoover had difficulty securing the disinterested cooperation of individual politicians. He also encountered problems with factions of the Republican party, including both the conservatives, who could never quite forgive Hoover's dalliance with the Wilson administration, and the progressives, who expressed their agrarian sympathies by endorsing legislation to increase farm income. Hoping to avoid intraparty squabbling, at least until after he moved into the White House, Hoover followed the advice of Elihu Root, and left Washington until the inauguration. The president-elect and his wife, Lou Henry Hoover, boarded the *USS Maryland* on 19 November for a two-month tour of Latin America. Taking care to say that his visit symbolized the friendliness of one good neighbor toward another, Hoover was able to establish a basis for hemispheric cooperation in the future. Yet his tour could not dispel all Latin American doubts about the United States, and it also could not wondrously produce congeniality within the Republican party.

## SELECTING A CABINET

Hoover wished his presidency to begin harmoniously, to be sure, and he recognized that traditional practices could be reassuring. He therefore turned to the time-tested device of balancing particular interests in his selection of a cabinet. He asked Andrew Mellon to stay on as secretary of the treasury, an appointment that pleased the old guard because Mellon stood for opposition to radical economic change. To calm agricultural interests that had not fully shared in the prosperity of the 1920s, Hoover wanted Senator Charles L. McNary as secretary of agriculture. Coauthor of the McNary-Haugen bill, a measure to raise farm prices that Hoover had opposed, McNary would have had strong support in rural areas, but he declined the post. Hoover then settled for Arthur Hyde, a car dealer and the governor of Missouri, who initially aroused limited enthusiasm but eventually won Hoover's respect. In recognition of his support during the campaign, Hoover named James W. Good as secretary of war, and Walter Brown as postmaster general. Good died in December, and his undersecretary, Patrick J. Hurley took his place.

Hoover used his appointments as a way of building support among diverse interests, but he also expected cabinet members to perform their jobs effectively. Foremost in the development of domestic programs was Hoover's close friend since their student days at Stanford, Ray Lyman Wilbur, who accepted appointment as secretary of interior. Turning to foreign affairs and a person he trusted to head the Department of State, Hoover chose Henry Stimson, then serving as governor general of the Philippines. Though Hoover's opposite in personality and temperament, and privately irritated by the cloud of gloom that seemed to settle on the White House, Stimson respected the president and worked dutifully with him. The remainder of the cabinet included William D. Mitchell as attorney general, James J. Davis as secretary of labor, Charles Francis Adams as secretary of the navy, and Robert P. Lamont as secretary of commerce. In addition to selecting heads of departments with care, Hoover paid particular attention to the undersecretaries and the staff members who carried out much of the real

work after departmental policies had been established.

With his administration in place, Hoover was eager to be under way. In his inaugural address he called for reform of the judicial system, enforcement of the Eighteenth Amendment, coordination of government and business, increases in educational opportunities, the improvement of public health, and renewed efforts to ensure peace in the world. More specifically, he announced that he would request a special session of Congress to develop programs for agricultural relief and for modification of the tariff. He had conceded during the campaign that chronic farm problems were a major concern, and he now proposed to carry out his pledge of agricultural reform.

## AGRICULTURAL AND TARIFF REFORM

Few people disagreed with the president on the need for changes in the U.S. agricultural system. For years farmers had suffered economic hardship because technology had changed the means by which they made a living. Modernization in agriculture had, for example, increased the need for heavy investment in agricultural machinery and in trucks for transporting agricultural commodities to market. Many farmers favored raising farm prices to meet increased costs, and they tended to support the McNary-Haugen bill or some other form of agricultural subsidy. Hoover, however, opposed direct payments to farmers and favored incentives to increase their efficiency. Thus, instead of subsidies, he urged the formation of marketing cooperatives, through which farmers working together might arrive at a businesslike resolution of their difficulties. He also favored high tariffs on farm products to protect U.S. farmers from agricultural imports produced more cheaply abroad.

Fulfilling the pledge in his inaugural address, Hoover called for a special session of Congress to work out farm and tariff legislation. After a lengthy debate, Congress passed the Agricultural Marketing Act, and Hoover signed it on 15 June 1929. The act sought to reduce speculation, to eliminate waste in distribution, to encourage cooperative marketing associations, and to stabilize prices by controlling surpluses. A Federal Farm Board of eight members appointed by the president was to supervise the program. In signing the bill, Hoover proudly identified it as "the most important measure ever passed by Congress in aid of a single industry." Rural folk, however, were confident neither of its salience nor of its merit. Later, under the stress of economic depression, the persistence of agricultural problems seemed to justify the farmers' doubts.

Tariff revision, the other legislative action that Hoover regarded as necessary for improvement of the rural economy, became lost in struggles over the Agricultural Marketing Act and had to be deferred. When Congress finally passed the Smoot-Hawley Tariff in 1930, the Great Depression had begun. The new tariff not only helped increase the severity of hard times by raising the price of food for consumers but also angered other nations that believed the U.S. import policies would harm other economies abroad.

Although Hoover's difficulties at the beginning of his presidency were to have unfortunate long-term effects, students of the period should avoid concluding that after his 1928 victory he somehow lost his administrative skills, his humanitarian concerns, and his ability to accomplish his goals. Close examination of Hoover's first year in the White House reveals a record of significant performance that in the absence of the massive economic disasters of the early 1930s might have enhanced his reputation as a conscientious and effective public servant.

## A LIST OF ACCOMPLISHMENTS
President Hoover liked compiling lists of his achievements—just as baseball players keep track of their batting averages—and his accomplishments during the first three quarters of 1929 were as impressive as in years past. Hoover had scarcely assumed office when he ordered that large refunds of income, estate, and gift taxes become public information, a measure that progressives had long sought. He then moved on to implement other reform measures. He revealed the names of people involved in promoting judicial appointments. He went out of his way to support the civil liberties of individuals involved in labor disputes or accused of political subversion or charged with liquor law violations or subjected to racial and other forms of discrimination.

He supported conferences dealing with children's health and housing reform. He concerned himself with the welfare of American Indians and, like some of his Quaker associates and relatives, he sought in many ways to improve the conditions under which Native Americans lived. He set about updating the National Park Service and took an enlightened position on preservation of the natural environment. He used his influence as president to support international agreements on the limitation of armaments. Finally, in an action that followed naturally from Hoover's eagerness to have reliable information on conditions he confronted, he appointed a committee of distinguished social scientists and gave them carte blanche to study recent social trends. Although they published their report in 1933, too late to be of value to the Hoover administration, the study remains a useful document for historians of the 1920s.

## ECONOMIC DISASTER
The Great Depression that began with the stock market crash in October 1929 destroyed the reputation Hoover was building as one of the most intelligent, innovative, and knowledgeable presidents of modern times. Hoover was not alone, of course, in having to confront disgrace and humiliation. In two days, 28 and 29 October, the depreciation of stock amounted to an aggregate of between $15 billion and $18 billion, and an average stock lost about 25 percent of its value. That last week of October was only a beginning. By 1933, the wholesale price index (based on 1929 equaling 100) fell to 69 for all commodities, to 56 for raw materials, and to 75 for manufactured

goods. The money supply and credit operations contracted sharply, and every economic sector slumped as the gross national product, in 1929 prices, declined 31 percent. The most worrisome data of all showed rapidly rising rates of unemployment and rapidly declining wages. By 1931, nearly 15 percent of the labor force was unemployed, and by the time Hoover left office in 1933 one worker in four was looking for a job.

For years Hoover had known that an economic disaster of such proportions was a possibility, for his understanding of current economic theory at least equaled that of most professional economists. Having witnessed the fall of governments and the collapse of nations in Europe, he knew from experience what he was about. With his theoretical knowledge and his practical experience, he believed that he could guide Americans back to prosperity, and so avert an upheaval such as the one that had occurred in Russia after 1917. When the stock market collapsed that fateful October in 1929, then, the president perceived himself not as prophet of doom but as the savior of a way of life Americans held dear.

As President Harding's secretary of commerce, Hoover had been largely responsible for the conference on unemployment the president convened in 1921 to deal with some of the consequences of the postwar recession. The recommendations of that conference had helped overcome economic difficulties in the early 1920s, and they had helped ensure prosperity during the New Era. In 1929, confronted with an economic disaster more severe than the one eight years earlier, Hoover again prepared to move briskly into action. Indeed it was Hoover, not his successor, who became the first president to meet a recession with forceful government intervention. He did not prevail over adversity—after all, the depression that followed the crash of 1929 turned out to be the most devastating national trauma since the Civil War—but Hoover's response to it was more focused and more theoretically sound than most of his critics realized. Furthermore, it must be

said that while his policies did not overcome the Great Depression, neither did those of the New Dealers who came to power after Hoover's defeat in 1932.

Hoover's initial reaction to the Wall Street debacle was, predictably, to hold a series of conferences with business leaders and public officials. On 15 November, he reported on the preliminary assessment of experts he had consulted. Prior to the crash, they agreed, capital had been diverted into securities. That development had in turn created a pressing need for investment in productive enterprise, as well as a need to preserve jobs and maintain wages. Seeking means to meet those needs, Hoover offered a comprehensive plan in his State of the Union message to Congress in December 1929. He proposed new programs for banking reform, conservation of resources, public works, and housing. With these progressive measures, he linked programs more attractive to the old guard, programs for reductions in government expenditure, for a balanced budget, and for tax cuts. Enactment of that agenda would restore the nation's confidence, he predicted, and he urged the vigorous pursuit of his program "until normal conditions are restored."

## HOOVER'S PROGRAM
## FOR RECOVERY

In the effort to reinvigorate the economy, Hoover did not rest content with steps taken in the immediate aftermath of the Crash. During 1930, he devoted more and more attention to an expanded public works program. His object, of course, was to increase the number of jobs available to workers in the building trades generally, and especially to veterans who were unemployed. By the time fiscal year 1931 opened, estimates of expenditure had been revised upward by about $200 million over actual expenditures for the previous year. Then, in the fall, Hoover announced that investment expenditures of railroads and public utilities for the first eight months of 1930 had exceeded the expenditures for the same months of 1929 by $500 million. Those were encouraging signs, to be sure, but

Hoover, in what was almost a frenzy of optimism, took them to be more reliable indicators of a resurgent prosperity than they actually were. "I am convinced we have passed the worst," he told the U.S. Chamber of Commerce on 1 May 1930, and his conviction led him to reject proposals for unemployment relief submitted by a cabinet committee that he, himself, had established. While he agreed that increases in government spending could provide a desirable economic stimulus, he would not commit himself to a program lasting more than a year. Persuaded that his policies were working, Hoover thought that by midsummer of 1931 unemployment relief would no longer be necessary.

Unhappily, however, Hoover's program for recovery was less effective than he thought. Expenditures for public works were extensive, but they were paltry compared with the decline in expenditures for private construction. In 1930, the whole recovery program that Hoover had so commended was floundering—not because it was wrongheaded but because it was too limited. Expectations of economic revival encouraged revenue estimates that were much higher than the taxes actually collected. With lower revenue extractions and with greater emergency expenditures, the possibility of tax relief faded, and so also did the possibility of expanding programs for public works. Then Congress passed the Smoot-Hawley Tariff, and in June the president signed it into law despite the protests of professional economists. Hoover's popularity went into a tailspin, and in the midterm elections held later that year he lost much of what remained of his support in Congress.

At issue in the congressional elections of 1930 was, of course, the condition of the U.S. economy. Few observers anticipated the devastating defeat of Republican candidates in November. The president's program, although it had failed to meet the expectations of voters, nevertheless appeared to have been in large part successful. Democratic victories were a measure of the nation's discontent, as the triumphant opposition party made the most of high Smoot-Hawley tariff rates, the continuing agricultural depression, Hoover's rejection of proposals to provide relief for farmers in drought-stricken areas of the West, his continued support of prohibition, his internationalism as expressed in his recommendation that the United States join the World Court, and, most important, his apparent failure to exercise leadership in meeting the needs of people experiencing severe economic hardship.

To be sure, Hoover had formed the National Drought Committee to develop community relief programs, and the President's Emergency Committee for Employment (PECE) to coordinate community programs providing jobs and relief. When economic indicators showed improvement early in 1931, Hoover asserted that organized voluntary action had demonstrated its effectiveness. Again his wish had proven father to the thought, however, and again his claims of success turned out to be premature. In the early summer of 1931, Europe experienced severe economic distress, and with that development the Great Depression became an international reality. As conditions worsened at home and abroad, Hoover attempted to halt the global economic landslide with a one-year suspension of international debt payments. At home, he replaced PECE with POUR (the President's Organization for Unemployment Relief). The new agency proved no more effective than the old one, however, and popular pressure for direct relief increased greatly during the fall and winter of 1931.

## IDEOLOGY AND (UNDISCIPLINED) ACTION

Hoover sympathized with the unemployed, but he disliked proposals for direct government relief because he thought that such measures would do irreparable harm to the American character. He had seen other nations sacrifice individual freedom in exchange for economic security, and he was convinced it was a bad bargain. Hoover therefore turned to another measure, which was to become central in his program for countering the depression. In his State of the Union address on 8 December 1931, he proposed creation of the Reconstruction Finance Corporation (RFC), modeled on the War Finance Corporation of the Wilson administration. The RFC, which received congressional approval in January 1932 and was expanded later that year, made loans to banks, railroads, local relief projects, and public works programs. Hoover argued that a revival of credit would help restore confidence and that confidence, in turn, would overcome hard times. Again he met disappointment. Though the economy improved during the summer of 1932, recovery was by no means complete. Despite the RFC, economic conditions continued to deteriorate during Hoover's final months in office.

The saddest spectacle of those last months occurred when the Bonus Army—about 20,000 veterans of World War I—gathered in Washington to lobby for immediate payment of bonuses Congress had promised it would provide in 1945. In response to the veterans' pleas, the House of Representatives passed such a bill, but the Senate rejected it. Defeated, a number of the bonus marchers returned home; others, with no better place to go, remained in makeshift encampments on the Anacostia Flats and in vacant structures, many within sight of the nation's capitol. Trouble began on 28 July, as police were clearing buildings scheduled for demolition. Hoover turned to Secretary of the Army Patrick J. Hurley, and Hurley gave Army Chief of Staff Douglas MacArthur the task of forcing the veterans out. With battle-equipped troops and tanks, MacArthur drove the veterans from the city and into their encampment, which by midnight had been consumed in fire. The president had obviously let matters get out of control.

As Hoover agonized over violence in the District of Columbia, Franklin Delano Roosevelt, in the company of Felix Frankfurter, listened to news of the Bonus Army.

Smiling, Roosevelt remarked, "Felix, this will elect me." He was right. On 8 November, citizens cast ballots for FDR by overwhelming margins. After the 1932 election, memories of the New Day faded from the minds of citizens as they welcomed a New Deal for the American people.

## BIBLIOGRAPHY

Arnold, Perry E. *Making the Managerial Presidency, 1905–1980* (Princeton University Press, 1986).

Burner, David. *Herbert Hoover: A Public Life* (Knopf, 1979).

Chandler, Lester V. *America's Greatest Depression, 1929–1941* (Harper & Row, 1970).

Fausold, Martin. *The Presidency of Herbert Hoover* (University Press of Kansas, 1985).

Hamilton, David. *From New Day to New Deal: American Farm Policy from Hoover to Roosevelt, 1928–1933* (University of North Carolina Press, 1991).

Karl, Barry. *The Uneasy State: The United States from 1915 to 1945* (University of Chicago Press, 1983).

Lichtman, Allen J. *Prejudice and the Old Order: The Presidential Election of 1928* (University of North Carolina Press, 1979).

Lisio, Donald. *Hoover, Blacks, and Lily-Whites: A Study of Southern Strategies* (University of North Carolina Press, 1985).

———. *The President and Protest: Hoover, Conspiracy, and the Bonus Riot* (University of Missouri Press, 1974).

Lloyd, Craig. *Aggressive Introvert: A Study of Herbert Hoover and Public Relations Management* (Ohio State University Press, 1972).

Nash, George H. *The Life of Herbert Hoover,* 3 vols. (Norton, 1983–1996).

Peel, Roy V., and Thomas C. Donnelly. *The 1920 Campaign: An Analysis* (Richard R. Smith, 1931).

Robinson, Edgar Eugene, and Vaughn Davis Bornet. *Herbert Hoover: President of the United States* (Hoover Institution Press, 1975).

Stein, Herbert. *The Fiscal Revolution in America* (University of Chicago Press, 1969).

★★★ 32 ★★★

# FRANKLIN DELANO ROOSEVELT
## 1933–1945

*Sidney M. Milkis*

*Born 30 January 1882 in Hyde Park, New York, to James Roosevelt and Sara Delano Roosevelt; educated at Harvard College, Cambridge, Massachusetts (B.A. 1903) and Columbia Law School (left without degree); admitted to the bar; married (Anna) Eleanor Roosevelt, 17 March 1905, New York, New York; six children; elected to the presidency in 1932 on the Democratic ticket with John Nance Garner, receiving 22,821,857 popular votes and 472 electoral college ballots, over the Republican slate of Herbert Clark Hoover of Iowa and Charles Custis of Kansas (15,761,845 votes and 59 electoral ballots); reelected with Garner in 1936 with 27,476,673 votes and 523 electoral ballots, over the Republican ticket of Alfred Mossman Landon of Kansas and Frank Knox of Illinois (16,679,583 votes and 8 electoral ballots); reelected in 1940 with Henry Agard Wallace of Iowa, receiving 27,243,466 votes and 449 electoral ballots to the Republican tallies for Wendell Lewis Willkie of New York and Charles Linza McNary of Oregon (22,304,755 votes and 82 electoral ballots); reelected in 1944 with Harry S Truman of Missouri, receiving 25,602,505 popular votes and 432 electoral ballots, over Thomas Edmund Dewey of New York and John William Brickman of Ohio (22,006,278 popular votes and 99 electoral ballots); died 12 April 1945 in Warm Springs, Georgia; buried in Hyde Park, New York.*

Franklin Delano Roosevelt (FDR) is one of those rare occupants of the White House whose name defines not just a presidency but also an era. Like the other contenders for presidential greatness in American history—Thomas Jefferson, Andrew Jackson, and Abraham Lincoln—FDR left more than a record of achievement; he left a legacy. Arguably, the most enduring contribution of Roosevelt's presidency was the consolidation of "modern" executive leadership. Many of the most important characteristics of the executive date from the Constitutional Convention and the earliest days of the Republic; during the nineteenth century, too, significant patterns and practices took shape. Still, prior to FDR, the executive office was not yet the center of politics and government in the United States.

Until the 1930s, the presidency was the captive of principles and institutions dedicated to limited and decentralized government. The foundation of this decentralized polity was the political party, rooted in the states and localities; at the national level Congress, the most decentralized federal institution, reigned supreme. Before Roosevelt's New Deal, presidents who sought to exercise power expansively or who perceived a need for the expansion of the national government powers were thwarted, as Stephen Skowronek has written, "by the tenacity of this highly mobilized, highly competitive, and locally oriented democracy."

What distinguished the modern presidency was the emergence of the president, rather than the Congress or the party organization, as the leading instrument of popular rule. Acting on this concept of presidential power, Theodore Roosevelt and Woodrow Wilson inaugurated the practices that strengthened the president as popular and legislative leader, as "the steward of the public welfare." It fell to FDR, however, to consolidate or institutionalize the changes in the executive office that were initiated during the Progressive era. Roosevelt's leadership was the principal ingredient in a full-scale partisan realignment of the political parties, the first in history that placed presidential power at the heart of its approach to politics and government. After Roosevelt's long tenure, the new understanding of executive responsibilities would lead even conservative Republican presidents to embrace the powers and responsibilities of modern executive leadership.

## BREAKING "FOOLISH TRADITIONS"

So great an impression did Franklin Roosevelt make on the U.S. political system that in the most recent survey of historians, he ranked as the second-greatest president in history, surpassed only by Abraham Lincoln. Above all, FDR's ranking can be attributed to his efforts to lead the American people through the Great Depression. As Roosevelt prepared to take the oath of office on 4 March 1933, the ranks of the unemployed numbered 15 million, about one-third of the work force. In thirty-two states, every bank had been closed by state government edict, and in the remaining sixteen states, bank operations were severely curtailed. On the morning of the inauguration, the New York Stock Exchange closed.

The national despair notwithstanding, Roosevelt's arrival in Washington was greeted with hope. Although "a cloud of worry . . . hung over the vast throngs" who came to see FDR inaugurated as the nation's thirty-second chief executive, the New York Times reported, "the new President's recurrent smile of confidence, his uplifted chin and the challenge of his voice did much to help the national sense of humor to assert itself." In truth, the country was ready to be enthusiastic over any display of leadership; the people were eager to be convinced that FDR would exhibit the kind of bold and energetic initiative they had demanded but had not received from Hoover.

Unlike Hoover, Roosevelt was admirably well suited to lead by personality and background. "The essence of Roosevelt's Presidency," the political scientist Clinton Rossiter has written, "was his airy eagerness to meet the age head on." His confidence stemmed not only from a privileged, albeit challenging, upbringing in Hyde Park, New

York, but also from an admirable political education: state senator, assistant secretary of navy in the Wilson administration, vice-presidential candidate in 1920, and two-term governor of New York, then the largest state in the Union.

Roosevelt's faith in his own abilities was accompanied by a willingness to experiment, which he displayed throughout his presidency. The nation became aware of that willingness when, shattering precedent, he hired a small plane to take him to the Democratic national convention in Chicago to make his acceptance speech. In the past, major party nominees had stayed away from the convention, waiting to be notified officially of their nomination. But FDR wanted to demonstrate dramatically that his physical disability (the year after the 1920 campaign he had been stricken with poliomyelitis) would not hinder him as a candidate or a president. "The convention rose enthusiastically to the voyager of the skies," marvelled one reporter, "and accepted his method of travel and the fact that he endured its rigors so well as a proof of his venturesome spirit and fine physical equipment for the office of the President of the United States."

Roosevelt also wanted to show his party and the nation that he would not hesitate to break revered traditions that stood in the way of his vision of progress. "I have started out on the tasks that lie ahead by breaking the absurd traditions that the candidate should remain in professed ignorance of what has happened . . . until he is formally notified of that event many weeks later," Roosevelt told the convention on 2 July 1932. "Let it also be symbolic that in so doing I broke traditions. Let it be from now on the task of our party to break foolish traditions."

Implicit in this bold call for experimentation was a challenge to the dominance of the party organization by leaders in the states and the Congress. The only previous presidential candidate to attend a convention was Theodore Roosevelt (TR), who having bolted from the Republican party appeared before the gathering in Chicago

that launched the Bull Moose campaign in 1912. TR's personal control of the Progressive party was extraordinary. The Progressive party thus foretold not only of the emergence of a more active and expansive federal government but also of presidential campaigns conducted less by parties than by individual candidates. FDR's feelings for his cousin were as competitive as they were pious. As one of his aides, Ernest Cuneo, observed, "FDR ran against only one opponent in his life—Teddy Roosevelt, his relative. He admired Teddy's maverick tactics and his bold attacks on his own party. He did the same thing."

It fell to FDR to institutionalize the challenge to regular party practices represented by TR's 1912 campaign. Roosevelt was the first nominee to address a regular national convention, signaling the subordination of parties to candidate-centered campaigns in presidential elections. The closing remarks of his nomination speech, pledging a "New Deal for the American people," foreshadowed not just novel experiments in government activism, but also unprecedented challenges to institutional arrangements that had dominated the country since the early days of the republic.

## REDEFINING THE SOCIAL CONTRACT

The consolidation of the modern presidency was closely associated with a transformation of the country's governing philosophy. FDR's victory in 1932, in which he won 42 states to the incumbent Herbert Hoover's 6, was greeted with "a note of jubilation," according to *New York Times* columnist Arthur Krock, "that the day had come when the new philosophy was to replace the rejected theories of the old." Roosevelt nurtured and shaped this change. "Government includes the art of formulating a policy and using the political technique to attain so much of the policy as will receive general support," FDR said during the 1932 campaign, "persuading, leading, sacrificing, teaching always, because the great duty of a statesman is to educate." This paean to civic education was not perfunctory.

As Harvard Law School Professor Felix Frankfurter put it, FDR had a rare gift for taking "the country to school," for giving the American people "a full dress exposition and analysis" of principles and policies he supported.

Roosevelt's talent for mass education stood in sharp contrast to the recalcitrance of his predecessor. Hoover was comfortable in dealing with facts, which he could marshall to support a course of action. But, as Walter Lippman wrote, the Great Engineer was "diffident in the presence of the normal irrationality of democracy." In contrast, FDR cultivated the art of popular leadership; he saw his task as teaching the American people that a strong national government and executive were not alien to their values. Roosevelt's leadership involved, as presidential scholar Elmer Cornwell has written, "a careful process of grafting the new responsibilities of government onto the stalk of traditional American values."

Roosevelt first spoke of the need to modernize the elements of the old faith in his famous Commonwealth Club address, delivered during the 1932 campaign and appropriately understood as the New Deal manifesto. This speech has its origins in a memorandum that Adolph Berle, a principal member of FDR's "Brain Trust," sent the Democratic candidate in September of 1932. The focus of such an address, Berle suggested, should be the idea of individualism. Hoover claimed that individualism was served by a hands-off approach to social problems, that "government shall keep clear of the entire economic system, confining itself to emergency relief, keeping the peace, and the like." Observing that this laissez-faire doctrine could hardly foster liberty "when nearly 70 percent of American industry is concentrated in the hands of six hundred corporations," Berle offered the outline of a new concept of individual rights:

> I can see the opposite view, which is a far truer individualism, and might be a policy by which the government acted as a regulating and unifying agency, so that within

the framework of this industrial system, individual men and women could survive, have homes, educate their children, and so forth.

The theme of the Commonwealth Club address was that the time had come—indeed, that it had come three decades earlier—to recognize the "new terms of the old social contract." It was necessary to rewrite the social contract to take account of a national economy remade by industrial capitalism and the concentration of economic power, a new contract to establish countervailing power—a stronger national state—lest the United States steer "a steady course toward economic oligarchy." Protection of national welfare must shift from the private citizen to the government; the guarantee of equal opportunity required that individual initiative be restrained and directed by the national state.

> Clearly all this calls for a reappraisal of values. Our task is not discovery or exploitation of natural resources or necessarily producing new goods. It is the soberer, less dramatic business of administering resources and plants already in hand, of seeking to reestablish foreign markets for our surplus production, of meeting the problem of under consumption, of adjusting production to consumption, of adjusting wealth and products more equitably, of adapting existing organizations to the service of the people. The day of enlightened administration has come.

The creation of a national state with expansive supervisory powers would be, FDR noted, a long, slow task. The Commonwealth Club address was sensitive to the uneasy fit between energetic central government and the Constitution, and it specified that it was imperative that the New Deal be informed by a public philosophy in which the new concept of state power would be carefully interwoven with earlier conceptions of U.S. government. The task of modern government, FDR announced, was "to assist the development of an economic declaration of rights, an economic constitutional order." The traditional emphasis in U.S. politics on individual self-reliance should therefore give way to a new understanding of the social contract, in which the government guaranteed individual men and women protection from the uncertainties of the marketplace. Security was to be the new self-evident truth of political life in the United States.

## STRONG GOVERNMENT AS A PROTECTOR OF RIGHTS

Most significant in this shift from natural rights to programmatic liberalism is the association of constitutional rights with the expansion (rather than the restriction) of the role of the national government. The defense of progressive reform as an extension of rights in the Constitution was critical to the development of a positive understanding of government responsibility in the United States. To be sure, reformers in the Progressive era anticipated many elements of this understanding of government. But the distinction between progressives and conservatives, as most boldly set forth by the New Nationalism of Theodore Roosevelt during the 1912 Progressive party campaign, calling for "the substitution of frank social policy for the individualism of the past," all too visibly placed reformers in opposition to constitutional government and the self-interested basis of U.S. politics. Franklin Roosevelt's "liberalism" gave legitimacy to the nationalist principles of TR, embedding them in the language of constitutionalism as an extension, rather than the transcendence, of the natural rights tradition.

The need to construct an economic constitutional order was reaffirmed repeatedly throughout the Roosevelt presidency; in fact, each key rhetorical moment represented an effort to elaborate on this theme. The new understanding of the Constitution was the principal message of Roosevelt's first reelection bid in 1936, a decisive triumph that established the Democrats as the majority party in U.S. politics for a generation. The Democratic party's platform for that campaign, drafted by Roosevelt, was written as a pastiche of the Declaration of Independence. As the platform claimed with respect to the Social Security Act, enacted in 1935,

> We hold this truth to be self-evident—that the test of representative government is its ability to promote the safety and happiness of the people. . . . On the foundation of the Social Security Act we are determined to erect a structure of economic security for all our people, making sure that this benefit shall keep step with the ever increasing capacity of America to provide a high standard of living for all its citizens.

As Roosevelt would later detail in his 1944 State of the Union address, constructing a foundation for economic security meant that the inalienable rights secured by the Constitution—free speech, free press, trial by jury, freedom from unreasonable searches and seizures—had to be supplemented by a "second bill of rights . . . under which a new basis of security and prosperity can be established for all—regardless of station, race, or creed."

## PROGRAMMATIC RIGHTS AND THE NEW DEAL

Historians have generally divided Roosevelt's first term into two periods, each identified by a flurry of legislative activity lasting approximately one hundred days. The first (1933–1934) responded to FDR's call for "bold, persistent experimentation" to meet the great emergency at hand. Among these measures were the Emergency Banking Relief Bill and other legislation establishing the Works Progress Administration, the Public Works Administration, and the National Recovery Administration. The second period (1935–1936) brought laws such as the Social Security Act and the National Labor Relations Act that converted emergency programs into ongoing obligations of the national government.

As the 1936 platform made clear, the programmatic initiatives of the Second New Deal were not simply viewed as policy but were also considered tantamount to rights—the embodiment of the economic constitutional order. The centerpiece of Roosevelt's program was the Social Security Act, which proposed to create a comprehensive federal system of old age and unemployment insurance. To sell Social Security was no easy task. Remarking on the unusual commitment in the United States to individual self-reliance, Senator Hugo Black of Alabama wrote to a member of the Roosevelt administration on 19 June 1934, "The public in our country has little conception of the possibilities of social insurance," and "there are few people in this country who realize such systems of social insurance have been adopted in most of the civilized countries in the world."

Fourteen months after Black's letter, the Social Security Act sailed through Congress and was ceremoniously signed into law by the president. In the interim, FDR had nurtured public opinion carefully. The development of a national industrial society, Roosevelt argued, made it no longer possible for individual financial security to be achieved within the familiar bonds of the small community and the family. Rather, the complexities of great communities and of organized industry required that the federal government help people to secure their welfare in time of need. To bring this lesson home, the president's fireside chat of 28 June 1934 included a folksy yet effective illustration: the remodeling of the White House office building (the West Wing), which he likened to the adoption of social insurance. After describing the wiring and plumbing that were being installed, and the modern means of keeping offices cool in the hot Washington summers, Roosevelt noted: "It is the combination of the old and new that marks orderly peaceful progress, not only in building buildings, but in building government itself. Our new structure is part of and a fulfillment of the old. . . . All that we do seeks to fulfill the historic traditions of the American people."

With the enactment of the Social Security program, FDR had gone far in moving the nation beyond the traditional idea that rights embody only guarantees against government oppression, to the new understanding, articulated in his Commonwealth Club address and championed by the 1936 Democratic platform, that government also has the obligation to ensure economic security. When Roosevelt committed the government in 1935 to an uncompromising policy of financing Social Security by payroll tax financing rather than by general revenues, he did so believing that such policy would make the protection an earned right. To those who complained of the regressive nature of financing Social Security by a contributory program, Roosevelt stressed the *political* importance of linking welfare programs as closely as possible to the traditional principles and practices of American constitutional government. As FDR put it to one such critic,

> I guess you're right on the economics, but those taxes were never a problem of economics. They are politics all the way through. We put those payroll contributions there so to give contributors a legal, moral, and political right to collect their pensions. . . . With those taxes in there, no damn politician can scrap my social security program.

The National Labor Relations Act (NLRA; the Wagner Act), also enacted in 1935, was organized labor's Magna Carta. The Wagner Act established the National Labor Relations Board, which not only recognized but also protected the right of unions to bargain collectively. When Roosevelt became president, few factory workers belonged to a labor union. By the time he left office, industrial unionism was firmly established, largely because of the Wagner Act, which empowered the government to enter factories to conduct elections so that workers could decide whether to join a union.

### THE NEW DEAL AND ITS CRITICS
Although hitching the New Deal to a new understanding of rights helped to make the emerging national state more acceptable in

the United States, not everyone was enthusiastic about FDR's proposals. Besides the Social Security Act and the NLRA, the Second New Deal also included a progressive revision of the tax codes, and a public utility holding company antitrust law. In pushing these measures, Roosevelt appeared deliberately to accept a policy course that sharpened class conflict. As Otis Graham notes, this brought FDR "more enemies among businessmen in return for more friends among those without significant property."

Like his progressive predecessors TR and Wilson, FDR fashioned himself as a conservative reformer who sought not to oppose private enterprise but to strengthen it by curbing the most abusive business practices and by ameliorating the most extreme conditions of economic inequality. But the president was opposed in this effort by an unreconstructed segment of the business community that denied that the federal government had any right to regulate commercial activity. As Roosevelt complained in a letter to Felix Frankfurter in February 1937, "It is the same old story of those who have property to fail to realize that I am the best friend the profit system ever had, even though I add my denunciation of unconscionable profits." Roosevelt's resentment of his critics in business was intense. As he told a roaring crowd at the 1936 Democratic convention in Philadelphia,

> These economic royalists complain that we seek to overthrow the institutions of America. What they really complain of is that we seek to take away their power. Our allegiance to American institutions requires the overthrow of this kind of power. In vain they seek to hide behind the flag and the Constitution. In their blindness they forget what the flag and the Constitution stand for. Now, as always, they stand for democracy, not tyranny; for freedom, not subjection; and against a dictatorship by mob rule and the overprivileged alike.

The phrase *economic royalists* was coined by White House aide Stanley High. Since December 1935, he had been urging Roo-

sevelt "to redefine the New Deal in those fundamentally American terms in which the [Commonwealth Club] speech first defined it." In doing so, High suggested comparing the battle for an economic constitutional order with various U.S. crises, beginning with "the Tory record in the revolution and following the Tory thread right on down through our history to the present." How well such a historical comparison would reveal, High enthused, "the New Deal as the real Americanism."

In the Commonwealth address of 1932, Roosevelt had warned that without reform, the country would come under the grip of "princes of property." Four years later, he pressed a more dire message, telling the convention that "privileged princes of these new economic dynasties" had used their political fortunes and legal legerdemain to create a new form of despotism. As a result, the average man once more confronted the problem that faced the Minute Man:

> Against economic tyranny such as this, the American citizen could appeal only to the organized power of government. . . . The royalists of the economic order have conceded that political freedom was the business of government, but they have maintained that economic slavery was nobody's business. They granted that the Government could protect the citizen in his right to vote, but they denied that Government could do anything to protect the citizen in his right to work and his right to live.
>
> Today, we stand committed to the proposition that freedom is no half-and-half affair. If the average citizen is guaranteed equal opportunity in the polling place, he must have equal opportunity in the market place.

Although it sharpened political conflict along class lines, the Second New Deal and the message of the 1936 campaign were not really based on class. Rather, as Marc Landy has noted, "It was a promise to overthrow a monarchy in the name of the commoners. In a nation where nearly everyone fancies himself a commoner the breadth of appeal was enormous." More important, FDR provided a means for partisan identification with the New Deal based on a powerful and enduring understanding of rights. In the final analysis, FDR enlisted New Deal supporters in a war against privilege that reaffirmed the social contract. As the peroration of Roosevelt's militant nomination speech conveyed, this was not simply a cause for labor and the dispossessed but a challenge for a generation. Among these final passages, emphasizing "faith, hope, and charity," come the words for which this address would be remembered: "There is a mysterious cycle in human events. To some generations much is given. Of other generations much is expected. This generation of Americans has a rendezvous with destiny."

The merits of this important public message were recognized beyond the throngs in Philadelphia's Franklin Field. "Now that I have read the full text," an admiring Frankfurter wrote Roosevelt a few weeks later, "I find in the speech enduring quality which makes it a classic. You have given us something not only to win with, but to win for."

Frankfurter sensed correctly that the parties had gotten caught up in something big, and that Roosevelt's convention speech had helped clarify the fundamental struggle under way. As the *New York Times* reported in February 1936, "Liberalism and all it stands for is coming forward as an issue in the national campaign. Both New Deal and anti-administration spokesmen declare their devotion to the liberal ideal of freedom and democracy; both assail each other as opponents of true liberalism." The struggle's conclusion suggested a great triumph for Roosevelt and his understanding of the Constitution.

FDR's victory in 1932 had expressed the public resentment of Hoover more than its approval of FDR and the Democrats. But sweeping confirmation of Roosevelt and the New Deal program came in 1936, when he won 60 percent of the popular vote—the largest plurality ever by a presidential candidate—and carried all but two states. The 1936 election, which also strengthened the Democratic hold on both houses of Congress, marked the Democrats' emergence as the majority party. Yet the victory of Roosevelt and the New Deal was hardly complete. Indeed, after 1937, the Roosevelt administration became embroiled in struggles that raised anew severe doubts about the future of the economic constitutional order.

## THE THIRD NEW DEAL

Roosevelt's reappraisal of values is important in understanding the New Deal, but it is also important in understanding the consolidation of the modern presidency. The "economic constitutional order" presupposed a stronger national government, a significant expansion of national administrative power, anchored by a dominant and dominating executive. As Roosevelt had said in his Commonwealth Club address, "The day of enlightened administration has come."

Just as the first term was dedicated to the formulation of a new social contract and to the enactment of legislation called for by the economic constitutional order, so Roosevelt pursued a program during his second term that would thoroughly reconstruct the institutions and practices of U.S. constitutional government. This program was pursued with the understanding that programmatic rights, such as Social Security, would not amount to anything unless new institutional arrangements were established that would reorganize the powers and redistribute the functions of government. It included three controversial initiatives, marking Roosevelt's second term as one of the most tempestuous in U.S. political history: the executive reorganization bill, sent to Congress in January, 1937; the "court-packing" plan, sent to Capitol Hill some three weeks after the administrative reform measure; and the "purge" campaign, undertaken during the 1938 Democratic primary campaigns.

## THE EXECUTIVE
## REORGANIZATION BILL

Taken together, the institutional reforms of the second term signified the emergence of a political program that would establish a modern bureaucratic state in U.S. politics, one with a managerial capacity characteristic of modern states elsewhere, but absent in the United States because of the extraordinary antipathy to centralized administration in this country. The various battles that took place over the Courts, executive reorganization, and the Democratic party after FDR's reelection are usually not viewed as part of a systematic effort to remake American politics. Rather, the period from 1937 to 1939 is generally portrayed as a time when the reformist aspirations aroused by the electoral outcomes of 1936 were frustrated not only by the revival of adamant and unreasonable conservatives but also by the president's ill-advised efforts to punish them. According to the historian Barry Karl, however, "Roosevelt had a plan for his second term, a Third New Deal . . . that would have involved a dramatic transformation of American presidential administration."

So characterized, Roosevelt's political program was a serious effort, as the historian Ellis Hawley has written, to fill the "hollow core" in the American state's bureaucratic apparatus. The centerpiece of the Third New Deal was the executive reorganization bill, which would strengthen the administrative power and capacity of the president. Significantly, the bill proposed to create a number of new administrative tools and support staff, not just for Roosevelt but for the office as an institution. "No measure was closer to Roosevelt's heart," the *New York Times* reported in August 1938, and none aroused "more determination to force it through Congress than the reorganization bill."

Roosevelt is often criticized for his inattention to the institutional problems of administrative management; in fact, he had thought about administration for a long time and had a coherent understanding and program for reconstituting the executive. He first developed an appreciation of the importance of executive branch structure while he was assistant secretary of the navy in the Wilson administration. In his testimony before the House Select Committee

on the Budget of 1 October 1919, Roosevelt expressed dismay at the inability of the president to formulate and carry out a coordinated public policy. He put much of the blame for this failure on the chaotic organization of the bureaucracy and the lack of administrative personnel available to the president. Responding especially to the lack of presidential authority to hold the various departments and agencies to a comprehensive budget plan, Assistant Secretary Roosevelt called for the creation of a budget office, directly under the president and "charged with coordinating the various estimates into one budget and transmitting it to Congress."

The Budget Act of 1921 created a budget bureau but placed it in the Treasury Department rather than directly under the supervision of the president. This structure tended to circumscribe the administrative power of the president and to retain the autonomy of executive departments and agencies from the oversight of the White House.

But the Great Depression and Roosevelt's extraordinary leadership seemed to justify the president's more ambitious idea of administrative reform. As Americans increasingly came to regard the presidency as the preeminent source of moral leadership, legislative guidance, and public policy, pressure mounted to increase the size and professionalism of the president's staff. A modest office from the time of its creation, the presidency developed after the 1930s into a full-blown institution.

Roosevelt hastened this development when he named three of the country's foremost scholars of public administration— Louis Brownlow, Charles E. Merriam, and Luther Gulick—to a newly formed presidential committee on administrative management. Concluding that the more activist president—the steward of the new economic constitutional order—"needs help," the Brownlow committee, as it came to be called after its chair, proposed that the Executive Office of the President (EOP) be established. This presidential institution would include not just the bureau of the budget, but a new White House Office, to be staffed by loyal and energetic presidential aides whose public influence would be limited by their "passion for anonymity."

The committee also proposed to enhance the president's control of the expanding activities of the executive branch. By 1937, the Roosevelt administration confronted a bewildering array of sometimes autonomous agencies that offended its vision of a unified and energetic executive. Roosevelt even remarked shortly after the 1936 election that administrative management was the least successful aspect of his first term, and he was glad that the Republicans had not hit on this weakness during the campaign. The Brownlow committee called for an overhaul of the executive branch, recommending that the more than 100 government agencies then in existence be integrated into twelve major departments, each under the virtually complete authority of the president. Thus would "the national will be expressed not merely in a brief, exultant moment of electoral decision, but in a persistent, competent, day-by-day administration of what the nation has decided to do."

When presented to Congress, the Brownlow committee's recommendations provoked one of the more intense political controversies of FDR's presidency. The president's assurances that this reform was merely a nonpartisan, businesslike effort to infuse public administration with sound business practices could not camouflage the challenge that the White House's plans posed to the influence Congress and the traditional party organizations had historically exercised over administration. Roosevelt's two-year battle for comprehensive administrative reform wrote a new chapter in the long-standing struggle between the executive and the legislature for control of administration.

What gave the battle special intensity was that it occurred just as administration was becoming an important arena of public policy. As Gulick reported approvingly, the expansion of welfare and regulatory programs during the New Deal meant that the complex responsibilities of government increasingly were set forth in discretionary statutes, each of them little more than "a declaration of war, so that the essence of the program is in reality in the gradual unfolding of the plan in actual administration." Thus, the struggle between the White House and Congress for control of the departments and agencies was no longer simply a squabble about patronage and prestige. The right to shape the direction and character of American public life was also at stake.

Indeed, soon after the triumphant 1936 election, which seemed to justify the New Deal understanding of liberalism, Roosevelt told the committee that he viewed the PCAM as a surrogate constitutional convention. As Gulick's notes between the committee and the president for November 1936 read, Roosevelt noted that "since the election he had received a great many suggestions that he move for a constitutional convention for the United States," so as to codify the changes brought by the New Deal. But he feared that there "was no way of keeping such an affair from getting out of hand," what with the sharp conflict aroused by the New Deal program and its critics on the extreme right and left.

Roosevelt's hope for a quiet revolution was disappointed by the Seventy-fifth Congress (1937–1938). Although the bill passed the Senate, what emerged was a shadow of the original proposal. His opponents raised the cry of *dictator*, a charge that had special meaning because of the rise of fascism in Germany and Italy. So intense did the campaign against the reorganization bill become that in March 1938, Roosevelt felt compelled to issue a public letter to an unnamed respondent, denying that the reorganization bill would make the president a dictator. James Farley, the head of the Democratic National Committee, lamented, "Apparently because of the situation that exists in Europe, the people have become fearful of such a possibility in this country. The people are unnecessarily disturbed about . . . the Reorganization Bill."

Arguably, however, Congress would have been abnegating its constitutional responsibility by forfeiting control of administrative organization just at a time in U.S. political history when administration was becoming the center of government action. Roosevelt did not effectively disabuse legislators of this possibility. Indeed, the fact that he thought it necessary to disavow dictatorial ambitions only lent credence to the opposition's accusation.

In April 1938, the House rejected the compromise version of executive reorganization. Nearly one-third of the president's party brethren abandoned him, joining Republicans in voting to recommit the legislation. "For Franklin D. Roosevelt, this was absolute treason," Farley reported. "He felt that they had ridden into office on his coattails in 1936, that he was the man who got them there and that they were now running on false principles—that he had made representations to the country and they had no business doing this."

The furious struggle over administrative reform revealed that the Third New Deal and the international crisis had combined to provoke a serious constitutional crisis. Roosevelt argued that his vision of modern executive power, like the welfare state, was in keeping with sound constitutional principles. "The only thing that has been happening," he told the nation in a fireside chat of 7 May 1933, "has been to designate the President as the agency to carry out certain of the purposes of Congress. This was constitutional and in keeping with past American traditions."

Such was not the view of New Deal opponents. "As they saw it," Hawley has written, "the balance and separation of powers established by the Constitution was being destroyed by a power-seeking presidency gathering into itself the power that should be exercised by Congress and the states."

## THE COURT-PACKING PLAN

The ranks of the New Deal critics included not just Roosevelt's enemies in Congress and business but also, until 1937, a majority of the Supreme Court. That Court had struck down more important national laws in 1935 and 1936 than in any comparable period in history. Roosevelt's judiciary reorganization bill, sent to Congress in 1937, was an act of retaliation against that record. The bill provided that for every justice who failed to retire within six months of reaching the age of 70, the president would appoint a new justice. Since six of the nine justices already were 70 or older, Roosevelt would be able to enlarge the court to fifteen members by making new appointments. Presumably, these new justices would overcome the Court's resistance to the New Deal.

Like the executive reorganization bill, the proposed court-reform legislation was an integral component of administrative reform. Roosevelt's plan would restaff the judiciary with jurists who would not stand in the way of expanding executive administration. Significantly, the two Supreme Court decisions that enraged FDR the most were *Humphrey's Executor v. United States* and *Schechter Poultry Corporation v. United States*, both of which imposed constraints on the president's personal authority. These decisions which were handed down on 27 May 1935 (soon known to New Dealers as "Black Monday"), threatened—no less than the Congress's rejection of the executive reorganization bill—to derail the institutional changes Roosevelt believed were necessary to solve the underlying problems of the depression.

The *Humphrey* case denied the president the right to remove appointees from the independent regulatory commissions, a legal power Roosevelt thought had been settled by *Myers v. United States* (1926). The *Schechter* ruling was a direct challenge to the modern state. It declared that the discretionary authority that Congress had granted, at Roosevelt's request, to the National Recovery Administration (NRA), the leading economic agency of the early New Deal, was an unconstitutional delegation of legislative power to the executive.

Roosevelt initially responded to the *Schechter* challenge at a news conference in May 1935, holding forth for an hour and twenty-five minutes on a decision he considered "more important than any decision since the infamous Dred Scott case." It was bad enough, he argued, that the Court rejected the National Recovery Act's delegation of power to the executive, but the judiciary profoundly compounded its constitutional impropriety by denying that the NRA was a proper exercise of the government's commerce power. The matter of delegation of power was not insurmountable—it could be gotten around, the president intimated. But when linked with such a narrow construction of the national government's commerce power, the *Schechter* decision represented an outmoded defense of limited government that would have the consequence of preventing the political system from assuming its essential role in supervising the political economy. The New Deal had set the United States on the course of joining the community of nations in solving its social and economic crises, claimed FDR, but "now it has been thrown right back in our faces." Then, in words that amounted to a declaration of war on the Supreme Court—words that would anticipate the court-packing plan and give this press conference an enduring notoriety—Roosevelt concluded his constitutional lecture to the press: "We have been relegated to a horse-and-buggy definition of interstate commerce."

Roosevelt's controversial press conference had identified the issues sharply and made inevitable the open struggle with the Court that would occur some eighteen months later. Although the court-packing bill failed in Congress, Roosevelt claimed he had lost the battle but won the war, for the Court never struck down another New Deal law. In fact, since 1937—with the exception of the line item veto—the Supreme Court has not invalidated any significant federal statute to regulate the economy, nor has the Court judged any law to be an unconstitutional delegation of authority to the president. Most of the judicial barriers to national and presidential power had fallen.

But the bitter fight over the court-packing plan entailed a considerable political cost. Like the executive reorganization bill, the plan served as a lightning rod for the New Deal's opponents. As such, it sparked a resurgence of congressional independence and the formation of an enduring bipartisan conservative coalition, consisting mainly of Republicans and southern Democrats, which would block nearly all presidential reform initiatives until the mid-1960s.

## THE PURGE CAMPAIGN OF 1938

The 1938 purge campaign, in which the president attempted to rid his party of those who failed to support his programs, was Roosevelt's first response to the new ideological fissure within Congress. The campaign marked the culmination of party reform that complemented the other two initiatives of the Third New Deal and that would mold an executive-centered party, free of the obstructive power of state and local leaders. The president intervened in one gubernatorial and several congressional primary campaigns in a bold effort to replace recalcitrant Democrats with candidates who were "100 percent New Dealers." Although William Howard Taft and Woodrow Wilson had made limited efforts to rid their parties of uncooperative members, Roosevelt's campaign was conducted on an unprecedentedly large scale and, unlike the previous efforts, bypassed the regular party organization. The extent to which his action was regarded as a shocking departure from the norm was indicated by the label—*the purge*—that the press gave it. The term evoked Adolf Hitler's attempt to weed out dissenters from the German Nazi party and Joseph Stalin's elimination of suspected opponents from the Soviet Communist party.

Although the so-called elimination committee—the White House aides who helped plan the 1938 campaign—urged FDR to undertake a full-scale assault on the party, using Democratic legislators' support for the judicial and executive reorganization bills as a litmus test, the president preferred a more selective strike. His special concern was the South, a Democratic stronghold since the Civil War whose commitment to states' rights represented, as the journalist Thomas Stokes put it, "the ball and chain that hobbled the party's forward march."

The Roosevelt administration won an important victory in the campaign for a more national and programmatic party at the 1936 Democratic convention, where it led a movement to abolish the two-thirds rule. This rule required backing from two-thirds of the delegates to Democratic national conventions for the nominations of president and vice president. The South had long regarded the rule as a vital protection against the nomination of candidates unsympathetic to its problems. Elimination of the rule weakened the power of southern Democrats. It also removed an important obstacle to the transformation of a decentralized party—responsible only to a local electorate—into an organization more responsible to the will of a national party leader (the president) and to the interests of the national electorate.

Roosevelt's command of the party, as the rise of the conservative coalition in the Seventy-fifth Congress attests, did not overcome the factionalism within the Democratic ranks. But New Deal programs and party reforms did alter the structure of conflict within the party. Historically a multifactional party dominated by sectional interests, the Democrats after 1936 became a bifactional party with durable ideological and policy divisions.

Roosevelt knew that if the Democrats were to become a national liberal party, conservative southern Democrats would have to be defeated. He did not confine his efforts to the South during the 1938 purge attempt, but his most outspoken and unequivocal opposition was directed against his party brethren below the Mason-Dixon line. His fireside chat to the nation of June 1938, which launched the purge campaign, compared recalcitrant Democrats to "copperheads," who, FDR reminded the nation, "in the days of the war between the States tried their best to make Lincoln and his Congress give up the fight, let the Nation remain split in two and return to peace—peace at any price." The president's reference to the events of the Civil War and the fact that he most actively sought to unseat the incumbent Democrats in the South conjured images of a renewed northern assault on the region, one that "would precipitate another reconstruction era for us," as Virginia's conservative senator Carter Glass wrote a friend.

The purge campaign failed. All but two of the incumbent Democrats whom Roosevelt opposed were renominated. Moreover, the campaign, which was widely condemned as an assault on the constitutional system of checks and balances, galvanized Roosevelt's political opposition, apparently contributing to the heavy losses the Democrats sustained in the 1938 general elections. Ironically, then, FDR's campaign to purge party dissidents only strengthened the conservative coalition. Peter Gerry, a conservative Democratic senator from Rhode Island, wrote to North Carolina's senator Josiah Bailey in September 1938:

> The victories of [conservative Democrats] have had even a greater effect than I had hoped for. They show that Roosevelt cannot control Senators for he does not have the weight with voters in his party that the New Dealers thought he possessed. They have also destroyed the picture of his being invulnerable. The Senate and the House will stiffen and the opposition to the New Deal has had a great stimulation to its morale.

## THE EXECUTIVE REORGANIZATION ACT OF 1939

Although the purge failed at the polls, conservative Democrats did think carefully before crossing Roosevelt after 1938. Given FDR's personal popularity, which had been little damaged by the 1938 elections, the continuation of open party warfare would be disastrous in the 1940 election. As Senator Bailey wrote to a friend in early 1939, "We must restrain him in essential matters, but in non-essential matters, we may well afford to let him have his way, lest he go on the radio and tell the people their present condition is not due to the failure of his policies, but to the obstructive tactics of the Senate and House."

The Executive Reorganization Act of 1939, which was considerably weaker than

Roosevelt's original proposal, represented one of these nonessential matters. For example, it restricted FDR's authority to overhaul the bureaucracy to two years and exempted twenty-one of the more important government agencies from reorganization. Nevertheless, the implementation of the 1939 statute by Executive Order 8248 put many of the Brownlow recommendations into effect. The order created the Executive Office of the President and moved several agencies under its umbrella. Also included were the National Resources Planning Board (a long-term planning agency, which first proposed the concept of a second bill of rights to FDR) and a refurbished and strengthened Bureau of the Budget, which was transferred from the Treasury Department. Newly housed, the Budget Bureau began to acquire much greater powers, eventually attaining the responsibility to oversee the formation of the president's domestic program.

The 1939 reforms enhanced the capacity of the president to manage the expanding activities of the executive branch. Most significant, the creation of the Executive Office of the President hastened the development of the "administrative presidency," which exercised extensive domestic power on behalf of the president through rule making and policy implementation. To be sure, the absence of detail of Article II of the Constitution had always left the door open for independent presidential action. But the institutionalization of the presidency established a formal organizational apparatus with which presidents and their appointees could short-circuit the separation of powers, ratifying the transfer of authority from Congress to the executive, which originally occurred on FDR's watch.

But the purpose of New Deal reforms was not to strengthen presidential government per se. Rather, the presidency was strengthened under the assumption that as the national office, it would be an ally of progressive reform. Consequently, executive power was refurbished in a way compatible with the objectives of programmatic liberalism, and administrative reform was intended to insulate reform and reformers from the presidential election cycle. By executive orders issued with the authority granted by the Executive Reorganization Act of 1939, most of the emergency programs of the New Deal were established as permanent institutions.

Moreover, in the 1940 Ramspeck Act the Roosevelt administration obtained legislative authority to extend civil service protection to New Deal loyalists who were brought to Washington to staff the newly created executive department. New Deal civil service, therefore, did not replace politics with administration, nor did it replace patronage practices with civil service procedures dedicated to scientific management or neutral competence. Rather, it transformed the political character of administration. Previously, the choice was posed as one between politics and spoils on the one hand and nonpartisan and nonpolitical administration on the other.

The New Deal celebrated an administrative politics that denied nourishment to the regular party apparatus but instead fed an executive department oriented toward expanding liberal programs. Thus, FDR's influence on national administration was profound. Arguably, as Herbert Emmerich, a member of the Brownlow committee support staff, would write many years later, the passage of the 1939 Executive Reorganization Act "converted the immediate 1938 defeat into a victory over the long term and laid the basis for [an] extraordinary series of administrative management reforms."

## DRAFTING ROOSEVELT FOR A THIRD TERM

Roosevelt's success in inspiring and managing the recasting of the executive in the New Deal image might not have happened had he not taken the extraordinary step of running for a third term in 1940. Congress might have been willing to resist the Ramspeck Act had it been championed by a "lame duck," but legislators found it difficult to forestall a popular president during an election year, especially on an issue trumpeted by the Roosevelt administration and the press as an assault on the spoils system.

The approach of World War II gave Roosevelt the opportunity to stand for an unprecedented third term. But FDR and his political allies had begun working for Roosevelt's renomination in the summer of 1938. The decision to try for the third term was made in the midst of the woeful beating Roosevelt suffered in the 1938 elections. "They are already casting lots for the cloak of the Master," Thomas Corcoran, a member of the "elimination committee," told Roosevelt that summer. But while Democratic leaders were discussing FDR's possible successor, the White House was planning his precedent-shattering try for a third term. Apparently a decision was made by Corcoran and other New Dealers in July 1938 that the salvation of the New Deal required that Roosevelt run again. No liberal could get the Democratic nomination in 1940, they concluded, except for Roosevelt, and they were determined to draft him.

Just as it became apparent that the president was going to suffer a setback in the purge campaign, the "elimination committee" was shifting gears, planning for the Democratic convention to be held in Chicago in two years. The kickoff speech at that convention was made by a loyal New Dealer, Governor Frank Murphy of Michigan, in the course of his ill-fated try for reelection. Ernest Cuneo, who played a leading part in organizing the draft-Roosevelt movement in the states, flew to Michigan, where he helped ghost-write an address delivered in Traverse City, Michigan, on 26 July, in which Murphy told 2,000 supporters that it might be necessary for the president to accept a third term. "The New Deal must go on," said the governor, "and we may have to draft the President for four more years of leadership." The speech was duly reported in the *New York Times*, thus initiating the national speculation and suspense that both encouraged the draft-Roosevelt drives in the various states and kept other potential Democratic candidates at bay. The suspense the White House created, Cuneo observed, "was in the essence of [FDR's] campaign."

Although he did not personally participate in his aides' efforts to draft him, Roosevelt certainly lent his tacit support. Not once did he make any effort to stop these activities, suggesting that even if the president had not determined to run by the summer of 1938, he was preparing the way should he decide to do so from that time forward. The failed experiment in party government convinced Roosevelt, no less than it did his aides, of the need to form a direct link between the executive office and the public. As Frank Friedel has written about Roosevelt's reaction to the 1938 elections, "One clear implication that may not have been lost upon Roosevelt was that, with his own popularity still at a high level, he could attain New Deal goals in future elections only if he himself headed the ticket. His glamour did not rub off on others." By early 1940, certainly, several months before the Democratic national convention, the president was apprised of, and engaged in, the draft-Roosevelt activities.

The White House bid for a third term, unlike the purge campaign, was hidden from public view, but it was no less energetic and perhaps better organized. In important respects, Roosevelt's nomination for a third term in Chicago in July 1940 reversed the bitter defeats the White House suffered during the Seventy-fifth Congress and the 1938 primaries. Despite spirited competition from Farley and Vice President Garner (the first time an incumbent vice president challenged his "chief" for a party's nomination), Roosevelt was easily renominated. "For the first time since 1932 Franklin Roosevelt was in absolute command of the party," *Time* magazine reported after the convention. "The purge that had failed in 1938 was being carried through in 1940."

But the purge of 1940 did not secure the liberalism of the Democratic party, not by a long shot. Roosevelt did not take over the party in shattering the two-term precedent; instead this development ratified the displacement of party politics by executive administration. As Cuneo put it, Roosevelt had "pistol whipped" the Democratic party chieftains into nominating him for a third term and into accepting Secretary of Agriculture Henry Wallace, a militant liberal with virtually no organized support in the Democratic organization, as his running mate.

Indeed, since 1937 Roosevelt had distanced himself from the regular party, turning to a new group of advisers, dubbed the "palace guard." At the center of this group were New Dealers such as Harry Hopkins, Thomas Corcoran, and Benjamin Cohen, who wrote the speeches, formulated the program, and administered most of the policies of the New Deal. This created a schism; on one side were the White House advisers who surrounded the president; on the other were the orthodox Democrats—James Farley, most of the representation of the party in both houses of the Congress, and the foot soldiers in the state and municipal machines.

The initiatives of the Third New Deal gave institutional form to the independence of the executive from party politics, undermining the latter's importance. In effect, personnel in the Executive Office of the President transformed the presidency into an alternative political organization that gradually preempted party leaders in many of their significant tasks: linking the president to interest groups, staffing the executive department, developing policy, and, most important, generating campaign support. As the 1940 Democratic convention revealed, presidents no longer won election and governed as the head of a party. Now they would be elected and would govern as head of a personal organization they created in their own image.

It is little wonder, then, that in spite of Roosevelt's nomination and his election to a third term as the Democratic standard-bearer, Samuel Lubell's postmortem on the 1940 campaign bespoke of a New Deal—rather than a Democratic—triumph: "The Republicans do not know what hit them; the Democrats, certainly, as distinguished from the New Dealers, do not know what they hit the Republicans with. The New Deal

aimed at a bloodless revolution. In 1940 it went a long way toward accomplishing it."

## THE APPROACH OF WAR

The economic crisis that dominated Roosevelt's first two terms as president was displaced in the late 1930s by the approach and then the outbreak of World War II. Even before the United States declared war in December 1941, the growing United States involvement in the European and Asian conflicts intensified the concentration of power in the national government, its administrative apparatus, and the president. Roosevelt's control of foreign policy was far from complete, however. Americans' exceptional celebration of the individual and locality, which had led them to resist the welfare state well after it had become a fixture in other nations, was also a longstanding bulwark of isolationism in the United States.

The progressive leadership of Theodore Roosevelt and Woodrow Wilson had promised a new role for the United States in the world. They subscribed to the view, held by most reformers prior to World War I, that to extend U.S. territory was not imperialism but its opposite. As the progressive writer Herbert Croly put it, "Peace will prevail in international relations, just as order prevails within a nation, because of the righteous use of superior force—because the power which makes for pacific organization is stronger than the power which makes for warlike organization."

But this progressive dream of strengthening the national resolve abroad foundered on the rock of the failed League of Nations treaty. The raw and disruptive conflict over the Versailles Treaty led the nation to what Wilson's successor, Warren Harding, called a "return to normalcy"—an era of Republican dominance that signaled an end not only to domestic reform but to progressive internationalism as well.

In 1937, Roosevelt began to confront the mood of isolationism that had dominated the polity since the end of World War I. Speaking in Chicago, he strongly attacked the aggression of Germany and Japan, whose armies had recently invaded the Rhine and China, respectively:

> The peace, the freedom and the security of ninety percent of the population of the world is being jeopardized by the remaining ten percent who are threatening a breakdown of all international order and law. Surely the ninety percent who want to live in peace under law and in accordance with moral standards that have received almost universal acceptance through the centuries, can and must find some way to make their will prevail.

Although the immediate reaction to the president's speech was positive, it was soon followed by a severe backlash demonstrating clearly that neither Congress nor the American people were yet prepared to intervene in Europe or the Far East. A resolution sponsored by Representative Louis Ludlow from Indiana threatened to cripple the executive's conduct of foreign affairs. The Ludlow resolution would have amended the Constitution to provide that, save in the case of an invasion, the United States could engage in war only when a majority so voted in a national referendum. The amendment had wide support, including an isolationist cross-section in the House, ranging from the liberal Texas Democrat Maury Maverick to the standpat Republican Hamilton Fish. Only an all-out campaign of pressure by the White House and Farley prevented House approval of the resolution, which was defeated 209 to 188 in January 1938. The 188 votes in favor of the Ludlow amendment, William Leuchtenburg has written, testified both to "the President's tenuous control of foreign policy and, as late as 1938, [to] the bedrock strength of isolationist sentiment in America."

In the face of this opposition, the president resolved to move cautiously, to educate rather than arouse public opinion of the need, as he put it in a fireside chat, "[to abandon] once and for all the illusion that we can ever isolate ourselves from the rest of humanity." That task was complicated by shifting alliances on Capitol Hill; most con-

servative Democrats supported the president's moves to aid the Allies, whereas many liberals and Midwestern progressives, fearing that U.S. involvement in Europe or Asia would bring an end to reform, joined the isolationist cause. Ironically, Roosevelt's efforts to control foreign policy were fortified by the very Court that had been such an obstacle to his domestic program.

In late 1936, in the case of *United States v. Curtiss-Wright Export Corp.*, the Supreme Court had upheld a 1934 law that authorized the president to place an embargo on the sale of U.S.-made weapons to countries engaged in armed conflict. The law had been passed with the so-called Chaco war between Bolivia and Paraguay in mind, and Roosevelt quickly forbade the sale of arms to both countries. Weapons merchants challenged the measure as an unlawful delegation of legislative authority to the president; a federal district court agreed. But the Supreme Court, in an opinion written by the conservative justice George Sutherland, laid down a sweeping doctrine of presidential authority in foreign affairs.

The Court held that the president's powers in domestic and foreign matters differ fundamentally: "The broad statement that the federal government can exercise no power except those specifically stated in the Constitution, and such implied powers as are necessary and proper to carry into effect the enumerated powers," Justice Sutherland wrote, "is categorically true only in respect to internal affairs." In foreign affairs, the actions of the federal government and, more specifically, the president as the government's "sole organ" in international relations, do not depend on a specific grant of power from either the Constitution or Congress. Because the executive's authority in foreign policy is "plenary and exclusive," the president enjoys a freedom from statuary restriction that "would not be admissible were domestic affairs alone involved."

Along with the 1937 *United States v. Belmont* case, which justified the president's right to reach executive agreements with other countries (that is, quasi-treaties that are forged without the participation of the

Senate), *Curtiss-Wright* made it virtually impossible to challenge on constitutional grounds Roosevelt's increasingly internationalist policies. Relying on this broad, Court-sanctioned understanding of the president's foreign policy authority, Roosevelt unilaterally concluded the agreement with Great Britain that became the controversial Lend-Lease Act of 1941. The agreement, which paved the way for the United States to send fifty naval destroyers to help England in its desperate battle with Nazi Germany, marked a departure from the official U.S. policy of neutrality. The constitutional scholar Edward Corwin charged that Roosevelt's conduct in this matter usurped authority that rightfully belonged to the legislature. "As a departure from neutral status," he wrote in a letter to the *New York Times*, "the President's action was a step towards war—and as such was an invasion of Congress's constitutional 'power to declare war.'"

Corwin's argument was belied by Court rulings such as *Curtiss-Wright* and *Belmont*, but it raised objections that continued to have strong political support in the United States. None of the major programs that came before Congress before the attack on Pearl Harbor passed without a struggle: from the repeal of the arms embargo in 1939 to the passage of the Selective Service Act of 1940 and the Lend-Lease Act of 1941, Congress was bitterly divided. When Roosevelt requested an extension of the Selective Service Act of 1940 beyond the one year initially allowed, it passed the House by a margin of a single vote. This division within Congress reflected the striking ambivalence of the American people as war approached. Indeed, polls on the eve of Pearl Harbor showed a majority against involvement.

### PEARL HARBOR
Japan's attack on Pearl Harbor on 7 December 1941—a day, FDR proclaimed, that would "live in infamy"—swept away isolationist sentiment. Roosevelt's aides recalled that when the president appeared before the legislature to deliver his State of the Union address at the beginning of the year, his pro-

posals had been met with a deafening silence—they were "heartbroken" at the lack of response. The atmosphere in Congress was quite different on 8 December. As the *New York Times* reported, "At the moment the President appeared . . . he received an ovation unmatched in his eight years as Chief Executive. Applause broke into cheering and lasted over a minute." Without debate and with only one dissenting vote in the House, Congress approved Roosevelt's resolution of war in the record time of 33 minutes. (By comparison, Wilson's resolution in World War I was debated for 6 days.) The new feeling of unity that was suddenly displayed in Congress and the common purpose that now formed behind Roosevelt were typical of what was taking place in the country. What took place would endure, allowing the president to assert an inherent executive prerogative far more boldly than he could prior to the attack on Pearl Harbor. For the first time in U.S. history, the presidency had become indelibly an office of world significance.

This foray into world affairs had important consequence for the separation of powers. As James Madison had warned in his 1793 critique of Alexander Hamilton's defense of broad executive discretion in foreign affairs, "War is the nurse of executive aggrandizement." Under conditions of total war, Roosevelt believed, the president was empowered not only to direct military operations abroad but to manage economic and social affairs at home. In a bold—critics said brazen—expression of his theory of power, Roosevelt demanded that an effective program of price and wage controls be created. "I ask the Congress," FDR said in his Labor Day message of 7 September 1942, "to take . . . action by the first of October. Inaction on your part by that date will leave me with an inescapable responsibility to the people of this country to see to it that the war effort is no longer imperiled by threat of economic chaos." If Congress did not act, Roosevelt warned, "I shall accept the responsibility and I will act."

Congress enacted the economic controls the president demanded, and Roosevelt never had to follow through on his threat. The legislature's acquiescence, however reluctant, indicated, as Hawley has noted, that "as depression gave way to war, another expansion of presidential authority was under way, linked chiefly now to the creation of a national security state rather than a welfare one."

## DR. NEW DEAL AND
## DR. WIN THE WAR

The old saw of the historical literature on the New Deal is that the national security state displaced domestic reform, that the economic constitutional order had to be abandoned in order to unite the nation and mobilize for war. Roosevelt himself gave the most recognized expression to such an imperative. To a correspondent who lingered after his 28 December 1943 press conference, the president confessed that he was weary of the phrase *New Deal.* Ten years earlier, he said, "Dr. New Deal," an internist, had treated the country for an acute internal illness. After recovery, however, the patient had "suffered a very bad accident" on 7 December 1941. Dr. New Deal, knowing nothing about curing such afflictions, had referred his patient to "an orthopedic surgeon, Dr. Win the War."

The news of "Dr. Win the War" replacing "Dr. New Deal" set off a celebration among the nation's conservatives. Editorial writers, most of whom shunned the New Deal, rejoiced. "Death revealed," read a banner headline in *Time* magazine. The obituary read as follows: "The New Deal, 10, died [on 28 December] after a long illness. Child of the 1932 election campaign, the New Deal had four healthy years. Last week its father, Franklin Roosevelt, pronounced it dead."

The news of the New Deal's death was premature. Roosevelt, in fact, went on to say at this same press conference that the New Deal reforms had become a permanent part of American life. "That old Dr. New Deal," the president told reporters, "he put in things like old age insurance, he put in unemployment insurance." The American people were hardly ready to give up these programs, although FDR granted that "there are a lot of people in the country who would like to keep us from having them." To be sure, the president acknowledged, the principal emphasis had to be on winning the war; when victory came, however, the New Deal program would have to be continued. Returning to "economic isolation" and revising laissez-faire policies made no more sense than returning to "military isolation."

In truth, the condition of total war gave FDR the authority he needed to further shape the reconstructed executive as an agent of New Deal politics. Woodrow Wilson had put business leaders such as Bernard Baruch in charge of industrial mobilization during World War I; in contrast, FDR staffed key positions during World War II with New Dealers who were committed to his perception of the nation's needs. With loyal New Dealers such as Harold Smith, who headed the Bureau of the Budget, and Chester Bowles, who directed the Office of Price Administration, organizing industrial mobilization, "Dr. Win the War" never truly eclipsed "Dr. New Deal." Rather, the Roosevelt revolution and the war effort were melded in such a way to irrevocably establish the government's responsibility for the welfare of the American people.

With the organizational and programmatic tools created by New Deal legislation, the United States finally completed the passage from deep depression to full employment with the help of strenuous wartime mobilization. Unemployment still stood at 14.6 percent in December 1940, but by 1942, Washington was pumping $3 million a day into U.S. wallets and purses. By 1945, the stubborn tumor of jobless men and women had disappeared; the total cost of the war—calculated at $245 billion—was more than the merged annual budgets of the United States from 1789 to 1940, a period that included the financing of five previous wars. This had a profound effect on the American mind, establishing the government as part of the stream of life.

The change was more than economic; Roosevelt's leadership elevated it into a new creed. Roosevelt had nurtured a new public philosophy throughout his presidency, but with his 1944 State of the Union message, in which he proclaimed the Second Bill of Rights, FDR gave the most detailed account of the economic constitutional order. It was the nation's duty, he announced in that address, to begin to lay the plans and determine the strategy for winning a lasting peace—and eternal peace would not be possible without a program dedicated to the economic truths that the American people now accepted as self-evident: the right to a useful and remunerative job; the right to earn enough to provide adequate food, clothing, and recreation; the right of every family to a decent home; the right to adequate medical care and the opportunity to achieve and enjoy good health; the right to adequate protection from the economic fears of old age, sickness, accident, and unemployment; and the right to a good education. The Second Bill of Rights appeared to resonate with the American people, and FDR made these economic rights the centerpiece of the 1944 presidential campaign.

These new programmatic rights were never formally ratified as part of the Constitution, but they became the foundation of political dialogue, redefining the role of the national government. Nearly every public policy today is defined as a right, as an entitlement, routinely conferring constitutional status on programs like Social Security, Medicare, and food stamps. The new social contract heralded by Roosevelt marked the beginning of the so-called "rights revolution"—a transformation of the governing philosophy of the United States that has brought about major changes in American political institutions.

## ROOSEVELT'S LEGACY

Franklin Delano Roosevelt's extraordinary stewardship of the nation came to an end in April 1945. "As word spread from city to town, politicians and reporters struggled to come to terms with Roosevelt's death," Doris Kearns Goodwin has written. "For the millions who adored him and for those who despised him, an America without Roosevelt seemed almost inconceivable." Most Americans wept, openly and unashamedly, for the passing of a mighty leader. "Even so," Barry Karl has noted, "they hoped they would never need such heroic presidential leadership again." Roosevelt's victory in 1940 made him the only president in U.S. history to break the two-term tradition; in 1944, during the latter stages of World War II, he also won a fourth term. Only death cut short his protracted reign. Soon thereafter the people would initiate and approve a constitutional amendment limiting future presidents to two terms. There would be no more Roosevelts.

But the New Deal and the changes it brought to U.S. political life would endure. Roosevelt had transformed politics in the United States permanently; he had taught most Americans to expect that the federal government would remain active in domestic and world affairs and that, within government, the president would take the lead. To be sure, Roosevelt did not overcome the antibureaucratic tradition in the United States, which has continued to play an important role in the nation's political life. Indeed, Roosevelt's championing of a Second Bill of Rights showed him to be ambivalent about this tradition. Roosevelt did not abolish the obstacles in the United States to the creation of a strong national state; in giving rise to new rights—which came to be called entitlements—he unintentionally created new obstacles that would continue to deny the "national will." Still, FDR and the New Deal led to a redefinition of the social contract—to an understanding of rights that required, rather than constrained, a strong federal presence—and gave rise to an executive that would nurture this new public philosophy.

After the Third New Deal, the presidency was no longer simply an office but was an institution. As a result, as Robert Eden has written, "what Roosevelt did by improvisation could henceforth be done deliberately and regularly." It was said of Harry S Truman, who had the unenviable task of succeeding Roosevelt, that "for a time he walked, as completely as the smallest laborer who had been a 'Roosevelt man,' in the shadow of the dead president." In truth, all presidents since FDR have dwelt in his shadow. After Roosevelt's long tenure, the expectations and institutions that sustained the modern presidency would lead even conservative presidents to wield executive power according to FDR's vision of the office. Indeed, even as he challenged some of the core New Deal principles, the conservative Republican Ronald Reagan referred so frequently to FDR in his 1980 campaign for the White House, that the *New York Times* dubbed him "Franklin Delano Reagan." Notwithstanding his opposition to New Deal liberalism, Reagan's identification with Roosevelt also expressed his desire to lead as FDR had led, exploiting fully the powers of the modern presidency to move the nation toward a new "rendezvous with destiny."

The modern presidency that arose from the Roosevelt revolution was hardly imperial, as some scholars and pundits frequently asserted by the end of Richard Nixon's ill-fated reign. Congress, the courts, and the states remained central to the structure and activities of U.S. politics and government. Roosevelt's legacy included a more powerful and prominent executive office; at the same time, this office would continuously arouse serious concerns about the dangers of concentrating too much power in the White House. "Dynamic presidents who symbolize the vitality of the democratic ideal can use the federal government to do a great many things," Karl has written, "but when they touch the nerve centers that register a threat to individual autonomy, they inevitably arouse the protests that lead, in turn, to reaction."

The president's uneasy and unsettled place in U.S. political life is accentuated by the decline of party. Roosevelt invested the executive with what Woodrow Wilson called an "extraordinary isolation." Since FDR, presidents have been freed from the constraints of party, only to be enslaved by a volatile political environment that can rapidly undercut popular support. At the end of the day, modern presidents bask in the honors of the more formidable office that emerged from the New Deal, but they find themselves navigating a treacherous and lonely path, subject to a volatile political process that makes popular and enduring achievement unlikely.

## BIBLIOGRAPHY

Brinkley, Alan. *The End of Reform: New Deal Liberalism in Recession and War* (Knopf, 1995).

Burns, James MacGregor. *Roosevelt*, 2 vols. (Harcourt Brace Jovanovich, 1956–1978).

Dallek, Robert. *Franklin D. Roosevelt and American Foreign Policy, 1932–1945*, rev. ed. (Oxford University Press, 1995).

Davis, Kenneth S. *FDR*, 4 vols. (Random House, 1972–1993).

Farley, James A. *Jim Farley's Story* (McGraw-Hill, 1948).

Freidel, Frank. *Franklin D. Roosevelt: Rendezvous with Destiny* (Little, Brown, 1990).

Goodwin, Doris Kearns. *No Ordinary Time: Franklin and Eleanor Roosevelt—The Home Front in World War II* (Simon & Schuster, 1994).

Karl, Barry. *Executive Reorganization and Reform in the New Deal* (University of Chicago Press, 1963).

———. *The Uneasy State* (University of Chicago Press, 1983).

Lash, Joseph P. *Dealers and the Dreamers* (Doubleday, 1988).

———. *Eleanor and Franklin: The Story of Their Relationship* (Norton, 1971).

Leuchtenburg, William E. *Franklin D. Roosevelt and the New Deal* (Harper & Row, 1963).

———. *In the Shadow of FDR: From Harry Truman to Ronald Reagan* (Cornell University Press, 1983).

———. *The Supreme Court Reborn: The Constitutional Revolution in the Age of Roosevelt* (Oxford University Press, 1995).

Lichtenstein, Nelson. *Labor's War at Home: The CIO and World War II* (Cambridge University Press, 1982).

Milkis, Sidney M. *The President and the Parties: The Transformation of the American Party System Since the New Deal* (Oxford University Press, 1993).

Patterson, James T. *Congressional Conservatism and the New Deal: The Growth of the Conservative Coalition in Congress* (University of Kentucky Press, 1967).

Perkins, Frances. *The Roosevelt I Knew* (Viking, 1946).

Polenberg, Richard. *Reorganizing Roosevelt's Government, 1933–1939* (Harvard University Press, 1966).

Roosevelt, Eleanor. *This I Remember* (Harper, 1949).

Rosenman, Samuel J. *Working with Roosevelt* (Harper & Bros., 1952).

Schlesinger, Arthur M., Jr. *The Age of Roosevelt*, 3 vols. (Houghton Mifflin, 1957–1960).

Schwarz, Jordan A. *The New Dealers: Power Politics in the Age of Roosevelt* (Knopf, 1993).

Sitkoff, Harvard. *Fifty Years Later: The New Deal Evaluated* (Temple University Press, 1978).

Weiss, Nancy. *Farewell to the Party of Lincoln: Black Politics in the Age of FDR* (Princeton University Press, 1983).

★★★ 33 ★★★

# HARRY S. TRUMAN
## 1945–1953

*Alonzo L. Hamby*

*Born 8 May 1884 in Lamar, Missouri, to John Anderson Truman and Martha Ellen Young Truman; graduated Independence, Missouri, high school 1901; studied at Kansas City School of Law, 1923–25; married Bess (Elizabeth Virginia) Wallace, 28 June 1919, Independence, Missouri; one child; succeeded to the presidency upon the death of Franklin Delano Roosevelt, 12 April 1945; elected president in 1948 on the Democratic ticket with Alben William Barkley of Kentucky, receiving 24,105,695 popular votes and 303 electoral college ballots, over the Republican ticket of Thomas Edmund Dewey of New York and Earl Warren of California (21,969,170 popular votes and 189 electoral ballots), the States Rights party ticket of James Strom Thurmond of South Carolina and Fielding Lewis Wright of Mississippi (1,169,021 popular votes and 39 electoral ballots), and the Progressive party slate of Henry Agard Wallace of Iowa and Glen Hearst Taylor of Idaho (1,156,103 popular votes and no electoral ballots); died 26 December 1972 in Independence, Missouri; buried in Independence, Missouri.*

Speaker of the House Sam Rayburn said of Harry Truman that he was right on all the big things, wrong on all the little ones. The remark became the most oft-quoted summary of the Truman presidency. The most frequent personal characterization of Truman himself, "the little man," somehow passed over the fact that he was an uncommonly vigorous individual of average physical stature. During his last years in office he was widely scorned and unpopular. Yet a decade later, he was voted a "near-great" chief executive in a poll of leading professional historians. By the time of his death Truman was a widely revered figure. His experience strongly validates the widespread recognition that the twentieth-century presidency is an intensely personal office, subjected to a scrutiny that magnifies the strengths and weaknesses of its incumbents. It also provides a strong argument that presidents, although forced to play with the cards dealt them by history, possess a measure of free agency that requires biographical analysis.

## ROOTS OF CAREER
## AND CONVICTIONS

Truman was first and always a product of turn-of-the-century, rural, small-town mid-America. Almost all of the first thirty-three years of his life were spent in an environment of face-to-face, first-name relationships that venerated democracy while systematically ignoring those rudimentary class distinctions that existed within it. His education instilled in him the values and cultural assumptions of the Victorian age: the inevitability of progress, the inflexibility of moral codes, the ideals of duty to one's family and nation. His society, scarcely a generation removed from the frontier experience, presented strong, unambiguous messages about gender roles. A woman's sphere was in domestic life. Men, preferably self-employed and entrepreneurial, were providers; ideally, they were also tough and aggressive, capable of settling disputes with fists if need be.

Young Harry accepted the values of his community without question, but from a very early point in his childhood on into early middle age, he had persistent difficulties exemplifying them. Myopia forced him to wear thick glasses as a child and made him a sissy in the eyes of his peers. His mother steered him toward the piano, rather than sports, as his major spare-time activity. (He excelled at it, developing a love of good music that stayed with him for the rest of his life.) Told by his parents to run away from a fight if need be, he learned to avoid confrontations and honed his skills as a conciliator. He surely sensed that his hot-tempered, two-fisted father had less interest in him than in his younger brother, John Vivian. One consequence of this rather difficult childhood was the development of interpersonal skills that served him well as a politician. But he paid a heavy price. Uncertain of his father's affection, inhibited in his relations with the opposite sex, forced to repress anger at others, young Harry Truman clearly was affected by self-doubt. As late as 1913, he was capable of describing himself as "a guy with spectacles and a girl's mouth."

As an adult well into his thirties, Truman also had to deal with repeated experiences of failure in business. His eight years as a junior partner with his father on the family farm were emotionally and financially unrewarding. A misconceived zinc- and lead-mining venture in 1916 was a fiasco in which he lost heavily. A subsequent oil exploration partnership failed to produce a big strike. A postwar Kansas City haberdashery, his most-remembered business enterprise, failed spectacularly. A small-scale effort at real estate speculation ended ignominiously with a tax foreclosure. These experiences weighed heavily on a man who, having hoped to join the local establishment, found himself instead without even the means to maintain a country club membership. Like many small businessmen, Truman went into one undertaking after another with insufficient capital, no strategic plan, and no distinctive product. In 1922, at the age of 38, broke and with no viable business prospects, he turned to politics to make a living.

During the first four decades of his life, Truman experienced only one major success. In 1917, although he was beyond military age, he rejoined a National Guard unit to which he had once belonged and went off to fight as an artillery captain in World War I. Capable, resourceful, and courageous under fire, he functioned for the first time in his life as a leader, admired by most of the men who served under him and by his fellow officers. The experience was an invaluable confidence-building counterpoint to the pervasive sense of inadequacy and repeated failures that characterized the first four decades of his life. It also left him convinced of the virtue of the citizen soldier. After the war, he became an enthusiastic member of the reserve officers corps and took a keen interest in national defense issues. Perhaps because his combat experience was relatively brief and culminated in a decisive victory, he never doubted the need for military power in a world that settled important issues by force.

## STATE AND LOCAL POLITICS

In 1922, Truman was elected eastern district judge (county commissioner) on the Jackson County court. Since the Civil War, both sides of his family had been intensely committed to the Democratic party. His father briefly had held minor office as a local road overseer. The young Truman had unquestioningly accepted a family tradition in which Thomas Jefferson was a fount of ideology, Andrew Jackson an exemplar of democracy's energy, Jefferson Davis more revered than Abraham Lincoln, and William Jennings Bryan a heroic spokesman for the hard-pressed common folk of the heartland. To this pantheon, Truman would add Woodrow Wilson, whom he venerated as a reformer and an eloquent advocate of America's international mission.

It is essential to understand Truman's worldview in order to make sense of his presidency, but ideas had little relevance to his early political career. For a dozen years (1922–1934), affiliated with the powerful Thomas J. Pendergast, Truman lived in a world of machine politics characterized by widespread corruption, an unapologetic spoils system, and open alliances between government and organized crime. As presiding judge (chief executive) of Jackson County, Missouri (1927–1934), he won a merited reputation as an honest administrator who built a fine road system, capably managed other important construction projects, advocated good government reforms, and appeared destined for greater things.

Success gave Truman new reasons for pride and confidence, but it also added to psychic tensions generated by earlier identity crises and failures. His personal refusal to line his own pockets notwithstanding, he could not avoid passive acquiescence in raids on the public treasury, election fraud, and other machine affronts to democratic ideals that clearly left him uneasy and defensive. He resolved these new stresses unsatisfactorily by persuading himself that loyalty to his benefactor Boss Pendergast was a paramount duty, that most antimachine reformers were hypocritical frauds no better than the bosses they criticized, and that some degree of corruption was an inevitable by-product of democratic politics. Stubbornly held, these attitudes would persist through his presidency, with uniformly negative consequences.

The initial phase of Truman's career affected his political outlook in other, mostly positive, ways. Because his constituency included a large metropolitan area (Kansas City, Missouri), he had to make room in his politics for a significant African-American vote and the concerns of numerous ethnic minorities; his situation essentially activated a fundamental tolerance he always had possessed. The conciliatory characteristics he had been forced to develop as a child helped him develop broad coalitions of interests in support of his projects. Presiding over a county government that long had run a chronic fiscal deficit, he developed a strong concern with budget balancing and public finance. Most revealingly, he consistently assumed every iota of power to which he might lay claim and constantly strove for more. In all these ways, his county government experience foreshadowed his years in the White House.

## THE U.S. SENATE

Truman's race for the U.S. Senate in 1934 and his subsequent decade of service in that body forced self-definitions on a much wider range of issues than he had ever before confronted. He emerged from the experience as a fairly representative example of a midwestern "insurgent progressive" in the mold of Robert La Follette, Sr., George W. Norris, or Burton K. Wheeler, who became Truman's friend and mentor in the Senate. Creations of the early twentieth century, the insurgent progressives typically voiced neopopulist resentments of Wall Street, the "trusts," and the "interests." Although most of them appealed to urban labor, they fundamentally expressed the entrepreneurial outlook of the farmer and small businessman. Reflexive trust-busters, they preferred an America of small economic units and sought to legislate in that direction whenever possible. From the early years of the century, however, they had come to realize that the regulatory state was frequently the only practical way of dealing with economic concentration. Consequently, they valued independent professional expertise as a tool of reform government. By virtue of background and experience, Truman fit the profile to near-perfection.

Insurgency faced challenges in the world of the 1930s. Much more than progressivism, the emerging New Deal was heavily based on the labor movement and urban ethnic and religious minorities. Ideologically, the New Deal tilted much farther toward social democracy. Perhaps because of his local metropolitan political experience, Truman easily resolved the tensions that existed between the insurgent progressive tradition and the emerging New Deal, effortlessly adding New Dealism to his ideological base. In large measure, the two traditions were rhetorically compatible. Little more was required than an attentive concern for the labor unions and minority groups. Although not in the front ranks of New Deal senators, Truman was a reliable supporter of Franklin D. Roosevelt and unquestionably a New Dealer. Two high-profile investigations defined his ideology and advanced his career.

The first, undertaken in 1937 and 1938 in cooperation with Burton K. Wheeler, probed the critical condition of most U.S. railroads. Discounting the impacts of the Great Depression and competitive modes of transportation, Truman asserted that many of the rail lines had been looted by Wall Street financiers, whom he intemperately denounced. Pursuing a classic insurgent-progressive objective, he backed legislation to rewrite the interstate commerce code with the objective of providing comprehensive, rationalized regulation of all forms of transportation. (The final outcome, the Transportation Act of 1940, was far more limited.) He also established a close relationship with the powerful railway unions, inflexibly backing their opposition to layoffs or wage cuts.

The second high-profile investigation was his ongoing examination of the national defense program, which occupied most of his time from early 1941 to mid-1944. It made him one of the leading members of the Senate and thereby established a basis for his vice-presidential nomination in 1944. At times, he indulged his insurgent prejudices, making ill-founded charges against giant corporations. But he also uncovered much actual waste and mismanagement, along with occasional criminal behavior. As in his early career in Jackson County, Truman achieved an image as a relatively nonpartisan advocate of the public interest and won admiration across a wide spectrum of political opinion.

By the time Truman established his wartime committee, insurgent progressivism was fading into irrelevance, less because of its domestic worldview than because of the isolationism to which so many of its representatives were prone. Truman was a notable exception. A Wilsonian since World War I, he was unshakable in his belief that the United States had an international mission. His wartime experience and military interests had made him a prewar advocate of military preparedness and a vocal critic of appeasement. During World War II, he had spoken out strongly in behalf of U.S. world leadership, and in so doing he completed the process of making himself compatible with the new liberalism that began to emerge in the 1930s.

He also had established himself as a formidable electoral politician. In 1934, he had won election to the Senate largely because he had the backing of the powerful Pendergast machine. By 1940, Pendergast was in prison and his organization in shreds. Truman (who foolishly, if loyally, had defended his patron to the end) seemed a sure loser for renomination. Instead, he honed his reputation as a military expert at a time of national crisis, waged an exhausting campaign, forged a New Deal–style coalition (labor, African Americans, rural Democratic loyalists, and St. Louis machine politicians), and defeated Governor Lloyd Stark in the Democratic primary. That fall, Truman was narrowly reelected, and by 1944, he was the most important and respected Democrat in his home state.

In Washington, Truman was likewise a power. One of the half-dozen or so leaders of the Senate, he had warm friendships in all factions of a sharply divided Democratic party. In 1944, when President Roosevelt acceded to pressure to replace the controversial Henry A. Wallace as vice president, Truman was a consensus choice, acceptable to labor, liberal activists, and conservative southerners. On 12 April 1945, not three months into his vice presidency, he became president following Roosevelt's sudden death.

## LIVING WITH THE PRESIDENCY

Less than a month short of his sixty-first birthday when he became president, Truman was acutely aware that many Americans, including a substantial majority of those in the administration he inherited, regarded him as an inadequate successor to one of the most imposing presidents in U.S. history.

Actually, his assets were substantial. They included practical experience at all levels of U.S. politics, an instinctive identification with ordinary Americans, an optimism that sustained him in difficult times, a keen intelligence, and a willingness to draw on the advice of men who at times had not only greater specialized expertise but also greater stature than he. He not only respected the power of the presidency, he worked zealously to increase and institutionalize it. And, for all his partisanship, he possessed a shrewd sense of when and how to work with his opposition in quest of greater goals.

But from the beginning Truman had to cope with major liabilities. His very commonness created doubts in the minds of those accustomed to Roosevelt's extraordinary leadership. His myopia made it difficult for him to deliver a prepared speech, and his voice—a blend of upper South and heartland Midwest—contrasted unfavorably with Roosevelt's patrician tones. Most fundamentally, years of achievement that might have been expected to leave Truman with a sense of confidence had, if anything, heightened the sense of self-doubt that had plagued him since childhood. Never at ease with the presidency, he betrayed his discomfort in numerous ways—gaffes at press conferences, temperamental outbursts, excessive loyalty to friends who lowered the tone of his administration. In good times, he could win the affection of the nation, but when the going was hard, even many Americans who had voted for him thought him inadequate as a leader.

Moreover, Truman had the misfortune to be president in difficult times. He not only had to bring World War II to a conclusion but also would be a major player in defining the shape of the postwar world. At home, his administration would have to deal with the uncertain economic consequences of the transition from war to peace, cope with an emergent civil rights movement, and set the nation on a postwar course that would either extend or implicitly repudiate Roosevelt's New Deal. The future of the Democratic party as the nation's continuing majority party would depend largely on Truman's success or failure.

## THE END OF WORLD WAR II AND THE ORIGINS OF THE COLD WAR

When Truman became president, victory in Europe was near. The war against Japan, however, still raged fiercely. Its focus for the first two months of his presidency was the battle of Okinawa, which cost some 45,000 American casualties. The endgame of the conflict, as envisioned by military planners, would be an invasion of the Japanese home islands with estimates of 225,000 to 250,000 casualties. As Truman contemplated this possibility, he faced also an increasingly difficult relationship with the Soviet Union. The USSR had been the West's indispensable ally against Nazi Germany. As it moved to establish dominance over the eastern European nations its armies had occupied, however, the USSR systematically violated the ideals of national self-determination and individual liberties that the United States and Great Britain had proclaimed as war objectives. Western protests were unavailing; a meeting of the Big Three leaders at Potsdam, Germany, in July 1945 resolved little. The diplomatic tangle was further complicated by western need for Soviet entry into the war against Japan and by Soviet ambitions in Manchuria.

The just-tested atomic bomb offered a way to cut through many of these dilemmas, but Truman, heavily motivated by his own World War I combat experience, viewed it primarily as a way to bring the war to a speedy conclusion. He, his secretary of state James F. Byrnes, and other administration figures assumed that the new weapon would give the United States substantially enhanced leverage in relations with the USSR, and they hoped (vainly) that a quick end to the war would forestall Soviet dominance of Manchuria. That said, they clearly would have used the bomb anyway. Evidence that Japan was prepared to surrender unconditionally before the Hiroshima bomb on 6 August 1945 is not merely unconvincing, it is nonexistent. (Whether the rapid use of the second bomb against Nagasaki on 9 August was necessary is a much more difficult issue.) Of course, the war could have been concluded eventually without use of the atomic bomb and perhaps without even the invasion of the home islands, but not without tens of thousands of casualties—American and Japanese, British and Asians throughout the Pacific theater. By agreeing to use of the bomb, Truman did what he believed he had to do to end the fighting quickly; the Japanese surrendered on 14 August. Despite his repeated protestations of no regret, however, he was shaken by the horror he had unleashed. For the remainder of his presidency, he not only refused to consider use of the bomb in warfare, he rejected military requests for physical custody over atomic weapons.

Relations with the Soviet Union deteriorated steadily throughout 1945 and 1946. The core issue was the extent of Soviet territorial ambitions, but other considerations took the conflict well beyond a classical sphere-of-influence dispute. The most fundamental of these was the ideological clash between Soviet totalitarian communism and American liberal capitalism. Encompassing vital matters of principle, it also produced worldviews so different that on both sides rational understanding of one's enemy became difficult. The character and personality of Soviet dictator Josef Stalin greatly exacerbated the problem. Utterly ruthless, convinced that he was surrounded by enemies or potential enemies at home and abroad, Stalin was incapable of believing any reassurances the West might give him. Certain that he was locked in a long struggle with an implacable enemy, he sought not simply to consolidate his wartime gains but to extend them, with no discernible sense of limits.

Truman possessed his own ideological imperatives—a sense of U.S. destiny, a fervent commitment to liberal values, and an attachment to capitalism—but he tempered these with a practical attachment to the ideal of an amicable, if imperfect, world order. Having matured politically in an environment that combined corruption and criminality with public service and civic progress, he had no illusions about the attainability of global perfectionism. His initial impulse, not unlike that of many

Americans who had met Stalin, was to see the Soviet dictator as a tough political boss with whom one could make deals on a man-to-man basis.

In 1946 the United States attempted to assuage Soviet fears of American atomic weapons by offering the Baruch plan for international control of atomic energy. Critics fairly enough observed that the plan would allow the United States to retain control of its atomic capability until the Soviet Union had turned all of its nuclear resources over to a United Nations agency. Still, no pragmatic observer could believe that the United States, once committed, could back away from the commitment to international control. Possibly flawed in detail, the Baruch plan nevertheless offered an unprecedented voluntary rejection of international power and a chance to remove nuclear weapons from international conflict. The Soviet Union rejected it because Stalin and his associates could not comprehend *any* U.S. proposal as being in good faith. They felt secure only by developing their own atomic bombs.

Although the United States vociferously criticized the steady, heavy-handed progress of Soviet dominance throughout eastern Europe, U.S. foreign policy offered no counterthreat to Stalin's regional hegemony. Neither Truman nor his policymakers had any objection to Soviet demands for friendly governments on the USSR's western borders. What they protested was the relentless purging of all dissenting opinion, the establishment of communist economic systems, and the imposition of communist dictatorships. These protests were sincere; still, through the winter of 1945–46, the dominant theme of U.S. foreign policy was a consistent search for areas of agreement with the USSR.

American policy took on a harder edge only after Soviet expansionism appeared to have ambitions that impinged more directly on U.S. interests. In the early spring of 1946, Truman authorized strong protests against a continued Soviet military presence (counter to wartime agreements) in northwestern Iran; the USSR withdrew, aban-doning a separatist movement it had nurtured. Through the spring and summer of 1946, the administration supported Turkey against Soviet demands for de facto control of the Turkish straits. Speaking at Stuttgart in early September, Secretary of State Byrnes assured anti-Nazi German leaders that the United States would remain on the European continent and support the establishment of German democracy. Soon thereafter, Truman fired Secretary of Commerce Henry A. Wallace when Wallace publicly protested the administration's "hard line" toward the USSR.

By the end of 1946, Truman and his foreign policy advisers had undergone a fundamental reorientation in their attitude toward the Soviet Union. Convinced that Stalin had designs on the oil-rich and strategically important Middle East, that he wanted to make his country into a Mediterranean power, and that he sought dominance of all of western Europe, the Truman administration abandoned the quest for a general postwar agreement and began the practice of containment. The new policy awaited only a defining moment.

## LIBERALISM, ECONOMIC RECONVERSION, AND THE DEFEAT OF 1946

Truman's most urgent political task upon becoming president was to define himself politically. Given his friendships with both liberals and conservatives and given the waning of New Deal liberalism during World War II, his course was by no means easily predictable. Although he never would fully satisfy the liberals who had revered Franklin Roosevelt, Truman followed his natural inclinations and pursued a program of neo–New Deal liberalism. The choice made political sense; as Truman would demonstrate in 1948, he had correctly gauged the Democratic party's ideological center of gravity. He also had guaranteed himself one domestic controversy after another. The Democratic congressional delegation was deeply divided between liberals, predominantly urban, and conservatives, usually southerners with a rural worldview.

Conservative Democrats and almost all Republicans on Capitol Hill tended to work together in an informal conservative coalition that blocked much of Truman's legislative program throughout his presidency. From the beginning, the president would be whipsawed between two imperatives that were both of great importance to him: his instinctive, deeply felt liberalism and his need to hold the Democratic party together.

The conservative coalition was sustained by an underlying public indifference. If the end of World War II had been followed by a return to the depression conditions of the 1930s, Truman might have built a far more impressive legislative record. Instead, he served as president during an era of steadily growing prosperity, in which a new middle class began the move to suburban subdivisions, raised families, purchased automobiles, and felt little need for government intervention. A decade or so earlier, "liberalism" had meant government assistance to hard-pressed Americans in need of a job or mortgage refinancing or agricultural subsidies. In the wake of World War II, it was far more likely to conjure up images of price controls, rationing, higher taxes, meddlesome economic management, or disruption of a racial status quo that most Americans accepted unquestioningly.

The debacle of postwar economic reconversion illustrated the point perfectly. A statistical examination of the period from 1945 to 1946 demonstrates effective full employment and economic prosperity, marred to be sure by an irritating but tolerable spurt of inflation. The much-feared specter of depression and deflation never materialized. Instead of receiving credit for that development, Truman wound up being blamed not only by consumers for every shortage and labor stoppage but also by farmers and businessmen for supporting continued price controls that were poorly administered, economically ill-advised, and often violated. The president compounded his difficulties by veering back and forth between his liberal commitments, which led him ultimately to come down in favor of economic controls, and his instincts as a small businessman,

which told him that they amounted to an unjustified interference with one's livelihood.

He likewise zigged and zagged in his relationship with a labor movement that expected unconditional backing from a Democratic president; the situation reached a low point when he forced settlement of a national rail strike by asking Congress for authority to draft the strikers into the army. Having demanded full continuance of the price control system, he ultimately had to settle for legislation that gutted it. When he attempted to use his remaining authority to hold the line on meat prices, producers refused to ship their livestock to market; in many urban areas, fresh meat all but disappeared from the shops. Consumers held the president and his party responsible. In 1946, in what Sam Rayburn called the "damned beefsteak election," the American people swept the Republicans back into Congress by a stunning margin.

## THE TRUMAN DOCTRINE AND THE MARSHALL PLAN

In early 1947, events allowed Truman to convert the practice of containment into a formal doctrine that established the tone of U.S. foreign policy for decades to come. Britain, exhausted and near-bankrupt, informed the United States that it could no longer support the right-wing government of Greece in its struggle against a Soviet-backed insurgency. To many liberals within Truman's own party, the appropriate response would have been inaction—the Greek government was corrupt and reactionary, the traditional British imperial role there discreditable. Some believed that a leftist government would be a progressive change in Greece. Many others simply did not want the United States to incur the taint of association with an unsavory regime. Administration foreign policy officials with a geopolitical outlook offered a very different vision. To allow a pro-Soviet government in Athens, they warned, would be to give the USSR a foothold in the eastern Mediterranean, make the position of Turkey untenable, and jeopardize western influence throughout the Middle East.

It tells one much about the nature of Truman's liberalism that he accepted their position. His experience in war and politics had taught him that in an imperfect world ideals often collide with reality. As he neared the end of his second year as president, Truman had come to believe that in addition to his official duty to protect U.S. interests, he could act on a higher moral imperative, that of blocking the spread of totalitarianism. His decision was a catalyst that forced American liberals to confront the challenge of the Soviet Union, just as conservatives had been forced to make decisions about Nazi Germany a decade earlier. Ultimately, most would choose what Arthur Schlesinger, Jr., described as the "vital center" option of anti-communist liberalism.

On 12 March 1947, Truman went before Congress to request $250 million in aid to Greece and $150 million for Turkey. Admitting the imperfection of the beneficiaries, he nonetheless argued from a larger vision of a world torn between two ways of life—totalitarianism and freedom. "I believe," he declared, "that it must be the policy of the United States to support free peoples who are resisting attempted subjugation by armed minorities or by outside pressures." The statement, quickly dubbed the Truman Doctrine, stopped short of being a blanket commitment to help anyone at any time, but it was not without universalistic implications. Assuredly, it expressed a sense of America's mission that Truman long had carried with him. After two months of emotional debate, the aid bill passed Congress, with 3-to-1 margins in both houses.

The Greek-Turkish aid program was simply the first step in the program of containment. Three months later, Truman's new secretary of state, George C. Marshall, dramatically urged a vast program of American aid for the postwar economic reconstruction of Western Europe. The Marshall Plan—a name chosen because Marshall was a revered nonpartisan figure—reassured many liberal Democrats who had been taken aback by the negative aspects of the Truman Doctrine. It also envisioned for the United States an international role unlike any it had ever before taken in peacetime. Truman and his foreign policy advisers wanted no less than the commitment of a historically isolationist nation to a role of continued active involvement with Europe and other important parts of the world. This involvement would include military assistance, economic reconstruction, an open international trading system, and ultimately a military alliance. Not intrinsically hostile to democratic varieties of socialism, the new foreign policy was nonetheless based primarily on a view of the world that valued liberalism and capitalism, both of which had reached their greatest development in the United States.

Among the most telling revelations of the new policy was Truman's success in getting it through a Congress controlled by the opposition. While he lashed out intemperately at the Republican Congress on most matters of domestic policy, he established a close relationship with its more moderate foreign policy leaders and constantly talked up the virtues of bipartisanship. By refusing to personalize his initiatives, he made it easier to have them considered on their own merits. Along the way, the Soviet Union, reacting to the specter of freedom and open markets, gave him considerable help. In mid-1947, communists seized absolute power in Hungary. In early 1948, they took over Czechoslovakia, apparently assassinating the Czech foreign minister in the process. A few months later, Soviet authorities in East Germany began to impede western access to Berlin. By the time they had established a full-scale blockade around the German capital, Congress had authorized large appropriations for the Marshall Plan. Opposition came primarily from the fringes of U.S. politics—the reactionary isolationist right and the pro-Soviet left. Truman had displayed shrewdness as a tactician, but ultimately his policy was successful because he had seized the center ground and had spoken to impulses deep within the American character.

In the meantime, Truman had embarked, hesitantly and erratically, on another fateful foreign policy commitment. In May 1948, he overruled virtually every foreign policy adviser and recognized the new state of Israel. Like many liberals, Truman felt that European Jews, horribly victimized by the Nazis, deserved a place of refuge and a national identity; moreover, he had a long history of good relationships with Zionist organizations and leaders. At the same time, he understood the fears, strongly imparted to him by Secretary of Defense James Forrestal and Secretary of State Marshall, that U.S. alignment with a Jewish state would irreparably damage American interests in the Middle East. In the end, after prolonged indecisiveness that contrasted markedly with his stance toward western Europe, he clearly decided that a core Democratic constituency and a prime source of campaign funds could not be alienated. Somewhat improbably, he became the father of an often difficult but fundamental international relationship.

In early 1949, the United States, responding primarily to the initiatives of its European allies, took the final step in the structure of containment. The North Atlantic Treaty, a mutual defense pact with the western European democracies, formally ended a policy of disengagement from European international entanglements that stretched back to 1793. After soul-searching debate, the Senate ratified it by a vote of 82 to 13. It was quickly followed by the establishment of the North Atlantic Treaty Organization (NATO) and passage of a large military assistance program for NATO member states. Separately, the United States, Britain, and France merged their military occupation zones into the Federal Republic of Germany and moved toward making their rehabilitated former enemy a full-fledged member of the alliance. With U.S. encouragement, moreover, the western Europeans moved steadily toward an open trading system that would complement their diplomatic alliance and undergird an emerging economic recovery.

Soviet expansionism had been stymied at every point. In the spring of 1949, the Russians abandoned their blockade of Berlin, which had been rendered ineffective by a western airlift. Henceforth, they concentrated on consolidating their own sphere of dominance, already a bit diminished by the ostentatious independence of Marshal Josef Tito's Yugoslav regime. Soviet influence, unable to move beyond the World War II advance of its military power, would be stalled for the next forty years.

## THE POLITICS OF LIBERALISM AND THE 1948 ELECTION

As a result of the 1946 election, Truman faced a Republican Congress that assumed that it had been elected to halt the momentum of New Deal liberalism and take at least a step or two back toward the world of the 1920s. Although apparently repudiated, Truman moved shrewdly in ways that enhanced his political position. He could no longer be held responsible for leading a Congress of his own party, an endeavor that had been a losing game for him in 1945 and 1946. Successful in making foreign policy a bipartisan endeavor, he could afford to concentrate on domestic controversies, where he understood that the Democratic party had great residual strength. Moreover, he and his aides increasingly understood how to use the visibility of the presidency to frame issues and set the tone of public debate. From the beginning of 1947 through the election of 1948, he followed a classical strategy of mobilizing key groups in the Democratic coalition and using the public relations power of the presidency to cast himself in the role of a defender of the interests of ordinary Americans.

In the 1930s, organized labor had become the most important of the Democratic interest groups. Given strong bargaining power and considerable affluence by postwar prosperity, labor was near the peak of its influence in American politics. Yet in the first two years of his presidency, Truman had distanced himself from it in a number of ways, most notably his harsh action in the rail strike of 1946. After the 1946 election he had ordered the prosecution of the United Mine Workers for going on strike against coal operations that (by provision of wartime legislation) were under federal control; the result was a heavy fine against the union.

With such a record, Truman might have been expected to take a benign attitude toward Republican efforts to restrict the unions. In fact, however, his attitude was far more ambivalent than that of many Republicans. While he still possessed enough of a small-business mentality to resent the excesses of labor, he also thought of himself as a friend of all "working people"—individual business owners, farmers, *and* industrial workers. In his Senate years, he had gone out of his way to cultivate union support, both because he identified with responsible labor organization and because he understood labor's increasing centrality in the Democratic party.

By June, the Republican Congress had sent the Taft-Hartley bill to his desk. Originally harshly antilabor, the bill had been considerably moderated in the Senate by Robert A. Taft of Ohio, a vehement ideological conservative who nevertheless approached issues on a practical problem-by-problem basis, his pragmatism perhaps encouraged by his presidential ambitions— it seemed entirely possible that he would be the 1948 Republican presidential candidate. The legislation, moreover, had enormous symbolic significance as an attack on both the legacy of the New Deal and labor's enhanced status in American life. It presented no real challenge to the existence of unions, but it did place significant restrictions on their activities. Most important, it outlawed the closed shop (which made possession of a union card a prerequisite for being hired), specifically allowed states to pass right-to-work laws prohibiting the union shop (compulsory union membership after a probationary period), and allowed the president to obtain injunctions requiring strikers to return to work for 80 days if a work stoppage threatened the national interest. Unions attacked the last provision, denouncing Taft-Hartley as a slave-labor bill.

It was a measure of labor's unpopularity after all the strikes of 1945 and 1946 that the bill had passed Congress by enormous margins. Most southern Democrats had voted for it, along with almost all Republicans. Nonetheless, Truman issued a stinging veto in which he called Taft-Hartley "a shocking piece of legislation" that would "take fundamental rights away from our working people." The House overrode his veto 331 to 83 and the Senate by 68 to 25. Appreciative of Truman's efforts and shocked into awareness that the Republicans were far more of a threat, the unions lined up behind the president; their efforts would be a critical part of his 1948 campaign.

Taft-Hartley established a model for Truman's strategy of reassembling the New Deal coalition for the 1948 election. Through policy declarations and vetoes, he both appealed to key interest groups and attempted to establish himself as a tribune of ordinary Americans. No longer saddled with a gridlocked Democratic Congress, Truman could attack the Republicans on Capitol Hill for tolerating inflation, pushing tax cuts mainly beneficial to the rich, failing to solve the postwar housing crisis, and rejecting needed social welfare advances. Intent on establishing a platform for the 1948 campaign, the president had no interest in negotiating compromise legislation with Republican leaders; his objective was to pillory them. By September 1947, his approval rating had climbed to 55 percent.

However, Truman faced one issue extraordinarily difficult to finesse or use in any way to his advantage: black civil rights. From Reconstruction to the Great Depression, African Americans had been relegated to the fringes of life in the United States. Most were poor. Segregation—generally informal in the North, rigidly established by law throughout the South—kept them out of the mainstream of American life and visible to most whites only as servants, manual laborers, or marginal farmers. Politically, this large group of Americans wielded the vote only in the North, where they had faithfully supported a Republican party that appeared largely indifferent to them; in the South, they were almost wholly disfranchised.

During the Great Depression, benefits received from Roosevelt's New Deal and the real sympathy of many members of his administration had brought the African-American vote into the Democratic party. World War II had encouraged a substantial black migration to the North. As a crusade against Nazism it also had highlighted ideals of equal justice regardless of race or ethnicity. Although the armed forces remained segregated, Roosevelt had established by executive order a Fair Employment Practices Committee (FEPC) to work for equal employment opportunity in industry. The FEPC and lesser gestures exposed a growing rift among Democrats: Northern urban liberals supported it wholeheartedly; Southerners, committed to segregation and white supremacy, opposed it monolithically.

Truman had inherited an issue that could no longer be postponed. The northern black vote was larger, better organized than ever, and an important Democratic constituency. African-American leadership, militant and independent, operating in an era of prosperity, made it clear that economic relief was no longer a top priority and pressed for action on civil rights. With Roosevelt gone and a man of the upper South sitting in his place, their very allegiance to the Democratic party was in doubt. White southerners—the largest, most identifiable, and hitherto most reliable Democratic constituency—remained rigidly opposed to any change in the racial status quo.

With the end of the war, the president lost the executive authority under which FEPC had been established, and a coalition of small-government Republicans and southern Democrats blocked legislation to make the agency permanent. Scattered episodes of ugly racial violence spread across the South. In some cases, the victims were returning black servicemen, still in uniform. In September 1946, Truman, genuinely horrified by such incidents and conscious of the need to appeal to an important interest group, appointed a committee, stacked with liberals sympathetic to civil rights issues, to study the problem of civil

rights in America. Its report, delivered a year later, urged the first comprehensive civil rights program for black Americans since Reconstruction.

Truman's decision could not have come without inner turmoil. He was, after all, a man of the upper South, and at heart at least a bit of a white supremacist—as a senator, he had frankly stated that he did not believe in "social equality." But equal opportunity was one of his most fundamental values; and, although the political gains were speculative at the time, he acted strongly on the committee's recommendations. The Justice Department began to argue on behalf of civil rights plaintiffs in important federal court cases. The White House sent an omnibus civil rights bill up to Congress. On the eve of the 1948 campaign, Truman issued an executive order mandating a policy of "equal opportunity" in the U.S. armed forces, the last major bastion of outright segregation in the federal government. The order, given special impetus by the Korean War, would lead to a process of desegregation that was well along by the time he left the presidency.

Nonetheless, by mid-1948, Truman seemed a sure bet to be a defeated incumbent. Indecision on Palestine and advocacy of civil rights had damaged him. Henry Wallace had announced his own candidacy for president as leader of the Progressive party, a third party composed of anti-Cold War activists from the Democratic left and the U.S. Communist party. Wallace damaged himself with maladroit attacks on the Marshall Plan and rationalizations of such events as the Czech coup and the Berlin blockade; nonetheless, analysts believed he could draw millions of votes away from Truman. Moreover, after a bruising civil rights platform battle at the Democratic convention, losing southern Democrats formed the States Rights party, nominating Governor J. Strom Thurmond of South Carolina as their candidate. Truman, who had taken the South's loyalty for granted, now faced the loss of at least some states in what had been a monolithic Democratic region. In the meantime, Republicans, united and confident, had nominated a dream ticket—Governor Thomas E. Dewey of New York and Governor Earl Warren of California. Probably the two best-known state chief executives in the nation, both men were highly capable and personally popular. Dewey had given Franklin Roosevelt a very close presidential race in 1944.

Truman responded to the challenge with an ultimately appealing blend of style and substance. Deficient at delivering a formal speech, he remained a master of retail politics, good at talking off the cuff to small groups. In the summer and fall of 1948, he criss-crossed the country by train, making a number of formal speeches but appearing most often before small crowds clustered around the rear platform at one whistle-stop after another. He committed a few embarrassing gaffes, but more often he came across as an ordinary man of the people, not much different from his listeners and able to understand their problems.

To this impression, Truman added a fiery denunciation of the Republican Congress, which he accused of wanting to repeal the New Deal. At one stop after another, always pitching his remarks to his specific audience, he reminded his listeners of what the Democratic party had done for them: backing of unions for the workers, price supports for farmers, major water and electrical power programs for the Western states, efforts to relieve the housing shortage in the cities. Dewey, the president asserted, would collaborate with the Republican Congress to undo all that had been done for the American people in the past sixteen years. Meanwhile, confident of victory, Dewey spoke in bland generalities; wanting to preserve party unity, he took no notice of Truman's exaggerated rhetoric.

On election day, Truman surprised the nation, taking 49.5 percent of the vote to 44.5 for Dewey and 2.5 each for Wallace and Thurmond. Truman won 303 electoral votes, Dewey 189, and Thurmond 39. The Democrats also regained control of Congress. With enormous effort and a little bit of luck, Truman had resuscitated the Roosevelt coalition and won yet another endorsement for the New Deal. It remained to be seen, however, whether his mandate ran beyond preservation of a status quo with which most Americans were comfortable.

## THE FAIR DEAL AND THE GRIDLOCKED POLITICS OF LIBERALISM

Truman did not hesitate to test the limits of the possible. He not only called for increases in numerous New Deal programs that had been established in the 1930s, he also offered his own Fair Deal program, a collection of proposals designed to speak to the problems of postwar America. Among them were a major housing bill that included public housing for the poor, large-scale federal aid to education, national health insurance, repeal of Taft-Hartley, comprehensive civil rights legislation, and a revolutionary overhaul of the agricultural program.

Historians who pass over the Fair Deal as simply a group of failed initiatives fail to grasp its importance as an effort to adapt Democratic liberalism to a period of prosperity and economic growth. Its most innovative initiative, the Brannan Plan (named for Secretary of Agriculture Charles F. Brannan), proposed to let the free market determine agricultural prices while the government delivered direct subsidies to family farms. It would thus support the income of most individual farmers while encouraging maximum production and allowing the price of food and other goods derived from agricultural commodities to drop. Truman and others hoped that the result would be a farm and labor political coalition that would provide a stronger base for Democratic liberalism and securely undergird future reform initiatives.

However visionary the conception, the Fair Deal faced enormous obstacles from the beginning. The public was largely indifferent to most of the Fair Deal, save for action to ease the middle-class housing squeeze. As a result, Truman got the Housing Act of 1949, with its large middle-class subsidies and a sizable public housing component.

But one by one, the other proposals went down. Although the Democrats had superficially healthy majorities in Congress, the old conservative coalition remained dominant on most domestic issues. The civil rights program galvanized unanimous opposition from southern Democrats, and died during a Senate filibuster. Efforts to develop cooperative relationships between the unions and liberal-inclined farm organizations failed to bridge the vast cultural gap between rural entrepreneurial farming and urban wage labor. The Taft-Hartley repeal was defeated by the continued widespread hostility toward the unions. Aid to education was a casualty in an emotional argument among Democrats about support for private parochial schools. National health insurance disappeared under the onslaught of an American Medical Association campaign condemning the proposal as "socialized" medicine. The Brannan plan went down as most farm organizations expressed their preference for the subsidies they knew rather than the ones they didn't. Truman himself enjoyed considerable public popularity through 1949 and into early 1950, but in a time of prosperity he was unable to invoke the sense of crisis that Roosevelt had used to hold the Democrats together at the peak of the New Deal. The Democratic party, and the liberalism associated with it, had become the aggregate of a group of diverse interests with little sense of common purpose.

Such a situation did not favor breakthrough legislation, but it did support existing programs, with their own constituencies and momentum. The administration secured increases for a number of them, including publicly generated electrical power, western reclamation projects, the minimum wage, and, above all, Social Security, which was substantially enhanced in 1950. The results fell far short of what Truman had wanted, but they were consistent with the national mood. The outbreak of the Korean War in the summer of 1950 would effectively end any hope of enacting the Fair Deal and deny Truman his dream of being remembered as one of the top-ranking reformist presidents.

## COLD WAR REVERSES AND THE RISE OF MCCARTHYISM

The passage of the North Atlantic Treaty and consequent beginnings of a European defense force marked the high point of Truman's foreign policy successes. From mid-1949 on, international events moved against the administration and stimulated angry partisan politics of anticommunism that increasingly eclipsed the president's domestic objectives. The pivotal event was the collapse of Chiang Kai-shek's Nationalist government in the Chinese civil war and the coming to power of a communist regime under Mao Zedong. During World War II, millions of Americans had come to believe that Chiang was a great leader who embodied the democratic hopes of the Chinese common people. In fact, his government had fallen less from communist military pressure than from internal corruption and decay. Truman's State Department, seeing China as a bottomless pit, had given up on Chiang two years earlier and had decided to concentrate limited foreign aid resources in Europe. A thoroughly defensible course, the policy was never explained to the American people, in part because support for Chiang was so great among Republicans, in part because the U.S. foreign policy establishment was much better at dealing with Europe than with Asia.

In contrast, the USSR gave Mao ample rhetorical support and some tangible aid. When Chinese communists took control of the world's most populous nation, it was natural—and not altogether inaccurate— for ordinary Americans to interpret the event as a severe reversal for the United States and a victory for Soviet ambitions. Many Republicans, their distress stoked by partisan rage, saw it as a betrayal perpetrated by State Department officials who were soft on communism. And Chiang, although he abandoned the mainland, managed to transfer his government to the offshore island of Formosa (Taiwan), securely beyond the reach of communist military capability. The continued existence of an anticommunist Republic of China provided a rallying point for administration critics and made diplomatic relations with Mao's new government impossible. Truman found himself not only unable to renounce Chiang (whom he privately detested) but also blamed for the "loss of China" and effectively blocked from realistic recognition of the facts of life on the mainland.

Truman's foreign policy suffered another severe setback in August 1949, with the first successful Soviet test of an atomic bomb. The implications, for both the short term and long term, were ominous. By ending the U.S. atomic monopoly, the Soviet bomb left many Americans feeling insecure in a world that was more dangerous than ever. The suspicion (now known to be correct) that espionage had facilitated the Soviet effort encouraged a widespread spy hunt inside and outside government. It also left the administration vulnerable to charges of laxness on national security issues. In early 1950, after two sensational trials, former State Department official Alger Hiss was found guilty of perjury for having denied he engaged in espionage for the USSR during the 1930s. Quickly thereafter, Klaus Fuchs was arrested in Britain, and Julius and Ethel Rosenberg in the United States; all were charged with atomic spying for the Soviets.

Taking advantage of this backdrop of loss in China, atomic insecurity, and revelations of espionage, the administration's critics (primarily Republican) asserted it was soft on communism—or worse. In February 1950, Senator Joseph McCarthy of Wisconsin asserted that over 200 "card-carrying communists" had positions in the State Department; subsequently, he charged specific individuals. McCarthy never uncovered a single communist in government, but his tenacity was as determined as his mendacity. Superbly exploiting widespread public apprehension, he attracted great attention and considerable support from his fellow Republicans. "McCarthyism"—a politics of false accusation, not to be confused with responsible anticommunism—has been interpreted as a symptom of an underlying social instability in American life. It probably is more accurate, however, to see it largely as a blunt partisan instrument that was politi-

cally effective because it spoke, however hysterically, to widespread fears.

The Soviet bomb also presented a fundamental challenge to U.S. national security strategy. The U.S. atomic monopoly, although not a deployable bargaining card in day-to-day diplomacy, had been an effective deterrent against Soviet moves that might present a frontal challenge to fundamental U.S. interests. Through the early years of the Cold War, Truman had used economic aid effectively and had steadily increased the nation's foreign commitments while cutting the military budget. In short, the U.S. bomb had facilitated peacetime prosperity *and* a global competition with communism. Until late 1949, Truman had not been forced to face the prospect of a militarized economy as the price of national security. The new secretary of state, Dean Acheson, a clear-eyed realist who believed in negotiation from strength, responded to the Soviet bomb by urging a comprehensive reevaluation of the nation's military policy. The result, forwarded to Truman in the spring of 1950 as National Security Council Document No. 68 (NSC-68), posited a long, hard struggle with the USSR and advocated a drastic military build-up.

By June 1950, Truman was still pondering NSC-68, but he was inclined against full implementation. He also expected that a congressional investigation of McCarthy's charges would discredit the Wisconsin senator and his more extreme Republican colleagues. The outbreak of war in Korea dashed both hopes.

## KOREA: THE DOWNWARD SPIRAL AT HOME AND ABROAD

The unexpected North Korean attack on South Korea on 25 June 1950 laid bare all the weak spots of Truman's national security policies. His military cuts had stretched U.S. forces thin everywhere, and they had been withdrawn from South Korea. Moreover, administration diplomats still dealt with eastern Asia absent-mindedly; in January 1950, Secretary of State Acheson had publicly drawn a U.S. security zone in the Pacific that excluded South Korea. Yet in a prevailing climate of opinion that vividly re-called pre-World War II appeasement, acquiescence to an attack across borders was unthinkable. The administration secured a United Nations resolution authorizing defense of South Korea, and Truman ordered U.S. troops there as the main international component of a United Nations force.

In the interest of haste, Truman acted without congressional authorization. It quickly became clear, moreover, that any Capitol Hill debate, while likely to end with a resolution of support, would be acrimonious. The president, perhaps primarily for that reason, asserted that he had acted on his inherent authority as commander-in-chief of the armed forces. He never requested legislative authorization either for his decision to intervene or for his decision to do so under the flag of the United Nations. He could make a respectable case in terms of constitutional theory, historical practice, and the practicalities of modern warfare. He also left himself exposed and vulnerable if things went wrong.

The administration assumed, with unmerited optimism, that the North Koreans could be easily repelled. Instead, the well-equipped and well-trained invaders came close to throwing the more poorly prepared Americans off the Korean peninsula. In mid-September, the tide turned abruptly and apparently decisively when the U.S./U.N. commander General Douglas MacArthur engineered a stunning amphibious landing at Inchon. Easily defeating a surprised enemy, MacArthur advanced into North Korea with the objectives of occupying the entire aggressor country, right up to the Yalu River boundary with China, and unifying the Korean peninsula. Reassured by MacArthur that total victory was in sight, neither Truman nor any of his advisers imposed caution upon him. Instead, they refused to take seriously explicit warnings of intervention from China. Two months after Inchon, the Chinese struck hard into North Korea, sent the United Nations forces reeling, and initiated a bloody stalemate that would endure for the remainder of the Truman presidency.

In September, Truman had approved NSC-68—the National Security Council document advocating a U.S. military build-up—thereby launching the nation on a drastic reversal of his previous low-level defense program. The Chinese intervention in November created a sense of crisis that gave greater urgency to that military build-up. Ironically, however, the sense of crisis, fueled by a widespread fear of global communist aggression, made it impossible to fight the Korean War to a finish, in part because the defense of western Europe remained a necessary first priority. The NATO allies were possessed by the fear of Soviet attack and intensely apprehensive of a possible U.S. shift in focus to Asia. The administration quickly concluded that most of the fruits of the U.S. build-up would have to be deployed across the Atlantic, not the Pacific. Given these circumstances, the best the administration could hope for was stabilization of the Korean front at approximately the old North-South boundary (achieved by March 1951) and a negotiated end to the war.

Viewed from a global perspective, the new policy of limited war and peace without victory in Korea possessed a certain inexorable logic. However, for an American population with vivid memories of total triumph in World War II, it was an emotional shock, accepted by some as a grim necessity, reviled by others as a product of administration incompetence or worse. General MacArthur, who had spent the past fourteen years in the Pacific and East Asia, was convinced that *his* part of the world was more important than Europe; he was equally certain that there was no substitute for victory. He publicly criticized the president's policy. Truman, after weeks of hesitation, relieved him of all his commands on 11 April 1951. An emotional binge of angry criticism followed, and—although public opinion moderated after a bit—the president's public approval ratings remained abysmally low for the balance of his presidency. Truman displayed great courage in staving off the most significant threat to civilian control of the military since McClellan faced off against

Lincoln. He would pay an equally great price for his act of courage: During his remaining twenty-one months in office, he was too wounded politically to be a fully effective president.

As the war dragged on with no end in sight, the political atmosphere at home became poisonous. Senator McCarthy and McCarthyism moved to the forefront of American politics. Even before the Chinese intervention in Korea, Congress had passed the McCarran Internal Security Act, a wide-ranging effort to suppress internal subversion in general and the Communist party in particular. Truman, believing it a blunderbuss that threatened civil liberties, issued an eloquent veto that Congress swiftly overrode by huge majorities. After the Chinese intervention and the dismissal of MacArthur, the Republican opposition routinely accused Truman and administration leading officials of pro-communist sympathies. McCarthy's voice was the loudest, but many other more responsible members of the opposition chimed in with little sense of restraint.

## SHELVING THE FAIR DEAL

Democratic reversals in the 1950 congressional elections already had undermined Truman's authority and narrowed his options. The losses were not great, but even in peacetime they would have ended hopes for the Fair Deal. With the nation in a state of de facto war, Truman had no choice but to devote his energies to uniting the Democratic party behind his foreign policy and his management of the national defense build-up. He was more successful in the former endeavor than in the latter.

The war in Korea required domestic efforts at economic management similar to those of World War II but much less stringent. Economic mobilization gave rise to a relatively mild inflation, with shortages, high prices, credit controls, production regulations, wage and price ceilings, and higher taxes, which in combination alienated almost every group of Americans. Truman was put in the position of asking Americans to make sacrifices and to do so in a situation

very different from the stark threat to national survival that had been posed by World War II. In a very real sense, this latest request reproduced all the national dissatisfaction and no-win politics that had plagued him during the reconversion period following World War II.

In the meantime, the administration was further damaging itself by lax and complacent responses to revelations of numerous instances of internal corruption—influence-peddling by associates of government figures, favoritism by federal lending agencies, tax-fixing by some Internal Revenue Service officials, unwarranted leniency by Justice Department prosecutors. Truman's initial reaction to such revelations was to view them as attacks on himself; his second was to rely too long on appointees who had looked the other way. In the early spring of 1952, he fired his laid-back attorney general, J. Howard McGrath, and finally began a real clean-up, but the political damage was beyond repair by that time. Although many of the offenses were relatively petty, they had offended Americans who were at that time being asked to make personal sacrifices for the good of the nation.

The president also involved himself in a labor dispute that would culminate in a major constitutional controversy. On 8 April 1952, Truman moved to avert a nationwide steel strike that posed a threat to defense production; he announced that, under his authority as chief executive, he was seizing the steel industry. (Having convinced the steelworkers union to stay on the job without a contract for three months, he did not feel he could invoke the Taft-Hartley Act, a move that also would have been politically dangerous in an election year.) Such a massive seizure of private property on vague claims of authority was an enormous gamble, and on 2 June the Supreme Court ruled it unconstitutional. The 53-day strike that followed fortunately did no perceptible damage to defense production.

By summer of 1952, Truman already had publicly rejected another run for the presidency; exhausted and widely unpopular, he turned the Democratic party over to Adlai

Stevenson. The following January, he would turn the presidency over to Republican Dwight D. Eisenhower. Truman's achievements were remarkable. Few presidents served in such epochal times, and few "made" so much history. He will be remembered foremost for establishing the policy of containment that largely defined U.S. diplomacy for a generation. As the architect of the national agenda, he also kept both the New Deal liberal tradition and the Democratic party alive—indeed, he revitalized them in many respects by his commitment to civil rights. And now that the intense partisan controversies of his administration have lost their salience, most Americans think of Harry S. Truman as, above all, an authentic and plain-speaking representative of democracy, who demonstrated the strength of the common man.

## BIBLIOGRAPHY

Donovan, Robert J. *Conflict and Crisis: The Presidency of Harry S. Truman, 1945–1948* (Norton, 1977).

———. *Tumultuous Years: The Presidency of Harry S. Truman* (Norton, 1982).

Ferrell, Robert, ed. *Dear Bess: The Letters from Harry to Bess Truman, 1910–1959* (Norton, 1983).

———, ed. *Off the Record: The Private Papers of Harry S. Truman* (Harper & Row, 1980).

———. *Harry S. Truman: A Life* (University of Missouri Press, 1994).

Hamby, Alonzo L. *Beyond the New Deal: Harry S. Truman and American Liberalism* (Columbia University Press, 1973).

———. *Man of the People: A Life of Harry S. Truman* (Oxford University Press, 1995).

Hillman, William, ed. *Mr. President* (Farrar, Straus, & Young, 1952).

Kirkendall, Richard, ed. *The Truman Encyclopedia* (G.K. Hall, 1989).

Lacey, Michael, ed. *The Truman Presidency* (Woodrow Wilson Center, 1989).

McCoy, Donald R. *The Presidency of Harry S. Truman* (University Press of Kansas, 1984).

McCullough, David. *Truman* (Simon & Schuster, 1992).

Miller, Merle. *Plain Speaking: An Oral Biography of Harry S. Truman* (Berkley Publishing, 1974).

Poen, Monte M., ed. *Strictly Personal and Confidential: The Letters Harry Truman Never Mailed* (Little, Brown, 1982).

Truman, Harry S. *Memoirs*, 2 vols. (Doubleday, 1955–1956).

———. *Mr. Citizen* (Columbia University Press, 1960).

Truman, Margaret. *Where the Buck Stops: The Personal and Private Writings of Harry S. Truman* (Warner Books, 1989).

★★★ 34 ★★★

# DWIGHT DAVID EISENHOWER
## 1953–1961

*Nancy Beck Young*

---

*Born 14 October 1890 in Denison, Texas, to David Jacob Eisenhower and Ida Elizabeth Stoever Eisenhower; educated at the U.S. Military Academy at West Point (B.S. 1915); married Marie (Mamie) Geneva Doud, 1 July 1916 in Denver, Colorado; two children; elected president in 1952 on the Republican ticket with Richard Milhous Nixon of California, with 33,778,963 popular votes and 442 electoral college ballots, over the Democratic slate of Adlai Ewing Stevenson of Illinois and John Jackson Sparkman of Alabama (27,314,992 votes and 89 electoral ballots); reelected with Nixon in 1956 with 35,581,003 popular votes and 457 electoral ballots over the Democratic team of Adlai Ewing Stevenson of Illinois and Estes Kefauver of Tennessee (25,738,765 popular votes and 73 electoral ballots); died 28 March 1969 in Washington, D.C.; buried in Abilene, Kansas.*

---

The circumstances of Dwight David Eisenhower's birth and early life in Denison, Texas, were modest. Originally from Kansas, his father, David Eisenhower, worked briefly on the railroad in Denison until a better opportunity emerged back home. The family settled in Abilene, Kansas, and David worked at the Belle Springs Creamery, a job that—unlike his earlier failures in the retail trade—

provided a steady income for his growing family. Frugal management of personal finances and strong family ties became the cornerstone for Dwight's early years. His family derived from the Pennsylvania Dutch and worshipped with the Brethren in Christ sect of the Mennonites. The future president's early life required hard work and acceptance of stern discipline, and it posed no deep questioning of the established order.

## ARMY CAREER

In June 1911, at the age of 20, Dwight Eisenhower boarded a train for West Point, where he had been admitted as a student. His interest in military history, combined with his close friendship with Everett "Swede" Hazlett, a student at Annapolis, had guided Eisenhower's decision to apply to one of the military academies instead of the University of Michigan, where his brother Edgar was a student. As a plebe, Eisenhower became enamored with the tradition of duty and service, and his boyhood love of sports continued at the academy, where he played varsity football.

Eisenhower's 1915 graduating class was the most famous in West Point's history. Of the 164 cadets, 59 went on to achieve the rank of brigadier general or higher. West Point had ignored all the social and educational reforms of the Progressive era and continued to drill its cadets according to old-fashioned methods, one of which was unquestioning rote memorization of established knowledge. As a cadet, Eisenhower had also learned to subordinate the individual to the interests of the group. He developed an apolitical outlook on life, believing that the military and the government should not intermingle. In this worldview, the president as commander-in-chief, not politician, played the dominant role.

After graduation, Eisenhower almost missed receiving an officer's commission because of an injury to his knee suffered while playing football. However, because he retained a sense of responsibility and had no other great plans, he took a spot in the infantry. World War I found Eisenhower deskbound; he spent the duration of the fighting in the United States drilling other troops for overseas combat. He thus retained his zest for battle and accumulated no bad memories of the carnage.

Eisenhower remained in the army during the 1920s and 1930s despite few prospects for advancement. During a tour of duty in the Panama Canal Zone, Eisenhower received much encouragement and guidance from General Fox Connor, his commanding officer. Yet he sometimes found his assignments tedious, most notably between 1936 and 1939 in Manila under General Douglas MacArthur. Eisenhower returned to the States in 1940 and helped ready the army for war with Germany. He sought greater efficiency in the training of troops and the preparation of budgets, of which growth in the latter concerned him.

Five days after the attack on Pearl Harbor, General George C. Marshall summoned Colonel Eisenhower to Washington, D.C., and asked him what the United States should do in the Pacific. Eisenhower prepared a response that recognized both the political and the military imperatives for defending the Philippines. His answer impressed Marshall, who then assigned Eisenhower strategic responsibility for defending that archipelago. With that assignment, an obscure colonel moved quickly to the center of the U.S. military effort.

In the early months of 1942, Eisenhower began spending more time planning U.S. actions in the European theater. Marshall, ever impressed with Eisenhower's ability, appointed him to command the European theater of operations on 11 June 1942. This assignment catapulted Eisenhower from obscurity to the headlines, a position he retained for the remainder of his life. Eisenhower proved popular with the press and the American public, who enjoyed reading the circumstances of his childhood. Building unity with the British proved the most difficult aspect of his work, and he was very disappointed when the British vetoed a cross-channel invasion for 1942 and 1943.

## LESSONS OF THE WAR

Eisenhower's experiences in the European theater colored the understanding of world affairs that he would take to the White House in the 1950s. Eisenhower contented himself with the opportunity to command forces in the field in northern Africa, the alternative campaign to a European continental invasion. However, the Soviets reacted suspiciously to the delayed second front. These tensions intensified in the postwar era. Eisenhower later thought that an earlier invasion of the continent might have kept Soviet troops out of eastern Europe.

The North African campaign provided Eisenhower with valuable field experience that served him well when the attack was made on the continent. By 1943, Eisenhower had high marks for mending disagreements among the Allies, and President Franklin D. Roosevelt named him supreme commander of the Allied Expeditionary Force. In 1944, he led the Allied forces in the D-Day landing at Normandy in France, and saw the troops on to victory in Europe on 7 May 1945.

## LOOKING FOR
## A POSTWAR CAREER

At war's end, General Eisenhower remained in Europe, serving as head of the U.S. occupation zone in Germany until December 1945, when he replaced General George C. Marshall as army chief of staff. Eisenhower held that position until June 1948, when he assumed the presidency of Columbia University. His tenure there would be short-lived; even while serving as Columbia's president Eisenhower made numerous trips to Washington to advise on military and diplomacy issues. When war broke out in Korea, civilian life paled, and Eisenhower readily accepted President Harry S Truman's offer of an appointment as the supreme commander of the recently formed North Atlantic Treaty Organization. This new position included responsibility for the rearmament of Europe in a defensive posture against the Soviet Union. Taking a leave of absence from Columbia, Eisen-

hower journeyed to Europe on 1 January 1951.

While working in Europe with NATO, Eisenhower faced increased pressures to offer himself as a presidential candidate. "Ike" as he was by then called, had grown irritated with Republican Senator Joseph McCarthy's increasingly vitriolic language in opposing the charges of domestic communism, and with Republican Senator Robert Taft's demands for isolation from the world. Eisenhower had even less sympathy for the spending programs of Truman and the Democrats. Although politics and the presidency held no great allure for him, Eisenhower had a great sense of duty. When friends and colleagues suggested a career change, he chose his words carefully so as to neither ensure nor prevent such a move. In January 1951, he recorded in his diary a response he made to General Ed Clark, an army friend and ready supporter for a presidential run: "I hope always to do my duty to my country; but I cannot even conceive of circumstances as of this moment that could convince me I had a duty to enter politics."

## "I LIKE IKE"

By the summer of 1951, pressure was mounting as "Ike" clubs emerged nationwide. Still unsure of Eisenhower's political affiliation, both Democrats and Republicans vied for his allegiance. Even President Truman promised the general his full support if he ran on the Democratic ticket. Eisenhower responded that he opposed the domestic agenda of the Democrats, especially with regard to labor legislation, and had always considered himself a Republican. Personal preference and a desire to counter the extreme tendencies within the Republican party dictated his choice, but he refused to make a public pronouncement of his political affiliation or plans until early 1952. Even then, a sense of duty more than the desire for political power propelled him into the race.

Eisenhower returned to the United States on 1 June 1952 and prepared for his presidential bid. Candidate Eisenhower found himself in the difficult position of explaining to undecided Republicans his role in implementing the Democratic party's foreign policy over the preceding twenty years. As a leading figure during World War II and as chief of staff of the army after the war, Eisenhower was directly linked to the foreign policies and politics of the Roosevelt and Truman years, including Yalta and the fall of mainland China to the communists in 1949. Eisenhower successfully explained his opposition to both isolation and the results of these past actions, thereby satisfying Republican party regulars and separating himself from his former Democratic party bosses.

While he would have preferred nomination by acclamation, Eisenhower was nine votes short of defeating Taft on the first vote, and he received the GOP nod on the second ballot. As the general election approached, Eisenhower conducted a thorough campaign in which he ignored the professionals and campaigned across the entire country, including the Democratic strongholds of the South. His running mate, Senator Richard Nixon, took responsibility for the direct attacks on the Democrats, labeling the Democratic nominee Adlai Stevenson "a graduate of Dean Acheson's 'Cowardly College of Communist Containment.'" Even charges that Nixon had wrongly accumulated a secret fund proved too little to prevent a Republican victory that November.

## THE GENERAL IN THE WHITE HOUSE

Eisenhower was the first Republican to hold the office in twenty years. Many adult Americans wondered what type of president he would be—many could not remember the last Republican president, and those who did remembered Herbert Hoover and the Great Depression. Eisenhower, the career military officer who had disdained partisan politics, now found himself at center stage. During this period he was well served by the valuable political lessons about the delegation of power he had gained while organizing the army during World War II. He would need all the talent he could muster to govern a nation in which postwar prosperity caused some Americans to demand even more guarantees from the federal government while equally loud voices asked that Washington curtail its involvement in the economy. Wartime declarations about the human rights of people abroad had increased the demands among African Americans for civil rights at home.

Although the Republicans had recaptured Congress along with the White House in 1952, the caustic and strident appeals of the far right did not abate easily. As president and party leader, Eisenhower bore the responsibility for halting the anticommunist witch hunt headed by Joe McCarthy while still standing firm on containing the spread of communism abroad. Foreign policy concerns intensified, especially among peoples of less-developed countries hungry for independence. Eisenhower also had to cope with the expanding Cold War with the Soviet Union, fueled in part by the administration's refusal to differentiate between communism and indigenous nationalism within developing nations. Concurrently, the president found himself responsible for setting policy with regard to military budgets.

An analysis of Eisenhower's organization and management of the presidency must address several key points. Two of the most important are his style of leadership and the nature of his relationship with the legislative branch. Leadership for Eisenhower emphasized teamwork that respected hierarchy and authority. Concomitantly, the new president disdained any display of partisanship. Eisenhower's hatred for politics played a key role in his presidency because he was the first modern chief executive to encounter the phenomenon of divided government, with Republicans controlling the White House and Democrats controlling Congress after 1954.

While positioning himself as being above partisanship, Eisenhower actually elaborated a more conservative theory of government. He viewed Harry Truman's Fair Deal as an abdication of the federal government's responsibility to broker among the various interests within the polity. Instead, Eisenhower believed, Truman had without question accommodated every demand of the interest groups beseeching government assistance—labor, minorities, agriculture, and the aged. Although the former general never advocated a reversal of the New Deal era reforms, he did attempt to check further growth of government, calling for more volunteer efforts and less reliance on an overly strong federal government. The new president strengthened ties to corporate America and emphasized private initiative. These statements placed him in line for controversy with Democrats, who found his views anathema.

Eisenhower's ideas about the functioning of the executive branch are reflected in the appointments he made. Eschewing patronage and the Republican power structure, the president instead sought the best-qualified individuals, although his critics noted that he limited his search to America's boardrooms. Eisenhower added a White House staff position, assistant to the president, and chose Sherman Adams to fill it. Adams performed procedural tasks with a firm hand so that Eisenhower could concentrate on weightier matters. This teamwork philosophy led many Washington observers to conclude that Eisenhower was incapable of independent action, yet a careful reading of his diaries indicates otherwise. His regular writings demonstrate a sophisticated and analytical approach to the country's problems that contrasts readily with his often boring or convoluted public statements, which were in reality constructed in a way to confuse the listener and perhaps deflect criticism.

## RELATIONS WITH CONGRESS
Popular accounts of Eisenhower's congressional relations alternate between two conflicting and incorrect ideas: Either Eisenhower wanted nothing to do with Congress, or, conversely, Eisenhower, Senate Majority Leader Lyndon B. Johnson, and House Speaker Sam Rayburn worked together with a shared purpose and agenda. In reality, Eisenhower paid close attention to congressional matters because he believed their actions mattered. Furthermore, the president worried that Congress, more than the executive branch, was likely to act outside of the national interest, which he believed he represented. He held weekly meetings with the leaders on Capitol Hill and exerted his influence in a quiet fashion.

Even for the two years that Republicans held power in both houses of Congress (1953–1955), the majority was thin, leaving Eisenhower between a divided GOP and a largely hostile opposition. Early in that period, he found Robert Taft agreeable as Senate majority leader, but their collaboration was short-lived because Taft died in July 1953. William Knowland, Taft's successor, never impressed Eisenhower, who once remarked in his diary that "in [Knowland's] case there seems to be no final answer to the question 'How stupid can you get?'" However, Everett McKinley Dirksen, Knowland's successor and Senate Republican leader for the last two years of Eisenhower's term, did impress the president. He also respected the House leaders, Speaker Joseph W. Martin, Jr., and later Charles A. Halleck. The president enjoyed good relations with his leadership team and enjoyed several legislative victories during the 83rd Congress, which was in session from 1953 through 1954. His relations with Congress deteriorated when dealing with the Democrats. Lyndon Johnson and Sam Rayburn—first as leaders for the minority, then after 1955 as leaders of their respective houses—played key roles in the Eisenhower presidency.

## THE EISENHOWER AGENDA
The general-turned-president favored an agenda that limited the federal government's role in the working of the economy. Instead of creating federal mandates to ensure fiscal responsibility, Eisenhower sought cooperation between public and private spheres toward that end. Eisenhower worried so much about budgets and excessive

spending that in 1953 he lobbied for deficit reduction instead of tax cuts. When the economy responded with a mild recession, Eisenhower advocated passage of a tax cut on corporate dividends the following year. His agenda did not include New Deal–style programs, except in a few politically calculated cases. For example, he believed there was significant public demand for the expansion of Social Security to take in more workers, and that any attempt to destroy Social Security would be political suicide for the party responsible. Similarly, Eisenhower advocated some increased federal responsibility for health-care costs in the form of subsidies to private concerns providing coverage for their workers.

Eisenhower almost always sided with the interests of the business community when environmental and economic policy concerns intersected. For example, the state of Texas had lobbied for years to retain title to its oil-rich offshore drilling rights in the Tidelands. Other states had no ownership rights for similar territory, but the administration cited the unique circumstances of Texas's brief history as an independent republic as grounds for its conflicting claims. In the West, Eisenhower similarly advocated dam construction instead of environmental protections for fragile ecosystems. When private economic interests faced direct competition with federal programs, as in the case of the Tennessee Valley Authority (TVA), the president usually sided with private interests. He wanted the TVA to become self-sufficient and even pushed for a private power company to provide electrical services for Memphis, a TVA city. That deal fell through when a series of charges were made public about conflict of interest between the bidding firm, Dixon-Yates, and their ties to the administration. TVA nevertheless lost some of its control over the region because the city of Memphis opted to build its own power plant. With regard to agricultural subsidies, Eisenhower pushed for a reduction of these payments on the grounds that they encouraged overproduction of farm goods.

## PRESIDING OVER A DIVIDED GOVERNMENT

In the 1954 congressional elections, voters handed control of Congress to the Democrats, and Eisenhower led a divided government. In the House, Democrats enjoyed a 30-seat advantage over the president's party, but they held the Senate by only a 1-seat majority. Eisenhower hoped the large number of powerful and conservative southern Democrats would at times cross party lines and weaken the opposition's position in the upper chamber.

Eisenhower took the position with the 84th Congress that his agenda corresponded with the interests of the nation. Nevertheless, the presence of Democratic majorities generated some worries for the president. Given his difficulties with old guard Republicans, how would his program for modern Republicanism fare in the new Congress? His worries were realized in several areas of disagreement and inaction in that Congress. Eisenhower sought a moderate program of federal moneys for school construction, but liberal Democrats wanted even more funds for increasing teacher salaries and linkage of funding provision to compliance with the recent ruling in *Brown v. Board of Education*, the 1954 school desegregation case. In the area of public health, Eisenhower sought more federal subsidies for private health insurance. He believed the federal government should play a role in highway construction, but was able to enact that belief only after a year of legislative wrangling, when in June 1956 he signed the Federal Aid Highway Act, providing for the modernization of roads.

Perhaps the most heated example of the president's discontent with legislative matters was Sam Rayburn's effort to give every American taxpayer a $20 tax credit. The Texas Democrat, enraged with the president's passage of high-end tax relief in 1954, sought benefits for working Americans and for his own party in the 1956 elections. Rayburn maneuvered the $20 tax credit through the House in February 1955, and from there the measure became the object of a month-long legislative struggle in the Senate. Although the bill was eventually defeated, it was symbolic of the difficulty Eisenhower had with Congress and lays bare the fiction of harmonious bipartisan cooperation during the last six years of his administration. According to James C. Hagerty, an aide to the president, Eisenhower remarked in the midst of a White House strategy meeting that "it's about time that I personally went after Rayburn. I know many of his constituents and have a lot of good friends in Texas. I think I should get those friends to go after him and ask him what the hell he is trying to do up here in Washington."

## ECONOMIC UPS AND DOWNS

By 1955, the domestic economy was booming and Eisenhower enjoyed favorable public ratings. Furthermore, Eisenhower and Congress created a budget that included a $4.1 billion surplus for fiscal year 1956. Inflation was nonexistent and unemployment was below 5 percent. Yet in 1957 the economy again endured a mild recession, and the interaction it precipitated between the executive and legislative branches provides another barometer for measuring Eisenhower's congressional difficulties. The focus was Eisenhower's budget for fiscal year 1958, which, although balanced, included an increase in spending over fiscal year 1957. The leading historians of the Eisenhower presidency have called the ensuing debate about spending priorities the "Battle of the Budget" because congressional relations worsened in the process. Part of the fault lay with the legislators; the other part lay with Eisenhower, who did a poor job of explaining his spending agenda to Congress and the nation. The administration seemed at odds over budgetary priorities even within itself when George Humphrey, the secretary of the treasury, described the Eisenhower spending plan as too generous. The situation became more complicated when the president quoted Humphrey in an attempt to beat back congressional attempts to increase federal spending.

Two disparate congressional groups—moderate Democrats and old guard Republicans—pushed for a more frugal budget. Eisenhower disagreed with the old guard Republicans, who wanted to roll back all of the New Deal; the president approved funding for programs like Social Security, which he believed held a public mandate. The Democrats, holding majorities in Congress, took the lead in cutting the budget for fiscal year 1958, which ultimately came in $4 billion under Eisenhower's original request.

As the 1958 midterm elections drew near, Eisenhower's approval ratings fell. The budget battle and the recession had caused Americans to worry about the decline in industrial and corporate profits, the rise in unemployment, and the rise in interest rates. The Little Rock school desegregation crisis of 1957 had angered many Americans. On the international front, the Soviet launching of Sputnik on 4 October 1957 generated fear that the United States had fallen behind in its knowledge of science and technology and that Eisenhower was losing the Cold War. (Top-secret intelligence reports proved otherwise, but Eisenhower could not make that evidence public since it originated in U.S. espionage efforts.)

Eisenhower prepared his fiscal year 1959 budget against the background of all these public concerns, yet he refused to consider any form of economic intervention in the economy because he feared it would bring about inflation. The Democrats countered with a different strategy. Instead of attempting to demonstrate their own fiscal conservatism in the 1958 budget talks, the opposition introduced and passed through Congress several measures for generating economic gains, including housing and highway expenditures and more unemployment insurance. Congress also passed the National Defense Education Act, with funding for training American students in the sciences, mathematics, engineering, and foreign languages.

## THE 1958 MIDTERM ELECTIONS

Conducted against the backdrop of ethical problems within the administration, the 1958 congressional elections proved a disaster for Eisenhower and the Republicans. Sherman Adams, Eisenhower's key adviser, was accused of trading government influence for private favors. His partisanship made him a target for Democrats, and old guard Republicans viewed Adams as an unwanted liberal influence on the president. When the final votes were counted, the Democrats had won a sweeping victory, gaining 13 Senate seats and 46 House seats. Conservative Republicans blamed the president for the debacle, while Eisenhower found himself even more in need of bipartisan cooperation. Instead of criticizing the Democrats for partisanship as he had in the past, Eisenhower highlighted his willingness to work with the opposition.

The election provided Eisenhower with the impetus for demanding internal party reform within Republican ranks. Nevertheless, he built a strong working relationship with the new Republican congressional leadership team—Charles Halleck in the House and Everett McKinley Dirksen in the Senate. The president wanted a face-off with liberal Democrats, themselves chafing under what they saw as outdated leadership from Johnson and Rayburn. Indeed, the Democratic divisions proved more significant than the Republican ones in 1959. Eisenhower benefited with easier wins for his agenda.

## TRYING TO DEAL WITH CIVIL RIGHTS

The area of Eisenhower's presidency in which he showed the most apparent contradictions among thought, speech, and action was the burgeoning civil rights movement. Demands for an end to the Jim Crow caste system within the South and discrimination in much of the rest of the country had intensified in the aftermath of World War II. Wartime rhetoric had promised human rights for people suffering from German, Italian, and Japanese oppression and had left African Americans reeling from the dissonance between U.S. policies overseas and those at home. Harry Truman had established a federal role for civil rights when he ordered the desegregation of the military. Eisenhower supported the concept of immediate reform at the same time that he cautioned African Americans to be patient.

Ultimately, Eisenhower remained sympathetic with what he believed was the plight of the white South. As a result, he never used federal power to ameliorate conditions for black Americans living in the South. His gradualist approach to reform produced a disparate legacy. He sent federal troops to Little Rock not for the purpose of integration but for the maintenance of public order. Furthermore, the civil rights legislation passed during his administration resulted as much from the efforts of Lyndon Johnson in the Senate as from any public presidential lobbying. While a precedent for federal action emerged, no major corresponding changes in the southern social structure unfolded.

As early as the 1952 campaign, Eisenhower had set a tone for his civil rights policy. He suggested that the president had precious little authority over the problem of racial justice. Fearing the creation of an excessively powerful central state, Eisenhower opposed such programs as the Fair Employment Practices Commission, and he insisted that job discrimination was a local matter. Furthermore, he actively campaigned for votes among white southern Democrats and carried Florida, Tennessee, Texas, and Virginia. One cannot understand the paradox of Eisenhower's racial views without some knowledge of his background. He had lived most of his adult life in segregated communities, and he did not worry about the moral implications of segregation. Most of his service in the military had been logged before any appreciable effort at integration took place. Furthermore, he had trained and lived in the South. Eisenhower pushed the idea that thoughts and attitudes were beyond the realm of legislation. Despite his publicly pronounced hopes for a better world, he did little to convert those hopes to actual plans for large-scale change.

Eisenhower focused on gradual change at the level of the individual, but the Supreme Court had other ideas. Knowing that a decision in the case *Brown v. Board of Education* was imminent, Eisenhower arranged for a stag dinner at the White House where Earl Warren, the new chief justice and an Eisenhower appointee, could meet with the attorney for the defense, John W. Davis. According to his biographer, Eisenhower himself lobbied Warren on behalf of the South: "These are not bad people. All they are concerned about is to see that their sweet little girls are not required to sit in school alongside some big overgrown Negroes."

Warren ignored this overt manipulation and led his Court to a unanimous decision upholding the NAACP (National Association for the Advancement of Colored People) suit and overturning *Plessy v. Ferguson*, an 1896 case that had established the precedent for separate-but-equal facilities. Eisenhower in turn ignored the 17 May 1954 decision in his public statements. Supporters of civil rights criticized his failure to provide moral leadership in the post-*Brown* era. In the 1960s Eisenhower became very critical of Warren's decisions with regard to criminal rights and often remarked that the Warren appointment was "the biggest damn fool mistake I ever made." Although many students of the Eisenhower years have misapplied this sentiment to the *Brown* case, Eisenhower's regrets about the Warren appointment appeared later. Despite his personal views on integration, Eisenhower endorsed the separation of power between the executive and judicial functions and hoped for slow enactment of civil rights legislation, in part because he feared the South would close the public schools entirely.

## THE FAILURE OF LEADERSHIP
Even extreme examples of southern resistance to African-American demands for civil rights did not affect Eisenhower's attitudes about gradualism. For example, he did nothing when Autherine Lucy was suspended and expelled from the University of Alabama in the wake of mob protest. When southerners in Congress drafted the Southern Manifesto, a statement of resistance, the president explained their good intentions. And when Texas governor Allan Shivers quietly used the Texas Rangers to prevent integration in the Texarkana and Mansfield public schools, Eisenhower did nothing.

The one area Eisenhower was willing to address was voting rights. Such a strategy appealed to his belief in gradualism. In 1956 and again in 1957 he sent legislation to Congress that gave the attorney general enforcement power over African-American voting rights and that formed within the Justice Department a division in charge of civil rights. The legislation produced few results in an election year despite support from northern liberal Democrats. Lyndon Johnson, then the Senate majority leader with presidential ambitions, not only understood the imperatives for change but also realized the benefits that such legislation would provide on the campaign trail. He also knew that a strong measure would never survive a filibuster from southern Democrats in the Senate. The substitute measure that ultimately passed replaced Justice Department enforcement with local jury trials.

## SHOWDOWN AT LITTLE ROCK
From the perspective of what Eisenhower was willing to do, it mattered little where enforcement rested because the president seemed reticent to use federal authority in the South. His conflicting statements on the matter have led some to argue that Eisenhower established the mood for Governor Orval Faubus to defy the law mandating school desegregation and make his stand in Little Rock, Arkansas. Privately, Faubus consented to a plan for gradual integration in Little Rock, with Central High scheduled to be the first school reformed. When vociferous segregationists noted their opposition, Faubus backpedaled, and with an eye to reelection concerns he sought a judicial postponement. When that failed, Faubus called in the National Guard and asked Eisenhower for support. The president sought a compromise between the

Arkansas governor on the one extreme and the federal court on the other. After meeting with Faubus, Eisenhower believed he had a deal which would permit the governor to change the National Guard's orders to protect the public safety and ensure the orderly integration of Central High. Faubus reneged, saying he had no responsibility for maintaining public order.

When a mob turned out at Central High on 23 September, Eisenhower described the scene as a disgrace, sent troops from the 101st Airborne Division, and federalized the Arkansas National Guard. Eisenhower explained his actions from the perspective of enforcing the law and maintaining order, not as an instance of supporting integration. He emphasized the point that citizens cannot pick and choose which laws they will obey, and he addressed the shock and fear of white southerners with assurances that Little Rock was not a precursor for a heightened federal presence in southern affairs. When Faubus closed the public schools in 1958, the president did nothing. While Eisenhower let it be known that he would not tolerate violence, he also made clear that public order was more important than integration.

## PRESSURE FROM THE RIGHT— THE BRICKER AMENDMENT

Problems with right-of-center ideologues haunted Eisenhower throughout the early years of his presidency. In many ways these challenges exacerbated his dilemmas with Congress because his conservative antagonists hailed from the legislative branch. Republican Senator John Bricker of Ohio and fellow Republican Senator Joseph McCarthy from Wisconsin vied with the president in their own ways for increased congressional authority—Bricker over the country's foreign policy, and McCarthy over domestic security. The president used what one scholar of his administration has termed "hidden-hand leadership" to deal with these rivals without alienating their constituent bases within the Republican party.

In September 1951, Bricker introduced legislation that would protect U.S. sovereignty in world affairs. Worried about the relationship between the United States and international agencies such as the United Nations and the North Atlantic Treaty Organization, Bricker attacked perceived presidential excesses achieved at the expense of Congress in the deliberation of foreign policy. Specifically, Bricker and the old guard Republicans who supported his endeavors reacted against what they perceived as weaknesses resulting from Franklin D. Roosevelt's World War II negotiations with the Soviet Union and from Harry S Truman's enactment of containment. In reality, the measure—which came to be known as the Bricker amendment—would have limited the range of action open to the executive branch in the execution of foreign policy and international treaties. Bricker and his cohorts worried that international treaties would limit congressional freedom with regard to domestic policy. As written, the Bricker amendment provided that no foreign policy could be enacted if it would interfere with constitutional rights or domestic affairs.

Eisenhower hated the measure and the handicap it would place on the conduct of foreign policy, but he acknowledged the domestic political land mine of outright condemnation. Most Republicans in the Senate were on record favoring Bricker's agenda. Thus, Eisenhower opted for subtle negotiations that would quietly defeat the measure. Silent on the matter in public, Eisenhower was loud in his private commentary, writing in his diary that Bricker was "almost psychopathic on the subject" of the amendment. Not until 1954 was Eisenhower able to defeat the Bricker amendment and similar companion bills. After almost two years of effort, the president and former general finally won the right to control the foreign policy of his administration. However, he paid a price for presidential supremacy in the exertion of effort that could better have been directed to other matters. The combined frustrations led Eisenhower to exclaim that the Bricker amendment was the biggest domestic problem of his administration.

## McCARTHY AND McCARTHYISM

As noted earlier, Bricker was not the only troublesome Republican Eisenhower encountered. Senator Joseph McCarthy completely disgusted Eisenhower's sense of morality. The Wisconsin Republican had become prominent with his 1950 speech to a women's club in Wheeling, West Virginia, in which he claimed there were communists in the State Department. The following year McCarthy's charges seemed outlandish to all but the true believers; yet the problem remained how to silence his attack without sounding procommunist at the height of the Cold War. In his diary in 1951 Eisenhower called McCarthy one of the "disciples of hate" in America.

After he assumed the office of the president in 1953, Eisenhower adopted a strategy of silence, arguing that the best way to fight McCarthy's charges was to ignore them. The president believed that publicity was McCarthy's main objective, making the failure to respond all the more damaging to the generation of media attention. Instead, Eisenhower privately maneuvered to attain his goal of checking McCarthy's attacks on private citizens and the government. Since McCarthy's presence at the center of the anticommunist crusade in the United States made him a public figure, he garnered more headlines than Bricker's sometimes confusing attack on the development of foreign policy. But this time the strategy proved inadequate to the task because of one major problem—the tactic was too slow to resolve the crisis before significant damage had been done. Public denunciation might have produced an earlier showdown and could have saved innocent people from slander and loss of livelihood.

As Eisenhower worked behind the scenes, McCarthy continued his assault with scatter-shot attacks on numerous Eisenhower nominees, including General Walter Bedell Smith (undersecretary of state), James B. Conant (American high commissioner of Germany), and Charles E. Bohlen (ambassador to the Soviet Union). When Eisenhower refused to withdraw his nominees, McCarthy backed down. Yet Eisenhower did not challenge the basic issue of communism as a domestic threat, or the basic policy objectives of the anticommunist crusade. He instituted his own strict internal security program. Eisenhower also refused all demands to commute to life imprisonment the death sentence for Ethel and Julius Rosenberg, who had been accused and convicted of trading atomic secrets to the Soviet Union. Their case had become an international cause célèbre for liberals and human rights activists who argued that the couple had not received a fair trial, and that they had been falsely accused and were victims of the McCarthy-inspired anticommunist hysteria.

Eisenhower's opposition to McCarthy rested on distaste for the methods used, not the ends desired. It was a difference of style, not substance. Delineating this difference involved what were at times slight distinctions. Nevertheless, Eisenhower would not denounce McCarthy publicly.

The senator's downfall resulted from his attacks on the U.S. Army, which led to the Army-McCarthy Hearings in 1954. Charging that high-ranking military officials were disloyal to the U.S. government, McCarthy went too far. Eisenhower used the claim of executive privilege to deny the congressional inquiry access to administration sources. Nevertheless, televised hearings had commenced. Eager to damn officials in high places, McCarthy urged that his prospective witnesses defy the president's orders and testify anyway. When no administration witnesses were willing to cooperate, the hearings collapsed. After that defeat, McCarthy's style of questioning deteriorated from its already questionable plane, and in the aftermath, he was left without major allies.

Most government officials and Americans finally recognized the senator's lack of decency. Later in the year the Senate censured McCarthy, imposing on him a forced silence on all matters pertaining to his red-baiting tactics. Scholars remain divided over whether Eisenhower, using more forceful action, could have controlled McCarthy's outbursts. Some praise the president for the effectiveness of his hidden-hand leadership, but others charge that his behind-the-scenes efforts indicate at best a president lacking control of the major issues of his administration and at worst a president out of touch with reality.

## SEARCHING FOR A FOREIGN POLICY—THE "NEW LOOK"

Eisenhower believed there were major problems with the U.S. approach to foreign policy when he entered office in 1953. Two issues dominated much of the Eisenhower presidency and therefore the search for a new foreign policy: the development of new weapons systems, and movements for independence among the peoples of Asia, the Middle East, Africa, and Latin America who had been colonized before World War II. Among Eisenhower's spoken priorities was a reduction in defense spending, which had almost quadrupled under Truman's administration, and a major overhaul of the containment policy with regard to the Soviet Union. Liberals contended that U.S. application of containment had become overly reliant on military solutions; conservatives argued that the country had lost the ability to dictate policy on international matters.

Eisenhower's foreign policy was popularly dubbed the "New Look." It provided for a decline in the number of troops deployed around the globe and an increase in air power, including nuclear weapons. As a result, the air force gained precedence over the army and navy in budgetary matters. However, in several key areas the "New Look" strongly resembled the foreign policy of Eisenhower's predecessors. Architects of the New Look were no more sanguine than previous policy makers about the willingness of the Kremlin to participate in meaningful peace talks. Nevertheless, Eisenhower's key speech, "The Chance for Peace," noted that moneys spent for defense equaled moneys not spent on food and shelter for the poor. In other ways, the New Look relied on past Cold War assumptions, especially with regard to the importance of collective security and the liberation of peoples oppressed by communism. Another component of the New Look, though, contained a startling break from past Cold War assumptions. The Atoms for Peace program originated from fears of nuclear destruction. It called for nations with atomic capabilities to deposit nuclear material into a program that would devote its attention to peaceful ends. The attempt to bring about arms control, though, produced little in the way of substantive gains.

The president mixed air strength with other strategies, notably covert operations, especially when handling problems in developing nations. For example, when Prime Minister Mohammed Mossadegh of Iran nationalized oil production, the United States and other western nations took this action as a direct threat and suspected communist connections. Early in his presidency, Eisenhower approved a Central Intelligence Agency (CIA) plan to overthrow Mossadegh and install a government friendly to the West. Eisenhower again used the CIA in Guatemala against Jacobo Arbenz Guzman. Ostensibly Arbenz's brand of nationalism seemed like communism to the United States. Perhaps more important, however, were Arbenz's land reforms, which took acreage away from the United Fruit Company, an American-owned business with legal representation from the firm in which Eisenhower's secretary of state, John Foster Dulles, had been a partner. U.S. ties to the overthrow were kept quiet, but the Eisenhower administration celebrated Arbenz's replacement by a military junta.

## POLICY IN ASIA

Southeast Asia proved an equally challenging locale for the effort to contain communism in developing nations. In 1950 a rebellion and civil war began in French Indochina. Truman and Eisenhower shared the fear that if communism became established in Indochina, it would spread throughout southeast Asia, and each administration funded French efforts to prevent this result. In 1954, the French were still fighting to maintain their position in the region at Dien Bien Phu. They asked for further U.S. support, this time in the form of weapons and air strikes. The United States opted not to provide air cover, and the fortress fell, just one day before a major conference in Geneva about southeast Asian problems. Timing proved key; the conference would play a key role in shaping the future of the region. Cambodia and Laos became independent countries, and Vietnam was divided along the 17th parallel, into a communist North Vietnam and an anticommunist South Vietnam.

The division of Vietnam was part of a strategy for the ultimate reunification of the country under leadership friendly to the West. Free elections were required within two years of the accords. Out of concern for political harmony in his own party, Eisenhower never officially approved the arrangement, but neither did he hinder its application in Vietnam. Eisenhower and Secretary of State Dulles did other things to ensure the success of the accords, most notably the creation of the Southeast Asia Treaty Organization (SEATO) and the image of a united western presence in southeast Asia. Yet SEATO really meant that the United States had made a commitment to South Vietnam and an independent future for that region. Indeed for the remainder of his presidency, Eisenhower focused on a program of nation building in South Vietnam, to the point that the United States fabricated North Vietnamese treaty violations, overturned the free elections, and committed further resources to South Vietnam.

## POLICY IN THE MIDDLE EAST

In the midst of his campaign for reelection, Eisenhower faced a serious foreign policy problem in the Middle East. President Gamel Abdel Nasser's Egyptian nationalism presented the State Department with a situation officials could not easily dissect. Calling Nasser a communist, U.S. officials sought to isolate him from his peers in the region and from the world community. U.S. funds for completion of a dam on the Aswan River—which would provide cheap electric power and irrigation facilities to

Egyptian small farms—became a bargaining chip in this process. Yet the administration missed its guess on how Nasser would respond. Instead of backing down, he nationalized the Suez Canal, prompting the British and the French to call for military action. The Israelis joined with England and France in their attack on Egypt despite Eisenhower's calls for diplomacy.

That fall other diplomatic problems arose. In October Premier Imre Nagy of Hungary separated his country from the Warsaw Pact nations. Immediately the Soviet Union responded with troops. Cold War rhetoric had made Nagy think U.S. support would be imminent. Eisenhower worried about the implications of the Soviet invasion, but he refused to commit troops to the region.

## THE EISENHOWER DOCTRINE

In early January 1957, Eisenhower called for military and economic aid to stop the spread of communism in the Middle East. This declaration led to the formulation of the Eisenhower Doctrine, which provided $200 million for Middle East countries, with Nasser the main target of the program. This foreign policy decision resulted from flawed assumptions that communism, not nationalism, was the biggest threat in the region. Nasser soon became a leading spokesman for the nationalistic impulses in other Middle Eastern countries. Furthermore, Eisenhower and his advisers failed to gauge the effect of the Arab-Israeli conflict on peace within the region.

Turmoil in Lebanon proved the most difficult challenge for Eisenhower. He ultimately ordered troops to the region, but in doing so he unintentionally highlighted weaknesses in his Middle East foreign policy. As problems within Lebanon's multisectarian government emerged in the spring of 1958, civil war seemed likely, and Eisenhower dispatched the Sixth Fleet to the region. When a faction hostile to the pro-Western government in Iraq successfully executed a coup and instituted a government friendly to Nasser, Eisenhower ordered two battalions of marines into

Lebanon to prevent the fall of another Middle East nation. Eisenhower likened his action to the prevention of World War III, but the accessibility of Middle East oil also influenced his decision. The marines encountered almost no hostile reaction to their presence.

The new Lebanese government ultimately resembled a plan that Nasser had suggested and that Eisenhower had rejected some months earlier. Nevertheless, Eisenhower approved the new government because it averted criticism of the U.S. invasion and because Nasser had little to do with its enactment. President Eisenhower's actions met with criticism on several fronts. The USSR attacked the intervention. Democrats noted the hypocrisy since Eisenhower had reacted much as the British and French had during the Suez crisis. The real problem with the Lebanon intervention evolved from the continuing difficulty of U.S. diplomats to detect the difference between nationalism and communism in the Middle East and elsewhere.

## RELATIONS WITH
## THE SOVIET UNION

In the middle of 1955, Eisenhower held the first summit with the Soviet Union since the end of World War II. At that meeting, he suggested several proposals for disarmament—mutual air inspections, the exchange of information about military facilities, and the establishment of surveillance parameters—but Soviet Premier Nikita Khrushchev rejected them all. Although the summit produced no substantive accomplishments, it did help establish an environment for debate. Discussions about bans on nuclear testing intensified in the latter years of the Eisenhower administration. Since Eisenhower moved slowly on the issue, critics of testing faulted the president for lack of decision. Ultimately the administration announced a unilateral ban that carried little international weight.

During the last years of his presidency, Eisenhower put even greater emphasis on establishing détente with the Soviet Union. Khrushchev juxtaposed the benefits of fur-

ther summit meetings—most notably the enhancement of his international reputation—against potential criticisms from Kremlin hardliners. The American use of U-2 planes in espionage flights over the USSR provided the greatest stumbling block to the meetings. Nevertheless, Eisenhower approved two flights for 1960 (one scheduled two weeks before the Paris summit), knowing that the pilot, the plane, and the collected data would not survive if a U-2 plane was shot down. His approval of the flights apparently was a response to Democratic criticisms of the "missile gap" and knowledge that the Soviets would soon have nuclear intercontinental ballistic missile capabilities.

Frances Gary Powers's U-2 flight proved much more newsworthy than anyone hoped. When shot down over Soviet air space, the plane and the pilot survived. Eisenhower's first reaction was to cover up the incident, but Soviet announcements about possession of the plane and the pilot forced a new version of the American story. Denying prior knowledge of the flight, Eisenhower conceded that Powers's mission had been espionage. When enormous public criticism forced the president to take even more responsibility, Eisenhower justified the flights for security reasons.

The U-2 flight also proved harmful for the pending summit. Although French and British diplomats advised Khrushchev to be practical, and to remember that everyone employed some form of espionage, Khrushchev could not negotiate with Eisenhower in the face of what had happened and remain in control of the Kremlin. The one-day meeting between the two men proved tense. As a result of the U-2 situation, the end of Eisenhower's presidency was marked by the deterioration of summit diplomacy and the disintegration of hopes for peace.

## EVALUATION OF
## EISENHOWER'S PRESIDENCY

Eisenhower's legacy as president was mixed. He enacted some of the policies he advocated, such as funding for highways and science education, but his largest domestic accomplishment resulted from his rule as a Republican over the New Deal welfare state that Franklin D. Roosevelt had created in the 1930s. Eisenhower's acceptance of the basic tenets of government responsibility for at least some aspects of the economy and social welfare policy made it more difficult for future generations of Republicans to roll the country back to a free market economy. His greatest failures as president resulted from his unwillingness to provide stronger moral leadership for the civil rights movement and against the human rights abuses of the McCarthy period.

As a diplomat, Eisenhower most of all sought a peaceful resolution of the Cold War. His foreign policy record contains statesmanlike efforts juxtaposed against human failures. For example, Eisenhower's Farewell Address has been termed both the shining accomplishment of his administration and its greatest irony. In it, the president warned that the military-industrial complex posed the greatest threat to peace and prosperity at home, and he cautioned against ballooning defense budgets. Yet critics charged that the apparent statesmanship of this address had never appeared previously in Eisenhower's administration. More to the point, Eisenhower tried to achieve peace, but he, the country at large, and the Soviet Union all lacked an understanding of Cold War dynamics sophisticated enough to permit any real consideration of programs like Atoms for Peace or a nuclear test ban.

When Dwight Eisenhower's second term ended in January 1961, he transferred leadership of the country to a younger man from the opposition party—John F. Kennedy. Even then, Eisenhower's influence on matters of state did not completely dissolve. During his retirement to Gettysburg, Pennsylvania, he advised the Democratic presidents of the 1960s, wrote his presidential memoirs in an effort to preserve his reputation as an active president, and functioned as an elder statesman within his own party.

## BIBLIOGRAPHY

Ambrose, Stephen E. *Eisenhower,* 2 vols. (Simon & Schuster, 1983–1984).

Brands, H. W., Jr. *Cold Warriors: Eisenhower's Generation and American Foreign Policy* (Columbia University Press, 1988).

Burk, Robert Fredrick. *The Eisenhower Administration and Black Civil Rights* (University of Tennessee Press, 1984).

Chandler, Alfred D., Jr., Stephen Ambrose, and Louis Galambos, eds. *The Papers of Dwight David Eisenhower,* 13 vols. (Johns Hopkins University Press, 1970– ).

Divine, Robert A. *Eisenhower and the Cold War* (Oxford University Press, 1981).

Eisenhower, Dwight D. *The White House Years,* 2 vols. (Doubleday, 1963–1965).

Ferrell, Robert H., ed. *The Diary of James C. Hagerty: Eisenhower in Mid-course, 1954–1955* (Indiana University Press, 1983).

———, ed. *The Eisenhower Diaries* (Norton, 1981).

Greenstein, Fred I. *The Hidden-Hand Presidency: Eisenhower as Leader* (Basic Books, 1982).

Griffith, Robert, ed. *Ike's Letters to a Friend, 1941–1958* (University Press of Kansas, 1984).

Hughes, Emmet John. *The Ordeal of Power: A Political Memoir of the Eisenhower Years* (Atheneum, 1963).

Pach, Chester J., Jr., and Elmo Richardson. *The Presidency of Dwight D. Eisenhower* (rev. ed., University Press of Kansas, 1991).

Parmet, Herbert S. *Eisenhower and the American Crusades* (Macmillan, 1972).

★★★ 35 ★★★

# JOHN FITZGERALD KENNEDY
## 1961–1963

*Barbara A. Perry*

*Born 29 May 1917 in Brookline, Massachusetts, to Joseph Patrick Kennedy and Rose Elizabeth Fitzgerald Kennedy; educated at Harvard College (B.S. cum laude 1940); married Jacqueline Lee Bouvier, 12 September 1953, Newport, Rhode Island; three children; elected president in 1960 on the Democratic ticket with Lyndon Baines Johnson of Texas, receiving 34,227,096 popular votes and 303 electoral college ballots, over the Republican slate of Richard Milhous Nixon of California and Henry Cabot Lodge of Massachusetts, with 34,107,646 popular votes and 219 electoral ballots (Harry Flood Byrd of Virginia, although not an announced candidate, received 15 electoral votes); assassinated 22 November 1963 in Dallas, Texas; buried in Arlington National Cemetery, Virginia.*

My introduction to John F. Kennedy (JFK) came at the tender age of four. On a fall day in October 1960, my mother loaded my brothers, a neighbor, and some cousins into our 1956 Chevy and drove to downtown Louisville, Kentucky, to attend a Kennedy campaign rally at the county courthouse. Alas, not recognizing what the experience would mean to my future career as a political scientist, all I can remember is that my mother lost an earring, which was later discovered by my cousin in a pile of confetti and slightly bent from having been trodden upon by the throng of people.

I relate this personal anecdote to illustrate the hold John Kennedy had on the average American. My mother abhors crowds, despises contentious debates over the details of public policy, and to this day avoids driving downtown whenever possible. Yet, also to this day, she tells the story—as if it happened yesterday—of how we arrived early at the rally and took our places directly in front of the platform where JFK ultimately addressed the crowd. Like so many Americans, she was utterly captivated by the personality, looks, charm, wit, and youth of the 1960 Democratic candidate for president. As a Roman Catholic, she was also inspired by Kennedy's religious affiliation.

After his assassination, our parish church distributed holy cards with the slain president's portrait on the front and traditional Catholic prayers for the dead on the back. My mother still keeps that card in her missal—the long-defunct prayerbook of pre-Vatican Catholic worshipers. And like so many other Americans, she can relate in minute detail where she was and what she was doing when she heard that her political hero had been shot in Dallas on 22 November 1963.

## THE KENNEDY MYTH
## AND THE RACE
## FOR THE WHITE HOUSE

The fundamental problem of assessing the Kennedy presidency is attempting to disengage myth from reality, image from substance. In fact, the endeavor is almost impossible because Kennedy and his supporters perfected the art of presidential image making to such an extent that it is linked inextricably with the essence of his administration. Therefore, while one can provide an assessment of the Kennedy presidency based on his successes and failures in foreign and domestic policy, his most abiding legacy (for good or bad) was making image a crucial component of governing— so much so that his successors have often

been judged on whether they have attained the "Camelot" standard. Sotheby's spring 1996 auction of Jacqueline Kennedy Onassis's estate proved once more how wedded to the Kennedy legend America continues to be. Americans flocked to New York to bid on Kennedy memorabilia, or at least to view it in the pre-auction exhibition. The outpouring of grief over John Kennedy Jr.'s fatal plane crash in 1999, and the endless recollections of how he had poignantly saluted his father's casket as a three-year-old, once again transported Americans back to the tragedies of Camelot.

Joe Kennedy was quite adept at image making long before his second son, John (known by his nickname Jack), ran for president in 1960. (His more handsome and talented older brother, Joseph Kennedy, Jr., had been groomed for public office but died tragically when his plane exploded over the English Channel during World War II.) In his first bid for public office in the 1946 race for the U.S. House of Representatives from Massachusetts, young Jack Kennedy ran a campaign that emphasized his war record, including his heroic rescue of his crew of the ill-fated PT-109 after it was sliced in two by a Japanese destroyer. His father, Joseph P. Kennedy, Sr., commissioned author John Hersey to write the story of JFK's remarkable World War II exploits and publish it in the *New Yorker.*

Although he suffered from chronic back pain and took daily medications for Addison's disease (malfunction of the adrenal glands), John Kennedy presented himself to the American public in 1960 as a hale and hearty 43-year-old U.S. senator who would lead the country into the "New Frontier." The contrast with the elderly incumbent president, Dwight Eisenhower, and by extension, his controversial vice president, Richard Nixon, was a key component of the Kennedy campaign for president.

Despite the benefits of a youthful image, an enormous family fortune, and a superb campaign organization run by his younger brother Robert, John Kennedy's nomination as the Democratic candidate for president in 1960 was not a foregone conclusion when he tossed his metaphorical hat into the ring. (In fact, Kennedy despised how he looked in hats and usually refused to wear them—despite howls of protest from haberdashers whose hat sales took a precipitous downturn in the 1960s. Kennedy's bucking the tide of traditional men's wear provided another point of contrast between him and older politicians, who were usually seen in public sporting fedoras or homburgs.)

JFK faced his stiffest primary election challenge from Senator Hubert H. Humphrey of Minnesota. He also had to contend with a host of anti-Catholic bigots who argued that members of a faith owing allegiance to the Pope should never serve in the White House. Indeed, only one Catholic, Governor Al Smith of New York, had ever run for president, and he had lost decisively to Republican Herbert Hoover in 1928. Yet Kennedy's victories in Humphrey's neighboring state of Wisconsin and, significantly, in the Protestant state of West Virginia, derailed Humphrey's nomination bid. Lingering support for Senate Majority Leader Lyndon Johnson of Texas and the sentimental favorite Adlai Stevenson, the two-time loser as the Democratic presidential nominee in 1952 and 1956, ultimately evaporated as JFK and his well-oiled campaign machine engineered a first-ballot victory at the Democratic nominating convention in Los Angeles in the summer of 1960.

Conducted at the height of the Cold War, the 1960 presidential campaign between Richard Nixon and John Kennedy focused in the foreign policy realm on U.S. preparations for thwarting communist regimes around the world. Kennedy accused the Eisenhower administration, with Nixon's participation, of allowing a "missile gap" to develop between the United States and the Soviet Union, which allegedly put the former at a distinct disadvantage in the arms race. (Subsequently, it was discovered that the Soviets had been bluffing about the size of their arsenal.) Moreover, under Eisenhower, the United States had failed to prevent the establishment of Fidel Castro's communist dictatorship in Cuba, a mere 90 miles from the nation's shores.

In the domestic realm, JFK was also on the offensive, portraying the eight years of the Eisenhower administration as a period of economic stagnation for the United States. The Kennedy campaign theme was a call to "get America moving again." Once more, image and message meshed perfectly for the Kennedy candidacy. His World War II heroism seemingly prepared him to lead a new generation of Cold Warriors. And the constant swirl of activity around Kennedy, from those now-famous family touch-football games to afternoons sailing off the family compound at Cape Cod, portrayed JFK as an energetic leader who could indeed get the country moving again.

Nonetheless, Nixon, with his authoritative bearing, was an able opponent. He offered breadth of knowledge and the invaluable experience he gained from occasionally substituting for Eisenhower, who had suffered from frail health during much of his presidency. As in all campaigns, several turning points probably shifted the tide in Kennedy's favor. One was his definitive response to anti-Catholic bias against his candidacy, which he made at the Greater Houston Ministerial Association in September 1960. There Kennedy declared he would not be elected either despite or because of his religious affiliation. Sounding a separationist theme, he argued, "I believe in an America where the separation of Church and State is absolute, where no Catholic prelate would tell the President (should he be a Catholic) how to act and no Protestant minister would tell his parishioners for whom to vote." He concluded dramatically, "If this election is decided on the basis that 40 million Americans lost their chance of being president on the day they were baptized, then it is the whole nation that will be the loser in the eyes of Catholics and non-Catholics around the world, in the eyes of history, and in the eyes of our own people."

By all accounts, a more determinative event in the 1960 campaign was the series of four debates broadcast on radio and television between Nixon and Kennedy in September and October. Kennedy boosted his chances by holding his own with Nixon in exchanges on foreign and domestic policy issues. Polls of voters who listened to the debates on radio gave the victory to Nixon, based on his demonstrated knowledge and the pleasant bass quality of his speaking voice, which, due to his California roots, was accentless. Some radio listeners found Kennedy's rather high-pitched voice and highly accented Boston English grating. But the balance shifted among those who watched the debates on TV. Kennedy, appearing handsome, tanned, and relaxed, projected a positive image. Nixon, who had been ill before the first debates, appeared haggard and nervous, and he perspired heavily in the initial broadcasts. Even at the peak of health, Richard Nixon, with his perpetual five-o'clock shadow, dark eyes, ski nose, and awkward gestures, was never a match for the urbane attractiveness of young John Kennedy. It is impossible to know how many votes were decided by the Nixon-Kennedy debates, but in an election won by Kennedy's slim margin of 118,550 ballots, every vote counted. The final tally was 34,227,096 votes for Kennedy (49.7 percent) and 34,108,546 votes for Nixon (49.5 percent). JFK received 303 electoral votes to Nixon's 219.

Perhaps the rhetorical apogee of Kennedy's style and image was reached in his inaugural address. Appearing before the cameras and throngs of spectators, who braved freezing temperatures and the effects of a January snowstorm, JFK stood without hat or coat and delivered one of the most stirring messages ever imparted by a new president. The rhythm, the cadence, the delivery, were sheer perfection. And the language and message, so skillfully fashioned by Kennedy's chief speech writer, Ted Sorensen, would inspire an entire generation to devote their lives to public service or, at least, to aspire to improve the human condition in the United States and around the world. (Hundreds of Americans eagerly enlisted in one of Kennedy's first creations—the Peace Corps, which established a volunteer force to teach and provide technical assistance to less developed coun-

tries.) Plucking a key theme from the campaign, Kennedy declared "that the torch has been passed to a new generation of Americans." With a deliberate staccato delivery, he warned the world that

> we shall pay any price, bear any burden, meet any hardship, support any friend, oppose any foe in order to assure the survival and success of liberty. . . . The energy, the faith, the devotion which we bring to this endeavor will light our country and all who serve it—and the glow from that fire can truly light the world.

Then came the line for which he is most famous, "And so, my fellow Americans: Ask not what your country can do for you—ask what you can do for your country."

## BAY OF PIGS—
## THE PRICE OF INEXPERIENCE

Yet all the inspirational rhetoric could not save Kennedy from his first major blunder as president. Although he tried to portray his youthfulness as an asset, his relative lack of preparation for serving as president of the United States at the age of 43 was evident from the beginning of his administration. (Indeed, he was the youngest man ever elected president of the United States; Teddy Roosevelt was one year younger when he assumed the presidency, but he did so by succession upon the assassination of William McKinley, under whom he had served as vice president.) Kennedy's inexperience, combined with his vow to stem the tide of communism, were a recipe for disaster in the Bay of Pigs invasion.

JFK simply did not know how to react to the briefings he received early in his presidency from the Central Intelligence Agency (CIA), which had begun to plan an invasion of Cuba during the Eisenhower administration. Seemingly with no viable alternatives, and relying too heavily on the advice of the CIA, the president approved the plan to establish a beachhead at the Bay of Pigs using 1,500 Cuban exiles, who were to precipitate a popular uprising against Castro. Without the necessary support of the U.S. military, the operation was an unmitigated disaster when it was attempted in April 1961, just three months after Kennedy took office.

Yet, in the aftermath of his first major crisis and failure, Kennedy displayed a strength that would stand him in good stead for the rest of his presidency. The young president addressed the American people and accepted complete responsibility for the failed operation. Indeed, his public approval ratings actually rose in the wake of the disaster. Still, Castro would remain a national embarrassment to the United States and a personal and political albatross for Kennedy. His administration became obsessed with the Cuban leader's removal from power, even to the extent of an alleged CIA attempt to assassinate him through the use of an exploding cigar!

## THE BERLIN WALL

Kennedy's Cold Warrior image was at stake in several other foreign policy crises of his presidency. Youthful enthusiasm once more affected his judgment and proved ineffective in his first meeting with Soviet premier Nikita Khrushchev in Vienna in 1961. JFK apparently thought his sharp intellect, wit, and charm would match Khrushchev's guile and experience. They did not, and even Kennedy himself admitted that the Soviet premier "savaged me." The young president now determined to stand firm at future flashpoints around the world.

The first one Kennedy encountered occurred just two months after his disastrous meeting with Khrushchev. Berlin, isolated in communist East Germany and a divided city since the victorious Allies had carved it up after World War II, was becoming increasingly tense. East Germans were streaming into free West Berlin by the thousands. Finally, in August 1961, the East German government began erecting a wall to stem the tide of emigrants. Kennedy clearly signaled Khrushchev that the West's will should not be tested in Berlin and that the leader of the free world would fight to keep West Berlin out of the Soviet sphere. Khrushchev did not press the issue further, but the Berlin Wall was now in place and a constant reminder that the Iron Curtain had fallen on yet another territory in the Soviet orbit.

Berlin, however, would provide JFK with an additional symbolic high point in his presidency. He journeyed to West Berlin in June 1963 and stood on a platform overlooking the menacing barrier, with its formidable stones, barbed wire, and constant military surveillance. He confessed that democracy was not a perfect form of government, but he taunted the communists with the fact that the United States had never had to erect a wall to prevent its people from leaving. To roars of approval from the German crowd, Kennedy recited one of his most memorable speeches, "Two thousand years ago the proudest boast was *'Civis Romanus sum.'* [I am a Roman.] Today, in the world of freedom, the proudest boast is, *'Ich bin ein Berliner.'* [I am a Berliner.]" He continued, "There are many people in the world who really don't understand, or say they don't, what is the great issue between the free world and the Communist world. *Lass sie nach Berlin kommen!* [Let them come to Berlin!]" With a blockbuster finish, Kennedy stirred the mass of humanity to delirium, "All free men, wherever they may live, are citizens of Berlin, and therefore, as a free man, I take pride in the words, *'Ich bin ein Berliner.'*" Even with these ponderous thoughts and words, Kennedy found a moment to display his wit for the German people. After the translator relayed his message to the crowd—including the dramatic German passages that JFK spoke phonetically in his Boston accent—Kennedy paused and ad-libbed, "I appreciate the interpreter translating my German!" The crowd broke into gales of laughter as Kennedy flashed his engaging smile.

## THE MISSILES OF OCTOBER

President Kennedy stood firm and avoided an escalation of hostilities in Berlin, but Khrushchev would test him more severely in Cuba by placing missiles aimed at the United States on that communist island stronghold in 1962. A repeat of Kennedy's ineffectual decision making leading up to the Bay of Pigs could have spelled disaster in the form of a nuclear war with the Soviet Union over the Cuban missiles. In this crisis, however, JFK's strengths came to the fore. He may have been inexperienced initially, but he was a quick study and had learned his hard lessons from the Bay of Pigs fiasco and his embarrassing meeting with Khrushchev in 1961. The president gathered his "best and brightest" advisers for secret meetings at the White House over the tense thirteen days in October 1962 that would come to be known as the Cuban missile crisis. On October 22, Kennedy finally took the crisis public and announced on television in the strongest terms possible that the United States would not tolerate offensive missiles 90 miles from its coast. He excoriated the Soviets for their prevarications that the missiles were purely for defensive purposes; U.S. aerial intelligence photos showed otherwise. His primary tactical maneuver was to impose a blockade of Cuba, in which all ships bound for the island would be inspected by U.S. naval forces and turned back if they were found to carry offensive weapons. In an update of the Monroe Doctrine, Kennedy alerted the Soviets that "it shall be the policy of this nation to regard any nuclear missile launched from Cuba against any nation in the Western Hemisphere as an attack by the Soviet Union on the United States, requiring a full retaliatory response upon the Soviet Union." The final demand to the Soviets was that they immediately dismantle and withdraw all offensive weapons from Cuba.

Khrushchev's reaction to Kennedy's stern ultimatum was mixed at best and confused at worst, indicating factional infighting within the Kremlin. The Soviet leader's first response to Kennedy's public statement was more favorable than the reply that followed it the next day. A strategic gamble on the part of the president to respond to Khrushchev's first letter paid off and the crisis ended with a U.S. victory. By the end of 1962, the "missiles of October" had been withdrawn from Cuba. Former secretary of state Dean Acheson wrote to congratulate Kennedy on his "leadership, firmness and judgment over the past tough week. We

have not had these qualities at the helm in this country at all times. It is good to have them again." Yet privately, Acheson thought the young president had taken a reckless gamble, which had succeeded through "plain dumb luck." Acheson's official assessment seems closer to the truth; Kennedy displayed leadership and sound judgment during the Cuban missile crisis. The incident also finally merged his Cold War rhetoric with decisive action. Image and reality were united in October 1962.

## BARRING NUCLEAR WEAPONS TESTS

Not surprisingly, the nuclear brinkmanship experienced during the crisis appalled Kennedy and his advisers. As his secretary of state Dean Rusk had put it, "We were eyeball to eyeball, and the other fellow just blinked." But what if for want of a blink the nation had been sent over the brink? Each member of the administration had to contemplate during those thirteen agonizing days in October what he and his family would do and where they would go in the event of a nuclear war. These contemplations led Kennedy to another foreign policy victory in the summer of 1963 when the USSR, Great Britain, and the United States signed a nuclear test ban treaty, pledging to stop the testing of nuclear weapons in the atmosphere. The treaty did not prevent underground testing, and China and France refused to ratify it. Nevertheless, the first ban on nuclear testing was a step toward recognizing and attempting to prevent the horrors associated with this new age of weaponry.

Once more, Kennedy's rhetoric matched the import of the act. In a television address to the American people on the day after Congress ratified the treaty, JFK told the nation,

> I speak to you tonight in a spirit of hope. . . . Yesterday a shaft of light cut into the darkness. . . . A full-scale nuclear exchange, lasting less than 60 minutes, with the weapons now in existence, could wipe out more than 300 million Americans, Europeans, and Russians. . . . Let us . . . step

back from the shadows of war and seek out the way of peace. And if that journey is a thousand miles, or even more, let history record that we, in this land, at this time, took the first step.

## CONFLICT IN SOUTHEAST ASIA

The ultimate test of the nation's will to stop the spread of communism occurred in southeast Asia, and Kennedy appeared as stumped for a solution there as his successors would be. Kennedy increased the number of U.S. military advisers in Vietnam from less than 1,000 to over 16,000. He implicitly approved a coup by a Vietnamese general that ousted and murdered President Ngo Dinh Diem. He refused to commit combat forces to Vietnam. And he is quoted as saying shortly before his own assassination,

> In the final analysis it is their [the Vietnamese] war. They are the ones who have to win it or lose it. We can help them, we can give them equipment, we can send them our men out there as advisers, but they have to win it, the people of Vietnam against the Communists.

Yet the record also shows that the Kennedy administration was obsessed with the Vietnam problem and worried about looking soft on the communist expansion there, lest the issue come back to haunt JFK in his 1964 reelection bid. After his death, several Kennedy advisers argued that he had intended to disengage completely from Vietnam after his reelection, but such speculation remains just that. At the very least, it is obvious that President Kennedy was as stymied by the intractable foreign and military policy questions raised by Vietnam as his successors would be. Whether he would have pursued a different and more successful course than they will never be known.

## THE HOME FRONT: SPACE TRAVEL AND CIVIL RIGHTS

In the domestic realm, Kennedy is remembered for two primary contributions: creation of the modern space program with a goal of landing a man on the moon before the end of the 1960s and the promotion of civil rights. Here, too, image and substance merged inextricably. The space race was a boon for U.S. science, technology, and military development. Nevertheless, another outcome for Kennedy was to have the United States catch up to and surpass the Soviet Union, whose launching of the Sputnik satellite in 1957 had proved such a shocking event for American scientists and the public at large.

On the issue of civil rights, some observers have credited President Kennedy and his brother, Attorney General Robert Kennedy, with converting the quest for equal rights for African Americans into a moral issue, much as Abraham Lincoln is praised for opposing the moral degradation attached to the institution of slavery. Yet if the Kennedys can be given such credit, they were slow in recognizing the ethical core of the civil rights quest. Perhaps they should not be blamed for their "deliberate speed" in eventually embracing the right position on the "Negro issue," for their life of privilege in New England had offered them virtually no contact with black Americans or their plight. Civil rights simply was not an issue for either Kennedy brother when JFK embarked on his administration in 1961. Moreover, when they eventually recognized it as an issue, they were far more concerned with its political ramifications for their relations with Congress and the 1964 presidential election. That approach may be praised as wise political pragmatism or condemned as amoral opportunism.

After attempting to keep the lid on race relations through the tense period of integration of the Universities of Mississippi and Alabama, and the violence-plagued Freedom Rides in the South, JFK finally injected the moral suasion of the presidency into the debate in June of 1963. In another of his memorable television addresses, he asked the American people,

> If an American, because his skin is dark, cannot eat lunch in a restaurant open to the public, if he cannot send his children to the

best public school available, if he cannot vote for the public officials who represent him, if in short, he cannot enjoy the full and free life which all of us want, then who among us would be content to have the color of his skin changed and stand in his place?

With that eloquent and poignant query, he announced his introduction of comprehensive civil rights legislation to the Congress. He and his brother had accurately assessed the potential obstacles that senior southern members of the legislature would create to thwart their proposal. Indeed, it took the drama of Kennedy's assassination and the legislative skills of his successor, Lyndon Johnson, finally to push the landmark 1964 Civil Rights Act through Congress. In LBJ's first address to a joint session of the legislature in the numb days after Kennedy's murder, he told his former colleagues that nothing would honor their slain leader more than passage of the civil rights legislation that he had introduced before his death.

## THE CAMELOT IMAGE
Thus, even president Johnson, so diametrically opposite to the youthful, suave, debonair Kennedy, did not fail to call on the image and memory of the nation's fallen leader in order to achieve a greater goal. The shock of Kennedy's death—the cutting down of a charismatic president in the prime of life, leaving behind his stoic young widow and two adorable children—was enough to ensure his heroic image in the American popular conscience. In addition, the recent release of author Theodore White's papers shows that the Camelot mythology, which has grown up around the Kennedy legend, was calculatingly planted in the public mind when a grieving Jackie Kennedy summoned White to Hyannisport a few days after JFK's funeral. She stated that she did not want bitter old men who had opposed her husband to shape and distort the history of his life and truncated administration. So she did some shaping of her own, relating how she and the president had enjoyed listening to the music from the pop-

ular Broadway show, *Camelot*, in the evenings before they went to sleep. She recounted Jack's favorite line, "Don't let it be forgot, that once there was a spot, for one brief shining moment that was known as Camelot."

While the loyal widow's maneuvers after her husband's tragic death provided a memorable label for the Kennedy era, John Kennedy himself was a master at creating images during his life and presidency. He pored over photographs of himself and carefully considered the camera angles used in his press conferences, seeking his most flattering media portrayals. He turned the televised news conference into high political art and sparkling entertainment. It presented him to the public exactly as he wanted to be perceived: knowledgeable, authoritative, witty, and handsome. These positive images were reflected in his Gallup Poll ratings: Kennedy often ranked in the 70 percent range, converting many opponents to his side during his first year in office. At the end of 1961, a poll of Californians reported that 59 percent of respondents stated that they had voted for Kennedy in 1960, and 32 percent said they had voted for Nixon—impossible numbers, since Nixon had carried California in the 1960 presidential race against JFK! Despite the tarnishing that the Camelot image suffered in the decades after Kennedy's death, JFK outpolled all other presidents by a large margin when Americans were asked in 1983 which chief executive they would like to have as president at that time. Kennedy received the nod from 30 percent of the respondents; Franklin Roosevelt was a distant second with 10 percent; Harry Truman earned 9 percent; and then-incumbent Ronald Reagan received 8 percent.

The same 1983 public opinion poll revealed that 31 percent of those questioned ranked JFK as "a great president," 44 percent rated him as "good," 18 percent said he was "fair"; only 3 percent rated him as "poor." The plurality's response in that poll was accurate: Although sentiment leads many Americans to rank Kennedy in the highest category, a more objective reading of the record during his 1,000 days as president reveals a mixture of successes and failures. At best, JFK was a good or above average president.

Nevertheless, how are we to judge the "image thing," as George Bush might have referred to the more superficial aspects of the presidency? To the extent that a positive image bolsters confidence in the president's leadership and the well-being of the country, it is a necessary component of successful governance. No president since Kennedy has possessed his panache, eloquence, wit, and joie de vivre. Reagan established his own brand of popularity, but what is one of his most memorable lines? "Mr. Gorbachev, tear down this wall!" Although uttered at the Berlin Wall, it hardly had the flair of *"Ich bin ein Berliner."* Bill Clinton has cultivated his association with his hero JFK and the Kennedy legacy, right down to displaying the moving video footage and photographs of the sixteen-year-old Clinton shaking hands with JFK in a 1963 Rose Garden ceremony at the White House. Yet for all its own youthful charisma, the Clinton White House has never reached the pinnacle of style displayed by the Kennedys. Moreover, who can remember any line of a Clinton speech? His public relations strength is an informal, empathetic link that he develops with an audience, not a memorable eloquence or wit.

Therefore, in some sense, Kennedy and his mythical legacy created an unattainable standard for most of his successors in the White House. Nonetheless, he also established a model for charismatic leadership that could be the basis for effective governance. The media's current sport of ravaging political figures, however, may never allow Americans to have such admiring faith in their president again. Gloria Steinem, the feminist writer and editor, once described her feeling after Kennedy's death as being "like the future died." Perhaps the generations who recall John Kennedy so fondly will have to pass away before Camelot itself dies and America can recapture a new future.

## BIBLIOGRAPHY

Brown, Thomas. *JFK: History of an Image* (Indiana University Press, 1988).

Chase, Harold W., and Allen H. Lerman. *Kennedy and the Press* (Crowell, 1965).

Goodwin, Doris Kearns. *The Fitzgeralds and the Kennedys: An American Saga* (Simon & Schuster, 1987).

Hamilton, Nigel. *JFK: Reckless Youth* (Random House, 1992).

Kennedy, Rose. *Times to Remember* (Doubleday, 1974).

Martin, Ralph G. *A Hero for Our Time: An Intimate Story of the Kennedy Years* (Macmillan, 1983).

O'Donnell, Kenneth P., and Dave Powers. *Johnny, We Hardly Knew Ye: Memories of John F. Kennedy* (Little, Brown, 1970).

Reeves, Richard. *President Kennedy: Profile of Power* (Simon & Schuster, 1993).

Schlesinger, Arthur M., Jr. *A Thousand Days: John F. Kennedy in the White House* (Houghton Mifflin, 1965).

Sorensen, Theodore. *Kennedy* (Harper & Row, 1965).

★★★ 36 ★★★

# LYNDON BAINES JOHNSON
## 1963–1969

*Steven F. Lawson*

*Born 27 August 1908 near Stonewall, Texas, to Sam Ealy Johnson, Jr., and Rebekah Baines Johnson; educated at Southwest Texas State Teacher's College, San Marcos, Texas (B.S. 1930); married Lady Bird (Claudia Alta) Taylor, 17 November 1934; two children; succeeded to the presidency 22 November 1963 upon the assassination of John Fitzgerald Kennedy; elected president in 1964 on the Democratic ticket with Hubert Horatio Humphrey of Minnesota, with 42,825,463 popular votes and 486 electoral college ballots, over the Republican ticket of Barry Morris Goldwater of Arizona and William Edward Miller of New York (27,175,770 popular votes and 52 electoral ballots); died 22 January 1973 at the Johnson ranch, Texas; buried in Johnson City, Texas.*

On 22 November 1963, Lyndon Baines Johnson (LBJ) became the eighth vice president to enter the White House following the death of the president. No previous "accidental president" had more political training for moving into the position than had Johnson. As a youngster, he had soaked up politics from his father, Sam Ealy Johnson, a Texas state legislator, and some thirty years of public service provided LBJ with as much practical experience as the nation could have hoped for in a chief executive. His political career spanned three of the twentieth century's most crisis-filled decades and placed him at pivotal points in efforts to combat the Great Depression, win World War II, and fight the Cold War. A proud southerner with deep ancestral roots in the soil of Texas history, Johnson nevertheless operated for most of his adult life within the geographical confines of Washington, D.C. Nobody understood the political culture of the nation's capital better, or practiced its main business with greater intensity and shrewdness, than did this scion of the Texas hill country.

## SON OF THE NEW DEAL

The New Deal propelled Johnson's early political development. In 1931, he became a legislative assistant to a Texas congressman and went to Washington; in 1937, he won the first of six elections to the House of Representatives; and in between, he headed the Texas division of the National Youth Administration. Throughout his upward climb, Johnson identified with President Franklin D. Roosevelt's reform efforts, including attempts to supply work-relief for the unemployed, extend electric power to rural dwellers, and reshape the Supreme Court.

Johnson came away from the New Deal with an ideology that sustained him without straightjacketing him for the next three decades. Like Roosevelt, Johnson was neither rigid nor doctrinaire but held a core set of beliefs that guided him through the legislative tangle of bargaining and compromise. A New Dealer who believed in the federal government's obligation to help ordinary citizens in distress, he also thought the government should provide opportunities for business interests to expand their profits. World War II and the Cold War offered rich prospects for defense contractors and oil companies, industries that a politically ambitious Texas lawmaker had to satisfy in the 1940s and 1950s. Johnson did not move consistently in a liberal direction. Serving two terms in the Senate beginning in 1949, he initially took anti–civil rights

and anti-labor positions that endeared him more to conservative Texans than to orthodox guardians of the New Deal. Yet as his support for later civil rights acts suggests, Johnson came to see the federal government as essential for removing the stain of racial discrimination from the South and for lifting his native region out of the impoverishment that caused it to lag behind the rest of the country.

## THE CONSUMMATE POLITICIAN

The Johnson who trimmed his views to fit shifting political circumstances nevertheless remained constant in his practice of politics. Throughout his long career, he attempted to govern through consensus. Abhorring conflict, he pursued political solutions that produced many winners and few losers. Johnson, Paul Conkin has commented, "hated subtraction and division; he loved addition and multiplication." His experience in the Senate during the 1950s reinforced his preference for moderation. Having closely observed Joseph McCarthy and assisted in the Senate condemnation of him in 1954, Johnson concluded that the greatest threat to American democracy came from unbridled demagogues who wreaked havoc by playing upon popular fears and emotions. Johnson worried that militants, from either the right or left wings of the political spectrum, created instability and chaos; because of such hazards, he considered himself a "consensus man." As he explained to one of his biographers: "The biggest danger to American politics is the politics of principle, which brings out the masses in irrational fights for unlimited goals."

To maintain order and balance within his legislative universe, Johnson as Senate majority leader in the 1950s attempted to leave little to chance. George Reedy, who worked for him as a congressional and presidential aide, remarked in awe that Johnson "could predict votes other senators did not even know they were going to cast." With tireless energy, Johnson built ruling coalitions by flattering, cajoling, manipulating, and twisting the arms of his senatorial colleagues. He believed the successful practitioner had to establish an "almost incestuous" relationship with lawmakers and come to know them "even better than they know themselves." Presidential Assistant Joseph Califano remembered the first time he told Johnson he thought he had a congressman's vote on a bill. His boss huffed: "Don't ever *think* about those things. Know, know, know. You've got to *know* you've got him, and there's only one way you know." Raising his right hand and curling his fingers into a fist, Johnson said with a smile, "And that's when you've got his pecker right here."

To guarantee legislative results, which Johnson considered the true measure of his political worth, he drove both himself and his staff to, and often beyond, the point of exhaustion. Throughout his career, Johnson conducted himself as a patriarch of an extended family of assistants and legislative colleagues. A father who was in turn strict and generous, pleading and lecturing, somber and amusing, analytical and cornpone, he presided, in Conkin's phrase, as the "Big Daddy from the Pedernales."

Maintaining control and order lay at the heart of Johnson's relationship with people. He wore out staff members with his demands on their time and fidelity. "To work for this man," an aide declared, "you've got to remember two things: You're never as good as he says you are when he praises you and you're never as bad as he says you are when he chews you out." Despite his harsh demands, Johnson succeeded in attracting bright, talented, and dedicated people to his staff. Looking back, most of them would probably agree with Califano that this surrogate political father "had drawn from most of us far more than we ever realized we had to give."

With character traits that tended toward the exaggerated, Johnson functioned best in private, out of the public limelight, when he faced people one on one. The Senate proved an ideal setting because the relatively small size of the body facilitated Johnson's kind of deal making and fostered his penchant for secrecy. Though devoted to political moderation, Johnson sported a personality filled with extremes and contradictions that were unflattering when exposed to the public by the media. As Harry McPherson, one of Johnson's ablest and most loyal aides acknowledged, Johnson's style invited ridicule. "Sometimes it took off into the clouds," he observed, " . . . sometimes it was as grave as a bishop's; sometimes it was impatient, quick with the hustle of a man who had much to do in a little time."

## TRANSITION TO THE WHITE HOUSE

The day John F. Kennedy was assassinated, Johnson lost much of his ability to separate public and private worlds, to detach political accomplishments from personal weaknesses. Kennedy had elevated charm, wit, and sophistication into trademarks of the television-age presidency. The first telegenic chief executive, he became the definition of charisma. With the ascendancy of style over substance, rhetoric over achievement, glamour over rumpled leadership, Johnson assumed office seriously handicapped. Not only did he have a well-deserved reputation for crudeness, he came from the South, a region the rest of the nation considered economically backward, racially bigoted, and culturally deprived. If the shock of Kennedy's murder was not enough, to many nonsouthern Americans it looked like someone out of Li'l Abner's Dogpatch was moving in to replace Camelot's elegant King Arthur. "I don't hate Johnson," a distinguished reporter told McPherson, "I just hate the fact that all the grace and wit has gone from what the American Presidency says."

Johnson had spent the previous one thousand days hidden in the shadow of the Kennedy White House. As vice president, his relations with the chief executive, a former senatorial colleague, remained cordial, but for the first time in several decades Johnson functioned on the periphery of power. The president's brother Robert, his attorney general and closest adviser, had little respect for Johnson, and the feeling was mutual. President Kennedy's staff occasionally neglected to invite Johnson to important meetings, and they rarely sought his advice. The unhappy vice president tried to make the best of his situation, playing a major role in supervising activities related to the space program and equal employment opportunities for African Americans. In fact, six months before Kennedy's death, in a magnificent speech commemorating the centennial of the Battle of Gettysburg, Johnson eloquently threw his moral support behind the black freedom struggle.

The circumstances of his taking office stirred caution in Johnson. On the one hand, few people knew their way around Washington better than he did. On the other, he had not been elected president and, indeed, had failed to win his party's nomination for the top spot on the ticket in 1960. A complex man, Johnson juggled a large ego and an overbearing personality with spasms of self-doubt. Cast as the accidental president, Johnson had to deal with the justifiable insecurity he felt having vaulted unexpectedly into the White House. "I am not the best man in the world at this job, and I was thrown into it through circumstances," the new president confided to a meeting of state governors shortly after taking over, "but I am in it and I am not going to run from it." Nevertheless, Johnson recalled that the "whole thing was almost unbearable."

## ESTABLISHING A
## PRESIDENTIAL IDENTITY

Though the presidency of his patron, Franklin D. Roosevelt, provided the standard for success, Johnson initially identified more with FDR's successor, Harry Truman, who became accidental president after the death of the beloved Roosevelt. Like Truman, Johnson had to establish himself as legitimate heir to the office. This politician who thrived on campaigning, deriving pleasure from shaking hands and mixing with people, had to overcome the liability of not having obtained a "mandate from the voters." He frequently sought Truman's advice, no more so than in eliciting "many good suggestions and wise counsel from his own experience of being suddenly thrust into the Presidency." Also like Truman, Johnson intended to carry out what he considered to be his predecessor's policies at home and abroad. By doing so he gained the political respect that would allow him to govern successfully and then win election to the presidency on his own record.

In the aftermath of the assassination, Johnson adroitly handled the transition by stressing continuity. He committed himself to Kennedy's initiatives on a tax cut, an antipoverty program, and civil rights. He also reaffirmed the country's involvement in Vietnam, although concerns with domestic matters initially loomed far larger than did foreign conflicts on the other side of the globe. "I knew," LBJ recalled, "when [Kennedy] selected me as his running mate that I would be the man required to carry on if anything happened to him. I did what I believed he would have wanted me to do." Furthermore, cloaking himself more securely in Kennedy's mantle, Johnson chose to retain his predecessor's cabinet and White House staff, most of whom consented to stay on. Unless he held onto this direct link with the martyred president, Johnson reasoned, he would be unable to secure the support of those Kennedy backers who had the greatest doubts about him: easterners, liberal intellectuals, and civil rights leaders.

His first days and weeks in office witnessed a succession of meetings and telephone calls with representatives of liberal, labor, and civil rights organizations in which the president asked them to join him in fulfilling Kennedy's legacy. To skeptics who worried that Johnson had wandered a long way from his days as a Roosevelt enthusiast, he assured them that he was still a New Dealer at heart. Accordingly, he informed Walter Heller, whom he kept as chair of the Council of Economic Advisers, that "John F. Kennedy was a little too conservative to suit my taste." Attributing previous disagreements to misunderstandings, Johnson declared to Joseph Rauh, the labor union and civil rights lawyer: "Let's let bygones be bygones. If I've done anything wrong in the past, I want you to know that's nothing now.

We're going to work together." And he meant it, even though he had to reinvent himself as a liberal.

Despite his desire to cement ties with liberal Democrats, Johnson worked to fashion a consensus that included Republicans, whose votes were needed to pass Kennedy's legislative proposals then stalled in Congress. During his tenure as Senate majority leader, Johnson had worked closely with President Eisenhower, whom he now brought to Washington for advice. At the same time, he held intense conversations with Republican congressional leaders, especially Senator Everett Dirksen of Illinois. Likening the situation to other postassassination crises, he implored the Republican minority leader to forget partisan politics. The country witnessed a virtuoso performance by a man whose instincts and training had prepared him to persuade Congress to honor the fallen Kennedy not with touching eulogies and token memorials (though there were plenty of those), but with concrete legislation. Within ten months, Johnson had helped heal the aching numbness of a grieving citizenry mourning for its deceased president and had restored faith in the ability of government to address long-unresolved and seemingly irreconcilable problems.

## ENACTING THE KENNEDY PROGRAM—THE TAX CUT

Johnson quickly compiled an impressive record surpassing that of most presidents who had served before him, including Kennedy. He inherited the Kennedy administration's tax cut and civil rights bills, which lay trapped in congressional committees, and a proposal for a war on poverty that had scarcely gotten off the drawing board. Playing on the sympathy aroused by Kennedy's murder went only so far; he still had the heavy task of convincing a previously reluctant Congress to endorse the sweeping measures. Obtaining any of the pending major pieces of legislation would have been a proud achievement; securing all three proved nothing less than stunning.

In chalking up victories, Johnson showcased his legendary bargaining powers. To get the frugal watchdog of federal spending, Senator Harry Byrd of Virginia, to release the tax-cut bill from his powerful clutches, Johnson shaved Kennedy's budget recommendations to come in under the $100 billion figure Byrd demanded. While Kennedy had performed "much of the educational work," Walter Heller observed, "Johnson used his incomparable techniques to get the thing done." A year after the tax cut took effect leading indicators of economic health—the gross national product, disposable personal income, median family income—skyrocketed. Little wonder then that *Fortune* magazine praised what Johnson had so cleverly achieved: "Without alienating organized labor or the antibusiness intellectuals in his own party, he has won more applause from the business community than any president in this century."

## THE CIVIL RIGHTS ACT OF 1964

With business leaders in tow on his right flank, Johnson moved to his left. As a Texas senator in 1949, he had opposed Truman's far-reaching civil rights proposals, helping to defeat them. At that time, the former Roosevelt aide James Rowe had chided the Texan for voting on the wrong side of the civil rights issue and suggested that if he reversed his position and spent the next twenty years trying to solve the racial problem he would "be one of the great men of American history." Johnson's transformation proceeded slowly if not surely. During the following decade, with the dexterity of a surgeon the Senate majority leader carved up two strong civil rights bills, stitched them back up, and assured their passage in acceptable, albeit weakened, form. Boosting his political stock nationally and preserving Democratic party harmony, President Johnson had embraced civil rights as one of his top priorities. Displaying the moral fervor of the recently converted did not stop him from calculating the political advantages in taking charge on this matter. He recalled that unless he got "out in front on this issue," the liberals who in the past had criticized him for compromising the civil rights cause would attack his credibility as president. Thus, he had to outperform Kennedy on civil rights or, Johnson contended, his administration would "be dead before I could even begin."

The Civil Rights Act of 1964 exceeded Kennedy's original bill and enhanced Johnson's image as a proponent of racial equality. The omnibus measure strengthened federal power to enforce school desegregation orders; outlawed racial discrimination in public accommodations; prohibited bias in public and private employment and established a commission to enforce it (a provision missing from Kennedy's bill); and set standards for judging whether literacy tests were being manipulated to prevent black voter registration. Having helped prepare the foundation for legislation by leading demonstrations in Birmingham, Alabama, the Reverend Martin Luther King, Jr., asserted that with respect to civil rights, Johnson's "emotional and intellectual involvement were genuine and devoid of adornment." Characteristically, the president constructed consensus for the measure by rallying labor unions and business organizations behind it. Religious leaders swarmed on Washington to highlight the moral dimensions of the bill. Reinforced by labor, capital, and clergy, Johnson applied careful and sustained political pressure on Senate Republican chieftain Everett Dirksen to ally his troops with administration supporters and successfully break the longest southern filibuster in history.

The bruising battle did not end without long-term partisan consequences, which the politically astute Johnson recognized. In destroying legally sanctioned segregation, the Johnson administration cemented the loyalty of African Americans to the Democratic party. At the same time, it stimulated electoral realignment in the South to the detriment of the Democrats. As Johnson presciently confided to one of his assistants following passage of the law, "I think we just delivered the [white] South to the Republican Party for my lifetime and yours." Indeed, since 1964, no Democratic candidate for president has captured a majority of white southerners.

## LAUNCHING THE WAR ON POVERTY

The final triumph in Johnson's spectacular first year came with the launching of the War on Poverty. Johnson did not hesitate for a moment in approving plans to develop the antipoverty assault that Kennedy had left unfinished. "This is my kind of program," Johnson revealed to Heller, "it will help people." In designing the Economic Opportunity Act (EOA), the administration assembled an assortment of projects providing for job training, remedial education (later to include preschool Head Start), a domestic Peace Corps (VISTA—Volunteers in Service to America), and community action programs that empowered the poor to help shape policies locally. Johnson typically wanted to provide something for everyone: offering the poor "a hand up, not a handout" while giving more affluent Americans a stake in this effort. Johnson intended to achieve this conflict-free objective through the engine of economic growth fueled by the income tax cut. As the economy expanded and the country reached maximum employment, the poor would prosper, but not at the expense of the wealthy. Increasing tax revenues, not tax rates, would make funding possible for antipoverty agencies. The logic of expansion rather than redistribution guided General Johnson's War on Poverty.

Like the two other major pieces of legislation adopted in 1964, the enactment of the EOA required Johnson's sure legislative touch. Perhaps his most important tactical decision came in selecting Representative Philip Landrum of Georgia to sponsor the recommendation. Ordinarily, Johnson would have tapped Adam Clayton Powell, chair of the House Education and Labor Committee, to direct the floor fight. However, the leadership of the controversial African American congressman from Harlem would have flagged the antipoverty measure as primarily a racial issue, something that Johnson sought to avoid as he attempted to keep conservative southern Democrats from gutting the proposal. In choosing Landrum, the president removed some of the liberal stigma from the bill and appealed to northern moderates and Republicans for support. The Georgia lawmaker had proposed a law in the late 1950s that restricted organized labor practices, and it is striking testimony to Johnson's power of persuasion that he induced George Meany, head of the AFL-CIO, to "put the interests of his country first" and back Landrum's efforts. It took only five months for the antipoverty bill to become law, and what makes this triumph even more amazing is that it occurred alongside passage of the pathbreaking Civil Rights Act of 1964.

### THE 1964 ELECTION

Fresh from impressive legislative victories, LBJ ran successfully for president. The nomination of Barry Goldwater by the Republicans all but assured Johnson's win. The archconservative Arizona senator had opposed both the Civil Rights Act and the EOA, and campaign slogans such as "Extremism in defense of liberty is no vice" targeted him as unreasonable and unbalanced. With Goldwater on his far right, Johnson easily positioned himself not so much as a liberal but as part of the broad political center, where he always felt more comfortable.

The president who had fostered national unity and reconciliation in the wake of tragedy would have beaten any of the potential Republican contenders for the nomination, but Goldwater's candidacy ensured a victory of landslide proportions. Running at the head of the ticket and garnering less than 40 percent of the popular vote, Goldwater dragged down to defeat numerous Republicans seeking congressional seats. As a result of the election, the Democrats increased their majority in the Senate by 2 (68 to 32) and in the House by 37 (295 to 140), giving Johnson the legislative muscle to expand upon Kennedy's program and inaugurate one bearing his own personal brand.

### LAUNCHING THE
### GREAT SOCIETY

In 1965, Johnson had no intention of slowing down the momentum built up in the legislative and presidential triumphs of the previous year. "You've got to give it all you can that first year," he instructed members of his legislative team about dealing with Congress. "Doesn't matter what kind of majority you come in with. You've got just one year when they treat you right, and before they start worrying about themselves." For Johnson, the window of opportunity would last for two years until first-term Democratic House members of the unusually liberal Eighty-ninth Congress stood for reelection. In 1965 and 1966, the president had comfortable majorities to work with; however, 61 House seats were occupied by Democratic lawmakers who in 1964 had carried their districts with less than 55 percent of the vote and whose reelection prospects were far from secure. Consequently, Johnson admonished his assistants "to get off your asses and do everything possible, before the aura and the halo that surrounds me disappear."

On 22 May 1964, even before Johnson had won reelection, he had issued a summons for a "Great Society," an expansive slogan that would identify his forthcoming administration. Not accustomed to thinking small, the president once exclaimed to his cabinet, "There is nothing this country can't do." Johnson's passion for the grand gesture, for surpassing the performance of presidential predecessors, for dominating people through sheer force of personality, only partially explain his choice of the sweeping phrase to describe his program. Johnson's excessive character traits notwithstanding, his vision of the Great Society squared with the expectations that President Kennedy had raised with his New Frontier rhetoric. Far-reaching in scope, the Great Society descended from Kennedy's inaugural address in 1961, which according to *Newsday* called upon "the American people and the world to move forward into a new era in which peace will overcome war, plenty will replace poverty, and true self-government will obliterate tyranny." Richard

Goodwin, a liberal holdover from the Kennedy administration, principally authored the signature speech delivered by Johnson, furnishing tangible evidence that the ideological similarities between the two regimes were more significant than the contrasting styles of their titular heads.

The words Goodwin crafted and Johnson eloquently spoke accurately mirrored growing concerns of millions of Americans. Most important, since the mid-1950s and especially after 1960, African Americans led a powerful social movement for racial equality and justice. Adding to the complaints voiced by the civil rights movement, the primarily white New Left, consisting mainly of college students, issued a manifesto from Port Huron, Michigan, that criticized America as an affluent society filled with "loneliness, estrangement, isolation." Indeed, Goodwin did not consider this 1962 statement from the Students for a Democratic Society (SDS) radical; rather, he understood the "sense of estrangement," the loss of community people felt amid economic abundance. Adults joined young people in articulating these anxieties. Michael Harrington and Rachel Carson wrote bestselling books, Harrington exposing the persistence of hard-core poverty, and Carson exposing the environmental dangers of chemical pollution. Against this backdrop and emerging out of the swirling currents for social change, a half year before Johnson began his second term, he challenged the graduating class of the University of Michigan to "join in the battle to build the Great Society, to prove that our material progress is only the foundation on which we will build a richer life of mind and spirit."

**ENACTING THE GREAT SOCIETY**
Unlike civil rights protesters and student activists, the president pursued these ideals through conventional political means. Though he proclaimed that this was not a time for "timid souls," he launched the fight against poverty, racism, substandard education, and "soulless wealth" in the only way he knew how—through an outpouring of legislation. Whereas members of SDS and

the Student Nonviolent Coordinating Committee (SNCC), a militant civil rights group, called for "participatory democracy" and massive direct-action protests to transform the relationship of ordinary citizens to their government, Johnson kept his faith in the traditional political system to produce the Great Society. The task of improving the quality of life for all Americans—and Johnsonian consensus meant that everyone, not just the poor and racial minorities, should benefit—would be charted in the number of bills Congress passed.

Indeed, the results were impressive. To give only a few examples, the Eighty-ninth Congress provided federal aid to public schools; subsidized health care for the elderly and poor; guaranteed voting rights to African Americans in the South and gave the Justice Department adequate powers to enforce those rights; authorized funds to cities for housing, jobs, education, crime prevention, and recreation; created national endowments for both the fine arts and the humanities; and adopted regulations to preserve clean air and water supplies. According to presidential assistant Joseph Califano, of the 200 items of major legislation the administration requested in 1965 and 1966, it managed to obtain a whopping 181. Johnson liked to quote the *New York Times* columnist Tom Wicker, who could hardly believe his eyes as they rolled "the bills out of Congress these days the way Detroit turns super-sleek, souped-up autos off the assembly line." Of course this begged the question of whether the Great Society's products would prove more reliable than those of the Motor City.

The War on Poverty and civil rights occupied center stage of the Great Society and can be used to evaluate its effectiveness and staying power. Divisions of race and class as well as gender have long tested the limits of the nation's willingness to extend equality of opportunity to the majority of citizens. By the mid-1960s little doubt existed that despite rising living standards and the expansion of black citizenship rights, the quality of life remained depressing for the approximately one-fifth of Americans who lived without hope of ever sharing the fruits of prosperity and felt excluded from civic participation. The War on Poverty raised serious questions as to how far the Johnson administration and its liberal allies would go in challenging inequality and to what extent the democratic capitalist system would accommodate them. The struggle for civil rights posed a similar dilemma, as African Americans began to demand compensatory treatment to overcome the enduring effects of past discrimination. Compared with these two issues, women's concerns for fair treatment received only a preliminary hearing within government circles.

Under Johnson's generalship, the War on Poverty attempted to relieve the suffering of the poor with little pain to the rest of the population. Following in the tradition of Truman and Kennedy before him, Johnson did not believe that the capitalist economy required a structural overhaul to reduce poverty. Through fiscal and monetary tinkering, Johnson's economic managers hoped to make technical adjustments that would maximize employment while minimizing inflation. The economic boom following the 1964 tax cut encouraged their optimism. Unfortunately, conceiving of the War on Poverty as an exercise in social engineering, subject to rational decisionmaking by experts—a notion that characterized liberal thinking in the 1960s—proved inadequate. Government mobilization of technical experts to solve problems required the kind of internal discipline and organizational control that the sprawling War on Poverty, with its many field commanders and unruly troops, could never muster.

## THE PROBLEMS OF THE GREAT SOCIETY

Many of the shortcomings in the antipoverty fight stemmed from political considerations, not from technical mistakes in fine-tuning the economy. The community action programs provide a salient example. Based on the theory that poor people need to have both a stake in shaping the political decisions affecting their lives and a decent job, the Equal Opportunity Act called for "maximum feasible participation" by the residents of local communities where projects were established. Under its provisions, involvement in public affairs for those hitherto excluded sharply increased. Initially, Johnson had no qualms about taking this unconventional approach. He viewed the community action programs as "the first building block in our program to attack poverty" and welcomed the chance to "shake up" existing institutions and challenge local governments. The president declined to start out small by carefully setting up pilot projects to test the idea. His sense of political timing convinced him he should get as much as he could out of Congress, as quickly as possible.

The results proved disappointing and forced a political retreat by the administration. The overextended number of community action programs did not allow for adequate controls and safeguards, and well-publicized scandals in several of them aroused opposition in Congress. More important, the poor aggressively engaged in political organizing, something they were supposed to do. But when they challenged Democratic party machines in key urban areas, Johnson reverted to customary thinking and ordered his aides, "For God's sake get on top of this and put a stop to it at once." Congress followed suit and passed legislation reining in local participation by the poor.

Political considerations also severely affected the financing to conduct the necessary operations. "The War on Poverty," Mark Gelfand has commented, "produced a classic instance of the American habit of substituting good intentions for cold, hard cash." It would have taken an annual appropriation of about $11 billion to lift every needy person above the poverty line. Johnson, hoping to lessen opposition from cost-minded legislators who desired to starve his programs if they could not stop them, asked Congress for just under $1 billion a year. Furthermore, he refused to press lawmakers harder for money because to do so he would have had to acknowledge that problems existed, and "then the wolves who never wanted us to be successful in the first place would be down upon us all at once." In short, Johnson fought the War on Poverty with one hand tied behind his back.

Political problems mainly beyond his control also plagued the president. Unquestionably, Johnson did more to promote first-class citizenship for African Americans than did any other occupant of the White House before or since. The measures he signed into law placed the considerable power of the federal government behind the elimination of Jim Crow laws and black disfranchisement. A steadfast presidential ally of civil rights, Johnson nevertheless could not determine the direction of the freedom movement. When urban revolts erupted in the mid-1960s mainly in the North, the Johnson administration, so closely identified with the cause of African Americans, felt the sting of white political backlash. Polls showed that 45 percent of white Americans attributed the outbreak of rioting to outside agitators and communist conspirators rather than to frustrated black Americans with legitimate economic grievances that remained unaffected by civil rights reforms. Racial animosity surfaced at ballot boxes during the 1966 congressional elections. Republicans riding the wave of white hostility gained 47 House seats and 3 Senate seats. The activist Eighty-ninth Congress was replaced by the Ninetieth, which, while retaining Democratic majorities, had a far less liberal cast to it.

## THE CRUMBLING COALITION

The consensus that Johnson had constructed for racial equality was clearly crumbling. In June 1965, in a commencement address at Howard University, the president argued that the next stage in the struggle for black advancement involved moving beyond equality of opportunity toward achieving equality of results. To this end, the government and private employers would have to take affirmative action to help African Americans compete for jobs and admission to colleges and universities from which they had been historically excluded. Under ordinary circumstances, this ap-

proach would have been hard to sell to white Americans who viewed such compensatory measures as reverse discrimination based on unfair racial preferences. But circumstances were not ordinary. The outbreak of black rioting heightened racial polarization and threatened further white support. The president himself recognized the political peril, and in characteristic coarse language groaned to Califano: "Negroes will end up pissing in the aisles of the Senate."

Although hurt by what he considered ingratitude from people he had done so much to help, Johnson refused to back away from supporting civil rights and affirmative action even after the 1966 elections, which were followed by more rioting in black urban neighborhoods. He distanced himself from black militants such as SNCC's Stokely Carmichael and H. Rap Brown, whose style and rhetoric he deplored, and from Martin Luther King, Jr., who increasingly attacked the War on Poverty as inadequate and the war in Vietnam as murderous. Still, Johnson continued to cooperate with such traditional civil rights leaders as Roy Wilkins of the NAACP and succeeded against all odds in getting Congress to pass a fair housing law in 1968. Notwithstanding this victory, the tense political atmosphere and the more conservative climate in Congress checked the president from requesting the funds necessary to attack the root causes of poverty that had sparked the riots.

## RACE, CLASS, AND GENDER

Class conflict reinforced the legislative constraints imposed by the highly charged racial politics. As early as 1964, a Johnson aide had warned the president that his efforts on behalf of the poor and blacks were alienating white middle-class Americans, the nation's "real majority [which] is suffering a minority complex of neglect." Evidence indicated that the number of poor and middle-class whites who benefited from the Great Society programs as recipients and administrators was much larger than the number of black Americans who were helped. Such evidence nevertheless failed to remove the class and racial lenses through which whites increasingly looked at the problem. In 1966, John Gardner, secretary of health, education, and welfare, reported that people still did not believe that "this Administration has much interest in the middle-class, middle-income family." What Bruce Schulman has identified as Johnson's "liberal universalism"—his belief that every American had a stake in eradicating poverty and racism—was collapsing under the weight of economic and social programs increasingly perceived as pitting blacks against whites, the unemployed against working people. The strain of achieving the unfinished business of liberal reform—which FDR had first sketched out and which LBJ had done more than any other president to accomplish—tore apart the fragile New Deal coalition of African Americans, white ethnic-Americans, and white southerners that had so delicately held together for thirty years.

Besides the race and class concerns that interfered with the extension of the Great Society, Johnson's conventional thinking about gender issues also limited the prospects for further success. The chief executive appointed more women to key government positions than any previous president, and his administration expanded the fight against sex discrimination. However, although single mothers and their children accounted for the largest share of the welfare rolls, Johnson aimed his antipoverty efforts mainly at men. "The architects of the war on poverty," Susan Hartmann has noted, "persistently looked upon poor women as 'dependents,' whose problems stemmed from the lack of a male breadwinner or male relatives' inadequate income-earning opportunities." Like most men of his era, Johnson's traditional views toward women ran deep. When he wanted to line up Representative Edith Greene of Washington for a congressional vote he instructed an aide to wine and dine her, spend some time in bed with her, and then "she'll support any Goddamn bill he wants." His preoccupation with masculinity often found

an outlet in the gendered language he spoke in private. He insulted a senatorial critic as a "frustrated old woman"; dismissed antiwar protesters as "very limp young men"; and sprinkled his policy discussions with metaphors of seduction, rape, fornication, and castration.

## GUNS AND BUTTER

Johnson compounded his problems by trying to fight one war at home while escalating another abroad. Although Vietnam will be discussed later in this essay, it must be pointed out here that Johnson's decision to pursue "guns and butter" without fully rallying Americans simultaneously behind both objectives guaranteed that neither would succeed. The legitimacy that he had tried so hard to obtain in succeeding Kennedy in 1963 was by 1968 shattered by the frustrations of attempting to sustain a two-front war.

Johnson's reasons for thinking he could be "a leader of war and a leader of peace" were understandable but misguided. Johnson believed he could master any situation once he put his mind to it and applied his will. Combining optimism about the ameliorative effects of economic growth with faith in reason and technical expertise to manage the economy, the president concluded that the government could adequately finance the cost of both domestic and foreign wars without seeking a politically risky income tax increase and "without denying our cities, our poor, our aged, our sick, our children, and our minorities the assistance they sorely needed." Moreover, Johnson's congressional experience with McCarthyite attacks on the Truman administration during the Korean War only strengthened his resolve. He refused to choose between "the Great Society woman I loved and that bitch of a woman in Southeast Asia." Instead, he concluded that unless he stood up to communist aggression ten thousand miles away, conservative lawmakers would succeed in red-baiting him and close down the Great Society. In so reasoning, however, he produced the very outcome he feared most.

In this instance, Johnson's political instincts undermined him. Whatever the efficacy of fighting such a two-front war—and historical precedent warned against it—the president refused to level with either the American people or Congress about the scope of his plans and the price the country would have to pay for them. However impressive the nation's economic growth in the early 1960s, it could not underwrite two wars without running a huge budget deficit and soaring inflation, which especially hurt the middle class. The longer Johnson hesitated to propose a tax hike to raise revenues and slow down rising prices, the worse the situation grew. Not even his successful effort at negotiating a wage settlement in the steel industry in 1965 could stem the problem for long. By 1967, when he finally recommended a 10 percent surcharge on individual and corporate income taxes, it was too late. Fiscal conservatives led by congressman Wilbur Mills of Arkansas, chair of the House Ways and Means Committee, exacted as their price for agreement huge cuts in spending for already underfunded Great Society social welfare programs. Johnson had incorrectly believed that he could manage an overheated economy, hide the costs from the public, and postpone indefinitely asking the American haves to make sacrifices with their pocket books for the have-nots.

Yet had Johnson not wielded guns in Vietnam, it is doubtful that Congress would have been considerably more generous in supplying butter for the War on Poverty. Despite the widely held view that Johnson's preoccupation with Vietnam destroyed his Great Society, the reality is more complex. Even before the chief executive escalated the Vietnam War in 1965, legislators had balked at appropriating anything close to the necessary funds. There is little reason to expect that Congress would have loosened its purse strings. In the absence of Vietnam, the white backlash and rising conservative sentiment would probably have hampered necessary expansion of antipoverty programs. As several British politicians found after visiting the United States following the 1966 congressional elections, there existed "an undercurrent of resentment concerning civil order and gains made by the Negro population." Both Richard Nixon and George Wallace capitalized on this disaffection in 1968, forcing the Democrats out of the White House and installing Republicans in their place. Although presidential memoirs are typically self-serving and Johnson's is no exception, one can still agree with the chief executive's judgment in *The Vantage Point:* "I was never convinced that Congress would have voted appreciably more funds for domestic programs if there had been no struggle in Southeast Asia."

## THE GREAT SOCIETY—EXPECTATIONS AND ACCOMPLISHMENTS

The Great Society failed to meet Johnson's expectations, but overall it accomplished a great deal. It virtually eliminated officially sanctioned racial segregation and disfranchisement. Public awareness of sexual bias rose, as did opportunities for women. Access to health care and education expanded. Even the weakened community action programs offered an important training ground for minority men and women, many of whom would go on to hold elective office in their towns and cities and work for change within the system. Poverty did not disappear, but it declined dramatically from 22 percent of the population to 12 percent. Even with the Vietnam War, social service expenditures during the Johnson years doubled, increasing from 4.6 to 6.1 percent of the gross national product. Although the wars against poverty and racism foundered on political tensions, overblown rhetoric, and conventional solutions, LBJ will go down in history for marshaling government as a weapon of compassion and refusing to withdraw unilaterally when the problems proved intractable.

## JOHNSON, VIETNAM, AND COLD WAR LOGIC

This same quality of stubborn commitment had disastrous consequences when applied to fighting the Vietnam War. The president who hoped to leave the Great Society as his historical legacy instead drew the country more deeply into a battleground that severely tarnished his presidential image. His difficulties did not stem primarily from a lack of experience. Johnson entered the White House knowledgeable about foreign affairs. Having been a legislator for twenty-five years, Johnson had participated in deliberations on critical policies related to World War II and the Cold War. As vice president, he travelled around the world, including a stop in Vietnam in 1961 to assess the situation for President Kennedy. The provincial Texan lacked personal sophistication in his approach to international relations, but he took over the Oval Office firmly grounded in the assumptions that had buttressed the conduct of U.S. foreign policy for nearly a quarter of a century.

These beliefs revolved around the principle that national security would be jeopardized unless the United States combatted foreign aggression posed by totalitarian rulers. Appeasement at Munich in 1938, which emboldened Adolf Hitler to further his plans for world conquest, greatly affected the thinking of Johnson's generation about the necessity of standing up to expansionist-minded dictators. The Cold War reaffirmed this outlook among U.S. political leaders who viewed the Soviet Union as conspiring to spread communism internationally, undermine the freedom of independent nations, and overthrow democratic capitalism. The policy of containment that shaped American responses to perceived communist challenges throughout the globe represented the unshakable consensus within the foreign policy establishment that Johnson shared.

Early on, Johnson recognized the risks that Vietnam posed. During his vice-presidential trip to South Vietnam, he concluded that if the United States expanded its military involvement in the conflict, it would mean "very heavy and continuing costs . . . in terms of money, of effort, and . . . prestige." He also recognized "that at some point we may be faced with the de-cision of whether we commit major United States forces to the area or cut our losses and withdraw should our efforts fail." At the beginning of November 1963, when the Kennedy administration backed the coup that led to the assassination of South Vietnam's president Ngo Diem, a skeptical Johnson worried that this action would lead to political destabilization in the embattled country. Troubled about the consequences for South Vietnam, Johnson only three weeks later had to face the fallout at home from Kennedy's murder.

## EXPANDING THE U.S. PRESENCE

When Johnson assumed the presidency, some 16,000 military advisers operated in South Vietnam, and although Kennedy had kept the nation's combat participation small, he seemed committed to defending South Vietnam from communist aggression. In the final months of his life, Kennedy expressed ambivalent sentiments about how far he was prepared to go in stepping up the war, but he did not explicitly reject the containment premises behind U.S. involvement. Whatever Kennedy may have intended to do had he lived, his successor firmly believed that he was carrying out his wishes. "My first major decision in Vietnam," Johnson remembered, "had been to reaffirm President Kennedy's policies." Just as he sought to preserve continuity in domestic matters, he likewise aimed to stay the course in Vietnam and uphold Kennedy's pledge not to "permit Southeast Asia to fall into the hands of the Communists."

Nor did the foreign policy counselors he inherited from the late president suggest otherwise. Secretary of State Dean Rusk, Secretary of Defense Robert McNamara, and National Security Adviser McGeorge Bundy reinforced the president's perception of the war as an outgrowth of communist aggression originating in Moscow. They added their support to his belief that if the United States did not come to the rescue, South Vietnam's Asian and Pacific neighbors would topple like dominoes to communism and eventually threaten America's security closer to home, and they affirmed that unless it fulfilled its obligation to pre-serve the independence of South Vietnam, the United States would lose credibility with its allies, especially those in Europe.

Johnson and his advisers did not seri-ously consider that the struggle in Vietnam failed to conform to their containment views. They did not entertain the possibility that, rather than a war inspired by the Soviet Union as the latest in its bid for world con-quest, the struggle in Vietnam was really a civil war between indigenous forces that held competing political and economic ide-ologies. Neither did they fathom that North Vietnam had a legitimate stake in the out-come of the war—not as an outsider, but as the other half of the nation to whom the Geneva Accords of 1954 had promised uni-fication through free elections, an agree-ment the United States had thwarted. The Kennedy and Johnson administrations, like Eisenhower's and Truman's before them, chose to see Ho Chi Minh's North Vietnam and its Vietcong allies in the South merely as proponents of communism. They never viewed them as nationalists whose primary objective was to rid their land of the forces of colonialism, whether Chinese, Japanese, French, or American, for that view of the war in Vietnam would have conflicted with the entrenched Cold War assumptions long held by Johnson. His unwillingness to ex-tricate himself from those assumptions re-sulted in catastrophe.

Johnson certainly did not consider the United States as the last in a long line of colonial powers dominating Vietnam. To the contrary, the president sincerely saw his role as providing South Vietnam with the economic and political means to build an independent, democratic nation. Whereas other U.S. presidents had shared this goal, none approached it with more gusto and confidence than did Johnson. Embracing the Cold War orthodoxy on Vietnam, John-son implemented it in his own personal style, and in doing so he exacerbated the problems. Throughout his political career, LBJ held that ordinary people everywhere, at home or abroad, wanted the same things, peace and prosperity, and that government

should see that they got them. In pater-nalistic fashion, Johnson said he felt a "special rapport" with Asians who are "just like you and I are," sharing "the same hopes and dreams." Holding such universalistic notions, the president could not see that American values might be unsuitable for transporting to foreign cultures. Further-more, like an austere father, he would not tolerate any misbehavior from an independent-minded North Vietnam, which he referred to as a "damn pissant country . . . a raggety-ass little fourth-rate country."

## LYNDON JOHNSON'S WAR

From 16,000 military advisers in 1965 to over 500,000 ground forces five years later, the conflict the president inherited ulti-mately became Lyndon Johnson's war. Se-crecy and deception characterized his handling of that war from the beginning. Under questionable circumstances, he per-suaded Congress in August 1964 that North Vietnamese naval attacks on U.S. ships in the Gulf of Tonkin required passage of a resolution authorizing open-ended retalia-tion, thereby providing the basis for future escalation. Yet LBJ did not operate blindly, unaware of the risks. Those like McGeorge Bundy who favored heightened military en-gagement did not hide the dangers. In Feb-ruary 1965, the National Security chief predicted that "defeat appears inevitable" but that if the United States stepped up its efforts it could wear down the communist forces and their will to wage war in the South. Warning that "no early solution is possible," Bundy, along with McNamara and Rusk, believed that U.S. manpower would prevail. Those who disagreed made their reservations plain. Confronted with a guerrilla war ten thousand miles away, Un-dersecretary of State George Ball predicted that "the mightiest power in the world [would be] unable to defeat" the enemy, a view seconded by Johnson's friend and Sen-ate Democratic leader, Mike Mansfield of Montana.

Taking these concerns and misgivings se-riously, the president nonetheless decided to widen the war in July 1965. A dedicated practitioner of centrist politics, Johnson steered Vietnam escalation down the middle of the road, attempting to combat the North Vietnamese and Vietcong with measured, graduated responses. He personally supervised the choice of bombing targets in North Vietnam and deliberately restricted extension of military activities in ways that might have drawn in Soviet or Chinese troops. Overall, his aide Harry McPherson concluded, Johnson tried "to summon up just enough martial spirit and determination in the people to sustain a limited war, but not so much as to unleash the hounds of passion that would force him" to expand it, thus precipitating the nuclear holocaust that a third world war would bring.

However much firepower the United States discharged, it proved no match for the willpower of its Vietnamese enemies. Neither the millions of tons of bombs dropped on North Vietnam nor the napalm and chemical defoliants deployed could flush out the Vietcong from their jungle hideouts in the South or force the insurgents to abandon their long struggle to create an independent nation free from outside interference. Despite routine administration claims that the war would soon end, the Tet offensive that began in late January 1968 graphically showed that the Americans did not control the situation. Enemy troops overran provincial capitals and took the fighting right up to the gates of the U.S. embassy in Saigon. Though U.S. and South Vietnamese troops eventually recaptured the seized territory and gained a military victory, the psychological damage was irreversible. Tet shattered what was left of Johnson's credibility.

## GIVING IN TO THE INEVITABLE

By the end of March 1968, Johnson was ready to stage a tactical retreat from the war. Only five months earlier in October 1967, key members of the foreign policy establishment whom Johnson respected, including former secretary of state Dean Acheson, former ambassador to the Soviet Union Averill Harriman, and McGeorge Bundy, who had left the administration to head the

Ford Foundation, counseled the president to hold the line in Vietnam. When Secretary of Defense Clark Clifford, who replaced McNamara, reconvened these so-called Wise Men five months later, they had changed their minds. Their abrupt turnabout in March resulted from the Tet offensive and their concern that prolonging the war was polarizing the country politically and ruining the economy. They urged Johnson to halt the bombing over North Vietnam, to decline the U.S. military's request to send in 200,000 additional troops, and to step up efforts to enter peace negotiations. Whereas the president had remained unmoved by antiwar protesters, he heeded the advice of the Wise Men, who represented elite policymakers, not militant activists. Unhappy but shaken by what he was hearing, Johnson expressed surprise that Tet "produced such a dismal effect on various people inside government and others outside whom I had always respected as staunch and unflappable."

On March 31, the president informed a national television audience that he was suspending the bombing of Hanoi and its environs and seeking peace, essentially following the Wise Men's suggestions. He further surprised his listeners and many of his political associates by announcing that he would not seek reelection and that he intended to spend his remaining time in office pursuing an honorable end to the fighting without partisan distractions. To seek renomination would have meant participating in bruising Democratic primary battles against such antiwar candidates as Senator Eugene McCarthy of Minnesota and his old nemesis, Senator Robert Kennedy of New York. Though the president's advisers expressed confidence that he could win, LBJ did not have the stomach for it.

The relentlessness of the war and his unaccustomed inability to shape the outcome to his wishes had taken an emotional toll. Lady Bird Johnson, who in 1967 had noted in her diary that a "miasma of trouble" hung over the White House, a year later worried that her husband was "bone weary" and "unable to sleep." However, Johnson's decision to withdraw was a rational choice, not the product of any emotional imbalance or what his former speechwriter Richard Goodwin believed was growing paranoia. LBJ's periodic ranting and raving to subordinates about conspiracies to undermine his foreign and domestic policies were not evidence of clinical pathology but a series of catharses by which he blew off large gusts of steam. Whatever psychological demons he wrestled with, the president's March 31 announcement was not only rational but also wise and appropriate, indicating he had not lost touch with reality.

However, good sense did not mean that Johnson had abandoned his deep-seated Cold War assumptions. Even after his decision not to seek another term, the president remained convinced that the United States should not withdraw quickly from its obligations in Southeast Asia. He had declared only a partial bombing halt and not until the end of October did he extend it to all of North Vietnam. All through the presidential campaign from April to November, peace negotiations faltered and fighting persisted, piling up casualties at an alarming rate. Taking advantage of the continued stalemate, the Republican candidate, Richard Nixon, captured the presidency.

## A DIFFERENCE IN OUTLOOKS

Had another chief executive sat in the White House from 1963 to 1969, the Vietnam War most likely would have turned out much the same. Presidents Kennedy and Nixon, like President Johnson, never understood that the United States was fighting on the wrong side of a nationalist, anticolonial war, a civil war in which the insurgents could outlast America's resolve to wage combat. The important question is not whether some other president would have kept the country out of war or would have fought that war to a more successful conclusion. The real anomaly is why Johnson could do neither. Much of the answer rests in an examination of the very talents that won him acclaim as the greatest legislative leader of the twentieth century.

What worked so well for LBJ in managing congressional lawmakers failed him in conducting foreign affairs. "I always believed," he told Doris Kearns, "that as long as I could take someone into a room with me, I could make him my friend." Johnson expected Ho Chi Minh to react as his Washington colleagues had, and he conceived of the war as "a filibuster—enormous resistance at first, then a steady whittling away, then Ho hurrying to get it over with." After all, this gradual application of pressure had worked in wearing down southern opposition to passage of the 1964 Civil Rights Act; why not against the North Vietnamese president? The ultimate dealmaker, Johnson believed every person had his price. Presidential assistant Bill Moyers recalled LBJ's exclaiming: "My God, I've offered Ho Chi Minh $100 million to build a Mekong Valley. If that'd been [the labor leader] George Meany, he'd have snapped it up."

Johnson's bargaining skills did serve him well in diplomatic settings that followed established rules and recognized conventions. He successfully held bilateral meetings with Soviet leaders, who operated in very traditional ways, and he reached agreements with them on extending trade and lessening Cold War nuclear confrontation. However, Johnson's legislative legerdemain was not so useful in convincing unconventional leaders to stop waging social and political revolutions. The North Vietnamese found his promises of building Mekong Valley dams and supplying hydroelectric power unacceptable trade-offs for abandoning their nationalist goals. Actually, LBJ could deal no better with Vietnamese insurgents who held different values and ideology than with militants in his own country who refused to play by the established rules of the game. It was one thing to negotiate with labor leader George Meany or NAACP leader Roy Wilkins or even Georgia's Senator Richard Russell, who battled him on civil rights but whose loyalty stood above reproach. It was quite another to communicate with Ho Chi Minh, who more closely resembled the black militant Stokely Carmichael or the New Left's Tom Hayden, foes whom Johnson considered illegitimate and beyond the pale of reasonable dialogue.

Johnson's political instincts failed to carry over in another area. In hammering out domestic legislation, LBJ elevated compromise to the highest plane, rejecting unyielding idealism. He often mocked liberals for taking extreme positions and refusing to back down. On Vietnam he reversed roles, swapping his customary realism for ideals that he refused to surrender. Had he encountered on legislative matters the same kind of opposition he faced on the war from such influential senators as Mike Mansfield and J. William Fulbright (chair of the Foreign Relations Committee), Johnson would have forged a face-saving compromise. But no such compromise emerged as the president downplayed the political warning signals flashing in Congress and across the country; instead, he stubbornly held onto a set of nonnegotiable principles that trapped him in the Vietnam quagmire.

## EVALUATION OF LYNDON JOHNSON'S PRESIDENCY

Overall, for better and worse, the Johnson presidency was extraordinary. The culmination of twentieth-century liberalism, the Great Society expanded the power of the national state to provide both compassionate government and bureaucratic regulation. Whereas the former permitted greater freedom for racial minorities and women, expanded educational opportunities for the disadvantaged, reduced poverty, extended health care, and began to clean up the environment, the latter imposed a degree of federal oversight that seemed to many Americans excessively restrictive and expensive. As contradictory as its creator, the Great Society produced unparalleled accomplishments while simultaneously planting the seeds for its own unraveling by generating a conservative counterattack that would gain political prominence over the next twenty-five years.

LBJ's handling of Vietnam plunged the nation into despair and damaged many of the domestic achievements he most cherished. But even here the Johnsonian paradox was played out: In fighting a hopeless, divisive war, the president made it less likely that in the future the United States would intervene and become bogged down at great human and economic expense in unmanageable civil wars across the far corners of the world.

The Lyndon Johnson who came into public view during his presidency was not a pretty picture. The worst aspects of his personality—obsessive secrecy, crudeness, masculine bravado, and overweening paternalism—were on display. Television did not treat him kindly. Joseph Califano remarked that LBJ "learned too late that the manipulative and devious behavior commonplace in the back alleys of legislative politics appalled the American people when exposed in their president." He did not look presidential, lacking the personal charm and grace of Franklin Roosevelt and John Kennedy, the straightforward honesty of Harry Truman, and the soothing geniality of Dwight Eisenhower. In an era increasingly oriented toward youth culture, this product of the 1930s looked as modern in the 1960s, Eric Goldman quipped, "as padded shoulders, a night at the radio, and Clark Gable."

It remains debatable whether the Johnson administration could have fulfilled the goals of the Great Society had the government not become mired in Vietnam. The society Johnson envisioned can be judged good but not great, falling short of satisfying the heightened expectations he raised. Yet, putting aside the shortcomings of the president's reform agenda, what does seem clear is that Johnson's accomplishments would have shone more brightly had Vietnam not intruded. The fact that Franklin Roosevelt's New Deal proved an insufficient economic remedy has not kept him from commanding a top spot in the ranks of presidential greatness. In stark contrast to Johnson, however, FDR led the United States to its greatest military triumph in the twentieth century. Without the Vietnam disaster, LBJ would have left office and taken his place in history having earned the respect of the American people, surely an admired if not a beloved president.

## BIBLIOGRAPHY

Berman, Larry. *Planning a Tragedy: The Americanization of the War in Vietnam* (Norton, 1983).

Bernstein, Irving, *Guns or Butter: The Presidency of Lyndon Johnson* (Oxford University Press, 1996).

Beschloss, Michael R., ed. *Taking Charge: The Johnson White House Tapes, 1963–1964* (Simon & Schuster, 1997).

Bornet, Vaughn Davis. *The Presidency of Lyndon Johnson* (University Press of Kansas, 1983).

Califano, Joseph A., Jr. *The Triumph and Tragedy of Lyndon Johnson: The White House Years* (Simon & Schuster, 1972).

Caro, Robert *The Years of Lyndon Johnson*, 2 vols. (Knopf, 1982–1990).

Conkin, Paul K. *Big Daddy from the Pedernales* (Twayne, 1986).

Dallek, Robert. *Lone Star Rising: Lyndon Johnson and His Times, 1908–1960* (Oxford University Press, 1991).

———. *Flawed Giant: Lyndon Johnson and His Times, 1961–1973* (Oxford University Press, 1998).

Divine, Robert A., ed. *The Johnson Years*, 3 vols. (University Press of Kansas, 1981–1994).

Dugger, Ronnie. *The Politicians: The Life and Times of Lyndon Johnson* (Norton, 1982).

Goldman, Eric F. *The Tragedy of Lyndon Johnson* (Dell, 1969).

Goodwin, Richard N. *Remembering America: A Voice from the Sixties* (Little, Brown, 1988).

Herring, George. *America's Longest War: The United States and Vietnam, 1950–1975*, 2d. ed. (Temple University Press, 1986).

Hunt, Michael. *Lyndon Johnson's War: America's Cold War Crusade in Vietnam, 1945–1968* (Hill & Wang, 1996).

Johnson, Lady Bird. *A White House Diary* (Holt, Rinehart, & Winston, 1970).

Johnson, Lyndon B. *The Vantage Point: Perspectives of the Presidency, 1963–1969* (Holt, Rinehart, & Winston, 1971).

Kearns, Doris. *Lyndon Johnson and the American Dream* (New American Library, 1976).

Lawson, Steven F. *In Pursuit of Power: Southern Blacks and Electoral Politics, 1965–1982* (Columbia University Press, 1985).

Leuchtenburg, William E. *In the Shadow of FDR: From Harry Truman to Ronald Reagan* (Cornell University Press, 1983).

Matusow, Allen J. *The Unraveling of America: A History of Liberalism in the 1960s* (Harper & Row, 1984).

McPherson, Harry. *A Political Education* (Little Brown, 1972).

Miller, Merle. *Lyndon: An Oral Biography* (Putnam, 1980).

Schulman, Bruce J. *Lyndon B. Johnson and American Liberalism* (Bedford Books, 1995).

Stern, Mark. *Calculating Visions: Kennedy, Johnson, and Civil Rights* (Rutgers University Press, 1992).

Wicker, Tom. *JFK and LBJ: The Influence of Personality upon Politics* (Penguin, 1968).

# RICHARD MILHOUS NIXON
## 1969–1974

*Joan Hoff*

---

*Born 9 January 1913 in Yorba Linda, California, to Francis Anthony Nixon and Hannah Milhous Nixon; educated at Whittier College (B.A. 1934) and Duke University Law School (LL.B. 1937); married Thelma Catherine (Patricia) Ryan, 21 June 1940, Riverside, California; two children; elected president on the Republican ticket in 1968 with Spiro Theodore Agnew of Maryland, with 31,710,470 popular votes and 301 electoral college votes, over the Democratic ticket of Hubert Horatio Humphrey of Minnesota and Edmund Sixtus Muskie of Maine (30,898,055 popular votes and 191 electoral ballots), and the American Independent party ticket of George Corley Wallace of Alabama and Curtis Emerson LeMay of Ohio (9,446,167 popular votes and 46 electoral ballots); reelected with Agnew in 1972 with 46,740,323 popular votes and 520 electoral ballots over the Democratic slate of George Stanley McGovern of South Dakota and Robert Sargent Shriver of Maryland (28,901,598 popular votes and 17 electoral ballots); resigned 9 August 1974; died 22 April 1994; buried at Richard M. Nixon Library and Birthplace, Yorba Linda, California.*

---

Richard Nixon became president of the United States at a critical juncture in American history. Following World War II there was general agreement between popular and elite opinion on two things: the effectiveness of most New Deal domestic policies, and the necessity of most Cold War foreign policies. During the 1960s, however, these two crucial postwar consensual constructs began to break down; and the war in Indochina, with its disruptive impact on the nation's political economy, simply hastened the disintegration of both of these consensuses. By 1968 the traditional bipartisan Cold War approach to the conduct of foreign affairs had been seriously undermined. Similarly, the "bigger and better" New Deal approach to the modern welfare state had reached a point of diminishing returns, even among liberals.

In 1968, when Nixon finally captured the highest office in the land, he inherited not only Lyndon Johnson's Vietnam War but also LBJ's Great Society. This transfer of power occurred at the very moment when both endeavors had lost substantial support among the people at large and, most important, among a significant number of the elite group of decision makers and leaders of opinion across the country. As early as 1966, Nixon himself began to sense "serious flaws," especially in the social programs of the Great Society. When such a breakdown had occurred within policy- and opinion-making circles on previous occasions—as it had before the Civil War, the Spanish-American War, and in the early years of the Great Depression—domestic or foreign upheavals had followed.

## A MAN FOR HIS TIME— THE 1968 ELECTION

Nixon had risen to national prominence as a fierce anticommunist congressman in the late 1940s and had then served as vice-president during both terms of Dwight Eisenhower's administration. He had then run for the top office in 1960, losing by a highly questionable razor-thin plurality to John F. Kennedy. Despite this defeat, Nixon remained one of the most perceptive of all politicians in the latter part of the twentieth century. A man less in tune with popular *and* elite attitudes might have responded more cautiously than he did in 1968 to the various manifestations of domestic discontent with the war and welfare. Nixon's sense of timing was all the more acute in 1968 and 1972 as a result of his close loss to Kennedy and his overwhelming defeat in the California gubernatorial race in 1962. Nixon had learned that old Republican campaign slogans and traditional anticommunist shibboleths would not carry him into office. During the 1968 presidential campaign he deliberately kept his domestic policy statements quite palatable to the masses by vaguely talking about dispersing power and ending the war. All in all, however, he gave few concrete clues to establishment decision makers or to the American people about how he as president would initiate new policies at home or abroad, let alone what those policies might be.

In 1968, unlike in 1960, Nixon faced a Democratic party hopelessly divided over the Indochinese war and haplessly led by Hubert Humphrey in the wake of LBJ's unexpected refusal to run again. During the campaign, Humphrey, the more liberal candidate, appeared to be defending past American efforts to win the war in Vietnam more than was Nixon, whom many considered to be an original Cold Warrior. The Republican candidate talked more about diplomacy and less about military escalation, and therefore seemed to be stressing less use of U.S. forces in bringing about a victory in Vietnam than Humphrey was. This left Humphrey wearing the very tattered military mantle of LBJ. Had President Johnson halted the bombing of North Vietnam and renewed the Paris peace talks before the end of October, Humphrey might have been able to squeeze by Nixon, for the election results proved to be almost as close as they had been in 1960, but without the same charges of ballot fraud against the Republicans as had been raised against the Democrats eight years earlier. Nixon won by 500,000 popular votes, receiving 301 electoral votes, compared to 191 for Humphrey and 46 for third-party candidate George C. Wallace.

Sensing the transitional mood of the country as it drifted away from consensus, and convinced that presidents can only accomplish significant deeds in their first administration, Nixon moved quickly on several fronts even before his inauguration. He gave his approval for reopening the Warsaw talks with China; privately decided on a gradual, unilateral withdrawal of American troops from Vietnam; made Henry Kissinger his national security adviser; approved a plan for reorganizing the National Security Council system; and concluded that Roy Ash, president of Litton Industries, should initiate a massive reorganization of the executive branch of government. At the same time, however, president-elect Nixon contacted Arthur Burns about becoming his deputy for domestic affairs, while simultaneously deciding to place Daniel Patrick Moynihan as head of a new Urban Affairs Council (WAC) to formulate domestic policy, although Burns and Moynihan were at opposite ends of the political and economic spectrum. These early private pre-inauguration actions, as detailed in his *Memoirs*, clearly indicate that Nixon fully intended to restructure the executive branch of government in order to accomplish his domestic and foreign policy goals.

The press and public, however, had almost completely misperceived what kind of president Richard Nixon would make. Perhaps no man has ever been so misjudged as an incoming president. The media, both the right- and left-of-center publications, ranging from *Ramparts* to the *National Review*, and commentators across the political spectrum all mistakenly anticipated an inactive and silent Nixon administration, reminiscent of the Eisenhower years—an administration that would allow the country to rest and superficially recuperate by not confronting its many foreign and domestic problems. At the same time Nixon was making it clear during the interregnum to those whom he was appointing to head task forces that he planned to be an "activist" president.

In April 1969 the *Wall Street Journal* printed a story that seemed to confirm these widespread impressions about the new president's mediocrity and caution. Interviewing people about Nixon's first hundred days in office, the *Journal* found among voters of all political persuasions "a rising chorus of apprehension that the new President won't act decisively," concluding that "among a significant minority there is suspicion that the President's deliberate pace masks a poverty of ideas and programs." Many of those interviewed expressed relief that Nixon appeared to be doing nothing. One Ph.D. candidate quoted in the *Wall Street Journal* said: "If you'd asked me six months ago, I'd have said I was scared to death to have Nixon as president. But now I can function in the morning and feel the world will be there that night." Another graduate student quipped: "Well, he's shown up for work every day. Otherwise I don't see where he's done much." A physician expressed disappointment. "I think I expected more. I feel there has been too much given to committees to do, and not enough action by Nixon himself." Finally a housewife remarked: "I still can't figure out what Nixon's going to do. He's neutral, and you have to be kind of neutral about him."

The conservatives within Nixon's own party were the first to criticize him, primarily for being too liberal or, worse yet, for being "the complete pragmatist without any political philosophy at all—a man who can be conservative on one issue, liberal on another, who will act however he reads the national need and national mood of the moment." The *National Review* summed up this position by saying: "You cannot define or predict Mr. Nixon's basic policy line because he doesn't have one." Congressmen of both parties, on the other hand, generally approved of Nixon's cautiousness, remarking, "There seems to be less hysteria in this Administration compared to that of Johnson . . . he is going out of his way not to rock the boat . . . Nixon's approach is slow and cautious, which is good . . . in the last Administration we had too much of a hurry. . . . Nixon is doing very well. He's going slow, and that's what he ought to do."

## THE "BORN AGAIN" CONSERVATIVE

Despite criticisms from conservatives within his own party, Nixon enjoyed an extended eleven-month honeymoon with the press—longer than any of the last five presidents with the exception of Lyndon Johnson. Much to everyone's surprise, especially the men closest to Nixon, the new administration basked in unexpected "praise for moderation and restraint" well into the winter of 1969–1970, despite continuing fears about the never-ending war in Vietnam. This response occurred partially because neither the president's friends nor his enemies could conceive of him doing anything significant, and partially because, except for welfare and civil rights issues, it was not until 1970 that he clearly publicized his intentions to make major changes in domestic policy. Moreover, Vietnamization (the replacement of American troops by Vietnamese soldiers), accompanied by the slow withdrawal of U.S. troops and the president's "Silent Majority" speech in November 1969, kept the antiwar movement at bay. For example, from January 1969 through March 1970 around 58 percent of those polled thought the war was a mistake, but only 21 to 36 percent favored outright withdrawal.

Thus, both the press and public alike misjudged the new president because they were misled not only by Nixon's penchant for appointing committees while keeping his own counsel, but also by their own intellectual and emotional biases about his previous reputation as nothing more than a Republican hatchet man. Since Nixon had not lived up to their worst expectations in his first months in office, they precipitously concluded that he could not be doing much of anything.

Reality proved otherwise. Instead of a "reborn" New Dealer, as Nicholas von Hoffman asserted in the *New Republic* in 1984, Nixon was a "born again" conservative. "A 'true' conservative," he once told

this author, "abhors reaction (in the sense of going backwards); preserves the best of the past; abhors demagoguery; is skeptical of too much concentration of power; has faith in progress; exhibits compassion; and is both an innovative pragmatist and activist." Thus, he began his presidency determined to reform the country's foreign and domestic policies using a mélange of administrative actions and public policy planning concepts—all of which ultimately came to be loosely tied together with the slogan "New Federalism."

## LAST OF THE JACKSONIAN DEMOCRATS

Aside from Nixon's own shifting positions on a few issues, there are two basic reasons for the misperceptions which continue to abound about him. The first has to do with aspects of his personality and his administrative style that led to Watergate. The second is not as obvious. It is related to the gradual breakdown of the extraconstitutional, party-dominated political system inherited from the 1830s, known as the "Age of Jackson." Although Andrew Jackson and Richard Nixon are not usually compared, in many ways their administrations (and even their personalities) are similar. It is not too farfetched to say that the Republican Nixon—not Kennedy, Johnson, Carter, or Clinton—is the last of the Jacksonian Democrats, as well as one of the last effective modern presidents. At the very least, both Jackson and Nixon had abrasive, combative personalities, disdained by certain intellectuals in their respective time periods. Both occupied the White House in a time of transition—when one set of domestic political values and socioeconomic philosophy was evolving into a new synthesis. As consummately pragmatic presidents, they were often criticized for their lack of moral or philosophical consistency. Both represented the beginning of realignment in the political party system and were considered anti-eastern establishment, in part because of their southern or southwestern support and interests. Accused of paranoid behavior and attitudes by the very eastern forces of power that fed their paranoia, both personalized their imagined and real enemies. Each wrestled with questions of national power versus states' rights, often enhancing the former while praising the latter.

While president, they surrounded themselves with a small, dedicated group of unelected advisers who on occasion became as controversial as the man they served. Interestingly, Jackson in the 1830s, no less than Nixon in the 1960s, viewed the spoils system and corrupt campaign tactics as a normal part of American politics. Both dealt aggressively, if sometimes misguidedly, with economic as well as with foreign policy. Finally, Nixon's persona, like Jackson's, dominated American politics for several generations of voters.

The political forces set in motion by Jackson ended in establishing a two-party system even though the Jacksonians lost their battle with burgeoning market capitalism. The permanent political results of Nixon's abortive presidency are still not completely known. Unlike Jackson who was on the wrong side of a major national economic shift, Nixon set in motion significant economic policies such as cost of living adjustments (COLAs) affecting all entitlement programs; and floating international exchange rates that in the 1990s continued to contribute to cut-throat regional economic competition and currency instability. But like Jackson, Nixon also had a long-term impact on U.S. politics. Had Nixon not resigned in disgrace, he would have been replaced, in all likelihood by another progressive Republican in 1976. Instead, Watergate made a viable presidential candidate out of Jimmy Carter, who was then perceived to have failed as president, throwing Democrats into a state of disarray until 1992. This allowed for the influence of neoconservatives and fundamentalists to increase in the ranks of the GOP, resulting in the election of Ronald Reagan when 1980 should have been a Democratic year after three terms of Republican presidents. In fact, this is probably the most important (and negative) political legacy of Richard Nixon—all because he was forced to resign over Watergate.

Without belaboring the point, it is possible that future historians will speak of the "Age of Nixon" as they speak today of an "Age of Jackson," because both left an indelible stamp on U.S. politics that far exceeded their time in the Oval Office. The major difference between "Tricky Dick" and "Old Hickory" was not so much a matter of party affiliation or charges of unconstitutional or corrupt actions, as it was of personality and personal popularity. John Quincy Adams once wrote that Jackson's personality explained "in large part the historical appeal of the era [he came] to symbolize and dominate," and the "base and dirty tricks" which he practiced. The same could be said of Nixon. While both men had enraging personalities, according to their enemies, Jackson's was also engaging to his supporters. Despite Nixon's consistently high rating as president in popularity polls until his very last months in office, he never exhibited the endearing characteristics that Jackson's followers found so irresistible. Nixon's popularity among Americans was always more partisan than personal. This explains to a greater degree than is usually acknowledged why Jackson (and Reagan) survived all the charges about their unconstitutional actions and Nixon finally succumbed to them.

Since 1974 the modern presidency has less and less reflected the basic tenets and practices of Jacksonian democracy, evolving gradually into a postmodern perversion of its nineteenth century origins. Even a popular old Indian fighter like Jackson would have thought twice in the face of such formidable bureaucratic power (and in Nixon's case, considerable bureaucratic opposition). Ever unpopular, Nixon did not. At one level he chose to try to beat the established liberal issue networks at their own game—and lost. At another level both parties since Nixon have failed to offer presidential candidates who reflected the ideological beliefs of a broadly based progressive coalition. At all levels U. S. politics since Nixon has become more professionalized and less substantive— a pattern confirmed by the MTV campaign levels to which all major candidates were reduced in 1992, and by the infomercial convention in 1996—a cross between revival meetings, the academy awards, and tell-it-all talk shows.

What the country has lost from this silent and seldom mentioned death of Jacksonian Democracy goes far beyond the personal and political tragedy that Watergate represented for Nixon and the major national trauma that it caused. Watergate was supposed to have confirmed the accountability of elected officials to the American people and greater access to information. Neither hope has been realized, despite some hastily enacted reforms in the 1970s. Instead, the electoral process has degenerated into nasty, single-issue campaigns in which candidates with the most money usually win and Congress has assiduously shunned the opportunity to salvage the American political system. Americans no longer expect constitutional behavior and accountability on the part of American presidents. In fact, the Clinton administration seems to prove (as the Reagan one did less obviously) that a popular president can get by with just about any personal or public behavior while in office. The country, in a word, needed a successful Age of Nixon to shore up badly bruised and battered political principles from the Age of Jackson. Instead, it suffered the angst of Watergate without learning that Nixon was not the "problem" but rather a symptom of a sick political system. Consequently, since 1974 there has occurred an unimpeded rush toward an increasingly undemocratic American megastate based on media-money-driven politics and scandal mongering.

Nixon's death in 1994 reminded us of what was and what might have been had it not been for Watergate's unintended political consequences and the insistence by Nixon critics that its constitutional importance cannot be separated from his personality. Nixon is not so much an *eminence grise*, as his detractors would like us to believe, but rather a symbol of opportunity lost because, as the last "Jacksonian" president, his resignation is an object lesson in first personal and then national political suicide. Therefore, the Nixon presidency remains more important than any that have followed in its wake and most which preceded it in this century. If this is true, then why does he continue to be so disliked and his achievements so underrated? If Nixon were no more than Watergate, we would have long since swept him under the rug with most other ex-presidents.

## FREE THINKERS AND POLITICAL BROKERS

After taking office in 1969, Nixon surrounded himself with two types of advisers: "free-thinking" outsiders who brainstormed with the president about new ideas and comprehensive programs, and the "political-broker" insiders who worked to draft and implement his legislative and administrative priorities. The initial momentum for change in domestic and foreign affairs came primarily from such free-thinking outsiders as Robert Finch, "Pat" Moynihan, Henry Kissinger, and later John Connally. All of these men appealed to Nixon's preference for bold action and, with the exception of Robert Finch, none had been closely associated with him prior to his election as president. During the first administration Moynihan and Kissinger influenced certain crucial details about, but not usually the broad outlines of, domestic and foreign policies. Encouraged by such advisers during his first years in office, Nixon embarked on a systematic risk-taking course in both foreign and domestic policy that attempted to update American federalism through government organization and revenue sharing, to revamp the entire welfare system with the idea of a guaranteed annual income (which he preferred to call a negative income tax), to expand dramatically spending for both environmental and social service programs, to set in motion a "grand design" for U.S. diplomacy based on the Nixon Doctrine, on devaluation of the dollar and other foreign economic policies, on ending (after widening) the war in Vietnam, and on establishing rapprochement with China and détente with the USSR.

The impact of the free-thinking outsiders on Nixonian policies is easy to trace. Moynihan and Finch greatly influenced specific legislation on welfare; Kissinger carried out the president's foreign policy, initially as national security adviser, and later as secretary of state; and Connally, whom Nixon appointed secretary of the treasury in 1971, almost single-handedly talked the president into both wage and price controls and devaluation of the dollar. Connally also played a crucial role in two of Nixon's most innovative environmental proposals—the Environmental Protection Agency and a department of natural resources—both against the wishes of the farm bloc. Perhaps of all his free-thinking outsider advisers, Nixon was most impressed by Connally, who usually does not figure prominently in books about his presidency. Nixon wanted Connally for his vice president in 1968, when he was still a Democrat and governor of Texas, and from the time they first met Nixon thought Connally understood him better than any of his other political associates. In turn, from the time that this apostate Democrat became secretary of the treasury in 1971, Nixon apparently hoped that Connally would succeed him as the Republican standard bearer in 1976.

Nonetheless, it was the political-broker insiders who increasingly gained ascendancy over the free-thinking outsiders within the first Nixon administration; and Nixon's plans to reorganize the federal government became more corporate in nature and more central to his thinking. Gray flannel types, many of whom he had known for many years—John D. Ehrlichman and H.R. Haldeman, the president's two closest aides; Leonard Garment, the liberal Democratic counterpart to Moynihan among Nixon's inside advisers; Arthur Burns, counselor to the president and later head of the Federal Reserve Board; Melvin Laird, secretary of defense; John Mitchell, attorney general; George Shultz, secretary of labor and later head of the Office of Management and Bud-

get; and businessman Roy Ash, chair of the president's Council on Executive Reorganization—all played the role of political-broker insiders.

In Nixon's first years in office Ehrlichman, Garment, Laird, and Shultz became dominant insiders on policy, while Haldeman and Roy Ash concentrated on organizational matters. For example, Ehrlichman, aided by John Whitaker, deputy assistant to the president and later under secretary of the interior, significantly influenced the content of Nixon's environmental legislation, especially in connection with land-use policies. Ehrlichman and Garment were instrumental in the formulation of both his civil rights and Native American Indian policies. Arthur Burns became the unexpected champion of revenue sharing within the administration. Shultz confined his advice largely to economics and labor but proved surprisingly influential in desegregation matters and countering discrimination in the workforce as well. Before Kissinger's ascendancy, Laird could be seen brokering on a wide variety of topics from foreign policy to such diverse issues as the volunteer army, revenue sharing, government reorganization, and Vietnamization.

Prior to Watergate, journalists, scholars, and numerous politicians had predicted that Nixon would be a cautious, if not a "do-nothing," president. Moreover, few listened in 1969 when he said that he intended "to begin a decade of government reform such as this nation has not witnessed in half a century." There was much scoffing when in 1971 his speech writers came up with the grandiose phrase "the New American Revolution" to describe his domestic programs. Contrary to these low expectations, in his first term Nixon actively pursued five areas of domestic reform: welfare, civil rights, economic and environmental policy, and reorganization of the executive branch of government. Ultimately, these domestic programs may be remembered longer than his currently better known activities in the realm of foreign policy, and they may even minimize his negative Watergate image.

## THE DOMESTIC AGENDA

With much of the press and Congress suspicious of him, Nixon's least obstructed route to significant domestic reform was through administrative action. This approach naturally prompted criticism from those who already distrusted his policies and priorities. If he had ended the Vietnam War during his first or second year in office, Nixon might have diffused some of this distrust; however, the manner in which he expanded and prolonged the war during his first two years in office simply reinforced existing suspicions about his personality and political ethics. (Significantly, liberal paranoia about his domestic programs fueled Nixon's paranoia about liberal opposition to the war, and vice-versa.)

Nixon considered his success in desegregating southern schools and his Supreme Court appointments (Warren E. Burger, Harry Blackmun, Lewis Powell, and William H. Rehnquist) his most important achievements in domestic policy, still insisting that Clement Haynsworth would have been his best choice had he been approved by the Senate. Nixon also included on his list of significant "firsts" his initiatives on the environment and space and his declared (and well-financed) wars against cancer, illegal drugs, and hunger. Nixon's closest aides usually placed revenue sharing and environmental and land-use policies higher on the list of his domestic achievements than the former president did himself.

According to John Ehrlichman, this continuing difference of opinion arose from the fact that Nixon paid more personal attention during his first term to those domestic issues with "political juice," such as cancer research, labor legislation, drugs, crime, taxes, desegregation, and welfare, than he did to economic matters involving revenue sharing, housing, hunger, transportation, and consumer protection, or environmental and general health concerns. On those "gut" issues that Nixon considered "potent political medicine," he became actively involved in policy formulation; the rest he delegated to others, especially Ehrlichman—even the controversial subjects of

campus unrest and antiwar demonstrations. By 1972, according to his *Memoirs*, Nixon recalled that his own list of "gut issues" was much smaller than it had been in 1969, including only "cost of living, busing, drug abuse, and possibly tax reform as it relates to property taxes."

As for his domestic mistakes, Nixon cited wage and price controls, which he later said he supported at the time only because it looked as though Congress would take this initiative to control inflation if the White House did not, and the automatic cost of living adjustments (COLA) for Social Security recipients. He said in 1983 that COLAs made sense at the time but not in light of the runaway inflation after he left office. Of course, many have logically claimed that wiretaps, the creation of the "plumbers" unit within the White House to plug information leaks and ultimately conduct break-ins, the harassment of individuals on an "enemies" list, and even the mere consideration of the "Houston Plan" for institutionalizing surveillance of suspect groups and individuals, were all domestic mistakes.

Although Nixon and both sets of his insider and outsider advisers realized that the odds were stacked against the administration's domestic programs receiving serious attention by a Democrat-dominated Congress, at end of his first term as president he had taken strong action in several major domestic reform areas, especially with respect to welfare and environmental legislation. Even in the area of civil rights, it was Nixon—not Eisenhower, Kennedy, or Johnson—who actually desegregated southern schools rather than simply talk about it. His administration also enforced such affirmative action programs as the Philadelphia "set asides" in the construction industry (an early form of affirmative action reserving a fixed percentage of contracts for minority-owned businesses) and it increased funding so the Equal Employment Opportunity Commission could effectively implement the 1964 Civil Rights Act, making his civil rights record with respect to women and Native Americans one of the best. With respect to the environment, Nixon both led and accepted from Congress the first concrete federal legislation on this issue. His administration was also impressive in retrospect for its reorganization of the executive branch of government—which most of his successors in office simply emulated or tinkered with, but did not basically change—including his restructuring of the National Security Council. Nixon failed to achieve welfare and health care reform, but his bold attempts in both areas (opposed by liberals and conservatives alike at the time) remain the most comprehensive suggestions made by any president after FDR and before Bill Clinton and the 104th Congress.

## THE OPENING TO CHINA

Nixon had become a foreign policy expert while he served as vice president under Eisenhower. By the time he became president Nixon had decided to establish a new policy toward the People's Republic of China in several stages. First, American anti-Chinese rhetoric had to be toned down in order to bring about a more rational discussion than had prevailed in the previous fifteen years. Second, trade and visa restrictions should be reduced; and third, U.S. troop levels at bases surrounding China and in Vietnam would be reduced. Finally, Nixon wanted the communist leaders to know that he would personally consider revising the rigid Cold War position of the United States on Taiwan. All of these changes in attitude and low-level diplomatic actions initially took place quietly and without fanfare. The Chinese ignored all of these private and public signals until 1970. The stage was set for a breakthrough in Sino-American relations. It came in April of 1971, after the United States terminated all restrictions on American travel to the China mainland and the twenty-year-old embargo on trade. Following the highly publicized ping-pong games between Chinese and American teams in both countries at the end of that same month, the Pakistani ambassador to the United States delivered a message from Chou En-lai to Nixon on April 27 (replying to one from the president on January 5), asking him to send a repre-sentative to China for direct discussions. Despite the obvious importance and success of rapprochement with the People's Republic of China, Nixon never believed that the media gave it as much credit as he would have liked.

Although various government officials denied that Nixon courted China in order to bring pressure to bear on the Soviet Union, the president's triumphant visit to the People's Republic of China in February 1972 (with its attendant joint communique) was clearly part of a triangularization policy. After he announced in July 1971 that he would visit China in 1972, there is some indication that possible Sino-American rapprochement made the Soviets more amenable to moving ahead with détente in the fall of 1971. However, the major purpose behind improved relations with both China and the USSR was to bring leverage to bear on both nations to improve the situation for the United States in Vietnam. This particular attempt at "linkage" did not prove successful.

There is no direct evidence, however, that because of Soviet concern over the results of Nixon's trip to China, rapprochement became indirectly "linked" to the success of negotiations leading to détente between the United States and the Soviet Union. The formal agreements signed in Moscow between the two nations provided for: prevention of military incidents at sea and in the air; scholarly cooperation and exchange in the fields of science and technology; cooperation in health research; cooperation in environmental matters; cooperation in the exploration of outer space; facilitation of commercial and economic relations; the interim agreement on the limitations on strategic arms (SALT I); and, most important, the anti-ballistic missile treaty—in short, the basic principles of U.S.-Soviet relations. In the area of arms control, the "Nixinger" détente policy contained the potential not only to substitute for containment (the standard way the United States had fought the Cold War against the Soviet Union since the late 1940s), but also to transcend the procrustean ideological constraints which were at the very heart of the post–World War II conflict between these two nations.

## GETTING OUT OF VIETNAM

According to his 1985 book, *No More Vietnams*, Nixon viewed that conflict as military, moral, and multinational in scope. Consequently, he first sought to bring military pressure to bear on the North Vietnamese in order to speed up the negotiating process. This process failed because the Viet Cong were ideologically committed to holding out, regardless of enormous loss of life, and because they correctly counted on increased antiwar opposition in the United States to the announced bombing and invasion of Cambodia in April 1970 and of Laos in February 1971. Likewise, Nixon's commitment to the war as a "moral cause" did not ring true as the carnage in that civil war increased despite American troop withdrawals. Finally, the president never succeeded in convincing the country that quick withdrawal from Vietnam would "damage American strategic interests" all over the world. So ending the draft and bringing U.S. troops home did not end opposition to the Vietnam War in Congress (although these actions did diminish the size of antiwar demonstrations beginning in 1971) because Nixon had failed to convince that branch of government (and many in the country at large) that the conflict in this tiny third world country warranted the military, moral, and multinational importance he attributed to it. Neither he nor Kissinger ever admitted that their policies destablized most of Indochina and led to horrific events in Cambodia, Laos, and Vietnam in which hundreds of thousands lost their lives.

Instead, Nixon allowed Henry Kissinger, first as head of the NSC and, after October 1973 as his secretary of state, to become egocentrically involved in secret negotiations with the North Vietnamese from August 4, 1969, to January 25, 1972 (when they were made public). As a result, only marginally better terms were finally reached in 1973 which had not been agreed to in 1969. The trade-off between Hanoi's agreement

that President Nguyen Van Thieu could remain in power in return for allowing its troops to remain in place in South Vietnam pales when compared to the additional 20,000 American lives lost during this three-year period—especially when the inherent weaknesses of the Saigon government by 1973 are taken into consideration. The most embarrassing evidence of this weakness occurred when President Gerald Ford was forced to order an emergency evacuation of the last remaining U.S. troops from Saigon in April 1975.

## THE ROGERS PLAN

One of the most important foreign policy discussions that took place during Richard Nixon's first year as president concerned National Security Study Memorandum 2, dated January 21, 1969. This represented the first full review of U.S. Middle East policy since the 1967 Six-Day War. The long overdue full-scale NSC debate over American Middle East policy took place at an all-day session on February 1, 1969, and resulted in the approval of the "Rogers plan," named after Secretary of State William Rogers and noted for its even-handed approach to Middle Eastern problems (meaning a less pro-Israeli policy than previous administrations).

From the very beginning the Rogers plan was based on three untenable assumptions for that time: (1) that the USSR would agree to become a joint peacemaker with the United States (by the time Moscow was willing to accept this role in 1973, Washington had abandoned the idea), and would pressure Nasser into accepting a compromise peace based on UN Resolution 242; (2) that a publicly impartial stance toward Israelis and Arabs would enhance the American bargaining position with both sides in a way that previous pro-Israeli statements by the United States had not; and (3) that Israel would comply with Roger's endorsement of a substantial withdrawal from occupied territory in return for a contractual peace.

But Nixon waited too long to focus systematically on Middle Eastern problems—by the fall of 1973 he was preoccupied with unfolding Watergate events. Obviously, Nixon could not have equally addressed all diplomatic fronts at once, and he clearly chose to concentrate on Vietnam, China, and the USSR during his first term in office. So it made sense for him personally to have put the Middle East on a back burner until some of his other foreign policy initiatives were achieved. In October 1969, the Soviet Union officially rejected the Rogers plan, leaving the new Republican administration with no apparent positive alternative until after the October 1973 war—aside, that is, from the Nixon Doctrine, represented by excessive arms sales to the Shah of Iran. From the 1970 crisis in Jordan through the October War, the United States appeared to pursue a policy of stalemate. The October War broke the stalemate that had substituted for American policy in the Middle East. By the time this breakthrough occurred, the stalemate had cost the United States more than Kissinger could ever gain back, even though it freed him to play hopscotch diplomacy among Middle Eastern countries.

## THE FAILURE OF FOREIGN POLICY

In the Middle East in particular, and in the third world in general, Nixon's foreign policy was dominated by geopolitical considerations that actually had little to do with the economic reality or the political and personal lives of people in already established or emerging small nations. This can be seen in such actions as the tilt toward Pakistan in 1971 in its war with India, the misguided intervention in the Angolan civil war, the use of the CIA and American businesses to destabilize the democratically elected communist regime in Chile and to overthrow Allende, and the refusal to aid starving Biafrans during the Nigerian civil war in 1969–1970.

Nixon's diplomatic legacy is weaker than he and many others have maintained. For example, the pursuit of "peace and honor" in Vietnam failed; because of Kissinger's shuttling, his Middle East policy ended up more show than substance; he had no systematic third world policy (outside of

Vietnam); détente with the USSR soon floundered in the hands of his successors; likewise the Nixon Doctrine did not prevent use of U.S. troops abroad. Only rapprochement with China, because it laid the foundation for recognition, remains untarnished by time, even though Nixon failed to achieve a "two China" policy in the United Nations. This summary is not meant to discredit Richard Nixon as a foreign policy expert both during and following his presidency. It is simply a reminder that the lasting and positive results of his diplomacy, especially after the end of the Cold War in 1989, may be fading faster than some aspects of his domestic policies. During the quarter century following his resignation as president, the event that forced him to leave office in disgrace also dimmed as a memory in the minds of most Americans.

## THE WATERGATE BREAK

"Watergatitis" swept the country in 1973 and 1974 as no scandal involving the highest officials of government had since the Teapot Dome scandal in the 1920s. And for good reason. The cover-up by the president and his top aides of the original break-in and bugging at Democratic National Committee (DNC) headquarters (located in Washington, D.C.'s, Watergate complex) on June 17, 1972, and the related corrupt or criminal political activities, ultimately resulted in the indictment, conviction, and sentencing of twenty men. These included the top White House aides to Nixon (John Ehrlichman and H. R. Haldeman), counsel to the president (John W. Dean III), a special assistant to the president (Charles Colson), one former cabinet member (Attorney General John Mitchell, Jr.), and others who worked for the Committee for the Re-election of the President (CRP, but usually derogatorily referred to as CREEP) and/or the White House special investigative unit known more commonly as the "Plumbers," whose members engaged in break-ins before Watergate occurred.

Most of these men functioned as Republican election officials or presidential advisers in whom public trust had been placed. A few "plumbers" such as E. Howard Hunt, James McCord, and G. Gordon Liddy—all former CIA or FBI agents—were specifically employed by the White House with private funds to carry out political espionage. They in turn hired the four Cubans arrested in the Watergate complex. All served time for their participation in the original burglary and bugging of the national offices of the Democratic Party. Despite multiple investigations and detailed studies of the events, many factual questions remain unanswered about Watergate, and its historical significance is still disputed.

The arrest of James McCord, Bernard Baker, Virgilio Gonzalez, Eugenio Martinez, and Frank Sturgis after the night watchman at the Watergate, Frank Wills, discovered adhesive tape not once, but twice, on basement doors of the expensive office and apartment complex in Washington, D.C., set off a series of events and investigations unprecedented in U.S. history. This break-in culminated a series of political dirty tricks authorized by CRP beginning in the fall of 1971, although it is still disputed whether the two Watergate break-ins were approved by Attorney General Mitchell or presidential counsel John Dean. President Nixon learned of the burglars' connections with CRP and White House personnel on June 20, 1972, and on June 23 he privately agreed with a recommendation that he thought came from Mitchell and Haldeman, but which, in fact, probably originated with Dean, that the CIA be used to prevent an FBI investigation of the Watergate break-in on grounds of national security. The CIA did not comply with the president's attempt to obstruct justice in a criminal matter and the investigation moved forward, after being delayed until the 1972 presidential election took place.

Even before the "smoking gun" tape of June 23, 1972 (which was not released by the White House until August 5, 1974) revealed how early Nixon had been involved in the cover-up, the Watergate special prosecution task force (WSPF) headed by Texas attorney Leon Jaworski had concluded in February 1974, that "beginning no later than March 21, 1973, the President joined an ongoing criminal conspiracy to obstruct justice, obstruct a criminal investigation, and commit perjury (which included payment of cash to Watergate defendants to influence their testimony, making and causing to be made false statements and declarations, making offers of clemency and leniency, and obtaining information from the Justice Department to thwart its investigation) and that the President is also liable for substantive violations of various criminal statutes."

All of these actions had taken place in the space of two years—from the summer of 1972 to the summer of 1974. Early in 1973, federal judge John J. Sirica, using heavy-handed legal tactics, threatened the Watergate defendants with tough sentences unless they told the truth. As McCord and others began to talk about payoffs from the White House, evidence of illegal campaign contributions (unassociated with the Watergate break-in) began to surface and be investigated by the WSPF. The WSPF ultimately set up five different task forces to investigate the variety of charges surfacing against the administration, ranging from the Watergate cover-up, campaign contributions, and the IT&T antitrust suits, to the other "Plumber" break-ins, Nixon's tax returns, and mistreatment of demonstrators.

Nixon essentially fired Haldeman, Ehrlichman, Dean, and Mitchell by formally accepting their resignations on April 30 and announced on May 22 that they had been involved in a White House cover-up without his knowledge. Dean then decided to testify before the Senate select committee on presidential campaign activities (the Ervin committee), and on June 25–29 accused the president of being involved. Among other things, testimony before this committee disclosed the existence of a White House "enemies list" of prominent politicians, journalists, academics, and entertainers, who had been singled-out for various types of harassment, including unnecessary IRS audits. In July 1973, Alexan-

der Butterfield, a former White House assistant, revealed, in a suspiciously inadver-
tent way when responding to questions
from staffers from the Ervin committee,
that Nixon had installed a voice-activated
taping system in the Oval Office in 1971.

From this point forward various attempts
to obtain unedited transcripts of these tapes
from the White House failed, until July 24,
1974 when the Supreme Court ruled in
*United States* v. *Nixon* that the president
could not retain subpoenaed tapes by claiming executive privilege. During this year-
long protracted legal struggle, Archibald
Cox, the first special prosecutor appointed
to investigate Watergate, acting on behalf
of a federal grand jury, also tried to gain access to the tapes. When Cox rejected a compromise proposed by Nixon, the president
ordered both Attorney General Elliot
Richardson and Deputy Attorney General
William D. Ruckelshaus to fire the special
prosecutor. Refusing to do so, they resigned.
On October 20, 1973, Acting Attorney
General Robert Bork (later unsuccessfully
nominated by President Reagan to the
Supreme Court in such controversial Senate
hearings that the verb "to be Borked" entered the American lexicon) finally carried
out Nixon's order, but this "Saturday Night
Massacre" was subsequently ruled an illegal
violation of Justice Department procedures
in *Nader* v. *Bork*.

This incident also created such negative
public opinion that the president agreed to
turn over nine subpoenaed tapes to Judge
Sirica, only to announce on October 31 that
two of the tapes did not exist and on November 26 that a third had an unexplained
eighteen-and-one-half minute gap in it—an
erasure which remains unexplained to this
day. Finally, on October 30, 1973, the
House Judiciary Committee, headed by
Peter Rodino, began preliminary investigations and in April 1974 launched a full-scale
impeachment inquiry which led on July 27
to a vote recommending the impeachment
of the president to the entire House of Representatives, even before the release of the
"smoking gun" tape on August 5. Nixon resigned from office on August 9, rather than
face almost certain conviction in a Senate
impeachment trial. Reasons for the Watergate break-in remain in dispute. None of
the many investigations has ever proved beyond reasonable doubt the motivation behind the original burglary.

## EVALUATION

The lingering negative perceptions regarding Richard Nixon personally, as well as
many of his international and national initiatives, have gone through several stages
since August 1974. At first liberals in particular and Democrats in general had a hey-
day castigating the former president for
fulfilling their most dire prophecy about
him as the most evil, venal, lying, potentially
dictatorial aberration ever to occupy the
White House. In the course of the 1980s,
this view of Nixon, which had ostracized
him from mainstream politics, began to be
replaced by a more nostalgic view of the
man—not among mainstream Republicans
who, if anything, became more conservative
under Reagan than Nixon ever thought
of being—but among some of his long-
standing left-of-center opponents. Finding
themselves in a state of disarray over how
to combat the conservative backlash of the
1980s—the length and depth of which they
had not foreseen in 1974 when Nixon resigned in disgrace—many liberals began
openly praising his legacy of "rational and
systematic pursuit of a new world order,"
and wishing that they had his farsighted domestic legislation, especially on welfare and
environmental issues, "to kick around"
again. Nixon's progressive stance on many
of the country's domestic problems remained in the 1990s one of the most positive aspects of his administration as both
parties moved far to the right of Nixon's
reforms.

During the last two decades of the twentieth century Watergate also became less of
a benchmark for judging his presidency for
that quarter of the population who were not
born when Nixon resigned in 1974. For
these young Americans, Nixon was at best
an oddity; at worst, someone their parents
either strongly opposed or supported. On

these two divergent points of view—that of aging liberals and teenagers—Nixon's gradual rehabilitation rested and continued in Phoenix-like fashion to grow in the 1990s. Moreover, this rehabilitation process found fertile ground for growth abroad where his resignation and disgrace over Watergate had never been understood in constitutional terms or thought to be as important as his foreign policy record. But there is a final reason for the partial current rehabilitation of Richard Nixon. In the last decade of the twentieth century, his longevity made him one of the few surviving ex-presidents in the United States who could still arouse passion—for or against him. Nixon remained until the end of his life the most controversial American political figure since World War II, one of the most important presidents of the twentieth century, and not only the last of the Jacksonian Democrats, but the last of the "big spenders" for domestic social services.

Nixon, of course, hoped to resolve the "problem" he posed for his political enemies in his own lifetime. "What history says about this administration will depend upon who writes history," he told David Frost in 1977. "Winston Churchill once told one of his critics that history would . . . treat him well, and his critic said: 'How do you know?' And, he said, 'Because I intend to write it.' And he did and he treated himself quite well." So did Nixon—in the eight books he wrote after resigning the presidency. But he was far from having rehabilitated himself before his death in 1994.

## POSTSCRIPT: THE NIXON TAPES

Evaluations of almost all major presidents change over time, because history is written to interpret the past in light of contemporary needs and views. But essentially historians rework and reinterpret a set body of materials; the words of the Emancipation Proclamation remain the same, only their meaning changes. Very rarely does a major cache of presidential documents suddenly surface altering our whole view of the available evidence. In recent years, the DNA tests pointing to Jefferson's paternity of children begotten on his slave Sally Hemings comes to mind. But while that information may affect our explanation of Jefferson as a man and as a philosopher of liberty, it will have little impact on our assessment of him as a president.

With Richard Nixon, however, we know that there is a large body of material relating to his presidency that is still closed, namely, the secret but not illegal tapes he made from February 1971 to July 1973. All told, there are 4,000 hours of original tapes. Less than 300 relating to the abuse of governmental powers have been released, as have 278 hours of cabinet meeting recordings. Another 820 have been designated as relating to exclusively private matters and will remain closed for the foreseeable future. That leaves some 2,600 hours that, in accordance with a recent court decision, will be made available to researchers over the next few years.

The information in these tapes may alter our interpretation of some aspects of the Nixon presidency and no doubt will confirm accounts based on other materials. We already know from some of the released tapes that the memoirs of leading Nixon aides such as Henry Kissinger are less than trustworthy in some respects. The tapes, for example, confirm that, contrary to his own account, Kissinger had indeed been present at a meeting in which a break-in of the Brookings Institution was discussed following Daniel Ellsberg's release of the purloined Pentagon papers.

We also know that some of the more lurid incidents from previously released tapes have to be reinterpreted. Nixon, like other presidents, had a tendency to pop off in what John Ehrlichman has called Nixon's "Queen of Hearts" syndrome, meaning that his "off with their heads" statements usually amounted to venting and nothing more. What has been called "Nixon's paranoid antisemitism" consisted of a verbal pattern condemning various ethnic (but not racial) groups and ordering IRS or other investigations of them which were almost never carried out.

I am not condoning the atmosphere that existed in the White House that these tapes underscore. I am only suggesting that Nixon should be given the same benefit of the doubt for talking of anger and frustration as other modern presidents have been given (albeit they were wise enough not to tape their ventings or to write so many of them in marginal notations). Nonetheless it is shocking to have such specific confirmation of previous hearsay and anecdotal evidence about the embattled mind-set within the White House that led to even the discussion of, let alone the president's ordering, black-bag jobs.

People who have rushed in to the most recently released tapes have grabbed the headlines with incidents seeming to confirm the worst rumors about the Nixon administration. In most cases, these events had already been known and the information available. There is no question that whatever else comes to light, Nixon's tenure as chief executive will be seen through the lenses of Watergate. But there is still much to come, and while the Watergate scandals and Nixon's resignation will never be erased, it is possible in those 2,600 hours of yet-to-be-released tapes we will find material that will significantly alter our overall impression of the man. The final story of Richard Nixon is yet to be told.

## BIBLIOGRAPHY

Aitken, Jonathan. *Nixon: A Life* (Regnery, 1993).

Ambrose, Stephen E. *Nixon*, 3 vols. (Simon & Schuster, 1987–1991).

Ball, Howard. *"We Have a Duty": The Supreme Court and the Watergate Tapes Litigation* (Greenwood, 1990).

Burke, Vincent, and Vee Burke. *Nixon's Good Deed: Welfare Reform* (University Press, 1974).

Crowley, Monica. *Nixon Off the Record* (Random House, 1996).

———. *Nixon in Winter* (Random House, 1998).

Emery, Fred. *Watergate: The Corruption of American Politics and the Fall of Richard Nixon* (Time Books, 1994).

Friedman, Leon, and William F. Lenvantrosser, eds. *Richard M. Nixon: Politician, President, Administrator* (Greenwood, 1991).

Garthoff, Raymond L. *Détente and Confrontation: American-Soviet Relations from Nixon to Reagan* (Brookings Institution, 1985).

Graham, Hugh Davis. *The Civil Rights Era: Origins and Development of National Policy, 1960–1972* (Oxford University Press, 1990).

Hersh, Seymour M. *The Price of Power: Kissinger in the Nixon White House* (Summit Books, 1983).

Hess, Stephen. *Organizing the Presidency* (Brookings Institution, 1988).

Hoff, Joan. *Nixon Reconsidered* (Basic Books, 1994).

Isaacs, Arnold. *Without Honor: Defeat in Vietnam and Cambodia* (Johns Hopkins University Press, 1983).

Isaacson, Walter. *Kissinger: A Biography* (Simon & Schuster, 1992).

Kimball, Jeffrey. *Nixon's Vietnam War* (Kansas University Press, 1998).

Kutler, Stanley I. *The Wars of Watergate: The Last Crisis of Richard Nixon* (Knopf, 1990).

Litwak, Robert. *Détente and the Nixon Doctrine: Foreign Policy and the Pursuit of Stability* (Cambridge University Press, 1984).

Lukas, J. Anthony. *Nightmare: The Underside of the Nixon Years* (Viking, 1976).

Matthews, Christopher. *Kennedy and Nixon: The Rivalry That Shaped Coldwar America* (Simon & Schuster, 1996).

Matusow, Allen J. *Nixon's Economy: Booms, Busts, Dollars, & Votes* (Kansas University Press, 1998).

Morris, Roger. *Richard Milhous Nixon: The Rise of an American Politician* (Holt, 1990).

Nixon, Richard M. *RN: The Memoirs of Richard Nixon* (Grosset & Dunlap, 1978).

———. *Six Crises* (Doubleday, 1962).

Obst, David. *Too Good To Be Forgotten: Changing American in the '60s and '70s* (John Wiley and Sons, 1998).

Oeste, Bob. *The Last Pumpkin Paper* (Random House, 1996).

O'Reilly, Kenneth. *Nixon's Piano: Presidents and Racial Policies from Washington to Clinton* (The Free Press, 1995).

Osgood, Robert, et al. *Retreat from Empire? The First Nixon Administration* (Johns Hopkins University Press, 1973).

Parmet, Herbert. *Richard Nixon and His America* (Little, Brown, 1990).

Reichley, A. James. *Conservatives in an Age of Change: The Nixon and Ford Administrations* (Brookings Institution, 1981).

Rochvarg, Arnold. *Watergate Victory: Mardian's Appeal* (University Press of America, 1995).

Rudenstein, David. *The Day the Presses Stopped: A History of the Pentagon Papers Case* (University of California, Berkeley Press, 1997).

Terriff, Terry. *The Nixon Administration and the Making of U.S. Nuclear Strategy* (Cornell University Press, 1995).

Thornton, Richard E. *The Nixon-Kissinger Years: Reshaping America's Foreign Policy* (Paragon House, 1989).

Wicker, Tom. *One of Us: Richard Nixon and the American Dream* (Random House, 1991).

Woodward, Bob, and Carl Bernstein. *All the President's Men* (Simon & Schuster, 1975).

———. *The Final Days* (Simon & Schuster, 1976).

Zeifman, Jerry. *Without Honor: The Impeachment of President Nixon and the Crimes of Camelot* (Thunder's Mouth Press, 1996).

★★★ 38 ★★★

# GERALD RUDOLPH FORD
## 1974–1977

*William C. Berman*

---

*Born 14 July 1913 (original name Leslie Lynch King, Jr.) in Omaha, Ne-*
*braska, to Leslie Lynch King and Dorothy Ayer Gardner King; name*
*changed when mother married Gerald Ford; educated at the University of*
*Michigan (B.A. 1935) and at the Yale Law School (LL.B. 1941); married*
*Elizabeth (Betty) Bloomer Warren, 15 October 1948, Grand Rapids,*
*Michigan; four children; nominated by Richard Nixon under the terms of*
*the Twenty-Fifth Amendment to be vice president upon the resignation of*
*Spiro T. Agnew, and confirmed 6 December 1973; became president upon*
*the resignation of Richard M. Nixon, 9 August 1974.*

---

When Vice President Gerald Ford became president of the United States on 9 August 1974, he declared that "our long national nightmare is over. Our Constitution works. Our great Republic is a government of laws and not men." With those reassuring words, he indicated that a new and better day had dawned for America and that the miasma that had covered the White House for well over a year had finally lifted. The American people responded to his message with a sense of relief and hope because they wanted to believe that he would restore the country's faith in its most important political office, which had lost so much credibility and respect as a result of the Watergate scandal. Perhaps with a new president in the White House, Americans could again focus on matters of far greater import, such as the state of the economy or relations with the Soviet Union, rather than criminal misdeeds in the Oval Office.

## BACKGROUND AND LOYALTIES

It is ironic that Ford, a longtime Republican congressman with no national following or presidential ambitions, was the first person in American history to serve as both an unelected vice president and an unelected president of the United States. As chief executive he sought to restore the power, prestige, and honor of his office to ensure that the vilified "imperial presidency" did not leave in its wake a permanently impaired or imperiled presidency. Ford managed to restore some dignity and character to the office before leaving it in January 1977, thanks to his more open and relaxed style of governing and to his staunch resistence to congressional challenges to his authority. That was his most important success as the caretaker of the Constitution.

The House of Representatives had been Ford's political home since 1948. As a moderately conservative congressman from Michigan he pursued a legislative career and acquired important political skills. He greatly admired President Dwight Eisenhower and embraced his political and economic views. Like Eisenhower, Ford was both a staunch fiscal conservative and a strong supporter of a foreign policy of containment. A fierce party loyalist, Ford also moved so successfully through the ranks of his fellow Republicans in the House that he was elected minority leader in 1965. In that position, Ford became a persistent critic of Lyndon Johnson's policy in Vietnam and frequently called on him to take tougher measures to win the war.

After Richard Nixon was elected president in 1968, Ford worked hard in support of his legislative agenda on Capitol Hill. Nixon was a friend of long standing, and Ford not only respected his political acumen and skill but also embraced his poli-

cies. Following Nixon's reelection in 1972, Ford decided to retire from politics in 1977, as his hope of becoming Speaker of the House now seemed permanently dashed in the face of the continuing Democratic control of Congress. Yet fate intervened in Ford's favor. Nixon, operating within the framework of the Twenty-fifth Amendment, selected him to replace Vice President Spiro Agnew, who had resigned his office in October 1973 due to financial improprieties. Nixon chose Ford in part because he knew the nomination would easily be approved by Congress. But by making Ford vice president, Nixon also thought he would help to ensure his own political survival, gambling that Congress would judge Ford unqualified to hold the office of president. Nixon bet on the wrong horse: Congressional Democrats liked and respected Ford, which made it easier for them to launch impeachment proceedings against Nixon.

## WATERGATE AND THE PARDON OF NIXON

Without the Watergate scandal, Gerald Ford would never have become president. Watergate inextricably tied the lives, careers, and policies of Nixon and Ford together during the full 895 days Ford occupied the country's most important and powerful political office. That connection did much to determine the ultimate political character and fate of his presidency. It is ironic that Ford had to bear the burden of Watergate, for he was a decent and likable person. And if he had not granted a pardon to Richard Nixon on 8 September 1974, for whatever crimes he commissioned or committed, Ford's standing with the American people would not have plummeted so precipitously, a factor that surely contributed to his defeat in the closely contested election in 1976.

Ford probably pardoned Nixon to prevent a trial of the former president from becoming such a public spectacle that it would have been impossible for the new president to focus the country's attention on its current difficulties. Nevertheless, Ford's action angered millions of Americans, who now believed that the pardon itself was a product of a secret deal arranged between Nixon and his successor. By failing to consult in advance with the leadership in Congress, and by failing to extract from Nixon a statement of contrition—which most Americans might have accepted as the bare minimum required in exchange for the pardon Nixon was about to receive—Ford thoughtlessly weakened the strong bond of trust he had established with the American people upon taking office. The political cost of that pardon came due quickly: Using Watergate as their key issue, the Democrats swept the 1974 midterm election, adding to their already sizable majority in Congress in an era of tarnished and weakened presidential power resulting from Watergate and the Vietnam War.

## A PLAIN-STYLE MAN

The fact that Ford came into office without a transition period or the time to articulate the key themes and priorities of a newly incoming administration complicated his political situation. And he found his largely legislative managerial style incompatible with pushing an agenda as a strong leader operating in an executive manner. Moreover, his lack of pretense and plain political style reminiscent of Harry Truman did not generate the media appeal that might have translated the country's personal affection for him and his family into political support for future policy initiatives. Worse yet, throughout his presidency, he suffered from a stream of television jokes and newspaper stories that portrayed him as a person of middling intelligence–or a first-class klutz who was prone to periodic pratfalls on golf courses, airplane ramps, or ski resorts.

Gerald Ford sought to gain respect and support from the American people, but First Lady Betty Ford won their admiration. She displayed a refreshing candor about her mastectomy, and publicly defended abortion rights and the Equal Rights Amendment. She dared to imply that those who had smoked marijuana, or had engaged in premarital sex, including possibly her own daughter, were not necessarily bad people.

The president was quick to suggest that her positions were not his, yet he himself was not as rigid or as outspoken in the defense of conservative social values as many Republicans wanted or demanded.

## ECONOMIC PROBLEMS AND POLICIES

The First Lady's social values were far less politically damaging to Ford than was his own tendency to flip-flop on economic policy. His apparent indecision reflected not only the confusion and misdirection inside the administration but also the nature of the problems Ford faced. By 1974, the economy was under assault from the gale force winds of "stagflation." Unlike past economic behavior, rising rates of inflation and unemployment now moved in tandem, creating a difficult domestic situation for the Ford White House. Looking for a fresh economic strategy to cope with this new condition, Ford turned to advisers such as Alan Greenspan, chair of the Council of Economic Advisers, and Treasury Secretary William Simon, who counseled him to fight the perils of inflation, not unemployment. They reinforced his belief that inflation was indeed America's number-one domestic enemy. As Ford himself said, only 8 percent of the work force experienced unemployment, but everyone suffered from inflation.

Ford's efforts to cope with a newly stressed economy severely tested his leadership. Ruling out price and wage controls, he proposed in October 1974 a 5 percent surcharge on individual and corporate incomes to rein in inflation, along with a voluntary program called "Whip Inflation Now" (WIN). After the disaster of the 1974 midterm election, and after unemployment reached 7.2 percent in December 1974, Ford shifted his ground and pushed for a tax cut of $16 billion. In early 1975, he and Congress finally agreed on the terms of a deal that contained a tax cut of $22.8 billion. Outraged, however, by the size of the cut and worried about the growing federal deficit, Ford was determined to veto future Democratic spending bills and to check what he saw as an irresponsible congressional spending spree. Thus, when Congress appropriated $5.3 billion dollars to create a million new jobs after unemployment had reached 9.2 percent, Ford vetoed it—a veto that reflected his strong ideological commitment to market forces and fiscal restraint. (By the same token, he also refused to support a federally financed bail-out of a nearly bankrupt New York City; he held that position until state and city officials produced evidence of significant budgetary cutbacks and institutional checks on spending.)

By the end of 1975, the general economic situation had improved. The gross national product was growing at the rate of 6.2 percent. Four million jobs had been created, and the inflation rate had declined, mainly as a result of a slowing in fuel and food prices. At the same time, Ford sought to limit the size of the deficit by making a deal with Congress calling for a permanent tax reduction of $28 billion that would be tilted toward middle-income earners and would be matched by a comparable cut in federal spending. Congress agreed only to a $9 billion cut, with a promise to cut spending in fiscal year 1977. As the 1976 election approached, Ford accepted these terms. He failed, however, to prevent a sizable increase in the federal deficit, which had climbed from $5 billion in 1974 to $66 billion in 1976. Nor could Ford engineer a decline in the unemployment rate in time to take the issue away from the Democrats. The rate remained at a perilously high 7.9 percent as late as August 1976, having risen from the previous May's 7.3 percent. Much to the president's intense discomfort, the twin specters of stagflation and the growing federal deficit now began to haunt the U.S. political landscape.

## FOREIGN AFFAIRS— VIETNAM AND THE BOMBING OF CAMBODIA

If domestic issues and concerns, such as the Nixon pardon and the state of the economy, handicapped Ford's presidency, foreign policy gave him an opportunity to strengthen his position. As was often the case with domestic policy, Ford followed in the footsteps of his predecessor both in Vietnam and in relations with the Soviet Union, by continuing the plan worked out in the Nixon administration. A longstanding supporter of Vietnam intervention, Ford had embraced Nixon's efforts to avoid defeat via the policy of "peace with honor." Thus, Ford and Secretary of State Henry Kissinger, whom he greatly admired and whose advice he rarely ignored, tried to preserve an economic commitment to the beleagured Saigon government. In April 1975, Ford implored Congress to appropriate fresh funds for a regime that appeared doomed, but there was the strong feeling everywhere in the country that it was time to forget about Vietnam, and the president's request went unheeded. Kissinger argued that it was the fault of Congress that this U.S. ally faced oblivion, but few Americans really cared, eager as they were to repress as quickly as possible the memories of the self-imposed disaster produced by the nation's longest war.

Smarting from the American defeat in Vietnam, Ford and Kissinger were eager to reestablish a fresh foundation for U.S. military credibility. In May 1975, they used force against Cambodian Khmer Rouge troops who had seized the American merchant ship *Mayaguez*, claiming it was in their territorial waters. Although the ship and its crew were eventually freed, the cost of the operation was high: Fifteen Marines died and eight helicopters were downed in an attack on a small island where the ship's crew was thought to be held. Ford, however, looked presidential by taking both that action and the bombing of the Cambodian mainland. The two contributed to an immediate 11-point jump in the polls, the biggest of his presidency.

## DÉTENTE AND ITS PROBLEMS

Ford's dealings with the Soviet Union were complicated and serious, given the nature of the intense and dangerous rivalry between the two nuclear-armed superpowers.

Building on Nixon's initiatives, Ford sought to preserve the framework of détente by engaging Moscow in talks leading to a new arms-control deal and a comprehensive agreement defining security arrangements in Europe. Although his face-to-face meetings with President Leonid Brezhnev in December 1974 produced some progress in a joint effort to rationalize the arms race, the two leaders failed to complete their work and produce a treaty that Ford could submit to the Senate for approval. More time, more discussions, and more compromises were needed to overcome the sticking points that remained. But the continued talks were held against a background of howls of protest from hard-line Democrats like Senator Henry Jackson of Washington, and from Ronald Reagan, the former governor of California and spokesperson of the Republican right. Notwithstanding the mounting criticism of détente—which had already been voiced during the Nixon years—Ford attended the 1975 Helsinki meeting of the Conference on Security and Cooperation in Europe. Out of that meeting came a diplomatic agreement of historic importance. The frontiers established in Eastern Europe at the end of World War II were accepted as permanent, to be changed only by peaceful means. Moscow was committed by the language of the agreement to recognize the centrality of human rights in the political life of the region.

The Republican right and many congressional Democrats remained firm in their opposition, accusing Ford and Kissinger of a sell-out and a betrayal of American values and interests. The political controversy generated by the Helsinki accords and détente revealed the extent of Ford's vulnerability to critics. His own political weakness and the concomitant strength of a bipartisan Cold War bloc eventually forced him to remove the very word *détente* from his public vocabulary. After the disaster in Vietnam, Ford—like Kissinger—had recognized that no president could manage a successful foreign policy without proper support and grounding at home.

## CONFINING THE CENTRAL INTELLIGENCE AGENCY

In the aftermath of Watergate, President Ford did not command the automatic respect that customarily went with his office. Many Americans were upset with him for having pardoned Nixon; many were opposed to his program of conditional clemency for draft resisters and deserters; and many viewed him as nothing more than a caretaker president. Still, Ford was determined to protect the presidency from any congressional effort to weaken its power and authority. Encouraged by Kissinger, he strongly resisted efforts by Senator Frank Church and Representative Otis Pike to expose the Central Intelligence Agency's (CIA) criminal behavior at home and abroad. He had good reason to oppose those investigations, knowing only too well that the CIA's illegal activity flowed directly from past presidential directives and orders, and fearing that such revelations would damage, in his words, "the reputation and foreign policy of the United States."

Hence, Ford authorized the creation of a commission headed by Vice President Nelson Rockefeller to examine the CIA's activity in an effort to preempt precisely those investigations that Church and Pike later undertook. As a result of Ford's intervention, Rockefeller's public report removed all references to CIA efforts to assassinate foreign leaders, including Fidel Castro. Despite White House objections, the Church committee went ahead and published the names of those foreign leaders the CIA had targeted for assassination while acting on orders from the Oval Office. Its report, containing those and many other revelations, reflected the enormous institutional and ideological differences separating congressional liberals from a president seeking to protect his arm of government from what some observers now called an "imperial Congress."

Ford managed to overcome much of the initial congressional mistrust of the CIA with the help of the *Washington Post* and the *New York Times*, which rallied to his side in the name of national security. He was successful in his exercise in damage control, which had included firing CIA Director William Colby for having given frank and open testimony about the agency's more sordid activities to the Church committee. As a result of Ford's action, Congress failed to alter or challenge the scope of the agency's covert activities and its various functions outside the United States. That failure later set the stage for William Casey, director of the CIA in the Reagan administration, to get away with his high-handed and ruthless disregard of Congress—with consequences that led directly to the Iran-Contra scandal in the 1980s.

## CLEANING UP THE JUSTICE DEPARTMENT

Although Ford ensured that the CIA would be kept under the dominant control of the president, he moved quickly to clean up the Justice Department in the aftermath of Watergate. It was one of his most successful undertakings, for which he deserves high praise. He appointed Edward Levi, the president of the University of Chicago, as attorney general. In so doing, Ford made it clear that this extremely sensitive position had been filled not by a partisan politico but by a person who was professionally qualified to manage the Justice Department and who would also show a proper respect for due process and civil liberties. During his tenure, Levi provided the leadership and direction needed in a period racked by the loss of credibility in public institutions, and his actions restored a degree of trust and confidence in the administration of justice by the chief legal officer of the United States.

Characteristically, other Ford appointments were also guided by strict professional standards, as the president sought to restore confidence in and respect for the integrity of his office. Eschewing ideological criteria as his sole guide, he took the advice of Attorney General Levi by selecting John Paul Stevens, a Northwestern University law professor and Chicago lawyer, to fill a vacant position on the Supreme Court created by the retirement of Justice William O. Douglas. Stevens was judicious, thoughtful, and fair-minded, and he represented in outlook and perspective the president who appointed him to the high bench.

## APPOINTMENT OF NELSON ROCKEFELLER AS VICE PRESIDENT

Ford also selected New York's Governor Nelson Rockefeller as his replacement as vice president. Rockefeller had years of experience in government, and he was a respected public figure among many Democrats and Republicans alike. Ford hoped his presence would add credibility and stature to a weak administration saddled with the fallout from Watergate. That hope failed to materialize. Rockefeller was the prime symbol of the Republican "Eastern Establishment," and as such was anathema to most Sun Belt conservatives, who had become a powerful force in the Republican ranks since the early 1960s. In an effort to placate them, Ford removed Rockefeller from the 1976 Republican ticket, but he admitted years later that "It was the biggest political mistake of my life. And it was one of the few cowardly things I did in my life."

## THE CHALLENGE FROM THE REPUBLICAN RIGHT

In reality, the opposition to Rockefeller was actually directed at Ford. Republican conservatives viewed him as a bumbling president who lacked consistency on domestic issues, and—even worse—one who supported détente. In their view, former California governor Ronald Reagan had the requisite political stature and ideological firmness to lead the party to victory. When Reagan announced in November 1975 that he would seek the 1976 GOP presidential nomination, he already had the support of enough Republican voters to lead Ford by 12 points in the polls. Standing directly in Ford's path, Reagan left no doubt that a bitter intraparty struggle for the nomination would now take place between two men who neither liked nor respected each other.

Domestic differences and personal ambition notwithstanding, foreign policy remained the most important issue separating Ford and Reagan. Reagan denounced Ford's attempt to negotiate an arms control agreement with Moscow as damaging to vital U.S. security interests. Reagan questioned Ford's political priorities, citing the president's refusal to meet at the White House with exiled Russian writer Aleksandr Solzhenitsyn. Reagan also viewed Ford's efforts to negotiate a treaty with Panama over the future status of the Panama Canal as tantamount to throwing away what had always rightfully belonged to the United States.

Ford was caught between Reagan's challenge, which greatly limited his options and forced him to move right, and the efforts of the Democratic Congress to throttle him by circumscribing his power and authority while passing legislation he found unacceptable. Ford's prospects for reelection were further dimmed by an economy, which was still in the grip of stagflation, and by the collapse of détente. As these various events were unfolding, a December 1975 Gallup Poll revealed that 61 percent of the American people could not think of anything Ford had done to impress them. He was in a shaky position with voters even before the start of the 1976 presidential campaign. Unlike Reagan, or even Nixon before Watergate, Ford lacked a grassroots base or a national constituency loyal to him. Thus, it now appeared that Gerald Ford, having become a somewhat better president than politician, was in the fight of his life to retain an office he was eager to return to for a full term.

President Eisenhower had also had difficulties with members of the Republican right, led by Senator Barry Goldwater, but no one had dared to challenge his position or authority in the way Reagan now challenged Ford. Ford managed to win the GOP nomination, narrowly defeating Reagan on the first ballot. After selecting Kansas senator Robert Dole as his running mate, he faced former Georgia governor Jimmy Carter, the Democratic nominee, who led him in the polls by 20 points.

## THE ELECTION OF 1976

Having experienced the pride and pleasure of being president on the day of the American bicentennial, Ford now had to face the grim reality that his pardon of Richard Nixon would haunt him until election day, making his task of overcoming Carter's big lead even more difficult. In addition, he had to cope with the image, fostered by Reagan and many others, that he was an error-prone loser. In reality, Ford was a hard-working, intelligent, and well-informed chief executive who had steadily matured on the job. But the constant media spoofing of his pratfalls and intellectual ability made him appear to many Americans, however much they liked him personally, to lack the right stuff to be president.

Despite those handicaps, Ford managed to make it a competitive race, aided not only by a thoroughly reorganized campaign staff headed by James Baker but also by Carter's various political gaffes. But just as he was beginning to catch up to the Democratic nominee, Ford blew it with a monumental gaffe of his own that contributed to a significant slowing of his momentum. During his second nationally televised debate with Carter, Ford remarked that "there is no Soviet domination of Eastern Europe, and there never will be under a Ford administration." A major verbal miscue, it provided Carter with a huge opening, allowing him to say that "I would like to see Mr. Ford convince Polish-Americans and Hungarian-Americans in this country that those countries don't live under the domination of the Soviet Union." Although Ford later admitted that he had made a "mistake," the damage was done. His comment probably cost him some votes among ethnic Catholics of Eastern European descent whose support he needed to ensure victory in a closely contested election. In more general terms, it seemingly vindicated the view of Reagan and Carter alike that Ford was not smart enough to be president. Seen from their perspective, he was more like an Edsel than a Ford or Lincoln.

More significant in shaping the outcome of the election was the decline in economic activity during the key third quarter, and the accompanying rise in the unemployment rate to 7.9 percent. By refusing to pump more money into the economy to stimulate growth, Ford rejected a short-term view, which hurt him on election day. Although Ford's stance was politically foolish, it was consistent with his general economic outlook. He believed that the future well-being of the economy depended on the prevention of a sharp increase in the federal deficit. Ford, like a majority of Americans, wanted the private sector to assume the major share of the responsibility for moving the economy ahead. Because of Ford's failure to respond to the unemployment problem, Carter was able to use the economic issue to unify otherwise disparate interest groups inside the Democratic party, which contributed to his narrow victory in 1976.

Ford's pardon of Nixon also played a role in determining the outcome of the election; at least 6 percent of the electorate voted against him for that reason alone. Although the pardon was politically costly, Ford never had any regrets about what he had done. Many years later, he remarked, "My feelings are even stronger today than they were at the time. It was the right thing to do." Although Ford undoubtedly did the "right thing," he botched it in a procedural sense. There is not, however—despite rumors and allegations to the contrary—any evidence to suggest that he made a deal to pardon Nixon in exchange for his resignation. Historians will continue to ponder the question of what else Ford might have done to avoid the stigma associated with the pardon he felt obliged to grant.

## EVALUATION OF GERALD FORD'S PRESIDENCY

The Nixon pardon overshadows everything else that occurred while Ford was in the White House. Ford's presidency nevertheless marks an important transitional period

in the life of the nation. Many complex problems, including an energy crisis, stagflation, and a shattered foreign policy consensus emerged full-blown during this period. But if a budget-minded conservative like Ford was unable to address them with much success, it was not because he lacked the will or intelligence. Few others could have done much better, given the magnitude of those problems and the institutional constraints that then prevailed. If Ford had won in 1976, he would have had a fresh chance to tackle the deficit problem, such as it was, as well as the option of finishing work on an arms-control agreement with Moscow. Along with those future possibilities, a Ford victory would probably have denied Ronald Reagan his opportunity to become president. Without Jimmy Carter in the White House, struggling with problems similar to those that Ford confronted, it is hard to imagine Reagan winning both the GOP nomination and the election in 1980.

Although Ford deeply lamented his defeat at the hands of Jimmy Carter, he took satisfaction in knowing that he had protected the presidency as an institution and helped restore confidence in it. Thus, whatever his limitations and mistakes, Ford did make a historic contribution to the well-being of the American political system. Thanks to his straightforward style and open personality, he went far to repair the damage that a former president who had waged war in Vietnam and against the Constitution had left in his wake. Such was Gerald Ford's most important accomplishment and greatest success as president.

## BIBLIOGRAPHY

Berman, William C. *America's Right Turn: From Nixon to Clinton*, 2nd ed. (Johns Hopkins University Press, 1998).

Cannon, James. *Time and Chance: Gerald Ford's Appointment with History* (HarperCollins, 1994).

Firestone, Bernard J., and Alexej Urginsky. *Gerald R. Ford and the Politics of Post-Watergate America*, 2 vols. (Greenwood Press, 1993).

Ford, Gerald. *A Time to Heal* (Harper & Row, 1979).

Greene, John Robert. *The Presidency of Gerald R. Ford* (University Press of Kansas, 1995).

Kutler, Stanley. *The Wars of Watergate: The Last Crisis of Richard Nixon* (Knopf, 1990).

Reichley, A. James. *Conservatives in an Age of Change: The Nixon and Ford Administrations* (Brookings Institution, 1981).

Schulzinger, Robert. *Henry Kissinger: Doctor of Diplomacy* (Columbia University Press, 1989).

★★★ 39 ★★★

# JAMES EARL (JIMMY) CARTER, JR.
## 1977–1981

### William E. Leuchtenburg

*Born 1 October 1924 in Plains, Georgia, to James Earl Carter and (Bessie) Lillian Gordy Carter; educated at the U.S. Naval Academy, Annapolis, Maryland (B.S. 1946); married Rosalynn Smith, 7 July 1946, Plains, Georgia; four children; elected president in 1976 on the Democratic ticket with Walter Frederick Mondale of Minnesota, with 40,830,763 popular votes and 297 electoral college ballots, over the Republican ticket of Gerald Rudolph Ford of Michigan and Robert Joseph Dole of Kansas (39,147,793 popular votes and 240 electoral ballots).*

No man in the twentieth century entered the White House more of an outsider than did Jimmy Carter. Born and raised in a dusty south Georgia town remote from the sinews of power, he was, if one excepts the Texan Lyndon Johnson who often identified with the West rather than the South, the first resident of a southern state elected president since Zachary Taylor. He had almost no connection to the Washington establishment. Unlike many other chief executives, he had not spent long years reconnoitering legislative corridors but was an agribusinessman engaged in marketing peanuts. He had served briefly in the Georgia legislature and one term as governor, but at the time of his election, he held no public office whatsoever. A born-again Christian in an increasingly secular age, he approached his duties with earnest piety. These circumstances and characteristics would account for a number of his successes—without them, he would never have been elected—but they also contributed to not a few of his difficulties and even failures.

## FROM PLAINS TO
## THE STATE HOUSE

James Earl Carter, Jr., who preferred to be called Jimmy, was born on 1 October 1924 in Plains, Georgia, son of the head of a prosperous brokerage in peanuts and of a registered nurse, "Miz Lillian," who would later volunteer for the Peace Corps at the age of 68 and serve in an Indian village. (He was the first president born not at home but in a hospital.) After graduating from the U.S. Naval Academy in 1946, Carter spent seven years in the Navy, the last of them in the prestigious atomic submarine program under the stern tutelage of Captain (later Admiral) Hyman Rickover, before he was called back to Plains to take over the family's peanut business from his dying father. In 1962, he campaigned for a seat in the Georgia senate. Counted out in a fraudulent contest, he tried again and won. In 1966, following two terms in the state senate where he earned a name for himself as a conscientious good-government legislator, he made a bid for the governorship. He ran respectably but was crushed by the defeat. Only his experience as an itinerant evangelist brought him out of a deep depression.

In 1970, Carter made another attempt for the governorship, and this time he was successful. In what his supporter Andrew Young said was the meanest county in Georgia, Carter had shown quiet courage in combating racism, but in his campaign he indulged in covert racial appeals. Hence, he caught the state by surprise when he announced in his inaugural address, "The time for racial discrimination is over," and when he hung a portrait of Martin Luther King, Jr., in the state capitol where only white faces had been featured before. As governor, he showed more zeal for arid solutions

such as zero-based budgeting than for liberal causes, but as successor to Lester Maddox—who had gained notoriety by driving blacks from his restaurant with a pick axe handle—Carter came to symbolize to the national media a new kind of modern southern statesman.

## THE EVANGELIST AS CANDIDATE

Yet when in December 1974, his tenure as governor drawing to a close, Jimmy Carter offered himself as a presidential candidate, the country responded (if it responded at all) "Jimmy Who?" (Earlier, when he told his mother he was planning to run for president, she replied, "President of what?") No more than a blip on the screen when polling on the Democratic presidential nomination began, Carter confronted a large field of well-known hopefuls, for, given the travail of Watergate, 1976 was not expected to be a Republican year. (One Democrat said, "We could run an aardvark and win.")

Carter, though, proved to be an indefatigable campaigner. Grinning ear to ear, his right hand outstretched, he would approach strangers saying, "My name is Jimmy Carter and I'm running for president." He shrewdly sensed that as an outsider, in no way tainted by anything that had happened in Washington, he had a unique appeal to a nation in revolt against the imperial presidency. He pledged, "I will never tell a lie to the American people," and, in the style of a revivalist preacher, informed spellbound audiences, "I want a government that is as good, and honest, and decent, and truthful, and fair, and competent, and idealistic, and compassionate, and as filled with love as are the American people." Then, in the phrase of one reporter, "this peanut-farmer Billy Graham" would descend from the platform and lay his hands on people in the crowd. In addition to seizing the moral issue, Carter as a centrist succeeded in positioning himself between George Wallace on his right and aspirants to his left who divided liberal support. By the time of the 1976 Democratic convention, Jimmy Carter—no longer Jimmy Who?—had put together a winning coalition. A southern moderate, he chose the northern liberal, Senator Walter F. "Fritz" Mondale of Minnesota, as his running mate, a ticket dubbed "Fritz and Grits."

Carter left the convention with an enormous 33-point lead over President Gerald Ford, but he almost blew all of it, in part because this Sunday school teacher and Baptist deacon gave an ill-advised interview to the sexually oriented magazine *Playboy* in which he used words such as *screw* and divulged that, although he had remained faithful to his wife, he had committed adultery in his heart many times. Moreover, he seemed so fuzzy on issues that liberals accused him of deserting them at the same time that Ford's running mate, Senator Robert Dole of Kansas, was jeering at him as "Southern-fried McGovern." Carter's statements were so vague, so insufferably moralistic, and so contradictory that one wit said, "They wanted to put Carter on Mount Rushmore—but they didn't have room for two more faces," and Gerald Ford said of him, "He wavers, he wanders, he wiggles, and he waffles and he shouldn't be President of the United States."

In the end, thanks largely to Ford's own blunders, Carter won, but barely—with 40.8 million votes (50.1 percent) to Ford's 39.1 million (48 percent) and so narrow a margin in the electoral college that a switch of less than 9,000 votes in Ohio and Hawaii would have spelled defeat for him. Alienated by Watergate and two unimpressive candidates, nearly half of the electorate stayed home on election day. As one journalist said, "Neither Ford nor Carter won as many votes as Mr. Nobody." With so fragile a mandate, Carter, if he was to succeed as president, would have to take special pains not to alienate any of the elements of his diverse coalition, ranging from labor union leaders and black activists to suburban independents.

## A NEW STYLE OF PRESIDENT

Jimmy Carter established his governing style on his very first day in office. Instead of wearing a cutaway to the inauguration ceremonies, as his predecessors had, he took the oath of office in an ordinary business suit, and he asked to be sworn in not as James but as Jimmy. Afterward he traveled the distance from the Capitol to the White House not by riding regally in the traditional black bulletproof limousine but by strolling up Pennsylvania Avenue with First Lady Rosalynn Carter and hand-in-hand with his 9-year-old daughter Amy, who skipped along as the president beamed and waved. Behind them followed other members of his family, including his 15-month-old grandson perched on the shoulder of his father.

In the ensuing months, Carter continued this simple republican mode. When he gave his first televised address, a fireside chat, he wore a modest cardigan. He forbade even high-ranking aides the convenience of government limousines, and after Congress gave him the authority he had sought to reorganize the government, he promptly reduced the White House staff by 28 percent. He stayed in the homes of ordinary Americans, held town meetings, carried his own luggage on and off planes, and even ran a phone-in talk show to make the White House seem more accessible. Carter's low-keyed manner deflated the pretensions of the imperial presidency, and he brought to the White House a rectitude that had been largely absent in the Nixon era.

## STAFFING THE ADMINISTRATION

Carter also sought to open up the government to groups that had been underrepresented. He named blacks to high posts: Patricia Harris as secretary of housing and urban development (HUD) and Andrew Young as ambassador to the United Nations. (When Carter subsequently dismissed Young because of the ambassador's unauthorized initiatives to the Palestine Liberation Organization, he replaced him with another African American, Donald F. McHenry.) Carter also appointed a black secretary of the army, solicitor general, head of the civil rights division of the Department of Justice (the first to hold that post), U.S. attorneys in five large states (including the first ever in a southern state), U.S. marshals in twelve states, and six black ambassadors. He chose three times as many African Americans for U.S. district court judgeships as Lyndon Johnson had. Carter also selected two women for his first cabinet—Secretary of Commerce Juanita Kreps and HUD Secretary Harris—and in 1979 he picked another woman, Shirley Hufstedler, to head the newly created Department of Education. To the dismay of men who could not stand the thought that a woman might exert influence, he also heeded the advice of First Lady Rosalynn Carter.

Most comfortable with those he knew well and determined to bring to Washington people with roots in the countryside, he elevated several persons from his home state to positions of importance. The "Georgia Mafia" included his Atlanta buddy Bert Lance as director of the Office of Management and Budget (OMB); another Atlantan, Judge Griffin Bell, as attorney general; and a conspicuous cadre in the White House—notably his chief aide, Hamilton Jordan; his press secretary, Jody Powell; and, as his domestic policy adviser, the bright, resourceful Stuart Eizenstat. His solicitude for his fellow Georgians did not carry far enough, however, to allow him to name even so trusted a lieutenant as Jordan to be chief of staff, for he wanted to avoid any association with the sort of concentrated power that had characterized the Nixon reign. As a consequence, critics said, Carter's programs lacked coordination.

Yet if Carter's manner and some of his appointments led the media to call him a populist, he turned to the establishment, especially Washington insiders and the corporate world, to fill the most important posts. He named to the cabinet the former government official and Washington, D.C. attorney, Cyrus Vance (secretary of state); the president of the California Institute of Technology, Harold Brown (secretary of defense); and Michael Blumenthal from the Bendix Corporation (secretary of the treasury). For his chief energy adviser, he chose James R. Schlesinger, who had been secretary of defense under Nixon and Ford. Even some of the Georgians fit into this pattern. Attorney General Bell was a conservative with racist associations, and Budget Director Lance was a well-connected banker.

## CUTTING EXPENDITURES

In truth, Carter, for all his desire to put a new face on government, pursued economic policies that did not diverge greatly from those of Nixon and Ford. In a lengthy postelection memo, his pollster, Patrick Caddell, dismissed figures such as Ted Kennedy, George McGovern, and Morris Udall as "traditional Democrats . . . in many ways . . . as antiquated and anachronistic a group as are conservative Republicans." He warned the incoming president against "resort to old Democratic dogmas" and recommended that he cut "across traditional ideology." Carter thought the memo was excellent, and, in good part, made it the basis for his emphases as president.

Liberals, union officials, and black leaders anticipated that Carter would make up for eight years of Republican neglect by enacting ambitious social welfare programs, but Carter concluded that, with the $66 billion deficit he had inherited from Ford, he could not meet the demand for big spending projects, even if he wanted to. Although he had campaigned on a promise to expand the economy, he decided that the main problem confronting the country was not unemployment but inflation, and that government deficits were driving up prices. Consequently, he submitted a series of lean and mean budgets that doomed liberal aspirations. In addition, he broke with the New Deal tradition and promoted the deregulation of major industries.

Carter's policies, while never conservative enough to appease Republican critics, set him on a collision course with liberal Democrats. He had hardly taken office when he enraged labor leaders and others by abandoning an economic stimulus program and refusing to go along with a minimum-wage hike. "It sometimes seems difficult to remember who won last fall," commented George McGovern, who charged that Carter was seeking to balance the budget on the backs of the poor. When in the fall of 1978 the Carter administration proposed to slash activities in education, housing, health, adult employment, and aid to cities, liberals exploded. At a midterm party conference in

Memphis in December, Carter evoked little enthusiasm, but Senator Edward Kennedy drew a rousing ovation from the assembled Democrats when he urged them to resist the "drastic" cuts. Unchastened, Carter early in 1979 offered a budget taking $400 million away from school lunches, $600 million from Social Security, and more than $2 billion from social services, while, to the exasperation of liberals, boosting spending by the Pentagon.

## RAMPANT INFLATION
The president and his circle countered criticism by commenting that the national concern about soaring prices could not be ignored. Mondale, though he had been counseling Carter against abandoning liberal programs, warned the Memphis gathering that if Democrats "don't end the ever-increasing cost of living, we will be driven out of office as we were by the Vietnam War." He told his fellow liberals: "If we don't solve inflation, this society will suffer terribly. Everything we stand for will be eroded. Inflation can destroy everything we believe in. When we press for real income improvement, inflation burns up the increase; when we push for growth, our standard of living deteriorates; when we expand personal opportunity, inflation lays its damp hand on our dreams of a more prosperous future."

Carter's anxiety about inflation derived in good part from the doubling of oil prices, a problem that became critical after Iran cut off supplies at the end of 1978. By the spring of 1979, lines at gas pumps stretched for more than a mile as shortages became an even more pressing matter than cost. In a major address to the nation in April 1977, Carter had warned that, unless the American people began to conserve energy by embracing a program that would be, in the philosopher William James's phrase, "the moral equivalent of war," the country would confront a "national catastrophe." Two days later, he asked Congress for a panoply of measures, including a large tax on gasoline to reduce consumption, a windfall profits levy on oil companies, the development of

synthetic fuels, and the establishment of a Department of Energy. Congress quickly agreed to create the new department but balked at other recommendations, especially the gasoline tax, which voters would be certain to resent. Not until November 1978 would Congress approve a watered-down version of Carter's original proposals, including the deregulation of natural gas.

## DETERIORATING RELATIONS WITH CONGRESS
The president's difficulties in rallying the nation, and more particularly Congress, to cope with the energy crisis stemmed partly from his shortcomings as a leader. In the words of one historian, "Jimmy Carter brought to the White House an honest grin, a disarming candor, and lots of inexperience." A technocrat who approached Congress with a slide-rule mentality, he did not have much feel for the nuances of Capitol Hill. The best that his friend Griffin Bell could summon up to say was that "Jimmy was about as good a president as an engineer can be." He not only failed to establish relationships with the power brokers on the Hill but in his speeches to the nation too often seemed less like the tribune of the people than the manager of an accounting firm. "Carterism does not march and it does not sing," said the historian and former Lyndon Johnson aide, Eric Goldman. "It is cautious, muted, grayish, at times even crabbed."

Congress and the president eyed one another with mutual suspicion. Since Carter had campaigned against the Washington establishment, congressional insiders did not cotton to him. Moreover, after its bruising experience with the domineering Lyndon Johnson and the arrogant Richard Nixon, Congress was determined to reassert itself. Carter aggravated this unpromising situation by inundating Congress with proposals, instead of establishing priorities, and by leaving veteran legislators with a hint that he felt superior to them. He immediately got himself into hot water by eliminating funds for nineteen water projects that certain House members cherished. Arguably, he was correct in saying that they were unnecessary and expensive, but his righteousness did not sit well and he spent valuable political capital over a relatively minor goal. The Senate lashed back by voting 65 to 24 to restore the projects, and Carter did not dare to veto the stipulation.

Alienating the Democratic leadership contributed to Carter's troubles in getting legislation enacted, despite his party's sizable majorities in both houses. His aides sometimes did not return phone calls from committee chairs, and when the leaders came to breakfast at the White House, the president, to save a few pennies, served them meager fare. "I didn't get this way eating sweet rolls," the big-bellied Speaker of the House, Tip O'Neill, told Mondale afterward. "I want a breakfast and I'm not coming back unless I get a meal!" When legislators did turn up, Carter, instead of listening to them and stroking their egos, harangued them on their duties. On leaving one such gathering, Mondale muttered, "Carter's got the coldest political nose of any politician I ever met."

Surfeited with White House moralizing, legislators took sly comfort in July 1977, when Senate investigators accused the president's closest adviser, Budget Director Bert Lance, of improper behavior in his Georgia banking business, and Carter, despite his high-toned emphasis on ethics in government, stood by his friend, "a man of honesty" of whom he was "proud." Even when the comptroller of the currency and the Internal Revenue Service created additional doubts about Lance, Carter remained stubborn. When in late September, the president at last accepted Lance's resignation with "regret and sorrow" while insisting that his friend had "exonerated himself completely," Carter's reputation for integrity was badly damaged. In the ensuing weeks, his approval rating plummeted. "If the Carter Administration were a television show," the columnist Russell Baker said, "it would have been canceled months ago."

## THE "DOMESTIC SUMMIT"

By the early summer of 1979, Carter's tribulations were so great that he concluded that nothing less than a "domestic summit" was required. That spring prices had risen to their highest level since the postwar inflation of 1946, with fears of worse to come as OPEC (the Organization of Petroleum Exporting Countries) announced its fourth, and biggest, price hike in five months. As supplies fell dramatically, exasperated motorists queued up on ever longer lines for the privilege of buying ever more costly gasoline. Over the Fourth of July weekend in the New York metropolitan area, 90 percent of all filling stations were shut down. The president responded not by offering a solution but by canceling the energy speech he had scheduled and repairing to his mountain retreat at Camp David in Maryland.

Carter had become persuaded by Pat Caddell that the American people had lost faith in their institutions and that the president had to reinvigorate them. Mondale, who thought that what the country needed was not sermonizing but viable programs, denounced this diagnosis, but Carter told his inner circle, "We're irrelevant and people don't listen to us." The national sense of despair would not be alleviated by "passing programs." Years later, Mondale observed sourly, "We said we needed a government as good as her people, now we discovered we need a people as good as their government." So for more than a week leaders from the public and private sphere, nearly 150 of them, went up to the mountain to tell the president what they thought had gone wrong.

When Carter finally came down from the mountain to speak to the nation on 15 July, he delivered an address that combined Caddell's and Mondale's approaches. The country, he said, echoing Caddell, was undergoing a "crisis of confidence" that "strikes at the very heart and soul and spirit of our national will." (Though the president never used the word *malaise*, his pollster did speak of a "national malaise" and the address has become known as the "malaise speech.") Carter also offered, as Mondale had urged, specifics of an energy conservation plan to end the "intolerable dependence" on OPEC. "Beginning this moment," he asserted, "this nation will never use more foreign oil than it did in 1977." The president had believed that "drama and mystery" were required if the American people were going to pay attention to him, and he turned out to be right, as the positive response to his eloquent address sent his approval rating soaring.

But Carter, who had earlier demonstrated a well-developed capacity for shooting himself in the foot, then destroyed all of this good will in a moment by telling the members of his cabinet that he wanted their written resignations. Frightened foreign chancelleries, unable to comprehend such a move, thought that the U.S. government was disintegrating, and critics at home raised serious doubts about the president's judgment. Carter followed up this action by firing, or accepting the resignations of, no fewer than five cabinet officials, including Energy Secretary Schlesinger (replaced by Charles Duncan), Attorney General Bell (Benjamin Civiletti), Treasury Secretary Blumenthal (George Miller), and, to the distress of Ted Kennedy and the liberal wing of the party, HEW Secretary Joseph Califano, one of the architects of Lyndon Johnson's Great Society (replaced by Patricia Roberts Harris). Within three weeks, Carter's approval rating had fallen to the lowest ever recorded, worse even than Nixon's when he resigned in disgrace.

## FOREIGN POLICY INITIATIVES

Carter had considerably greater latitude for change in foreign affairs, where he was determined to break away from the rigidities of the Cold War and develop new initiatives. In 1978 Carter became the first U.S. president ever to visit the black-ruled nations south of the Sahara. His appointee Andrew Young established cordial relations between the United States and the new black regimes in Africa; helped turn the white government of Rhodesia over to the new black-ruled state of Zimbabwe; and cast the American vote in the United Nations Security Council for a mandatory arms embargo on South Africa. Carrying to fulfillment a process begun under Nixon, Carter

on 1 January 1979 established full diplomatic relations with China. (Not realizing that he was speaking close to a live microphone, Carter, after announcing the action, murmured, "Massive applause throughout the nation!") In defiance of hawks in the Pentagon and in his own party, he opposed production both of the B-1 bomber and the neutron bomb (a nuclear weapon that would kill multitudes of people but spare buildings), and he vetoed a bill to add a very expensive nuclear aircraft carrier to the fleet.

He also conducted foreign policy with a sensitivity to democratic principles, notably by establishing an Office of Human Rights in the State Department. Carter brought pressure on the white supremacist governments of Rhodesia and of South Africa. He also hectored the Soviet regime, personally answering a letter from the Russian dissident and Nobel laureate Andrei Sakharov. The president cut off aid to despotisms that treated their citizens brutally, even when they were anticommunist—including the dictatorships of Argentina and Uruguay—and he not only withdrew support from the Somoza tyranny in Nicaragua but also helped sustain the successor Sandinista regime, despite its tilt toward the communists. Carter drew criticism both at home and abroad as a do-gooder ignorant of the imperatives of power politics, but some governments did, in fact, release political prisoners.

## THE PANAMA TREATIES

In 1978 Carter, with great courage and no little skill, carried to success an unpopular venture against very long odds. After the government completed negotiations to yield the Panama Canal to the Republic of Panama, a survey revealed that only 8 percent of the country approved, with 78 percent opposed. During the 1976 campaign Ronald Reagan had declared, "We bought it, we paid for it, we built it and it is ours, and we intend to keep it," and another California Republican, Senator S. I. Hayakawa, later insisted, "We stole it fair and square." But marshaling a public relations effort, Carter and his aides won over skeptical senators, including even Hayakawa on one key vote. As a consequence, the Panama treaties were ratified on two roll calls, each time by just one vote more than the required two-thirds. He gained approval, however, only after the treaties were amended to sanction U.S. armed intervention to keep the thoroughfare open, if that proved necessary.

## THE CAMP DAVID ACCORDS

Carter's boldest venture came in the Middle East, where he took the great risk of inviting Prime Minister Menachem Begin of Israel and President Anwar el-Sadat of Egypt to meet with him at Camp David in September 1978. So fierce was the hostility between the two nations that President Carter seemed to be courting almost certain humiliation. Only indefatigable effort on his part prevented Sadat from breaking off talks with the abrasive Begin and going home. But after thirteen wearying, enervating days at his mountain retreat, Carter emerged with the happy news that the two antagonists had agreed in principle on a pact. Afterward, though, it appeared that the compact would fall apart, with Begin characterizing it as a "sham document." Selflessly, Carter flew to the Middle East in March 1979, and for nearly a week shuttled between Cairo and Tel Aviv to preserve the accord. When Sadat and Begin signed the treaty at the White House on 26 March 1979, the ceremony marked the greatest triumph of the Carter presidency.

## RUSSIA: SALT II
## AND AFGHANISTAN

Though most Americans approved of his endeavors in the Middle East, Carter learned during his attempt to thaw relations with the Soviet Union and to slow down the arms race that he had to keep domestic pressures constantly in mind. At a summit meeting in Vienna with USSR President Leonid Brezhnev in June 1979, the president signed SALT II (Strategic Arms Limitation Talks, Treaty II), the climax of seven years of negotiations started under Nixon. The treaty established limits on each country's nuclear arsenals, but Carter—attempting to appease

opponents—agreed to endorse the controversial MX intercontinental missile system that would operate through 2,000 miles of underground tunnels. Liberals, in turn, were dismayed that the president, who would not countenance relatively small sums for social spending, would consent to a $33 billion project of doubtful utility.

Carter's desire to reach an understanding with the Kremlin sustained a serious setback in late December 1979 when the USSR invaded Afghanistan. Though it probably did so with limited aims, Carter chose to perceive the invasion as a Soviet move on the Persian Gulf and called it the "gravest threat to peace" since 1945. In reprisal, he revived registration for the draft, embargoed grain sales to the USSR (an unpopular move in the wheat belt), banned U.S. participation in the forthcoming Olympic games in Moscow, accelerated production of the Cruise missile, and—in a disappointing denouement—withdrew the SALT II treaty. In what became known as the Carter Doctrine, he announced, "Any attempt by any outside force to gain control of the Persian Gulf region will be regarded as an assault on the vital interests of the United States of America and such an assault will be repelled by any means necessary, including military force."

## EXPLOSION IN TEHERAN

Carter's preoccupation with the Persian Gulf owed much to a development that had begun a month before the Afghanistan invasion, detonating an explosion that would reverberate through all of the president's final year in office. Early in 1979, revolutionaries in Iran had overthrown the Shah, who had been catapulted to power by the Central Intelligence Agency (CIA) in 1953 and ever since had been a staunch U.S. ally. For more than twenty-five years, his country had been a reliable source of oil and a substantial buyer of U.S. arms. The use of torture by his CIA-trained secret police, however, had become an embarrassment to Carter's human rights policy. American diplomats in Iran warned the president that if the Shah was permitted to enter the

United States, the followers of the new Iranian leader, the Ayatollah Khomeini, would strike back. Pushed by the banker David Rockefeller and by Henry Kissinger, Carter allowed the critically ill former ruler to come to New York for medical treatment he could have received elsewhere, and on 4 November 1979, as predicted, the Iranians retaliated by overrunning the U.S. embassy in Teheran and seizing 53 Americans as hostages. Americans were infuriated when a howling mob paraded the blindfolded prisoners through the streets, with threats to hang them if the Shah was not returned to Iran for swift justice.

More than any other episode, the Iranian captivity fixed in the public mind the image of Carter as an inept leader. In the early stages, Carter's approval rating jumped—in the wake of the seizure of the embassy, his rating doubled to 61 percent, the biggest one-month leap in the history of polling. In part this happened because the country always rallies to its president in a time of crisis; moreover, Carter took a number of steps, such as freezing Iranian assets in the United States, that conveyed an impression of firmness. But when Carter wisely preferred diplomatic channels to military action, his critics increasingly charged him with indecisiveness. Carter then uncharacteristically approved an ill-conceived commando raid to liberate the captives, only to wind up announcing, early on the morning of 25 April 1980, that the effort had been botched, at the cost of the lives of eight servicemen in the Iranian desert. Faultfinders asked whether the Three Stooges were now running the government. Thereafter, Carter had nothing to offer save patience, and as Americans were reminded each night on the evening news of the number of days the embassy staff had been incarcerated (444 at the end), Carter came to seem the very symbol of diminished U.S. national power.

Foreign policy, a terrain on which Carter had registered not a few successes, had by 1980 become quicksand, with the president unable to impose his will on those closest to him. His younger brother, Billy, who had been raising eyebrows by his good ole boy behavior and his self-promoting marketing of Billy Beer, further tarnished the president's reputation in foreign affairs by taking a $200,000 retainer as agent for Libya, a haven for terrorists headed by the despot, Maummar Qaddafi. Within Jimmy Carter's own administration, Secretary of State Cyrus Vance, an experienced diplomat who sought to avoid confrontation, feuded with National Security Adviser Zbigniew Brzezinski, the hard-nosed son of a Polish exile, who believed that force commanded respect. Vance viewed Brzezinski as trigger-happy; Brzezinski thought Vance revealed the feebleness of a WASP elite going into eclipse. "The tussling is Jimmy Carter's fault," wrote one reporter. "He jumps around like a water spider on a June afternoon." After Carter chose force in the Iranian rescue mission, Vance resigned. (Carter replaced him with Senator Edmund Muskie of Maine.)

### THE KENNEDY CHALLENGE

Troubles at home competed with those overseas in Carter's dreadful last year. In November 1979, the same month in which the invasion of the U.S. embassy had taken place in Teheran, Senator Edward Kennedy of Massachusetts announced he was a candidate for the presidential nomination in 1980. Though, in truth, the two Democrats differed less than either of them claimed, "their rivalry," as the historian Leo Ribuffo has said, "came to symbolize a seemingly unbridgeable gap between those Democrats, led by Senator Kennedy, who wanted primarily to expand the welfare state, and those Democrats, led by President Carter, who placed a higher priority on government efficiency and fiscal prudence." When Kennedy raised his challenge, Carter told a gathering of congressional representatives, "I'll whip his ass," and, after months of nasty crossfire, he did—but at a cost. So bitter did the rivalry become that when Carter sought to grasp Kennedy's hand at the Democratic national convention in a gesture of upraised arms signaling reconciliation and party unity, the senator deliberately eluded him. With the added handicap of a party now badly fractured, Carter entered the 1980 race against the Republican nominee, Ronald Reagan, as one commentator said, "dogged by the captivity of hostages he could not free, an economy he could not seem to improve, a brother he could not disown, and an opponent he could not shake."

## STAGFLATION AND THE 1980 CAMPAIGN

Carter's economic woes plagued him at least as much as did the national obsession with the captives in Teheran. Early in 1980, inflation and the prime interest rate approached 20 percent, and when the government began to note some progress in reducing inflation, unemployment figures soared: Nearly 2 million were added to the jobless rolls in only five months. With mortgage rates at an astronomic 15 percent, home ownership was beyond the reach of millions of Americans, especially young families, and once again the president got the blame. After it was all over, Carter told Hamilton Jordan, "1980 was pure hell—the Kennedy challenge, Afghanistan, having to put the SALT Treaty on the shelf, the recession, Ronald Reagan, and the hostages . . . always the hostages! It was one crisis after another."

In the 1980 campaign, Carter sought reelection by exposing the incompetence of his opponent, but—though Reagan obliged him with a number of gaffes—the president could not persuade the country that his own record had earned him another term. Reagan called the Vietnam war "a noble cause"; shared a platform with a man who said, "God doesn't hear the prayers of a Jew"; and insisted that trees caused more pollution than cars or factories. (College students hung signs on trees saying, "Chop me down before I kill again.") But in a critical debate, the Republican candidate asked the American people, "Are you better off than you were four years ago?" With the country reeling under the effects of "stagflation," the answer to that question was not in doubt. Furthermore, Carter, who had had little but bad luck in his four years in office, encountered the misfortune of having the country go to the polls on a November day that was precisely the anniversary of the takeover in Teheran one year before.

In the 1980 election, Reagan trounced Carter, who won only six of the fifty states. With 51 percent of the ballots to Carter's 41 percent, Reagan outpolled the president 43.9 million to 36.4 million. John B. Anderson, a Republican representative to Congress from Illinois running as an independent, got 5.7 million (7 percent), in good part from people who had voted for Carter in 1976 but who had soured on him. Only one previous incumbent (William Howard Taft in 1912 when his party divided) had received so few electoral votes when he sought reelection—Carter's 49, contrasted with Reagan's 489. Despite his dismaying defeat, Carter worked indefatigably in the final weeks of his term to liberate the hostages. In a bitterly ironic stroke, his goal was achieved as Reagan was delivering his inaugural address, the credit thereby accruing to his opponent.

## EVALUATION: A FAILED PRESIDENCY?

Historians have rendered a harsh verdict on Jimmy Carter. A poll of scholars in 1981 ranked him as one of the country's ten worst presidents, and a well-respected *Washington Post* columnist termed Carter's tenure a "tragedy." In a fair-minded appraisal, the historian Burton I. Kaufman observed "that while Carter viewed himself as a trustee of the public good, he never adequately articulated an overarching purpose and direction for his administration." Kaufman, author of the most judicious history of the Carter period, concluded that "the events of his four years in office projected an image to the American people of a hapless administration in disarray and of a presidency that was increasingly divided, lacking in leadership, ineffective in dealing with Congress, incapable of defending America's honor abroad, and uncertain about its purpose, priorities, and sense of direction. In my view, this contemporary image of the Carter presidency was, unfortunately, all too accurate and helped assure a mediocre, if not a failed, presidency."

In years to come, historians may take a somewhat more benign view of Carter, for he did chalk up some achievements: the Camp David agreement, his human rights policy, the Panama Canal treaties, his appointments of women and blacks to high positions, the creation of a Department of Energy—and these do not exhaust the list. On his very first full day in office, he showed courage by pardoning some ten thousand Vietnam-era draft evaders, most of them living in exile in Canada. He created a new cabinet-level agency, the Department of Education, and he achieved the first reform of the civil service since Chester Arthur. He overcame the objections of timber, mineral, oil, and gas interests and preserved one-third of the enormous state of Alaska from exploitation, thus doubling the area of the country's national parks and wildlife refuges in one of the most important pieces of environmental legislation in American history. The same month that he approved that measure—December 1980—he signed a bill establishing a "superfund" to rid the environment of dangerous chemicals that had been dumped or spilled.

Historians are also beginning to acknowledge that, although Carter had serious shortcomings, he operated under severe constraints and was a wise counselor to the nation. The historian Steven Gillon has concluded that a "schism in the public mind" of citizens who wanted both a balanced budget and more federal spending for education and health care "made effective leadership in the late 1970s nearly impossible." Though voters preferred Reagan's cheery demeanor to his rival's hectoring, scholars may one day perceive Jimmy Carter as the first U.S. president with the foresight to tell the American people what they did not want to hear—that the nation had to adapt to an age of limits. Highly intelligent, studious, and well-informed, Carter gave the country a government of integrity and high-mindedness. He also showed a commitment to civic duty that was to earn him respect in his post–White House years for his service as a mediator of disputes abroad and a leader of Habitat for Humanity at home.

Yet one-termers do not loom very large in the history books, and, for all of his accomplishments and good intentions, Carter will probably be remembered best as the first of the Democratic chief executives to reject the legacy of the New Deal and the one associated forever with the unsavory image of tormented American captives dragged through the streets of Teheran—a beleaguered president who had become, as the Senate majority leader said, the Ayatollah's fifty-fourth hostage.

## BIBLIOGRAPHY

Abernathy, Glenn, Dilys M. Hill, and Phil Williams, eds. *The Carter Years: The President and Policy Making* (Pinter, 1984).

Carter, Jimmy. *Keeping Faith: Memoirs of a President* (Bantam, 1982).

Fink, Gary. *Prelude to the Presidency: The Political Character and Legislative Leadership Style of Governor Jimmy Carter* (Greenwood, 1980).

Germond, Jack W., and Jules Witcover. *Blue Smoke and Mirrors: How Reagan Won and Why Carter Lost the Election of 1980* (Viking, 1981).

Gillon, Steven M. *The Democrats' Dilemma: Walter F. Mondale and the Liberal Legacy* (Columbia University Press, 1992).

Glad, Betty. *Jimmy Carter: In Search of the Great White House* (Norton, 1980).

Hargrove, Erwin C. *Jimmy Carter as President: Leadership and the Politics of the Public Good* (Louisiana State University Press, 1988).

Jones, Charles O. *The Trusteeship Presidency: Jimmy Carter and the United States Congress* (Louisiana State University Press, 1988).

Kaufman, Burton I. *The Presidency of James Earl Carter, Jr.* (University Press of Kansas, 1993).

Miller, William Lee. *Yankee from Georgia: The Emergence of Jimmy Carter* (Time Books, 1978).

Smith, Gaddis. *Morality, Reason, and Power: American Diplomacy in the Carter Years* (Hill & Wang, 1986).

Witcover, Jules. *Marathon: The Pursuit of the Presidency, 1972–1976* (Viking, 1977).

★★★ 40 ★★★

# RONALD WILSON REAGAN
## 1981–1989

*Richard M. Pious*

*Born 6 February 1911 in Tampico, Illinois, to John Edward Reagan and Nelle Clyde Wilson Reagan; educated at Eureka College, Eureka, Illinois (B.A. 1932); married Jane Wyman (Sarah Jane Fulks) 24 January 1940, Glendale, California; two children; divorced 19 July 1949; married Nancy Davis (Anne Frances Robbins) 4 March 1952, Los Angeles, California; two children; elected president on the Republican ticket in 1980 with George Herbert Walker Bush of Texas, with 43,901,812 popular votes and 489 electoral college ballots, over the Democratic slate of James Earl Carter of Georgia and Walter Frederick Mondale of Minnesota (35,483,820 votes and 49 electoral ballots); reelected in 1984 with 54,451,521 popular votes and 525 electoral ballots over the Democratic ticket of Walter Frederick Mondale of Minnesota and Geraldine Anne Ferraro of New York, with 37,565,334 votes and 13 electoral ballots.*

At the time of his election in 1980, Ronald Reagan was the oldest person to have been elected president and the first to have entered that office after having been divorced. Perhaps more important, he was the first president to have come out of Hollywood, with its emphasis on vivid imagery, dramatic narrative, and simplified versions of history.

## FROM HOLLYWOOD
## TO THE WHITE HOUSE

Ronald Reagan's origins were modest. His father worked in a shoe store and his mother was a store clerk employed by the Works Progress Administration during the New Deal. Reagan played football and was elected student government president in high school. At Eureka College he also played football, participated in student government, and was in the dramatics society. After graduating in 1932 with a major in economics and sociology, he got a job as a radio sports announcer in Iowa. In 1936 Reagan went to Hollywood, where his good looks caught the eye of movie producers. He signed as a contract motion picture actor at Warner Brothers, where he starred in action dramas and comedies such as *Knute Rockne—All American*, *King's Row*, and *Bedtime for Bonzo*. During this period he also married actress Jane Wyman, from whom he was later divorced. Reagan joined the army and made military films during World War II; after the war, he served as president of the Screen Actors Guild from 1947 to 1952 and was involved in efforts to remove communists and their sympathizers from the guild.

Active in Democratic politics, Reagan supported Harry Truman in his election bid in 1948. Like much of Hollywood, he also supported Helen Gahagan Douglas against Richard Nixon in a bitter senatorial contest in 1950. Two years later, Reagan married Nancy Davis, a contract actress at MGM Studios. Between 1954 and 1962, with his movie career in the doldrums, Reagan hosted two series on television, first the "General Electric Theater" and then "Death Valley Days." In 1959 he served another term as president of the Screen Actors Guild, this time leading a strike that gave actors a share in the profits from movies shown on television.

During the 1950s Ronald Reagan abandoned his New Deal roots and became a conservative. He supported the presidential candidacies of Dwight Eisenhower in 1952 and 1956 and backed Richard Nixon in 1960. Two years later he switched his voter registration from Democrat to Republican. He actively and effectively campaigned for Barry Goldwater in 1964, making a televised speech for the Republicans that catapulted him immediately into the ranks of leading conservative spokespersons. Reagan was elected governor of California in 1966 and in 1970 as the contender from the most conservative wing of the state party. A formidable campaigner, Reagan managed to defeat incumbent Democrat Edmund ("Pat") Brown in 1966, although California at the time seemed inhospitable to conservatives in statewide elections.

For six of his eight years as governor, Reagan confronted a Democratic legislature. He cut welfare rolls, increased income taxes to prevent a projected budget deficit, and lowered property taxes. He more than doubled the funding for California's top-ranked system of public universities, colleges, and community colleges, but he took a strong stand against antiwar student demonstrators on the campuses. Reagan instituted the Medi-Cal program to pay medical bills for the poor under the federal Medicaid program. His unyielding opposition to Cesar Chavez's attempts to organize migrant workers, and his opposition to the California Rural Legal Assistance Program (providing legal aid to the poor, particularly migrant workers), made him the archenemy of the state's liberals. Nevertheless, Reagan as governor demonstrated flexibility in compromising with political opponents and an affability that left even his political enemies willing to come to agreement with him.

Reagan ran as a dark-horse contender for the Republican presidential nomination in 1968, which Nixon won on the first ballot with 692 votes. Centrist New York Governor Nelson Rockefeller received only 277 votes that year, and Reagan received 182 votes—almost half from his favorite-son control of California's delegation. The remaining Reagan votes came from scattered delegates in the Sunbelt states, where Reagan's brand of conservative Republicanism was popular. Reagan declined to run for a third term as California's governor; instead, free of the encumbrances of running the state, he challenged President Gerald Ford for the Republican nomination in 1976. Reagan did well in the Sunbelt primaries, but lost the nomination by a slim margin of 117 votes of the 2,259 cast. Nevertheless, his conservative followers managed to dominate the platform-writing phase of the convention, saddling Ford with foreign policy planks that repudiated the initiatives of Secretary of State Henry Kissinger, particularly his attempts at détente with the Soviet Union.

In 1980 Reagan made his third try for the Republican presidential nomination. He defeated George Bush handily, receiving more than 7.7 million votes in presidential primaries, to Bush's nearly 3 million and John Anderson's approximately 1.6 million. In all, Reagan won 60.8 percent of the primary vote. At the nominating convention held in Detroit, Reagan tried to get ex-president Gerald Ford to join the ticket, but Ford insisted on a novel "co-presidency" arrangement that would have given the vice president independent authority in foreign affairs. Reagan rejected the idea and instead put Bush on the ticket. In a three-candidate contest (John Anderson ran as an independent), Reagan won 44 states with 489 votes in the electoral college. In popular votes he won a majority over incumbent president Jimmy Carter, gaining 43.9 million votes (50.7 percent) to Carter's 35.5 million (41 percent), and Anderson's 5.7 million (6.6 percent). The election itself did not mobilize a large electorate: 52.6 percent of voting-age Americans turned out, and Reagan received the support of only 26.7 percent of the voting age population—hardly a popular mandate.

Although the Democrats retained control of the House in the 97th Congress (242 to 192), Reagan's victory coincided with a 33-seat Republican gain. His coattails may

have added 2 percent to the Republican column. In 134 districts, however, the winning Republican had more votes than Reagan did, and in 149 districts, the Republican had a larger percentage of the two-party vote. Total votes for the 192 Republicans in the House topped 24.9 million compared with the 22.6 million cast for Reagan in these districts—any coattails that existed clearly belonged to the congressional party, not to Reagan. The pattern was not so clear in the upper house. Republicans gained 12 seats to capture the Senate (53 to 46, with one independent) and would control it for the first time since 1956. Many of the newly elected senators were conservatives who did ride to victory on Reagan's coattails; only eight of the Republican senators received more votes than did Reagan.

Given the workings of the seniority system in the Senate, the results were not necessarily advantageous to Reagan. The party leaders were moderates, including Senate Majority Leader Howard Baker. Newly installed chairs of many committees, including Charles Percy of Illinois, Richard Lugar of Indiana, and Robert Dole of Kansas, were as moderate as the Democrats they replaced and were not inclined to move a highly divisive ideological agenda. Reagan entered the White House without a conservative mandate from the election, with a moderate Republican Senate inclined to forge a centrist coalition with Democrats, and with a House of Representatives controlled by liberal Northern Democrats. Reagan's prospects for a successful presidency seemed to depend on the answers to two questions: Could he gain enough influence in Congress to pass a conservative economic and social agenda and gain congressional acquiescence for his foreign policy initiatives, and could he win a realigning election in his second term that would finally make the Republicans the majority party in the nation?

## REAGAN AS A REALIGNING PRESIDENT
Did Reagan finally put an end to liberal and centrist government policies by putting an end to the post–New Deal political coalitions

of the period from 1960 to 1980? There is no definitive answer to this question. Counting his presidency, only four occupants of the Oval Office in the twentieth century had served two full terms or more; the other three were Woodrow Wilson, Franklin Roosevelt, and Dwight Eisenhower. Of these, only Reagan turned over his office to a successor of the same party in the next election after finishing his term (though Roosevelt might have done so had he not died in office). Reagan was an extraordinary politician, and his own electoral successes put him in extraordinary political company.

But Reagan did not realign Congress to create a conservative majority. He won a personal, not a party, victory in 1980. The percentage of House seats involved in split-party results (president from one party, representative from another) in that year, was 32.8, a figure exceeded only once by a Republican presidential victory—Nixon's 44.1 percent in 1972. In 1980, most Democratic voters were still splitting their tickets, not changing their party identifications when they voted for Reagan. In the first midterm election of 1982, Republicans picked up another Senate seat (but their margin decreased by one in the next presidential election). In the House, Democrats kept control in midterm (269 to 166). In 1984, as with almost all presidents who first came into power in a three-candidate race, Reagan reinforced his personal victory with a second-term landslide. He won with 59 percent of the vote over Walter Mondale, with 54.4 million popular votes to Mondale's 37.6 million. Reagan took the electoral college hands down, at 525 to 13. Had the nonvoters participated, his margin of victory would have been even higher.

In the 1986 midterm congressional elections, Democrats regained the Senate (55 to 45) and held control of the House (258 to 177). When Bush succeeded Reagan, Republicans had a lower percentage of seats in the House than at any time a Republican president had assumed office, with Democrats holding 260 and the Republicans 174. No president of either party had ever come

into office with so few seats controlled by his own party. Reagan had not been able to realign, except in the South. By 1989, when he left office, there were actually fewer Republican officeholders than in 1981.

There is a case to be made that Reagan was an important figure in a "rolling realignment" of party strength that had been occurring since the mid-1960s. Party identification changed during Reagan years. By the beginning of his second term, Republicans had drawn almost even with the Democrats (though not in formal party registration). In the South, Reagan's presidency coincided with a huge change in the party identification of white voters: from one-third Republican when Reagan took office to about two-thirds Republican when he left. Reagan was someone these voters could identify with—he himself had made the odyssey from New Deal Democrat to conservative Republican, and he spoke for many when he claimed, "I didn't leave the Democratic party; the party left me."

Reagan helped strengthen the Republican party organization. His extensive fundraising for the state parties raised millions of dollars and allowed them to install new media and computer technologies. He raised more than $9 million for the state parties in 1980 at "Unity Dinners." Reagan's appearances at congressional fundraisers in 1982 brought in $191 million, far more than the amount raised at their Democratic counterparts. The Republicans used those funds to develop coordinated polling, campaign management services, computerized links with national party headquarters, and a data base of large donors. In an election first, the party used teleconferences in 1982 and 1984 to link Reagan to top party donors to discuss upcoming elections and to appeal for funds. These organizational efforts did not result in increased electoral success in the 1980s, but one could argue that they laid the groundwork for the Republican successes of the mid-1990s.

Neither did Reagan realign the ideology of the American people. According to a New York Times/CBS poll, liberals comprised 20 percent of the public in 1981 and

21 percent when he left office in 1989. Conservatives comprised 33 percent in 1981 and 34 percent in 1989. These shifts are within the margin of error. The real drop in liberal support occurred after 1992, with a decline from 22 percent to 18 percent through 1995. In the same period, conservative support increased from 32 percent to 37 percent; it took a Democratic president, Bill Clinton, to preside over the ideological shift that had eluded Ronald Reagan.

## WAS THERE A REAGAN REVOLUTION?

"Government is not the solution to our problem," Reagan told the nation in his inaugural address, "government is the problem." Was there a Reagan revolution? Did Reagan, like Franklin Roosevelt, establish a new and durable political regime? Did he put an end to the New Deal regime? Did he drive a stake through the heart of liberalism—or merely nick it?

Reagan's presidency stands apart from others in the twentieth century because only Reagan attempted to make fundamental changes from the vantage point of a minority party in a system of split-party government. Reagan attempted to institute his program by forging a national consensus about values and general principles. He was the first president to use media politics to define "valence issues," the fundamental values of the nation. Reagan broke with the Eisenhower-Nixon consensus policies based on fiscal probity, cutbacks in defense spending, and more efficient delivery of social welfare programs by emphasizing consolidation and managerial reforms. Instead, he proposed to redefine the role of the national government altogether, a redefinition that would lead to tax cuts, a reduction in domestic social and regulatory programs, and a large defense build-up—in each instance, policies that his Republican predecessors had opposed.

At the core of Reagan's program was supply-side economics, known as Reaganomics. According to Reaganomics, government would provide incentives for producers to invest in plant, equipment, research and development, and a better trained work force. Given this impetus, the economy would grow, inflation would be reduced, and employment would increase as the benefits "trickled down" to the rest of the population. Reagan abandoned Democratic demand-side macroeconomic stimulus in favor of his supply-side approach. In doing so, he also abandoned Republican fiscal orthodoxy, which emphasized a balanced budget as the prime macroeconomic goal. In his first year in office, Reagan got Congress to pass the Economic Recovery Tax Act, a huge tax cut (the largest in U.S. history) that benefited large investors and businesses—$749 billion in cuts over five years. The Tax Reform Act of 1986 continued the cuts, this time in personal tax rates: fourteen tax brackets were reduced to three, rates were cut, and many tax breaks were eliminated. Large numbers of poor Americans were eliminated from tax rolls altogether, and the earned-income tax credit redistributed income to the working poor. The Reagan tax cuts reduced taxes as a percentage of the gross national product from 20.1 percent when he took office to 19.4 percent. This was not much of a drop, but it was a revolutionary change of direction.

There is considerable controversy among economists over how much additional investment was stimulated by these cuts. Some argue that there was a great deal of new investment in technologically advanced industries, which bore fruit within the decade with extensive plant modernization. Others argue that the investments followed the economic recovery and were led by demand. But there is no doubt about the social consequences: Between 1981 and 1989 the wealthiest 1 percent of the population had its taxes lowered by almost one-quarter, and the wealthiest fifth had its taxes decreased more than 4 percent. During this same period, rises in Social Security levies (enacted in the Social Security Act Amendments of 1983) increased the taxes of the poorest fifth of the population by 2.6 percent, and of the middle fifth by 3.6 percent. Under Reaganomics, the wealthiest Americans increased their incomes, partly from the tax cuts and partly because of income received from corporate dividends and capital gains. The economy boomed for these wealthy individuals: The top 1 percent saw their real income (adjusted for inflation) rise by 80 percent and the wealthiest fifth saw a rise of almost 30 percent. In contrast, the poorest fifth had their incomes decline by 11.8 percent, continuing a trend that had started in the late 1970s and continued into the mid-1990s of declining wages for less-skilled and less-educated workers. Very little actually trickled down during the Reagan years. Between 1983 and 1989, the top 1 percent gained 62 percent of newly created wealth. The United States was on its way to greater class polarization, as the rich got richer while wages and benefits for American workers stagnated or declined.

To balance the tax cuts, Reagan proposed massive spending cuts in domestic programs. His first budget called for spending reductions of $130 billion in three years, with $42 billion proposed for the first year. Instead of submitting his 223 specific domestic program proposals piecemeal to the congressional committees controlled by House Democrats, Reagan proposed that Congress vote on the entire package in the spring, in an "early reconciliation" bill. Reagan wanted an early vote to capitalize on his popularity, which had soared following his successful recovery from a gunshot wound caused by an assassination attempt on 30 March 1981. He also wanted a vote on the entire package because that would focus the nation's attention on the single budget figure rather than the individual program cuts. If the Democrats had had their way, each program would have been voted on separately.

To get the vote for early reconciliation on the entire budget, Reagan had to win a majority vote in each chamber to change the rules for voting on bills. He knew that the Senate, controlled by his own party, would not be a problem, but he was unsure of winning in the House. He therefore wooed conservative Democrats, mostly from the South, promising that if they voted both for the rules changes and for his tax and spending package, he would not campaign on be-

half of Republicans running against them in the 1982 midterm elections. Using a combination of carrot and stick, Reagan induced sixty-three Democrats to defect and he retained the votes of every single Republican. The key votes took place in late spring, just after Reagan made a nationwide address. Just prior to the votes, a Gallup poll indicated that 68 percent of the public approved of Reagan's handling of the presidency and 58 percent approved of his economic plans. Given Reagan's mastery of public opinion, the conservative coalition in Congress enacted the Gramm-Latta II cuts of $35.2 billion for the first year.

## REAGANOMICS AND THE ECONOMY OF THE 1980s

Reaganomics initially led to a sharp recession, but beginning in 1983 Reagan's policies either ignited or coincided with one of the greatest booms in American history. Under Reagan the gross national product rose by almost one-quarter in the longest sustained period of expansion in American history. Inflation was cut from double digits under Carter to a negligible rate, inaugurating a period of price stability that benefited families at all income levels, particularly the elderly on fixed incomes. The economy produced millions of new jobs, particularly in the high-technology and service industries. Under Reagan the nature of job-creation changed; small companies and individual entrepreneurs, many of them women, created the new jobs, rather than large corporations, which began to downsize.

But there were several problems with Reaganomics. First, the president had promised that increased revenues from the economic expansion would result in a balanced budget. These forecasts turned out to be preposterous and involved manipulation of data by Reagan's budget director David Stockman when the initial projections indicated deficits would continue. By 1984 Reagan promised the budget would be in balance during his second term. In 1988 he predicted a balanced budget by 1991. In fact, the increase in defense spending and tax cuts in the Reagan program accounted for $1.5 trillion of deficits in his two terms, while the failure to reign in the "uncontrollable" spending on medical care and other programs accounted for most of the other $1.5 trillion in accumulated deficits over his two terms. Reagan did not reduce the size of government spending as a percentage of GNP, which actually rose fractionally from 22.7 to 22.8 percent. Fiscal policy remained out of balance. By the end of the Reagan presidency, the total debt of the United States had gone from $1 trillion to more than $3 trillion and remained out of control. The debt ballooned because the tax cuts did not generate the additional revenues that supply-side economists had initially forecast. These tax cuts proved politically advantageous to the president, but they saddled future generations with an enormous interest burden.

The high domestic deficit "crowded out" some domestic investment. The Treasury and the monetary authorities kept interest rates high enough to attract foreign investment, and until 1986 they also propped up the value of the dollar against foreign currencies. The result of this combination of macroeconomic and monetary policies was disastrous for American exporters. In part because of increasing price differentials, the United States began to run a large merchandise trade imbalance, which zoomed from $20 billion at the end of Carter's presidency into the $150 billion range during Reagan's. Moreover, the United States had consistently invested more in other nations than other countries had invested in the United States; in the Reagan years the situation reversed itself, and the United States became a net debtor for the first time since 1917. The "hollowing out" of the American industrial base continued during the Reagan years, with millions of industrial workers losing their jobs or facing reductions in pay and benefits.

A deregulation of financial institutions sponsored by a Democratic Congress near the end of Reagan's presidency allowed savings and loans associations to make questionable loans, particularly in real estate.

Reaganomics was partly to blame for the ensuing debacle, which began after the stock market crashed in 1987 and a speculative bubble in stocks and real estate burst. More than 200 banks and 200 savings and loans associations failed. By 1989 the Bush administration, in attempting to clean up the mess, had to place 318 savings and loans in conservatorships. The overall cost to taxpayers for the S&L reorganization was more than $100 billion.

The Reagan spending cuts had an enormous impact on the role of the national government, with outlays for discretionary domestic programs falling from 5.7 percent of the gross national product to 3.7 percent. In 1981, the federal programs provided one-quarter of the funds for state and local government programs; by 1989, that figure had declined to 18 percent. The Reagan administration made a sharp distinction between a "safety net" for the poor, which it pledged would be maintained, and provision of services or cash payments that it considered excessive, which it intended to cut or eliminate. "We will continue to fulfill our obligations that spring from our national conscience," Reagan told Congress in his first budget proposals in 1981. "Those who through no fault of their own must depend on the rest of us, the poverty-stricken, the disabled, the elderly, all those with true need, can rest assured that the social safety net of programs they depend on are exempt from any cuts."

In practice, few programs were spared. Reagan used the language of "reforming programs" to make severe cuts in the safety net programs, as the Office of Management and Budget took aim at people in families whose income exceeded 150 percent of the poverty level—a group that, according to government figures, was receiving 44 percent of the Medicaid funds and 14.2 percent of the welfare payments. These households, comprising 12.7 million people, were made ineligible for many programs. Funds for inner-city public housing were slashed, and the rent charged for the 2.4 million families living in public housing was increased from 25 to 30 percent of their income. Hundreds of thousands of homeless appeared in the streets, to be cared for in emergency shelters and fed in soup kitchens not seen since the Great Depression. There were cuts in funds for medical clinics for the poor, with more than 700,000 low-income children losing free health care because their family's income was just over the poverty line. For the same reason, more than 725,000 persons lost the services of community mental health centers. Rules were tightened for receiving food stamps, eliminating 21 percent of those receiving aid. More than 3.5 million children, including hundreds of thousands of low-income children, were made ineligible for school nutrition programs. Welfare payments and food-stamp allowances failed to keep up with inflation. Almost 500,000 children whose mothers held low-paying jobs lost some or all of their welfare benefits after the administration got Congress to repeal a 1969 law that had let welfare recipients keep the first $30 earned each month and one-third of any additional monthly wages.

For the first time since the 1960s, the absolute number as well as the percentage of poor people in the United States increased. During the Reagan years, more than 17 percent of American children were born into poverty, a rate higher than that of eleven other industrialized nations. In consequence, infant mortality rates increased: American children were more likely to die before their first birthday than were children in ten other industrial nations.

Reaganomics was conservative in ideology and partisan in execution. It benefited wealthier Republicans at the expense of the poorest Democrats. It favored geographic areas growing in the Sunbelt at the expense of urban areas in the Northeast. It benefited the politically organized at the top of American society, primarily at the expense of the unorganized and disorganized at the bottom. By the end of Reagan's first term, the Urban Institute concluded that cuts in benefit payments and other programs disproportionately affected those below the average income level, with programs benefiting the poor and working poor cut the

most, while programs and payments for the middle class were affected least. Overall, the Congressional Budget Office estimated that families with incomes below $10,000 lost $23 billion in after-tax income and benefits between 1981 and 1983, while families with incomes above $80,000 gained about $35 billion, primarily in tax benefits. In a television address on behalf of Barry Goldwater in 1964, Reagan had warned Americans that "the real destroyer of the liberties of the people is he who spreads among them bounties, donations, and benefits." Yet, that is just what Reagan had done, and even his budget director David Stockman was appalled at all the loopholes involving oil leases, real estate tax shelters, and corporate taxes. Stockman remarked in his postmortem of Reaganomics that "the greed level, the level of opportunism, just got out of control."

Most of Reaganomics was enacted in the first two years of the Reagan presidency. It would be a mistake to assume that for the remainder of his term Reagan was able to dominate fiscal policymaking or the budget process. By the fall of his first year he submitted a proposal for cuts in Social Security, and his measure was soundly defeated in the Senate, 98 to 2. After his first year, his budget proposals were usually pronounced "dead on arrival" on Capitol Hill.

## THE SOCIAL AGENDA

Although Reagan had been divorced, was not a regular church-goer, and had difficult relationships with his children, the president took conservative "pro-family" positions on all the divisive issues of social policy. He opposed passage of the Equal Rights Amendment to the Constitution, claiming it would weaken the family, and its seven-year time period for passage expired in 1982. He supported a constitutional amendment to permit prayer in the public schools, although he never pushed hard for it in Congress. At both the 1980 and 1984 Republican presidential nominating conventions, his followers inserted language in the party platform opposing *Roe v. Wade* (the 1973 Supreme Court decision that recognized a constitutional right to abortion), and his Department of Justice was sympathetic in court cases to state laws limiting abortion rights. Reagan's administration, like Nixon's before it, opposed busing to overcome racial segregation in public schools caused by prior state action, claiming that it would weaken neighborhood schools. It opposed affirmative action programs to end the past effects of discrimination against women and minorities, and the Justice Department filed friend-of-the-court briefs appealing federal court decisions upholding city hiring practices that involved racial targets, claiming that government action based on racial classifications violated the Fourteenth Amendment. When Congress passed the Civil Rights Restoration Act of 1988, a law requiring that all programs run by institutions receiving federal funds bar discrimination, Reagan vetoed the measure, which Congress then passed over his veto.

## LEGISLATIVE LEADERSHIP

Except in his first two years, Reagan was not an effective legislative leader, whether compared with his Republican contemporaries or their Democratic counterparts. His economic proposals were modified, his budgets were ignored, and his proposals for administrative reforms side-tracked. In his second term, during the Iran-Contra scandal, his support scores were lower than in any presidency since Eisenhower's.

In the House, although he had the support of a majority of Republicans, Reagan got less support from them on party-line votes than Nixon or Eisenhower had gotten, in large measure because his conservative agenda alienated party moderates. Most of his conservative programs were blocked or heavily amended by Democratic liberals and Republican defectors. In the Senate, Reagan could sometimes forge a bipartisan group to pass compromises based on his proposals, but that meant ignoring or selling out his most conservative (and recently elected) followers. Many of those new legislators would be defeated in the 1986 contests, giving the Democrats back control of the Senate. Until Reagan's presi-

dency, the number of major measures passed by Congress had been steadily climbing since Eisenhower. But a big plunge took place with Reagan: He got sixteen significant laws passed in his first term, compared with twenty-two for Carter, thirty-eight for Nixon, and thirty-eight for Johnson—only one more than Eisenhower's fifteen in his first term. In his second term, Reagan got twenty-one important measures passed, compared with thirty-six for the Nixon-Ford years, and sixteen for Eisenhower's second term.

When Reagan introduced his program, his opponents won their way by refashioning almost one-quarter of them. On almost a quarter more, there was no action. The president won a little over one-quarter, and in one-quarter a stalemate eventually gave way to a policy compromise. This record stands in sharp contrast to the greater successes of Nixon and Eisenhower, but it must be remembered that Reagan was not a centrist and did not introduce measures that a bipartisan centrist coalition would support. In contrast, according to studies by political scientist David Mayhew, Eisenhower had a consensus 31 percent of the time, dominated Congress 19 percent, compromised 17 percent, while his opponents won only 17 percent of the time. Nixon dominated only 5 percent, but found consensus 18 percent of the time, and compromised 23 percent. Nixon's opponents defeated him on only 13 percent of his initiatives, though there was considerable inaction on 41 percent of his program.

## RESHAPING THE JUDICIARY

Reagan's most enduring domestic legacy may well have involved promoting an ideological change in the federal judiciary—he appointed almost half of all sitting federal judges during his two terms. Reagan ended the practice used by Nixon, Ford, and Carter of permitting the American Bar Association to screen potential nominees; instead, he permitted screening only of announced nominees. Most of his nominees were white men, reversing Carter's emphasis on appointing more women and minorities.

Reagan abolished the panels Carter had established in each judicial district to identify potential female and minority nominees. (Reagan appointed more women, but fewer minorities, than Nixon and Ford had done.) Reagan created an Office of Legal Policy within the Justice Department to screen candidates. It used questionnaires on judicial philosophy and personal interviews to identify conservatives and those who favored judicial restraint. The president's committee on federal judicial selection, consisting of White House counsel, the attorney general, and the White House chief of staff, made the final recommendations to Reagan. Key conservative thinkers such as Richard Posner, Robert Bork, and Ralph Winter were put on the courts of appeal, and Reagan gained a conservative majority on the important Court of Appeals for the District of Columbia, which hears a majority of cases testing the validity of federal legislation.

He named William Rehnquist as chief justice of the United States in 1986 and put conservative Antonin Scalia onto the Court. But Sandra Day O'Connor, his first appointment to the Supreme Court (and the first woman ever to be appointed to the Court), kept conservatives from dominating by helping to fashion a centrist coalition that maintained most of the important precedents involving civil rights, abortion rights, and criminal law that had been established by the Warren and Burger Courts from the 1950s through the 1970s.

Nevertheless, Reagan kept trying for an ideological majority. He nominated Robert Bork, who failed to win nomination because of the bitter opposition in the Senate by liberals such as Joseph Biden and Edward Kennedy, who questioned Bork's judicial ideology and argued that the president should keep the Court in ideological balance. Reagan then nominated Douglas Ginsburg, another conservative, though without Bork's distinguished credentials. Ginsburg had to withdraw after admitting that he had smoked marijuana in law school. Finally Reagan nominated Anthony Kennedy, a noncontroversial moderate conservative who initially was disinclined to overturn precedent. Yet Reagan did lay the groundwork for a conservative majority on the Supreme Court, one that would move more aggressively in the Bush and Clinton years to overturn prior Warren and Burger court rulings in civil rights and criminal procedure, as well as the settled law of federalism established during the New Deal.

## DEFENSE BUILD-UP AND WAR POWERS

Reagan came to power intent on reversing what he believed to be a decline in U.S. military power. He proposed a three-year, 27 percent increase in defense spending, primarily for advanced new weapons systems and increased preparedness. Over his eight years in office, military spending increased from 5.3 percent to 6.4 percent of the GNP, at a time when GNP was growing rapidly. His "arm to parley" approach to the Cold War involved a massive build-up in strategic and tactical nuclear weapons. These included introduction of the Pershing II intermediate-range nuclear missile for Europe, development of the cruise missile, the MX intercontinental ballistic missile, and the B-1 bomber. Reagan accelerated development on neutron bombs and authorized production of 8,500 new nuclear warheads. He planned the deployment of 4,000 warheads for air-launched cruise missiles, and 1,000 new warheads for sea-launched missiles.

Although this was a huge build-up, Reagan provided less than what the joint chiefs of staff had called for. Reagan planned 16 divisions for the army; the joint chiefs had asked for 23. He authorized 15 carrier groups; the chiefs had asked for 24. And he planned 27 air force wings; the chiefs had proposed 44. During his first term, Reagan authorized construction for a 600-ship navy and for massive airlift capabilities that would project greater U.S. power farther and more quickly than at any time in U.S. history. Was Reagan's defense build-up a departure from existing plans? Carter had also authorized more defense spending and new weapons systems, but his proposed build-up would have occurred somewhat more slowly, and the overall spending target as of 1985 was $60 billion more annually under Reagan than had been projected by Carter.

Reagan used military force in a number of situations, but never when they involved the potential for a U.S.-Soviet confrontation. The administration followed the Weinberger Doctrine (developed by Secretary of Defense Caspar Weinberger and his military aide Colin Powell), which built on the lessons learned from Vietnam. The Pentagon's guidelines for the use of military force eschewed signaling diplomatic resolve or gradual escalation, and instead emphasized defining and following clear-cut military objectives, maintaining public and congressional support, and using overwhelming force to achieve the objectives and avoid getting bogged down. When military operations did not conform to these guidelines, or when they began to fail, Reagan had no hesitation in ending a mission and cutting his losses.

Reagan inserted a peace-keeping force in Lebanon in 1982 to disengage the Israeli army and the Palestine Liberation Organization forces in Beirut. Then he kept a marine force in Lebanon to prop up its pro-Western government against a coalition of militias backed by Syria. Although Reagan claimed that the forces were necessary to maintain the West's position in the Middle East, he withdrew the forces shortly after terrorists blew up a Marine Corps barracks, killing 250 troops. By doing so, he avoided not only a quagmire with further casualties but also congressional action to force a withdrawal.

Just prior to the bombing of the barracks in Lebanon, Reagan had diverted a carrier task force headed toward Lebanon and had ordered it to proceed to the island of Grenada, where fighting had erupted. A procommunist regime had split into two factions, and a military coup was in process. In a few days, using the presence of American medical students on the island as a pre-

text, U.S. forces invaded and installed a pro-American government. Reagan's popularity soared. The contrast between the open-ended and unpopular commitment of forces in Lebanon, which drained Reagan's political capital, and the successful and popular Grenada operation, was not lost on the administration. It remained leery of peace-keeping operations but willing to engage in low-risk, high-reward confrontations.

In 1986 Reagan took military action against Libya because it had sponsored a terrorist action that cost the lives of American soldiers stationed in West Germany. Reagan ordered navy and air force planes to mount bombing raids. One of the targets was Libya's mercurial leader Muammar Qaddafi; the bombs missed him but injured one of his children. Congress and the American public strongly supported the raids, which seemed to diminish Libyan terrorist activities.

In 1987, the war between Iraq and Iran spilled over, affecting neutral shipping in the Persian Gulf. The United States had tilted toward Iraq in this conflict and was supplying that country with intelligence information, food, weapons, and advanced communications technology. The Reagan administration therefore decided to protect the shipping lanes against Iranian attempts to blockade Iraq and Kuwait (a transit point for goods to Iraq). Kuwait asked the United States to convoy its tankers, and the administration agreed to do so if the ships were registered as American-flag ships. In several minor engagements, Iranian patrol boats were sunk and oil rigs were destroyed. Again, Reagan benefited from a rally-round-the-flag effect.

In none of these uses of the armed forces did Reagan consult beforehand with Congress, as required by the War Powers Act of 1973. Like Ford and Carter, Reagan neither followed the provisions of that resolution nor recognized its constitutionality. Nevertheless, Reagan was prepared to compromise with Congress to gain support for his military ventures. The War Powers Act, passed in the aftershock of the Vietnam War, requires the president to withdraw troops after sixty days unless Congress has authorized the engagement. After his peacekeeping force had been in Lebanon for almost a year and had suffered casualties from sniping and shelling, Congress and Reagan reached an agreement about continuing the mission. Congress passed a resolution to continue the mission, and Reagan agreed to sign the authorization, for the first time seemingly recognizing the constitutionality of the act. But he issued a "signing statement" declaring that Congress could not use the act to restrict or regulate his powers as commander in chief. Congress again invoked the War Powers Act after the invasion of Grenada, passing a resolution calling on Reagan to issue a report about the invasion and follow all procedures of the act. But the immediate success of the operation and its strong public support kept Congress from pushing its requests. By the third day of the Grenada invasion, Republicans and Democrats alike were applauding the president for evacuating the medical students and restoring peace on the island, and all talk of using the act ended.

Congress made no attempt to invoke the War Powers Act when Reagan bombed Libya. There was some complaint that the prior consultation with Congress on the use of force, as mandated by the act, occurred only while the planes were en route to their targets and was a briefing rather than a consultation. Nor did Congress attempt to invoke the act when Reagan provided navy escorts for reflagged Kuwaiti ships in the Gulf. Instead, opponents of the reflagging struck a deal with supporters in Congress: The legislature passed a nonbinding resolution supporting the president's actions and called for another vote either to authorize or to end the mission within a few months. All thoughts of the second vote faded once the mission was successful. By the time Reagan's presidency ended, both the administration and Congress considered the War Powers Act a dead letter. It is telling that its consultation procedures were not used either by President Bush during the Persian Gulf crisis or by Congress when it authorized hostilities against Iraq in 1991.

## PRESIDENTIAL DIPLOMACY

President Reagan laid out his foreign policy ideas in a speech at Notre Dame University in 1981, when he predicted that "the West will not contain communism; it will transcend communism." Reagan called communism "a sad, bizarre chapter in human history whose last pages are even now being written." Reagan had a clear vision about the current and future course of superpower relations and the eventual resolution of the Cold War. The West would put strong pressure on the Soviets in all areas, and eventually the Soviets would buckle under the pressure. He would negotiate with what he referred to as "the evil empire," but only from a position of strength, and he would always assume that the communist leaders could not be trusted to keep their word and must therefore be held to strict standards of verification.

Reagan's strategy went beyond traditional containment into the realm of hypercontainment. In his view, it was not enough simply to put military and diplomatic pressure on the Soviets to prevent them from expanding; rather, the West should impose relentless military pressure that could force communism to evolve or even collapse. The Soviets, Reagan believed, could not keep up with the West's economic growth or military technologies, and their efforts to do so would eventually force a crisis that their rulers would not be able to surmount. One aspect of his strategy involved the North American Treaty Organization (NATO): Reagan proposed to provide NATO with advanced nuclear ballistic and cruise missiles. Although the Soviets protested bitterly and mobilized an antinuclear movement in Western Europe, the missiles were deployed. The Soviets responded to the U.S. defense build-up by stockpiling their own new strategic weapons and deploying their next generation of missiles and submarines. In the end, Reagan was correct: They could not keep up with the West without grievously damaging their already fragile economy.

In 1985 Reagan embarked on summit diplomacy with the new Soviet leadership.

He had already been told by British Prime Minister Margaret Thatcher that Gorbachev was "someone we could deal with." Nevertheless, Reagan's Helsinki summit was a disaster. The Soviets asked Reagan to renounce his Star Wars program, which involved testing and eventually deploying an advanced antimissile defense against a surprise Soviet attack or attacks from rogue nuclear states or terrorists. The Soviets claimed that testing would violate provisions of the 1972 Anti-Ballistic Missile Treaty, a position Reagan's critics in the U.S. arms control community also took. Reagan refused to budge. He pressed Gorbachev on Poland, Nicaragua, Angola, and Afghanistan, and he asked if the Soviets were still seeking world domination. The exchanges between the two leaders grew intense, and the summit broke up with mutual recriminations. Negotiations did continue, however, and by the end of 1987 Reagan and Gorbachev had their first agreement, the Intermediate Nuclear Forces (INF) Treaty. Its provisions eliminated U.S. and Soviet intermediate nuclear weapons from Europe.

On regional issues, Reagan was determined to roll back Soviet gains in the 1970s. Covert aid to Afghanistan Muslim rebels enabled them within the decade to force a Soviet withdrawal. The leftist regime in Grenada was overthrown by direct U.S. military intervention. The U.S. discreetly encouraged Solidarity in Poland, the Protestant human rights movement in East Germany, Charter 77 in Czechoslovakia, and ethnic and nationalist movements throughout Eastern Europe. Aid to UNITA, a rebel movement in Angola, was resumed in 1986 to keep a pro-Soviet regime off balance.

## THE IRAN-CONTRA AFFAIR

In an attempt to free U.S. hostages held by pro-Iranian Shi'ites in Lebanon, President Reagan authorized the sale of weapons to Iran in an arms-for-hostages deal. The arms included three shipments of American-made weapons from Israel in 1985, and four shipments of weapons from the U.S. Defense Logistics Agency in 1986. The Central Intelligence Agency sold the weapons to arms dealers operating at the behest of the U.S. government, and those dealers sold the arms to Iran at a profit of over $15 million. On orders from Colonel Oliver North, a staffer at the National Security Council (NSC), more than $3.5 million of these residual profits were transferred to Nicaraguan counterrevolutionaries—the Contras—for use in a guerrilla war against the leftist Sandinista government. Reagan authorized the sales to Iran as an intelligence operation, in spite of grave doubts from his secretaries of defense and state. The sales were kept secret from the American public and from Congress.

The sale of weapons to Iran violated provisions of the Intelligence Oversight Act of 1980 requiring prior congressional notification of such activities. The operation remained covert because the overt policy of the U.S. government was to deny arms to Iran as a terrorist nation. The arms sales violated Executive Order 12333, promulgated by Reagan himself, which limited execution of covert operations to the CIA. They also violated a number of export licensing and arms export laws, and they violated laws requiring that funds received or controlled by U.S. officials must be transmitted to the Treasury Department. The diversion of funds to the Nicaraguan contras took place after Congress had passed the Boland Amendment to a defense appropriation act and had prohibited the CIA, Defense Department, "or any other agency or entity of the United States involved in intelligence activities" from supporting the Contras, either directly or indirectly. The NSC staff was, according to Executive Order 12333, the "highest intelligence entity" of the U.S. government.

On 3 November 1986, *As Shiraa*, a pro-Iranian news magazine in Beirut, broke the story of the arms sales. At first the White House denied everything, but as the revelations continued, the administration suggested it was an Israeli operation. Then President Reagan claimed only a small number of weapons had been transferred.

Finally, Reagan ordered Attorney General Meese to conduct an investigation. Reagan also appointed a commission headed by Senator John Tower to study improvements in national security policymaking. Reagan accepted the resignations of his national security adviser and of Oliver North, and his new aides implemented recommendations of the Tower Commission. These included dissolving the political–military affairs directorate of the National Security Council (which developed operational plans for covert operations), encouraging full debate on national security matters by the affected departments, and making the national security adviser a "custodian-manager" of policy proposals rather than an advocate or operations manager. Finally, Reagan announced a "double-safe" briefing method: When the national security adviser briefed the president, the White House chief of staff would be present; when the secretaries of state or defense met with the president, the national security adviser and White House chief of staff would attend.

The Iran-Contra affair deeply affected the second part of Reagan's second term. Both the policy and its cover-up cast grave doubts on the authority of the president to conduct a coherent foreign policy. Chief of Staff Donald Regan resigned and was replaced by Howard Baker, who as former leader of the Republicans in the Senate had the confidence of Congress. Reagan was deeply despondent for about a year and held no news conferences; meanwhile, his popularity plummeted more than 20 points, from the low 60s into the high 30s. The administration remained preoccupied while Congress conducted investigations and an independent counsel began preparations to try a number of senior aides. Policy initiatives were stalled, and the president's program languished in Congress. Once it became clear that there was no direct evidence tying Reagan to the diversion of funds to the Contras, Democrats in Congress turned their attention from Reagan to his aides and the arms dealers. Reagan gradually regained his popularity, but there were

few major initiatives during the remainder of his term.

## REAGAN'S GOVERNING STYLE

Many presidential scholars have viewed Reagan as lazy and inattentive, an intellectual lightweight who did not do his homework and who was easily manipulated by his aides. Yet officials such as Edwin Meese, Martin Anderson, Richard Pipes, and Oliver North claimed that Reagan worked hard, was attentive and knowledgeable, and was clearly in command. Although the Tower Commission seemed to hold the former view, transcripts of Reagan's comments at meetings discussing the sale of arms to Iran or the negotiations with the Soviets indicate that Reagan played an important role in discussions and was the decision maker in foreign policy. When there were serious disagreements among senior aides, Reagan made the final decision, and it always reflected his own priorities and values.

Reagan kept on his desk a plaque that said, "There's no limit to what you can do if you don't mind who gets the credit." He was willing to delegate great responsibility. His staff structure was detailed in theory but amorphous in practice, and there was a great deal of freelancing, lots of rivalries, and an extraordinary amount of backbiting, even by White House standards. "I believe that you surround yourself with the best people you can find, delegate authority, and don't interfere as long as the overall policy that you've decided upon is being carried out," Reagan told a reporter for *Fortune Magazine*. But his approach went beyond delegation: Reagan waited for people to bring things to him, and he almost never took the initiative. He was an innovative political campaigner, but once in the Oval Office he functioned as chief magistrate rather than chief executive.

To the public, the entire question of how involved Reagan was in running the government seemed beside the point. A large majority thought he had good judgment under pressure, except in the Iran-Contra affair. Although many Americans initially were afraid that Reagan would lead the nation into war, he dissipated that fear within his first two years in office, and voters gave Reagan credit for restoring respect for America abroad. Voters approved of his policies on budgets and national defense, and they generally supported his proposals for domestic cuts in social programs, though not in Social Security or Medicare. They gave him high marks for controlling inflation and for lowering taxes, and they blamed prior Democratic administrations for the country's economic problems, particularly the budget deficits. The public followed Reagan and, above all, recognized that he had brought a new spirit to the nation. They thought things were going in the right direction, that they personally were becoming better off, and that things would continue to improve throughout Reagan's term. *Public Opinion* magazine's gross national spirit index rose substantially—if erratically—during Reagan's two terms.

Reagan was called the "Great Communicator" by his aides, because of his early command of public opinion on key issues. His opponents called him the "Teflon president," in recognition that their sharp criticism of his performance was not sticking. Reagan preferred to think of himself as a latter-day Franklin Roosevelt: He would provide vigorous presidential leadership of party and public opinion for great purposes. And in many ways they were similar. A majority of the public could identify major national priorities with Reagan, and his performance in this area was matched by only one prior president—FDR. Reagan was a master at public rhetoric, perhaps a legacy of his Hollywood days. He could communicate his policies through simple slogans and ideas, dramatic anecdotes, and revealing metaphors that would resonate around the kitchen table. Like FDR, Reagan exuded confidence in himself and confidence in the American people—a welcome contrast from Carter, who seemed to struggle under the burdens of the office, and whose speeches seemed to blame the malaise of American society for the worsening economic problems.

Reagan and his aides made many innovations in American governance. His budget successes in 1981 occurred because he was able to invert the entire budget process through "early reconciliation," an approach later used with some success by President Clinton in his first year in office. He created the system in which the Office of Management and Budget had regulatory clearance for agency rules and regulations, and he required agencies to justify their proposals through cost-benefit analysis. Reagan established cabinet councils through which new proposals and initiatives would be funneled so that White House domestic policy aides could control initiatives coming from the departments. Reagan also initiated the signing statement, whereby he could claim that his interpretation of any law he signed should be the authoritative legislative history that federal courts should use for statutory interpretation.

Reagan gained more control over the permanent government—the bureaucratic structure—than any of his predecessors had exercised. In his first term, he filled more than 850 of the senior executive service positions with political appointees. With two-fifths of the senior executive personnel leaving in his first three years, Reagan was able to promote conservatives and cluster them in key agencies to ensure that his priorities were not hindered by lower-level bureaucratic resistance. Finally, Reagan developed the concept of "soft prerogative" constitutional claims. Unlike Nixon, who viewed as a direct challenge congressional attempts to develop framework legislation involving war powers, Reagan was willing to compromise with Congress and work within its statutory framework—all the while conceding nothing as to the constitutionality of the congressional statutes. George Bush would use the same "soft prerogative" approach in obtaining congressional authorization for the Persian Gulf War.

## REAGAN'S PLACE IN PRESIDENTIAL HISTORY

Reagan put an end to the New Deal paradigm of national government. He did so by returning to a traditional theme in U.S. history: Government is the problem, the governing establishment has grown unresponsive and bloated, and power must devolve back to the states and the people. Reagan liberated the Republican party from its eat-your-peas emphasis on balanced budgets and high taxes. He created a new version of politics based on old-fashioned values that overwhelmed the post–New Deal emphasis on programmatic politics. Reagan used rhetoric not so much to position himself along a liberal-conservative ideological dimension, but rather to soar above program politics: His language created a nostalgia for an American past that existed only in the movies, and it kindled an optimism about an American future that a majority of voters gratefully embraced.

When Reagan assumed office, the conventional wisdom in Washington was that presidents lacked the power to govern and that the imperial presidency—in which the president dominated the federal government—had given way to what Gerald Ford had called "the imperiled presidency." Since 1961, one president had been killed by an assassin, another booted out of office by his own party because of the Vietnam War, a third forced out by threat of impeachment, a fourth defeated in part for pardoning his predecessor, and a fifth defeated after a single term because of stagflation. Ronald Reagan was the first president since 1961 to complete two terms in office, and he was the first since Franklin Roosevelt to reorient his party around an ideological agenda. He began the process of making the Republicans the majority party in the nation. He gained much of his economic and domestic policy program in a single budget resolution and tax bill in his first year. He got his defense build-up, and his predictions about the course of the Cold War were vindicated (though experts differ on whether external pressure from the United States or internal contradictions within the Soviet system were primarily responsible for the implosion of the Soviet empire). Reagan retired from the White House as the most popular president since pollsters have taken measurements, with approval ratings topping 60 percent. Only the Twenty-Second Amendment prevented his supporters from trying to nominate him for a third term, and had he been nominated, he would almost certainly have won. During Reagan's two terms, at least, there was little talk of an imperiled presidency.

## BIBLIOGRAPHY

Anderson, Martin. *Revolution* (Harcourt, Brace, Jovanovich, 1988).

Cannon, Lou. *President Reagan: The Role of a Lifetime* (Simon & Schuster, 1991).

Draper, Theodore. *A Very Thin Line* (Hill and Wang, 1991).

Johnson, Haynes. *Sleepwalking Through History* (Norton, 1991).

Jones, Charles. ed. *The Reagan Legacy: Promise and Performance* (Chatham House, 1988).

Mayer, Jane, and Doyle McManus. *Landslide: The Unmaking of the President, 1984–1988* (Houghton Mifflin, 1988).

Reagan, Ronald. *An American Life* (Simon & Schuster, 1990).

———. *Speaking My Mind: Selected Speeches* (Simon & Schuster, 1989).

Regan, Donald T. *For the Record* (Harcourt, Brace, Jovanovich, 1988).

Schieffer, Bob. *The Acting President* (Dutton, 1989).

Schmertz, Eric J., Natalie Datlof, and Alexej Ugrinsky, eds. *Ronald Reagan's America* (Greenwood, 1996).

Shultz, George P. *Turmoil and Triumph: My Years as Secretary of State* (Macmillan, 1993).

Schweizer, Peter. *Victory: The Reagan Administration's Secret Strategy That Hastened the Collapse of the Soviet Union* (Atlantic Monthly Press, 1994).

Stockman, David *The Triumph of Politics* (Harper & Row, 1986).

Walsh, Lawrence E. *Iran-Contra: The Final Report* (Random House, 1994).

Wills, Garry. *Reagan's America: Innocents at Home* (Doubleday, 1987).

### ★★★ 41 ★★★

# GEORGE HERBERT WALKER BUSH
## 1989–1993

*Herbert S. Parmet*

*Born 12 June 1924 in Milton, Massachusetts, to Prescott Sheldon Bush and Dorothy Walker Bush; educated at Yale College, New Haven, Connecticut (B.A. 1948); married Barbara Pierce, 6 January 1945, Rye, New York; six children; elected president in 1988 with Dan Quayle of Indiana on the Republican ticket, receiving 48,881,278 popular votes and 426 electoral college ballots over the Democratic slate of Michael Stanley Dukakis of Massachusetts and Lloyd M. Bentsen, Jr., of Texas (41,805,374 votes and 111 electoral college ballots).*

Friends of Ronald Reagan feared from the outset that "the Gipper" had fumbled the ball by positioning George Bush to become the forty-first president. Bush was a "stranger," an outsider to "movement" conservatives—a Texan for the last four decades but still a Connecticut Yankee, a Republican from another generation and another culture.

George Bush, like his father before him, was an Episcopalian establishment man with family and ideological ties to a Republican party of the generation that honored Wendell Willkie, Robert Taft, and Dwight Eisenhower. He also fell into the internationalism of Theodore Roosevelt, Woodrow Wilson, and Henry L. Stimson. His Yale education, especially as an economics major, left him with few traces of populism. Bush's brand of conservatism, more fiscal than social, was also closer to the legacy of the Progressive and New Deal eras. Reaganites never got over how he had scoffed at the heart of their incipient revolution by dismissing supply-side theory as "voodoo economics."

## WINNING THE PRESIDENCY

George Bush carried both the assets and the liabilities of the Reagan presidency into the battle for his party's nomination in 1988. With the help of some deft political strategy, featuring an "air war" managed by media expert Roger Ailes and a "ground war" plotted by the youthful consultant Lee Atwater, he turned back all rivals. He then reached for the element of surprise by nominating as his running mate Senator J. Danforth Quayle of Indiana, a youthful conservative. Quayle's lack of preparation for the spotlight soon became obvious. Much more damaging in the long run was Bush's reiteration during his acceptance speech of a pledge he had made from the start of his candidacy. Following the advice of a speechwriter, he emphasized and further embellished the point with appropriate gestures: "The Congress will push me to raise taxes, and I'll say no. And they'll push, and I'll say no. And they'll push again, and I'll say to them, Read my lips: No new taxes." Given the role of taxes in recent presidential politics, especially in the aftermath of the climate created but artfully dodged by Reagan, the forceful statement was pleasing to the ears of right-wing Republicans. Less welcome, and later cited as a small heresy, was his call for a "kinder and gentler nation."

Bush found himself walking a tightrope between gaining credit as the successor to Reagan and suffering the liabilities for the administration's embarrassments—most notably, scandals and Bush's own involvement in the Iran-Contra affair. Constantly charging that the liberalism of the Great Society had failed, the Republican campaign tried to demonstrate that the Democratic candidate, Governor Michael Dukakis of Massachusetts, was an archetypal exponent of that repudiated ideology. They did so in part through the Willie Horton commercial.

While Dukakis was governor of Massachusetts, Willie Horton, a convicted murderer serving a life sentence, was granted a weekend furlough; during this brief period of freedom, Horton raped a woman and beat up her boyfriend. A widely used and often repeated Republican campaign commercial featured this story, illustrated by the menacing black face of Willie Horton, as a symbol of the monstrous consequences of uncontrolled social experimentation. The official Bush campaign commercials avoided suggestions of race; they depicted the "revolving-door justice" that conservatives had been using so effectively when throwing the crime issue at the feet of liberals. The widely seen television commercial that emphasized Horton's race was produced by independent filmmakers. "If ever there has been a distortion of fact or history," Bush complained nearly four years later, "it is making Willie Horton a race issue instead of a prison furlough issue." In the public mind, the two Horton ads merged into one, and localized Republican campaigns helped to fan the process of appealing to fear. By election day, Bush had overcome his 17-point deficit of late July. In a forty-state sweep, the Bush-Quayle ticket took 426 electoral votes and 53.4 percent of the popular vote.

## "HITTING THE GROUND CRAWLING"

Bush's independence became clear in the staffing of the new administration. Its basic composition consisted of an inner circle of long-standing Bush loyalists and an outer core of political veterans. Closest to Bush was his old friend from Texas, James Addison Baker III, who was also an experienced political tactician. Baker, who came closest to being Bush's alter ego, served him as secretary of state. Many of those who worked in the administration, including Baker and the adviser for national security affairs, General Brent Scowcroft, were veterans of the Ford White House. They confirmed Bush's preference for congenial advisers.

The most-asked question from early on was just what kind of president Bush would be, and he made it clear from the start that his term would not be "Reagan's third." "We're headed the right way," he told the nation, "but we cannot rest," and he outlined an array of desires from cutting the deficit to ending "barriers left by past discrimination," environmental controls (including a new Clean Air Act), child-care tax credits, and a one-year freeze in the military budget. He also called for balancing the budget, cutting the maximum tax rate on capital gains, and pursuing Reagan's Strategic Defense Initiative ("Star Wars").

Exactly what this all meant was not very clear, but to some Republican ears it sounded more like Rockefeller than like Reagan. Bush's critics began to complain about his lack of "vision" and about the absence of the easy-going rhetoric of the Reagan presidency. The new administration seemed to feel no urgency about compiling an impressive "first one hundred days" sense of action, but, explained Republican Minority Whip Newt Gingrich, such crash plans only provided a media scorecard of "what a liberal welfare state President would do." Bush was "hitting the ground crawling," complained critics. The index of the president's success rate for that first year, at least as measured by *Congressional Quarterly*, stood at 62.6 percent, the lowest since that publication began keeping score in 1953.

Bush's distaste for "inside baseball" combined with circumstances to weaken the administration's legislative record. Both houses of Congress were in the hands of the Democrats. Although Bush did establish good working relationships with such key opponents in the House as speaker Tom Foley and Ways and Means Chairman Dan Rostenkowski, he failed to do so with Senate Majority Leader George Mitchell. Even with the best working relationship, bold new initiatives would have been ruled out by the slim pickings left after the enormous budgetary deficits of the Reagan years. Taking note of the collapse of communism abroad and of the desired role of government at home, Bush said right after his swearing-in that "for the first time in this century, for the first time in perhaps all history, man does not have to invent a system by which to live."

The administration's stance vis-à-vis Congress began to resemble a veto strategy. Each side accused the other of creating a gridlock. Bush, in dealing with Democratic majorities, used his veto power forty-four times in all, killing legislation designed to achieve a wide array of policies on social, regulatory, tax, and spending issues. There was, in all this, just one congressional override of his veto, and that was on a bill to reregulate the cable television industry. He nevertheless compiled a low record of support from the Democratic Congress.

His achievements, however, left much of the Republican right unimpressed. One notable achievement, in spite of critics on both sides of the aisle, was the Americans with Disabilities Act of 1990. Another, in keeping with the president's self-proclaimed role as an "environmental president," was an updated and improved Clean Air Act. Bush also pushed for a North Atlantic Free Trade Agreement (NAFTA), but that would not be achieved until Clinton's presidency. By far the most controversial aspect of Bush's domestic record was the 1990 budget agreement, which called for a budget reduction plan but, alas, also called for new taxes.

### THE BUDGET "DEAL"
The budget agreement became the administration's Achilles heel. Bush's optimistic pledge of no new taxes served him well at a time when the polls showed him seriously behind his opponent. Once in office, facing the realities of the budget, he was unable to deliver as promised. Years earlier, Reagan himself had attempted to ease the damage caused by his original sharp cuts in 1981. Although he was unable to mitigate the damage, Reagan's popularity enabled him to escape the political consequences of his program. That administration also managed to raise rates using various means other than directly taxing incomes—primarily with fees that affected the wealthy. The Gramm-Rudman-Hollings deficit-reduction

scheme passed during the Reagan years was proving itself inadequate in the face of additional budgetary obligations. The savings-and-loan scandals had also left the government with another enormous financial problem.

Against this background, Bush was confronted with the need to act with minimal political pain. The only possible solution was to have the White House become the moving force in opening a round of negotiations with bipartisan congressional leaders. The group, committed to secrecy and mutual dedication to their responsibility, agreed to accept the White House initiative only if the president openly acknowledged his abandonment of the tax pledge, which he did on 26 June. At that time, he also asked the public to pressure Congress to endorse the bipartisan plan. The final package, with a schedule for a five-year deficit-reduction plan, seemed a reasonable compromise. The president kept his commitment to the Democrats by taking the responsibility for going out front and telling the country that the agreement was "balanced" and "fair." He urged the public to recognize its importance to the nation's long-term interest by pressuring their representatives to support the deal.

It was at that point that Minority Whip Newt Gingrich abandoned ship, deciding that his own best interests lay in opposing the work of the negotiating team, of which he was a member. The arrangement as constituted could, by its very concept, withstand no defections, but he nevertheless tore it apart. With congressional elections coming up, Gingrich did not have to work hard to convince his colleagues to oppose the package. They embarrassed the president by resisting White House lobbying and rejecting the plan by a vote of 254 to 179. With the Republican defectors having chosen politics over constructive action, the Democrats were forced to go along with the antitax rebellion.

Bush's troubles on the domestic front were exacerbated by developments in the Middle East. Saddam Hussein had marched into Kuwait in 1990. The Persian Gulf cri-

sis and the consequent effect on national security obligations and the economic impact of the potential oil crisis only increased the seriousness of the budgetary situation. Placed in a desperate position, the president passed on the pressure to Congress. His refusal to sign a budget forced government to temporarily close many popular tourist facilities.

As a result of all this, legislative initiative passed to the majority Democrats, who shaped a revised deficit-reduction plan— this time, with an increase in income taxes. Although Bush had little choice but to sign the measure, his approval ratings plummeted, dropping between 10 and 19 points within a month. The agreement, which actually did its work in the next two years, remained an albatross around the neck of the man who had promised "no new taxes," and he later disavowed the deal as the biggest mistake he had made in office. Republican right-wingers were not about to grant absolution, especially when they concluded that what they had in the White House was worth sacrificing for ideological purity.

### "THE SIGNS OF A PRESIDENT IN TROUBLE"

Bush's more moderate conservatism became increasingly difficult to sustain. His newly acquired reputation as a racist in the aftermath of the Willie Horton issue rendered him suspect to liberals, and his budget deal placed him in an equally untenable position with the party's social conservatives. He seemed unable to please either faction. He vetoed civil rights legislation in 1990 by calling it a "quota bill," but in 1991— following controversies over his nomination of Clarence Thomas to the Supreme Court and over the "Republican" candidacy of a former Klansman, David Duke, as Louisiana's governor—Bush signed a version that barely differed from the original. "The scent of late Carterism is wafting from Pennsylvania Avenue," wrote Paul A. Gigot in the *Wall Street Journal*. "The floundering, the abandonment of principles like used clothes—these are the signs of a president in trouble."

The White House was not much better off a few months later when rioting broke out in Los Angeles over the acquittal of four policemen indicted for the beating of a black motorist, Rodney King. Personally revolted by the televised pictures of the clubbing of the apprehended man, and then agitated about the racially charged urban disorders, Bush was caught in legalistic, conservative indecision. He saw the matter as the problem of local government; jurisdiction belonged to the Los Angeles Police Department and its chief, Darryl Gates, whom Bush had met and respected. "You see blacks going after Asians," he noted. "What does that have to do with Rodney King? It has to do with the turmoil in the ghetto."

After being chided for his absence by H. Ross Perot, Bush finally made a personal tour of the area on a prescheduled trip to the city. As though to balance his act with his own political need, he carefully attributed the disturbances to the failure of the social programs of the 1960s. Bush, the social liberal on matters of race, too often seemed representative of an enlightenment that belonged to an even earlier decade. "If Reagan was a coach, then Bush is a manager. The former is a leader, the latter an administrator," wrote columnist Richard Cohen in the *Washington Post*.

## THE END OF THE COLD WAR

Richard Cohen's comments were perceptive. Bush came to the presidency as the Cold War was dissolving, with the Berlin Wall itself collapsing just ten months after his inaugural and the Soviet Union going out of business two years later. He finessed the transition with just the right touch, steering a fine course between overreaction and underreaction and resisting the demands of hotter heads to intervene when Russian troops were sent into the Baltics to restore order. There was no need, indeed it would be counterproductive, he held, to gloat in public over the plight of the disintegrating Soviet Union. He continued the arms control initiations already begun, meeting with Gorbachev on the island of Malta, at Camp David, and in Moscow in 1991.

In the summer of that year, within three weeks after he had left the Soviet capital, a rebellion led by Red Army reactionaries and the Communist party began a coup. Bush did not hesitate to back Gorbachev. With material assistance from President Boris Yeltsin of the Russian Republic and an uprising of citizens in response to his call, the conspirators were put down. The event only sped up change. By the end of the year, the Soviet Union ceased to exist. Sovereignty went to the independent republics. It was hard to fault the way the president and his secretary of state had responded to the crisis.

## VARIATIONS ON A THEME OF REALPOLITIK

Nobody had anticipated the magnitude of the change. Chinese students, inspired by Gorbachev's reforms and having begun a prodemocracy movement in the spring of 1989, confronted government tanks in Beijing's Tiananmen Square in June of 1991. The number of protesters shot or killed by the crushing communist forces is still unknown. Bush, deploring what had happened, suspended further military sales to the People's Republic of China. But the event was more of a signal to the world than a determinant of the administration's foreign policy. No more ready to forego the prospect of relations with Beijing than was Nixon before him, Bush dispatched General Brent Scowcroft and Lawrence Eagleburger on a secret mission to China. For Bush, so concerned with commerce and foreign trade, it was the clearest example of realpolitik. The trip, he knew, would "enrage the Democrats and the right-wing Republicans," but they could not allow him to isolate China.

Other developments were variations on that theme. In Nicaragua, Marxist Sandinistas under Daniel Ortega now were fighting without Soviet backing but were still holding out against the American-backed Contras. That government collapsed, with the new U.S. administration doing hardly anything except continuing its assistance. Ortega, fully expecting to prevail in a popular election, was stunned as Nicaraguans turned to the opposition under Violeta Barrios de Chamorro, finally bringing democratic rule to a key part of Central America. By then, Bush had also moved against Panama dictator Manuel Noriega. Noriega had long been used by U.S. intelligence as a conduit to all sides, including Castro's Cuba, but he was far less valuable with no continuing Soviet threat to the region. Operation Just Cause, undertaken after an abortive coup two months earlier that Bush had shied away from backing, dispatched army and marine troops to Panama, where, after some difficulty, Noriega was captured, taken to Miami, and imprisoned for drug dealing.

## THE GULF WAR

In the region of the Persian Gulf, U.S. policy had continued unchanged since the 1980s until the moment of Saddam Hussein's invasion of Kuwait on 2 August 1990. Arms sales and loans that had been part of pitting the Iraqi regime against Iran during their long war had continued even after the cease-fire, since keeping the government as a deterrent against the fundamentalist rulers in Tehran was just as important as before. The policy, however, had ignored Saddam's saber-rattling against both the United States and Israel.

The timing of the invasion of Kuwait introduced an additional element: Bush was caught at a moment of personal frustration, one of those times when presidential "power" seems most elusive. He was disappointed at the lack of progress during his recent meetings with Gorbachev. GOP right-wingers were not being shy about expressing doubts about his nomination of David Souter to the U.S. Supreme Court. Republican political fortunes had been going downhill of late, with some party leaders attributing the decline to the absence of Republican National Committee Chairman Lee Atwater, whose hospitalization for a brain tumor gave Bush additional personal distress. Would Atwater have advised jump-starting the budget negotiations

by publicly accepting the inevitability of new taxes? "If I didn't have this budget deficit problem hanging over my head," Bush dictated for his diary, "I would be loving this job." Considering, too, that the press was reveling in one of his son's getting caught up in the savings-and-loan scandals, it was "not a good time."

The invasion changed all that. "It's probably been the most hectic 48 hours since I have been President and in terms of national security interest," he noted. By the evening of 3 August, the president had been on the phone incessantly, forging a coalition that would be needed to overcome the hesitation of King Fahd of Saudi Arabia and Hosni Mubarak of Egypt. He found King Hussein of Jordan succumbing to the regional fear of the Iraqi dictator and, as Bush put it, "simply out there apologizing for Saddam Hussein and being almost a spokesman for him."

The president was clearly the administration's chief hawk. On 5 August, he told newsmen that "this will not stand." In acting as he did, he upheld all the lessons he had learned about internationalism. For a man who had put in time, albeit briefly, as ambassador to the United Nations during the Nixon presidency, avoiding the mistakes of the League of Nations and the period preceding World War II came easily, collective action readily. His goal for the commitment in the Middle East, however, was to avoid the disasters of either another Vietnam or appeasement, as he explained to the nation on 8 August. Not only was Saddam's aggression unacceptable, but his troops must be withdrawn. Occupation of Kuwait, which produced some 7 percent of the world's oil, also threatened Saudi Arabia, a much greater supplier, because Saddam's control of the lesser source would suffice to drive up prices on the world market.

Bush did not emphasize this reasoning in his announcement to the nation on 8 August. Instead, he made more general references to "security and stability," legitimacy, and protection of lives. At the outset, the president had directed that Iraqi and Kuwaiti assets in the United States be frozen; in response to the Bush initiatives, the United Nations now would impose economic sanctions on Iraq. General Norman Schwarzkopf was placed at the head of coalition forces in what was quickly named Operation Desert Shield. The original force was steadily upgraded to 550,000, although that number was not announced until after the midterm American elections in the United States.

The best evidence holds that Bush never believed sanctions alone would be sufficient to get Saddam out of Kuwait. The history of sanctions, like the history of economic boycotts in general, was not encouraging. Yet, sanctions and diplomacy were politic prerequisites to actually going to war. In November, the United Nations handed Iraq a deadline of 15 January for getting out of Kuwait. Vigorous public debate formed around the question of whether to continue with sanctions alone (and if so, for how long) or to take military action. To address the qualms about the "unseemliness" of "taking lives for oil," Bush stressed the moral principles behind international order. Especially notable was his comparing Saddam to Hitler, which evoked the "unconditional surrender" goal of World War II. In the long run, that goal would cause Bush trouble, but in the short run Bush's leadership was as persuasive with the American public as it was in building an international coalition. Saddam, it became clear, was going to be held to the deadline with or without congressional approval. Both houses consented, however, the Senate 52 to 47 and the House 250 to 183, largely along party lines.

On 17 January, a powerful air war was launched from sites and bases in the Persian Gulf and Turkey. Saddam, in a move blatantly calculated to pull Israel into the fighting and thereby alienate such Arab powers as Egypt, Syria, and Saudi Arabia from the coalition, responded by firing Scud missiles at the Jewish state. Israel's refusal to intervene was both a notable act of self-discipline by the government in Tel Aviv and a key diplomatic coup for Bush. To make "neutrality" at least politically acceptable, the ad-

ministration sent Israel defensive Patriot missiles, which were then given excessive credit for their value in deterring missile attacks. Bush's military success was sufficient for him to reject a peace plan worked out by Saddam with Mikhail Gorbachev, who had backed the U.N. war until that point, and to launch a ground attack on 24 February to sweep the Iraqis out of Kuwait.

On 27 February, one hundred hours after the start of the ground war, the president called for an armistice at midnight. If, as Bush believed, "clarity of purpose" was the key to "kicking the Vietnam syndrome," the result was decidedly mixed. The coalition's forces had fulfilled the United Nation's mandate. But Saddam—whose withdrawal included torching Kuwait's oil wells while salvaging the core of his elite troops, the Republican Guard—remained as a vivid reminder that Bush, in addressing the dilemma of a past war, had encountered equally intractable matters in a new situation. Once again, fighting the lessons of the past deceived planners about the present. "We need a surrender—we need Saddam out," the president wrote in his diary. "And yet, our objectives are to stop short of all that." There never would be, as he had hoped, "a battleship Missouri surrender," with Saddam personally turning in his sword.

The U.S. military, from Joint Chiefs of Staff Chairman General Colin Powell on down, was loathe to expend additional lives. With 79 U.S. personnel killed and 213 wounded, there had been few deaths, considering the size of the encounter, and even those were disproportionately from friendly fire. The U.N. mandate had, moreover, called for no further advance, no invasion of Iraq itself. Saddam's demise would have to be achieved via an internal overthrow. In May, President Bush signed a secret order for the Central Intelligence Agency to undertake covert operations aimed at deposing Saddam, but Saddam remained in power.

A vital element that dictated the armistice were the Arab members of the coalition. Not only were Saddam's neighbors opposed to continuing the war beyond the liberation of Kuwait, but they abhorred risking destabilizing Iraq, which, with its Kurdish minority, could have negative consequences throughout the Middle East should a civil war break out. Moreover, consideration of the United Nation Arab members played a key role in the one aspect of the conclusion that Bush later conceded may have been an error—the failure to humble Saddam by having him personally lay down his sword at the 3 March signing of the armistice at the Iraq border town of Safwan. The Americans stopped short of trying to humiliate their enemy because of Arab concerns about forcing one of their own to surrender to Westerners. "It doesn't go over well with the Arabs," Bush noted for his diary as the war neared its unexpectedly rapid conclusion.

## "IT'S THE ECONOMY"

If euphoria from the Gulf War fallout was deceptive, it minimized domestic issues, and when Bush returned to "inside baseball," it was all downhill. The administration was suffering from the liabilities of the Reagan era and from its own weaknesses. Bush and his economic advisers were sensitive both to the burdensome deficit and to the Democratic majorities in Congress, who could, they feared, turn any stimulus program into partisan advantage. They were left with the faith that the economic recession would recover along the lines followed by the eight previous postwar downturns. Bush, much more sophisticated than Reagan about the workings of the economy, nevertheless lacked the latter's ability to convince the public that with such a big manure pile, there must be a pony. Even as conditions improved before election day, Bush later admitted, "I couldn't convince the American people we were no longer in a recession. That was my style."

Hints of trouble on the home front had preceded the Iraq invasion. Analyst Lou Harris had warned as early as May of that year that concern about the country's economic health and the growing disparity of income between rich and poor were becoming Bush's burdens. The recession was later calculated as beginning in the summer of 1990 and then compounded by increases in the price of oil and other dislocations caused by the Gulf crisis. Even as Bush was building up Desert Shield to its half-million strength, his standing in the polls began to decline. The slumping economy could produce "America's first wartime recession," wrote Kevin Phillips that October, and was "likely to be . . . decisive in the long run." Bush's break with his no-tax pledge, coupled with his inability to slash capital gains rates, helped to tag Bush himself as a cause of why the Reagan revolution had gone astray. It was, supply-side economist Jude Wanniski declared, a "Bush recession."

Bush was suddenly burdened, noted Eleanor Clift, by Jimmy Carter's triple problem: recession, rising oil prices, and hostages. "Passions are very high in the Republican Party," wrote Robin Toner in the *New York Times* at the end of the year. "Conservatives have not forgotten the fight over the budget and the Administration's embrace of higher taxes, which was simple heresy to the party's right wing." "We're enjoying sluggish times, and not enjoying them very much," Bush explained in January, when he also acknowledged that there really was a recession. He had been advised that conditions would improve by spring, but such hopes were dashed. Revised estimates indicated a weaker-than-expected recovery. Unemployment moved upward from 5.4 percent to 6.8 percent one year after the downturn began.

The national anxiety about taxes, debts, and deficits added an extra chill to the political climate as Pat Buchanan challenged Bush's nomination in the New Hampshire primary and walked away with 37 percent of the Republican vote plus 7 percent from write-ins by Democrats. As David Broder wrote, "New Hampshire signaled the seriousness of Bush's reelection problem. And he has not shifted his focus yet." In November 1991, the Dow Jones index dropped by 120 points, the worst since the crash of October 1987, amid widespread agreement within leading financial circles that "the economy is dead in the water." By June, as

Bush prepared to face a Democratic ticket headed by Governor Bill Clinton of Arkansas, unemployment stood at 7.8 percent, the budget deficit was at a record high, and wages were stagnant. Instead of recovery, the economy had gone into a secondary dip, leaving Bush "shell-shocked," according to his press secretary, Marlin Fitzwater.

The much-publicized slogan attributed to Clinton consultant James Carville, "It's the economy, stupid!" lent itself to various nuances. Bush was frustrated throughout the campaign by the numbers indicating continuing distress—certainly a slow recovery if not necessarily the deepest recession. He remained bitter ever after at what he regarded as the failure of the press to herald the start of an upturn. To some extent, he had a point, but it was exaggerated. Rosier figures showing an improved growth rate for the third quarter were released by the Commerce Department only one week before the election, hardly enough time for even a friendlier media to influence more than a small segment of public opinion. And the independent candidacy of H. Ross Perot, who repeatedly emphasized the importance of balancing the budget, may have hurt Bush more by placing the spotlight on economic problems than by costing him votes.

On the Friday before the election, Bush's credibility suffered another blow. A new indictment of Reagan's former defense secretary, Caspar W. Weinberger, revealed handwritten notes that seemed to rebut Bush's claim that as vice president he was "out of the loop" when arms were sold to Iran as part of an arms-for-hostages deal. The harm done to Bush's reelection effort by that election-eve strike by the federal grand jury working with the special prosecutor, Lawrence E. Walsh, cannot be calculated.

## THE CAMPAIGN OF 1992

Bush had made his concessions to the party's ultraconservatives. The religious right, notably Pat Robertson's Christian Coalition, cooperated by spearheading a powerful drive among evangelicals. Their power was surely

among the reasons he held on to Dan Quayle despite serious pressure within the administration to install another vice president. Bush ran on a conservative, antiabortion, prolife platform entitled "An American Vision: For Our Children and For Our Future"—a virtual replica of Reagan's 1984 platform. It also called for term limits for office holders, a balanced-budget amendment, reduction of capital gains taxes, and, above all, less government. The party's convention, held that year in Houston, was dominated by themes dedicated to "family values" and conservative government. An address by Pat Robertson kept the influence of the religious right at the forefront. Best remembered, however, was a controversial screed by Bush's primary election opponent, speechwriter Pat Buchanan, who set a harsh, supernationalistic, often xenophobic tone. Although much criticized later, the convention—and especially the Buchanan speech with its closing exhortation for Americans to "take back our cities, and take back our culture, and take back our country" (which Barbara Bush later described as "mean-spirited racist")—nevertheless boosted the standing of the Bush-Quayle ticket.

Unlike the campaign of 1988, the 1992 campaign was under the direction of a troika, a three-man directorship that was frequently criticized for its inefficiency. The president himself seemed more inclined to delay much of a personal effort, appearing to believe that it was more appropriate to be seen doing his job than to go begging for votes. His vow to do whatever it took to win failed to overcome reservations about his zest or even his energy, which seemed below the level of four years earlier. Even before the convention, Secretary of State Baker was asked to do as he had done in 1988, give up his cabinet post and direct the campaign.

Bush, finding Clinton a tenacious campaigner, went into his campaign mode more easily at the thought of his opponent as a "draft-dodger" and one whose patriotic credentials were made more questionable by his having demonstrated against the Vietnam War while he was a student in England. Riled by that thought, the decorated veteran of World War II found it hard to believe that the American public would prefer his "sleazy" opponent, whom he referred to as a "bozo." In two debates with Clinton and Perot, Bush held his own, but he struck many viewers as distracted and uninterested, especially when the camera caught him glancing at his wristwatch during the second one. Clinton thrived on a town meeting format. Bush, behind in the polls, nevertheless kept hoping that they were wrong about the outcome. He continued to believe that he would be appreciated for having been a good president, and he clutched at the hope that his superior personal qualities would be obvious to the American people and would see him through.

Bush came out with no better than 38 percent of the three-way popular vote, losing out to Clinton's 43. Perot, whose idiosyncratic, on-again, off-again candidacy was probably triggered by the combination of an old vendetta against Bush and personal ego, wound up with 19 percent, a strong showing for a third-party competitor. Perot won no electoral votes, however, while Clinton with his running mate, Senator Albert Gore, Jr., finished with 370 to 168 for the Bush-Quayle ticket.

The generational change was obvious. Although George Bush was succeeded by a Democratic "baby boomer," it was another contemporary of Clinton's, Republican Minority Whip Newt Gingrich, who had concluded that the president was expendable. The defeat of George Bush helped to squeeze life out of what remained of the party's moderately conservative component, culminating the rightward swing that predated Nixon's election. A new and remarkably monolithic radical right was poised finally to achieve the unfulfilled revolution of Ronald Reagan.

## BIBLIOGRAPHY

Bush, George, and Brent Scowcroft. *A World Tranformed* (Knopf, 1998).

Campbell, Colin, and Bert A. Rockman, eds. *The Bush Presidency: First Appraisals* (Chatham House, 1991).

Duffy, Michael, and Dan Goodgame. *Marching in Place: The Status Quo Presidency of George Bush* (Simon & Schuster, 1992).

Fitzwater, Marlin. *Call the Briefing! Bush and Reagan, Sam and Helen: A Decade of Presidents and the Press* (Time Books, 1995).

Kolb, Charles. *White House Daze: The Unmaking of Domestic Policy in the Bush Years* (Free Press, 1994).

Mervin, David. *George Bush and the Guardianship Presidency* (St. Martin's Press, 1996).

Parmet, Herbert S. *George Bush: The Life of a Lone Star Yankee* (Scribner/Lisa Drew, 1997).

Podhoretz, John. *Hell of a Ride: Backstage at the White House Follies, 1989–1993* (Simon & Schuster, 1993).

Powell, Colin. *My American Journey* (Random House, 1995).

★★★ 42 ★★★

# WILLIAM JEFFERSON (BILL) CLINTON
## 1993–

*Robert D. Holsworth*

*Born 19 August 1946, given name William Jefferson Blythe, IV, in Hope, Arkansas, to William Jefferson Blythe, III, and Virginia Cassidy Blythe; graduated Georgetown University, Washington, D.C. (B.S., 1968), Oxford University, England (Rhodes Scholar), Yale Law School, New Haven, Connecticut (J.D. 1973); married Hillary Diane Rodham, 11 October 1975, Fayetteville, Arkansas; one child; elected to the presidency in 1992 on the Democratic ticket with Albert A. Gore, Jr., of Tennessee, with 44,908,233 popular votes and 370 electoral college ballots, over the Republican ticket of George Herbert Walker Bush of Texas and J. Danforth Quayle of Indiana, with 39,102,282 popular votes and 168 electoral ballots and the independent candidacy of Henry Ross Perot of Texas and James B. Stockdale of California, with 19,721,433 popular votes; relected with Gore in 1996, with 45,590,703 popular votes and 379 electoral college ballots, over Bob Dole of Kansas and Jack Kemp of New York, with 37,816,307 popular votes and 159 electoral ballots.*

An assessment of a sitting president's historical importance is always a risky undertaking. It is often only the passage of time that provides the context in which we can judge the significance of the contribution that the individual has made to leading the nation. Presidents widely criticized and occasionally reviled in their own era can be rehabilitated by the judgment of history. But there have also been presidents who left office with broad public approval only to be viewed over time as mediocre chief executives.

The difficulty in assessing the historical impact of a sitting president is magnified in the case of William Jefferson Clinton. From the perspective of his strongest critics, Clinton's place in history will be captured by the reality that he was only the second American president ever to be impeached. Clinton's critics believe that history will vindicate the president's accusers and that he will ultimately be remembered as a leader who was willing to violate his constitutional oath to faithfully uphold the laws in order to perpetuate a cover-up of his personal transgressions. According to his critics, the character failings that became evident in the impeachment process infected his entire presidency. In their minds, it was a presidency driven more by polls than by principle, concerned more with campaigning than with governing, and one that continually pandered to the worst tendencies in American culture.

The president and his defenders, however, believe that the judgment of his administration is likely to be more balanced and generous. They believe that Clinton will be remembered as the president who eliminated the budget deficit, reformed welfare, reduced crime, and redefined the Democratic party. The president and his supporters hope that he will be recognized as a leader who established a third way of governing between an obsolete New Deal liberalism and an excessively harsh and punitive laissez-faire conservatism. The president's defenders suggest that the impeachment process will be seen in the future in much the same terms as the public views it today: as a partisan effort to transform an embarrassing and inappropriate private action into a matter of high constitutional principle.

The very uncertainty about who Bill Clinton is, what his political convictions are, and what his legacy will be provides an important clue to how his presidency should be viewed. In part, this uncertainty is related to the individual style, personality, and political history of the president himself. Clinton possesses an agile and synthetic intellect. He is a political figure of uncommon resilience who has, on more than one occasion, picked himself off the floor to overcome adversity. But while doubts have never been raised about his mind or his heart, troubling questions remain about his political soul. His friends as well as his critics have wondered about the solidity of his convictions and the extent to which he has sacrificed principle to expediency. Even those who were most impressed with his prodigious political skills had to acknowledge the utter recklessness that would place an entire presidency in jeopardy to pursue a furtive relationship with a former intern.

In part, however, the uncertainty surrounding the Clinton presidency is related to the era in which he has been elected and the changing nature of the challenges that the office must confront. Bill Clinton is our first postmodern president, engaged with defining a role for the nation, for the use of government, and for the presidency at a time when the frameworks that have shaped our economy, foreign policy, and culture are undergoing fundamental restructuring and when the American public is ambivalent about the appropriate role of government. In this sense, our doubts about Clinton are related to the broader uncertainties about American economic and political life.

## CREATING THE "NEW DEMOCRAT"

Bill Clinton's victories in 1992 and 1996 broke the cycle that had governed presidential elections for the previous quarter century. From 1968 to 1992, the Republicans had dominated American presidential elections, with the single exception of Jimmy Carter's 1976 triumph over Gerald Ford. The New Deal coalition of Franklin D. Roosevelt, which had made the Democrats the dominant presidential party from 1932 to 1968, was in tatters. In three of the elections during this period, the Republicans won by landslide proportions. By the end of the 1980s, journalists and academic pundits had begun to speak about the Republican "lock" on the electoral college and to wonder whether the Democrats could possibly recapture the White House in the foreseeable future.

Bill Clinton was a key participant in the effort initiated by some Democrats in the 1980s to modify the party's direction. As a Democratic governor from the South, Clinton and others such as Jim Hunt, Bob Graham, and Chuck Robb believed that they had demonstrated how Democrats could win elections in moderate to conservative environments. They maintained that their program of fiscal responsibility and social progressivism was a model that Democratic presidential candidates could emulate. Clinton and other Democratic governors from the South were also instrumental in establishing the Democratic Leadership Council (DLC) to serve as an institutionalized voice inside the party for this perspective.

Clinton's presidential run in 1992 applied the lessons that the southern Democratic governors and the DLC had been preaching. The campaign sought to recapture the Democrats' advantage on economic issues by portraying George Bush as "out of touch" with the concerns of American families. In addition, Clinton contrasted his pro-choice stance on abortion with what he labeled the extreme position of the Republican Party. Clinton also distanced himself in symbolic and highly visible ways from previous Democratic campaigns. He promised a middle-class tax cut and pledged to "end welfare as we know it." In his role as governor of Arkansas, he showed his support of the death penalty by allowing an execution to go forward in the middle of the campaign. And he castigated Rev. Jesse Jackson at a Rainbow Coalition event for not denouncing the racially inflammatory rhetoric that had been voiced at the meeting by a popular rap singer.

## REJECTION

Bill Clinton's first year in office was productive. Family and medical leave legislation was passed with dispatch. "Motor voter" legislation enabling citizens to register to vote more easily was signed. The president's economic package focusing on deficit reduction carried the day narrowly after extended debate. The earned income tax credit was expanded. A modified version of the president's national service legislation was passed by Congress. The "Brady bill" which required a waiting period for the purchase of a handgun, was passed. The North American Free Trade Agreement (NAFTA) was ratified as many Republicans voted with the president against a majority of Democrats. Executive orders reducing restrictions that the Republicans had put on counseling and funding for abortion were issued. By comparison to his predecessor George Bush and to most presidents who have served in the last twenty years, Clinton's first year accomplishments were substantial.

Paradoxically, Clinton's performance set the stage for his second year defeats and the repudiation of his leadership in the congressional elections of 1994. The ordering and timing of his priorities did little to reinforce and much to undermine the "New Democrat" message that had been delivered during the campaign. Clinton's announcement in his first week in office that he wanted to end the ban on gays in the military generated a firestorm of opposition in both parties and with high-ranking officials in the services. And the manner in which his economic package was crafted, debated, and passed also negated the moderate image that he had cultivated.

Clinton realized on taking office that he had to establish priorities among the competing promises (deficit reduction, a tax cut for the middle class, and a set of government investments intended to stimulate the economy) that he had articulated during the campaign. The choice provoked a vigorous debate inside the administration between individuals who wanted Clinton to maintain a populist orientation and those who argued that his long-term prospects were dependent on his capacity to show that Democrats were serious about addressing the budget deficit and entitlement reform. The package that the president announced in February 1993 placed its heaviest emphasis on deficit reduction. The proposal contained stimulus investments in the $230 billion range, but it also included more than $700 billion in spending cuts and tax increases and deferred the promise of a middle-class tax cut until deficit reduction was achieved.

Although the plan was initially well received, it was quickly subjected to a withering Republican attack. The GOP maintained that Clinton's proposal relied too much on tax increases and did not contain adequate spending cuts. Calling the new revenue sources "the largest tax increases in American history," Republicans suggested that it was possible to reduce spending more extensively and relatively painlessly. The Republicans also contended that the president's stimulus package had simply put a new name (investment) on an old staple (pork). Clinton's plan was not very popular on the Democratic side either. Democrats from oil-producing states angered by the energy tax included in the plan and deficit hawks who thought the stimulus program was unnecessary joined the chorus of Republican critics. And liberal Democrats were displeased with how many conservative assumptions were embodied in the plan's focus on deficit reduction. After an intense struggle, the president's program was passed (minus the stimulus investments) by one vote in each chamber, but without the support of a single Republican.

If Clinton had turned immediately from the economic plan to welfare reform, he might have been able to convince the public of his centrist intentions. But the political problems evident in the struggle to pass the economic package were simply exacerbated by his second major initiative, the health reform proposal. In 1993, the president had asked his wife, Hillary Rodham

Clinton, and Ira Magaziner, an aide for domestic policy issues, to manage the White House Task Force on National Health Care Reform in order to develop a plan that provided access to health care for Americans who presently did not have insurance and that controlled escalating costs.

The composition of the task force and the process it established to conduct its work were, in retrospect, disastrous. First, the group itself was extraordinarily large and unwieldy. Five hundred individuals were named to participate on the various working groups. Second, the secrecy in which the deliberations occurred and the decisions made about which groups to consult only raised suspicion about the nature of the end product. Third, the belief on the part of the task force that health care reform was best shaped by removing it, at least temporarily, from the political process by not consulting with congressional leaders later made passage extraordinarily difficult. Finally, the selection of the president's spouse to co-chair the task force may have highlighted the president's commitment, but at the cost of impairing the deliberations of the group and locking the president into supporting the outcome before he knew what it would be.

The task force ran months behind schedule and its recommendations were not officially handed to Congress until November 1993 in a 1,350-page bill. The tardiness of the proposal made it impossible to act on in 1993 and pushed it into the 1994 election cycle. Given the tremendous economic stakes involved in any program of health care reform, interest groups opposed to the plan mobilized all the forces at their disposal. While Clinton was the master of electoral politics, his team proved to be stunningly inept in its first public policy campaign. Public support for the proposal dissipated as the opposition publicized its least popular elements. In the end, much of the middle class became convinced that the plan could achieve its goals of increasing access and reducing costs only by putting the quality and/or convenience of their health care at risk. Rejecting Clinton's proposals,

Congress left the president with nothing on health care and his reputation as a New Democrat in shambles.

The congressional elections that followed the defeat of health care reform were devastating for Clinton and the Democrats. Republican-oriented voters angered with Clinton remained in a state of high mobilization. At the same time, core Democratic constituencies seemed relatively indifferent to the fate of the president and his party. Republicans found new instruments, including talk radio and the "Contract with America," a set of Republican-sponsored promises, to help nationalize the congressional races and reduce the traditional advantage that incumbents possessed. The combination of public disapproval of the president, effective mobilization of Republican-leaning voters, and a complacent Democratic base enabled the GOP to take control of the Senate and do the same in the House with an astounding switch of 52 seats.

## REINVENTION

The months following the 1994 disaster was the low point of Clinton's first term. Commentators and fellow Democrats laid the blame for the Republican's remarkable showing at his doorstep. Media attention was focused almost exclusively on the "Contract with America." The newly installed Republican speaker of the House, Newt Gingrich, was treated as if he were co-president. Scholars and journalists wrote about congressional resurgence and a shrinking presidency. In response to a question at an April 1995 press conference about whether Clinton could ensure that his "voice is heard in the coming months," the leader of the most powerful country in the world was compelled to assert that "the president is relevant here."

Shaking off his political depression, Clinton returned to his "comeback kid" mode of operation. He brought his former consultant Dick Morris to the White House, and Morris stressed the importance of Clinton reinventing his New Democrat identity. Although Clinton did not accept all of Morris's recommendations (especially to aban-

don affirmative action), he moved decisively to the center on a range of issues. Clinton's decision to introduce his own balanced budget angered many Democrats who believed that he would be forced to endorse unacceptable spending cuts. But it proved to be a stroke of political genius. As David Maraniss has written, it shifted the terms of political debate from "whether to balance the budget (to) how to do it."

On this question, Clinton completely outmaneuvered Gingrich and his fellow Republicans. Clinton and the Democrats argued that the Republicans were interested in imposing unacceptable cuts in the safety net, especially for Medicare recipients, in order to give a tax cut to the wealthiest Americans. They were successful in convincing a majority of Americans that it was Gingrich's intransigence that was responsible for the shutdown of the federal government (a brief period in 1995 when many federal offices shut down because spending authorization bills had not been passed). And they established Clinton's political identity as the one man in the nation strong enough to check Gingrich's radical excesses. By the summer of 1996, the Republicans were on the defensive and the "revolutionaries" of 1994 were unable to stop the passage of legislation that raised the minimum wage and increased spending on education.

In the 1996 presidential campaign, Clinton cruised to reelection against the Republican candidate, former Senate majority leader Bob Dole, and Ross Perot's weak Reform party bid. Clinton obtained 49 percent of the popular vote to Dole's 40.7 percent and Perot's 8.4 percent in the three-way race. This translated into an electoral vote landslide with Clinton beating Dole by a 379 to 159 margin. Clinton took credit for a prosperous American economy, the elimination of the budget deficit, and the initiation of welfare reform. Simultaneously, he presented himself as a check against the radicalism of the social conservatives. Clinton maintained that he had fulfilled the promises that were made in 1992 and was the only candidate capable of building a "bridge to the twenty-first century." Given the strong economy and public uneasiness with Republican congressional leaders, neither Dole nor Perot were ever able to mount a serious challenge.

## IMPEACHMENT

President Clinton hoped that he could translate the ease of his electoral victory into a productive second term. He spoke about developing a long-term solution to the problems of Social Security funding, dealing with problems in Medicare funding, and establishing a set of national standards for American education. In addition, Clinton outlined a "values agenda" in which he planned to utilize moral suasion to effect a larger measure of racial reconciliation and reduce the cynicism that Americans felt toward politics and the political order.

But Clinton's plans were irreparably damaged by another character scandal that polarized the Congress politically and resulted in his impeachment. During the government shutdown in 1995, the president had started an affair with Monica Lewinsky, an intern in the White House. Toward the end of 1997, Lewinsky was added to the witness list in a sexual harassment/civil rights law suit that had been filed against Clinton by a former Arkansas state employee named Paula Jones. In both the deposition he gave in the case and in a public statement to the American public, Clinton denied having a sexual relationship with Lewinsky. Through an unusual series of events, an independent counsel, Kenneth Starr, who had been appointed to investigate the Clintons' involvement in a failed real estate deal in Arkansas in the 1980s (the so-called Whitewater scandal), was given jurisdiction to examine whether any crimes had been committed in regard to the president's relationship with Lewinsky and the subsequent effort to prevent its disclosure.

In the summer of 1998, Starr furnished a referral to Congress claiming that there was credible and substantial evidence that the president had committed impeachable offenses. Although both public opinion polls and congressional election results in No-

vember 1998 indicated that the citizenry did not want the president removed, the House Judiciary Committee took up the Starr report and voted articles of impeachment against the president. On 19 December 1998 the full House voted to impeach the president for perjury before the Starr grand jury and obstruction of justice in attempting to prevent disclosure of his relationship with Lewinsky. The vote followed a bitter partisan debate about whether any of the offenses were truly impeachable and occurred almost entirely along party lines. The perjury charge passed the House by a 228–206 margin and the obstruction of justice charge by 221–212. In the Senate trial in early 1999, however, Clinton was acquitted as his opponents were unable to muster even a simple majority on either charge.

Throughout the impeachment debate and Senate trial, the majority of the public was unwavering in its belief that Clinton should not be removed. Moreover, congressional Republicans were clearly damaged in the process by the public perception that they were more intent on persecuting the president than on protecting the country's long-term interests. Still, impeachment exacted a major toll on President Clinton. During the process, the nation's attention was focused almost entirely on this issue and not on Clinton's second-term agenda. Moreover, the president's capacity to press forward on his issues was almost entirely diminished by the impeachment process. Even if the long-term historical judgment about the impeachment turns out to mirror what the public was thinking in 1998 and 1999, it will remain true that Clinton's political capital with the Congress was eroded by the battle and that his capacity to expand his legacy beyond the sound management of the economy was diminished.

## FOREIGN POLICY

At the end of the Cold War, the United States was the only superpower left standing. Yet the most significant feature of the foreign policy context that existed when Clinton arrived in office was the absence of a clear definition of American interests in the post–Cold War era. Indeed, a clear definition of the global situation, let alone U.S. interests, was also lacking. Larry Berman and Emily O. Goldman have written about three kinds of uncertainty that characterize the post–Cold War circumstances. First, a predictable adversary has been replaced by a set of unfamiliar and novel challengers— narco-terrorists, small states who possess nuclear capabilities, and powderkegs of ethnic violence—that have the potential to be very disruptive but do not hold the destructive capacity of the Soviet Union. In addition, the nature of international competition among major powers may be increasingly more economic than military. Second, the end of the Cold War poses fresh questions for the nature of American alliances: Should we focus on establishing firm alliances, or are we better off creating flexible partnerships that can be enhanced and dissolved as our interests demand? Third, how does the United States manage and distribute its resources to respond to the kind of challenges that it faces in the international arena?

During the 1992 campaign, Clinton did not seriously engage these questions. Promising to focus on the economy like a "laser beam," he pushed foreign policy to the back burner. There were good tactical reasons for Clinton to do so: He was inexperienced, and President George Bush's most formidable achievement was organizing the international coalition that undid Saddam Hussein's invasion of Kuwait. To the extent that Clinton discussed foreign policy matters in 1992, he typically offered idealistic criticisms of the policies pursued by the Bush administration. Clinton maintained that United States policy in China was "coddling dictators" and should be more concerned with protecting human rights and less interested in advancing momentary economic interests. He worried that the Bush administration had been excessively deferential to our European allies in Bosnia and contended that ethnic cleansing could not proceed unabated. Despite these occasional assertions, Clinton made it clear to the public that he would be, first

and foremost, a domestic president who attended to the economic anxieties that were afflicting American families.

## FOREIGN POLICY PERFORMANCE

Given this background, it is not surprising that the most decisive response that the Clinton administration offered in its early years to the questions about America's post–Cold War posture was its insistence that economic security was the key to international success. As Clinton's trade representative Mickey Kantor observed, "trade and international economics have joined the foreign policy table. . . . Clinton is really the first president to make trade the bridge between foreign and domestic policy." Clinton has included voices from the Commerce Department and the Treasury Department in the administration's internal discussion of foreign policy issues. Indeed, many foreign policy observers believe that the president's most substantial success has been his management of the international economy. With respect to regional trade agreements, he departed from Democratic orthodoxy to pass the North American Free Trade Agreement and succeeded in obtaining ratification of the Uruguay Round of the General Agreement on Tariffs and Trade (GATT). The president was able to garner modest concessions from Japan in the longstanding effort to open the Japanese market to goods produced in the United States and he negotiated a cooperative agreement on a yen-dollar adjustment.

The decision to emphasize American economic and trade interests ultimately compelled President Clinton to back away from positions that candidate Clinton had articulated. Trade relations with China was the paramount example. Running for office, the president had maintained that, unlike President Bush, he would make renewal of most-favored-nation (MFN) trade status for China dependent on its addressing seriously its record of human rights violations. In May 1993, President Clinton renewed China's MFN status for a year but also issued a report to Congress and an executive order that tied future renewal to specific progress on human rights. In May 1994, however, the president announced the renewal of China's MFN status despite his acknowledgment that China had failed to meet the human rights goals detailed in the 1993 executive order. Saying that he was starting to "delink" human rights from considerations of MFN status, Clinton maintained that we had "reached the end of the usefulness of that policy." The president listed a series of steps that would be taken in outside trade negotiations to continue our support for human rights advances. But it was evident that strategic concerns about Asian stability and, most important, economic considerations related to an ongoing trade relationship and the emerging Chinese market were now the driving forces behind U.S. policy.

But the first two years of the Clinton administration were marked by a series of missteps in responding to the noneconomic challenges in foreign policy. The president and his advisers allowed the Bush administration's humanitarian mission in Somalia to be transformed into the pursuit of a Somalian warlord that led to the death of eighteen Americans soldiers in a firefight. The administration was compelled to retreat and redefine the policy once again in reaction to congressional outrage. The administration's response to the crisis in Bosnia was, until 1995, hesitant and indecisive in the face of a situation that demanded clarity and purposefulness. An American ship, the USS *Harlan County*, sent to Haiti for the purpose of landing U.N. observers to monitor the restoration of the country's democratically elected government, decided not to land when met by a hundred rioters chanting "we will make this another Somalia." And the Clinton administration was largely indifferent in this period to the massacre occurring in Rwanda. William Hyland has described the record as a "two-year binge that ended in disaster and humiliation."

From 1994 to 1996, the administration's record in managing foreign policy challenges was considerably improved. It undertook a series of actions in the foreign policy arena, sometimes taken in defiance

of public opinion and congressional will, where the outcome was generally acknowledged to be positive. The United States helped to support Russian president Boris Yeltsin against an internal political threat from communists. The administration engineered a bailout that kept the Mexican economy from disintegrating despite opposition in Congress. The government eventually used military strength in Haiti to restore democracy from the military leaders who had hijacked it. Although the election of Benjamin Netanyahu as Israeli prime minister was a substantial setback in the Middle East, Clinton and Secretary of State Warren Christopher's encouragement of an agreement between Israel and the Palestine Liberation Organization (PLO) was handled relatively deftly. And when the president decided to detail an American presence in Bosnia to support a fragile peace, he finally demonstrated his willingness to step forward on the world stage and exhibit the kind of leadership that America's role in the world demands.

While President Clinton did become a better manager of foreign policy by the end of his first term, questions remained about the capacity of the administration to articulate a coherent framework for American interests in the post–Cold War era beyond the domestic economic agenda that was driving it. By most accounts, the president was only sporadically engaged in foreign policy. Colin Powell described National Security Council meetings during his time as chair of the Joint Chiefs of Staff as "graduate student bull sessions." Clinton's foreign policy team led by Warren Christopher seemed more concerned with managing foreign policy than with developing a conceptual underpinning to guide it. The doctrine of enlargement and engagement appeared to describe accurately the administration's intentions of expanding democracy and opening markets, but its vagueness made it a poor guide for decision making and for allocating scarce resources. It did not necessarily specify where engagements should occur, what criteria should lead to the utilization of American coercive power, and precisely how this power should be employed.

The practical consequences of attempting to develop a new framework for foreign policy became apparent during Clinton's second term. In 1999, the president and the NATO allies decided to intervene in Yugoslavia in order to stop the government of Slobodan Milosevic from carrying out its campaign of ethnic cleansing of Albanians in the Serbia province of Kosovo. Against those who suggested that American vital interests were not at stake in the Serbian assault on Kosovar Albanians, Clinton responded that we had entered a new era in foreign policy in which humanitarian concerns could not be entirely subordinated to narrowly confined conceptions of vital interests. He said that the United States and the world had been too slow to respond to the genocide in Rwanda and that it was crucial to prevent war criminals such as Milosevic from carrying out his designs unimpeded.

When negotiations with Milosevic failed, NATO began a campaign of bombing. The NATO airstrikes ultimately succeeded in making Milosevic retreat from his original stance. The Serb army pulled out of Kosovo and Milosevic was compelled to agree to a NATO peacekeeping force in Kosovo. These concessions were more substantial than many critics of the intervention ever thought would be exacted. At the same time, the extent of the "victory" achieved by Clinton and NATO was highly uncertain. The administration had suggested that the primary aim of the intervention in Yugoslavia was to prevent Milosevic from mistreating the ethnic Albanians in Kosovo. But while NATO bombing runs degraded Milosevic's industrial and military infrastructure, the Serbian military surprised American planners by escalating its campaign against the ethnic Albanians, driving them from their homes and creating hundreds of thousands of refugees. The extent to which a new principle of humanitarian intervention was established in Kosovo is also still uncertain and is likely to depend on how long the presence of the peacekeeping force is nec-

essary and whether political pressure is sufficient to oust Milosevic from power.

At the same that the intervention in Yugoslavia was occurring, a congressional report detailing Chinese spying in American nuclear weapons labs brought debate about American policy toward China to center stage. The report described almost twenty years of leaks of sensitive design information about nuclear weapons to the Chinese. This transfer of top-secret information had taken place during the Reagan, Bush, and Clinton presidencies. And while the Clinton administration argued that the longstanding nature of the problem was ample demonstration why it should not be viewed in partisan terms, administration critics believed that the lethargy with which the Clinton foreign policy team responded to the information it had received about Chinese spying was a dereliction of responsibility. The administration's harshest critics argued that campaign donations from China that were illegally funneled to the Democrats in 1996 led to the administration's slow response to information about possible Chinese spying. Charges about the influence of Chinese campaign dollars were probably grossly overstated. What was true, however, was that the administration had not provided Americans with a coherent framework for understanding China. Was it one of the world's worst violators of human rights and an emerging threat to American national security? Or was it the largest potential market and a trading partner that should be cultivated for the economic benefits that the relationship could provide?

Any evaluation of President Clinton's foreign policy must take note of the political context in which it has operated. The American public is apparently content for the nation to take, at least temporarily, a rest from its international leadership role. In neither the 1992 nor the 1996 elections did foreign policy ever become a major issue. Public opinion polls indicate that a majority of Americans approve of the manner in which the president has handled foreign policy. And many of Clinton's conservative political opponents have both abandoned their interest in the nation assuming an expansive international role and been content to watch the "miniaturization" of the presidency so long as someone who did not share their ideology occupied the position. In this milieu, President Clinton has frequently adopted a broader view of American interests than either the public or his Republican opponents have. But still it cannot be said that the president has successfully redefined a role for the United States in the postwar world that other nations can discern and that the public has embraced.

## CULTURE AND COMMUNITY

Throughout the 1970s and 1980s, Republicans successfully used values issues against Democrats in presidential elections. In 1984, Walter Mondale and the Democrats were accused of embracing an outlook that "blamed America first" for the world's problems. Four years later, the Bush campaign launched an attack on Michael Dukakis's patriotism and commitment to protecting Americans against crime from which he never recovered. Republican assaults on Dukakis's unwillingness to make the pledge of allegiance mandatory in Massachusetts's schools, his assertion that he was a "card carrying" member of the American Civil Liberties Union, and his use of a furlough program for prisoners that gave a committed rapist, Willie Horton, a weekend pass defined him as a liberal outside the American mainstream.

Clinton responded to the Democratic party's values dilemma in three ways during the 1992 campaign. First, he inoculated himself from Republican attacks by adopting positions different from previous Democratic contenders. Second, Clinton counterattacked by arguing that it was the Republicans, the party of Pat Buchanan, Pat Robertson, and Dan Quayle, who had adopted extreme positions. Finally, Clinton spoke about the need to establish a broad sense of community in which all Americans willing to play by the rules could participate.

But in his first six months in office, the president's mishandling of cultural issues palpably damaged him. His announcement that he planned to issue an executive order ending discrimination in the military against gays and lesbians and the perception that he associated with Hollywood stars undermined the centrist image that he had cultivated. By the end of his term, however, Clinton had became more skillful in turning cultural issues to his advantage by successfully redeploying the strategies he had used during the campaign.

## INOCULATION

Although he had endorsed the abolition of discrimination based on sexual orientation in the military during the 1992 campaign, the issue was never really discussed in the contest. But it became the central theme of national conversation when the president announced that he would issue an executive order lifting the military's ban on homosexuals. While the Clinton administration maintained that the president was simply delivering on a campaign promise, it was viewed by others as a radical departure from his New Democrat theme. Fellow "New Democrat" Sam Nunn opposed Clinton's position; Colin Powell noted how damaging it would be to the morale of the American services; and conservative commentators asserted that Clinton's intention to lift the ban confirmed their view of him as a liberal who had contempt for the military. Senator Chuck Robb, a former marine, was one of the few congressional officials to publicly endorse the president's position. Robb noted that he found "the specter of two girls dancing together unsettling to say the least" but still asserted that the "threat to morale comes not from the orientation of a few but the closed minds of the many."

Ultimately, the opposition of senior military officers and the threat by Congress to reverse the proposed executive order legislatively persuaded the president to back away from his pledge and support an alternative position, labeled "don't ask, don't tell." The compromise to which the president agreed came down largely on the side of those who opposed his original plan. It did contain a provision that new recruits to the service would not be asked if they were gay. But it continued the ban on homosexual conduct in which "conduct" was defined broadly to include the mere disclosure of homosexual orientation to a friend. The president's opponents also included in the defense authorization bill passed in the Senate the statement that "homosexuality poses an unacceptable risk" to morale, order, and discipline in the armed forces.

In 1996, gay rights surfaced again when it appeared that a pending court case in Hawaii was likely to legalize gay marriage in that state. Across the nation, other states became fearful that reciprocity in marriage laws would require them to recognize the unions established in Hawaii. Legislation was introduced in Congress (The Defense of Marriage Act) empowering states not to respect "a relationship between persons of the same sex that is treated as a marriage" by another state. The president claimed to find the bill objectionable, but let it be known that he would not veto it. To show his displeasure, he signed the bill at midnight.

Clinton's position on gay rights did not change between 1992 and 1996, but his political stance evolved. In 1992, he appeared willing to expend a portion of his political capital on an unpopular stance. But when it became evident that he could not follow through, he cut his losses and agreed to a compromise that was hardly face-saving. In 1996, he signed legislation vigorously opposed by most gay rights activists and in doing so took the issue off the table as a possible campaign liability. On the issue of equal treatment of gay men and lesbians, the politics of principle gave way to a strategy of inoculation.

## MARGINALIZING REPUBLICANS

Many political scientists now believe that abortion was as important to Clinton's election in 1992 as was dissatisfaction with George Bush's handling of the economy. Public wariness about the influence of Christian conservatives and abortion foes such as Pat Buchanan on the Republican party enabled Clinton to position himself advantageously on social issues. Analysis of the 1992 National Election Study indicated that pro-choice Republicans were much more likely to vote for Clinton than pro-life Democrats were likely to cast a ballot for Bush.

In contrast to the manner in which he retreated on gay rights, Clinton remained adamantly pro-choice on abortion. He issued executive orders easing the gag rules on abortion counseling by agencies receiving federal funding in his first week in office and removed the ban on giving U.S. aid to international organizations involved in the provision and promoting of abortion. He allowed the federal government to fund research that utilized fetal tissue. And he endorsed legislation making it a felony to obstruct access to abortion clinics and providing for Justice Department prosecution of violators. President Clinton's two appointees to the Supreme Court, Ruth Bader Ginsburg and Stephen Breyer, were both reliably pro-choice. In 1996, Congress passed legislation outlawing a procedure known as partial-birth abortion that could occur in the last trimester. The ban on partial-birth abortions had a wide range of supporters that extended beyond the circle of pro-life groups that might predictably support any restriction on abortion. Claiming that he had suggested some changes for medical purposes that the Republicans refused to put in the bill, Clinton vetoed the legislation.

## REBUILDING THE NATIONAL COMMUNITY

From the time he stepped on the national stage through his campaign for reelection in 1996, Clinton has called for Americans to establish a revitalized and more inclusive sense of national community. His boyhood political hero, John F. Kennedy, had inspired a generation of Americans with his call to national service and the creation of the Peace Corps. The Democratic Leadership Council in the late 1980s had endorsed a plan for national service that required individuals to perform service in order to receive college grants. And even while he was asking Dick Morris and a new set of pollsters to the White House in 1995 to salvage a besieged presidency, Clinton was also inviting prominent academic theorists of civic democracy to the White House to discuss how he might foster this broadened sense of community in the culture.

Clinton's efforts to reinvigorate civic community in the nation were both practical and rhetorical. On taking office, the president recommended passage of national service legislation that would provide funding for young people to perform service-oriented work in their communities. "A lot of the problems with this country are *intensely* cultural, personal, human. I believe that this national service project has the capacity, anyway, to make us believe that we don't have anybody to waste, to make us believe we are all in this together, to give us a chance to reach across racial and income lines to work together." Although Republicans attacked the program as an example of "tax and spend" government and an open-ended commitment that could not be scaled back in later years, a modified version of the president's proposal passed in September 1993. The bill created a Corporation for National and Community Service that enabled young people to work on locally defined projects administered by nonprofit organizations. Participants would be provided with a stipend of up to $7,400 a year and were also eligible to receive up to $4,725 a year in educational assistance for up to two years.

Since his miscalculation about how his position on gays in the military would be received, Bill Clinton has proven to be extremely adept in his handling of cultural politics. He has managed to avoid the dilemmas that have afflicted other Democratic national figures, place Republicans on the defensive, and capture almost perfectly the ambivalence that Americans seem to possess about cultural matters. In a nation divided between its libertarian and its moralistic instincts, Clinton has a capacity to strike the politically appropriate chord. The president has been an extraordinarily strong supporter of the right to privacy on almost all issues dealing with abortion. But on issues relating to children—especially to-

bacco, television viewing, guns in school, and school uniforms—he has endorsed government regulation and technological restrictions on behalf of the common interest in raising young people with appropriate values. And a number of Clinton's most eloquent speeches have focused on his beliefs that Americans need to care more about what unites them rather than what divides them, especially on the matter of race.

Clinton has certainly taught other Democrats that the politics of culture can potentially work to their advantage. But it is still not clear if Clinton's legacy in this regard will extend beyond recognition of his political skill in redefining the partisan stakes involved in cultural politics. He has certainly drawn attention to the communitarian side of American political life and cultural opinion. But his effort to make this a central element of his presidential legacy could be potentially undermined by his own difficulties in addressing the character issue.

## CHARACTER AND CORRUPTION IN THE CAMPAIGNS

The effort to raise questions about Clinton's character was a central feature of both the 1992 and 1996 campaigns. Clinton was almost derailed in 1992 by the claims of a woman in Arkansas, Gennifer Flowers, that they had carried on an affair over many years. In addition, media scrutiny of Clinton's Vietnam era draft record indicated that he had not been completely truthful about his efforts to avoid military service. While President Bush declined to discuss Clinton's extramarital activities, he felt that their respective war records were fair game. Bush believed that given a choice between a candidate who fudged his age when he was seventeen so he could fly fighter planes in World War II and another who avoided service and participated in antiwar rallies in the Vietnam era, the public would ultimately choose the individual who had sacrificed for his country.

In 1996, Bob Dole also decided to highlight Clinton's character after polling and focus group results indicated that the public believed that Dole was more trustworthy.

Like Bush, Dole mostly avoided any discussion of Clinton's alleged marital infidelities. But he argued that Clinton's own history of drug use and willingness to laugh about his "I didn't inhale" statement made him unsuitable to lead the war against drugs. Indeed, Dole argued that Clinton simply did not understand the seriousness of the problem and had made policy decisions to weaken the drug czar at a time when teenage drug use was rising. Moreover, Dole pointed to a record of indictments and special prosecutor investigations of Clinton's appointees that exemplified what he considered to be the administration's deplorable ethical standards. Finally, Dole maintained in the last days of the campaign that the Democratic fund-raising operation had engaged in practices that were legally questionable and morally objectionable.

## RECTITUDE AND EMPATHY

The 1992 and 1996 Republican campaign strategies were, in part, merely efforts to exploit a perceived weakness in their opponent. But these attempts ultimately raised a larger issue about character and the public's understanding of it. In outlining Clinton's inadequacies, both Bush and Dole articulated a traditional definition of character that encompassed virtues such as patriotism, honor, rectitude, dedication to principle, sincerity, and loyalty. They implied that Clinton operated according to a different set of values that elevated self-preservation over patriotism, expedience over honor, and popularity over principle. Both Bush and Dole apparently believed that Americans would not vote for a candidate who ordered moral priorities in this manner. By the end of the 1996 campaign, however, Dole was incredulous that the public had lost what he called its sense of "outrage" over the president's ethical lapses.

In political terms, neither of Clinton's Republican opponents were especially well-situated to take advantage of any weakness that he might have on the character question. Bush's reversal of his "read my lips, no new taxes" pledge in 1988 had forfeited his credibility on that issue. The belief held by a substantial portion of the public that Dole was too old to be president made it difficult for him to convince the public that he was a credible alternative to Clinton.

But their biggest mistake might have been their inability to discern the complexity embedded in the public's understanding of character. Most of the evidence does show that the American people had serious reservations about the sincerity of the president, about his capacity to follow through on his commitments, and even about his reliability to keep his word. Measured by a traditional standard of character—the possession of rectitude and integrity—the public doubts about the president's character never subsided. Gallup surveys during 1996 found that 59 percent of the public did not believe that Clinton kept his promises, 51 percent did not think that he was honest and trustworthy, and only a bare 51 percent majority agreed that he was a man of strong convictions.

Yet character judgments are more than assessments of probity. The public wants to know if a political figure can identify with their daily needs and concerns, if the candidate for office can articulate these concerns, and if that person will be actively engaged in trying to resolve their problems. Bill Clinton was rated much more favorably on these more affectional measures of character. Polling data indicated that Clinton held a substantial advantage in both 1992 and 1996 over his Republican opponents in terms of empathetic identification with the public. In 1996, for example, the public was evenly divided in its opinion about whether Bob Dole "cares about the needs of people like you," but it overwhelmingly believed by a 63 percent to 34 percent margin that Bill Clinton did.

In the last two years of his first term, Clinton's response to a series of public tragedies displayed the full range of his empathetic qualities. His reaction to the terrorist bombing of a federal building in Oklahoma City in 1995 in which he consoled individual families, led the nation's mourning, and denounced the "angry voices" that spewed hate was widely applauded.

Polls conducted in the aftermath of the tragedy showed that 80 percent of the public approved of how the president had responded to the event. After Secretary of Commerce Ron Brown died in an airplane crash, Clinton went to the family's home to offer consolation and spoke eloquently at public ceremonies honoring his life. Clinton himself was apparently aware of how important these affectional moments were to his presidency, noting in an interview that his presidency turned around as a result of his response not only to the Gingrich-dominated Congress but to the events in Oklahoma City.

Ultimately, the empathetic bond that Clinton had established with the public served him well during the impeachment process. The majority of citizens were steadfast in their belief that a president who was doing a good job and had the best interests of the public in mind should not be removed for personal ethical failings. At the same time, Clinton's ethical shortcomings undermined his ability to follow through on the agenda he had articulated at the start of his second term. He had said that he wanted to address the cynicism in American culture and politics. But Clinton not only lost the moral standing to do so, but had to rely on that cynicism—by casting aspersions on the motivations of his opponents, the independent counsel, and the media—to maintain his popularity with the public. In part, it was the public's belief that politicians should be last to throw ethical stones at one another that saved the Clinton presidency.

## CLINTON'S LEGACY?

In recent history, American presidents have not fared very well after being reelected. Ronald Reagan carried 49 states in 1984 but his second term was not nearly as successful as his first. Richard Nixon won a landslide victory in 1972 over George McGovern only to resign from office in 1974 to fend off impeachment and conviction. Despite a landslide victory over Barry Goldwater in 1964, Lyndon Johnson was so buffeted by Vietnam and domestic urban uprisings that he decided not to seek renomination. Although Dwight Eisenhower left office with very high public approval ratings, one probably has to go back to FDR to find a president whose second term was both successful politically and significant in terms of legislative impact. Bill Clinton will not be an exception to this trend. The politically divisive impeachment struggle eroded whatever political capital he might have had with a Republican Congress. And foreign policy crises over Serbian "ethnic cleansing" in Kosovo and Chinese nuclear spying are unlikely to be resolved in a manner that will burnish his reputation.

There will be, however, positive features to Clinton's legacy. At a minimum, Clinton has practiced the kind of pragmatic politics that has broken the Republican hold on the electoral college. Clinton has retained enough of the traditional Democratic commitment to economic uplift for ordinary Americans to bring significant numbers of working-class Americans back into the Democratic fold. During the 1970s and 1980s, the Democrats lost credibility with significant portions of the electorate on economic matters. Clinton has managed to regain, at least partially, what was lost. And he has managed to do this without appearing to be the kind of liberal that Americans found objectionable with previous Democratic party nominees for president. At the same time, he has skillfully exploited public concern about the ideological stance of the Republican party and the perception that the GOP is more interested in returning to an older America than in responding to the real needs of the emerging nation.

Bill Clinton has also framed the context of America's domestic challenges in a more compelling manner than any president since the time of Lyndon Johnson. His effort to educate Americans about the opportunities and demands of the emerging global economy has been perhaps the most constant feature of his leadership. He was willing to break ranks with many of his allies inside the Democratic party over both welfare reform and the North American Free Trade Agreement. And he has remained committed—against Republican opposition—to a vision of government that helps to provide individuals and families with the tools they need to be optimistic about their future possibilities. Moreover, Clinton has recognized that overcoming America's social divisions will be critical to the capacity of the nation to compete effectively in the new global marketplace.

But the shortcomings of the Clinton presidency will be difficult to ignore. He did not develop a record of legislative accomplishment which rivals that of the major American presidents in the last fifty years. He did not bequeath to his successors a compelling vision of America's foreign policy role in the post–Cold War era. And his effort to develop a values-based agenda was fatally compromised by the public airing of his own character flaws. Doris Kearns Goodwin has said that presidents ought to be judged, in part, by the things for which they are willing to risk their political capital. And President Clinton will never be able to escape the realization that perhaps the biggest risk he took—a relationship with a twenty-one-year-old intern—was in the service of self-gratification and not the national interest.

Reporters who covered President Clinton often wrote that he was extremely concerned with how he would be viewed in the future. There is little doubt that his intelligence, tenacity, and flexibility will be acknowledged in years to come. But the concerns about his basic political identity that have been present throughout his years in office will linger for decades. It may be fair to conclude that Bill Clinton is a president who did not run for history nearly as well as he ran for office.

## BIBLIOGRAPHY

Berman, Larry, and Goldman, Emily O. "Clinton's Foreign Policy at Midterm," in Colin Campbell and Bert A. Rockman (eds.), *The Clinton Presidency: First Appraisals* (Chatham House, 1995).

Campbell, Colin, and Bert A. Rockman, eds. *The Clinton Presidency: First Appraisals* (Chatham House Publishers, 1995).

Drew, Elizabeth. *Showdown* (Simon and Schuster, 1996).

———. *On the Edge: The Clinton Presidency* (Simon & Schuster, 1994).

Edsall, Thomas Byrne, with Mary D. Edsall. *Chain Reaction: The Impact of Race, Rights, and Taxes on American Politics* (Norton, 1992).

Maraniss, David. *First in His Class: A Biography of Bill Clinton* (Simon & Schuster, 1995).

O'Brien, David M. "Clinton's Legal Policy and the Courts: Rising from Disarray or Turning Around and Around?," in Colin Campbell and Bert A. Rockman (eds.), *The Clinton Presidency: First Appraisals* (Chatham House, 1995).

Quirk, Paul J., and Joseph Hinchliffe. "Domestic Policy: The Trials of a Centrist Democrat," in Colin Campbell and Bert A. Rockman (eds.), *The Clinton Presidency: First Appraisals* (Chatham House, 1995).

Sinclair, Barbara. "Trying to Govern Positively in a Negative Era: Clinton and the 103rd Congress," in Colin Campbell and Bert A. Rockman (eds.), *The Clinton Presidency: First Appraisals* (Chatham House, 1995).

Stanley, Harold W. "The Parties, the President, and the 1994 Midterm Elections," in Colin Campbell and Bert A. Rockman (eds.), *The Clinton Presidency: First Appraisals* (Chatham House, 1995).

Stewart, James B. *Blood Sport: The President and His Adversaries* (Simon & Schuster, 1996).

Stoesz, David. *Small Change: Domestic Policy Under the Clinton Presidency* (Longman, 1996).

Waldman, Steven. *The Bill* (Penguin Books, 1994).

Wilson, Graham K. "The Clinton Administration and Interest Groups," in Colin Campbell and Bert A. Rockman (eds.), *The Clinton Presidency: First Appraisals* (Chatham House, 1995).

Woodward, Bob. *The Choice* (Simon & Schuster, 1996).

———. *The Agenda* (Simon & Schuster, 1994).

# Appendix A

## PRESIDENTS AND THEIR CABINETS

### 1. George Washington (1789–1797)

| Department | | Assumed Office |
|---|---|---|
| State | John Jay | 1789 |
| | Thomas Jefferson | 1790 |
| | Edmund Randolph | 1794 |
| | Timothy Pickering | 1795 |
| War | Henry Knox | 1789 |
| | Timothy Pickering | 1795 |
| | James McHenry | 1796 |
| Treasury | Alexander Hamilton | 1789 |
| | Oliver Wolcott, Jr. | 1795 |
| Post. General | Samuel Osgood | 1789 |
| | Timothy Pickering | 1791 |
| | Joseph Habersham | 1795 |
| Atty. General | Edmund Randolph | 1790 |
| | William Bradford | 1794 |
| | Charles Lee | 1795 |

### 2. John Adams (1797–1801)

| Department | | Assumed Office |
|---|---|---|
| State | Timothy Pickering | 1797 |
| | Charles Lee | 1800 |
| | John Marshall | 1800 |
| War | James McHenry | 1797 |
| | Benjamin Stoddert | 1800 |
| | Samuel Dexter | 1800 |
| Treasury | Oliver Wolcott Jr. | 1797 |
| | Samuel Dexter | 1801 |
| Post. General | Joseph Habersham | 1797 |
| Atty. General | Charles Lee | 1797 |
| Navy | Benjamin Stoddert | 1798 |

### 3. Thomas Jefferson (1801–1809)

| Department | | Assumed Office |
|---|---|---|
| State | John Marshall | 1801 |
| | Levi Lincoln | 1801 |
| | James Madison | 1801 |
| War | Henry Dearborn | 1801 |
| | John Smith | 1809 |
| Treasury | Samuel Dexter | 1801 |
| | Albert Gallatin | 1801 |
| Post. General | Joseph Habersham | 1801 |
| | Gideon Granger | 1801 |
| Atty. General | Levi Lincoln | 1801 |
| | John C. Breckinridge | 1805 |
| | Caesar A. Rodney | 1807 |
| Navy | Benjamin Stoddert | 1801 |
| | Henry Dearborn | 1801 |
| | Robert Smith | 1801 |

### 4. James Madison (1809–1817)

| Department | | Assumed Office |
|---|---|---|
| State | Robert Smith | 1809 |
| | James Monroe | 1811 |
| War | John Smith | 1809 |
| | William Eustis | 1809 |
| | James Monroe | 1813 |
| | John Armstrong | 1813 |
| | Alexander J. Dallas | 1815 |
| | William H. Crawford | 1815 |
| | George Graham | 1816 |
| Treasury | Albert Gallatin | 1809 |
| | George W. Campbell | 1814 |

|                | Alexander J. Dallas | 1814 |
|                | William H. Crawford | 1816 |
| *Post. General* | Gideon Granger | 1809 |
|                | Return J. Meigs, Jr. | 1814 |
| *Atty. General* | Caesar A. Rodney | 1809 |
|                | William Pinkney | 1812 |
|                | Richard Rush | 1814 |
| *Navy*          | Robert Smith | 1809 |
|                | Charles W. Goldsborough | 1809 |
|                | Paul Hamilton | 1809 |
|                | William Jones | 1813 |
|                | Benjamin Homans | 1814 |
|                | Benjamin W. Crowninshield | 1814 |

## 5. James Monroe (1817–1825)

| *Department*    |                     | *Assumed Office* |
|-----------------|---------------------|---------|
| *State*         | John Graham | 1817 |
|                 | Richard Rush | 1817 |
|                 | John Quincy Adams | 1817 |
| *War*           | George Graham | 1817 |
|                 | John C. Calhoun | 1817 |
| *Treasury*      | William H. Crawford | 1817 |
| *Post. General* | Return J. Meigs, Jr. | 1817 |
|                 | John McLean | 1823 |
| *Atty. General* | Richard Rush | 1817 |
|                 | William Wirt | 1817 |
| *Navy*          | Benjamin W. Crowninshield | 1817 |
|                 | John C. Calhoun | 1818 |
|                 | Smith Thompson | 1818 |
|                 | John Rodgers | 1823 |
|                 | Samuel L. Southard | 1823 |

## 6. John Quincy Adams (1825–1829)

| *Department*    |                     | *Assumed Office* |
|-----------------|---------------------|---------|
| *State*         | Daniel Brent | 1825 |
|                 | Henry Clay | 1825 |
| *War*           | James Barbour | 1825 |
|                 | Samuel L. Southard | 1828 |
|                 | Peter B. Porter | 1828 |
| *Treasury*      | Samuel L. Southard | 1825 |
|                 | Richard Rush | 1825 |
| *Post. General* | John McLean | 1825 |
| *Atty. General* | William Wirt | 1825 |
| *Navy*          | Samuel L Southard | 1825 |

## 7. Andrew Jackson (1829–1837)

| *Department*    |                     | *Assumed Office* |
|-----------------|---------------------|---------|
| *State*         | James A. Hamilton | 1829 |
|                 | Martin Van Buren | 1829 |
|                 | Edward Livingston | 1831 |
|                 | Louis McLane | 1833 |
|                 | John Forsyth | 1834 |
| *War*           | John H. Eaton | 1829 |
|                 | Philip G. Randolph | 1831 |
|                 | Roger B. Taney | 1831 |
|                 | Lewis Cass | 1831 |
|                 | Carey A. Harris | 1836 |
|                 | Benjamin F. Butler | 1836 |
| *Treasury*      | Samuel D. Ingham | 1829 |
|                 | Asbury Dickins | 1831 |
|                 | Louis McLane | 1831 |
|                 | William J. Duane | 1833 |
|                 | Roger B. Taney | 1833 |
|                 | McClintock Young | 1834 |
|                 | Levi Woodbury | 1834 |
| *Post. General* | John McLean | 1829 |
|                 | William T. Barry | 1829 |
|                 | Amos Kendall | 1835 |
| *Atty. General* | John M. Berrien | 1829 |
|                 | Roger B. Taney | 1831 |
|                 | Benjamin F. Butler | 1833 |
| *Navy*          | Charles Hay | 1829 |
|                 | John Branch | 1829 |
|                 | John Boyle | 1831 |
|                 | Levi Woodbury | 1831 |
|                 | Mahlon Dickerson | 1834 |

## 8. Martin Van Buren (1837–1841)

| *Department*    |                     | *Assumed Office* |
|-----------------|---------------------|---------|
| *State*         | John Forsyth | 1837 |
| *War*           | Benjamin F. Butler | 1837 |
|                 | Joel R. Poinsett | 1837 |
| *Treasury*      | Levi Woodbury | 1837 |
| *Post. General* | Amos Kendall | 1837 |
|                 | John M. Niles | 1840 |
| *Atty. General* | Benjamin F. Butler | 1837 |
|                 | Felix Grundy | 1838 |
|                 | Henry D. Gilpin | 1840 |
| *Navy*          | Mahlon Dickerson | 1837 |
|                 | James K. Paulding | 1838 |

## 9. William Henry Harrison (1841)

| *Department*    |                     | *Assumed Office* |
|-----------------|---------------------|---------|
| *State*         | J. L. Martin | 1841 |
|                 | Daniel Webster | 1841 |
| *War*           | John Bell | 1841 |

| | | |
|---|---|---|
| *Treasury* | McClintock Young | 1841 |
| | Thomas Ewing | 1841 |
| *Post. General* | Selah R. Hobbie | 1841 |
| | Francis Granger | 1841 |
| *Atty. General* | John J. Crittenden | 1841 |
| *Navy* | John D. Simms | 1841 |
| | George E. Badger | 1841 |

## 10. John Tyler (1841–1845)

| Department | | Assumed Office |
|---|---|---|
| *State* | Daniel Webster | 1841 |
| | Hugh S. Legaré | 1843 |
| | William S. Derrick | 1843 |
| | Abel P. Upshur | 1843 |
| | John Nelson | 1844 |
| | John C. Calhoun | 1844 |
| *War* | John Bell | 1841 |
| | Albert M. Lea | 1841 |
| | John C. Spencer | 1841 |
| | John M. Porter | 1843 |
| | William Wilkins | 1844 |
| *Treasury* | Thomas Ewing | 1841 |
| | McClintock Young | 1841 |
| | Walter Forward | 1841 |
| | John C. Spencer | 1843 |
| | George M. Bibb | 1844 |
| *Post. General* | Francis Granger | 1841 |
| | Selah R. Hobbie | 1841 |
| | Charles A. Wickliffe | 1841 |
| *Atty. General* | John J. Crittenden | 1841 |
| | Hugh S. Legaré | 1841 |
| | John Nelson | 1843 |
| *Navy* | George E. Badger | 1841 |
| | John D. Simms | 1841 |
| | Abel P. Upshur | 1841 |
| | David Henshaw | 1843 |
| | Thomas W. Gilmer | 1844 |
| | Lewis Washington | 1844 |
| | John Y. Mason | 1844 |

## 11. James K. Polk (1845–1849)

| Department | | Assumed Office |
|---|---|---|
| *State* | John C. Calhoun | 1845 |
| | James Buchanan | 1845 |
| *War* | William Wilkins | 1845 |
| | William L. Marcy | 1845 |
| *Treasury* | George M. Bibb | 1845 |
| | Robert J. Walker | 1845 |
| *Post. General* | Charles A. Wickliffe | 1845 |
| | Cave Johnson | 1845 |
| *Atty. General* | John Nelson | 1845 |
| | John Y. Mason | 1845 |
| | Nathan Clifford | 1846 |

| | | |
|---|---|---|
| | Isaac Toucey | 1848 |
| *Navy* | John Y. Mason | 1845 |
| | George Bancroft | 1845 |
| | John Y. Mason | 1846 |

## 12. Zachary Taylor (1849–1850)

| Department | | Assumed Office |
|---|---|---|
| *State* | James Buchanan | 1849 |
| | John M. Clayton | 1849 |
| *War* | William L. Marcy | 1849 |
| | Reverdy Johnson | 1849 |
| | George W. Crawford | 1849 |
| *Treasury* | Robert J. Walker | 1849 |
| | McClintock Young | 1849 |
| | William M. Meredith | 1849 |
| *Post. General* | Cave Johnson | 1849 |
| | Selah R. Hobbie | 1849 |
| | Jacob Collamer | 1849 |
| *Atty. General* | Isaac Toucey | 1849 |
| | Reverdy Johnson | 1849 |
| *Navy* | John Y. Mason | 1849 |
| | William B. Preston | 1849 |
| *Interior* | Thomas Ewing | 1849 |

## 13. Millard Fillmore (1850–1853)

| Department | | Assumed Office |
|---|---|---|
| *State* | John M. Clayton | 1850 |
| | Daniel Webster | 1850 |
| | Charles M. Conrad | 1852 |
| | Edward Everett | 1852 |
| *War* | George W. Crawford | 1850 |
| | Samuel J. Anderson | 1850 |
| | Winfield Scott | 1850 |
| | Charles M. Conrad | 1850 |
| *Treasury* | William M. Meredith | 1850 |
| | Thomas Corwin | 1850 |
| *Post. General* | Jacob Collamer | 1850 |
| | Nathan K. Hall | 1850 |
| | Samuel D. Hubbard | 1852 |
| *Atty. General* | Reverdy Johnson | 1850 |
| | John J. Crittenden | 1850 |
| *Navy* | William B. Preston | 1850 |
| | Lewis Warrington | 1850 |
| | William A. Graham | 1850 |
| | John P. Kennedy | 1852 |
| *Interior* | Thomas Ewing | 1850 |
| | Daniel C. Goddard | 1850 |
| | Thomas M. T. McKennan | 1850 |
| | Alexander H. H. Stuart | 1850 |

## 14. Franklin Pierce (1853–1857)

| Department | | Assumed Office |
|---|---|---|
| State | William Hunter | 1853 |
| | William L. Marcy | 1853 |
| War | Charles M. Conrad | 1853 |
| | Jefferson Davis | 1853 |
| | Samuel Cooper | 1857 |
| Treasury | Thomas Corwin | 1853 |
| | James Guthrie | 1853 |
| Post. General | Samuel D. Hubbard | 1853 |
| | James Campbell | 1853 |
| Atty. General | John J. Crittenden | 1853 |
| | Caleb Cushing | 1853 |
| Navy | John P. Kennedy | 1853 |
| | James C. Dobbin | 1853 |
| Interior | Alexander H. H. Stuart | 1853 |
| | Robert McClelland | 1853 |

## 15. James Buchanan (1857–1861)

| Department | | Assumed Office |
|---|---|---|
| State | William L. Marcy | 1857 |
| | Lewis Cass | 1857 |
| | William Hunter | 1860 |
| | Jeremiah S. Black | 1860 |
| War | Samuel Cooper | 1857 |
| | John B. Floyd | 1857 |
| | Joseph Holt | 1861 |
| Treasury | James Guthrie | 1857 |
| | Howell Cobb | 1857 |
| | Isaac Toucey | 1860 |
| | Philip F. Thomas | 1860 |
| | John A. Dix | 1861 |
| Post. General | James Campbell | 1857 |
| | Aaron V. Brown | 1857 |
| | Horatio King | 1859 |
| | Joseph Holt | 1859 |
| Atty. General | Caleb Cushing | 1857 |
| | Jeremiah S. Black | 1857 |
| | Edwin M. Stanton | 1860 |
| Navy | James C. Dobbin | 1857 |
| | Isaac Toucey | 1857 |
| Interior | Robert McClelland | 1857 |
| | Jacob Thompson | 1857 |
| | Moses Kelly | 1861 |

## 16. Abraham Lincoln (1861–1865)

| Department | | Assumed Office |
|---|---|---|
| State | Jeremiah S. Black | 1861 |
| | William H. Seward | 1861 |
| War | Joseph Holt | 1861 |
| | Simon Cameron | 1861 |
| | Edwin M. Stanton | 1862 |
| Treasury | John A. Dix | 1861 |
| | Salmon P. Chase | 1861 |
| | George Harrington | 1864 |
| | William P. Fessenden | 1864 |
| | Hugh McCulloch | 1865 |
| Post. General | Horatio King | 1861 |
| | Montgomery Blair | 1861 |
| | William Dennison | 1864 |
| Atty. General | Edwin M. Stanton | 1861 |
| | Edward Bates | 1861 |
| | James Speed | 1864 |
| Navy | Isaac Toucey | 1861 |
| | Gideon Welles | 1861 |
| Interior | Moses Kelly | 1861 |
| | Caleb B. Smith | 1861 |
| | John P. Usher | 1863 |

## 17. Andrew Johnson (1865–1869)

| Department | | Assumed Office |
|---|---|---|
| State | William H. Seward | 1865 |
| War | Edwin M. Stanton | 1865 |
| | Ulysses S. Grant | 1867 |
| | John M. Schofield | 1868 |
| Treasury | Hugh McCulloch | 1865 |
| Post. General | William Dennison | 1865 |
| | Alexander W. Randall | 1866 |
| Atty. General | James Speed | 1865 |
| | J. Hubley Ashton | 1866 |
| | Henry Stanbery | 1866 |
| | Orville H. Browning | 1868 |
| | William M. Evarts | 1868 |
| Navy | Gideon Welles | 1865 |
| Interior | John P. Usher | 1865 |
| | James Harlan | 1865 |
| | Orville H. Browning | 1866 |

## 18. Ulysses S. Grant (1869–1877)

| Department | | Assumed Office |
|---|---|---|
| State | William H. Seward | 1869 |
| | Elihu B. Washburne | 1869 |
| | Hamilton Fish | 1869 |
| War | John M. Schofield | 1869 |
| | John A. Rawlins | 1869 |
| | William T. Sherman | 1869 |
| | William W. Belknap | 1869 |
| | George M. Robeson | 1876 |
| | Alphonso Taft | 1876 |
| | James D. Cameron | 1876 |
| Treasury | Hugh McCulloch | 1869 |
| | John F. Hartley | 1869 |
| | George S. Boutwell | 1869 |
| | William A. Richardson | 1873 |
| | Benjamin H. Bristow | 1874 |

| | | |
|---|---|---|
| | Charles F. Conant | 1876 |
| | Lot M. Morrill | 1876 |
| *Post. General* | St. John B. L. Skinner | 1869 |
| | John A. J. Creswell | 1869 |
| | James W. Marshall | 1874 |
| | Marshall Jewell | 1874 |
| | James N. Tyner | 1876 |
| *Atty. General* | William M. Evarts | 1869 |
| | J. Hubley Ashton | 1869 |
| | Ebenezer R. Hoar | 1869 |
| | Amos T. Akerman | 1870 |
| | George H. Williams | 1872 |
| | Edwards Pierrepont | 1875 |
| | Alphonso Taft | 1876 |
| *Navy* | William Faxon | 1869 |
| | Adolph E. Borie | 1869 |
| | George Robeson | 1869 |
| *Interior* | William T. Otto | 1869 |
| | Jacob D. Cox | 1869 |
| | Columbus Delano | 1870 |
| | Benjamin R. Cowen | 1875 |
| | Zachariah Chandler | 1875 |

## 19. Rutherford B. Hayes (1877–1881)

| Department | | Assumed Office |
|---|---|---|
| *State* | Hamilton Fish | 1877 |
| | William M. Evarts | 1877 |
| *War* | James D. Cameron | 1877 |
| | George W. McCrary | 1877 |
| | Alexander Ramsey | 1879 |
| *Treasury* | Lot M. Morrill | 1877 |
| | John Sherman | 1877 |
| *Post. General* | James N. Tyner | 1877 |
| | David M. Key | 1877 |
| | Horace Maynard | 1880 |
| *Atty. General* | Alphonso Taft | 1877 |
| | Charles Devens | 1877 |
| *Navy* | George M. Robeson | 1877 |
| | Richard W. Thompson | 1877 |
| | Alexander Ramsey | 1880 |
| | Nathan Goff, Jr. | 1881 |
| *Interior* | Zachariah Chandler | 1877 |
| | Carl Schurz | 1877 |

## 20. James A. Garfield (1881)

| Department | | Assumed Office |
|---|---|---|
| *State* | William M. Evarts | 1881 |
| | James G. Blaine | 1881 |
| *War* | Alexander Ramsey | 1881 |
| | Robert T. Lincoln | 1881 |
| *Treasury* | Henry F. French | 1881 |
| | William Windom | 1881 |
| *Post. General* | Horace Maynard | 1881 |
| | Thomas L. James | 1881 |

| | | |
|---|---|---|
| *Atty. General* | Charles Devens | 1881 |
| | Wayne MacVeagh | 1881 |
| *Navy* | Nathan Goff, Jr. | 1881 |
| | William H. Hunt | 1881 |
| *Interior* | Carl Schurz | 1881 |
| | Samuel J. Kirkwood | 1881 |

## 21. Chester A. Arthur (1881–1885)

| Department | | Assumed Office |
|---|---|---|
| *State* | James G. Blaine | 1881 |
| | Frederick T. Frelinghuysen | 1881 |
| *War* | Robert T. Lincoln | 1881 |
| *Treasury* | William Windom | 1881 |
| | Charles J. Folger | 1881 |
| | Charles E. Coon | 1884 |
| | Henry F. French | 1884 |
| | Walter Q. Gresham | 1884 |
| | Hugh McCulloch | 1884 |
| *Post. General* | Thomas L. James | 1881 |
| | Timothy O. Howe | 1882 |
| | Frank Hatton | 1883 |
| | Walter Q. Gresham | 1883 |
| *Atty. General* | Wayne MacVeagh | 1881 |
| | Samuel F. Phillips | 1881 |
| | Benjamin H. Brewster | 1882 |
| *Navy* | William H. Hunt | 1881 |
| | William E. Chandler | 1882 |
| *Interior* | Samuel J. Kirkwood | 1881 |
| | Henry M. Teller | 1882 |

## 22. Grover Cleveland (1885–1889)

| Department | | Assumed Office |
|---|---|---|
| *State* | Frederick T. Frelinghuysen | 1885 |
| | Thomas F. Bayard | 1885 |
| *War* | Robert T. Lincoln | 1885 |
| | William C. Endicott | 1885 |
| *Treasury* | Hugh McCulloch | 1885 |
| | Daniel Manning | 1885 |
| | Charles S. Fairchild | 1887 |
| *Post. General* | Frank Hatton | 1885 |
| | William F. Vilas | 1885 |
| | Don M. Dickinson | 1888 |
| *Atty. General* | Benjamin H. Brewster | 1885 |
| | Augustus H. Garland | 1885 |
| *Navy* | William E. Chandler | 1885 |
| | William C. Whitney | 1885 |
| *Interior* | Merritt L. Joslyn | 1885 |
| | Lucius Q. C. Lamar | 1885 |
| | Henry L. Muldrow | 1888 |
| | William F. Vilas | 1888 |
| *Agriculture* | Norman J. Colman | 1889 |

## 23. Benjamin Harrison (1889–1893)

| Department | | Assumed Office |
|---|---|---|
| State | Thomas F. Bayard | 1889 |
| | James G. Blaine | 1889 |
| | William F. Wharton | 1892 |
| | John W. Foster | 1892 |
| War | William C. Endicott | 1889 |
| | Redfield Proctor | 1889 |
| | Lewis A. Grant | 1891 |
| | Stephen B. Elkins | 1891 |
| Treasury | Charles S. Fairchild | 1889 |
| | William Windom | 1889 |
| | Allured B. Nettleton | 1891 |
| | Charles Foster | 1891 |
| Post. General | Don M. Dickinson | 1889 |
| | John Wanamaker | 1889 |
| Atty. General | Augustus H. Garland | 1889 |
| | William H. H. Miller | 1889 |
| Navy | William C. Whitney | 1889 |
| | Benjamin F. Tracy | 1889 |
| Interior | William F. Vilas | 1889 |
| | John W. Noble | 1889 |
| Agriculture | Norman J. Colman | 1889 |
| | Jeremiah M. Rusk | 1889 |

## 24. Grover Cleveland (1893–1897)

| Department | | Assumed Office |
|---|---|---|
| State | William F. Wharton | 1893 |
| | Walter Q. Gresham | 1893 |
| | Edwin F. Uhl | 1895 |
| | Alvey A. Adee | 1895 |
| | Richard Olney | 1895 |
| War | Stephen B. Elkins | 1893 |
| | Daniel S. Lamont | 1893 |
| Treasury | Charles Foster | 1893 |
| | John G. Carlisle | 1893 |
| Post. General | John Wanamaker | 1893 |
| | Wilson S. Bissell | 1893 |
| | William L. Wilson | 1895 |
| Atty. General | William H. H. Miller | 1893 |
| | Richard Olney | 1893 |
| | Judson Harmon | 1895 |
| Navy | Benjamin F. Tracy | 1893 |
| | Hilary A. Herbert | 1893 |
| Interior | John W. Noble | 1893 |
| | Hoke Smith | 1893 |
| | John M. Reynolds | 1896 |
| | David R. Francis | 1896 |
| Agriculture | Jeremiah M. Rusk | 1893 |
| | Julius Sterling Morton | 1893 |

## 25. William McKinley (1897–1901)

| Department | | Assumed Office |
|---|---|---|
| State | Richard Olney | 1897 |
| | John Sherman | 1897 |
| | William R. Day | 1898 |
| | Alvey A. Adee | 1898 |
| | John M. Hay | 1898 |
| War | Daniel S. Lamont | 1897 |
| | Russell A. Alger | 1897 |
| | Elihu Root | 1899 |
| Treasury | John G. Carlisle | 1897 |
| | Lyman J. Gage | 1897 |
| Post. General | William L. Wilson | 1897 |
| | James A. Gary | 1897 |
| | Charles Emory Smith | 1898 |
| Atty. General | Judson Harmon | 1897 |
| | Joseph McKenna | 1897 |
| | John K. Richards | 1898 |
| | John W. Griggs | 1898 |
| | Philander C. Knox | 1901 |
| Navy | Hilary A. Herbert | 1897 |
| | John D. Long | 1897 |
| Interior | David R. Francis | 1897 |
| | Cornelius N. Bliss | 1897 |
| | Ethan A. Hitchcock | 1899 |
| Agriculture | Julius Sterling Morton | 1897 |
| | James Wilson | 1897 |

## 26. Theodore Roosevelt (1901–1909)

| Department | | Assumed Office |
|---|---|---|
| State | John M. Hay | 1901 |
| | Francis B. Loomis | 1905 |
| | Elihu Root | 1905 |
| | Robert Bacon | 1909 |
| War | Elihu Root | 1901 |
| | William Howard Taft | 1904 |
| | Luke E. Wright | 1908 |
| Treasury | Lyman J. Gage | 1902 |
| | Leslie M. Shaw | 1902 |
| | George B. Cortelyou | 1907 |
| Post. General | Charles Emory Smith | 1901 |
| | Harry C. Payne | 1902 |
| | Robert J. Wynne | 1904 |
| | George B. Cortelyou | 1905 |
| | George von L. Meyer | 1907 |
| Atty. General | Philander C. Knox | 1901 |
| | William H. Moody | 1904 |
| | Charles J. Bonaparte | 1906 |
| Navy | John D. Long | 1901 |
| | William H. Moody | 1902 |
| | Paul Morton | 1904 |

|  |  |  |
|---|---|---|
|  | Victor H. Metcalf | 1906 |
|  | Truman H. Newberry | 1908 |
| *Interior* | Ethan A. Hitchcock | 1901 |
|  | James R. Garfield | 1907 |
| *Agriculture* | James Wilson | 1901 |
| *Comm & Labor* | George B Cortelyou | 1903 |
|  | Victor H. Metcalf | 1904 |
|  | Oscar S. Straus | 1906 |

## 27. William Howard Taft (1909–1913)

| Department | | Assumed Office |
|---|---|---|
| State | Robert Bacon | 1909 |
|  | Philander C. Knox | 1909 |
| War | Luke E. Wright | 1909 |
|  | Jacob M. Dickinson | 1909 |
|  | Henry L. Stimson | 1911 |
| Treasury | George B. Cortelyou | 1909 |
|  | Franklin MacVeagh | 1909 |
| Post. General | George von L. Meyer | 1909 |
|  | Frank H. Hitchcock | 1909 |
| Atty. General | Charles J. Bonaparte | 1909 |
|  | George W. Wickersham | 1909 |
| Navy | Truman H. Newberry | 1909 |
|  | George von L. Meyer | 1909 |
| Interior | James R. Garfield | 1909 |
|  | Richard A. Ballinger | 1909 |
|  | Walter Lowrie Fisher | 1911 |
| Agriculture | James Wilson | 1909 |
| Comm. & Labor | Oscar S. Straus | 1909 |
|  | Charles Nagel | 1909 |

## 28. Woodrow Wilson (1913–1921)

| Department | | Assumed Office |
|---|---|---|
| State | Philander C. Knox | 1913 |
|  | Wm. Jennings Bryan | 1913 |
|  | Robert Lansing | 1915 |
|  | Frank L. Polk | 1920 |
|  | Bainbridge Colby | 1920 |
| War | Henry L. Stimson | 1913 |
|  | Lindley M. Garrison | 1913 |
|  | Hugh L. Scott | 1916 |
|  | Newton D. Baker | 1916 |
| Treasury | Franklin MacVeagh | 1913 |
|  | William Gibbs McAdoo | 1913 |
|  | Carter Glass | 1918 |
|  | David F. Houston | 1920 |
| Post. General | Frank H. Hitchcock | 1913 |
|  | Albert Sidney Burleson | 1913 |

| Atty. General | George W. Wickersham | 1913 |
|---|---|---|
|  | James Clark McReynolds | 1913 |
|  | Thomas Watt Gregory | 1914 |
|  | A. Mitchell Palmer | 1919 |
| Navy | George von L. Meyer | 1913 |
|  | Josephus Daniels | 1913 |
| Interior | Walter Lowrie Fisher | 1913 |
|  | Franklin Knight Lane | 1913 |
|  | John Barton Payne | 1920 |
| Agriculture | James Wilson | 1913 |
|  | David Franklin Houston | 1913 |
|  | Edwin T. Meredith | 1920 |
| Commerce | Charles Nagel | 1913 |
|  | William C. Redfield | 1913 |
| Labor | Charles Nagel | 1913 |
|  | William Bauchop Wilson | 1913 |

## 29. Warren G. Harding (1921–1923)

| Department | | Assumed Office |
|---|---|---|
| State | Bainbridge Colby | 1921 |
|  | Charles Evans Hughes | 1921 |
| War | Newton D. Baker | 1921 |
|  | John W. Weeks | 1921 |
| Treasury | David F. Houston | 1921 |
|  | Andrew W. Mellon | 1921 |
|  | Albert Sidney Burleson | 1921 |
|  | Will H. Hays | 1921 |
|  | Hubert Work | 1922 |
|  | Harry S. New | 1923 |
| Atty. General | A. Mitchell Palmer | 1921 |
|  | Harry M. Dougherty | 1921 |
| Navy | Josephus Daniels | 1921 |
|  | Edwin Denby | 1921 |
| Interior | John Barton Payne | 1921 |
|  | Albert B. Fall | 1921 |
|  | Hubert Work | 1923 |
| Agriculture | Edwin T. Meredith | 1921 |
|  | Henry C. Wallace | 1921 |
| Commerce | Joshua Willis Alexander | 1921 |
|  | Herbert C. Hoover | 1921 |
| Labor | William Bauchop Wilson | 1921 |
|  | James J. Davis | 1921 |

## 30. Calvin Coolidge (1923–1929)

| Department | | Assumed Office |
|---|---|---|
| State | Charles Evans Hughes | 1923 |
|  | Frank B. Kellogg | 1925 |
| War | John W. Weeks | 1923 |
|  | Dwight F. Davis | 1925 |

| | | |
|---|---|---|
| *Treasury* | Andrew W. Mellon | 1923 |
| *Post. General* | Harry S. New | 1923 |
| *Atty. General* | Harry M. Dougherty | 1923 |
| | Harlan Fiske Stone | 1924 |
| *Navy* | Edwin Denby | 1923 |
| | Curtis D. Wilbur | 1924 |
| *Interior* | Hubert Work | 1923 |
| | Roy O. West | 1929 |
| *Agriculture* | Henry C. Wallace | 1923 |
| | Howard M. Gore | 1924 |
| | William M. Jardine | 1925 |
| *Commerce* | Herbert C. Hoover | 1923 |
| | William F. Whiting | 1928 |
| *Labor* | James J. Davis | 1923 |

### 31. Herbert C. Hoover (1929–1933)

| Department | | Assumed Office |
|---|---|---|
| *State* | Frank B. Kellogg | 1929 |
| | Henry L. Stimson | 1929 |
| *War* | Dwight F. Davis | 1929 |
| | James W. Good | 1929 |
| | Patrick J. Hurley | 1929 |
| *Treasury* | Andrew W. Mellon | 1929 |
| | Ogden L. Mills | 1932 |
| *Post. General* | Harry S. New | 1929 |
| | Walter F. Brown | 1929 |
| *Atty. General* | John G. Sargent | 1929 |
| | James DeWitt Mitchell | 1929 |
| *Navy* | Curtis D. Wilbur | 1929 |
| | Charles F. Adams | 1929 |
| *Interior* | Roy O. West | 1929 |
| | Ray L. Wilbur | 1929 |
| *Agriculture* | William M. Jardine | 1929 |
| | Arthur M. Hyde | 1929 |
| *Commerce* | William F. Whiting | 1929 |
| | Robert P. Lamont | 1929 |
| | Roy D. Chapin | 1932 |
| *Labor* | James J. Davis | 1929 |
| | William N. Doak | 1930 |

### 32. Franklin D. Roosevelt (1933–1945)

| Department | | Assumed Office |
|---|---|---|
| *State* | Cordell Hull | 1933 |
| | Edward R. Stettinius | 1944 |
| *War* | George H. Dern | 1933 |
| | Harry H. Woodring | 1936 |
| | Henry L. Stimson | 1940 |
| *Treasury* | William H. Woodin | 1933 |
| | Henry Morgenthau, Jr. | 1934 |
| *Post. General* | James A. Farley | 1933 |
| | Frank C. Walker | 1940 |

| | | |
|---|---|---|
| *Atty. General* | Homer S. Cummings | 1933 |
| | Frank Murphy | 1939 |
| | Robert H. Jackson | 1940 |
| | Francis Biddle | 1941 |
| *Navy* | Claude A. Swanson | 1933 |
| | Charles Edison | 1939 |
| | Frank Knox | 1940 |
| | James V. Forrestal | 1944 |
| *Interior* | Harold L. Ickes | 1933 |
| *Agriculture* | Henry A. Wallace | 1933 |
| | Claude R. Wickard | 1940 |
| *Commerce* | Daniel C. Roper | 1933 |
| | Harry L. Hopkins | 1938 |
| | Jesse H. Jones | 1940 |
| | Henry A. Wallace | 1945 |
| *Labor* | Frances Perkins | 1933 |

### 33. Harry S. Truman (1945–1953)

| Department | | Assumed Office |
|---|---|---|
| *State* | Edward R. Stettinius | 1945 |
| | James F. Byrnes | 1945 |
| | George C. Marshall | 1947 |
| | Dean G. Acheson | 1949 |
| *War* | Henry L. Stimson | 1945 |
| | Robert P. Patterson | 1945 |
| | Kenneth C. Royall | 1947 |
| *Treasury* | Henry Morgenthau, Jr. | 1945 |
| | Fred M. Vinson | 1945 |
| | John W. Snyder | 1946 |
| *Post. General* | Frank C. Walker | 1945 |
| | Robert E. Hannegan | 1945 |
| | Jesse M. Donaldson | 1947 |
| *Atty. General* | Francis Biddle | 1945 |
| | Tom C. Clark | 1945 |
| | J. Howard McGrath | 1949 |
| | James P. McGranery | 1952 |
| *Navy* | James V. Forrestal | 1945 |
| *Interior* | Harold L. Ickes | 1945 |
| | Julius A. Krug | 1946 |
| | Oscar L. Chapman | 1949 |
| *Agriculture* | Claude R. Wickard | 1945 |
| | Clinton P. Anderson | 1945 |
| | Charles F. Brennan | 1948 |
| *Commerce* | Henry A. Wallace | 1945 |
| | W. Averell Harriman | 1946 |
| | Charles Sawyer | 1948 |
| *Labor* | Frances Perkins | 1945 |
| | Lewis B. Schwellenbach | 1945 |
| | Maurice J. Tobin | 1948 |
| *Defense* | James Forrestal | 1947 |
| | Louis A. Johnson | 1949 |
| | George C. Marshall | 1950 |
| | Robert A. Lovett | 1951 |

## 34. Dwight D. Eisenhower (1953–1961)

| Department | | Assumed Office |
|---|---|---|
| State | John Foster Dulles | 1953 |
| | Christian A. Herter | 1959 |
| Treasury | George M. Humphrey | 1953 |
| | Robert A. Anderson | 1957 |
| Post. General | Arthur E. Summerfield | 1953 |
| Atty. General | Herbert Brownell, Jr. | 1953 |
| | William P. Rogers | 1958 |
| Interior | Douglas McKay | 1953 |
| | Frederick A. Seaton | 1956 |
| Agriculture | Ezra Taft Benson | 1953 |
| Commerce | Sinclair Weeks | 1953 |
| | Lewis L. Strauss | 1958 |
| | Frederick H. Mueller | 1959 |
| Labor | Martin P. Durkin | 1953 |
| | James P. Mitchell | 1953 |
| Defense | Charles E. Wilson | 1953 |
| | Neil H. McElroy | 1957 |
| | Thomas S. Gates, Jr. | 1959 |
| H.E.W. | Oveta Culp Hobby | 1953 |
| | Marion B. Folsom | 1955 |
| | Arthur S. Fleming | 1958 |

## 35. John F. Kennedy (1961–1963)

| Department | | Assumed Office |
|---|---|---|
| State | Dean Rusk | 1961 |
| Treasury | C. Douglas Dillon | 1961 |
| Post. General | J. Edward Day | 1961 |
| | John A. Gronouski | 1963 |
| Atty. General | Robert F. Kennedy | 1961 |
| Interior | Stewart L. Udall | 1961 |
| Agriculture | Orville L. Freeman | 1961 |
| Commerce | Luther H. Hodges | 1961 |
| Labor | Arthur J. Goldberg | 1961 |
| | W. Willard Wirtz | 1962 |
| Defense | Robert S. McNamara | 1961 |
| H.E.W. | Abraham A. Ribicoff | 1961 |
| | Anthony J. Celebrezze | 1962 |

## 36. Lyndon B. Johnson (1963–1969)

| Department | | Assumed Office |
|---|---|---|
| State | Dean Rusk | 1963 |
| Treasury | C. Douglas Dillon | 1963 |
| | Henry H. Fowler | 1965 |
| Post. General | John S. Gronouski | 1963 |
| | Lawrence O'Brien | 1965 |
| Atty. General | Robert F. Kennedy | 1963 |
| | Nicholas Katzenbach | 1965 |
| | Ramsey Clark | 1967 |
| Interior | Stewart L. Udall | 1963 |
| Agriculture | Orville L. Freeman | 1963 |
| Commerce | Luther H. Hodges | 1963 |
| | John T. Conner | 1965 |
| | Alexander B. Trowbridge | 1967 |
| | C. R. Smith | 1968 |
| Labor | W. Willard Wirtz | 1963 |
| Defense | Robert S. McNamara | 1963 |
| | Clark Clifford | 1968 |
| H.E.W. | Anthony J. Celebrezze | 1963 |
| | John W. Gardner | 1965 |
| | Wilbur J. Cohen | 1968 |
| H.U.D. | Robert C. Weaver | 1966 |
| Transport. | Alan S. Boyd | 1967 |

## 37. Richard M. Nixon (1969–1974)

| Department | | Assumed Office |
|---|---|---|
| State | William P. Rogers | 1969 |
| | Henry A. Kissinger | 1973 |
| Treasury | David M. Kennedy | 1969 |
| | John B. Connally | 1971 |
| | George F. Shultz | 1972 |
| | William E. Simon | 1974 |
| Post. General | Winton M. Blount | 1969 |
| Atty. General | John N. Mitchell | 1969 |
| | Richard G. Kleindienst | 1972 |
| | Elliot L. Richardson | 1973 |
| | William B. Saxbe | 1973 |
| Interior | Walter J. Hickel | 1969 |
| | Rogers C. B. Morton | 1971 |
| Agriculture | Clifford M. Hardin | 1969 |
| | Earl L. Butz | 1971 |
| Commerce | Maurice H. Stans | 1969 |
| | Peter G. Peterson | 1972 |
| | Frederick B. Dent | 1973 |
| Labor | George P. Shultz | 1969 |
| | James D. Hodgson | 1970 |
| | Peter J. Brennan | 1973 |
| Defense | Melvin R. Laird | 1969 |
| | Elliot L. Richardson | 1973 |
| | James R. Schlesinger | 1973 |
| H.E.W. | Robert H. Finch | 1969 |
| | Elliot L. Richardson | 1970 |
| | Caspar W. Weinberger | 1973 |
| H.U.D. | George W. Romney | 1969 |
| | James T. Lynn | 1973 |
| Transport. | John A. Volpe | 1969 |
| | Claude S. Brinegar | 1973 |

## 38. Gerald R. Ford (1974–1977)

| Department | | Assumed Office |
|---|---|---|
| State | Henry A. Kissinger | 1974 |
| Treasury | William E. Simon | 1974 |
| Atty. General | William B. Saxbe | 1974 |
| | Edward H. Levi | 1975 |
| Interior | Rogers C. B. Morton | 1974 |
| | Stanley K. Hathaway | 1975 |
| | Thomas S. Kleppe | 1975 |
| Agriculture | Earl L. Butz | 1974 |
| | John A. Knebel | 1976 |
| Commerce | Frederick B. Dent | 1974 |
| | Rogers C. B. Morton | 1975 |
| | Elliot L. Richardson | 1975 |
| Labor | Peter J. Brennan | 1974 |
| | John T. Dunlop | 1975 |
| | W. J. Usery, Jr. | 1976 |
| Defense | James R. Schlesinger | 1974 |
| | Donald H. Rumsfeld | 1975 |
| H.E.W. | Caspar W. Weinberger | 1974 |
| | F. David Mathews | 1975 |
| H.U.D. | James T. Lynn | 1974 |
| | Carla Anderson Hills | 1975 |
| Transport. | Claude S. Brinegar | 1974 |
| | William T. Coleman, Jr. | 1975 |

## 39. Jimmy Carter (1977–1981)

| Department | | Assumed Office |
|---|---|---|
| State | Cyrus R. Vance | 1977 |
| | Edmund S. Muskie | 1980 |
| Treasury | W. Michael Blumenthal | 1977 |
| | G. William Miller | 1979 |
| Atty. General | Griffin B. Bell | 1977 |
| | Benjamin R. Civiletti | 1979 |
| Interior | Cecil D. Andrus | 1977 |
| Agriculture | Bob Bergland | 1977 |
| Commerce | Juanita M. Kreps | 1977 |
| | Philip M. Klutznick | 1979 |
| Labor | F. Ray Marshall | 1977 |
| Defense | Harold Brown | 1977 |
| H.E.W. | Joseph A. Califano, Jr. | 1977 |
| | Patricia Roberts Harris | 1979 |
| H.U.D. | Patricia Roberts Harris | 1977 |
| | Moon Landrieu | 1979 |
| Transport. | Brock Adams | 1977 |
| | Neil E. Goldschmidt | 1979 |
| Energy | James R. Schlesinger, Jr. | 1977 |
| | Robert W. Duncan | 1979 |
| Health and Human Services | Patricia Roberts Harris | 1979 |
| Education | Shirley M. Hufstedler | 1979 |

## 40. Ronald Reagan (1981–1989)

| Department | | Assumed Office |
|---|---|---|
| State | Alexander M. Haig, Jr. | 1981 |
| | George P. Shultz | 1982 |
| Treasury | Donald T. Regan | 1981 |
| | Nicholas F. Brady | 1988 |
| Atty General | William French Smith | 1981 |
| | Edwin Meese 3d | 1985 |
| | Richard Thornburgh | 1988 |
| Interior | James G. Watt | 1981 |
| | William P. Clark | 1983 |
| | Donald P. Hodel | 1985 |
| Agriculture | John R. Block | 1981 |
| | Richard E. Lyng | 1986 |
| Commerce | Malcolm Baldrige | 1981 |
| | C. William Verity, Jr. | 1987 |
| Labor | Raymond J. Donovan | 1981 |
| | William E. Brock | 1985 |
| | Ann D. McLaughlin | 1987 |
| Defense | Caspar W. Weinberger | 1981 |
| | Frank D. Carlucci | 1987 |
| H.U.D. | Samuel R. Pierce, Jr. | 1981 |
| Transport. | Andrew L. Lewis, Jr. | 1981 |
| | Elizabeth Hanford Dole | 1983 |
| | James H. Burnley | 1987 |
| Energy | James B. Edwards | 1981 |
| | Donald P. Hodel | 1982 |
| | John S. Herrington | 1985 |
| Health and Human Services | Richard S. Schweiker | 1981 |
| | Margaret M. Heckler | 1983 |
| | Otis R. Bowen | 1985 |
| Education | William J. Bennett | 1985 |
| | Lauro F. Cavazos | 1988 |

## 41. George Bush (1989–1993)

| Department | | Assumed Office |
|---|---|---|
| State | James A. Baker, 3d | 1989 |
| | Lawrence S. Eagleburger | 1992 |
| Treasury | Nicholas F. Brady | 1989 |
| Atty. General | Richard Thornburgh | 1989 |
| | William P. Barr | 1991 |
| Interior | Manuel Lujan | 1989 |
| Agriculture | Clayton K. Yeutter | 1989 |
| | Edward Madigan | 1991 |
| Commerce | Robert A. Mosbacher | 1989 |
| | Barbara H. Franklin | 1992 |
| Labor | Elizabeth Hanford Dole | 1989 |
| | Lynn S. Martin | 1991 |
| Defense | Richard S. Cheney | 1989 |
| H.U.D. | Jack F. Kemp | 1989 |
| Transport. | Samuel K. Skinner | 1989 |

| | Andrew H. Card, Jr. | 1992 |
| --- | --- | --- |
| *Energy* | James D. Watkins | 1989 |
| *Health and Human Services* | Louis W. Sullivan | 1989 |
| *Education* | Lauro F. Cavazos | 1989 |
| | Lamar Alexander | 1991 |
| *Veterans Affairs* | Edward J. Derwinski | 1989 |

## 42. Bill Clinton (1993–)

| Department | | Assumed Office |
| --- | --- | --- |
| *State* | Warren M. Christopher | 1993 |
| | Madeleine K. Albright | 1997 |
| *Treasury* | Lloyd M. Bentsen, Jr. | 1993 |
| | Robert E. Rubin | 1995 |
| | Lawrence Summers | 1999 |
| *Atty. General* | Janet Reno | 1993 |
| *Interior* | Bruce Babbitt | 1993 |
| *Agriculture* | Mike Espy | 1993 |
| | Dan Glickman | 1995 |

| *Commerce* | Ronald H. Brown | 1993 |
| --- | --- | --- |
| | Mickey Kantor | 1996 |
| | William M. Daley | 1997 |
| *Labor* | Robert B. Reich | 1993 |
| | Alexis Herman | 1997 |
| *Defense* | Les Aspin | 1993 |
| | William Perry | 1994 |
| | William S. Cohen | 1997 |
| *H.U.D.* | Henry G. Cisneros | 1993 |
| | Andrew Cuomo | 1997 |
| *Transport.* | Federico F. Peña | 1993 |
| | Rodney E. Slater | 1997 |
| *Energy* | Hazel R. O'Leary | 1993 |
| | Federico F. Peña | 1997 |
| | Bill Richardson | 1999 |
| *Health and Human Services* | Donna E. Shalala | 1993 |
| *Education* | Richard W. Riley | 1993 |
| *Veterans Affairs* | Jesse Brown | 1993 |

# *Appendix B*

# VICE PRESIDENTS OF THE UNITED STATES

| | | | |
|---|---|---|---|
| 1. John Adams | (1789–1797) | 24. Garret A. Hobart | (1897–1899)* |
| 2. Thomas Jefferson | (1797–1801) | 25. Theodore Roosevelt | (1901)*** |
| 3. Aaron Burr | (1801–1805) | 26. Charles W. Fairbanks | (1905–1909) |
| 4. George Clinton | (1805–1812)* | 27. James S. Sherman | (1909–1912)* |
| 5. Eldridge Gerry | (1813–1814)* | 28. Thomas R. Marshall | (1913–1921) |
| 6. Daniel D. Tompkins | (1817–1825) | 29. Calvin Coolidge | (1921–1923)*** |
| 7. John C. Calhoun | (1825–1832)** | 30. Charles G. Dawes | (1925–1929) |
| 8. Martin Van Buren | (1833–1837) | 31. Charles Curtis | (1929–1933) |
| 9. Richard M. Johnson | (1837–1841) | 32. John Nance Garner | (1933–1941) |
| 10. John Tyler | (1841)*** | 33. Henry A. Wallace | (1941–1945) |
| 11. George M. Dallas | (1845–1849) | 34. Harry S. Truman | (1945)*** |
| 12. Millard Fillmore | (1849–1850)*** | 35. Alben W. Barkley | (1949–1953) |
| 13. William Rufus D. King | (1853)* | 36. Richard M. Nixon | (1953–1961) |
| 14. John C. Breckinridge | (1857–1861) | 37. Lyndon B. Johnson | (1961–1963) |
| 15. Hannibal Hamlin | (1861–1865) | 38. Hubert H. Humphrey | (1965–1969) |
| 16. Andrew Johnson | (1865)*** | 39. Spiro T. Agnew | (1969–1973)** |
| 17. Schuyler Colfax | (1869–1873) | 40. Gerald R. Ford | (1973–1974)*** |
| 18. Henry Wilson | (1873–1875)* | 41. Nelson A. Rockefeller | (1974–1977) |
| 19. William A. Wheeler | (1877–1881) | 42. Walter F. Mondale | (1977–1981) |
| 20. Chester A. Arthur | (1881)*** | 43. George Bush | (1981–1989) |
| 21. Thomas A. Hendricks | (1885)* | 44. J. Danforth Quayle | (1989–1993) |
| 22. Levi P. Morton | (1889–1893) | 45. Albert A. Gore Jr. | (1993– ) |
| 23. Adlai E. Stevenson | (1893–1897) | | |

*Died in office
**Resigned
***Succeeded to presidency

# *Appendix C*

## FIRST LADIES OF THE UNITED STATES

| Name | Dates as First Lady | Name | Dates as First Lady |
|---|---|---|---|
| Martha Dandrige Custis Washington (1731–1802) | 1789–1797 | Edith Kermit Carow Roosevelt (1861–1948) | 1901–1909 |
| Abigail Smith Adams (1744–1818) | 1797–1801 | Helen Herron Taft (1861–1943) | 1909–1913 |
| Dolley Payne Todd Madison (1768–1849) | 1809–1817 | Ellen Louise Axson Wilson (1860–1914) | 1913–1914 |
| Elizabeth Kortright Monroe (1768–1830) | 1817–1825 | Edith Bolling Galt Wilson (1872–1961) | 1915–1921 |
| Louisa Catherine Johnson Adams (1775–1852) | 1825–1829 | Florence Mabel Kling Harding (1860–1924) | 1921–1923 |
| Anna Tuthill Symmes Harrison (1775–1864) | 1841 | Grace Anna Goodhue Coolidge (1879–1957) | 1923–1929 |
| Letitia Christian Tyler (1790–1842) | 1841–1842 | Lou Henry Hoover (1874–1944) | 1929–1933 |
| Julia Gardner Tyler (1820–1889) | 1844–1845 | Anna Eleanor Roosevelt (1884–1962) | 1933–1945 |
| Sarah Childress Polk (1803–1891) | 1845–1849 | Elizabeth Virginia Wallace ("Bess") Truman (1885–1982) | 1945–1953 |
| Margaret Mackall Smith Taylor (1788–1852) | 1849–1850 | Mamie Geneva Doud Eisenhower (1896–1979) | 1953–1961 |
| Abigail Powers Fillmore (1798–1853) | 1850–1853 | Jacqueline Lee Bouvier Kennedy Onassis (1929–1994) | 1961–1963 |
| Jane Means Appleton Pierce (1806–1863) | 1853–1857 | Claudia Alta Taylor ("Lady Bird") Johnson (1912– ) | 1963–1969 |
| Mary Todd Lincoln (1818–1882) | 1861–1865 | Thelma Catherine Ryan ("Pat") Nixon (1912–1993) | 1969–1974 |
| Eliza McCardle Johnson (1810–1876) | 1865–1869 | Elizabeth Ann Bloomer ("Betty") Ford (1918– ) | 1974–1977 |
| Julia Dent Grant (1826–1902) | 1869–1877 | | |
| Lucy Ware Webb Hayes (1831–1889) | 1877–1881 | Rosalyn Smith Carter (1927– ) | 1977–1981 |
| Lucretia Rudolph Garfield (1832–1918) | 1881 | Nancy Davis Reagan (1921– ) | 1981–1989 |
| Frances Clara Folsom Cleveland (1864–1947) | 1886–1889 1893–1897 | Barbara Pierce Bush (1925– ) | 1989–1993 |
| Caroline Lavinia Scott Harrison (1832–1892) | 1889–1893 | Hillary Rodham Clinton (1947– ) | 1993– |
| Ida Saxton McKinley (1847–1907) | 1897–1901 | | |

# *Appendix D*

# PRESIDENTIAL LIBRARIES AND WEB SITES

The National Archives and Records Administration, by an act of Congress, is responsible for the preservation of the papers of all presidents since Herbert Hoover (1929–1933). The collections of presidents before Hoover are located in the Library of Congress. The list below gives the addresses and Web sites of the presidential Libraries built since the Hoover administration.

Herbert Hoover Presidential Library
211 Parkside Dr., P.O. Box 488
West Branch, IA 52358-0488
tel. 319-643-5301
http://www.nara.gov/nara/president/hoover

Franklin D. Roosevelt Library
511 Albany Post Rd.
Hyde Park, NY 12538-1999
tel. 914-229-8114
http://www.academic.marist.edu/fdr

Harry S. Truman Library and Museum
500 W. U.S. Highway 24
Independence, MO 64050-1798
tel. 816-833-1400
http://sunsite.unc.edu/lia/president/truman.
   html

Dwight D. Eisenhower Presidential Library
200 S.E. 4th St.
Abilene, KS 67410-2900
tel. 913-263-4751
http://sunsite.unc.edu/lia/president/
   eisenhower.html

John Fitzgerald Kennedy Library
Columbia Point
Boston, MA 02125-3398
tel. 617-929-4500
http://sunsite.unc.edu/lia/president/kennedy.
   html

Lyndon B. Johnson Library and Museum
2313 Red River St.
Austin, TX 78705-5702
tel. 512-916-5137
http://www.lbjlib.utexas.edu

Richard Nixon Library and Museum
18001 Yorba Linda Blvd.
Yorba Linda, CA 92886
tel. 714-993-3393
http://www.nixonlibrary.org

Gerald R. Ford Library
1000 Beal Ave.
Ann Arbor, MI 48109-2114
tel. 313-741-2218
http://www.lbjlib.utexas.edu/ford/index.html

Jimmy Carter Library
1 Copenhill Ave. N.E.
Atlanta, GA 30307-1406
tel. 404-331-3942
http://sunsite.unc.edu/lia/president/carter.
  html

Ronald W. Reagan Presidential Library
40 Presidential Dr.
Simi Valley, CA 93065-0666
tel. 805-522-8844
http://sunsite.unc.edu/lia/president/reagan.
  html

George Bush Presidential Library and
  Museum
701 University Dr. E., Ste. 300
College Station, TX 77840-9554
tel. 409-260-9552
http://www.csdl.tamu.edu/bushlib

# INDEX

BALDWIN PUBLIC LIBRARY

3 1115 00490 7290

NO LONGER THE PROPERTY OF
BALDWIN PUBLIC LIBRARY

973.099 A                    125.00
The American Presidents.

**BALDWIN PUBLIC LIBRARY**
2385 GRAND AVENUE
BALDWIN, N.Y. 11510
516-223-6228